International Rare
Book Prices

EARLY PRINTED
BOOKS

1992

International Rare Book Prices

EARLY PRINTED BOOKS

Series Editor: Michael Cole

1992

The Clique

International Rare Book Prices – Early Printed Books

ISBN 1 870773 29 2

Typesetting by Maxiprint, York, England
Printed and bound by Biddles Ltd., Guildford, England

Contents

Introduction and Notes

The annual *IRBP* series, now in its sixth year, provides annual records of the pricing levels of out-of-print, rare or antiquarian books within a number of specialty subject areas and gives likely sources and suppliers for such books in Britain and the United States of America. It is intended to be used by both the experienced bookman and the newcomer to book-collecting.

Sources of information:

The books recorded each year in the various subject volumes of *IRBP* have been selected from catalogues of books for sale issued during the previous year by numerous bookselling firms in Britain and the United States. These firms, listed at the end of this volume, range in nature from the highly specialized, handling books solely with closely defined subject areas, through to large concerns with expertise across a broad spectrum of interests.

Extent of coverage:

IRBP concentrates exclusively on books published in the English language and, throughout the series as a whole, encompasses books published between the 16th century and the 1970s.

The 30,000 or so separate titles recorded in the annual volumes of *IRBP* vary greatly from year to year although naturally there is a degree of overlap, particularly of the more frequently found titles. Consecutive annual volumes do not, therefore, merely update pricings from earlier years; they give substantially different listings of books on each occasion. The value of the *IRBP* volumes lies in providing records of an ever-increasing range of individual titles which have appeared for sale on the antiquarian or rare book market.

Emphasis is placed throughout on books falling within the lower to middle range of the pricing scale (£10 - £250; $20 - $500) rather than restricting selection to the unusually fine or expensive. In so doing, *IRBP* provides a realistic overview of the norm, rather than the exception, within the booktrade.

Authorship and cross-references:

Authors are listed alphabetically by surname.

Whenever possible, the works of each author are grouped together under a single form of name irrespective of the various combinations of initials, forenames and surnames by which the author is known.

Works published anonymously, or where the name of the author is not recorded on the title-page, are suitably cross-referenced by providing the main entry under the name of the author (when mentioned by the bookseller) with a corresponding entry under the first appropriate word of the title. In cases of unknown, or unmentioned, authorship, entry is made solely under the title.

Full-titles:
Editorial policy is to eschew, whenever possible, short-title records in favour of full-, or at least more complete and explanatory, titles. Short-title listings do little to convey the flavour, or even the content, of many books - particularly those published prior to the nineteenth century.

Descriptions:
Books are listed alphabetically, using the first word of the title ignoring, for alphabetical purposes, the definite and indefinite articles *the, a* and *an*. Within this alphabetical grouping of titles, variant editions are not necessarily arranged in chronological order, i.e., a 2nd, 3rd or 4th edition might well be listed prior to an earlier edition.

Subject to restrictions of space and to the provisos set out below, the substance of each catalogue entry giving details of the particular copy offered for sale has been recorded in full.

The listings have been made so as to conform to a uniform order of presentation, viz: Title; place of publication; publisher or printer; date; edition; size; collation; elements of content worthy of note; description of contents including faults, if any; description and condition of binding; bookseller; price; approximate price conversion from dollars to sterling or vice versa.

Abbreviations of description customary within the booktrade have generally been used. A list of these abbreviations will be found on page *x*.

Collations:
Collations, when provided by the bookseller, are repeated in toto although it should be borne in mind that booksellers employ differing practices in this respect; some by providing complete collations and others by indicating merely the number of pages in the main body of the work concerned. The same edition of the same title catalogued by two booksellers could therefore have two apparently different collations and care should be taken not to regard any collation recorded in *IRBP* as being a definitive or absolute record of total content.

Currency conversion:
IRBP lists books offered for sale priced in either pounds sterling (£) or United States dollars ($). For the benefit of readers unaccustomed to one or other of these currencies, an approximate conversion figure in the alternative currency has been provided in parentheses after each entry, as, for example, "**£100 [≃ $178]**", or, "**$60 [≃ £34]**". The conversion is based upon an exchange rate of £1 sterling ≃ US $1.78 (US $1 ≃ £0.562 sterling), the approximate rate applicable at the date of going to press.

It must be stressed that the conversion figures in parentheses are provided merely as an indication of the approximate pricing level in the currency with which the reader may be most familiar and that fluctuations in exchange rates will make these approximations inaccurate to a greater or lesser degree.

Acknowledgements:

We are indebted to those booksellers who have provided their catalogues during 1991 for the purposes of *IRBP*. A list of the contributing booksellers forms an appendix at the rear of this volume.

This appendix forms a handy reference of contacts in Britain and the United States with proven experience of handling books within the individual specialist fields encompassed by the series. The booksellers listed therein are able, between them, to offer advice on any aspect of the rare and antiquarian booktrade.

Many of the listed books will still, at the time of publication, be available for purchase. Readers with a possible interest in acquiring any of the items may well find it worth their while communicating with the booksellers concerned to obtain further and complete details.

Caveat:

Whilst the greatest care has been taken in transcribing entries from catalogues, it should be understood that it is inevitable that an occasional error will have passed unnoticed. Obvious mistakes, usually typographical in nature, observed in catalogues have been corrected. We have not questioned the accuracy in bibliographical matters of the cataloguers concerned.

The Clique

Abbreviations

advt(s)	advertisement(s)	intl	initial
addtn(s)	addition(s)	iss	issue
a.e.g.	all edges gilt	jnt(s)	joint(s)
ALS	autograph letter signed	lge	large
altrtns	alterations	lea	leather
Amer	American	lib	library
bibliog(s)	bibliography(ies)	ltd	limited
b/w	black & white	litho(s)	lithograph(s)
bndg	binding	marg(s)	margin(s)
bd(s)	board(s)	ms(s)	manuscript(s)
b'plate	bookplate	mrbld	marbled
ctlg(s)	catalogue(s)	mod	modern
chromolitho(s)	chromo-lithograph(s)	mor	morocco
ca	circa	mtd	mounted
cold	coloured	n.d.	no date
coll	collected	n.p.	no place
contemp	contemporary	num	numerous
crnr(s)	corner(s)	obl	oblong
crrctd	corrected	occas	occasional(ly)
cvr(s)	cover(s)	orig	original
dec	decorated	p (pp)	page(s)
detchd	detached	perf	perforated
diag(s)	diagram(s)	pict	pictorial
dw(s)	dust wrapper(s)	port(s)	portrait(s)
edn(s)	edition(s)	pres	presentation
elab	elaborate	ptd	printed
engv(s)	engraving(s)	qtr	quarter
engvd	engraved	rebnd	rebind/rebound
enlgd	enlarged	rec	recent
esp	especially	repr(d)	repair(ed)
ex lib	ex library	rvsd	revised
f (ff)	leaf(ves)	roy	royal
f.e.p.	free end paper	sep	separate
facs	facsimile	sev	several
fig(s)	figure(s)	sgnd	signed
fldg	folding	sgntr	signature
ft	foot	sl	slight/slightly
frontis	frontispiece	sm	small
hand-cold	hand-coloured	t.e.g.	top edge gilt
hd	head	TLS	typed letter signed
ill(s)	illustration(s)	unif	uniform
illust	illustrated	v	very
imp	impression	vell	vellum
imprvd	improved	vol(s)	volume(s)
inc	including	w'engvd	wood-engraved
inscrbd	inscribed	w'cut(s)	woodcut(s)
inscrptn	inscription	wrap(s)	wrapper(s)

Books published prior to 1800
1991 Catalogue Prices

A., D., Gent.
- The Whole Art of Converse ... With the Characters of the Four Humours ... London: for Joseph Hindmarsh, 1683. 12mo. [xii],128 pp. Marg wormhole 1st 20 ff. Sm tear in 1 leaf. Old calf, worn. Wing A3B.
(Hollett) **£175 [≈ $312]**
- The Whole Art of Converse: containing Necessary Instructions for all persons ... London: for Joseph Hindmarsh, 1683. [12],128 pp. Sm marg worm hole 1st few ff. Contemp sheep, spine sl rubbed. Wing 3A.
(C.R. Johnson) **£280 [≈ $498]**

Abbot, George
- A Brief Description of the Whole World ... London: John Marriott, 1620. 5th edn. 4to. [88] ff. Intl blank leaf. Stain lower margs of last few ff. Later half calf.
(Bookpress) **$450 [≈ £253]**

Abercrombie, John
- The Hot-House Gardener ... London: for John Stockdale, 1789. 1st edn. Roy 8vo. xvi, 238 pp. 5 hand cold plates inc frontis. Frontis lower marg sl trimmed. Contemp tree calf, rebacked.
(Vanbrugh) **£295 [≈ $525]**

Abercromby, David
- A Moral Discourse on the Power of Interest. London: Tho. Hodgkin for the author, 1690. 1st edn. 8vo. [xxiv],191 pp. Title sl dusty, sl damp stain some margs. Period calf, rebacked, crnrs sl worn. Wing A83 (variant imprint).
(Rankin) **£450 [≈ $801]**

Absalom Senior ...
- See Settle, Elkanah

Account ...
- An Account of Church-Government, and Governours ... see Brett, Thomas.
- An Account of Sweden ... see Robinson, John.
- An Account of Switzerland ... see Stanyan, Abraham.
- An Account of the late Establishment of Presbyterian Government ... see Sage, John.
- An Account of the Loss of His Majesty's Ship Deal Castle, commanded by Capt. James Hawkins, off the Island of Porto Rico, during the Hurricane ... in the year 1780. London: for J. Murray, 1787. 1st edn. 8vo. [ii],ii, 48,[2] pp inc final errata leaf. Rec cloth.
(Burmester) **£150 [≈ $267]**
- The Account of the Manner of Executing a Writ of Inquiry of Damages: Between His Royal Highness James Duke of York and Titus Oates ... London: 1684. 1st edn. Folio. 31 pp. Mod cloth backed bds. Wing A.320.
(Robertshaw) **£35 [≈ $62]**

Accurate ...
- An Accurate Description and History of the Cathedral and Metropolitical Church of St. Peter, York ... see Drake, Francis.
- An Accurate Description of the United Netherlands ... see Carr, William

Acherley, Roger
- Free Parliaments: or an Argument on their Constitution ... London: 1731. 1st edn. 8vo. 322 pp. Title sl spotted, sm tear without loss. Disbound. Anon. *(Robertshaw)* **£18 [≈ $32]**

Adams, George, the elder
- Essays on the Microscope ... A General History of Insects ... Configuration of Salts ... London: for the author, by Robert Hindmarsh ..., 1787. 1st edn. Stout 4to. Half-title. Frontis (spotted, offset), 32 plates (1-31,26 bis). Occas spot. New mrbld calf.
(Georges) **£1,600 [≈ $2,848]**
- A Treatise describing and explaining the Construction and Use of New Celestial and Terrestrial Globes ... London: for the author, 1766. 1st edn. 8vo. xxii,242,[8 advt] pp. 3 plates. Contemp calf, jnts cracked, hd of spine sl chipped. *(Burmester)* **£750 [≈ $1,335]**

Adams, George, the younger

- An Essay on Electricity, explaining the Theory and Practice of that useful Science ... Third Edition corrected and considerably enlarged. London: 1787. 8vo. 468 pp. Fldg frontis, title vignette, 7 plates. Mod half calf.
  (Robertshaw) **£180 [≈ $320]**

- Geometrical and Graphical Essays ... Mathematical Instruments used in ... Surveying, Levelling, and Perspective ... Second Edition ... enlarged by William Jones. London: 1797. 2 vols in one. 14 ctlg, 2 advt pp. Frontis, 34 fldg plates. Contemp calf, hd of spine v sl worn. *(Weiner)* **£175 [≈ $312]**

- Lectures on Natural and Experimental Philosophy ... Second Edition, with considerable Corrections and Additions, by William Jones ... London: 1799. 5 vols. 8vo. Frontis, 43 fldg plates. End ff sl foxed. Contemp half calf. *(Fenning)* **£450 [≈ $801]**

- Plates for the Essays on the Microscope. London: 1787. Oblong folio. 33 plates on 31 sheets. Sl water stain lower part early plates. Few old marg notes. Orig bds, uncut, v worn, front bd detached. *(Weiner)* **£375 [≈ $668]**

Adams, John

- Analysis of Horsemanship: Teaching the Whole Art of Riding ... Volume I [all published]. London: M. Ritchie ... for the author, & sold by Cadell & Davies, 1799. 1st edn. 8vo. 196 pp. Frontis port, 8 plates. Orig speckled calf, some shelf wear.
  (Chapel Hill) **$800 [≈ £449]**

Adams, John, Revd

- The Flowers of Ancient History ... Designed for the Improvement and Entertainment of Youth. Dublin: Zachariah Jackson, 1789. 1st edn. xii,290,[1] pp. Contemp calf, red label.
  (C.R. Johnson) **£65 [≈ $116]**

- The Flowers of Ancient History ... Designed for the Improvement and Entertainment of Youth. Second Edition, enlarged. London: 1790. 12mo. Contemp half calf.
  (Robertshaw) **£30 [≈ $53]**

- The Flowers of Modern Travels; being Elegant, Entertaining and Instructive Extracts selected from the Works of the most celebrated Travellers ... Boston: John West, 1797. 1st Amer edn. 2 vols. 8vo. 324; 312 pp. Contemp sheep, rubbed, scuffed, jnts cracked. *(Clark)* **£85 [≈ $151]**

Adams, Thomas

- The Works ... Being the summe of his Sermons, Meditations, and other Divine and Morall Discourses ... London: 1629. Folio. Title, x, 1240, index pp. Sl marg worm. Sm

marg reprs. Calf, rebacked.
  (Francis Edwards) **£350 [≈ $623]**

Addison, Joseph

- Cato. A Tragedy. London: for J. Tonson, 1713. 1st edn. Sm 4to. Half-title. Panelled calf gilt, rebacked, spine rubbed.
  (Ximenes) **$600 [≈ £337]**

- Miscellaneous Works in Verse and Prose ... Edinburgh: J. Robertson, 1769. 4 vols. 12mo. 32 plates in vol 3. Some browning. Contemp calf, extrs sl worn, lacks most labels.
  (Clark) **£30 [≈ $53]**

- Remarks on Several Parts of Italy. London: Tonson, 1705. 1st edn. Large Paper. 8vo. [xii], 534 pp. Some browning & spotting. Contemp calf in 'Cambridge Pane' pattern, reprd. *(Ash)* **£250 [≈ $445]**

- Remarks on Several Parts of Italy, &c. In the Years 1701, 1702, 1703. London: Tonson, 1718. 2nd edn. 12mo. [12],x,410,[5] pp. Sev text w'cuts. Lacks front blank flyleaf. Old calf, splits in jnt ends.
  (D & D Galleries) **$100 [≈ £56]**

- Remarks on Several Parts of Italy, &c. In the Years 1701 ... 1703. The Fifth Edition. London: Tonson, 1736. Lge 12mo. 304,[8] pp. Contemp calf gilt, sl worn.
  (Fenning) **£24.50 [≈ $45]**

- Remarks on Several Parts of Italy, &c. In the Years 1701, 1702, 1703. London: Tonson & Draper, 1745. 8vo. 303,[9] pp. Contemp calf, gilt spine. *(O'Neal)* **$75 [≈ £42]**

- The Resurrection: a Poem ... The Third Edition. London: for E. Curll, 1718. Latin & English text. 8vo. xii,13 pp. Sgntr 'a' is repeated. Frontis. Disbound.
  (Hannas) **£35 [≈ $62]**

- The Works. London: Tonson, 1721. 1st coll edn. 4 vols. 4to. Frontis vol 1. Contemp Cambridge style calf, mor labels.
  (Waterfield's) **£235 [≈ $418]**

Address ...

- Address to the Seamen in the British Navy. London: Richardson, 1797. 8vo. Stitched pamphlet. *(Rostenberg & Stern)* **$60 [≈ £34]**

Adlerfeld, Gustavus

- The Military History of Charles XII. King of Sweden ... Translated into English. London: Knapton, 1740. 1st edn in English. 3 vols. 8vo. Half-title in vol 2 (correctly). Frontis port, 6 fldg battle plans (2 sl used). Contemp calf gilt, sl worn. *(Blackwell's)* **£175 [≈ $312]**

Adrichem, Christiaan van

- A briefe description of Hierusalem and of the

suburbs thereof, as it flourished in the time of Christ ... Translated out of Latin into English by Thomas Tymme. London: Peter Short for Thomas Wight, 1595. 1st edn. 4to. [xvi],112,[4] pp. Lacks map. Contemp vellum, soiled. *(Claude Cox)* **£140 [≈ $249]**

The Adventurer ...
- See Hawkesworth, John (ed.)

Adventures ...
- The Adventures of Ferdinand Count Fathom ... see Smollett, Tobias.
- The Adventures of Five Hours ... see Tuke, Sir Andrew.
- The Adventures of Peregrine Pickle ... see Smollett, Tobias.
- The Adventures of Roderick Random ... see Smollett, Tobias.

Advice ...
- Advice from Farmer Trueman ... see Hanway, Jonas.

Aeneas and His Two Sons ...
- Aeneas and His Two Sons. A True Portrait ... London: J. Oldcastle, (1746). 1st edn. 8vo. xxxii,33-691 advt pp. 1 blank crnr torn away, 1 closed tear. Disbound.
(Young's) **£120 [≈ $214]**

Aesop
- Aesop's Fables. With Instructive Morals and Reflections ... and the Life of Aesop prefixed, By Mr. Richardson. London: [1760]. 12mo. xxxiv,[ii],192 pp. Engvd title, 25 plates (each with 10 vignettes). Contemp sheep, rubbed, sm split in jnt. *(Clark)* **£60 [≈ $107]**
- Fables of Aesop and others: translated into English. With Instructive Applications ... The Fourteenth Edition. London: Rivington ..., 1788. 8vo. [xxxiv],329,[vii] pp. Frontis, 196 w'cut vignettes. Minor marg damp stains. Contemp sheep, rubbed, some insect damage. *(Clark)* **£48 [≈ $85]**
- Fables ... see also L'Estrange, Sir Roger.

Aglionby, William
- Painting Illustrated in Three Dialogues ... London: John Gain for the author, 1685. 1st edn. 4to. [xxxviii],127,[i], 125-132, 129-367, (364)-375,[i] pp. Imprimatur leaf. Red & black title. Some wear & tear. Contemp calf, sl worn but sound. Wing A.764. Anon.
(Clark) **£300 [≈ $534]**
- Painting Illustrated in Three Dialogues. London: Gain for the author, 1685. 1st edn. 4to. Red & black title. Calf, rebacked,

recrnrd, scuffed. Wing A.764. Anon.
(Rostenberg & Stern) **$1,850 [≈ £1,039]**

Agrippa, Henricus Cornelius
- The Vanity of Arts & Sciences. London: 1684. 4th edn (?). Orig calf, worn but sound.
(Deja Vu) **£450 [≈ $801]**
- The Vanity of Arts and Sciences. London: R.E. for R.B. & sold by C. Blount, 1684. 8vo. [10],368 pp. Port frontis. Rec pigskin. Wing A.791. *(O'Neal)* **$400 [≈ £225]**

Aikin, John
- England Delineated; or, a Geographical Description of every County in England and Wales ... For the Use of Young Persons. Second Edition, With Additions and Corrections. London: Bensley, 1790. 8vo. 425, v],[2 advt] pp. 43 maps (1 fldg). Contemp sheep, rebacked.
(Gough) **£250 [≈ $445]**
- Essays on Song-Writing: with a Collection of such English Songs as are most eminent for Poetical Merit. The Second Edition, with Additions and Corrections. Warrington: William Eyres ..., 1774. 8vo. Contemp qtr calf, sl worn. *(Sanders)* **£80 [≈ $142]**
- Letters from a Father to his Son, on Various Topics, relative to Literature and the Conduct of Life ... Third Edition. London: for J. Johnson, 1796-1800. Vol 2 1st edn. 2 vols. 8vo. Final advt leaf vol 2. Contemp mottled caif gilt, fine.
(Hannas) **£110 [≈ $196]**
- Observations on the External Use of Preparations of Lead. With Some General remarks on Topical Medicines. London: 1771. iv,104 pp. Some foxing endpapers & title. Contemp polished calf, front hinge cracked but firm. *(Whitehart)* **£150 [≈ $267]**

Aitzema, Lieuwe
- Notable Revolutions: Being a true relation of what hapn'ed in the United Provinces of the Netherlands in the years MDCL and MDCLI ... London: William Dugard, 1653. Folio. Mod calf. Wing A.821.
(Hollett) **£250 [≈ $445]**

A Kempis, Thomas
- The Christian Pattern Paraphras'd: or, the Book of the Imitation of Christ, commonly ascribed to Thomas A Kempis. By Luke Milbourne. London: for Abel Roper, & Roger Clavel, 1697. 1st edn. 8vo. Frontis. Contemp calf, rebacked. Wing T.945.
(Ximenes) **$500 [≈ £281]**

Akenside, Mark
- Odes on Several Subjects. London: for R. Dodsley, & sold by M. Cooper, 1745. 1st edn. 4to. 54 pp. Engvd title vignette. Half-title sl dusty. Disbound. Anon.
(Burmester) **£35 [≈ $62]**
- The Poems ... London: Bowyer & Nichols, sold by Dodsley, 1772. 1st coll edn. 4to. Mezzotint port. Lacks intl blank leaf. Contemp tree calf, edges rubbed, rebacked.
(Hannas) **£120 [≈ $214]**
- The Poems. London: Bowyer & Nichols, 1772. 1st 8vo edn. xii,402 pp. Contemp mottled calf, elab gilt spine, ft of spine chipped.
(Karmiole) **$125 [≈ £70]**

Alanson, E.
- Practical Observations on Amputation and the After-Treatment ... London: 1782. 2nd edn. xxxii,296 pp. Occas sl foxing. Contemp leather, rebacked. *(Whitehart)* **£220 [≈ $392]**

Albin, E.
- A Natural History of Spiders, and Other Curious Insects. London: 1736. 4to. [viii],76 pp. Frontis, 40 (of 53) plates. Sl foxing & offsetting. A few plate margs trifle frayed. New half calf.
(Wheldon & Wesley) **£225 [≈ $401]**

Alcock, John
- Harmonia Festi, or a Collection of Canons; cheerful & serious Glees & Catches ... Never before published ... Lichfield: printed for the author ..., 1791. 1st edn. Oblong folio. Engvd title, 2 letterpress ff subscribers, engvd index leaf, 59 plates. Rec buckram.
(Burmester) **£200 [≈ $356]**

The Alcoran of Mahomet ...
- See The Koran

Alexander, William
- An Experimental Enquiry concerning the Causes which have generally been said to produce Putrid Diseases. London: Becket & De Hondt, 1771. 8vo. [8],256 pp. 1 clean tear. Orig bds, uncut, rebacked, crnrs worn.
(Spelman) **£120 [≈ $214]**

Algarotti, Francesco, Count
- An Essay on Painting written in Italian. London: for L. Davis & C. Remers, 1764. 8vo. Contemp calf, rebacked.
(Waterfield's) **£150 [≈ $267]**

Alleine, Joseph
- The Saints Pocket Book. London: for J. Drew

& H. Stead, 1774. 12mo. Contemp calf, rebacked. *(Waterfield's)* **£55 [≈ $98]**

Allestree, Richard
- The Art of Patience under all Afflictions. London: for W. Cademan, 1684. 1st edn. Cr 8vo. [x],206 pp. Frontis. Old calf, rebacked, few faint marks. Wing A.1095. Anon.
(Ash) **£250 [≈ $445]**
- The Gentleman's Calling ... London: R. Norton for Robert Pawlet, 1676. 8vo. [24], 165,[1 blank],[2 advt] pp. Addtnl engvd title. Contemp calf. Wing A.1125. Anon.
(O'Neal) **$200 [≈ £112]**
- The Ladies Calling. In Two Parts. By the Author of The Whole Duty of Man ... Oxford: at the Theater, 1673. 1st edn. 8vo. [xxiv], 141,[iii], "95" [ie 103],[i] pp. Frontis (1st state). Contemp calf, rebacked. Wing A.1140. Anon. *(Vanbrugh)* **£245 [≈ $436]**
- The Lively Oracles given to us ... Third Edition. Oxford: At the Theater, 1679. 8vo. Imprimatur leaf. Addtnl engvd title. Contemp calf. Wing A.1152. Anon.
(Waterfield's) **£50 [≈ $89]**
- The Works of the Learned and Pious Author of The Whole Duty of Man. Oxford: at the Theater, 1684. Folio. [xv],456,[xi], 1-'240' [ie 238],[vi], 241-'322" [ie 320], [i,iv] pp. Frontis. Sl marks & damp stains. Mod qtr mor. Wing A.1082. Anon. *(Blackwell's)* **£75 [≈ $134]**
- The Works of the ... Author of The Whole Duty of Man. The Second Impression. Oxford: at the Theater, 1687. Folio. [xvi],456, [xii], 322,[vi] pp. Frontis, title vignette. Frontis marg reprd. Rec cloth. Wing A.1083. *(Clark)* **£60 [≈ $107]**

Almon, John
- Literary and Political Anecdotes of Several of the most Eminent Persons of the Present Age ... With an Appendix ... London: Longman & Seeley, 1797. 1st edn. 3 vols. 8vo. xi,408; viii,373; ii,410 pp. Orig tree calf, rebacked. Anon. *(Hartfield)* **$245 [≈ £138]**

Alston, Charles
- A Third Dissertation on Quick-Lime and Lime-Water. Edinburgh: 1757. 8vo. iv,46 pp. Disbound. *(Weiner)* **£100 [≈ $178]**

Altieri, Ferdinando
- A New Grammar, Italian-English, and English-Italian ... London: for William Innys, 1728. 1st edn. 8vo. [viii],416 pp. Contemp calf, sm cracks in jnts.
(Burmester) **£150 [≈ $267]**

Ambler, Charles
- Reports of Cases argued and determined in the High Court of Chancery ... London: Strahan & Woodfall, for T. Whieldon ..., 1790. 1st edn. Folio. Half-title. Errata. Contemp calf, spine worn, bds detached.
(Vanbrugh) £135 [≈ $240]

Ambrose, Isaac
- Prima, Media & Ultima: The First, Middle, and Last Things; in three Treatises ... London: for Webb & Grantham, 1654. 2nd combined edn. 4to. 4 secondary titles. Some fraying & damp staining. Contemp calf, worn. Wing A.2962.
(Clark) £140 [≈ $249]

Amhurst, Nicholas
- The British General; a Poem, sacred to the Memory of his Grace John, Duke of Marlborough. London: for R. Franklin, [1722]. 1st edn. 8vo. [8],31 pp, inc half-title. Cropped sgntr of Amhurst at end. Disbound.
(Hannas) £100 [≈ $178]
- Oculus Britanniae: an Heroi-Panegyricall Poem on the University of Oxford Illustrated with Divers Beautiful Similes and Useful Digrations. London: for R. Francklin, 1724. 8vo. Title sl dusty. Disbound. Anon.
(Waterfield's) £60 [≈ $107]

Amory, Thomas
- The Life of John Buncle, Esq; ... London: J. Noon, 1756. 1st edn. 8vo. ix,[vii],511,[i] pp. Title & last leaf v sl foxed, minor extreme fore edge marg worm. Contemp half calf, crnrs rubbed. Anon. *(Blackwell's)* £130 [≈ $231]

Ample ...
- An Ample Disquisition into the Nature of Regalities and Heretable Jurisdiction, in that Part of Great Britain call'd Scotland ... By an English Gentleman. London: for M. Cooper, 1747. 1st edn. 8vo. 51 pp. Disbound.
(Hannas) £85 [≈ $151]

Anacreon
- The Works ... Translated into English Verse ... added ... Sappho. With the Original Greek plac'd opposite to the Translation. By Mr Addison. London: John Watts, 1735. Fcap 8vo. [22],279,[1] pp. Frontis. Old water stain at end. Lib stamp on endpaper. Contemp calf, backstrip relaid. *(Spelman)* £30 [≈ $53]

Anderson, James
- The New Book of Constitutions of the Antient and Honourable Fraternity of Free and Accepted Masons ... London: Ward & Chandler, 1738. 4to. x,230,[1],[1 advt] pp.

Title torn without loss. Lacks a blank. Contemp calf. *(Fenning)* £75 [≈ $134]

Andrewes, Lancelot
- The Devotions of Bishop Andrews. Translated from the Greek by Dean [George] Stanhope. New Edition. London: Rivington, 1778. Sm 8vo. xl,191 pp. Some foxing & dust marking. Contemp tree calf, ft of spine v sl worn. *(Blackwell's)* £80 [≈ $142]
- A Manual of Private Devotions and Meditations. Translated out of a fair Greek MS. of his Amanuensis. By R. D[rake]. London: for Will. Freeman, 1692. 12mo. Addtnl engvd title. Contemp crimson mor gilt, a.e.g., extrs sl worn. Wing A.3139.
(Sanders) £75 [≈ $134]
- The Moral Law Expounded ... London: M. Sparke ..., 1642. 1st edn. Sm folio. [v],440, 729-855, 136,[ii],59 pp, complete. Port (creased & discold). Contemp calf, 19th c reback. Wing A.3140.
(Blackwell's) £95 [≈ $169]
- XCVI. Sermons ... The second edition ... London: Richard Badger, 1632. Folio. Port frontis (trimmed & mtd with sl loss). Occas sl staining. 1 sm repr. *(Clark)* £250 [≈ $445]
- XCVI Sermons ... The Fifth Edition ... London: Printed in the Year of Our Lord God, 1661. Roy 4to. [xii],[40], 21-794,[xiv] pp. Contemp calf, sl wear to lower bd with loss of leather. This imprint not in Wing.
(Sotheran's) £485 [≈ $863]

Andrews, James Pettit
- The History of Great Britain connected with the Chronology of Europe. London: for T. Cadell, 1794. 2 vols in one. 4to. Title vignettes, 4 fldg tables. Mod qtr calf, red label. *(Waterfield's)* £120 [≈ $214]

Andrews, John, Vicar of South Newington
- The Kebla: or, a Defence of Eastward Adoration. In a Letter to the Author of Alkibla. [Bound with] The Kebla. Part II ... London: for J. Batley, 1728-29. 1st edns. 2 vols in one. 8vo. 39; [iv],68 pp. 19th c half calf, uncut. *(Burmester)* £58 [≈ $103]

Andrews, John
- A Comparative View of the French and English Nations, in their Manners, Politics, and Literature. London: Longman, Robinson, 1785. 488 pp. Orig calf, lacks label, spine rubbed. *(C.R. Johnson)* £125 [≈ $223]
- History of the War with America ... London: 1785-86. 4 vols. ii,448; 449; 445; 416,[70] pp. 6 fldg maps, 1 other map, 24 plates. Sl tanning & foxing, occas marg worming. Later

three qtr calf, jnts worn, hd of 2 spines sl chipped.   *(Reese)* **$1,250 [≃ £702]**
- Letters to a Young Gentleman, on his setting out for France ... Directions for Travellers ... London: for J. Walter & W. Brown, 1784. 1st edn. 8vo. [xvi],576 pp. Orig bds, uncut & unopened, minor reprs.
          (Burmester) **£150 [≃ $267]**
- Remarks on the French and English Ladies, in a Series of Letters. London: Longman & Robinson, 1783. Half-title, 360 pp. Contemp calf, lacks label, spine rubbed.
          (C.R. Johnson) **£140 [≃ $249]**
- Remarks on the French and English Ladies, in a Series of Letters ... Dublin: for Walker, Beatty ..., 1783. 1st Dublin edn. Half-title. Contemp calf, sl rubbed, leather torn away from 1 crnr.   *(Hannas)* **£140 [≃ $249]**

Anecdotes ...
- Anecdotes of the Life of the Right Hon. William Pitt, Earl of Chatham ... Dublin: P. Wogan ..., 1792. 1st Irish edn. 2 vols. xiv, 402; half-title, vi, 433 pp. Fldg table vol 2. Contemp calf, gilt spine, sl wear 1 jnt.
          (Jermy & Westerman) **£75 [≃ $134]**

Angelo, Domenico Angelo Malevote Trememondo
- The School of Fencing. With a General Explanation of the Principal Attitudes and Positions Peculiar to the Art. London: for S. Hooper, 1765. 1st edn in English. Oblong folio. English & French titles & text. 63,[5] pp. 47 engvs. Some foxing. 19th c cloth, rebacked.   *(Chapel Hill)* **$2,500 [≃ £1,404]**

Anglesey, The Earl of
- The King's Right of Indulgence in Spiritual Matters with the Equity thereof, asserted. London: 1688. 1st edn. 4to. 75 pp. Mod wraps. Wing A.3169. Anon.
          (Robertshaw) **£25 [≃ $45]**

Angus, W.
- The Seats of the Nobility and Gentry in Great Britain and Wales. Engraved by W. Angus. Islington: W. Angus, 1787. Oblong 8vo. 63 engvd views. Sl foxed. Contemp gilt dec straight grained mor, a.e.g., crnrs & extrs rubbed, jnts worn.
          (Hermitage) **$400 [≃ £225]**

Annals ...
- The Annals of King James and King Charles the First ... see Frankland, Thomas.

The Annual Anthology ...
- See Southey, Robert (editor).

Anstey, Christopher
- The New Bath Guide: Or Memoirs of the B-N-R-D Family. In a Series of Poetical Epistles ... London: Dodsley, 1784. 12th edn. 8vo. viii,175 pp. Frontis. Occas spotting. Calf backed bds. Anon.   *(Young's)* **£25 [≃ $45]**

Answer ...
- An Answer to Pereat Papa: or, a Reply by way of Letter from a Gentlewoman to a Person of Quality; commending to her consideration a Paper Entituled Pereat Papa ... [London: 1681?]. 1st edn. Folio. Drop-head title. 4 pp. Brown-stained. Disbound. Wing A.3372.
          (Hannas) **£35 [≃ $62]**

Anthologia Hibernica ...
- Anthologia Hibernica: or Monthly Collections of Science, Belles-Lettres, and History. Illustrated with Beautiful Engravings. Dublin: 1793-94. 4 vols. 8vo. Subscribers. Index. Plates. Contemp half calf, rebacked.   *(de Burca)* **£245 [≃ $436]**

The Anti-Jacobin ...
- Poetry of the Anti-Jacobin. London: for J. Wright, 1799. 1st edn. Sm 8vo. Lacks half-title. Early polished calf gilt, fine.
          (Hannas) **£95 [≃ $169]**

Anti-Machiavel ...
- See Frederick II, King of Prussia

Appeal ...
- An Appeal to the Public; in Relation to the Tobacco ***: And a Revival of the Old Project, to establish a General Excise. London: for W. Owen, 1751. 1st edn. 8vo. 63 pp. Disbound.   *(Hannas)* **£200 [≃ $356]**

Appeale ...
- An Appeale to the World in these Times of Extreme Danger. [London: 1642]. 4to. Caption title. Stitched. Wing A.3569.
          (Rostenberg & Stern) **$85 [≃ £48]**

Appian
- The History of Appian of Alexandria, in Two Parts ... Made English by J.D. [John Dancer]. London: for John Amery, 1679. 1st edn of this translation. 4to. [xiv],251, 273,[i advt] pp. Sm hole through H4 & 4F2. Rec qtr calf. Wing A.3579.   *(Sotheran's)* **£285 [≃ $507]**

An Arabian Tale ...
- See Beckford, William

Arbuthnot, J.
- Miscellaneous Works. With an Account of

the Author's Life. London: 1770. 2nd edn. 2 vols. xvi,246; 310 pp. Half mor, a.e.g., rather worn. *(Whitehart)* **£140 [≈ $249]**

Arbuthnot, John

- An Appendix to John Bull Still in His Senses: or, Law is a Bottomless-Pit. Printed from a Manuscript found in the Cabinet of the famous Sir Humphry Polesworth ... London: for John Morphew, 1712. 1st edn. 8vo. 22,[2 advt] pp. Trimmed close, no loss. Disbound. Anon. *(Young's)* **£85 [≈ $151]**

- An Essay concerning the Nature of Aliments, and the Choice of Them, according to the Different Constitutions of Human Bodies ... Third Edition, to which are added, Practical Rules of Diet ... London: 1735. 8vo. 436 pp. Contemp calf, sl rubbed.
  (Robertshaw) **£95 [≈ $169]**

- John Bull in his Senses: being the Second Part of Law is a Bottomless-Pit ... London: for John Morphew, 1712. 1st edn. 8vo. 24 pp. Cut close. Last page rubbed with sl loss. Disbound. Anon. *(Young's)* **£85 [≈ $151]**

- John Bull still in his Senses: being the Third Part of Law is a Bottomless-Pit ... London: for John Morphew, 1712. 1st edn. 8vo. 47,[1 advt] pp. Some page numerals cropped. Disbound. Anon. *(Young's)* **£85 [≈ $151]**

- Law is a Bottomless-Pit ... London: for John Morphew, 1712. 1st edn. 8vo. 24 pp. Head mrgs shaved close, some staining. Sm hole in last leaf affecting 2 letters. Disbound. Anon.
  (Young's) **£100 [≈ $178]**

- Law is a Bottomless-Pit ... London: for John Morphew, 1712. 2nd edn. 8vo. 24 pp. Disbound. Anon. *(Young's)* **£70 [≈ $125]**

- Lewis Baboon turned Honest, and John Bull Politician. Being the Fourth Part of Law is a Bottomless-Pit ... London: for John Morphew, 1712. 1st edn. 8vo. [vi],37,2 advt pp. Disbound. Anon.
  (Young's) **£140 [≈ $249]**

- Tables of Antient Coins, Weights, and Measures ... London: 1754. 327,43 pp. Fldg chart. Calf, worn. *(King)* **$125 [≈ £70]**

Archenholtz, Johann Wilhelm von

- A Picture of Italy. Translated from the Original German ... by Joseph Trapp. Dublin: W. Corbet for P. Byrne ..., 1791. 12mo. xii, 327 pp. Contemp calf, red label.
  (Frew Mackenzie) **£90 [≈ $160]**

Archer, James

- Sermons on Various Moral and Religious Subjects. Second Edition. London: Sampson Low for E. Booker, 1794. 4 vols. 8vo. Occas

foxing. Contemp qtr calf, vellum crnrs, some chipping to labels, minor rubbing.
  (Spelman) **£25 [≈ $45]**

Arderne, James

- A Sermon Preached at the Visitation of the Right Reverend Father in God, John Lord Bishop of Chester, at Chester ... London: 1677. 1st edn. 4to. [iv],19 pp. Disbound. Wing A.3625. *(Young's)* **£50 [≈ $89]**

Argument ...

- An Argument Concerning the Militia ... see Savile, George.

Aristophanes

- The Frogs, a Comedy. Translated from the Greek by C.D. [Charles Dunster]. Oxford: for J. & J. Fletcher, [1785]. 8vo. Disbound.
  (Waterfield's) **£100 [≈ $178]**

Aristotle

- Aristotle's Rhetoric; or the True Grounds and Principles of Oratory ... Made English by the Translators of the Art of Thinking. London: T.B. for Randal Taylor, 1686. 1st English edn. 8vo. [12],280,[7] pp. Intl licence leaf. Contemp calf, reprd. Wing A.3695.
  (Spelman) **£480 [≈ $854]**

- Aristotle's Rhetoric; or the True Grounds and Principles of Oratory ... The Second Edition ... London: S. Briscoe, 1693. 8vo. [12],280,[7] pp. Intl licence leaf. Title-leaf a cancel. Contemp calf, rebacked. Wing A.3696.
  (Spelman) **£320 [≈ $570]**

- A Treatise on Government. Translated from the Greek ... By William Ellis. London: for T. Payne ..., 1776. 1st edn of this translation. 4to. xviii,428,[14] pp. Contemp polished calf, gilt spine, hinges strengthened.
  (O'Neal) **$225 [≈ £126]**

Aristotle's Last Legacy ...

- Aristotle's Last Legacy: Unfolding the Mysteries of Nature in the Generation of Man ... London: for R.G. & sold by the booksellers, 1712. 1st edn. 12mo. [iv],112 pp. Frontis. Sm repr 1 leaf. Last leaf sl stained. Contemp sheep.
  (David White) **£150 [≈ $267]**

Arlington, Henry Bennet, 1st Earl of

- The Right Honourable the Earl of Arlington's Letters to Sir W. Temple, Bar. From July 1665 ... to September, 1670 ... London: sold by Tho. Bennet, 1701. 1st edn. 8vo. [viii],454 pp. Port. Occas minor crnr damp stain. Contemp calf, gilt dec spine, rubbed, gilt faded. *(Clark)* **£65 [≈ $116]**

Armstrong, John
- The Art of Preserving Health: a Poem. In Four Books. London: 1748. 3rd edn. 128 pp. Leather, front bd detached.
    (Fye) **$125 [≃ £70]**
- Miscellanies. London: for T. Cadell, 1770. 1st edn. 2 vols. 8vo. Contemp mottled calf, gilt spines, sl worn. *(Ximenes)* **$150 [≃ £84]**
- Miscellanies. London: for T. Cadell, 1770. 1st edn. 2 vols. Sm 8vo. Leaf O7 vol 1 is a cancel. Contemp polished calf.
    (Hannas) **£110 [≃ $196]**
- The Oeconomy of Love. A Poetical Essay. New Edition. London: 1756. Sm 4to. Contemp calf, rubbed, jnts cracked. Anon.
    (Robertshaw) **£20 [≃ $36]**

Arnauld, Antoine & Nicole, Pierre
- Logic; or, the Art of Thinking ... Done from the new French Edition. By Mr. Ozell. London: for William Taylor, 1717. 1st edn of this translation. 8vo. [xii],215, 240-452,[4 advt] pp. Frontis. Rec qtr calf. Anon.
    (Burmester) **£140 [≃ $249]**

Arnot, Hugo
- A Collection and Abridgement of Celebrated Criminal Trials in Scotland, from A.D. 1536, to 1784 ... Edinburgh: for the author by William Smellie, 1785. 1st edn. 4to. xxiii, [i],400 pp. 13 pp subscribers. Occas marks. 19th c half calf, sl worn.
    (Clark) **£120 [≃ $214]**

Art ...
- The Art of Cookery, made Plain and Easy ... see Glasse, Hannah.
- Art of Drawing and Painting in Water-Colours. Wherein the Principles of Drawing are laid down, after a Natural and Easy Manner ... Fifth Edition. London: G. Keith, 1779. Sm 8vo. 96 pp. 2 fldg plates. Some marg soiling & creasing. Contemp wraps.
    (Spelman) **£120 [≃ $214]**
- The Art of Manual Defence; or, System of Boxing: perspicuously explained ... By a Pupil both of Humphreys and Mendoza. London: for G. Kearsley, 1789. 3rd edn. 12mo. [v], 8-9, [iv], xiv-xxxv, [i], 133,[9] pp. 10 plates inc frontis. Contemp half calf, rebacked, rubbed. *(Burmester)* **£450 [≃ $801]**
- The Art of Painting in Miniature ... Translated from the Original French. The Sixth Edition. To which ... added ... London: for J. Hodges & M. Cooper, 1752. 12mo. x,150,[vi] pp. Frontis, 1 plate. Contemp sheep, spine worn but sound.
    (Burmester) **£110 [≃ $196]**

- The Art of Patience under all Afflictions ... see Allestree, Richard.
- The Art of Politicks, in Imitation of Horace's Art of Poetry ... see Bramston, James.
- The Art of Singing: or, a Short and Easy Method, for obtaining a Perfect Knowledge of the Gregorian Note. London: for T. Meighan, 1748. 1st edn. 12mo. Disbound, sl loose.   *(Ximenes)* **$900 [≃ £506]**
- The Art of Speaking ... see Lamy, Bernard

The Artificial Clock-Maker ...
- See Derham, William

Arwaker, Edmund (translator)
- Truth in Fiction: or, Morality in Masquerade. A Collection of ... Fables of Aesop, and Others. Done into English Verse ... London: for J. Churchill, 1708. 1st edn. 8vo. Final advt leaf. Sl worm lower marg. Contemp panelled calf, roughly rebacked.
    (Hannas) **£65 [≃ $116]**

Ascham, Roger
- The English Works ... Toxophilus ... The Schoolmaster ... With Notes ... Life, by James Bennett. London: Dodsley, 1761. 1st edn. 4to. 4,[4 subscribers],xvi,395 pp. Vertical crease title & dedic. Contemp calf, backstrip relaid.   *(Gough)* **£195 [≃ $347]**
- The Scholemaster ... Now revised a second time, and much improved, by James Upton. London: for W. Innys, 1743. 8vo. xxii,274 pp. Contemp calf, rebacked, sides rubbed.
    (Burmester) **£120 [≃ $214]**
- The Schoolmaster: or, a Plain and Perfect Way of teaching Children to understand, write and speak the Latin Tongue. Now corrected ... by the Reverend Mr. Kames Upton. London: Benj. Tooke, 1711. 8vo. [xii],xiii,[i], 212,[2], 40,[4] pp. Half-title. Contemp calf, jnts sl cracked.
    (Burmester) **£150 [≃ $267]**

Asgill, John
- An Argument proving, That according to the Covenant of Eternal Life revealed in the Scriptures, Man may be translated from hence into that Eternal Life, without passing through Death ... London: Anno Dom. 1700. 1st edn. 8vo. 106 pp. Contemp calf, extrs worn. Wing A.3926. *(Clark)* **£100 [≃ $178]**
- An Essay on a Registry for Title of Lands. London: printed in the year 1698. 34 pp. Rec wraps.   *(C.R. Johnson)* **£125 [≃ $223]**

Ash, John
- Grammatical Institutes: or, an Easy

Introduction to Dr. Lowth's Grammar: designed for the use of Schools ... New Edition, Corrected and Improved. London: C. Dilly ..., 1796. xxiv,171,[9] pp. Contemp sheep, rebacked.
(C.R. Johnson) £165 [≈ $294]

Ashdowne, William

- The Unitarian, Arian, and Trinitarian Opinion concerning Christ, examined and tryed by Scripture Evidence alone. Canterbury: J. Grove, 1789. 8vo. Disbound.
(Waterfield's) £40 [≈ $71]

Ashe, John

- A Second Letter sent from John Ashe Esquire ... to the Honourable William Lenthall ... London: A.N. for Ed. Husbands, 1642. 1st edn. Sm 4to. 8 pp. Faint marg browning. Mod wraps. Wing A.3946.
(Blackwell's) £45 [≈ $80]

Ashe, Thomas

- Le Primier [& Second] Volume del Promptuarie ... London: John Beale, 1614. 1st edn. 2 vols. Sl browned. Mod polished calf. STC 840.5.
(Meyer Boswell) $1,200 [≈ £674]

Ashley, John

- The Sugar Trade with the Incumbrances thereon Laid Open. By A Barbadoes Planter. London: Peele, 1734. 12mo. [6],22 pp. 2 fldg tables. Later half leather.
(McBlain) $185 [≈ £104]

Ashmole, Elias

- The Antiquities of Berkshire ... London: for E. Curll, 1719. 1st edn. 3 vols. 8vo. Errata leaf vol 2. Fldg port, fldg map, 1 plate, 11 fldg sheets vol 3. Some browning. Early 19th c blue mor gilt, a.e.g., v sl sunned & rubbed.
(Georges) £600 [≈ $1,068]
- The Institution, Laws & Ceremonies of the Most Noble Order of the Garter ... London: 1672. 1st edn. Lge folio. Privilege & errata ff. "29th of May 1674" leaf. Erratic pagination. 31 plates. Early 19th elab gilt c blue mor. Wing A.3983. *(Vanbrugh)* £755 [≈ $1,344]

Ashmole, Elias & Lilly, William

- The Lives of those Eminent Antiquaries ... With Several Occasional Letters, [edited] By Charles Burman. London: T. Davies, 1774. 1st edn thus. 8vo. 7,[i],399,[i] pp. Occas browning & foxing, sm piece torn from crnr of title. Rec qtr calf, untrimmed.
(Clark) £110 [≈ $196]

Astell, Mary

- An Essay in Defence of the Female Sex ... In a letter to a Lady. Written by a Lady. London: Roper, Wilkinson, Clavel, 1696. 1st edn. 8vo. Frontis (sl shaved at hd). Contemp mottled calf, lower jnt splitting. Wing A.4058. Anon. Also attributed to Judith Drake or H. Wyatt. *(Hannas)* £360 [≈ $641]
- An Essay in Defence of the Female Sex ... The Third Edition with Additions. London: Roper, Clavel, 1697. 8vo. Frontis. Name cut from blank marg of title. Contemp panelled sheep, somewhat worn. Wing A.4060. Anon.
(Hannas) £250 [≈ $445]

Astruc, John

- A Treatise of the Venereal Disease ... Translated from the Latin by William Barrow. London: for W. Innys, 1737. 1st English edn. 2 vols. 8vo. Contemp calf, backstrips relaid. *(Appelfeld)* $275 [≈ £154]

Atkins, John

- A Voyage to Guinea, Brasil and the West Indies ... London: for Ward & Chandler, 1735. 265,[i errata],[6 advt] pp. Title vignette. Some browning, minor soiling. 1 leaf loose. Rebound in half calf, v sl rubbed.
(Francis Edwards) £285 [≈ $507]

Atkinson, Frederick (compiler)

- The Banquet of Thalia, of the Fashionable Songsters Pocket Memorial ... York: from the Herald Office by Wilson, Spence & Mawman, 1790. Engvd title, 216 pp. Contemp tree calf, black label, spine sl rubbed. Anon.
(C.R. Johnson) £125 [≈ $223]

Atkyns, Sir Robert

- A Defence of the Late Lord Russel's Innocency, by way of Answer or Confutation of a Libellous Pamphlet ... London: 1689. 1st edn. Folio. 51 pp. Disbound. Wing A.4136.
(Robertshaw) £24 [≈ $43]

Atterbury, Francis

- The Rights, Powers, and Priviledges, of an English Convocation, Stated and Vindicated ... London: Tho. Bennet, 1700. 8vo. 1st edn. 8vo. [xxxii],272, (273)-(294), 273-516 pp. Fldg type-facs (sm tear). Contemp calf, worn, front bd detached. Wing A.4151. Anon.
(Clark) £40 [≈ $71]
- Sermons and Discourses on Several Subjects and Occasions. The Seventh Edition. London: Davis & Reymers, 1761. 4 vols. 8vo. Port. Contemp calf, gilt spines, labels chipped, hd of spines sl worn.
(Blackwell's) £85 [≈ $151]

Atterbury, Lewis

- A Sermon Preach'd at Whitehall, on Thursday, June 7, 1716 ... London: for J. Roberts, 1716. 1st edn. 8vo in 4s. Last leaf loose. Disbound, untrimmed.
(Sanders) £18 [≈ $32]

An Attorney's Practice Epitomized ...

- An Attorney's Practice Epitomized; or the Method, Time and Expences of Proceedings in the Courts of King's Bench and Common Pleas ... Ninth Edition. London: Catherine Lintot ..., 1759. 8vo. Some damp stains. Contemp qtr sheep.
(Meyer Boswell) $350 [≈ £197]

Aulnoy, Marie Catherine, Comtesse d'

- The Lady's Travels into Spain; or a Genuine Relation of the Religion, Laws, Commerce, Customs and Manners of that Country ... Written by the Countess of Danois ... New Edition ... London: 1774. 2 vols. 8vo. Sl wear & tear. Contemp half calf, sl worn.
(Burmester) £90 [≈ $160]
- The Prince of Carency; a Novel. Written in French ... Translated into English. London: W. Wilkins, for J. Peele, 1719. 1st edn in English. 8vo. [iv],382 pp. Contemp speckled calf.
(Burmester) £250 [≈ $445]
- Queen Mab: Containing a Select Collection of ... Tales of the Fairies ... Third Edition. London: Dodsley, 1782. 12mo. iv,368 pp. Engvd frontis, 9 w'cuts in text. Rebound in half calf, gilt spine. *(Karmiole)* $125 [≈ £70]

Ayloffe, Sir John

- Calendars of the Ancient Charters, and of the Welch and Scotish Rolls, now remaining in the Tower of London ... London: for Benjamin White, 1774. 4to. 4 engvd facs, 4 engvd medallions in the text. Contemp tree calf, elab gilt flat back, yellow edges, sl used.
(Blackwell's) £145 [≈ $258]

Ayscough, George Edward

- Letters from an Officer in the Guards to his Friends in England: containing some Account of France and Italy. London: T. Cadell, 1778. 1st edn. 8vo. [iv],234,[ii] pp. Half-title. Final advt leaf. Contemp sheep, crudely rebacked, extrs sl worn. Anon.   *(Clark)* £65 [≈ $116]

Ayscough, Samuel

- An Index to the Remarkable Passages and Words made use of by Shakspeare. Dublin: for William Jones, 1791. 1st Dublin edn. Title foxed. Contemp half calf, worn.
(Hannas) £35 [≈ $62]
- An Index to the Remarkable Passages and Words: made use of Shakspeare ... Dublin: for W. Jones, 1791. 1st Irish edn. Roy 8vo. [2], 1083-1754 pp. Contemp calf gilt, gilt spine, sl rubbed.   *(Fenning)* £45 [≈ $80]

B., A.

- A Letter from a Friend in Abingdon, to A Gentleman in London, concerning The Election of Burgesses for the ensuing Parliament [caption title]. No imprint, [1679]. Folio. 4 pp. Minor soiling. Disbound. Wing B.11.   *(Clark)* £65 [≈ $116]

B., A.J.

- What Kinde of Parliament will please the King; and how well he is affected to this present Parliament. Gathered out of his owne Papers ... London: printed, 1642. 1st edn. Sm 4to. [i],6 pp. Stitched into mod wraps. Wing B.35.   *(Blackwell's)* £45 [≈ $80]
- What kinde of Parliament will please the King. London: 1642. 4to. Stitched. Wing B.35.   *(Rostenberg & Stern)* $100 [≈ £56]

B., J.

- Some Reflections upon the Earl of Danby, in relation to the Murther of Sir Edmondbury Godfrey. In a Letter to a friend. [London: 1679]. 1st edn. Folio. Drop-head title. 4 pp. Disbound. Wing B.127.
(Hannas) £35 [≈ $62]

Babington, Gervase

- The Works ... Late Bishop of Worcester ... London: Miles Flesher, 1637. 3rd edn. Folio. General title & sev sep titles. Port frontis. Fldg table. Contemp calf, lacks label, sl worn, front hinge half cracked but firm. STC 1080.
(Vanbrugh) £275 [≈ $490]

Babington, Zachary

- Advice to Grand Jurors in Cases of Blood. London: for John Amery ..., 1677. 1st edn. Contemp sheep, rebacked. Wing B.248.
(Meyer Boswell) $450 [≈ £253]

Bacon, Sir Francis

- Certain Considerations touching the better Pacification and Edification of the Church of England: Dedicated to his most Excellent Majestie. N.p.: 1640. STC 1123. Anon.   *(Robertshaw)* £50 [≈ $89]
- Certaine Miscellany Works ... Published by William Rawley ... London: I. Haviland for Humphrey Robinson, 1629. 1st edn. Sm 4to. Intl blank. Sl browning. Rec antique style calf. STC 1124.   *(Georges)* £650 [≈ $1,157]
- The Elements of the Common Lavves of England ... London: assigns of John More,

1639. 3rd edn. Sm 4to. [xx],94, [viii],72 pp. General title & 2 sep titles. Minor worm affecting text of 3 ff. Contemp sheep, rebacked. STC 1136.
(Vanbrugh) **£375 [≃ $668]**

- The Historie of the Raigne of King Henry the Seventh ... London: Stansby for Lownes & Barret, 1622. 1st edn. Tall 4to. viii,248 pp. Intl blank. Port (remargd), engvd title (sl soiled). Contemp calf gilt, sl rubbed, crnrs worn, rebacked to style. STC 1159.
(Hollett) **£250 [≃ $445]**

- The Historie of the Reign of King Henry the Seventh ... London: ... sold by Philemon Stevens & Christopher Meredith, 1629. 3rd edn, 2nd issue. Folio. [xiv],248 pp. W"cut title (edges sl worn, sl dust soiled). Contemp vellum, sl distressed. STC 1161.
(Vanbrugh) **£425 [≃ $757]**

- The Historie of the Reigne of King Henry the Seventh. London: R.Y. & R.H., & sold by R. Meighan, 1641. 3rd edn. Sm folio. [14],248 pp. Frontis port (blank marg frayed), dec title. Contemp calf, rebacked to style. Wing B.229
(O'Neal) **£325 [≃ £183]**

- History Natural and Experimental, of Life and Death. Or of the Prolongation of Life ... London: John Haviland for William Lee, and Humphry Moseley, 1638. 24mo. Imprimatur leaf at beginning and at end. Some foxing & browning. New calf, old bds laid down.
(Goodrich) **$595 [≃ £334]**

- The History of Henry VII of England, Written in the Year 1616 ... London: for the editor at the Logographic Press, 1786. 1st edn thus 8vo. iv,288,4 pp. Rec half calf.
(Young's) **£42 [≃ $75]**

- Of the Advancement and Proficiencie of Learning ... Oxford: Leon. Lichfield ..., 1640. 1st complete edn in English. Translated by G. Watts. Folio. Port frontis (altered by a Victorian hand), addtnl engvd title. Lacks colophon leaf. Contemp sheep. STC 1167.
(Vanbrugh) **£525 [≃ $935]**

- Of the Advancement and Proficiencie of Learning ... Interpreted by Gilbert Wats. London: for Thomas Williams, 1674. 2nd Watts edn. Folio. Port frontis. Contemp calf, rebacked. Wing B.312.
(Vanbrugh) **£375 [≃ $668]**

- Of the Advancement and Proficiencie of Learning: or the Partition of Sciences. Nine Books. London: for Thomas Williams, 1674. Folio. Frontis. Contemp calf, crnrs worn, front jnt cracked. Buckram slipcase. Wing B.312. *(Waterfield's)* **£165 [≃ $294]**

- Of the Advancement and Proficiencie of Learning: or the Partitions of Sciences ... London: T. Williams, 1674. Sm folio.

[32],38, [14],322,[20] pp. Frontis port. Contemp speckled calf, rebacked. Cloth box. Wing B.312. *(O'Neal)* **$450 [≃ £253]**

- Sylva Sylvarum: or, A Naturall History ... London: J.F. for William Lee, 1651. Folio. Port frontis, addtnl engvd title. Occas sl damp stain, edges of 1st 2 ff brittle. Contemp calf, Victorian reback. Wing B.327.
(Vanbrugh) **£425 [≃ $757]**

- The Two Books ... Of the Proficiencie and Advancement of Learning, Divine and Humane. Oxford: 1633. 3rd edn. 4to. [ii],335 pp. 19th c calf backed bds, rebacked. STC 1166. *(Vanbrugh)* **£345 [≃ $614]**

Bacon, Sir Francis & Godwyn, Francis

- The History of the Reigns of Henry the Seventh, Henry the Eighth, Edward the Sixth, and Queen Mary ... London: 1676. 1st edn. Folio. [xii],138, [xii],151, [iii],155-201 pp. General title dated 1676, 3 sep titles dated 1675. Port frontis. Contemp calf, rebacked. Wing B.300. *(Vanbrugh)* **£395 [≃ $703]**

Bacon, Nathaniel

- An Historical and Political Discourse of the Laws and Government of England, from the First Times to the Reign of Queen Elizabeth ... London: for D. Browne, 1760. 5th edn. 4to. xix,203,185 pp. Last few ff sl soiled. Old cloth. *(Young's)* **£60 [≃ $107]**

- The History of the Life and Actions of St. Athanasius together with the ... Arian Heresie ... By N.B.P.C. Catholick. London: Maxwell for Eccleston, 1664. Frontis. Some crnr damage, sl browning. Mod qtr calf. Wing B.351. Anon. Attribution questioned.
(Waterfield's) **£90 [≃ $160]**

Bage, Michael

- Hermsprong; or, Man As He Is Not. A Novel ... London: for William Lane, at the Minerva-Press, 1796. 1st edn. 3 vols. 8vo. Half-titles. Some marg worm, marg tear. Occas browning. Contemp half calf, uncut, sometime rebacked, rubbed. Michael Sadleir's booklabels. *(Finch)* **£680 [≃ $1,210]**

Baglivi, Girogi

- The Practice of Physick, Reduc'd to the ancient Way of Observations ... The Second Edition. London: Midwinter ..., 1723. 8vo. xvi,431 pp. Occas browning. New qtr calf.
(Goodrich) **$250 [≃ £140]**

Bagshaw, Edward

- The Rights of the Crown of England as it is Established by Law. London: Miller, 1660. 8vo. 6 advt pp at end. Vertical title on last

page. Frontis. Calf. Wing B.397.
(Rostenberg & Stern) **$425 [≈ £239]**

Bailey, Nathaniel
- An Universal Etymological English Dictionary ... Third Edition, with large additions. London: for J. Darby, A Bettesworth ..., 1726. Thick 8vo. Title sl soiled with sm tear at ft. Last leaf creased. Lacks endpapers. Contemp calf, used.
(Burmester) **£60 [≈ $107]**
- An Universal Etymological Dictionary ... The Fourteenth Edition, with considerable Improvements. London: R. Ware ..., 1751. 8vo. Some use & pen-trials. Contemp reversed sheep, rubbed, sm nick in spine, lib mark on spine.   *(Clark)* **£50 [≈ $89]**
- An Universal Etymological English Dictionary ... Seventeenth Edition, with considerable improvements. London: 1759. Roy 8vo. Rear endpapers v sl wormed. Endpapers sl water stained. Calf gilt, crnrs worn, spine ends sl bumped with sm split at hd.   *(Francis Edwards)* **£50 [≈ $89]**

Baillie, John
- A Letter to Dr. ------- in Answer to a Tract in the Bibliotheque Ancienne & Moderne, relating to some Passages in Dr. Freind's History of Physick ... London: J. Roberts, 1728. 8vo. [iv],80 pp. Half-title & title browned. Rec bds. *(Goodrich)* **$295 [≈ £160]**

Baily, Thomas
- The Life & Death of that renowned John Fisher, Bishop of Rochester ... see Hall, Richard.

Baine, James
- The Theatre Licentious and Perverted. Or, a Sermon for Reformation of Manners ... Inscribed to Samuel Foote, Esq. Edinburgh: printed by J. Reid ..., 1770. 2nd edn. 8vo. 40 pp. Disbound.   *(Burmester)* **£125 [≈ $223]**

Baker, J.
- The History of the Inquisition as it subsists in the Kingdom of Spain, Portugal, &c. and in both the Indies to this day. London: Marshall, Davies, Spencer, 1734. 4to. 4 plates. Blank strip cut from title. Contemp calf, rebacked. *(Waterfield's)* **£145 [≈ $258]**

Baker, Sir Richard
- A Chronicle of the Kings of England ... London: for H. Sawbridge, 1684. 8th edn. Folio. [xlviii],750,42 pp. Addtnl engvd title (sl edgeworn). Old calf, rebacked. Wing B.509.   *(Young's)* **£85 [≈ $151]**

Baker, Thomas
- Reflections upon Learning ... The Fourth Edition. London: A. Bosvile, 1708. 8vo. [16], 295 pp. Minor marg browning. Contemp calf, backstrip relaid.   *(Spelman)* **£70 [≈ $125]**

Balcarres, Colin Lindsay, 3rd Earl of
- An Account of the Affairs of Scotland, relating to the Revolution in 1688 ... London: for J. Barker ..., 1714. 1st edn. 8vo. [iv],16,vi, 150,[2 advt] pp. B4v of the Key (for J. Moor) soiled. Disbound. Anon.
(Young's) **£95 [≈ $169]**

Balguy, Thomas
- Divine Benevolence asserted; and vindicated from the Objections of Ancient and Modern Sceptics. London: for Lockyer Davis, 1781. 8vo. Disbound. *(Waterfield's)* **£65 [≈ $116]**

Ball, John
- A Friendly Triall of the Grounds tending to Separation ... Cambridge: Roger Daniel, for Edward Brewster, 1640. 1st edn. 4to. [xvi],314,[4] pp. Minor stains. Contemp sheep, extrs worn, rubbed, minor loss hd of spine, no endpapers. STC 1313.
(Clark) **£90 [≈ $160]**

Balzac, Jean Louis Guez de
- New Epistles ... [bound with] A Svpply to the Second Part; or The Third Part of the Letters. London: Crooke, Eglesfield, & Serger, 1638. 4 parts in one vol. 8vo. Engvd title. Vellum. STC 12454.
(Rostenberg & Stern) **$300 [≈ £169]**

Bancroft, John
- The Tragedy of Sertorius. Acted at the Theatre-Royal. London: for R. Bentley & M. Magnes, 1679. 1st edn. 4to. Title cut short & mtd, some head-lines shaved. Paper v spotted & sl water stained. Lacks intl leaf (probably blank). Disbound. Wing B.636.
(Hannas) **£100 [≈ $178]**

Banks, John
- The History of the Life and Reign of the late Czar Peter the Great, Emperor of all Russia. London: 1740. 12mo. 346,index pp. Port. Contemp calf, spine ends sl worn. Anon.
(Robertshaw) **£32 [≈ $57]**
- The History of the Life and Reign of William III, King of England ... London: Marsh & Davies, 1744. 1st edn. 12mo. viii, [ii],1-96, 121-362,[xii] pp. Final advt leaf. Contemp calf, backstrip relaid, label defective, crnrs sl worn. Anon.   *(Clark)* **£45 [≈ $80]**

Banks, John, Lecturer in Experimental Philosophy
- A Treatise on Mills, in Four Parts ... Kendal: W. Richardson & W. Pennington, 1795. 1st edn. 8vo. [iii]-xxiv,172,[iv] pp. Lacks half-title. 3 fldg plates. Sm stain ft of 1 leaf. Extreme margs dusty. Rec qtr calf, rough trimmed. *(Blackwell's)* **£150 [≈ $267]**

The Banquet of Thalia ...
- See Atkinson, Frederick

Barbauld, Anna Laetitia, nee Aikin
- Poems. London: for Joseph Johnson, 1773. 1st edn. 2nd issue, with the errata crrctd & H3 a cancel. 4to. Blank crnr of title reprd. Mod qtr mor, vellum crnrs. Anon. *(Hannas)* **£160 [≈ $285]**

Barclay, Revd James
- A Complete and Universal Dictionary on a New Plan. London: Richardson & Urquhart, 1774. 1st edn. Frontis. Contemp calf, v worn, bds held by cords. *(Jermy & Westerman)* **£75 [≈ $134]**

Barclay, Robert
- The Anarchy of the Ranters, and other Libertines, the Hierarchy of the Romanists, and other pretended Churches, equally refused and refuted ... London: Mary Hinde, 1771. 8vo. viii,113,[3 advt] pp. Old qtr calf, rebacked. *(Young's)* **£40 [≈ $71]**
- An Apology for the True Christian Divinity ... Aberdeen: John Forbes, 1678. 8vo. Last leaf laid down with loss of a few words. Contemp calf, rebacked. Wing B.720. *(Waterfield's)* **£300 [≈ $534]**
- An Apology for the True Christian Divinity ... People called Quakers. Birmingham: 1765. 1st Baskerville printing. [xi],xiii, 504, [xvi] pp. Contemp calf, rebacked, some wear. *(Hartfield)* **£395 [≈ £222]**
- An Apology for the True Christian Divinity ... Doctrines of the People called Quakers. Eighth Edition. Birmingham: Baskerville, 1765. 4to. [xi],xiii,520 pp. Lacks errata leaf as usual. Sl foxing. Sl ink notes. Contemp calf, sl rubbed, jnts sl cracked, crnrs sl worn. *(Blackwell's)* **£210 [≈ $374]**
- Robert Barclay's Apology for the true Christian Divinity Vindicated from John Brown's Examination and pretended confutation thereof ... London: Benjamin Clerk, 1679. 8vo. Mod half calf. Wing B.724. *(Waterfield's)* **£75 [≈ $134]**

Bardwell, Thomas
- Practical Treatise on Painting in Oil-Colours. London: E. & J. White, 1795. Pirated edn. 8vo. xvi,246 pp. Occas browning & sl spotting. Rec half calf. Anon. *(Spelman)* **£300 [≈ $534]**

Baretti, Joseph
- Easy Phraseology, for the Use of Young Ladies, who intend to learn the colloquial part of the Italian Language. London: Robinson & Cadell, 1775. 1st edn. 8vo. Contemp calf gilt, spine & 1 crnr sl worn. *(Ximenes)* **$600 [≈ £337]**
- A Journey from London to Genoa, through England, Portugal, Spain, and France. The Third Edition. London: for T. Davies, & L. Davis, 1770. 4 vols. 8vo. Contemp mottled calf, gilt spines (sl bruised). John Cator b'plates. *(Hannas)* **£420 [≈ $748]**
- A Journey from London to Genoa, through England, Portugal, Spain, and France. London: T. & L. Davies, 1770. 1st 8vo edn. 4 vols. 8vo. Early speckled calf gilt, dble labels. *(Hartfield)* **$750 [≈ £421]**

Barford, Richard
- The Virgin Queen. A Tragedy ... London: for J. Watts, 1729. 1st edn. 8vo. Lacks half-title. Sl browned. Disbound. *(Hannas)* **£55 [≈ $98]**

Barker, Henry, translator
- The Polite Gentleman: or Reflections upon the several Kinds of Wit ... Done out of French. London: for R. Basset, 1700. 12mo. Sl browned, 1 sm closed tear. New calf. Wing P.2760. *(Sanders)* **£280 [≈ $498]**

Barker, Jane, & others
- Poetical Recreations: consisting of Original Poems, Songs, odes, &c. with several New Translations. In Two Parts ... London: for Benjamin Crayle, 1688. 1st edn. 8vo. Licence leaf. Mod calf, elab gilt spine, a.e.g. Wing J.770. *(Hannas)* **£850 [≈ $1,513]**
- Poetical Recreations ... London: for Benjamin Crayle, 1688. 1st edn. 8vo. Lacks licence leaf. Sl stains & browning throughout, sm marg tears (a few crudely reprd). Contemp panelled calf, roughly rebacked. Wing J.770. *(Hannas)* **£450 [≈ $801]**

Barlow, Joel
- Advice to the Privileged Orders in the Several States of Europe, Resulting from the Necessity and Propriety of a General Revolution in the Principle of Government ... London: for J. Johnson, 1792. 2nd edn. 8vo. 156 pp. Title sl creased. New bds. *(Young's)* **£45 [≈ $80]**

Barlow, Theodore
- The Justice of the Peace: a Treatise containing the Power and Duty of that Magistrate ... London: Henry Lintot ..., 1745. 1st edn. Folio. xxii,592,(136) pp. Contemp calf, crnrs sl worn.   *(Burmester)* **£250 [≈ $445]**

Barlow, William
- The Sermon Preached at Paules Crosse, the Tenth Day of November ... after the Discoveries of this late Horrible Treason ... London: for Mathew Lawe, 1606 [ie 1605]. Issue with 'Lawe' in imprint. 4to. [38] pp. No intl blank. Sl marg damp stain. Old half mor, sl rubbed.   *(Clark)* **£120 [≈ $214]**

Barn, Andrew
- The Christian Officer's Panoply: Containing Arguments in Favour of a Divine Revelation. By a Marine Officer with a Recommendation in favour of the work by Sir Richard Hill. London: Bensley, 1789. Sm 8vo. xvi,232,[8 advt] pp. Tree calf, upper jnt cracked. Anon.   *(Francis Edwards)* **£40 [≈ $71]**

Barnard, James
- The Life of the Venerable and Right Reverend Richard Challoner, D.D. ... London: J.P. Coghlan, 1784. 1st edn. 8vo. xii,284 pp. Contemp polished calf, black label, gilt rules on spine, blind motifs.   *(Young's)* **£55 [≈ $98]**

Barnard, Sir John
- A Defence of Several Proposals for raising Three Millions for the Service of Government, for the Year 1746. With a Postscript ... London: for J. Osborn, 1746. 1st edn. 8vo. [2],77 pp. Disbound.   *(Hannas)* **£60 [≈ $107]**
- A Present for an Apprentice: or, a Sure Guide to gain both Esteem and an Estate ... Second Edition, with great variety of Improvements. London: for T. Cooper, 1740. 8vo. [iv],76 pp. Rec qtr calf. Anon. *(Burmester)* **£45 [≈ $80]**
- Reasons for the more speedily Lessening of the National Debt, and Taking off the most Burthensome of the Taxes. London: for J. Roberts, 1737. 1st 8vo edn. 24 pp inc half-title. Sl foxed. Disbound. Anon.   *(Hannas)* **£45 [≈ $80]**

Barnard, Thomas
- An Historical Character relating to the Holy and Exemplary Life of the Right Honourable the Lady Elisabeth Hastings ... Leedes: James Lister, for John Swale, 1742. 1st edn. 8vo. xxviii,190 pp. Marg repr 2 ff. Rec calf.   *(Young's)* **£95 [≈ $169]**

Barnes, Joshua
- The History of that Most Victorious Monarch Edward III ... Together with ... The Black-Prince ... Cambridge: John Hayes for the author, 1688. 1st edn. Folio. [xvi],911 pp. Errata. 5 ports. Contemp calf, front hinge cracked. Wing B.871.
            (Vanbrugh) **£475 [≈ $846]**

Barrett, William
- The History and Antiquities of the City of Bristol; compiled from Original Records ... Bristol: William Pine, 1789. Subscribers. 30 plates. Mod qtr calf, old label.   *(Waterfield's)* **£200 [≈ $356]**

Barriffe, William
- Military Discipline: or the Young Artillary-Man ... The 4th Edition ... inlarged. London: 1643. 4to. [viii], 6, 61-261,iii pp (collates A4, C-O4, Aa-Nn4). Frontis port, 4 plates, num text ills. Some marking. Period calf, cvrs wormed. Wing B.918.
            (Rankin) **£335 [≈ $596]**

Barrow, Isaac
- A Treatise of the Pope's Supremacy. To which is added a Discourse concerning the Unity of the Church. London: Miles Flesher for Brabazon Aylmer, 1680. 8vo. Sm lib stamp on title. Contemp calf, sl worn, front jnt broken. Wing B.961.
            (Waterfield's) **£65 [≈ $116]**
- A Treatise on the Pope's Supremacy ... London: Miles Flesher for Brabazon Aylmer, 1680. 1st edn. 4to. viii,428, ii,49 pp. Red & black title. Frontis port. Contemp calf, worn but sound. Wing B.961.
            (Gaskell) **£200 [≈ $356]**

Barrow, John
- Dictionarium Polygraphicum: or, the Whole Body of Arts regularly digested. Containing the Arts of Designing, Drawing, Painting ... London: 1735. 1st edn. 2 vols. 8vo. [2], i, 556); [2], (512),[2 advt] pp. 1 frontis (sl shaved), 55 plates. Contemp calf, rebacked.   *(Spelman)* **£350 [≈ $623]**

Bartas, Guillaume de Saluste du
- See Saluste de Bartas, Guillaume de

Barton, Philip
- A Sermon Preached in Lambeth Chapel, at the Consecration of ... Robert Lord Bishop of Saint David's on Sunday, June 15, 1766. London: for Will. Sandby, 1766. 4to. Rec bds.   *(Sanders)* **£15 [≈ $27]**

Barwick, John
- Querela Cantabrigiensis: or, A Remonstrance By way of Apologie, for the Banished Members of the late flourishing University of Cambridge ... London: Anno Dom., 1647. 2nd edn. 8vo. [xii],28,[8] pp. Rebound in half calf. Wing B.1010. Anon.
(Vanbrugh) **£125 [≈ $223]**

Bate, George
- The Regal Apology: Or, The Declaration of the Commons, Feb. 11. 1647 ... London: printed in the yeare, 1648. 1st edn. 4to. [ii],92 pp. New wraps. Wing B.1090. Anon.
(Young's) **£45 [≈ $80]**

Bates, William
- A Funeral Sermon, Preached upon the Death of the Reverend and Excellent Divine Dr. Thomas Manton, Who deceas'd the 18th of October, 1677. London: J.D. for Brabazon Aylmer, 1678. 1st edn. 4to. 59,1 advt pp. Disbound. Wing B.1109 or 1110.
(Young's) **£45 [≈ $80]**
- The Harmony of the Divine Attributes ... London: J.M. for Ranew ..., 1675. 2nd edn, enlgd. 4to. Port. Few sl marks. 1 sm marg tear. Contemp calf, sl split front hinge. Wing B.1114.
(P and P Books) **£40 [≈ $71]**

Bath, William Pulteney, Earl of
- See Pulteney, William, Earl of Bath

Baxter, Richard
- The Crucifying of the World, By the Cross of Christ. London: R.W. for Nevill Simmons, 1658. 1st edn. Sm 4to. Lacks free endpapers. Some browning. Contemp calf, bds rubbed, spine sl rubbed, front hinge broken but firm.
(P and P Books) **£60 [≈ $107]**
- The Practical Works ... London: T. Parkhurst, 1707. 1st coll edn. 4 vols. Folio. Engvd port & title. Occas sl foxing. Contemp panelled calf, sometime rebacked, crnrs worn, 1 cvr almost detached.
(Blackwell's) **£375 [≈ $668]**

Bayly, Thomas
- Herba Parietis. Or, the Wall-Flower. As it grew out of the Stone-Chamber belonging to the Metropolitan Prison of London, called Newgate ... London: John Holden, 1650. 1st edn. Sm folio. [viii],130 pp. Crnrs of title reprd, 1 other tear reprd. Later sheep.
(Bookpress) **$575 [≈ £323]**

Beach, William Wither
- Abradates and Panthea: a Tale extracted from Xenophon. Salisbury: S. Collins for James

Fletcher, London, 1765. 4to. Half-title. Disbound.   *(Waterfield's)* **£60 [≈ $107]**

Bearcroft, Phillip
- An Historical Account of Thomas Sutton Esq; And of his Foundation in Charter-House. London: E. Owen, 1737. 1st edn. 8vo. xvi, 275, [1 errata] pp. Port frontis, 1 fldg plate. Occas v sm lib stamp. 18th c calf, rebacked.   *(Young's)* **£110 [≈ $196]**

Beattie, James
- An Essay on the Nature and Immutability of Truth, in opposition to Sophistry and Scepticism. London: Dilly, 1774. 5th edn. 8vo. 518 pp. Wide margs. Orig bds, uncut, rebacked.   *(Young's)* **£140 [≈ $249]**
- Essays: on Poetry and Music, as they affect the Mind; on Laughter, and Ludicrous Composition; on the Utility of Classical Learning. Edinburgh: Edward & Charles Dilly, 1778. Edinburgh reissue of London 1st edn, with cancel title. Contemp calf, rebacked.   *(C.R. Johnson)* **£245 [≈ $436]**
- The Minstrel; or the Progress of Genius: a Poem. London: Dilly, & Kincaid & Creech, Edinburgh, 1774. 1st book 4th edn, 2nd book 3rd edn. 4to. Disbound.
(Waterfield's) **£60 [≈ $107]**
- Poems on Several Occasions. Edinburgh: for W. Creech, 1796. vi,83 pp. Orig mrbld bds, uncut, respined.   *(C.R. Johnson)* **£45 [≈ $80]**

Beaufort, James
- Hoyle's Games Improved ... London: for Osborne & Griffin; & H. Mozley, Gainsborough, 1788. Sm 8vo in 6s. 216 pp. Sl browning at ends. Mod half calf gilt.
(Hollett) **£75 [≈ $134]**

Beaumont, Francis & Fletcher, John
- A King and No King. Acted at the Black-Fryars ... and now the fourth time Printed, according to the true Copie. London: Printed in the Year, 1661. 6th sep edn. 4to. [74] pp. No intl blank. Mod half calf, sl rubbed. Wing B.1590.   *(Clark)* **£225 [≈ $401]**
- The Maids Tragedy. As it hath been Acted at the Theatre Royal ... London: for R. Bentley & S. Magnes, 1686. 4to. Faint water stains. Stitched, uncut, as issued. Wing B.1597.
(Hannas) **£45 [≈ $80]**
- Philaster, or Love Lies a Bleeding. A Comedy ... London: for Bentley & Magnes, 1687. 4to. Few minor marg tears. Contemp mrbld wraps. Wing B.1600. *(Hannas)* **£65 [≈ $116]**

Beaumont, John

- An Historical, Physiological and Theological Treatise of Spirits, Apparitions, Witchcrafts, and other Magical Practices ... London: D. Browne ..., 1705. 1st edn. Frontis. Some water stains & foxing. 10 pp browned. Contemp calf, sl rubbed, ft of spine missing.
(P and P Books) **£325 [≈ $579]**

Beaumont, Sir John

- Bosworth-field: with a Taste of the Variety of other Poems ... London: 1629. 1st edn. Sm 8vo. [xxii],'208" [ie 206] pp. Lacks intl blank & as always N3 (suppressed). Title mtd & soiled. Some worm & soil. 19th c calf, reprd, rubbed. STC 1694.
(Blackwell's) **£400 [≈ $712]**

Beauty's Triumph ...

- Beauty's Triumph: or the Superiority of the Fair Sex invincibly proved ... In Three Parts ... London: J. Robinson, 1751. [2],306 pp. Contemp sheep, sl rubbed.
(C.R. Johnson) **£450 [≈ $801]**

Becket, Andrew

- A Concordance to Shakespeare ... London: for G.G.J. & J. Robinson, 1787. 1st edn. 8vo. viii,470 pp. Contemp half calf, worn but sound.
(Burmester) **£90 [≈ $160]**

Beckford, Peter

- Thoughts upon Hare and Fox Hunting. London: for Vernor & Hood, 1796. 1st illust edn. 8vo. 20 etchings & engvs. Contemp calf, rebacked.
(Ash) **£400 [≈ $712]**

Beckford, William

- An Arabian Tale, from an unpublished Manuscript: with Notes Critical and Explanatory. London: for J. Johnson, 1786. 1st edn of Vathek. 8vo. Contemp half calf, gilt spine, some rubbing.
(Ximenes) **$750 [≈ £421]**
- An Arabian Tale, from an Unpublished Manuscript: with Notes Critical and Explanatory. London: for J. Johnson, 1786. 1st edn in English, ordinary paper issue. 8vo. viii,334 pp. Lacks blank Y8. Sl spotting. Contemp half calf, gilt spine reprd at ends. Slipcase.
(Finch) **£550 [≈ $979]**
- An Arabian Tale, from an Unpublished Manuscript: with Notes Critical and Explanatory. London: J. Johnson, 1786. 1st (pirated) edn. 8vo. iv,334 pp. With errata on a4, blank Y8. Contemp half calf, upper jnt sm split at hd. Anon.
(Frew Mackenzie) **£210 [≈ $374]**
- Vathek. Lausanne: Isaac Hignou, 1787

[1786]. 1st edn in French. 8vo. iv,204 pp. Title border. Title vignette. 1 other vignette. Contemp pink bds, vellum label, sprinkled edges, spine sl darkened, crnrs & ft of spine sl rubbed. Anon.
(Finch) **£2,500 [≈ $4,450]**
- Vathek, Conte Arabe. Paris: chez Poincot, 1787. 1st Paris edn, 1st issue. 8vo. 190,[i advt] pp. W'engvd title vignette. Contemp tree sheep, smooth spine gilt, mor label, hd of spine sl worn, some insect damage to leather of spine. Slipcase. Anon.
(Finch) **£600 [≈ $1,068]**

Beckingham, Charles

- The Tragedy of Henry IV of France ... London: Curll, Fauncy, 1720. 1st edn. 8vo. Port frontis. Hole through frontis, title & next leaf. Disbound.
(Hannas) **£65 [≈ $116]**

Bedford, Arthur

- The Scripture Chronology demonstrated by Astronomical Calculations ... London: Knapton ..., 1730. 1st edn. Large Paper. Folio. [iv], vi,[ii], 774,[24] pp. 13 maps, 10 plates. 2 pp subscrs, num tables. Sl marg worm. Contemp panelled calf, sl worn, lacks label.
(Clark) **£200 [≈ $356]**

The Bee ...

- The Bee, a Selection of Poetry from the Best Authors. A New Edition. Dublin: John Gough, 1796. 1st Dublin edn. 12mo. 11,[3],191 pp. Engvd title with vignette. Contemp tree calf.
(Burmester) **£75 [≈ $134]**

Behmen, Jacob

- See Boehme, Jacob

Behn, Aphra

- Poems upon Several Occasions: with a Voyage to the Island of Love. London: for R. Tonson & J. Tonson, 1684. 1st edn. 8vo. Table misbound at end. A2 reprd. Mod calf. Wing B.1757.
(Hannas) **£450 [≈ $801]**

Bell, Henry

- The Perfect Painter: or, a Compleat History of the Original, Progress and Improvement of Painting ... London: printed in the year, 1730. Lge 12mo. [iv],138,[4] pp. Possibly lacks advt leaf at end. Sl foxing. Occas ink notes. Contemp calf, rebacked. Anon.
(Rankin) **£145 [≈ $258]**

Bell, John

- Travels from St. Petersburg in Russia to Diverse Parts of Asia. Glasgow: Robert & Andrew Foulis, 1763. 1st edn. 2 vols. 4to. xvii,[ii],357; 426,[i] pp. Fldg map. Sm reprs

to title margs. Titles soiled. Contemp calf
gilt, reprd, crudely rebacked, sl rubbed.
(Francis Edwards) **£150 [≈ $267]**

Beloe, William
- Poems and Translations. London: for J.
Johnson, 1788. 1st edn. 8vo. Sl browning.
Contemp half calf gilt, spine sl rubbed.
(Ximenes) **$450 [≈ £253]**

Belsham, William
- Memoirs of the Reign of George III. To the
Session of Parliament ending A.D. 1793.
London: Robinson, 1795. 2nd edn. 4 vols.
8vo. Half-titles. Occas foxing & dusting. Orig
bds, uncut, sl worn.
(Burmester) **£100 [≈ $178]**

Benezet, Anthony
- The Case of our Fellow-Creatures, the
oppressed Africans, respectfully
recommended to the serious consideration of
the Legislature of Great Britain ... London:
James Phillips, 1784. 2nd edn. 8vo. 15,[1] pp.
Disbound. Anon. *(Burmester)* **£150 [≈ $267]**
- A Caution to Great Britain and Her Colonies,
In a Short Representation of the Calamitous
State of the Enslaved Negroes in the British
Dominions. New Edition. London: 1784.
8vo. 46,[i advt] pp. Minor stains at start.
Disbound. *(Francis Edwards)* **£50 [≈ $89]**
- Some Historical Account of Guinea ... With
an Inquiry into the Rise and Progress of the
Slave Trade ... A New Edition. London: J.
Phillips, 1788. xvi,131,[i advt] pp. Half-title.
W'cut title vignette by Bewick. Orig bds,
backstrip defective, hinges cracked.
(Blackwell's) **£145 [≈ $258]**
- Some Historical Account of Guinea ...
Inquiry into the ... Slave Trade ... New
Edition. London: J. Phillips, 1788. 8vo. xv,
131,[i advt] pp. Half-title. Title-vignette by
Thomas Bewick. Later half mor, uncut,
rebacked. *(Gough)* **£110 [≈ $196]**

Bennett, John
- Letters to a Young Lady, on a Variety of
Useful and Entertaining Subjects ... The
Second Edition. London: Cadell & Davies,
1795. 2 vols. Half-titles. Advt leaf vol 2.
Contemp qtr calf.
(C.R. Johnson) **£120 [≈ $214]**

Bennett, Thomas
- A Short Introduction of Grammar ...
Knowledge of the Latin Tongue. London:
Will. Norton, 1707. 1st edn thus. 8vo. [70],
[ii], 130, [131-148] pp. Sep title to 2nd part.
1st leaf sgnd A4 with elab w'cut border. Sl

worn. Rec calf. Anon.
(Vanbrugh) **£155 [≈ $276]**

Bentham, Jeremy
- Defence of Usury ... [with] a Letter to Adam
Smith ... Dublin: D. Williams ..., 1788. 1st
Irish edn. 12mo. [6],232 pp. Sm marg
wormhole. Lacks half-title & blank fly ff.
Contemp calf. *(Fenning)* **£485 [≈ $863]**
- A Fragment on Government; Being an
Examination ... Introduction to Sir William
Blackstone's Commentaries ... Dublin:
Sheppard ..., 1776. 8vo. xli,132 pp. Some
browning & staining. Mod speckled calf.
Anon. *(Meyer Boswell)* **$3,500 [≈ £1,966]**

Berington, Joseph
- The Memoirs of Gregorio Panzani ...
Birmingham: Swinney & Walker, 1793. 1st
edn. 8vo. xliii,473,[1],2 advt pp. Orig bds,
uncut. *(Young's)* **£78 [≈ $139]**

Berkeley, George
- Alciphron: or, the Minute Philosopher. In
Seven Dialogues ... London: Tonson, 1732.
1st edn. 2 vols. 8vo. Engvd title vignettes.
Endpapers browned. Contemp calf, spines
rubbed. Anon.
(Frew Mackenzie) **£395 [≈ $703]**
- Alciphron or the Minute Philosopher ...
Second Edition. London: for J. Tonson,
1732. 2 vols. 8vo. Contemp calf, rebacked,
crnrs reprd. Anon.
(Waterfield's) **£260 [≈ $463]**
- Three Dialogues between Hylas and Philonus
... Second Edition. London: for William &
John Innys, 1725. 8vo. [x],166 pp. Closed tear
in 1 leaf. Contemp calf, rebacked, edges
rubbed. *(Burmester)* **£350 [≈ $623]**

Berkeley, George Berkeley, Earl of
- Historical Applications and Occasional
Meditations upon Several Subjects. Written
by a Person of Honour. London: J. Macock,
for R. Royston, 1670. 2nd edn. Sm 8vo. With
inserted dedic leaf. Lacks intl & final ff
(?blanks). Contemp calf, rebacked. Wing
B.1964. Anon. *(Hannas)* **£85 [≈ $151]**

Berkenhout, J.
- Clavis Anglica Linguae Botanicae; or, a
Botanical Lexicon; in which the Terms of
Botany, particularly those of ... Linnaeus ...
are explained. London: 1764. Sm 8vo. xii,
[215] pp. Lib b'plate. Contemp sheep.
(Wheldon & Wesley) **£35 [≈ $62]**
- Outlines of the Natural History of Great
Britain and Ireland. London: 1769-72. 1st
edn. 3 vols in 2. Contemp calf, sl worn, jnts

cracked but not broken.
(Wheldon & Wesley) **£200 [≃ $356]**

Berquin, Arnaud
- The Looking-Glass for the Mind ... Chiefly Translated from that much admired Work L'Ami des Enfans, or The Children's Friend. Dublin: John Jones, 1788. [4],212 pp. Frontis. Contemp tree calf.
(C.R. Johnson) **£225 [≃ $401]**

Bertramus, presbyter
- The Book of Bertram the Priest, concerning the Body and Blood of Christ in the Sacrament ... Translated into English ... London: 1686. 12mo. [xxxvi],96,[8 ctlg] pp. Cropped at foredge. Contemp calf, later mor reback, crnrs sl worn. Wing B.2049B.
(Clark) **£90 [≃ $160]**

Besnier, Pierre
- A Philosophicall Essay for the Reunion of the Languages, or The Art of Knowing all by the Mastery of One. Oxford: Hen. Hall for James Good, 1675. 8vo. Front endpaper adhering to gutter of title. Later panelled calf, rebacked. Anon. Old Wing (only) R.1934.
(Waterfield's) **£475 [≃ $846]**

Best ...
- The Best and Most Approved Method of Curing White-Herrings and all Kinds of White-Fish. Containing particular Directions how to Slit, Gut, Salt, Dry, and Barrel them ... London: Davidson, 1750. 1st edn. 8vo. [2], 28 pp, advt leaf.
(Hannas) **£140 [≃ $249]**

Bethel, Slingsby
- The Interest of Princes and States. London: 1680. 1st edn. 8vo. 354,advt pp. Lacks A1 (blank?). Old calf, roughly rebacked. Wing B.2064. Anon.
(Robertshaw) **£150 [≃ $267]**
- The World's Mistake in Oliver Cromwell ... London: Printed in the Year 1668. 1st edn. Sm 4to. [ii],20,[2 blank] pp. Title sl dusty. Rec half calf. Wing B.2079. Anon.
(Georges) **£250 [≃ $445]**

Bettesworth, John
- The New Universal Ready Reckoner; or Every Trader's Infallible Guide. London: [ca 1785]. 1st edn. 12mo. Frontis. Later cloth, roughly rebacked. *(Robertshaw)* **£25 [≃ $45]**

Beveridge, William
- The Great Necessity and Advantage of Publick Prayer, and Frequent Communion Designed to revive Primitive Piety. London: E.P. for R. Smith, 1708. 1st edn. 8vo.

[vii],109, 149,[6 ctlg] pp. Port. Contemp panelled calf, sm crack in jnt, wear hd of spine.   *(Blackwell's)* **£404 [≃ $71]**

Bewick, John (illustrator)
- Tales for Youth; in Thirty Poems ... Ornamented with Cuts, neatly designed and engraved on wood, by Bewick. London: E. Newbery, 1794. Fcap 8vo. x,158,[2 advt] pp. 30 ills. Occas sl marks. 19th c half calf, hd of spine reprd.   *(Spelman)* **£160 [≃ $285]**

Bewick, Thomas
- A General History of Quadrupeds. Newcastle: S. Hodgson, 1791. 2nd edn. x,483 pp. Contemp diced russia gilt, backstrip relaid.   *(Gough)* **£165 [≃ $294]**

Bibliotheca ...
- Bibliotheca Americana ... See Rede, Leman Thomas
- Bibliotheca Topographica Britannica ... see Nichols, J. (ed.); Orem, William.

Bilson, Thomas
- The Perpetual Government of Christes Church ... London: Deputies of Christopher Barker, 1593. 1st edn. Sm 4to. [xxviii], 414,[i] pp. Sl damp marking. Blank crnr torn from 1 leaf. 17th c calf, rebacked, crnrs worn. STC 3065.   *(Blackwell's)* **£180 [≃ $320]**
- The True Difference between Christian Subjection and Unchristian Rebellion ... Oxford: Joseph Barnes, 1585. 1st edn. 4to in 8s. [xxiv],820,[x] pp. Old calf, rebacked, jnts rubbed, crnrs sl worn. STC 3071.
(Clark) **£425 [≃ $757]**

Bingham, Joseph
- The Works ... London: Robert Knaplock, 1726. 1st coll edn. 2 vols. Folio. Map. Sl marg damp staining, sl worming chiefly to index vol 1. Contemp panelled calf, rebacked, sm reprs.   *(Frew Mackenzie)* **£98 [≃ $174]**

Biochimo the famous Italian
- See Greco, Gioachino

Biographia Britannica ...
- Biographia Britannica: or, the Lives of the most Eminent Persons who have flourished in Great Britain and Ireland ... London: for W. Innys, W. Meadows ..., 1747-66. 1st edn. 6 vols in 7. Folio. Contemp calf, gilt spines, mor labels, sm reprs & traces of wear.
(Burmester) **£400 [≃ $712]**

Birch, Samuel
- The Smugglers: a Musical Drama ... London:

C. Dilly, 1796. 1st edn. 8vo. 37 pp. Half-title. Rec wraps. *(Burmester)* £30 [≈ $53]
- The Smugglers; a Musical Drama, in Two Acts. London: C. Dilly, 1796. Half-title, 37 pp. Rec wraps. *(C.R. Johnson)* £30 [≈ $53]

Birch, Thomas
- The Life of Henry Prince of Wales, Eldest Son of King James I ... London: A. Millar, 1760. 1st edn. 8vo. [cvi],552,[xii] pp. L7 torn for cancellation. Cancellans bound in as A8. Contemp calf, rubbed, hd of spine frayed. *(Clark)* £65 [≈ $116]
- The Life of the Honourable Robert Boyle. London: Millar, 1744. 1st sep edn. 8vo. Advts. 2 lib stamps. Lib b'plate. Cloth. *(Rostenberg & Stern)* $150 [≈ £84]

Bird, William
- The Magazine of Honour: or, a Treatise of the severall Degrees of the Nobility ... enlarged ... by Sir John Doderidge. [London]: Sheares, 1642. 1st edn. Sm 8vo. [vi],158 pp (erratic pagination). Printer's mark 1st leaf. Rec half calf. Wing B.2955. *(Vanbrugh)* £175 [≈ $312]
- The Magazine of Honour ... see also Doddridge, Sir John.

Bishop, Matthew
- The Life and Adventures of Matthew Bishop of Deddington in Oxfordshire ... Written by Himself. London: J. Brindley ..., 1744. Only edn. 8vo. viii,[iv],283,[i errata] pp. Contemp calf, lacks label, rubbed, extrs worn, jnts cracking but holding. *(Blackwell's)* £300 [≈ $534]

Blackall, Offspring
- The Lord Bishop of Exeter's Answer to Mr. Hoadly's Letter ... London: J. Leake for W. Rogers, 1709. 1st edn (?). 8vo. 56 pp. Disbound. *(Young's)* £95 [≈ $169]

Blacklock, Thomas
- Poems on Several Occasions ... Edinburgh: Hamilton, Balfour & Neill, 1754. 8vo. xvi,181 pp. 4 ff with sm tear at hd. Contemp calf, mor label, front jnt sl tender. Anon. *(Finch)* £100 [≈ $178]

Blackmore, Sir Richard
- Prince Arthur. An Heroick Poem ... Appendix ... London: Churchill, 1696. 3rd edn. Folio. [xx],296,[2] pp. Contemp calf. Wing B.3082. *(Vanbrugh)* £225 [≈ $401]
- A Short History of the Last Parliament. London: 1699. 1st edn. 4to. Disbound. Wing

B.3088. Anon. *(Robertshaw)* £25 [≈ $45]

Blackstone, Sir William
- Commentaries on the Laws of England. Oxford: Clarendon Press, 1770-70-68-69. Vols 1 & 2 4th edns, vols 3 & 4 1st edns. 4 vols. 2 plates in vol 2. Occas sl foxing, sl marg damp stains. Ink notes. Later red half leather, gilt dec spines, rubbed & dull. *(Heritage)* $3,000 [≈ £1,685]
- Commentaries on the Laws of England ... Phila: Robert Bell ..., 1771-72. 1st Amer edn. 4 vols. Without subscriber leaf vol 4. Some browning & staining. Few blank margs torn away. Contemp sheep, sl worn, vol 1 rebound to style. *(Meyer Boswell)* $3,500 [≈ £1,966]

Blackwall, Anthony
- An Introduction to the Classics ... London: for George Mortlock, 1719. 2nd edn. 12mo. [viii],272, [7],[1 advt] pp. Contemp panelled calf, sl worn. *(Young's)* £90 [≈ $160]

Blackwell, Thomas
- An Enquiry into the Life and Writings of Homer. London: 1735. 1st edn. 8vo. [6], 335, [80] pp. Fldg map, frontis, 12 half-page plates. Single marg worm hole 1st 30 pp. Contemp calf, gilt spine, hinges broken but cords strong. Anon. *(Claude Cox)* £65 [≈ $116]

Blair, Hugh
- A Critical Dissertation on the Poems of Ossian, the Son of Fingal. London: Becket & De Hondt, 1763. 4to. Sl marg worm hole. Disbound. *(Waterfield's)* £125 [≈ $223]
- Lectures on Rhetoric and Belles Lettres. Phila: Robert Aitken, 1784. 1st Amer edn. 4to. viii,454,[12] pp. Some marks, marg worm. Period sheep, gilt spine, upper jnt cracked but firm, sl cracks lower jnt, cvrs scuffed. *(Rankin)* £165 [≈ $294]
- Lectures on Rhetoric and Belles-Lettres. The Third Edition. London: for A. Strahan, 1787. 3 vols. 8vo. Port. Some foxing. Period calf, 1 jnt cracked but holding, sm split in another jnt. *(Rankin)* £135 [≈ $240]
- Lectures on Rhetoric and Belles Lettres. The Sixth Edition. London: Strahan, Cadell, 1796. 2 vols. 8vo. Port frontis vol 1. Contemp speckled calf, gilt spines, 2 jnts sl cracked. *(Spelman)* £85 [≈ $151]

Blane, William
- Essays on Hunting ... Different Kinds of Hounds ... Choice of a Hunter ... Hare-Hunting ... Southampton: T. Baker ..., [1781]. 1st edn. 8vo. xvii,135 pp. Sl foxing &

browning. Later sheep, jnts reprd. Anon.
(Burmester) **£300 [≈ $534]**

- Essays on Hunting ... Southampton: T. Baker; London: Robson & Fielding; Oxford: D. Prince, (1781). 1st edn. 8vo. xvii,135 pp. Leather, jnts reprd. Anon.
(Bookline) **£300 [≈ $534]**

Blome, Richard

- The Present State of His Majesties Isles and Territories in America ... With New Maps of Every Place ... London: for Dorman Newman ..., 1687. [ii title],[6],262,[36] pp. 6 advt pp. Port, 7 fldg maps, 1 plate. Old calf, rebacked, extrs worn, no label. Wing B.3215.
(Reese) **$3,000 [≈ £1,685]**

Blondel, David

- A Treatise of the Sibyls. London: T.R. for the author, 1661. 1st English edn. Sm folio. Edges of title frayed. Qtr calf. Wing B.3220.
(Rostenberg & Stern) **$450 [≈ £253]**

Blount, Charles

- Anima Mundi: or, an Historical Narration of the Opinions of the Ancients concerning Men's Soul after this Life ... London: Will. Cademan, 1679. Sm 8vo. [viii],109 pp. Sl marg staining. Sev ff with sm marg hole. Contemp calf, rebacked, crnrs worn. Wing B.3298.
(Finch) **£90 [≈ $160]**

Blount, Thomas

- Glossographia; or, A Dictionary, interpreting the Hard Words ... By T.B. London: by Tho. Newcomb ... sold by Robert Boulter, 1674. 4th edn. Cr 8vo. [xvi],'706" [ie 708],[ii] pp. Occas sl marks. Old calf, rebacked. Wing B.3337.
(Ash) **£400 [≈ $712]**

Blundeville, Thomas

- Four Chiefest Offices belonging to Horsemanship ... of the Breeder, of the Rider, of the Keeper, and of the Ferrier ... London: Richard Yardley & Peter Short, [1593]. 5th edn. Sm 4to. [450] pp. 53 w'cut ills. Contemp calf, some ageing to spine & ends reprd.
(Chapel Hill) **$2,000 [≈ £1,124]**

Boate, Gerard, & others

- A Natural History of Ireland, In Three Parts ... Dublin: George Grierson, 1726. 1st Dublin edn. 4to. [vi],102,[ii], 105-186,[ii], 187-213 pp. 11 plates. Contemp calf gilt, label sl defective.
(Vanbrugh) **£755 [≈ $1,344]**

Boccaccio, Giovanni

- The Novels and Tales ... The Fifth Edition,

much Corrected and Amended. London: for Awnsham Churchill, 1684. Folio. [xvi],483 pp. Frontis port. Few sm marg reprs. Early 19th c russia, a.e.g., jnts worn, spine rubbed. Wing B.3378.
(Sotheran's) **£398 [≈ $708]**

Bodley, Thomas

- Reliquiae Bodleianae: or some Genuine Remains ... London: for John Hartley, 1703. 1st edn. 8vo. [xvi],383,[i errata] pp. Occas browning & spotting. Early 19th c speckled calf gilt, smooth spine gilt, contrasting labels, a.e.g.
(Finch) **£250 [≈ $445]**

Boehme, Jacob

- The Third Book of the Author being the High and Deep Searching Out of the Threefold Life of Man ... By Jacob Behmen ... Englished by J. Sparrow ... London: for H. Blunden, 1650. 1st English edn. Sm 4to. 1 text engv. Sl marked. Early 20th c qtr calf, gilt spine. Wing B.3422.
(Vanbrugh) **£555 [≈ $988]**

Boemus, Joannes

- The Manners, Lawes and Customs of All Nations ... Now newly translated into English, by Ed. Aston. London: G.Eld, sold by Francis Burton, 1611. 1st edn of this translation. 4to. Title soiled with lib stamp on verso. Minor stains. Early calf, rebacked. STC 3198.
(Hannas) **£750 [≈ $1,335]**

Boileau-Despreaux, Nicolas

- Boileau's Lutrin: a Mock-Heroic Poem. In Six Canto's. render'd into English verse ... London: for Sanger & Curll, 1708. 8vo. [xxii], 122 pp. Frontis. Contemp panelled sheep, rebacked.
(Sotheran's) **£125 [≈ $223]**

Bolingbroke, Henry St. John, Viscount

- A Collection of Political Tracts ... London: 1769. 1st edn. 8vo. 388,index pp. Occas spotting. Contemp half calf, new endpapers. Anon.
(Robertshaw) **£40 [≈ $71]**
- The Craftsman Extraordinary. Being Remarks on a late Pamphlet, intitled, Observations on the Conduct of Great Britain ... Published by Caleb D'Anvers ... London: for R. Francklin, 1729. 1st edn. 8vo. [4],28 pp. Disbound. Anon.
(Hannas) **£110 [≈ $196]**
- A Dissertation upon Parties ... London: H. Haines, 1735. 2nd edn. 8vo. xxxi,246, [1 erratum] pp. Old speckled calf, rebacked.
(Young's) **£40 [≈ $71]**
- A Final Answer to the Remarks on the Craftsman's Vindication ... London: for R. Francklin, 1731. 1st edn. 8vo. 32 pp.

Disbound. Anon. *(Young's)* **£55 [≈ $98]**
- The Freeholder's Political Catechism. London: for J. Roberts, 1733. 1st edn. 8vo. 24 pp. Disbound. Anon. *(Young's)* **£65 [≈ $116]**
- A Letter to Sir William Windham. II. Some Reflections of the Present State of the Nation. III. A Letter to Mr. Pope. London: A. Millar, 1753. 1st edn. 531 pp. Port. Contemp calf, rubbed, jnts tender, hd of spine & crnrs worn but sound.
(Jermy & Westerman) **£50 [≈ $89]**
- Letters, On the Spirit of Patriotism: On the Idea of a Patriot King: And On the State of Parties ... London: A. Millar, 1750. 1st authorised edn. 8vo. 338,[2 advt] pp. Contemp speckled calf gilt, fine. Anon.
(O'Neal) **£275 [≈ £154]**
- Letters on the Spirit of Patriotism: on the Idea of a Patriot King; and on the State of Parties ... New Edition. London: T. Davies, 1775. 8vo. xxxvi,243 pp. Frontis. Occas foxing, some paper discolouration. Contemp calf, upper jnt sl cracked.
(Spelman) **£40 [≈ $71]**
- Letters on the Study and Use of History. London: 1752. 1st edn. 2 vols. 8vo. Contemp calf, gilt crnrs sl worn, 1 label chipped.
(Robertshaw) **£50 [≈ $89]**
- Letters on the Study and Use of History ... Dublin: for John Smith, [1752]. 1st Dublin edn. 2 vols. 12mo. [vi],268; [iv],224 pp. Lacks collective half-title. Contemp calf, raised bands, red & black labels, gilt decs.
(Young's) **£140 [≈ $249]**
- The Misscellaneous [sic] Works ... prefixed, some Account of the Author. Edinburgh: for A. Donaldson, 1768. 4 vols. 12mo. Half-titles. Occas foxing. Contemp calf, labels, spines darkened, ft of vol 1 sl worn, some rubbing. *(Blackwell's)* **£175 [≈ $312]**
- The Philosophical Works. Published by David Mallet, Esq. London: printed in the Year 1754. 1st 8vo edn. 5 vols. 8vo. Lacks Preface vol 1. Contemp calf, rubbed, lacks labels. *(Clark)* **£35 [≈ $62]**
- The Works. Dublin: for P. Byrne, 1793. 5 vols. 8vo. Contemp speckled calf, twin labels (1 chipped), sl rubbed.
(Young's) **£85 [≈ $151]**

Bolton, Robert
- A Letter to a Lady on Card-Playing on the Lord's Day. London: 1748. 1st edn. 50 pp. Sl soiled. Disbound. Anon. *(King)* **£75 [≈ £42]**
- Letters and Tracts on the Choice of Company and Other Subjects. London: 1761. 1st edn. 8vo. 304 pp. Contemp gilt ruled calf, jnts cracked. Anon. *(Robertshaw)* **£50 [≈ $89]**

- Letters and Tracts on the Choice of Company and Other Subjects. London: for J. Whiston & B. White, 1761. 1st edn. 8vo. xxxii,304 pp. Rec contemp style half calf.
(Young's) **£185 [≈ $329]**
- Letters and Tracts on the Choice of Company and other Subjects. London: for J. Whiston & B. White; & R. & J. Dodsley, 1762. 2nd edn. 8vo. [ii],xxxii,304 pp. Errata leaf & advts. Contemp calf, gilt spine, sl rubbed. Anon.
(Burmester) **£150 [≈ $267]**

Bolton, Robert, probable author
- Letters to a Young Nobleman. London: for A. Millar, 1762. 1st edn. 8vo. [vi],230,[2 errata] pp. Half-title. Contemp speckled calf, spine a bit worn. Anon. *(Burmester)* **£110 [≈ $196]**

Bond, William
- A Description of the Four Last Things, viz. Death, Judgement, Hell and Heaven; in Blank Verse. London: John Clark, 1719. 1st edn. Lge 12mo. 154 pp, advt leaf. Intl & final blanks. Contemp calf, gilt borders, minor wear. Anon. *(Spelman)* **£340 [≈ $605]**

Bonnycastle, John
- An Introduction to Astronomy. In a Series of Letters from a Preceptor to a Pupil ... London: for J. Johnson, 1786. 1st edn. 8vo. vi,[ii], 431,[i] pp. Frontis, 20 plates (10 fldg, 1 misfolded). Contemp polished calf, flat back gilt, jnts starting, hd of spine chipped.
(Blackwell's) **£250 [≈ $445]**

Book ...
- The Book of Conversation and Behaviour. Written by a Person of Distinction. London: for R. Griffiths, 1754. vii,[1],302 pp. Contemp calf, jnts broken.
(C.R. Johnson) **£650 [≈ $1,157]**
- The Book of Martyrs: or, the History of Paganism and Popery ... Abstracted from the Best Authors, both Ancient and Modern. Coventry: ptd by T. Luckman; sold by J. Fuller, London, 1764. 1st edn. 8vo. 440,[8] pp. Frontis (sl spotted). Contemp qtr calf, rubbed, hd of spine worn.
(Burmester) **£55 [≈ $98]**

Booth, A.
- Examen Legum Angliae: or, the Laws of England Examined, By Scripture, Antiquity, and Reason. London: James Cottrel, 1656. Only edn. Sm 4to. Errata leaf at end. Sl browning & marg staining. Rec buckram. Wing B.3738. Anon. *(Georges)* **£200 [≈ $356]**

Borlase, William

- Observations on the Ancient and Present State of the Islands of Scilly ... Oxford: W. Jackson, 1756. 1st edn. 4to. 140 pp. Half-title. 5 plates (occas v sl spotting, 1 repr). Half calf, sometime renewed, some wear, lacks label.   *(Francis Edwards)* £380 [≈ $676]

Bossu, Jean Bernard

- Travels through that Part of North America formerly called Louisiana ... Catalogue of ... Plants ... London: 1771. 1st English edn. 2 vols. viii,407; 432 pp. Half-title vol 2. Foxed & tanned, old stamp on title versos. Contemp calf, rebacked.   *(Reese)* $1,500 [≈ £843]

Boswell, James

- An Account of Corsica. The Journal of a Tour to that Island; and the Memoirs of Pascal Paoli. The Third Edition. Dublin: J. Exshaw, 1768. Sm 12mo. xii,280 pp. Early polished calf, some wear.
       (Hartfield) $295 [≈ £166]
- An Account of Corsica, the Journal of a Tour to that Island; and Memoirs of Pascal Paoli. London: for Edward & Charles Dilly, 1768. 2nd edn. 8vo. xxii,[ii],384 pp. Half-title. Fldg map. Contemp calf, gilt spine, jnts sl cracked but firm, hd of spine rubbed.
       (Burmester) £150 [≈ $267]
- The Essence of the Douglas Cause. To which is subjoined, Some Observations on a Pamphlet lately Published ... London: for J. Wilkie, 1767. 1st edn. 2nd issue, without the Observations at the end. 8vo. [4],77 pp. Contemp qtr calf, spine reprd in cloth. Anon.
       (Heritage) $550 [≈ £309]
- The Journal of a Tour to the Hebrides with Samuel Johnson, LL.D. London: Henry Baldwin for Charles Dilly, 1785. 1st edn. 8vo. vii,[i],524 pp. Half-title. No errata leaf. Sm lib stamp on title. Contemp calf gilt, rubbed, extrs worn, jnts cracked.
       (Clark) £100 [≈ $178]
- The Journal of a Tour to the Hebrides, with Samuel Johnson, LL.D. London: 1785. 1st edn. 8vo. [viii],524 pp, errata leaf. Half-title. Sl aged & foxed. Old calf, backstrip relaid.
       (D & D Galleries) $500 [≈ £281]
- The Journal of a Tour to the Hebrides with Samuel Johnson ... Second Edition, Revised and Corrected ... London: Baldwin for Dilly, 1785. 8vo. [iii-xx],[ii],534 pp. Title vignette. Lacks half-title & final advt leaf. 19th c purple lib half calf.   *(Finch)* £130 [≈ $231]
- The Journal of a Tour to the Hebrides, with Samuel Johnson. Dublin: White, Byrne & Cash, 1785. 1st Irish edn. vii,[i],524 pp, advt leaf. Half-title. Contemp mottled calf,

rebacked.   *(Spelman)* £160 [≈ $285]
- The Life of Samuel Johnson ... London: Henry Baldwin ..., 1793. 2nd (1st 8vo) edn. 3 vols. 8vo. Port, Round Robin, facs plate. 19th c half calf, gilt spines, new labels.
       (Young's) £350 [≈ $623]
- A North Briton Extraordinary: Written by a young Scotsman, now a Volunteer in the Corsican Service ... Corte Printed ..., 1769. 1st edn. 8vo. [ii],85,[i] pp. Last leaf reprd. Title browned. Disbound. Anon. Formerly attributed to Boswell.   *(Clark)* £45 [≈ $80]

Bouhours, Dominic

- The Life of St. Ignatius, Founder of the Society of Jesus ... Translated into English by a Person of Quality ... London: Henry Hills, 1686. 1st edn in English. 8vo. [viii], 403,[vii] pp. 3 advt pp at end. Contemp calf, rubbed, crnrs sl worn. Wing B.3826.
       (Clark) £95 [≈ $169]

Boulainvilliers, Henri, Comte de

- An Historical Account of the Antient Parliaments of France ... Translated ... by Charles Forman. London: J. Brindley, 1739. 1st edn in English. 2 vols. 8vo. xxxvi, [i],[ii], 332,[vii],[i errata]; [iv],364, [ix], [i errata],[iv advt] pp. Contemp calf gilt, spines sl worn.
       (Blackwell's) £85 [≈ $151]

Boureau Delandes, Andre Francois

- An Essay on Maritime Power and Commerce; Particularly those of France ... London: for Paul Vaillant, 1743. 1st English edn. 8vo. xii, 163 pp. Disbound. *(Hannas)* £110 [≈ $196]

Bourget, John

- The History of the Royal Abbey of Bec, near Rouen in Normandy. Translated from the French. London: for John Nichols, sold by H. Payne ..., 1779. 1st edn in English. 8vo. viii, 140,[4 advt] pp. Half-title. Fldg frontis, fldg plate. Rec bds.   *(Burmester)* £50 [≈ $89]

Bourn, Benjamin

- A Sure Guide to Hell. By Belzebub. London: for Peter Imp, [1750]. 1st edn (?). 8vo. [ii], vi,9-96 pp. Half title. Sl water stained. Rec bds, uncut. Anon. *(Burmester)* £75 [≈ $134]

Bourne, Henry

- The History of Newcastle upon Tyne ... Newcastle upon Tyne, 1736. Only edn. Folio. [viii], v-viii, 245,[vii] pp. 3 pp subscribers. Fldg plan. Contemp calf, jnts reinforced, extrs worn, lacks label. *(Clark)* £285 [≈ $507]

Boutcher, William
- A Treatise on Forest Trees ... New and Useful Discoveries. Edinburgh: 1775. 1st edn. 4to. 4,xlviii,259,4 pp. Contemp mrbld bds, uncut, rebacked, new endpapers. Not sgnd by the author on title verso.
(Henly) **£125 [≈ $223]**

Bowdler, John
- Reform or Ruin; Take Your Choice! In which the Conduct of the King is considered ... Third Edition. Dublin: John Milliken, 1798. 32 pp. Rebound in bds. Anon.
(C.R. Johnson) **£25 [≈ $45]**

Bowles, John
- A Short Answer to the Declaration of the Persons calling themselves The Friends of the Liberty of the Press. London: Downes, 1793. 1st edn. Tall 8vo. Stitched.
(Rostenberg & Stern) **$185 [≈ £104]**

Bowles, William Lisle
- Sonnets, (Third Edition) with Other Poems ... Bath: R. Cruttwell, sold by C. Dilly, 1794. 8vo. 8,121,[i] pp. Title vignette. Contemp mottled calf gilt, rubbed, jnts cracking, crnrs worn. *(Finch)* **£35 [≈ $62]**
- Sonnets, and Other Poems. Bath: R. Cruttwell ..., 1796. 5th edn, enlgd. 8vo. 140 pp. Tinted aquatint frontis. Lacks half-title. Contemp green half mor, gilt dec spine, sl rubbed. *(Burmester)* **£120 [≈ $214]**

Bowlker, Charles
- The Art of Angling; or, Compleat Fly-Fisher ... Birmingham: Swinney & Walker, 1792. 12mo. xi,118,[2 advt] pp. Frontis. Sm marg stain title & frontis.
(Fenning) **£95 [≈ $169]**

Bownas, Samuel
- An Account of the Life, Travels, and Christian Experiences in the Work of the Ministry of Samuel Bownas. London: 1756. viii, 3-198,[2 advt] pp. 1 sm tear. Calf gilt, front jnt worn, sm chip hd of spine, crnrs bumped. *(Reese)* **$275 [≈ £154]**

Bowyer, William & Nichols, John (editors)
- The Origin of Printing. In Two Essays ... The Second Edition: With Improvements. London: Bowyer & Nichols, 1776. 8vo. viii,176 pp. Mod lib cloth, spine ends sl rubbed. Anon. *(Finch)* **£300 [≈ $534]**

Boydell, John & Josiah
- A Collection of Views, of Gentlemen's Seats, Castles, and Romantick Places in North Wales. Drawn and Engraved by Eminent Artists. London: 1792. Landscape 4to. 14 plates. Occas sl foxing. Later bds, sl worn & rubbed. *(Francis Edwards)* **£250 [≈ $445]**

Boyer, Abel
- The Compleat French Master, for Ladies and Gentlemen ... London: for R. Sare, & John Nicholson, 1699. 2nd edn, "corrected and much enlarged". 8vo. [vi],180,[2], 96,160 pp. 6 ff at end with music (not called for). Sl marg worm. Contemp sheep, sl worn. Wing B.3914. *(Burmester)* **£95 [≈ $169]**
- The Royal Dictionary Abridged. In Two Parts. (French & English). London: Innys ..., 1755. 8vo. Frontis. Minor stains lower edges. Mod cloth, soiled & worn.
(D & D Galleries) **$75 [≈ £42]**

Boyer, Jean Baptiste, Marquis d'Argend
- New Memoirs establishing a true Knowledge of Mankind, by discovering the Affections of the Heart ... London: for D. Browne ..., 1747. 1st English edn. 2 vols. 12mo. Plate on the weight of the air. Lib marks on titles. 3 ff torn in marg, no loss. Mod half roan.
(Hannas) **£140 [≈ $249]**

Boyle, Charles, Earl of Orrery
- Dr. Bentley's Dissertations on the Epistles of Phalaris and the Fables of Aesop examined ... The Second Edition. London: for Tho. Bennet, 1698. 8vo. red & black title. Contemp panelled calf, rubbed. Wing O.470.
(Waterfield's) **£105 [≈ $187]**

Boyle, John, Earl of Orrery
- Remarks on the Life and Writings of Dr. Jonathan Swift ... London: for A. Millar, 1752. 1st edn. 8vo. 339,[9] pp. Port frontis. Contemp calf, sl rubbed, jnts sl tender.
(Young's) **£75 [≈ $134]**
- Remarks on the Life and Writings of Dr. Jonathan Swift. Dublin: George Faulkner, 1752. 12mo. Port. Half-title with vignette port. Occas sl browning. Contemp dark red mor gilt, a.e.g., later amateur reback.
(P and P Books) **£45 [≈ $80]**

Boyle, Robert
- A Free Discourse against customary swearing and a Dissuasive from Cursing ... Published by John Williams. London: R.R. for Thomas Cockerill, 1695. 8vo. Title-page a cancel as usual. Frontis. Contemp panelled calf, rebacked. Wing B.3978.
(Waterfield's) **£375 [≈ $668]**
- A Free Discourse Against Customary Swearing. And a Dissuasive from Cursing.

London: R.R. for Thomas Cockerill ..., 1695.
1st edn. 8vo. [16],131, [3],[32],[2 advt] pp.
Frontis port (trimmed & mtd). Title worn &
soiled. Sl soil. Later calf. Wing B.3978.
(D & D Galleries) **$525 [≈ £295]**

- New Experiments and Observations touching
Cold ... With an Appendix ... London: 1683.
[xlii],325, 20,29 pp. 2 plates in facs. Contemp
leather, rubbed, hinges cracked, sl shaken.
(Whitehart) **£400 [≈ $712]**

- Occasional Reflections upon Several Subjects
... London: W. Wilson for Henry
Herringman, 1665. 1st edn. 8vo. [xxxviii],80,
161-264, [ii],229,[xi] pp. Imprimatur leaf.
Contemp calf, sl rubbed, scuffed. Wing
B.4005.   *(Clark)* **£680 [≈ $1,210]**

- The Origin of Formes and Qualities ...
Second Edition, augmented ... Oxford: H.
Hall for Ric. Davis, 1667. 8vo. [xxxii],262,
265-289, [1], 291-362 pp. F8 present, lacks
a4. Title sl creased. Contemp calf, shaken,
jnts cracked. Wing B.4015.
(Gaskell) **£600 [≈ $1,068]**

Bracton, Henry de
- De Legibus et Consuetudinibus Angliae,
Libri Quinque. London: Totell, 1569. 1st
edn. Folio. Title, 15 ff, [1]-172, 175-444 ff,
complete. Some dust & chipping at ends.
Occas foxing & sl browning. Later calf,
backstrip laid down. STC 3475.
(Meyer Boswell) **$7,500 [≈ £4,213]**

Braddon, Lawrence
- Essex's Innocency and Honour Vindicated ...
London: for the author, 1690. 1st edn. 4to.
[viii],62 pp. Frontis. Title dust stained, some
soiling. Later mrbld bds, worn. Wing B.4101.
(Finch) **£85 [≈ $151]**

Bradley, Richard
- New Improvements of Planting and
Gardening, Both Philosophical and Practical.
In Three Parts ... Fourth Edition ... added ...
Herefordshire-Orchards. London: W. Mears,
1724. 3 parts in one vol. 8vo. 11 plates.
Contemp calf, rebacked, sl worn.
(Heritage) **$450 [≈ £253]**

- New Improvements of Planting and
Gardening, both Philosophical and Practical.
In Three Parts. To which is added
Herefordshire Orchards, A Pattern for all
England. London: [1730-] 1731. 6th edn. 8vo.
[xiv],608,[23] pp. Frontis, 18 plates (on 13 ff).
Mod calf antique.
(Wheldon & Wesley) **£100 [≈ $178]**

- New Improvements of Planting and
Gardening, both Philosophical and Practical,
In Three Parts ... To which is added ...

Herefordshire Orchards ... London: 1739. 7th
edn. 8vo. [xvi],608,[xxiv] pp. Frontis, 13
plates (10 fldg). Contemp calf gilt, rubbed,
backstrip relaid.   *(Henly)* **£175 [≈ $312]**

- A Survey of the Ancient Husbandry and
Gardening collected from Cato, Varro,
Columella, Virgil, and others. London: 1725.
8vo. [xvi],373,[10] pp. 4 plates on 2 ff.
Contemp calf, rebacked with mor.
(Wheldon & Wesley) **£130 [≈ $231]**

Bramston, James
- The Art of Politicks, in Imitation of Horace's
Art of Poetry. London: 1729. 1st edn. 8vo.
Frontis. Orig wraps. Anon.
(Robertshaw) **£50 [≈ $89]**

Brand, John
- The History and Antiquities of the Town and
County of Newcastle upon Tyne. London:
White & Egerton, 1789. 2 vols. Folio.
Subscribers. 12 fldg & 21 other plates, text
ills. Inner marg worm end of vol 1. Orig bds,
shabby, some damage.
(Rostenberg & Stern) **$175 [≈ £98]**

Brand, John, of Lincoln College, Oxford
- On Illicit Love. Written among the Ruins of
Godstow Nunnery, near Oxford. Newcastle
upon Tyne: T. Saint ..., 1775. 1st edn. 4to.
[4],20 pp, inc half-title. Title engv by R.
Beilby. Disbound.   *(Hannas)* **£160 [≈ $285]**

Brandon, John
- Fifty Queries, Seriously Propounded to those
that Question, or Deny Infants Right to
Baptism. By J.B. ... London: for Nevil
Symonds, 1675. Only edn. 8vo. [vi],26 pp.
Title laid down. 1st 3 ff reprd in margs. New
bds. Wing B.4249A. *(Young's)* **£75 [≈ $134]**

Brathwaite, Richard
- A Comment upon the Two Tales of ... Sr.
Jeffray Chaucer ... The Miller's Tale, and
The Wife of Bath. London: W. Godbid, sold
by Robert Clavell, 1665. 1st edn. 8vo. Mod
calf, old style. Wing B.4260A. Anon.
(Hannas) **£320 [≈ $570]**

- Drunken Barnaby's Four Journeys to the
North of England. In Latin and English
Metre ... London: for S. Illidge, 1723. 3rd
edn. 12mo. [xxii],175, [9],[2 advt] pp. Frontis,
5 plates. Contemp calf, jnts cracked, label
chipped. Anon.   *(Burmester)* **£75 [≈ $134]**

- Drunken Barnaby's Four Journeys to the
North of England. In Latin and English Verse
... Dublin: for William Williamson, 1762.
12mo. 137,[7] pp. Some stains. Later green
calf. Anon.   *(Burmester)* **£140 [≈ $249]**

- A Survey of History: or, A Nursery for Gentry ... London: J. Okes for Jasper Emery, 1638. 2nd edn. 4to. Addtnl engvd title with port of the author. Upper blank marg of title & 3 prelim ff strengthened. Niger mor, a.e.g. STC 3583A. *(Hannas)* £650 [≈ $1,157]

Bray, William

- Sketch of a Tour into Derbyshire and Yorkshire ... London: for B. White ..., 1783. 2nd edn. vii,402 pp. 9 plates. Occas minor browning & offsetting. Half calf & bds, sl worn. *(Francis Edwards)* £45 [≈ $80]
- Sketch of a Tour into Derbyshire and Yorkshire ... Second Edition. London: B. White, 1783. viii,402 pp. 9 plates. Tears in title reprd. 19th c half calf, backstrip relaid, new endpapers.
(Jermy & Westerman) £95 [≈ $169]
- Sketch of a Tour into Derbyshire and Yorkshire ... London: 1783. 2nd edn. 8vo. viii,402 pp. 9 plates. Occas foxing. Contemp tree calf, gilt spine, extrs worn, upper bd detached, lower jnt cracked.
(Francis Edwards) £40 [≈ $71]
- Sketch of a Tour into Derbyshire and Yorkshire ... London: B. White, 1783. 2nd edn. 8vo. viii,402 pp. 9 plates. Orig half leather, worn.
(Bates & Hindmarch) £65 [≈ $116]

Brende, John

- The History of Quintus Curtius, contayning the Actes of the great Alexander. Translated out of Latine into English. London: Thomas Crede, 1614. Sm 8vo. Title rather soiled & weak with sm tears at lower edge. Later polished calf gilt. STC 6148.
(Hollett) £95 [≈ $169]

Brett, Thomas

- An Account of Church-Government, and Governours. London: for John Wyat, 1701. 1st edn. 8vo. [xii],260 pp. Contemp panelled calf, label chipped, front cvr just pulling. Anon. *(Young's)* £80 [≈ $142]
- A Collection of the Principal Liturgies, used by the Christian Church in the Celebration of the Holy Eucharist ... London: Richard King, 1720. 1st edn. 8vo. xvi, [vii], 160, 437,[3] pp. Title inner marg reprd. Mod qtr mor gilt.
(Blackwell's) £45 [≈ $80]

Breval, John Durant

- Mac-Dermot: or, the Irish Fortune-Hunter. A Poem By the Author of the Art of Dress. London: for E. Curll, 1717 [crrctd in ink to 1719]. 8vo. [8],48 pp. Sl browning. Disbound. Anon. *(Hannas)* £200 [≈ $356]

Brevint, Daniel

- Saul and Samuel at Endor, or the New Waies of Salvation and Service ... Represented, and refuted ... Oxford: at the Theater, 1674. 1st edn. 8vo. [xiv],413,[1 errata] pp. Frontis. Old calf, rebacked. Wing B.4423.
(Young's) £45 [≈ $80]

Brickell, John

- The Natural History of North Carolina. With an Account of the Trade, Manners, and Customs of the Christian and Indian Inhabitants ... Dublin: 1737. xv,[1],408 pp. Fldg map, 4 plates. Antique calf & mrbld bds.
(Reese) $3,000 [≈ £1,685]

Bridges, John & Foly, Thomas

- The Humble Petition of Many Thousands, Gentlemen ... of the County of Worcester, to the Parliament of the Common-Wealth of England ... London: Tyton & Underhill, 1652. 4to. Stitched. Wing B.4477.
(Rostenberg & Stern) $85 [≈ £48]

Bridges, W.

- Ioabs Counsell, and King Davids Seasonable Hearing It. Delivered in a Sermon before the Honourable House of Commons ... Feb 22. London: R. Cotes for Andrew Croke, 1643. Sm 4to. [viii],23 pp. 1 blank crnr torn. Later half calf. Wing B.4484A.
(Frew Mackenzie) £45 [≈ $80]

Bridoul, Toussaint

- The School of the Eucharist established upon the Miraculous Respects ... which Beasts, Birds, and Insects ... have rendred to the Holy Sacrament ... made English ... London: 1687. 1st edn in English. 4to. [ii], 45, [i] pp. Disbound, stitching broken. Wing B.4495.
(Clark) £50 [≈ $89]

Brief ...

- A Brief and true Representation of the Posture of Our Affairs: containing a Particular Account of the Dangers to be apprehended from the present Invasion ... London: for E. Owen, 1745. 1st edn. 8vo. 30 pp, blank leaf. Disbound.
(Hannas) £65 [≈ $116]

Brightland, John

- A Grammar of the English Tongue, with the Arts of Logick, Rhetorick, Poetry, &c. ... Third Edition. London: for John Brightland, 1714. Fcap 8vo. [16],264 pp, inc fldg table. Contemp calf, spine ends reprd, new label.
(Spelman) £120 [≈ $214]

Britannia in Mourning ...

- Britannia in Mourning: or, a Review of the Politicks and Conduct of the Court of Great Britain with regard to France ... Second Edition. London: for J. Huggonson, 1742. 8vo. 8vo. 72 pp. Disbound.
(Hannas) £65 [≈ $116]

British ...

- The British Librarian ... see Oldys, William
- The British Navy Triumphant! Being Copies of the London Gazettes Extraordinary; containing the Accounts of the Glorious Victories obtained ... Oxford: 1798. 8vo. 28 pp. Half-title. Sl dusty. Disbound.
(Clark) £35 [≈ $62]
- British Zoology Illustrated ... see Pennant, Thomas

Brodrick, Thomas

- A Compleat History of the Late War In the Netherlands. Together with an Abstract of the Treaty at Utrecht. London: for Thomas Ward, 1713. 1st edn. 1 vol bound in 2. 8vo. [xii], 23,[i], xvi,218, (219)-448, [xii] pp. Intl advt leaf. 15 plans. Sl marks. Rec half calf.
(Clark) £130 [≈ $231]

Brome, Alexander

- Songs and Other Poems. London: Henry Brome, 1661. 1st edn. 8vo. [i],[xvi], "202" [ie 328] pp. Without the errata slip sometimes found. Port. Few pen trials. Late 19th c mor, a.e.g., spine & jnts sl rubbed. Wing B.4852.
(Blackwell's) £400 [≈ $712]
- Songs and Other Poems. The Second Edition Corrected and Enlarged. London: Henry Brome, 1664. 8vo. [xxvi],350,[6] pp. 3 advt ff & transverse title label at end. No intl blank. Lib marks on title. Port frontis. Contemp calf, gilt spine, sl worn. Wing B.4853.
(Clark) £380 [≈ $676]

Bromley, William

- Several Years Travels through Portugal, Spain, Italy, Germany, Prussia, Sweden, Denmark, and the United Provinces. Performed by a Gentleman. London: for A. Roper ..., 1702. 1st edn. 8vo. Interleaved. Contemp calf, spine ends reprd. Anon.
(Hannas) £240 [≈ $427]

Brook, Abraham

- Miscellaneous Experiments and Remarks on Electricity, the Air-Pump, and the Barometer ... Norwich: Crouse & Stevenson, for J. Johnson, London, 1789. 1st edn. 4to. 3 plates. Old lib stamp. Contemp calf gilt, crudely rebacked in cloth.

(Ximenes) $500 [≈ £281]

Brooke, Henry

- The Fool of Quality; or, the History of Henry Earl Moreland. London: for W. Johnston ..., 1766-70. 1st edn. 5 vols. 12mo. Some browning to titles. Lacks fly-leaf vol 1. Vol 1 title mtd & stubbed. Rebound in half calf.
(Francis Edwards) £300 [≈ $534]
- The Fool of Quality, or the History of Henry Earl of Moreland ... The Second Edition. London: for W. Johnstone, 1767-69. 4 vols. 8vo. Contemp calf, somewhat worn but sound. *(Waterfield's)* £100 [≈ $178]
- The Fool of Quality: or, The History of Henry Earl of Moreland. London: for W. Johnston, 1767-70. 2nd edn vols 1 & 2, 1st edn vols 3-5. 5 vols. 12mo. Contemp calf.
(Hannas) £220 [≈ $392]
- Juliet Grenville: or, the History of the Human Heart. London: for G. Robinson, 1774. 1st edn. 3 vols. 12mo. Half-titles, final blank leaf vol 3. Contemp polished calf gilt, jnts weak. *(Hannas)* £350 [≈ $623]

Brooke, Nathaniel

- Englands Glory, or, an Exact Catalogue of the Lords of his Majesties Privy Councel. London: Brooke, 1660. 8vo. Compartmental frontis. Contemp calf. Wing B.4907.
(Rostenberg & Stern) $350 [≈ £197]

Brookes, R.

- The General Dispensatory. Containing a Translation of the Pharmacopoeias of the Royal Colleges of Physicians of London and Edinburgh. London: 1765. 2nd edn. x,390 pp. Endpapers & title sl torn. Foxing. Old leather, hinges sl cracked but firm.
(Whitehart) £90 [≈ $160]
- The General Practice of Physic ... London: 1754. 2nd edn. 332 pp. Occas sl foxing. Old calf, rebacked. *(Whitehart)* £180 [≈ $320]

Brooks, Catharine

- The Complete English Cook; or Prudent Housewife ... Fourth Edition. London: for the authoress, & sold by J. Cooke, [ca 1765]. 8vo. 132 pp. 'To the Ladies' advt between A1 & A2. Frontis, 3 w'engvd ills. Early 19th c limp vellum. *(Gough)* £295 [≈ $525]

Brooks, Jonathan

- Antiquity; or the Wise Instructor, being a Collection of the most Valuable Admonitions and Sentences ... Bristol: 1770. 1st edn. 12mo. Contemp calf, rubbed, lower cvr loose.
(Robertshaw) £35 [≈ $62]

Broome, Ralph

- The Letters of Simkin the Second, Poetic Recorder of all the Proceedings, upon the Trial of Warren Hastings, Esq. in Westminster Hall. London: 1791. 8vo. 368 pp. Contemp half calf, crnrs sl rubbed. Anon.
  (Robertshaw) **£40 [≈ $71]**

Brown, Edward (pseudonym)

- The Travels and Adventures ... see Campbell, John

Brown, John "Estimate"

- The Cure of Saul. A Sacred Ode. London: for Davis & Reymers, 1763. 1st edn. 4to. [vi],21,[3] pp. Half-title, final advt leaf. Sl marg water stains.
  (Burmester) **£150 [≈ $267]**
- An Essay on Satire: Occasion'd by the Death of Mr. Pope. London: for J. Dodsley, 1745. 1st edn. 4to. 32 pp. Title engv. Disbound. Anon.
  (Hannas) **£250 [≈ $445]**
- An Estimate of the Manners and Principles of the Times. London: for L. Davis & C. Reymers, 1758. 1st edn vol 2, 7th edn vol 1. 2 vols in one. 8vo. 221,[3]; 265,[5] pp. Crnr torn from an advt leaf with loss of 5 letters. Contemp calf, minor wear hd of spine. Anon.
  (Burmester) **£175 [≈ $312]**
- An Estimate of the Manners and Principles of the Times ... The Third Edition. London: for L. Davis & C. Reymers, 1757. 8vo. Contemp calf, ft of spine chipped, jnts cracked. Anon.
  (Waterfield's) **£75 [≈ $134]**
- An Explanatory Defence of the Estimate of the Manners and Principles of the Times being an Appendix to that Work, occasioned by the Clamours lately raised against it ... London: Davis & Reymers, 1758. 8vo. Half-title. B3 cancelled as usual. Disbound. Anon.
  (Waterfield's) **£105 [≈ $187]**
- The History of the Rise and Progress of Poetry through its Several Species. Newcastle: J. White & T. Saint, 1764. vii, [2], 10-266,[2] pp. Advts. Contemp calf, sl splits in jnts.
  (C.R. Johnson) **£250 [≈ $445]**
- Honour. A Poem. Inscribed to the Right Honble the Lord Viscount Lonsdale. London: Dodsley, Cooper, 1743. 1st edn. 4to. 23 pp, inc half-title. Some pp cut short at ft, cutting into imprint & 1 footnote. Disbound. Anon.
  (Hannas) **£300 [≈ $534]**
- Sermons on Various Subjects. London: Davies & Reymers, 1764. 1st edn. 8vo. Title-page not a cancel. Contemp calf, mor label, sl rubbed.
  (Waterfield's) **£80 [≈ $142]**

Brown, Thomas, of Shifnal

- The Lives of all the Princes of Orange; From William the Great. London: Thomas Bennet, 1693. 1st edn. 8,6,16, 305 pp. Port. Contemp calf, gilt dec spine, label chipped, rear bd loose, front bd detached.
  (Jermy & Westerman) **£30 [≈ $53]**

Brown, Thomas

- The Weesils. A Satyrical Fable: giving an Account of some Argumental Passages happening in the Lion's Court about Weesilion's taking the Oaths. London: ptd in the year 1691. Only edn. 4to. [ii],12,[2 postscript] pp. 2 sm worm holes. Rec bds. Wing B.5077. Anon. *(Clark)* **£120 [≈ $214]**
- The Works ... Serious and Comical, in Prose and Verse ... With the Life and Character of Mr. Brown ... by James Drake ... Ninth Edition. London: Wilde ..., 1760. 4 vols. 8vo. 4 frontis, 23 plates. Period calf, spine ends sl chipped. *(Rankin)* **£250 [≈ $445]**

Brown, Thomas & Ward, Edward

- Legacy for the Ladies. Or, Characters of the Women of the Age. With a Comical View of London and Westminster ... London: H. Meere, for S. Briscoe, sold by J. Nutt, 1705. 1st edn. 8vo. 4 advt pp. 19th c polished calf, gilt spine. *(Hannas)* **£550 [≈ $979]**

Brown, Thomas, & others

- Letters from the Dead to the Living. London: printed in the Year, 1702. 1st edn. 8vo. Contemp calf, rubbed, jnts cracking.
  (Waterfield's) **£200 [≈ $356]**

Browne, Sir John

- A Collection of Tracts, concerning the Present State of Ireland, with Respect to its Riches, Revenues, Trade, and Manufacture. London: Woodward & Peele, 1729. 1st edn of this compilation. 8vo. [2],144 pp inc half-title. Disbound. Anon.
  (Hannas) **£450 [≈ $801]**

Browne, Joseph

- St. James's Park. A Satyr. London: H. Hills, 1709. 8vo. 16 pp. Disbound. Anon.
  (Hannas) **£85 [≈ $151]**

Browne, Sir Thomas

- Christian Morals ... Published from the Original and Correct Manuscript ... by John Jeffery ... Cambridge: University Press ..., 1716. 1st edn. 12mo. [viii],127,[i] pp. Advt leaf at end. Lacks intl blank & half-title. Ink trials. Contemp calf, backstrip relaid.
  (Blackwell's) **£200 [≈ $356]**

- Posthumous Works ... Printed from his Original Manuscripts ... To which is prefix'd his Life. London: E. Curll & R. Gosling, 1712. 8vo. [iv],xl,[ii], 74,[iv],8, 16,56,64 pp. Port, 22 plates. Some plates damp stained. Contemp panelled calf, rebacked, crnrs rprd.
(Clark) **£225 [≈ $401]**
- Pseudodoxia Epidemica: or, Enquiries into very many received Tenets, and commonly presumed Truths. London: T.H. for Edward Dod, 1646. 1st edn. Sm folio. [xx],386 pp. Licence leaf. Sm wormhole. Contemp sheep, rebacked. Crack in upper jnt. Wing B.5159.
(Burmester) **£350 [≈ $623]**
- Pseudodoxia Epidemica: or, Enquiries into very many Received Tenets, and commonly presumed Truths ... London: Harper for Dod, 1646. 1st edn. Sm folio. [20],386 pp. Final blank. Text within double rules. Orig (?) panelled calf, v sl worn.
(Goodrich) **$1,250 [≈ £702]**
- Pseudodoxia Epidemica: or Enquiries into very many received Tenets, and commonly presumed Truths. London: T.H. for Edward Dod, 1646. 1st edn. Folio. A1 blank present. Title laid down & reprd. Minor marg fraying few ff. Mod qtr calf. Wing B.5159.
(Waterfield's) **£375 [≈ $668]**
- Pseudodoxia Epidemica ... The Second Edition, Corrected and much Enlarged by the Author ... London: Miller ..., 1650. Sm folio. [8],329,[5] pp. Sl browning. Later calf, gilt inner dentelles. *(Goodrich)* **$795 [≈ £447]**
- Religio Medici. The Seventh Edition, Corrected and Amended. With Annotations ... also Observations By Sir Kenelm Digby ... London: 1678. 8vo. [xvi],181, [ix], 185-371, [3] pp. Frontis (edges sl chipped). Contemp calf, rebacked, crnrs sl worn. Wing B.5177.
(Clark) **£110 [≈ $196]**
- The Works ... London: Bassett, Chiswell ..., 1686. 1st coll edn. Folio. [xviii], 316, [xii], [xiv],102,[viii], 52,[vi], "103" [ie 73],[v] pp. Port frontis, 2 engvd ills. Final index leaf sl frayed, no loss. Contemp calf, rebacked, extrs sl worn. Wing B.5150. *(Clark)* **£450 [≈ $801]**

Browne, William

- Britannia's Pastorals. London: John Haviland, 1625. 1st 8vo edn. 2 parts. Lacks sub-title to 2nd part. Some stains, 2 pp (with w'cuts) v finger marked. Contemp calf. STC 3916. Anon. *(Hannas)* **£220 [≈ $392]**

Bruys, Francois

- The Art of Knowing Women: or, the Female Sex Dissected, in a Faithful Representation of their Virtues and Vices ... By the Chevalier Plante-Amour. The Second Edition. London:

for E. Curll & T. Payne, 1732. 12mo. [16],244,[4 advt] pp. Frontis. Mod three qtr mor gilt.   *(D & D Galleries)* **$500 [≈ £281]**

Bryant, Jacob

- Observations and Inquiries Relating to the Various Parts of Ancient History ... Together with an Account of Egypt in its Most Early State ... Cambridge: J. Archdeacon, 1767. 1st edn. 4to. xvi,324 pp. 6 fldg maps, 1 plate. Contemp calf gilt, rebacked.
(Gough) **£185 [≈ $329]**
- Observations upon the Poems of Thomas Rowley: in which the authenticity of those Poems is ascertained. London: for T. Payne & Son, T. Cadell, P. Elmsly, 1781. 1st edn. 8vo. 2 fldg tables. Contemp calf gilt, spine rubbed & dry.   *(Ximenes)* **$175 [≈ £98]**

Brydall, John

- Jura Coronae. His Majesties Royal Rights and Prerogatives Asserted. London: Dawes, 1680. 8vo. Plate of Royal Arms. Calf, rebacked. Wing B.5260. Anon.
(Rostenberg & Stern) **$375 [≈ £211]**
- Jus Imaginis apud Anglos; or The Law of England relating to the Nobility & Gentry. London: for John Billinger ..., 1675. 1st edn. Fldg table. Browned. 1st blank defective. Mod half calf. Wing B.5261.
(Meyer Boswell) **$350 [≈ £197]**
- Jus Sigilli: or, The Law of England, Touching His Majesties Four Principal Seales ... London: E. Flesher, for Thomas dring & John Leigh, 1673. Only edn. 12mo. [ii], 129, [xv] pp. Edges trifle browned. Old calf, rebacked. Wing B.5263.
(Hollett) **£175 [≈ $312]**

Brydges, Sir Samuel Egerton

- Topographical Miscellanies ... Volume I [all published]. London: Robson & Symonds, 1792. Only edn. 4to. [ii],xx,[cxxxiv],66, 4,[ii] pp. Half-title, binder leaf at end. 13 plates inc fldg plan. Contemp qtr calf, mrbld bds renewed, sm reprs spine ends. Anon.
(Clark) **£160 [≈ $285]**

Brydges, Thomas

- A Burlesque Translation of Homer. London: for G.G. & J. Robinson, 1797. 1st edn. 2 vols. 8vo. [vi],360; [iv],432 pp. 24 etchings by Samuel Howitt. Contemp red half mor, gilt ruled spines. Anon. *(Gough)* **£295 [≈ $525]**

Brydone, Patrick

- A Tour through Sicily and Malta. In a Series of Letters to William Beckford ... London: Strahan & Cadell, 1776. New (4th) edn. 2

vols. 8vo. Contemp tree calf, gilt spines, contrasting mor labels (tiny rubbed spot on one label). *(Ximenes)* **$350 [≈ £197]**

- A Tour through Sicily and malta. In a Series of Letters to William Beckford ... London: 1776. 2 vols. 8vo. xvi,373; xi,355 pp. Fldg map. Tree calf, rebacked, vol 2 front jnt splitting. *(McBlain)* **$100 [≈ £56]**

Buch'hoz, Pierre Joseph
- The Toilet of Flora; or, a Collection of the most simple and approved Methods of Preparing Baths, Essences, Pomatums, Powders, Perfumes and Sweet-Scented Waters ... New Edition, improved. London: 1779. 12mo. Half-title. Frontis. Mod mor. Anon. *(Robertshaw)* **£165 [≈ $294]**

Buchan, William
- Domestic Medicine. or, a Treatise on the Prevention and Cure of Diseases ... The Second Edition, with considerable additions ... London: 1772. 8vo. xxxvi,758 pp. Contemp half calf, worn.
(Goodrich) **$250 [≈ £140]**
- Domestic Medicine ... Carefully Corrected from the latest (8th) London Edition ... Phila: Joseph Cruikshank, 1784. 8vo. 540 pp. Some foxing & browning. Contemp calf, worn, jnts weak, sm piece missing from spine.
(Goodrich) **$150 [≈ £84]**
- Domestic Medicine ... Fifteenth Edition: To which is added Observations concerning the Diet of the Common People ... London: Strahan & Cadell, 1797. 8vo. xl,746,(36) pp. Orig tree calf, sl rubbed.
(Goodrich) **$145 [≈ £81]**

Buchanan, George
- The History of Scotland ... Faithfully Rendered into English. London: Edw. Jones for Awnsham Churchill, 1690. 1st edn in English. Folio. [8],434, 286,[36] pp. Port. Occas sl browning. Contemp panelled calf, rebacked. Wing B.5283.
(O'Neal) **$475 [≈ £267]**

Buckingham, John Sheffield, Duke of
- The Character of a Tory [drop-title]. [Colophon] London: William Inghall the Elder Bookbinder, 1681. Folio. 2 pp. 19th c half calf, hd of spine rubbed. Old Wing B.5335. Anon.
(Frew Mackenzie) **£80 [≈ $142]**

Buckler, Benjamin (attributed author)
- A Philosophical Dialogue concerning Decency. To which is added a Critical and Historical Dissertation on Places of

Retirement for Necessary Occasions ... London: for James Fletcher ..., 1751. 1st edn. 4to. 47,[1] pp. Sl marg water stains. Qtr mor by Sangorski & Sutcliffe. Anon
(Burmester) **£400 [≈ $712]**

Buckley, Samuel
- A Letter to Dr. Mead, concerning a New Edition of Thuanus's History. London: ptd by Sam. Buckley ... sold by J. Roberts, 1728 [1729]. 1st edn. 8vo. Buckley's sgntr on p 38. Disbound. Anon. *(Young's)* **£125 [≈ $223]**

The Builder's Magazine ...
- The Builder's Magazine: or, a Universal Dictionary for Architects, Carpenters, Masons, Bricklayers, &c. ... By a Society of Architects ... New Edition. London: E. Newbery, 1788. [vi],345,100,8 pp. 185 plates. Old qtr leather, sl worn. Attributed to J. Carter. *(Hortulus)* **$900 [≈ £506]**

Bull, George
- A Vindication of the Church of England, from the Errors and Corruptions of the Church of Rome ... London: E. Curll, 1719. 1st edn. 8vo. [xiii],240 pp. Contemp sprinkled calf, spine gilt, sprinkled edges.
(Blackwell's) **£85 [≈ $151]**

Buller, Francis
- An Introduction to the Law relative to Trials at Nisi Prius ... London: for C. Bathurst, 1781. 3rd edn. 4to. viii,336, [337-380] pp. Contemp calf, label damaged.
(Vanbrugh) **£95 [≈ $169]**

Bullingbrooke, Edward (editor)
- The Duty and Authority of Justices of the Peace and Parish-Officers for Ireland ... Dublin: Boulter Grierson, 1766. 1st edn. 4to. [xviii],816 pp. No free endpapers. Minor soil. Contemp calf, some wear to edges & extrs.
(Clark) **£130£ [≈ $231]**

Bunbury, Henry W.
- An Academy for Grown Horsemen ... By Geoffrey Gambado ... London: for W. Dickinson ..., 1787. 1st edn. 4to. [20],38 pp. Hand cold engvs by Rowlandson. 19th c half mor, gilt spine. *(Chapel Hill)* **$1,200 [≈ £674]**

Bunbury, William
- Reports of Cases in the Court of Exchequer, from the Beginning of the Reign of King George the First ... In the Savoy: Lintot for Browne, 1755. 1st edn. Folio. viii,348,[349-394] pp. Licence leaf. Errata. Contemp calf. *(Vanbrugh)* **£125 [≈ $223]**

Bunyan, John

- The Acceptable Sacrifice: or, the Excellency of a Broken Heart ... London: Richard Janeway for John Gwillim, 1698. 3rd edn. 12mo. Crnr of title chipped. Some browning & foxing. Contemp sheep, worn, spine sometime reprd with 2 leather strips. Wing B.5482. *(Ximenes)* **$1,250 [≈ £702]**

- The Holy War ... [with his] The Heavenly Footman ... [and] An Authentic Account of the Life and Death of Mr. John Bunyan ... Birmingham: Robert Martin, 1789. 8vo. vii, [i], 347,[i], 36,35,[i] pp. Port frontis, 8 plates. Contemp sheep, extrs worn.
  (Clark) **£35 [≈ $62]**

- The Pilgrim's Progress ... Complete in Two Parts ... The Thirty-First Edition. Adorned with curious Sculptures, engraven by J. Sturt. London: for W. Johnston, 1766. 8vo. xvi,212, [xiv],196,[ii] pp. Frontis, 21 plates. Rebound in mottled calf, elab gilt spine.
  (Finch) **£225 [≈ $401]**

- The Works ... Second Edition, with Additions. London: for E. Gardner ..., 1736-37. 1st complete edn. 2 vols. Tall thick folio. Frontis port, plates. Early three qtr leather, elab gilt dec spines (reprd).
  (Hartfield) **$650 [≈ £365]**

Buonamici, Castruccio

- Commentaries on the Late War in Italy, Translated from the original Latin ... prefixed an Introduction. By A. Wishart, M.A. London: for A. Millar, 1753. 8vo. xxviii,547 pp. Lacks front free endpaper. Speckled calf, gilt spine. *(Rankin)* **£60 [≈ $107]**

Burbury, John

- A Relation of a Journey of the Right Honourable My Lord Henry Howard, from London to Vienna, and thence to Constantinople ... London: Collins & Ford, 1671. 1st edn. 12mo. [8],225,[1],[24 advt] pp. Later calf. Wing B.5611.
  (Spelman) **£200 [≈ $356]**

- A Relation of a Journey of the Right Honourable My Lord Henry Howard, from London to Vienna, and thence to Constantinople ... London: Collins & Ford, 1671. 12mo. [x], 225, [1],[29] pp, inc blank A & final blank. Old calf, edges sl worn, mor reback. Wing B.5611. *(Hollett)* **£250 [≈ $445]**

- A Relation of a Journey of the Right Honourable My Lord Henry Howard, from London to Vienna, and thence to Constantinople ... London: Collins & Ford ..., 1671. Only edn. 12mo. [8],225,[xxv] pp. Lacks A1 (blank?). Later calf, sl rubbed. Wing B.5611. *(Clark)* **£450 [≈ $801]**

Burchett, Josiah

- A Complete History of the Most Remarkable Transactions at Sea ... London: W. B. for J. Walthoe ..., 1720. 1st edn. Folio. [lvi],800, [801-832],[i] pp. Privilege & errata ff. 9 fldg maps, port frontis, frontis. Contemp calf gilt, elab gilt spine. *(Vanbrugh)* **£975 [≈ $1,736]**

Burgh, James

- The Art of Speaking. Containing, I. An Essay ... II. Lessons ... Second Edition. London: T. Longman, 1768. 8vo. [2],373,[16] pp. Half-title. Occas soiling. 19th c half calf, rubbed, new endpapers, jnts v sl cracked.
  (Spelman) **£100 [≈ $178]**

- The Art of Speaking. Containing, I. An Essay ... II. Lessons ... Sixth Edition. Dublin: 1784. Fcap 8vo. [2],308,[20] pp. Half-title. Contemp calf, worn. *(Spelman)* **£30 [≈ $53]**

Burgoyne, John

- The Maid of the Oaks: a new Dramatic Entertainment ... London: for T. Becket, 1774. 1st edn. 8vo. Title sl stained. Disbound. Anon. *(Hannas)* **£30 [≈ $53]**

- A State of the Expedition from Canada ... London: 1780. 2nd edn. ix,[1],191, [1],civ pp. 6 fldg cold maps. Contemp calf, outer hinges cracked, front bd loose.
  (Reese) **$1,500 [≈ £843]**

Burke, Edmund

- An Authentic Copy of Mr. Pitt's Letter to His Royal Highness the Prince of Wales, with his Answer. London: Stockdale, 1789. 1st edn (?). 8vo. 12,[4 advt] pp. Disbound.
  (Young's) **£90 [≈ $160]**

- A Letter ... to Sir Hercules Langrishe ... on the Subject of Roman Catholics of Ireland ... London: Debrett, 1792. 1st London edn, 1st imp. 8vo. 88 pp. Outer ff dust soiled. Disbound. Todd 59c.
  (Blackwell's) **£50 [≈ $89]**

- A Letter to a Noble Lord on the Attacks made upon him and His Pension. London: 1796. 7th edn. 8vo. Bds.
  (Rostenberg & Stern) **£60 [≈ $34]**

- A Letter to His Grace the Duke of Portland, on the Conduct of the Minority in Parliament containing the Fifty-Four Articles of Impeachment against the Rt. Hon. C.J. Fox. London: 1797. 8vo. Wraps.
  (Rostenberg & Stern) **£60 [≈ $34]**

- A Philosophical Enquiry into the Origin of our Ideas of the Sublime and Beautiful. The Fifth Edition ... Berwick: R. & J. Taylor, 1772. vii,[5],194, vii,62 pp. Contemp calf. Anon. *(C.R. Johnson)* **£145 [≈ $258]**

- A Philosophical Enquiry into the Origin of our Ideas of the Sublime and Beautiful. The Eighth Edition. With an Introductory Discourse ... and several other Additions. London: Dodsley, 1776. 8vo. Sl foxing, one marg repr. Contemp calf, rebacked. Anon.
(Spelman) £80 [≈ $142]
- A Philosophical Inquiry into the Origin of our Ideas of the Sublime and Beautiful. New Edition. Basel: J.J. Tourneisen, 1792. 8vo. 291,[1 advt] pp. Contemp calf, some rubbing. Anon. *(Robertshaw)* £100 [≈ $178]
- Reflections on the Revolution in France. London: Dodsley, 1790. 2nd edn. 8vo. Disbound. *(Rostenberg & Stern)* $140 [≈ £79]
- Reflections on the Revolution in France ... Dublin: for W. Watson, 1790. 1st Irish edn. 8vo. iv,356 pp. Some marg stains. Rec qtr calf gilt. *(Fenning)* £115 [≈ $205]
- Reflections on the Revolution in France. Dublin: W. Watson, 1790. 1st Dublin edn. iv,356 pp. Contemp tree calf, rubbed, bds almost detached.
(Jermy & Westerman) £100 [≈ $178]
- Reflections on the Revolution in France. London: Dodsley, 1790. 5th edn. 8vo. Disbound. *(Rostenberg & Stern)* $75 [≈ £42]
- A Vindication of Natural Society: or, A View of the Miseries and Evils arising to Mankind from every Species of Artificial Society. Third Edition. London: 1780. 8vo. 160 pp. Mod bds. Anon. *(Robertshaw)* £30 [≈ $53]

Burlesque ...
- A Burlesque Translation of Homer ... see Brydges, Thomas

Burn, Richard
- The Justice of the Peace, and Parish Officer ... continued ... by John Burn. The Seventeenth Edition ... Appendix. London: Strahan & Woodfall, 1793. 4 vols. 8vo. Contemp calf, gilt labels, fine.
(Spelman) £225 [≈ $401]

Burnaby, Andrew
- Travels through the Middle Settlements in North-America, in the Years 1759 and 1760. With Observations upon the State of the Colonies. London: 1775. 4to. viii,106 pp. Errata leaf. Sm hole in title, not affecting text. Later half calf. *(Reese)* $600 [≈ £337]
- Travels through the Middle Settlements in North America, in the Years 1759 and 1760 ... London: for T. Payne, 1775. 2nd edn. 8vo. 198,[1] pp. Contemp calf, gilt labels, jnts weak but holding.
(Chapel Hill) $375 [≈ £211]

- Travels through the Middle Settlements in North America ... London: 1798. 3rd edn. Lge 4to. xix,209 pp. 2 plates, 2 fldg tables. Occas damp stains & foxing. Contemp three qtr calf, untrimmed, sl worn.
(Reese) $950 [≈ £534]

Burnaby, William
- The Ladies Visiting-Day. A Comedy ... With the Addition of a New Scene. By the Author of The Reformed Wife. London: for Peter Buck & Geo. Browning, 1701. 1st edn. 4to. Browning, sl stains. Most head-lines cut into. Mod bds. Anon. *(Hannas)* £180 [≈ $320]

Burnet, Gilbert
- An Abridgement of Bishop Burnet's History of His Own Times. By the Reverend Mr. Thomas Stackhouse. London: J. Smith ..., 1724. 1st edn. 8vo. xvi,422,16 pp. Frontis, port vignette on title. Mod calf.
(Clark) £42 [≈ $75]
- An Essay on the Memory of the Late Queen. London: for Richard Chiswell, 1695. 1st edn. 8vo. 197,[3 advt] pp. Frontis. 18th c calf, mor label. *(Young's)* £110 [≈ $196]
- An Essay on the Memory of the late Queen. The Second Edition. London: Ric. Chiswell, 1696. 197,advt pp. Contemp panelled calf, rebacked. Wing B.5786.
(C.R. Johnson) £55 [≈ $98]
- History of his Own Time ... Together with the Author's Life, by the Editor, and some Explanatory Notes. London: A. Millar, 1753. 1st 8vo. edn. 4 vols. Port frontis vol 1. Contemp qtr calf, vellum leading edges to bds. *(Spelman)* £240 [≈ $427]
- The History of the Rights of Princes in the Disposing of Ecclesiastical Benefices and Church-Lands. Relating chiefly to the Pretensions of the Crown of France to the Regale ... London: for Richard Chiswell, 1682-81. 1st edn. 8vo. 328,[3],235 pp. Later half calf. *(Young's)* £95 [≈ $169]
- The Life and Death of Sir Matthew Hale, Kt. Sometime Lord Chief Justice of His Majesties Court of Kings Bench. London: for William Shrowsbery, 1682. Port. Mod leather.
(D & D Galleries) $145 [≈ £81]
- The Life of William Bedell, D.D., Bishop of Kilmore in Ireland ... London: John Southby, 1685. 1st edn. 8vo. [xxxviii],259,[i errata], [xii], 265-487 pp. Contemp calf, rubbed, some wear hd of spine. Wing B.5830.
(Blackwell's) £65 [≈ $116]
- The Memoires of ... James and William Dukes of Hamilton and Castleherald ... London: Grover for Royston, 1677. Only edn. Folio. [xviii],436,[437-448] pp. Errata

page & licence leaf. 3 ports inc frontis. Occas lib stamp in text. Rec qtr calf. Wing B.5832.
(Vanbrugh) £325 [≃ $579]

- Reflections on Mr. Varillas's History of the Revolutions that have happened in Europe in matters of Religion. Amsterdam: for P. Savouret, 1686. 1st edn. 12mo. Contemp mottled calf over wooden bds, jnts cracking. Wing B.5852.   *(Hannas)* £55 [≃ $98]

- Some Account of the Life and Death of John Wilmot, Earl of Rochester ... Written by his own Direction on his Death-Bed. Albany: M'Donald, 1797. 8vo. Calf.
(Rostenberg & Stern) $150 [≃ £84]

- Three Letters Concerning the Present State of Italy, Written in the Year 1687. [London]: 1688. 8vo. Calf. Wing B.5931.
(Rostenberg & Stern) $285 [≃ £160]

- Three Letters concerning the Present State of Italy ... Being a Supplement to Dr. Burnets letters. [London]: Printed in the Year, 1688. 1st edn (?). 'Present State' on title in roman letters. Sm 8vo. [16],191,[1] pp. Contemp calf, rebacked. Wing B.5931.
(Hannas) £45 [≃ $80]

- Three Letters Concerning the Present State of Italy, written in the Year 1687. London: 1688. 1st edn. Fcap 8vo. [16],191,[1 errata] pp. Minor worm to 1 marg just affecting some text. Rec half calf. Wing B.5931.
(Spelman) £85 [≃ $151]

- Three Letters concerning the Present State of Italy ... [London]: Printed in the Year, 1688. 2nd edn (?). 'Present State' on title in Black Letter. 12mo. [24],192 pp, inc intl blank leaf. Mod bds. Wing B.5932.
(Hannas) £30 [≃ $53]

Burnet, Gilbert (translator)

- The Letter writ by the last Assembly General of the Clergy of France to the Protestants, inviting them to return to their Communion ... Translated into English and Examined ... London: Chiswell, 1683. 8vo. [xx], 179,[i] pp. Old sheep, some wear & tear. Wing L.1759.
(Clark) £50 [≃ $89]

Burnet, Thomas

- The Sacred Theory of the Earth ... Sixth Edition, to which is added the Author's Defence of the Work ... London: 1726. 2 vols. 8vo. Frontis port, addtnl engvd title, fldg plate, text ills. Ex-lib. Contemp calf, v worn, 1 bd detached.   *(Weiner)* £100 [≃ $178]

Burney, Charles

- A General History of Music ... London: for the author, 1776-89. 1st edn. 4 vols. 4to. Num plates, engvd music. Sm lib blind

stamp. B'plates. Early elab gilt three qtr leather, backstrips laid down.
(Hartfield) $1,950 [≃ £1,096]

Burney, Frances (Fanny), Madame D'Arblay

- Camilla: or, a Picture of Youth. By the Author of Evelina and Cecilia. London: for T. Payne, Cadell & Davies, 1796. 1st edn. 5 vols. 12mo. Subscribers. Final advt leaf vol 1. 2 sm reprs. Contemp half calf. Anon.
(Hannas) £180 [≃ $320]

- Evelina, or a Young Lady's Entrance into the World. In a Series of Letters. London: for T. Lowndes, 1779. 2nd edn. 3 vols. 12mo. B'plates removed. Contemp half calf, gilt spines, sl rubbed, 1 jnt cracked. Anon.
(Ximenes) $600 [≃ £337]

- Evelina, or the History of a Young Lady's Entrance into the World. London: T. Lowndes, 1779. 3 vols. 8vo. 3 frontis. Orig tree calf, rebacked. *(Hartfield)* $495 [≃ £278]

- Evelina, or the History of a Young Lady's Entrance into the World. A New Edition. London: for T. & W. Lowndes, 1784. 2 vols. 8vo. Lacks a free endpaper vol 1. Contemp calf, contrasting labels. Anon.
(Waterfield's) £75 [≃ $134]

Burns, John

- An Historical and Chronological Remembrancer of all remarkable Occurences, from the Creation to this Present Year of Our Lord, 1775 ... Dublin: for the author, 1775. 1st edn. 8vo. 504,[8] pp. Subscribers. Contemp calf, new label.
(Young's) £85 [≃ $151]

Burns, Robert

- Poems, Chiefly in the Scottish Dialect ... Third Edition ... London: 1787. 1st London edn. 8vo. xlviii,(13)-372 pp. Half-title. 38 pp subscribers. Port frontis. Occas sl foxing. 1 gathering advanced. Contemp calf, gilt spine, rubbed, spine ends worn.
(Clark) £120 [≃ $214]

- Poems, chiefly in the Scottish Dialect. A New Edition, Considerably Enlarged. Edinburgh: for T. Cadell, London, & William Creech, 1794. 2 vols. Lge 12mo. xii,237; [iv], 283 pp. Half-titles. Port. Lacks final blank vol 2. V sl marg soil. Contemp calf, rebacked.
(Blackwell's) £165 [≃ $294]

Burnyeat, John

- The Truth Exalted in the Writings of ... Collected ... as a Memorial to his faithful Labours in and for the Truth. London: for T. Northcott, 1691. 1st coll edn. 4to. [10],20,

72,[2], 73-257, 260-264 [ie 262] pp. 1 sm repr.
Contemp calf, worn but sound. Wing B.5968.
(Fenning) £85 [≈ $151]

Burroughes, Jeremiah
- Moses His Choice, with His Eye Fixed upon
Heaven: Discovering the Happy Condition of
a Self-Denting Heart. Delivered in a Treatise
upon Hebrews ... London: 1641. 1st edn.
Title, [13],754 pp. Sm crnr reprs. Sl foxed.
Green polished calf, faded, hinges rubbed.
(D & D Galleries) $125 [≈ £70]

Burton, John
- A Treatise on the Non-Naturals ... subjoin'd,
A Short Essay on the Chin-Cough ... York:
ptd by A. Staples ..., 1738. 1st edn. 8vo.
[ii],xxiii, [i],367 pp. Contemp calf, rebacked
to style, new endpapers. *(Finch)* £400 [≈ $712]

Burton, R.
- Wonderful Prodigies of Judgment & Mercy
Discovered in above 300 Memorable
Histories. Edinburgh: 1762. 6th (?) edn. Orig
calf, rear bd detached.
(Deja Vu) £85 [≈ $151]

Burton, Robert
- The Anatomy of Melancholy ... The Fourth
Edition, corrected and augmented by the
author. Oxford: Henry Cripps, [1632]. Folio.
Engvd border to title. Title sl cropped at ft
with loss of date. 18th c diced calf, sl worn.
STC 4162.
(Frew Mackenzie) £650 [≈ $1,157]

**Burton, Robert (pseudonym of Nathaniel
Crouch)**
- A New View, and Observations ... of London
and Westminster ... London: Bettesworth,
Hitch, Batey, 1730. 1st edn thus. 8vo. [vi],
312, 145-240, 385-468 pp, complete. Num
w'cuts, some full-page. Contemp calf,
rebacked. *(Vanbrugh)* £175 [≈ $312]

Burton, William
- A Commentary on Antoninus his Itinerary, or
Journies of the Romane Empire, so far as it
concerneth Britain ... London: Roycroft for
Twyford, 1658. 1st edn. Sm folio. [22],
266,[6] pp. Frontis port, dble page map.
Contemp calf, rebacked, rubbed. Wing
B.6185. *(O'Neal)* £300 [≈ £169]
- A Commentary on Antoninus his Itinerary, or
Journies of the Romane Empire, so far as it
concerneth Britain ... London: 1658. 1st edn.
Sm folio. [xxii],266,[vi] pp. Port, dble page
map. Contemp sheep, rebacked, edges sl
worn. Wing B.6185. *(Clark)* £145 [≈ $258]

- The Description of Leicester Shire ...
London: for Iohn White, (1622). 1st edn.
Earlier issue with Oo1 not a cancel. Sm folio.
Usual mispagination. Port, engvd title, fldg
map (laid down). Sl age marks, few sm reprs.
Calf antique, new endpapers. STC 4179.
(Bow Windows) £300 [≈ $534]

Busnot, F. Dominick
- The History of the Reign of Musey Ismael,
The Present King of Morocco ... London: for
A. Bell ..., 1715. 12mo. [12],250,[2 advt] pp.
Some soiling. Early calf, somewhat rubbed &
worn. *(Francis Edwards)* £140 [≈ $249]

Bussy, Roger de Rabutin, Comte de
- The Amorous History of the Gauls. Written
in French ... and now translated into English.
London: for Sam Illidge, 1725. 1st edn of this
translation. 12mo. [ii],viii, [xxxviii], 189,
192-234,[4 advt] pp. Frontis. Rebound in half
mor, gilt spine. *(Burmester)* £375 [≈ $668]

Butler, Hillary
- The Mayor of Wigan, a Tale. To which is
added, the Invasion, a Fable. London: Owen,
Wilcox ..., 1760. Half-title, [4],40 pp. Rec
wraps. *(C.R. Johnson)* £350 [≈ $623]

Butler, John
- Some Account of the Character of the Late
Right Honourable Henry Bilson Legge.
London: for J. Almon, 1764. 1st edn. 4to.
19,[1 advt] pp. Disbound. Anon.
(Young's) £85 [≈ $151]

Butler, Joseph
- The Analogy of Religion ... London:
Knapton, 1736. 1st edn. 4to. [xi],i-x,11-320
pp. V sl marg staining to half-title. Mod qtr
calf. *(Blackwell's)* £200 [≈ $356]
- The Analogy of Religion ... London:
Knapton, 1736. 1st edn. 4to. [xi],i-x,11-320
pp. Half-title & title foxed, some spotting
throughout. Mod qtr calf.
(Blackwell's) £175 [≈ $312]
- The Analogy of Religion Natural and
Revealed ... Seventh Edition. Aberdeen: John
Boyle, 1775. 12mo. Contemp calf, front jnt
broken. *(Waterfield's)* £40 [≈ $71]
- Fifteen Sermons Preached at the Rolls
Chapel. London: W. Botham for James &
John Knapton, 1726. 1st edn. 8vo. Contemp
panelled calf, front jnt cracked but sound.
(Waterfield's) £110 [≈ $196]

Butler, Samuel, author of Hudibras
- Butler's Ghost: or, Hudibras. The Fourth
Part ... see D'Urfey, Thomas

- The Genuine Remains in Verse and Prose ... With Notes by R. Thyer ... London: Tonson, 1759. 2 vols. 8vo. [xl],429; 512 pp. Subscribers vol 1. Contemp calf, mor labels gilt, spines worn, jnts sl tender.
(Finch) **£50 [≈ $89]**
- Hudibras. The First and Second Parts ... [bound with] The Third and last Part ... London: 1674, 1678. 1st combined edn of 1st 2 parts; 1st edn, 2nd issue of part 3. 8vo. [ii], 202],[iv], 223-412; [ii],285,[i] pp. Contemp calf, rebacked. Wing B.6311, 6314. Anon.
(Clark) **£90 [≈ $160]**
- Hudibras. The Third and last Part. London: Simon Miller, 1678. 1st edn. 2nd issue, with licence on reverse of title, & no final errata leaf. 8vo. [ii],285,[i] pp. Contemp calf, old reback, jnts rubbed. Wing B.6314. Anon.
(Clark) **£40 [≈ $71]**
- Hudibras, in Three Parts ... London: D. Midwinter ..., 1739. Lge 12mo. Port, 9 plates by Hogarth. Occas sl browning. Contemp calf gilt, hinges splitting, sl worn.
(P and P Books) **£80 [≈ $142]**
- Hudibras, in Three Parts ... With large Annotations, and a Preface, by Zachary Grey ... The Second Edition. London: C. Hitch, 1764. 2 vols. 8vo. [2],xxvi, 424,[16]; [2], 446,[23] pp. Frontis port, 16 plates after Hogarth. Contemp calf, elab gilt spines.
(Spelman) **£140 [≈ $249]**
- Hudibras. With Large Annotations and a Preface by Zachary Grey LL.D. Edinburgh: Bell & Murray, 1779. 2 vols. Contemp calf, rubbed.
(Glyn's) **£25 [≈ $45]**
- Hudibras ... With Large Annotations and a Preface, by Zachary Gray. London: Bensley for Vernor & Hood ..., 1799. 2 vols. 8vo. [ii],lii, [ii],436; [iv],446, [xiii],[iii] pp. Inserted fly-titles. Port, 16 plates, text decs. Some foxing. Early russia gilt, sl worn
(Blackwell's) **£75 [≈ $134]**
- A Letter from Mercurius Civicus to Mercurius Rusticus: or, Londons Confession but not Repentance ... [Oxford]: Printed, 1643. 1st edn. 4to. 33 pp. Disbound. Wing B.6323. Anon.
(Young's) **£220 [≈ $392]**
- The Posthumous Works ... The Third Edition, Corrected. London: R. Reily, 1730. 12mo. Contemp calf, jnts cracked, label defective.
(Waterfield's) **£40 [≈ $71]**

Butt, George
- Isaiah Versified. London: Cadell, 1785. Half-title, xxxi,[2],316 pp. Contemp tree calf, red label.
(C.R. Johnson) **£125 [≈ $223]**

Byrom, John
- The Universal English Short-Hand ... Manchester: L. Harrop, 1767. 1st edn. 8vo. [4],x,92 pp. 12 engvd plates, engvd table in text. Later half calf. *(O'Neal)* **$425 [≈ £239]**

Byron, John
- The Narrative of the Honourable John Byron, (Commodore in a Late Expedition round the World) ... London: Baker, Leigh, Davies, 1768. 2nd edn. 8vo. viii,257 pp. Half-title. frontis. Contemp sprinkled calf gilt, trifle rubbed. *(Hollett)* **£150 [≈ $267]**

Bysshe, Edward
- The Art of English Poetry ... The Eighth Edition, Corrected and Enlarged. London: F. Clay, 1737. 2 vols. 8vo. [8],280; 288,x,40 pp. Interleaved throughout. Orig grey paper bds, respined to style. *(Spelman)* **£160 [≈ $285]**

C., S.
- Lex Custumaria ... see Carter, Samuel

Cabala ...
- Cabala, Mysteries of State, in Letters of the great Ministers of K. James and K. Charles ... London: for Bedell & Collins, 1654. 1st edn. 4to. [xvi],347,[xxi] pp. Blank before title. 7 advt pp at end. Contemp sheep, scuffed. Wing C.183. *(Clark)* **£140 [≈ $249]**
- Cabala: sive Scrinia Sacra. Mysteries of State & Government: in Letters of Illustrious Persons ... In Two Parts ... London: for Bedel & Collins, 1654. 1st edn. 2 parts in 1 vol. Sm 4to. xvi,347,[13], "355" [ie 255],[13] pp. 4 advt ff. Contemp calf, sl worn. Wing C.183. *(Burmester)* **£120 [≈ $214]**
- Cabala, sive Scrinia Sacra, Mysteries of State and Government: in Letters of Illustrious Persons ... London: Bedel & Collins, 1663. Folio. [vi],12, (11)-(14), 13-56,(49)-(56), 57-416,[x] pp. Imprimatur leaf. Contemp calf, gilt spine worn, jnt ends split. Wing C.185. *(Clark)* **£65 [≈ $116]**
- Cabala, sive Scrinia Sacra, Mysteries of State and Government: In Letters of Illustrious Persons and Great Ministers of State ... London: Bedell & Collins, 1663. Folio. [15],416,[10] pp. Later half leather. *(O'Neal)* **$275 [≈ £154]**

Cade, Anthony
- A Justification of the Church of England ... Or a Counothercharme against the Romish Enchantments ... London: for George Lathum, 1630. 1st edn. Sm 4to. [40],315,112 pp. Contemp vellum. STC 4327. *(O'Neal)* **$275 [≈ £154]**

Cadogan, William

- A Dissertation on the Gout, and all Chronic Diseases ... Addressed to all Invalids. The Third Edition. London: Dodsley, 1771. 8vo. x,[1],12-99 pp. Lacks half-title. Later wraps.
(Spelman) **£45 [≈ $80]**
- A Dissertation on the Gout, and all Chronic Diseases ... Seventh Edition. London: Dodsley, 1771. 8vo. 100 pp. half-title. Contemp calf backed bds, some worming hd of spine extending to last gathering, extrs rubbed. *(Frew Mackenzie)* **£110 [≈ $196]**

Caesar, Julius

- The Commentaries of Caesar, Translated ... [with] a Discourse ... by William Duncan. London: Tonson, 1753. 1st edn thus. Folio. [12],civ, 335,[10] pp. 86 on 85 engvd plates. 2 plates defective. Some sm marg tears. Contemp calf, old reback, worn & rubbed but strong. *(Fenning)* **£145 [≈ $258]**

Calamy, Edmund

- An Abridgment of Mr. Baxter's History of His Life and Times ... The Second Edition ... Vol.I. [only]. London: for John Lawrence ..., 1713. 8vo. [24],726,82,[32] pp. Port. Contemp calf, rebacked.
(Fenning) **£45 [≈ $80]**

Caldwell, Sir James

- Debates relative to the Affairs of Ireland; in the Years 1763 and 1764 ... London: 1766. 1st edn. 2 vols. 8vo. [iv], x, iii, [i],404; [ii],[405]-853 pp. Contemp calf, red mor labels, gilt bands, spines worn at hd, sl stripping to sides. Anon.
(Finch) **£240 [≈ $427]**

Calet, Jean Jacques

- A True and Minute Account of the Destruction of the Bastile ... London: ptd by W. Browne & J. Warren, & sold for the author ..., 1789. 1st edn. 8vo. [vi],61 pp. Few sm marks, tear reprd (no loss), sm hole. Disbound. *(Burmester)* **£50 [≈ $89]**

Callander, John

- Two Ancient Scottish Poems; The Gaberlunzie-Man, and Christ's Kirk on the Green. With Notes and Observations ... Edinburgh: J. Robertson, 1782. 1st edn. 8vo. 11,179 pp. New bds. *(Young's)* **£58 [≈ $103]**

Callimachus

- The Works of Callimachus, Translated into English Verse ... Notes ... By H.W. Tytler. London: T. Davison, sold by Charles Dilly, 1793. 1st edn. 4to. viii,268,[6 subscribers] pp.

19th c half calf, gilt spine, sl scuffed, sl worn.
(Rankin) **£50 [≈ $89]**

Calvin, Jean

- A Commentarie of M. John Calvin upon the Epistle to the Philippians ... Translated out of Latine by W. B. [Beckett]. London: Nicolas Lynge, 1584. 4to. [iv],95 pp. Occas old underlining. Rebound in qtr calf. STC 4402.
(Frew Mackenzie) **£250 [≈ $445]**

Calvin, John

- A Harmonie upon the Three Evangelists ... with the Commentarie of M. John Calvine: faithfully translated out of Latine into English by E.P. ... London: Bishop, 1584. 1st English edn. 8vo. Title, [lxiii], 806, [4 blank], 464, [xxi] pp. Contemp bndg, rebacked, worn. STC 2962.
(Frew Mackenzie) **£350 [≈ $623]**

Cambridge, Richard Owen

- An Account of the War in India, Between the English and the French, on the Coast of Coromandel ... Second Edition. London: T. Jefferys, 1762. 8vo. lvi,357,[1 blank],[26] pp. 9 fldg maps, plates, plans. Contemp calf, gilt spine. *(O'Neal)* **$300 [≈ £169]**

Camilla: or, a Picture of Youth ...

- See Burney, Frances, Madame D'Arblay

Campbell, George

- The Philosophy of Rhetoric. London: W. Strahan, 1776. 1st edn. 2 vols. 8vo. xv,[i], 511,[1 errata]; vi,errata leaf,445,[i],[2 advt] pp. Contemp tree calf, gilt spines, v sl reprs.
(Spelman) **£300 [≈ $534]**

Campbell, John

- Lives of the Admirals and Other Eminent British Seamen ... London: Ewing ..., 1748. 4 vols. 8vo. 322,[25]; 314,[20]; 316,[22]; 329, [19] pp. Sl foxed. Contemp calf, extrs rubbed.
(Heritage) **$300 [≈ £169]**
- A Political Survey of Britain being a series of Reflections on the Situation, Lands, Inhabitants, Revenues, Colonies, and Commerce of this Island. London: for the author, 1774. 2 vols. 4to. Mod qtr calf.
(Waterfield's) **£350 [≈ $623]**
- The Spanish Empire in America. Containing a Succinct relation of the Discovery and Settlement of the Several Colonies ... By an English Merchant. London: for M. Cooper, 1747. 8vo. viii,[iv], 330,[2 advt] pp. Possibly lacks half-title. Sl marg worm. Contemp calf, sl worn. *(Burmester)* **£250 [≈ $445]**
- The Travels and Adventures of Edward

Brown, Esq; [pseudonym] ... Observations on France and Italy; his Voyage to the Levant ... London: for A. Bettesworth ..., 1739. 1st edn. 8vo. xvi,434,[xiv] pp. Browned. Rec half calf.
(Clark) **£200 [≈ $356]**

- The Travels and Adventures of Edward Brown ... Observations in France and Italy ... the Levant ... Malta ... Egypt ... Abyssinian Empire ... London: for A. Bettesworth ..., 1739. 1st edn. 8vo. xvi, 434,[14] pp. Faint water stain. Contemp calf, rebacked. Fiction.
(Burmester) **£350 [≈ $623]**

Campbell, R.
- The London Tradesman. Being a Compendious View of all the Trades, professions, Arts, both Liberal and Mechanic, now practised ... London: T. Gardner, 1747. 1st edn. 8vo. xii,340 pp. Sl soiling, sl wear. Contemp calf, spine ends worn.
(Burmester) **£450 [≈ $801]**

Campbell, Thomas
- A Philosophical Survey of the South of Ireland in a Series of Letters to John Wilkinson, M.D. London: Strahan, 1777. 1st edn. 8vo. 6 plates (2 fldg). Rec half mor. Anon.
(de Burca) **£225 [≈ $401]**

Campe, J.H.
- Pizarro; or, the Conquest of Peru; as related by a Father to his Children ... Translated from the German ... London: Sampson Low ..., 1799. 1st edn in English. 2 vols in one. 12mo. 136; 136 pp. Fldg map (v sm tears). Contemp calf gilt, spine v sl rubbed. Translated by Elizabeth Helme.
(Burmester) **£95 [≈ $169]**

Candid ...
- A Candid Examination of the Mutual Claims of Great-Britain and the Colonies ... see Galloway, Joseph.

Canne, John
- A Seasonable Word to the Parliament-Men. London: Chapman, 1659. 4to. Wraps. Wing C.442.
(Rostenberg & Stern) **$140 [≈ £79]**

Capel, Arthur, Baron
- Excellent Contemplations, Divine and Moral ... London: for Nath. Crouch, 1683. 1st edn. 3 parts. 12mo. Port. Black bordered title. Sm tear in C9. Contemp calf gilt, jnts weak. Wing C.469.
(Hannas) **£150 [≈ $267]**

Capel, Arthur, Earl of Essex
- Letters ... Prefixed an Historical Account of his Life, and deplorable Death in the Tower

of London. Dublin: Boulter Grierson, 1770. 1st Irish edn. 8vo. xxxix,367 pp. Contemp calf, worn, lacks label, jnts cracked.
(Fenning) **£75 [≈ $134]**

Capper, James
- Observations on the Passage to India, through Egypt, and across the Great Desert ... London: Faden, 1783. 1st edn. 4to. xx,120 pp. 2 fldg maps. Rec qtr leather gilt.
(Bates & Hindmarch) **£225 [≈ $401]**

The Card ...
- See Kidgell, John

Care, Henry
- English Liberties, or the Free-born Subject's Inheritance; containing Magna Charta ... Continued ... by W.N. ... London: Eliz. Nutt ..., 1719. 4th edn. 8vo. [xii],356 pp. Marg wormholes not affecting text. Contemp legal calf, lacks label. *(Burmester)* **£60 [≈ $107]**

Carew, Bampfylde-Moore
- The Life and Adventures. London: for J. Hodges, W. Millar, R. Tonson ..., 1788. Post 12mo. 222,[vi] pp. Sl soiled & creased. Mod qtr calf. *(Ash)* **£75 [≈ $134]**
- The Life and Adventures of Bampfylde-Moore Carew, commonly called the King of the Beggars ... and a Dictionary of the Cant Language, used by the Mendicants. London: for John Taylor, 1789. 8vo. 204 pp. Frontis. Some browning & foxing. Orig wraps, uncut, worn. *(Spelman)* **£40 [≈ $71]**

Carew, Richard
- The Survey of Cornwall. London: S.S. for John Jaggard, 1602. 1st edn. 4to. Intl blank leaf, errata leaf, table at end. Marg repr to title, clean tear in 1 leaf. Single worm-hole through last qtr of book. Minor stains. Contemp limp vellum. STC 4615.
(Hannas) **£750 [≈ $1,335]**

Carey, Henry
- The Dramatic Works ... London: S. Gilbert, 1743. 1st coll edn. Sm 4to. 6 pp subscribers. S2 uncancelled. Sm worm hole in title & next 3 ff. Contemp calf, rebacked, crnrs reprd.
(Georges) **£200 [≈ $356]**
- The Dramatick Works ... London: S. Gilbert, 1743. 1st coll edn. 4to. Subscribers. Half mor, gilt spine, sl used. *(Hannas)* **£150 [≈ $267]**
- The Dramatick Works. London: S. Gilbert, 1743. Only coll edn. 4to. [xvi],254,[2] pp. 6 pp subscribers. Sl browning & spotting. 19th c half sheep, jnts rubbed.
(Clark) **£200 [≈ $356]**

Carleton, George
- The Memoirs ... see Defoe, Daniel

Carlile, James
- The Fortune-Hunters: or, two Fools well met. A Comedy ... London: for James Knapton, 1689. 1st edn. 4to. Final leaf of 'Song' with advts on verso. Browned. Half calf, upper cvr detached. Wing C.590.
(Hannas) £110 [≈ $196]

Carr, George
- Sermons. Second Edition. Edinburgh: for Cadell, London, & Elliot, Edinburgh, 1778. 2 vols. 8vo in 4s. Half-title. Final advt leaf. Contemp half calf, red labels, green edges, crnrs v sl rubbed. *(Blackwell's)* £50 [≈ $89]

Carr, William
- An Accurate Description of the United Netherlands, and of the most considerable Parts of Germany, Sweden & Denmark ... London: for Timothy Childe, 1691. 1st edn. 2 parts. Sm 8vo. 5 fldg plates. Half calf, rebacked, crnrs worn. Wing C.632. Anon.
(Hannas) £160 [≈ $285]

Carre, Thomas
- Sweete Thoughts of Jesus and Marie ... see Pinkney, Miles

Carte, Thomas
- An Account of the Numbers of Men able to bear Arms in the Provinces and Towns of France, taken by the King's Orders in 1743 ... London: for M. Cooper, 1744. 1st edn. 8vo. [4],51 pp. Disbound. Anon.
(Hannas) £85 [≈ $151]
- A Full and Clear Vindication to A Letter from a Bystander. In which all the Cambridge Gentleman's Cavils and Misrepresentations of that Book ... are exposed and refuted ... London: for J. Robinson, 1743. 1st edn. 8vo. [4],122,[23] pp. Disbound. Anon.
(Hannas) £75 [≈ $134]

Carter, Matthew
- A most trve and exact Relation of that as Honourable as unfortunate Expedition of Kent, Essex and Colchester. N.p.: 1650. 1st edn. 8vo. Contemp calf. Wing C.662.
(Rostenberg & Stern) $125 [≈ £70]

Carter, Samuel
- Lex Custumaria: or, a Treatise of Copy-hold Estates, in respect of the Lord, Copy-holder ... By S.C. Barrister at Law. London: assigns of Richard & Edward Atkins ..., 1701. 2nd edn. 8vo. [xxiv],392,[24] pp. Half-title. Sm marg wormholes. Contemp calf.
(Burmester) £150 [≈ $267]
- Reports of Sevral [sic] Special Cases Argued and Resolved in the Court of Common Pleas ... London: for Bassett & Keble, 1688. 1st edn. Folio. viii,243, [244-284] pp. Licence leaf. Occas browning & foxing, sm marg worm prelims. Contemp calf, spine worn. Wing C.666. *(Vanbrugh)* £165 [≈ $294]

Carteret, John, Earl Granville
- The State of the Nation for the Year 1747, and respecting 1748 ... The Third Edition. London: for M. Cooper, 1748. 8vo. xvi,68 pp. Disbound. Anon. *(Hannas)* £65 [≈ $116]

Cary, John
- Cary's New and Correct English Atlas. London: for John Cary, 1793. 2nd edn, early issue, with maps dated 1787. Cr folio. [vi], [90],[18 pp. 47 hand cold maps. Few sl marks. Contemp diced calf gilt, sl wear to jnts.
(Ash) £1,000 [≈ $1,780]

Cary, Robert
- Memoirs of the Life of Robert Cary, Baron of Leppington, and Earl of Monmouth. Written by himself ... London: 1759. 1st edn. 8vo. 200, index pp. Frontis. Contemp calf, rebacked. John Cator b'plate.
(Robertshaw) £40 [≈ $71]

Casaubon, Meric
- Of Credulity and Incredulity in Things Natural, Civil, and Divine. London: 1668. 2 parts in one vol. 8vo. Lacks Al (blank leaf). Some stains at ends. Mod cloth. Wing C.808. *(Robertshaw)* £25 [≈ $45]

Case, Thomas
- A Sermon Preached before the Honourable House of Commons at Westminster, August 22. 1645 ... London: Ruth Raworth, for Luke Fawne, 1645. 1st edn. 4to. [iv],34 pp. Disbound. Wing C.842.
(Young's) £35 [≈ $62]

Cassandra: The Fam'd Romance ...
- See La Calprenade, Gaultier de Coste

Castelnau, Michael de
- Memoirs of the Reigns of Francis II. and Charles IX, of France ... Done into English by a Gentleman ... London: Printed in the Year, 1724. 1st English edn. Folio. [iv],426 pp. Errata. Contemp calf, spine sl worn, hinges cracked but firm.
(Vanbrugh) £275 [≈ $490]

Castillo Solorzano, Alonso del

- The Spanish Pole-Cat: or the Adventures of Senora Rufina ... London: Curll, Taylor, 1717. 1st edn of this translation (by L'Estrange & Ozell). 12mo. Final advt leaf. Frontis. Sl marg tear 2 ff. Contemp calf, spine sl worn.   *(Hannas)* **£550 [≈ $979]**

Catalogue ...

- Catalogue of Five Hundred Celebrated Authors of Great Britain, now living ... London: R. Faulder ..., 1788. Only edn. 8vo. viii,(276) pp. Contemp half sheep, uncut, worn.   *(Bookpress)* **$550 [≈ £309]**

Catullus

- Catulli, Tibulli et Propertii. Opera. Birmingham: Baskerville, 1772. 12mo. [2],276 pp. A2 uncancelled. Contemp polished calf, sometime rebacked.
 (Claude Cox) **£42 [≈ $75]**

Caussin, Nicholas

- The Holy Court in Five Tomes ... Translated into English by Sr. T.H. [Thomas Hawkins] and Others. The Third Edition. London: John Williams, 1663. Folio. [xxiv], 855,[xv] pp. Addtnl engvd title, ports in text. Half title reprd. Contemp calf, sl rubbed. Wing C.1548A.   *(Clark)* **£140 [≈ $249]**
- The Unfortunate Politique, first written in French by C.N. Englished by G.P. Oxford: L. Lichfield for Joseph Godwin, 1638. 1st edn. 12mo. [viii],218 pp. Lacks the 2 final blank ff. 19th c calf backed bds, gilt spine, rubbed. STC 4876.
 (Burmester) **£350 [≈ $623]**

Cauty, William, cabinet-maker

- Natura, Philosophia, & Ars in Concordia ... An Essay. In Four Parts ... London: for the author; sold by Nicoll, Taylor, Jones, 1772. 1st edn. 8vo. xvi,110,[2 errata] pp. Fldg plate. Rec bds.   *(Burmester)* **£300 [≈ $534]**

Cave, William

- Apostolici: or, the History of the Lives ... of those who were Contemporary with ... the Apostles ... Primitive Fathers ... Fourth Edition Corrected. London: for J. walters ..., 1716. Folio. [xxiv],xxii,738 pp. Addtnl engvd title, ports in text. Contemp calf, rebacked.
 (Clark) **£48 [≈ $85]**

Cavendish, George

- The Negotiations of Thomas Wolsey, the great Cardinall of England, containing his Life and Death ... London: Sheres, 1641. 1st edn. 4to. [viii],60, 57-118,[iv] pp. Final blank.

Later port substituted (laid down). Sm repr with sl loss. Rec vellum. Wing C.1619. Anon.   *(Blackwell's)* **£100 [≈ $178]**

Cavendish, William, Duke of Devonshire

- The Charms of Liberty: a Poem. By the late Duke of D---- ... London: Printed [by Henry Hills] in the Year, 1709. 1st edn (?). 8vo. 16 pp. Worm holes in lower marg. Mod bds.
 (Hannas) **£45 [≈ $80]**

Cavendish, William, Duke of Newcastle

- A New Method and Extraordinary Invention to dress Horses and work them ... London: 1667. Folio. [xii], "352" [ie 360],[iv] pp. Extra pp 001-008 after p 342. Sm marg repairs. Damp staining, some head margs partly disintegrated. Contemp calf, some time rebacked, sl worn. Wing N.887.
 (Blackwell's) **£300 [≈ $534]**

Cawdrey, Daniel

- A Sober Answer, to A Serious Question. Propounded by Mr. G. Firmin Minister of the Church in Shalford in Essex ... London: for Christopher Meredith, 1652. 1st edn. 4to. [viii], 31 pp. First & last ff sl soiled. Disbound. Wing C.1636.
 (Young's) **£40 [≈ $71]**

Cayley, Cornelius

- The Seraphical Young Shepherd. Being a very remarkable Account of a Shepherd in France ... London: for the author; sold by M. Lewis ..., 1762. 1st edn. 2 parts in one vol. 12mo. xvii,[iii], 214,[6] pp, inc errata & advts. Contemp calf, rebacked.
 (Burmester) **£110 [≈ $196]**

Cellini, Benvenuto

- The Life of Benvenuto Cellini: a Florentine Artist ... Written by himself ... and Translated from the Original by Thomas Nugent. London: T. Davies, 1771. 1st English edn. 2 vols. 8vo. x,512; [2],403,[1 errata], [44 contents] pp. Port frontis. Contemp calf, jnts sl worn.
 (Blackwell's) **£125 [≈ $223]**
- The Life of Benvenuto Cellini: a Florentine Artist ... Written by himself ... and Translated from the Original by Thomas Nugent. London: T. Davies, 1771. 1st edn in English. 2 vols. 8vo. x,512; [2],403, errata,[42] pp. Port frontis vol 1. Contemp qtr calf, sl rubbed.   *(Spelman)* **£150 [≈ $267]**

Cennick, John

- The Good Shepherd being the substance of a Discourse delivered at St. Ginnis in

Cornwall, in the year 1744. Dublin: S. Powell, 1754. 8vo. Disbound.
(Waterfield's) **£20 [≈ $36]**

- Simon and Mary being the substance of a Sermon preach'd in Exeter in the year 1744. London: John Hart, 1754. 8vo. Disbound.
(Waterfield's) **£20 [≈ $36]**

Cerdan, Jean Paul, Comte de

- The Kingdom of Sweden restored to its True Interest. A Political Discourse. London: M. Flesher, for Joanna Brome, 1682. 1st English edn. 4to. [4],32 pp. Title & last page dust soiled. Disbound. Old Wing K.581 (variant imprint). Anon.
(Hannas) **£35 [≈ $62]**

Certaine Sermons ...

- Certaine Sermons or Homilies appointed to be read in Churches ... [Bound with] The Second Tome of Homilies ... London: John Bill, 1623. Sm folio. [vi],98, [iv],320,[ii] pp. Some wear & tear, lacks final blanks. Old sheep, roughly rebacked. STC 13659, 13675.
(Clark) **£45 [≈ $80]**

Cervantes Saavedra, Miguel de

- The History of the Valorous and Witty Knight Errant, Don Quixote of the Mancha. Translated out of the Spanish [by Thomas Shelton]; now newly Corrected and Amended. London: for R. Scot ..., 1675-72. 2 parts. Folio. Sl used. Contemp calf, rebacked & reprd. Wing C.1777.
(Hannas) **£500 [≈ $890]**

- Novellas Exemplares: or, Exemplary Novels, in six books ... Translated by Mr. Tho. Shelton ... New Edition, revised ... by Mr. Mendez ... London: C. Hitch ..., 1743. 12mo. [ii],144, 147-396,[2] pp. Contemp calf, fine.
(Burmester) **£250 [≈ $445]**

- Persiles and Sigismunda: a celebrated Novel ... Translated into English from the Original. London: for C. Ward & R. Chandler ..., 1741. 1st edn of this translation. 2 vols. 12mo. Intl advt leaf vol 2. Port. Mottled calf gilt, by W. Nutt.
(Hannas) **£280 [≈ $498]**

Challoner, Richard

- The Grounds of the Old Religion: or, Some General Arguments in Favour of the Catholick, Apostolick, Roman Communion ... By a Convert. Printed at Augusta [London?]: 1742. 1st edn. 8vo. v,[vi],213 pp. Rec half calf. Anon. *(Young's)* **£85 [≈ $151]**

- Memoirs of Missionary Priests ... that have suffered Death in England ... from 1577 to 1684 ... London: 1741-42. 1st edn. 2 vols. 8vo. [xxviii],450; [xvi],496 pp. Some marg worm vol 1. Lib blind stamps on endpapers.

Contemp calf, rebacked.
(Blackwell's) **£280 [≈ $498]**

Chalmers, George

- The Abridged Life of Thomas Paine, the Author of the Seditious Writings, entitled Rights of Man. By Francis Oldys, A.M. of the University of Pennsylvania [pseudonym]. The Eighth Edition, Corrected. London: Stockdale, 1793. 8vo. [ii],32 pp. Disbound.
(Burmester) **£35 [≈ $62]**

- An Estimate of the Comparative Strength of Great Britain, during the Present and Four Preceding Reigns ... London: for John Stockdale, 1786. 2nd edn. 8vo. xi,[i], 238,[xv] pp. Half-title, final blank R8. 2 sm marg tears. Contemp calf, flat back gilt, sl rubbed.
(Blackwell's) **£275 [≈ $490]**

Chamberlayne, John

- Magnae Britanniae Notitia: or, the Present State of Great Britain ... In Two Parts ... London: for A. Ward ..., 1745. 8vo. [xiv], 440, 292,70 pp. Port frontis. Contemp calf gilt, extrs rubbed, lacks label, hd of spine worn. *(Finch)* **£30 [≈ $53]**

Chambers, Ephraim

- Cyclopaedia: or, an Universal Dictionary of Arts and Sciences ... With the Supplement ... by Abraham Rees. London: Rivington, 1786-79-81-83. 4 vols. Folio. Port frontis, 146 plates, 10 pp of printing types inc 2 fldg type specimens. Sl used. Contemp calf, rebacked.
(Frew Mackenzie) **£600 [≈ $1,068]**

Chandler, G.

- A Treatise on the Diseases of the Eye and their Remedies to which is prefixed the Anatomy of the Eye; the Theory of Vision; and the Several Species of Imperfect Sight. London: Cadell, 1780. Only edn. v,[v],191 pp. 3 plates. Occas sl marg water stain. New bds, uncut. *(David White)* **£65 [≈ $116]**

Chandler, Richard

- Travels in Asia Minor: or an Account of a Tour made at the expense of the Society of Dilettanti. London: 1776. 2nd edn. 4to. xiii,283,[i advt,i errata] pp. Fldg map frontis (sev sm splits). Minor soiling. Later half calf.
(Francis Edwards) **£300 [≈ $534]**

Chandler, Samuel

- A Paraphrase and Critical Commentary on the Book of Joel. London: for J. Noon, R. Hett & J. Gray, 1735. 4to. Mod qtr calf, vellum tips. *(Waterfield's)* **£65 [≈ $116]**

- A Second Treatise on the Notes of the

Church; As a Supplement to the Sermon Preach'd at Salters-Hall, January 16, 1734 ... London: for T. Cox, 1735. 1st edn. 8vo. 60 pp. Disbound. *(Young's)* **£26 [≈ $46]**

Chapman, George
- A Treatise on Education. With a Sketch of the Author's Method. Edinburgh: Kincaid & Creech, 1773. 1st edn. 8vo. viii,256 pp. Contemp calf, jnts tender, some wear.
(Burmester) **£400 [≈ $712]**

Chapman, Thomas
- An Essay on the Roman Senate. Cambridge: J. Bentham, 1750. 1st edn. 8vo. 398,index pp. Mod bds, leather label.
(Robertshaw) **£25 [≈ $45]**

Chapone, Hester
- Miscellanies in Prose and Verse. A New Edition. London: C. Dilly, 1783. Fcap 8vo. x,[3],216 pp. Intl & final blanks. Contemp calf, gilt spine with onlay & gilt label, minor rubbing hd of spine. *(Spelman)* **£45 [≈ $80]**

Chaptal, M.I.A.
- Elements of Chemistry. Translated from the French. Phila: 1796. 3 vols in one. 8vo. 673 pp. Title mtd. Lib stamp on title. Old calf, rebacked. *(Goodrich)* **$195 [≈ £110]**

Charles I, King of England
- Bibliotheca Regia ... see Heylyn, Peter
- His Majesties Answer to a Printed Book, Entituled, A Remonstrance ... May 26, 1642 ... concerning the businesse of Hull. London: Barker & assigns of John Bill, 1642. 1st edn. Sm 4to. [ii],30 pp. Mod wraps. Wing C.2103.
(Blackwell's) **£45 [≈ $80]**
- His Majesties Answer to the Declaration of Both Houses Concerning Hull. Sent 4 May 1642 ... London: for S.E., 1642. Sm 4to. [8] pp. Centre of pp sl creased. Stitched into mod wraps, untrimmed, partly unopened. Variant of Wing C.2112 (imprint differs).
(Blackwell's) **£45 [≈ $80]**
- His Majesties Answer, To a Booke, intituled, The Declaration, remonstrance of the Lords and Commons, of the 19. of May. 1642. Imprinted at Yorke. London: reptd, for R. Lownes & H. Tuckey, 1642. 2nd edn. 4to. 16 pp. Sm hole affecting occas letter. Bds. Wing C.2095. *(Young's)* **£60 [≈ $107]**
- His Majesties Declaration to all His loving Subjects, Occasioned by a false and scandalous Imputation laid upon His Majestie ... London: Barker & the assigns of John Bill, 1642. 1st edn. Sm 4to. [ii],13,[i] pp. Top edges sl shaved. Mod wraps. Wing

C.2237. *(Blackwell's)* **£45 [≈ $80]**
- His Majesties Declaration, concerning His Proceedings with His Subjects of Scotland, Since the Pacification in the Camp neere Berwick. London: Young & Badger, 1640. 4to. Frontis port. Royal Arms on B1. Stitched. STC 22006.
(Rostenberg & Stern) **$150 [≈ £84]**
- His Majesties Declaration, to all His loving Subjects. Published with the advice of His Privie Council. London: Printed, 1641. 1st edn. 4to. [2],6 pp. Marg rust hole in 2 ff. Disbound. Wing C.2249A.
(Young's) **£90 [≈ $160]**
- His Majesties declaration: To All His Loving Subjects, Of the causes which moved him to dissolve the last Parliament. London: Robert Barker ..., 1640. Sm 4to. [ii],55 pp. Royal Arms on title & verso. Old ink notes. Contemp limp vellum, sl dusty. STC 9262.
(Georges) **£150 [≈ $267]**
- His Majesties Message to both Houses of Parliament, January 20 ... London: Barker & the assigns of John Bill, 1641. 1st edn. Sm 4to. [ii],24 pp. Disbound. Wing C.2450.
(Blackwell's) **£50 [≈ $89]**
- His Majesties Speech and Protestation, Made in the Head of His Armie, between Stafford and Wellington, the 19th of September, 1642 ... London: Robert Barker ..., 1642. Sm 4to. 4 ff. Disbound. Wing C.2776.
(Georges) **£85 [≈ $151]**
- His Majesties Speech spoken to the Mayor, Aldermen, and Commonaltie of the Citie of Oxford and Berks ... Oxford [really London]: Leonard Lichfield, 1643. 1st edn. 4to. 8 pp. Later wraps. Wing C.2796.
(Clark) **£85 [≈ $151]**
- His Majesties Two Speeches, One to the Knights ... of Nottingham and Newark, the other to the Knights of Lincoln. London: Barker & Assigns of Bill, 1642. 4to. Title within typographical border. Royal arms on title verso. Stitched. Wing C.2866.
(Rostenberg & Stern) **$75 [≈ £42]**
- The King's Most Gracious Messages for Peace, and a Personal Treaty. Published for His Peoples Satisfaction ... London: Printed in the Yeare, 1648. 1st edn. 4to. [viii],138 pp. New bds. Wing C.2520. *(Young's)* **£50 [≈ $89]**
- The Kings Declaration to all his Subjects, Of whatsoever Nation, Quality, or Condition ... London: Printed in the Year, 1648. Sm 4to. 4 ff. Sl soiled. Disbound. Wing C.2264.
(Georges) **£85 [≈ $151]**
- The Papers which passed at New-Castle betwixt His Sacred Majesties and Mr. Al: Henderson: Concerning the Change of

Church-Government ... London: R. Royston, 1649. 1st edn. [ii],58,[2] pp. Final errata leaf. No A1 (blank?). Sl soil. Disbound. Wing C.2535. *(Clark)* £85 [≈ $151]

- Reliquiae Sacrae Carolinae, or the Works of that Great Monarch and Glorious Martyr ... Hague: Samuel Browne, 1650. Thick 8vo. [xvi], 280,12, [iv],361 pp. Sep title to Eikon dated 1649. Errata. Port. Contemp sheep, gilt spine sl worn. Wing C.2072.
(Vanbrugh) £175 [≈ $312]

- The Workes ... [Bound with] Eikon Basilike. The Pourtraicture of His Sacred Majesty in his Solitudes and Sufferings. The Hague: Sam. Browne, 1648. 8vo. 355,374, 9-119,[8] pp. Port frontis. Contemp calf gilt, rubbed, spine worn. Wing C.2070.
(Hollett) £130 [≈ $231]

Charleton, W.

- Enquiries into Human Nature in VI. Anatomic Praelections in the New Theatre of the Royal College of Physicians in London. London: 1680. [xl],149, 369-544,[4] pp. Frontis, 6 text figs. Lacks port. Wear & tear. Contemp calf, new label, crnrs reprd. Wing C.3676. *(Whitehart)* £180 [≈ $320]

Charlevoix, Pierre Francois Xavier de

- The History of Paraguay ... London: for Lockyer Davis, 1769. 1st edn in English. 2 vols. 8vo. vii,[i],463; viii,415 pp. Contemp dark calf, elab gilt spines, mor labels, spines sl worn, gilt faded, jnts cracked but firm.
(Finch) £240 [≈ $427]

Charlton, Lionel

- The History of Whitby and of Whitby Abbey ... York: 1779. 4to. xvii,[i errata],379 pp. Fldg map frontis (crease tear), 3 plates. Sl worming at end sl affecting text. Title sl soiled. Rebound in cloth.
(Francis Edwards) £75 [≈ $134]

Chastellux, Francois J.

- Travels in North America, in the Years 1780, 1781, and 1782. London: 1787. 1st British edn. 2 vols. 8vo. xv,462; xii,432 pp. 2 fldg maps, 3 fldg plates. Contemp calf, vol 1 backstrip relaid, wear at outer hinges.
(Reese) $1,200 [≈ £674]

Chatterton, Thomas

- Poems, supposed to have been written at Bristol in the Fifteenth century, by Thomas Rowley ... With a Commentary ... by Jeremia Milles. London: T. Payne & Son, 1782. 1st Milles edn. Large Paper. 4to. Plate. Mod calf gilt. *(Hannas)* £85 [≈ $151]

- Poems, supposed to have been written at Bristol, by Thomas Rowley ... London: T. Payne & Son, 1777. 1st edn. With the cancel signed c4 containing reworded 'Advertisement'. 8vo. xxviii,307,[i] pp. Engvd plate. Contemp half calf, front jnt worn, spine ends worn. *(Finch)* £110 [≈ $196]

- Poems supposed to have been written at Bristol by Thomas Rowley and Others, in the Fifteenth Century. Cambridge: B. Flower for the editor ..., 1794. 5th edn. Large Paper. 8vo. xxix,329 pp. Title vignette, 1 plate. Sm lib marks. Rebound in half mor gilt.
(Hartfield) $285 [≈ £160]

Chaucer, Geoffrey

- The Canterbury Tales ... Notes ... by the late Thomas Tyrwhitt. The Second Edition. Oxford: Clarendon Press, 1798. 2 vols. 4to. Port frontis. Contemp mottled green calf gilt, dec backstrips relaid, some wear.
(Sotheran's) £250 [≈ $445]

- The Works ... [edited] by John Urry ... London: Lintot, 1721. Folio. 2 ports, title vignette, 27 engvs of the Pilgrims. 1 sm tear, sl browning, occas marg stain. Contemp calf, jnts broken but holding, crnrs bumped.
(P and P Books) £160 [≈ $285]

Chesterfield, Philip Dormer Stanhope, Earl of

- The Case of the Hanover Forces in the Pay of Great Britain, Impartially and Freely Examined ... London: for T. Cooper, 1743. 1st edn. 8vo. Half-title. Disbound. Anon.
(Young's) £65 [≈ $116]

- Characters of Eminent Personages of his Own Time ... Never before Published. London: for William Flexney, 1777. 1st edn. 12mo. [2],54 pp. Disbound. *(Hannas)* £75 [≈ $134]

- Characters of Eminent Personages of his Own Time ... never before published. London: for William Flexney, 1777. 1st edn. 12mo. [ii],54 pp. Contemp half calf, sl rubbed.
(Burmester) £200 [≈ $356]

- Characters of Eminent Personages ... Second Edition. London: for William Flexney, 1777. 12mo. [2],54 pp. Faint water stains. Disbound. *(Hannas)* £35 [≈ $62]

- Letters written ... to his Son ... The Tenth Edition ... London: Dodsley, 1792. 4 vols. 8vo. Half-titles. Port. Contemp tree calf, pale calf spines gilt, contrasting labels, fine.
(Burmester) £130 [≈ $231]

Chesterfield, Philip Dormer Stanhope, Earl of, & Waller, Edmund

- The Case of the Hanover Forces in the Pay of Great Britain, Impartially and freely

examined ... London: for T. Cooper, 1743. 1st edn. Todd's B issue. 8vo. [4],83 pp, inc half-title. Disbound. Anon.
(Hannas) £95 [≈ $169]

Chetwood, William Rufus

- The Voyages, Dangerous Adventures, and Imminent Escapes of Capt. Rich. Falconer ... Second Edition Corrected. London: for J. Marshal ..., 1724. 12mo. [vi],224,[vi] pp. Frontis. 1st few ff sl stained. Contemp calf, mor label, jnts beginning to crack ft of spine.
(Finch) £480 [≈ $854]

Cheyne, George

- The English Malady: or, a Treatise of Nervous Disorders ... London: Strahan & Leake, 1733. 1st edn. 8vo. [vi],xxxii,[ii], 370,[6 advt] pp. Contemp calf, upper jnt cracked. *(Gaskell)* £600 [≈ $1,068]
- The English Malady: or, A Treatise of Nervous Diseases of all Kinds; as Spleen, Vapours,   Lowness   of   Spirits, Hypochondriacal, and Hysterical Distempers ... The Fourth Edition. London: Strahan, 1734. 8vo. xxxi, 370, advt pp. Some foxing. Contemp calf, jnts cracked.
(Goodrich) $195 [≈ £110]
- An Essay of the True Nature and Due Method of Treating the Gout ... and Quality of Bath-Waters ... London: Strahan, 1738. 9th edn, enlgd. Title reprd. Rec calf.
(P and P Books) £115 [≈ $205]
- An Essay on Health and Long Life. London: 1724. 1st edn. 8vo. Contemp calf, jnts cracked. *(Goodrich)* $295 [≈ £166]
- The Natural Method of Cureing the Diseases of the Body, and the Disorders of the Mind depending on the Body. London: 1742. 1st edn. 8vo. 316 pp. Lib stamp on title & at end. Contemp calf, worn, upper cvr detached.
(Robertshaw) £125 [≈ $223]
- A New Theory of Acute and Slow Continu'd Fevers ... Second Edition, with many Additions. London: Strahan, 1702. 8vo. [viii], 37, 166,[1 advt] pp. W'cut text diags. Minor marg worm. Contemp sprinkled sheep, jnts worn. Anon. *(Gaskell)* £450 [≈ $801]
- Philosophical Principles of Religion: Natural and Revealed: in Two Parts ... Elements of Natural Philosophy ... Nature and Kind of Infinites ... London: Strahan, 1715. 1st complete edn. Large Paper. 8vo. Occas sl browning. Contemp mor gilt, a.e.g., v sl rubbed. *(Gaskell)* £850 [≈ $1,513]

Child, Sir Josiah

- A New Discourse of Trade ... London: John Everingham, 1693. 8vo. [liv],37, 234,[2] pp,

inc licence leaf & final blank. F4 a cancel. E2 & F8 supplied in facs. Old calf, rebacked. Wing C.3860.   *(Hollett)* £525 [≈ $935]
- A New Discourse of Trade ... Second Edition. London: 1694. 8vo. 238 pp. Occas sl browning, sl marg staining. 18th c mrbld bds, roughly rebacked. Wing C.3861.
(Robertshaw) £245 [≈ $436]
- A New Discourse of Trade ... To which is added, a Small Treatise against Usury, by the Same Author. The Fifth Edition. Glasgow: Robert & Andrew Foulis, 1751. Sm 8vo. xxix, [iii], 184 pp. Blank leaf b8. Title dust soiled. Contemp sheep, rebacked, crnrs worn.
(Burmester) £85 [≈ $151]

Chillingworth, William

- The Religion of Protestants a Safe Way to Salvation ... The Fourth Edition. London: Andrew Clark for Richard Chiswell, 1674. Folio. [xxx],447,[i] pp. Imprimatur leaf. Contemp panelled calf, extrs sl worn, lacks label. Wing C.3891.   *(Clark)* £55 [≈ $98]
- The Works ... Tenth Edition, with a Preface. London: D. Midwinter ..., 1742. Folio. [viii],394, 199,[ix] pp. Sm closed tear in 1 leaf. Contemp calf, rebacked, recrnrd.
(Clark) £60 [≈ $107]

Chippendale, Thomas

- The   Gentleman   and   Cabinet-Maker's Director ... London: for the author, 1754. 1st edn. Folio. Title, half-title, engvd dedic leaf, Preface iii-vi, subscribers vii-x, 27, [1 blank] pp. 161 plates (I-CLX, XXV bis). Few sm marks & reprs. 19th c calf, rebacked.
(Spelman) £3,800 [≈ $6,764]

Christian ...

- The Christian Officer's Panoply ... see Barn, Andrew

The Christmas Treat ...

- The Christmas Treat: or Gay Companion. being a Collection of Epigrams, Ancient and Modern ... Dublin: for Will. Whitestone, 1767. 1st edn. 8vo. xxxviii,192 pp. 1 leaf reprd (no loss). Orig wraps, uncut, lacks backstrip, crnr torn from front wrapper.
(Burmester) £150 [≈ $267]

Chrysal: or, the Adventures of a Guinea ...

- See Johnstone, Charles

Church, John

- The Divine Warrant of Infant-Baptism. or VI Arguments for Baptism of Infants of Christians ... London: for George Calvert, 1652. 2nd edn. 4to. [vi],50 pp. Stain in crnr

of title. 1 leaf cropped at outer edge.
Disbound. Wing C.3988.
(*Young's*) **£75 [≈ $134]**

Churchill, Charles

- The Candidate. A Poem. London: for the author, 1764. 1st edn. 4to. [ii],38 pp. Lib label. Three qtr calf. (*Young's*) **£32 [≈ $57]**
- The Conference. A Poem. London: for G. Kearsley ..., 1763. 1st edn. 4to. [ii],19 pp. Sm flaw in last leaf. Lib label. Three qtr calf.
(*Young's*) **£32 [≈ $57]**
- Poems. In Two Volumes. The Fourth Edition. London: John Churchill & W. Flexney, 1769. 2 vols. 8vo. [iv],369,[iii]; [iv],330 pp. Contemp sheep, minor wear, sl scuffed. (*Clark*) **£32 [≈ $57]**

Churchill, Sir Winston

- Divi Britannici: Being a Remark Upon the Lives of All the Kings of this Isle, from the Year of the World 2855 ... London: Roycroft for Eglesfield, 1675. 1st edn. Folio. [6], 362, [2] pp. Title vignette, num engvd coats of arms. Old calf, spine ends worn. Wing C.4275. (*O'Neal*) **$475 [≈ £267]**

Churchman, John

- An Account of the Gospel Labours, and Christian Experiences of ... John Churchman, Late of Nottingham, in Pennsylvania ... London: 1780. 8vo. vii,351,1 pp. V occas sl spotting. New endpapers. Title sl thumbed. Rec qtr calf. (*Francis Edwards*) **£75 [≈ $134]**
- An Account of the Gospel Labours and Christian Experiences of ... John Churchman, late of Nottingham in Pennsylvania, now deceased ... Philadelphia printed. London: reptd, 1780. 8vo. Contemp calf, rebacked.
(*Waterfield's*) **£40 [≈ $71]**
- An Account of the Gospel Labours, and Christian Experiences ... added, a Short Memorial of the Life ... of ... Joseph White. Philadelphia, and London, printed. Dublin: reptd by Robert Jackson, 1781. 1st Irish edn. 8vo. vii,351,[1 advt] pp. Rec qtr calf.
(*Fenning*) **£45 [≈ $80]**

Churchyard, Thomas

- The Worthines of Wales, a Poem ... London: Thomas Evans, 1776. Reprinted from the edition of 1587. 8vo. xv,128 pp. Half-title. Occas trivial browning. Contemp qtr calf, vellum tips, rebacked, sides sl rubbed.
(*Frew Mackenzie*) **£70 [≈ $125]**
- The Worthines of Wales: a Poem ... London: Thomas Evans, 1776. Reprinted from the edition of 1587. 8vo. Later qtr roan.
(*Waterfield's*) **£60 [≈ $107]**

Cibber, Colley

- An Apology for the Life of Colley Cibber, Comedian. The Fourth Edition. London: Dodsley, 1756. 2 vols. 12mo. [xiv],324; [ii], 303,[xxxi] pp. Port frontis. Contemp calf, gilt spines, extrs sl worn, lacks 3 labels.
(*Clark*) **£32 [≈ $57]**
- The Careless Husband. A Comedy ... Second Edition. London: for W. Davis, 1705. 4to. Bottom line of prologue & some catchwords cut into. Sm hole in 1 leaf. Ex-lib. Qtr roan, worn. (*Hannas*) **£110 [≈ $196]**
- The Careless Husband. A Comedy. London: for J. Tonson, 1725. 6th edn. 8vo. 94,[2] pp. Frontis. Orig blue wraps, uncut.
(*Young's*) **£20 [≈ $36]**
- A Letter from Mr Cibber to Mr Pope, inquiring into the Motives that might induce him in his Satyrical Works, to be so frequently fond of Mr Cibber's Name. The Second Edition. London: W. Lewis, 1742. 66 pp. Half-title. Rec bds.
(*C.R. Johnson*) **£65 [≈ $116]**
- Papal Tyranny in the Reign of King John. A Tragedy ... London: for J. Watts ... sold by B. Dod, 1745. 1st edn. 8vo. [xii],70,[2] pp. Disbound. (*Georges*) **£50 [≈ $89]**
- Plays ... London: Jacob Tonson ..., 1721. 1st coll edn. 4to. 2 vols. [x],219, [ix], 249-324, [viii],329-406,[ii]; [xii],8,17-181, [v],179-463,[i] pp. 2 pp subscribers. Half-title vol 2. Minor browning. Contemp calf, rebacked, crnrs sl worn. (*Clark*) **£200 [≈ $356]**

Cicero, Marcus Tullius

- Tully's Five Books De Finibus ... Done into English by S.P. [Samuel Parker] ... Revis'd ... by Jeremy Collier ... London: Tonson, 1702. 1st edn. 8vo. [lxxiv],368 pp. Port. Some foxing. Period panelled calf, upper jnt cracked. (*Rankin*) **£65 [≈ $116]**
- Tully's Offices. In Three Books. Turned out of Latin into English. By Ro. L'Estrange. London: for Henry Brome, 1680. 1st edn of this translation. 8vo. [xvi],208 pp. 19th c half calf, dec gilt spine, jnts rubbed.
(*Sotheran's*) **£148 [≈ $263]**

The Citizen of the World ...
- See Goldsmith, Oliver

The Civil Warres of Great Britain and Ireland ...
- See Davies, John

Claggett, William
- The Difference of the Case, Between the Separation of the Protestants from the

Church of Rome, and the Separation of Dissenters from the Church of England. London: 1683. 1st edn. 4to. [ii],71,[i] pp. Closed tear, sm hole in errata. Disbound Wing C.4377. Anon.   *(Clark)* £20 [≈ $36]

Claims ...
- The Claims of the People of England, Essayed. In a Letter from the Country. London: for A. Baldwin, 1701. 116 pp. Sm repr to title. Contemp sheep, rebacked.
                    (C.R. Johnson) £135 [≈ $240]

Clanricarde, Marquis of
- Memoirs of the Right Honourable the Marquis of Clanricarde, Lord Deputy General of Ireland ... Dublin: Powell, 1744. 8vo. cxxvi,152 pp. Lib stamp on title. Contemp calf, jnts split but firm.
                    (de Burca) £160 [≈ $285]

Clare, Peter
- An Essay on the Cure of Abscesses by Caustic, and on the Treatment of Wounds and Ulcers ... London: Cadell, 1779. 1st edn. 154 pp. Contemp calf, red label, rubbed, scuffed. *(Jermy & Westerman)* £275 [≈ $490]

Clarendon, Edward Hyde, Earl of
- An Answer to a Pamphlet, Entit'led, A Declaration of the Commons of England in Parliament assembled ... London: Printed in the yeare, 1648. 1st edn. 4to. [ii],13 pp. New wraps. Wing C.4417. Anon.
                    (Young's) £38 [≈ $68]
- A Collection of several Tracts ... Published from his Lordship's Original Manuscripts. London: Woodward & Peele, 1727. Folio. [iv],770 pp. Minor marg damp stain. Contemp calf, worn, lacks label
                    (Clark) £90 [≈ $160]
- A Full Answer to An Infamous and Trayterous Pamphlet, Entituled, A Declaration of the Commons of England in Parliament assembled ... London: for R. Royston, 1648. 1st edn. 4to. [vi],188 pp. Title crnr stained. New contemp style calf. Wing C.4423.   *(Young's)* £100 [≈ $178]
- The Life of Edward Earl of Clarendon ... [with] The Continuation of the Life. Written by himself. Oxford: Clarendon Printing House, 1759. 1st 8vo edn. 3 vols. 8vo. Contemp mottled calf, gilt spines, red & black labels.   *(Frew Mackenzie)* £220 [≈ $392]
- The Life of Edward Earl of Clarendon ... [with] The Continuation of the Life. Written by himself. Oxford: 1759. 3 vols. 8vo. Contemp calf, backstrips relaid, 1 new label.
                    (Spelman) £140 [≈ $249]

- The Life ... Oxford: Clarendon Printing House, 1760. 2nd 8vo edn. 2 vols. [x],512; 525,[28] pp. Contemp calf, rebacked.
                    (Young's) £56 [≈ $100]

Clark, James
- A Treatise on the Prevention of Diseases incidental to Horses ... subjoined, Observations on some of the Surgical and Medical Branches of Farriery. Phila: William Spotswood, 1791. 1st Amer edn. 12mo. 2 advt ff. Contemp sheep, split in spine. Half mor slipcase.   *(Ximenes)* $600 [≈ £337]

Clarke, James
- A Survey of the Lakes of Cumberland, Westmorland, and Lancashire ... London: for the author, 1787. 1st edn. 1st issue. Tall folio. xlii,194 pp. 11 fldg plans, 2 plates. Occas sl spotting or browning, few sm reprs. Mod half mor gilt.   *(Hollett)* £950 [≈ $1,691]

Clarke, Samuel, 1599-1683
- The Life and Death of Hannibal ... as also the Life and Death of Epaminondas the Great ... London: William Miller, 1665. 1st edn. 4to. [iv],1-68, 93-137,[i] pp. Some browning, few marg marks. Disbound, outer ff dusty. Wing C.4528.   *(Clark)* £100 [≈ $178]
- The Marrow of Ecclesiastical History ... Third Edition, corrected and somewhat Enlarged. London: for W.B., sold by Tho. Sawbridge & William Birch, 1675. Folio. Port, frontis to 2nd part, 89 vignette ports in text. Minor marg worm. Old calf, sl worn. Wing C.4545.   *(Clark)* £65 [≈ $116]

Clarke, Samuel, 1675-1729
- A Collection of Papers, which passed between the late learned Mr Leibnitz, and Dr Clarke ... relating to the Principles of Natural Philosophy and Religion ... London: Knapton, 1717. 8vo. xiii,[4],416,46 pp, advt leaf. Sl dusty. Vellum over calf, sl soiled.
                    (Spelman) £120 [≈ $214]
- A Discourse concerning the Being and Attributes of God ... Being Sixteen Sermons ... Fifth Edition, corrected. London: Botham for Knapton, 1719. 8vo. [xxxii],135, [xxiv], 344,42 pp, advt leaf. Contemp calf, spine worn, jnts cracked but holding.
                    (Blackwell's) £45 [≈ $80]

Clarke, William
- The Undoubted Heir: and He Must Reign. Dedicated to The Pretender. London: London: J. Baker, 1714. [6],40 pp. Rec wraps.
                    (C.R. Johnson) £65 [≈ $116]

Clarkson, David

- The Practical Divinity of the Papists Discovered to be Destructive of Christianity and Mens Souls ... London: for Tho. Parkhurst & Nath. Ponder, 1676. 1st edn. 4to. [xxxvi], 413,[1 errata] pp. Usual mispagination pp 210 onwards. Old calf. Wing C.4575. Anon.

(*Young's*) £120 [≈ $214]

Clarkson, Thomas

- An Essay on the Impolicy of African Slave-Trade. In Two Parts. London: J. Phillips, 1788. Orig blue bds, paper spine, uncut, old ink title on spine.

(*C.R. Johnson*) £280 [≈ $498]

Classical ...

- A Classical Dictionary of the Vulgar Tongue ... see Grose, Francis

Clavering, Robert

- An Essay on the Construction and Building of Chimneys. London: I. Taylor, 1779. 1st edn. 8vo. vii,[1],100,[4 advt] pp. Fldg frontis (reprd), fldg table. Mod qtr calf.

(*Sotheran's*) £195 [≈ $347]

Clement, S.

- Faults on both Sides: Or, An Essay Upon the Original Cause, progress, and Mischievous Consequences of the Factions in this Nation. London: the booksellers, 1710. 2nd edn. 8vo. 56 pp. Title soiled. Anon.

(*Young's*) £45 [≈ $80]

Cleveland, John

- Clivelandi Vindiciae; or, Clieveland's Genuine Poems, Orations, Epistles, &c ... many Additions ... Account of the Author's Life. London: Obadiah Blagrave, 1677. 1st edn. 8vo. [xxiv],239,[i] pp. Port frontis. Rec half calf. Wing C.4670.

(*Clark*) £280 [≈ $498]

- The Idol of the Clownes, or, Insurrection of Wat the Tylor ... London: Printed in the Year, 1654. 1st edn. Sm 8vo. Title dust soiled, minor stains. Title border & some numerals cut into. 19th c half calf, worn. Wing C.4672. Anon.

(*Hannas*) £220 [≈ $392]

- The Works ... With the Life of the Author. London: Holt for Blagrave, 1687. 1st edn. 8vo. [xxii],177,[i], [ii],181-384, [ii], 387-514, [515-528] pp. Port. Titles double box-ruled. Occas v sl foxing. Contemp style calf. Wing C.4654.

(*Vanbrugh*) £495 [≈ $881]

Clifford, Martin

- A Treatise of Humane Reason. London: for Henry Brome, 1675. 12mo. Licence leaf. Some soiling. Contemp calf, worn, rebacked. Anon. Wing C.4708.

(*Waterfield's*) £185 [≈ $329]

Clinton, Sir Henry

- A Letter ... to the Commissioners of Public Accounts, relative to ... censure on the late Commanders in Chief of His Majesty's Army in North America. London: Debrett, 1784. 8vo. 31,[i] pp. Orig wraps stitched as issued, unopened, cvrs soiled.

(*Frew Mackenzie*) £100 [≈ $178]

- Observations on Mr. Stedman's History of the American War. London: 1794. 34 pp. Sev sm holes on title & last leaf, no loss of text. Disbound.

(*Reese*) $300 [≈ £169]

Cobden, Edward

- A Persuasive to Chastity. A Sermon Preached before the King at St. James's, On the 11th of December, 1748. London: for J. Lodge, 1749. 1st edn. 4to. [iv],20 pp. Title sl soiled. Stitched as issued.

(*Young's*) £40 [≈ $71]

- A Persuasive to Chastity. A Sermon Preached before the King at St. James's, On the 11th of December, 1748. London: for J. Lodge, 1749. 2nd edn. 8vo. iv,24 pp. Disbound.

(*Young's*) £20 [≈ $36]

- Poems on Several Occasions ... London: for the benefit of a Clergyman's Widow ..., 1748. 1st edn. 8vo. x,352,[vi] pp. Contemp calf, worn, rebacked, new endpapers.

(*Finch*) £125 [≈ $223]

- Poems on Several Occasions. London: for the benefit of the Clergyman's Widow ..., 1748. 1st coll edn. 8vo. Sl spotting. Contemp calf, rebacked.

(*Hannas*) £140 [≈ $249]

Cochin, Charles Nicholas & Bellicard, Jerome Charles

- Observations upon the Antiquities of the Town of Herculaneum ... The Second Edition, with Additions. London: for Wilson & Durham, 1756. 8vo. [iv],43, 236,[iii] pp. 42 plates (occas sl foxing). Free endpapers removed. Period speckled calf, gilt spine.

(*Rankin*) £250 [≈ $445]

Cockburn, W.

- The Nature and Cures of Fluxes ... London: for John Clarke, 1724. 3rd edn. xlii,[iv],344 pp. Lacks fldg table. Crnr of a few pp chipped, not affecting text. Sl marg spotting. Few margs thumbed. Contemp calf, rebacked, hinges reprd.

(*Francis Edwards*) £65 [≈ $116]

Cocker, Edward
- The Young Clerks Tutor Enlarged: Being a most useful Collection of the best Presidents of Recognizences, Obligations, Conditions, Acquittances ... The Sixth Edition. London: Bassett, 1670. 208 pp, 4 pp plates. Sl used. Rebound in panelled calf. Wing C.4859.
(C.R. Johnson) **£165 [≈ $294]**

Code ...
- A Code of Gentoo Laws ... see Halhed, N.B.
  - A Code of Laws for the Island of Jersey. [St. Helier]: 1771. 8vo. 335,index pp. Title detached. Contemp vellum, soiled.
(Robertshaw) **£225 [≈ $401]**

Cogan, Henry, translator
- The Court of Rome ... and a Direction for such as shall travell to Rome ... Curiosities, and Antiquities ... Translated out of Italian. London: 1654. 1st English edn. Fcap 8vo. [8],199,[1], sectional title-leaf, [6], 199-275 pp. Contemp calf, sl worn. Wing C.6591.
(Spelman) **£320 [≈ $570]**

Coghan or Cogan, Thomas
- The Haven of Health. London: Anne Griffin, 1636. Sm 4to. [xvi],321,[1 blank],[22 index] pp. Later mor.   *(Bookpress)* **$475 [≈ £267]**

Cohausen, Johann Heinrich
- Hermippus Redivivus; Or, the Sage's Triumph over Old Age and the Grave ... London: J. Nourse, 1744. 1st edn in English. 8vo. [8],168 pp. Orig bds, rebacked. Translated by J. Campbell. Anon.
(O'Neal) **$200 [≈ £112]**
- Hermippus Redivivus; Or, the Sage's Triumph over Old Age and the Grave ... London: 1748. Sm 8vo. 124 pp. Contemp calf, lacks label. Translated by J. Campbell. Anon.   *(Robertshaw)* **£56 [≈ $100]**

Coke, Sir Edward
- The Complete Copy-Holder; Being a Learned Discourse of the Antiquity and Nature of Manors and Copy-Holds ... London: E. Flesher ..., 1673. 8vo. Sl browning. Mod mor. Wing C.4916.
(Meyer Boswell) **$500 [≈ £281]**
- The Fift Part of the Reports ... London: for the Company of Stationers, 1624. Some staining & browning. Mod half calf. STC 5508.   *(Meyer Boswell)* **$500 [≈ £281]**
- The First Part of the Institutes of the Laws of England ... London: Society of Stationers, 1628. 1st edn. Folio. 7,395,[1] ff. Lacks port. Title backed & reprd. Sl stains. Contemp calf,

worn, jnts cracked. STC 15784.
(Meyer Boswell) **$2,250 [≈ £1,264]**
- The First Part of the Institutes of the Laws of England, or a Commentary upon Littleton ... London: 1703. 10th edn. Folio. [10],88 pp, 394 ff, [64] pp. Frontis, port, fldg chart (torn without loss). Sl spots & marg worm. Mod three qtr leather.   *(O'Neal)* **$400 [≈ £225]**
- The First Part of the Institutes of the Laws of England ... London: for E. & R. Brooke, 1794. Edited by Hargrave & Butler. 8vo. Unpaginated. Contemp calf, worn, spines sl worn, 1 bd detached.
(Vanbrugh) **£125 [≈ $223]**
- The Lord Coke His Speech and Charge. With a Discourse of the Abuses and Corruptions of Officers. London: for Nathaniell Butter, 1607. Browned & foxed. Mod three qtr calf. STC 5492.4. *(Meyer Boswell)* **$550 [≈ £309]**
- Le Quart Part des Reports ... London: 1635. Sl dusty. Mod three qtr calf. STC 5503.7.
(Meyer Boswell) **$500 [≈ £281]**
- Les Reports [Parts 1-6] d'Edward Coke L'attorney generall le Roigne ... London: Companie of Stationers, 1618-24. 6 vols. Some browning & staining. Mod three qtr calf. STC 5494.3, 5498, 5501, 5503.4, 5508, 5510.   *(Meyer Boswell)* **$2,500 [≈ £1,404]**
- Les Reports de Edward Coke ... [Part 1]. London: 1636. Sl dusty. Mod qtr calf. STC 5494.8.   *(Meyer Boswell)* **$500 [≈ £281]**
- Les Tierce Part des reports ... London: Assignes of John More, 1635. Mod three qtr calf. STC 5501.5.
(Meyer Boswell) **$500 [≈ £281]**

Coker, John
- A Survey of Dorsetshire ... London: for J. Wilcox ..., 1732. 1st edn. Sm folio. Fldg map by Seale, 6 plates. Contemp calf, leather label, fine.   *(Georges)* **£650 [≈ $1,157]**

Cole, Benjamin, engraver
- Select Tales and Fables with Prudential Maxims and other little Lessons of Morality in Prose and Verse ... London: for F. Wingrave ..., [ca 1780]. 2 vols in one. 12mo. iv,80; iv,80 pp. Engvd title & frontises, 60 engvd ills. 19th c half calf, rebacked.
(Burmester) **£150 [≈ $267]**

Colepeper, William
- A True State of the Difference between Sir George Rook and William Colepeper, together with an Account of the Tryal of Mr. Nathanael Drew ... London: 1704. Part 1, all published. 1st edn. Folio. 44 pp. Mod cloth backed bds.   *(Robertshaw)* **£75 [≈ $134]**

Coleridge, Samuel Taylor

- Poems, by S.T. Coleridge. Second Edition. To which are now added Poems by Charles Lamb, and Charles Lloyd. Bristol: N. Biggs, for J. Cottle, & Messrs. Robinson, London, 1797. Sm 8vo. Lacks errata slip (as always). Blue crushed mor. *(Hannas)* **£480** [≈ $854]

Collection ...

- A Collection of all the Wills, known to be extant, of the Kings and Queens of England ... London: J. Nichols, 1780. 4to. x,434 pp. Occas contemp MS notes. Half calf, crnrs worn, hd of spine sl worn.
  (Francis Edwards) **£60** [≈ $107]
- A Collection of Articles, Injunctions, Canons, Orders, Ordinances, & Constitutions Ecclesiastical, With other Publick Records of the Church of England ... London: for Blanch Pawlet, 1684. 4th impression. 4to. [xiv], 406, [12] pp. Contemp calf, sometime rebacked.
  (Young's) **£70** [≈ $125]
- A Collection of Cases and other Discourses lately written to recover Dissenters to the Communion of the Church of England by Some Divines of the Church of England. London: Basset & Tooke, 1685. 1st coll edn. 2 vols. 4to. Contemp calf, labels chipped, sl rubbed. Wing B.5114.
  (Blackwell's) **£85** [≈ $151]
- Collection of Odes, Songs, and Epigrams, against the Whigs, alias the Blue and Buff; in which are included, Mr. Hewardine's Political Songs. London: J. Bell, 1790. 1st edn. 8vo. viii,98 pp. Half-title. Rec bds, uncut, largely unopened.
  (Burmester) **£145** [≈ $258]
- Collection of Poems relating to State Affairs from Oliver cromwell to this Present Time: By the Greatest Wits of the Age ... London: [no publisher] 1705. Pirated edn. Tall 8vo. [3],[10],591 pp. Title sl worn & mtd. Rebound in calf gilt.
  (Hartfield) **$345** [≈ £194]
- A Collection of Scarce and Valuable Papers, Some whereof were never before Printed. London: Sawbridge, 1712. 8vo. Irregular pagination. Some browning. Qtr calf.
  (Rostenberg & Stern) **$235** [≈ £132]
- A Collection of Welsh Tours; or, a Display of the Beauties of Wales. Selected principally from Celebrated Histories and Popular Tours ... added, a Tour of the River Wye.. London: Sael, 1798. 3rd edn. Fcap 8vo. xix,[i],456 pp. 7 plates. Contemp half calf, backstrip relaid.
  (Spelman) **£85** [≈ $151]

Collier, Jeremy

- A Defence of the Reasons for Restoring some

Prayers and Directions of King Edward the Sixth's First Liturgy ... London: for John Morphew, 1718. 8vo. Disbound. Anon.
  (Waterfield's) **£50** [≈ $89]
- Essays upon Several Moral Subjects ... The Fourth Edition. London: for Richard Sare, & H. Hindmarsh, 1700. 2 vols in one. 8vo. Final advt leaf vol 2. Minor stains. Contemp panelled calf. Wing C.5255.
  (Hannas) **£65** [≈ $116]
- Miscellanies: in Five Essays [with Miscellanies upon Moral Subjects. The Second Part]. London: Keble & Hindmarsh, 1694-95. 1st edns. 2 vols. 8vo. Contemp calf, not entirely uniform, 1 spine sl defective. Wing C.5256, 5257. *(Hannas)* **£120** [≈ $214]
- A Short View of the Immorality and Profaneness of the English Stage ... Third Edition. London: Keble, Sare & Hindmarsh, 1698. 8vo. [xvi],288 pp. 3 advt pp after Contents. Contemp calf, rubbed, lacks label, sm splits jnt ends. Wing C.5265.
  (Clark) **£75** [≈ $134]
- A Short View of the Immorality and Profaneness of the English Stage ... Third Edition. London: for S. Keble ..., 1698. 8vo. [xvi],288 pp. Contemp calf, 19th c reback.
  (Gough) **£125** [≈ $223]

Collier, John

- A View of the Lancashire Dialect; By Way of Dialogue; between Tummus o'Willioms, o'f Margit o'Soase, and Meary o'Dicks, o'Tummy o'Peggy's ... London: for the author, 1775. 1st edn. 8vo. 203, Battle of Dragon 33 pp. General title dated 1793. 10 engvs. New bds, uncut.
  (Young's) **£80** [≈ $142]

Collignon, Charles

- The Miscellaneous Works of Charles Collignon, M.D. ... Cambridge: Hodson, 1786. 4to. Half-title, subscribers, [5],345 pp, errata leaf. Calf, jnts weak.
  (Goodrich) **$175** [≈ £98]

Collingwood, Francis & Woolams, John

- The Universal Cook, and City and Country Housekeeper ... Second Edition. London: Noble for Scatcherd, 1797. 8vo. [viii],[xx],451,[i advt] pp. 13 (of 14, lacks port) plates. Plates sl browned. Sl later diced russia, later reback. *(Gough)* **£250** [≈ $445]

Collins, Anthony

- A Discourse concerning Ridicule and Irony in Writing, in a Letter to the Reverend Dr. Nathanael Marshall. London: for J. Brotherton ..., 1729. 1st edn. 8vo. 77,[1] pp.

Title dust soiled. Some catchwords shaved. Rec qtr calf. Anon. *(Burmester)* **£120 [≈ $214]**

- A Discourse of Free-Thinking occasion'd by the Rise and Growth of a Sect call'd Free-Thinkers. London: printed in the Year, 1713. 8vo. Mod qtr calf. Anon.
(Waterfield's) **£200 [≈ $356]**

Collins, William
- The Poetical Works ... With Memoirs of the Author; and Observations on his Genius and Writings. By J. Langhorne. A New Edition. London: for T. Evans, 1781. Sm 8vo. Contemp tree calf, gilt spine, lacks label.
(Hannas) **£30 [≈ $53]**

Colman, George, the elder
- The Dramatick Works. London: T. Becket, 1777. Only coll edn. 4 vols. 8vo. Half-titles. Sl used. Early 19th c half calf, gilt spines, dble labels, crnrs sl worn, few sm splits in jnts.
(Clark) **£150 [≈ $267]**
- The Man of Business, a Comedy ... Dublin: Exshaw, Sleater, 1774. 1st Irish edn. Lge 12mo. 69,[3] pp. Rec wraps.
(Fenning) **£38.50 [≈ $69]**
- Some Particulars of the Life of the late George Colman, Esq. Written by himself ... London: Cadell & Davies, 1795. 1st edn. 8vo. [2],23 pp. Port. Lacks half-title. Port & title sl spotted. Disbound. *(Hannas)* **£240 [≈ $427]**

Colson, Nathaniel
- The Mariner's New Calendar. London: for W. & J. Mount, T. & T. Page, 1753. Pott 4to. 136 pp. Ills. Thumbed. Contemp sheep, rebacked, reprd. *(Ash)* **£200 [≈ $356]**

Columella; or, the Distressed Anchoret ...
- See Graves, Richard

Colvill, Samuel
- The Grand Impostor Discovered: or an Historical Dispute of the Papacy and Popish Religion ... Part I [apparently all published]. Edinburgh: for the author, 1673. 1st edn. 4to. [lxiv],226, 92,[2] pp. Contemp calf, sl worn. Anon. Wing C.5425. *(Clark)* **£60 [≈ $107]**

Comazzi, Giovanni Battista
- The Morals of Princes ... Done into English by William Hatchett ... London: for T. Worrall, 1729. 8vo. xvi,391,[i] pp. Subscribers. Frontis. Contemp panelled calf, spine ends worn, jnts rubbed, crnrs bumped, upper hinge cracked. *(Finch)* **£30 [≈ $53]**
- The Morals of Princes ... Done into English, by William Hatchett ... London: for T.

Worrall, 1729. 1st edn. 8vo. xvi,391,[1 advt] pp. Subscribers. Frontis. Contemp calf, rebacked. *(Young's)* **£75 [≈ $134]**

Combe, William
- The Diaboliad, A Poem. Dedicated to the Worst Man in His Majesty's Dominions ... London: for G. Kearsly, 1677 [1777] 2nd edn. 8vo. 4to. [iv],iv,24 pp. Disbound. Anon.
(Young's) **£20 [≈ $36]**
- The Diaboliad, A Poem. Dedicated to the Worst Man in His Majesty's Dominions ... London: for G. Kearsley, 1777. New edn. 4to. [iv],24 pp. Half-title. New bds. Anon.
(Young's) **£45 [≈ $80]**
- The First of April: Or, the Triumphs of Folly: A Poem ... London: for J. Bew, 1777. 1st edn. 4to. iv,38 pp. New bds. Anon.
(Young's) **£45 [≈ $80]**
- The First of April: Or, the Triumphs of Folly: A Poem ... By the Author of the Diaboliad. Dublin: J. Mehain ..., 1777. 1st Dublin edn. 8vo. 36 pp. Disbound. Anon.
(Young's) **£95 [≈ $169]**
- Letters supposed to have been written by Yorick and Eliza. London: for J. Bew, 1779. 1st edn. 2 vols. 12mo. Possibly lacks half-titles. Polished calf, gilt spines, contrasting labels, hd of 1 spine v sl chipped. Anon. A spurious continuation of Sterne's Letters.
(Burmester) **£150 [≈ $267]**
- A Word in Season to the Traders & Manufacturers of Great Britain. N.p.: 1792. 7th edn. 8vo. Stitched. Anon.
(Rostenberg & Stern) **$60 [≈ £34]**

Comberbach, Roger
- The Report of Several Cases Argued and Adjudged in the Court of King's Bench ... From the First Year of King James the Second ... In the Savoy: for J. Walthoe, 1724. 1st edn. Folio. [xiv],484,[485-535] pp. Errata. Contemp calf, spine sl worn.
(Vanbrugh) **£135 [≈ $240]**

Comines
- See Commines

Commerell, Abbe de
- An Account of the Culture and Use of the Mangel Wurzel, or Root of Scarcity, Translated from the French. London: 1787. 3rd edn. 8vo. xxxix,51 pp. Cold plate. Half calf, somewhat worn.
(Wheldon & Wesley) **£60 [≈ $107]**

Commines, Philippe de
- The Historie of Philip de Commines Knight,

Lord of Argenton. London: I. Norton, 1596. 1st edn in English. Folio. [xvi],396,[1] pp. Later half calf.   *(Bookpress)* **$500 [≈ £281]**

- The History of Philip de Commines, Knight, Lord of Argenton. London: A. Hatfield for I. Norton, 1596. 1st edn in English. Sm folio. [16],396,[1 errata] pp. W'cut title border. Closely trimmed. Rebound in qtr calf. STC 5602.   *(O'Neal)* **$550 [≈ £309]**

- The Historie. London: A. Hatfield for J. Norton, 1601. 2nd edn. Translated by Thomas Danett. Sm folio. [xvi],364 pp. W'cut title (guarded). New endpapers. Contemp sheep, gilt spine. STC 5603.
    (Vanbrugh) **£325 [≈ $579]**

- The Historie. London: Bill, 1614. Sm folio. Marg repr to L2 with sl loss of text. Dec title border. Goat, gilt medallion on cvrs, front cvr detached. STC 5604.
    (Rostenberg & Stern) **$525 [≈ £295]**

A Compendious Library of the Law ...

- A Compendious Library of the Law, necessary for Persons of all Degrees and Professions. In the Savoy: Nutt, Gosling, for Osborn, 1740. 1st edn. 2 parts in one vol. 12mo. Contemp calf, later label, sl rubbed, jnts sl tender.   *(Ximenes)* **$200 [≈ £112]**

Compleat ...

- The Compleat Clark, containing the best forms of all sorts of presidents ... Third Edition. London: T.R. for N. Brook, 1671. Some browning. Mod polished half calf. Wing C.5636. *(Meyer Boswell)* **$450 [≈ £253]**

- The Compleat Clerk, containing the best forms of all sorts of presidents ... London: W. Rawlins, S. Roycroft, H. Sawbridge ..., 1683. 5th edn. 4to. [vi],936,[80] pp. Engvd title. Rec calf backed bds. Wing C.5636B.
    (Burmester) **£375 [≈ $668]**

Complete ...

- A Complete Body of Divinity ... see Stackhouse, Thomas

- A Complete Collection of Protests from the Year MDCXLI to the Present Year MDCCXXXVII. London: W. Webb, 1737. 1st edn. 8vo. [xii],470 pp. Sm piece torn from crnr of title. Contemp calf gilt, sl rubbed, ft of spine sl chipped. The Colquhoun copy.
    (Clark) **£85 [≈ $151]**

- A Complete Collection of State-Trials, and Proceedings for High-Treason, and other Crimes and Misdemeanours ... Second Edition, with great Additions. London: J. Walthoe ..., 1720.. 6 vols. Folio. Contemp reversed calf, few minor blemishes.
    (Frew Mackenzie) **£600 [≈ $1,068]**

- The Complete English Farmer ... see Henry, David

- The Complete Family-Piece: and, Country Gentleman, and Farmer's Best Guide ... Second Edition. London: Bettesworth, Hitch ..., 1737. Lge 12mo. xii,520,[lxi] pp. Generally cropped at hd. Sm worm hole at start. Contemp style panelled calf.
    (Gough) **£450 [≈ $801]**

- The Complete Farmer: or, a General Dictionary of Husbandry, in all its Branches ... The Second Edition, Corrected and Improved. By a Society of Gentlemen. London: 1769. 4to. (A)1-2,B1-4R4, 4S1-2,*A1-*O4, *P1-2. 29 plates. Sl worn. Contemp calf, sl worn. *(Clark)* **£220 [≈ $392]**

- A Complete History of the Origin and Progress of the Late War ... London: J. Knox, 1764. 1st edn. 2 vols. 8vo. [iv],358,[ii]; [ii],(359)-771,[i] pp. Occas minor foxing. Contemp calf, extrs worn, lacks labels, jnts cracked but secure.   *(Clark)* **£65 [≈ $116]**

- The Complete Parish-Officer ... see Jacob, Giles, possible author

Concanen, Matthew
- See under Flower-Piece ...

The Conduct of the Allies ...
- See Swift, Jonathan

Congreve, William
- The Mourning Bride, a Tragedy ... London: for Jacob Tonson, 1697. 1st edn. 4to. Lacks half-title. Edges browned. Mrbld bds. Wing C.5856.   *(Hannas)* **£450 [≈ $801]**

- Poems upon Several Occasions. Glasgow: R. & A. Foulis, 1752. 8vo in 4s. 189,[iii] pp. Occas minor browning. Mod mor, a.e.g., by Gray of Cambridge.   *(Clark)* **£65 [≈ $116]**

Consett, Matthew
- A Tour through Sweden, Swedish-Lapland, Finland and Denmark ... London: J. Johnson, 1789. 1st edn. 4to. [16],157 pp. Half-title. Engvd frontis & 7 engvd plates by Thomas Bewick. Sl browning & foxing, 1 clean tear. Orig bds, early cloth spine, uncut, crnrs worn.   *(Spelman)* **£180 [≈ $320]**

Considerations ...
- Considerations on the Present State of Affairs in Europe, and particularly with regard to the Number of Forces in the Pay of Great Britain. London: for J. Roberts, 1730. 1st edn. 8vo. 55 pp. Lacks half-title. Disbound.
    (Young's) **£60 [≈ $107]**

- Considerations on the Definitive Treaty,

Signed at Aix la Chapell, October 7/18th, 1748 ... London: for J. Roberts, 1748. Only edn. 8vo. 55 pp. Disbound.
(Young's) £90 [≈ $160]
- Considerations relating to a New Duty upon Sugar. The Second Edition. To which is now added, a Supplement. London: for M. Cooper, 1746. 8vo. Disbound.
(Hannas) £85 [≈ $151]
- Considerations upon Wit and Morals ... see Meilhan, Gabriel Senac de

Constable, John
- The Conversation of Gentlemen Considered in most of the Ways, that make their Mutual Company Agreeable, or Disagreeable. In Six Dialogues. London: J. Hoyles, 1738. 1st edn. 12mo. viii,272,[8] pp. Frontis. Contemp sheep, jnts cracked but firm. Anon.
(Burmester) £180 [≈ $320]

Cook, James, Captain
- A Voyage towards the South Pole, and around the World ... in the Years 1772, 1773, 1774, and 1775 ... London: Strahan & Cadell, 1777. 1st edn. 2 vols. 4to. 378; 396 pp. Port frontis, 63 plates & maps (sl damp stain to 2). Contemp calf, backstrips laid down.
(Chapel Hill) $2,300 [≈ £1,292]

Cook, John
- King Charles his Case: or, An Appeal to all Rational Men, Concerning His Tryal at the High Court of Justice ... London: Peter Cole, 1649. 1st edn. 4to. 43 pp. Title trifle soiled, lower marg crnrs sl browned. Disbound. Wing C.6025.
(Young's) £140 [≈ $249]

Cook, M.
- The Manner of Raising, Ordering, and Improving Forest-Trees. London: 1724. 3rd edn. 8vo. xx,273 pp. Frontis, fldg plate. Lacks half-title. Calf, reprd.
(Wheldon & Wesley) £120 [≈ $214]

Cook, Revd Thomas
- The Universal Letter-Writer: or, New Art of Polite Correspondence. London: A. Millar, 1794. 1st edn. xii,13-228 pp. Frontis. Contemp calf, rubbed, hd of spine worn.
(Jermy & Westerman) £35 [≈ $62]

Cooke, Alexander
- Pope Joane. A Dialogue betweene a Protestant and a Papist. London: for John Haviland & William Garrat, 1625. 2nd edn. 4to. Title dust soiled & outer edge strengthened. Occas faint water stains. Mod limp reversed calf, yapp edges. STC 5660.

(Hannas) £75 [≈ $134]

Cooke, Thomas
- The Universal Letter-Writer; or, New Art of Polite Correspondence ... London: for Osborne & Griffin; & H. Mozley, Gainsborough, 1788. 240 pp. Frontis. Contemp sheep, rebacked.
(C.R. Johnson) £95 [≈ $169]

Cooke, William
- Poetical Essays on Several Occasions. London: for S. Smith, 1775. 4to. Subscribers. Orig wraps, lacks backstrip, 1 crnr frayed & stained.
(Waterfield's) £125 [≈ $223]

Copywell, J.
- The Shrubs of Parnassus ... see Woty, William

Corbet, Richard
- Poems. London: J.C. for William Crook, 1672. 3rd edn. 12mo. Occas v sl soiling. Lacks 1st blank. 119th c olive mor gilt, a.e.g., by Riviere, fine. Slipcase. Wing C.6271.
(P and P Books) £675 [≈ $1,202]

Cordiner, Charles
- Antiquities & Scenery of the North of Scotland, in a Series of Letters to Thomas Pennant. London: 1780. Sm 4to. 173,[xi] pp. 21 plates. Occas sl spotting, title sl creased. Old qtr roan gilt, sl rubbed & defective, vellum crnrs.
(Hollett) £130 [≈ $231]

Cornaro, Luigi
- Discourses on a Sober and Temperate Life. Translated from the Italian Original. London: for Benjamin White, 1768. 1st edn of this translation. With the Italian text. 2 parts. 8vo. Some water stains. Contemp calf, rebacked, crnrs worn.
(Hannas) £45 [≈ $80]

Cornelius Nepos
- The Lives of Illustrious Men ... done into English by the Honourable Mr Finch, Mr Creech, and other eminent Gentlemen of Oxford. London: for Tho. Shelmerdine, 1723. Fcap 8vo. [36],250 pp. Half-title. Engvd title, dble-page plate. Some browning. Contemp calf ft of spine sl worn.
(Spelman) £35 [≈ $62]

Cornwallis, Sir Charles
- A Discourse of the most Illustrious Prince Henry, late Prince of Wales. London: 1641. 1st edn. 4to. 29 pp. Title marked. Mod half mor, t.e.g.. Wing C.6329.
(Robertshaw) £65 [≈ $116]

The Correspondents ...

- The Correspondents, an Original Novel; in a Series of Letters. London: for T. Becket, 1775. 1st edn. 12mo. Half-title. Sl water stains. Mod half calf.
(Ximenes) **$500 [≈ £281]**

- The Correspondents. An Original Novel; in a Series of Letters. London: for T. Becket, 1775. 1st edn. 12mo. Half-title. Contemp calf, rebacked.
(Hannas) **£320 [≈ $570]**

Corye, John

- A Cure for Jealousie, a Comedy ... London: for Richard Harrison, 1701. 1st edn. 4to. Title & following ff stained. Few marg reprs. Disbound. Anon.
(Hannas) **£75 [≈ $134]**

Cosens, John

- The Economy of Beauty; in a Series of Fables addressed to the Ladies. London: for J. Walter, 1777. 4to. Frontis, 20 vignettes. Mod qtr calf.
(Waterfield's) **£135 [≈ $240]**

Cosin, James (editor)

- The Names of the Roman Catholics, Nonjurors, and Others, who refused to take the Oaths to his late Majesty King George ... London: 1745. 1st edn. 151 pp. Disbound. Anon.
(Robertshaw) **£15 [≈ $27]**

Cotgrave, Randle

- A Dictionarie of the French and English Tongues ... Whereunto is also annexed a most copious Dictionarie of the English set before the French by R.S.L. [Robert Sherwood, Londoner]. London: 1632. 2nd edn. 2 vols in one. Folio. Contemp calf, crnrs rubbed, jnts cracked. STC.5831.
(Robertshaw) **£195 [≈ $347]**

Cotton, Charles

- Burlesque upon Burlesque: or, The Scoffer Scoft. Being Some of Lucian's Dialogues Newly Put into English Fustian ... The Second Edition Corrected. London: Charles Brome, 1686. 8vo. 200,[2] pp. Frontis. 19th c calf gilt, jnts rubbed. Wing C.6380A.
(Karmiole) **$200 [≈ £112]**

- The Genuine Poetical Works ... Containing I. Scarronides ... III. The Wonders of the Peake. The Second Edition, Corrected. London: for R. & J. Bonwicke ..., 1725. 12mo. 7 plates. Contemp calf, gilt spine, lacks label.
(Hannas) **£45 [≈ $80]**

- The Genuine Poetical Works ... Third Edition, Corrected. London: for J. Walthoe ..., 1734. 8vo. [iv],348,[8 ctlg] pp. 8 plates. Period calf, label chipped, upper jnt cracked.
(Rankin) **£45 [≈ $80]**

- The Genuine Works ... Containing I. Scarronides ... IV. The Planters Manual. London: for R. Bonwicke ..., 1715. 1st coll edn. 8vo. 10 plates (1 fldg). 4 lines in Scarronides inked out. Contemp calf.
(Hannas) **£120 [≈ $214]**

- Poems on Several Occasions. London: Bassett, Hensman, Fox, 1689. 1st edn. 8vo. Sl water stains at end. Contemp panelled calf, rebacked. Wing C.6389.
(Hannas) **£200 [≈ $356]**

- Scarronides: or, Virgil Travestie. A Mock Poem. In Imitation of the Fourth Book of Virgils Aeneis in English. London: 1665. 1st edn of the "Fourth Book". 8vo. 155,[2] pp. Mod half calf. Wing C.6392. Anon.
(Robertshaw) **£65 [≈ $116]**

- The Wonders of the Peak. London: for Joanna Brome, 1681. 1st edn. 8vo. [6],86,[2] pp, inc intl & penultimate blank ff. Lacks final blank. Contemp mottled calf, spine sl wormed. Wing C.6400.
(Hannas) **£220 [≈ $392]**

Cotton, John

- Gods Mercie mixed with his Justice, or, His Peoples Deliverance in Times of Danger. Laid Open in Severall Sermons. London: G.M. for Edward Brewster & Henry Hood, 1641. Sm 4to. [8],72 pp. Dark blue mor gilt, a.e.g., by Matthews (ca 1870), sl rubbed. Wing C.6433.
(Karmiole) **$650 [≈ £365]**

Cotton, Nathaniel

- Visions in Verse, for the Entertainment and Instruction of Younger Minds ... London: Dodsley, 1776. 9th edn. 12mo. 141,[2] pp. Frontis. Near contemp calf, gilt spine, front jnt partly worn. Anon.
(Young's) **£28 [≈ $50]**

Cotton, Sir Robert

- Cottoni Posthuma: Divers Choice Pieces wherein are discussed several important Questions concerning the Right and Power of the Lords and Commons in Parliament. London: 1679. 8vo. Port. Contemp calf, elab gilt spine. Wing C.6487.
(Robertshaw) **£55 [≈ $98]**

- An Exact Abridgement of the Records in the Tower of London ... Revised ... By William Prynne. London: for William Leake, 1657. 1st edn thus. Folio. [xxxvi],716,[717-854] pp, erratic but complete. V occas sl browning. Contemp calf, rebacked. Wing C.6489.
(Vanbrugh) **£275 [≈ $490]**

The Court of Rome ...

- See Cogan, Henry, translator.

Court, Pieter de la
- Fables, Moral and Political, with large Explications. Translated from the Dutch. London: Printed in the Year, 1708. 2 vols. 8vo. Frontis in vol 1. Contemp calf, 1 vol rebacked. Anon. *(Waterfield's)* **£250 [≈ $445]**

Courtenay, John
- A Poetical Review of the Literary and Moral Character of the late Samuel Johnson, L.L.D. with Notes. London: for Charles Dilly, 1768. 1st edn. 4to. [ii],27 pp. Lacks half-title. Half calf. Bound with 2 other minor pieces. *(Burmester)* **£375 [≈ $668]**

Courteville, Raphael
- Arguments respecting Insolvency. Dedicated to the Rt. Hon. Arthur Onslow. London: for M. Cooper, [1761?]. 1st edn. 8vo. vii,32 pp. Disbound. *(Hannas)* **£60 [≈ $107]**

Courtilz de Sandras, Gatien de
- The French Spy: or, The Memoirs of John Baptist De La Fontaine. London: Basset, 1700. Translated by Jodocus Crull. 8vo. Mor gilt. Anon. *(Rostenberg & Stern)* **$275 [≈ £154]**
- The Life of the Famous John Baptist Colbert, late Minister and Secretary to Lewis XIV ... Done into English from a French Copy. London: Bentley, Tonson ..., 1695. 1st English edn. 8vo. Frontis. Advt leaf & final blank. Contemp calf, jnts cracking. Wing C.6599. Anon. *(Hannas)* **£75 [≈ $134]**

Courtilz de Sandras, Gatien de (supposed author)
- The Memoirs of the Marquess de Langallerie ... The Second Edition. Translated from the French, and continued to this Present Time. London: for J. Round ..., 1710. 8vo. [xvi],416 pp. Contemp calf, sometime rebacked, spine ends worn, jnts cracked. Anon. *(Burmester)* **£175 [≈ $312]**

Coventry, Francis
- The History of Pompey the Little. London: for M. Cooper, 1751. 1st edn. 12mo. viii,272 pp. Frontis. Sl browning. Rec half calf gilt by Bayntun. Anon. *(Ash)* **£250 [≈ $445]**

Cowell, John
- The Interpreter: or Booke containing the Signification of Words. Wherein is set foorth the true meaning of all, or the most part of such words and termes, as are mentioned in the Law Writers ... London: Sheares, 1637. Sm 4to. Sl water stain. Contemp calf. STC 5901. *(Burmester)* **£375 [≈ $668]**

Cowell, John, gardener
- The Curious and the Profitable Gardener ... London: Weaver Bickerton, 1730. 1st edn. 8vo. iv,[iv],126, [11],67,[1] pp. Frontis, 1 fldg plate. Contemp sheep, worn. *(Bookpress)* **$650 [≈ £365]**

Cowley, Abraham
- Poems: viz. I. Miscellanies ... IV. Davideis ... London: for Humphrey Moseley, 1656. 1st coll edn. Folio. Sm repr to title. Mod pigskin to a cottage roof design. Wing C.6682. *(Waterfield's)* **£425 [≈ $757]**
- Poems: viz. I. Miscellanies. II. The Mistress, or Love Verses. III.. Pindarique Odes and IV. Davideis ... London: for Humphrey Moseley, 1656. Folio. Sm repr to title. Mod dec pigskin. Wing C.6682. *(Waterfield's)* **£425 [≈ $757]**
- Select Works ... in Two Volumes: with a Preface and Notes by the Editor [Richard Hurd]. London: Bowyer & Nichols, 1772. 1st edn thus. 2 vols. 8vo. Title vignette. Contemp calf, dble green labels, jnts rubbed. *(Waterfield's)* **£65 [≈ $116]**
- Select Works of Mr A. Cowley ... With a Preface and Notes by the Editor [R. Hurd]. Dublin: 1772. 2 vols. Fcap 8vo. xii,204; vii, [i],207 pp. Vignette title ports. Contemp calf, raised bands, gilt labels. *(Spelman)* **£60 [≈ $107]**
- The Works ... Third Edition. London: J.M. for Henry Herringman, 1672. Folio. Port. Contemp calf, crnrs sl worn. Wing C.6651. *(Hannas)* **£240 [≈ $427]**

Cowley, Hannah
- The Fate of Sparta: or, The Rival Kings. A Tragedy ... Dublin: William Porter, 1788. 1st Dublin edn. 8vo. [v],52 pp. Disbound. *(Young's)* **£20 [≈ $36]**
- The Poetry of Anna Matilda ... To which are added Recollections, printed from an Original Manuscript, Written by General Sir William Waller. London: J. Bell, 1788. 1st edn. 8vo. [viii],139,[i] pp. Contemp tree calf, gilt dec spine, mor onlays, sl chipped. *(Clark)* **£90 [≈ $160]**

Cowper, Henry
- Reports of Cases adjudged in the King's bench: from Hilary Term, the 14th of George III, 1774 to ... 1778 ... London: for E. Brooke, 1783. 1st edn. Folio. [xii],846, [847-888] pp. Errata. Contemp calf, spine sl worn, lacks label. *(Vanbrugh)* **£115 [≈ $205]**

Cox, N.
- The Gentleman's Recreation: In Four Parts

... London: Rolls, 1696. Fldg frontis, addtnl engvd title, 3 fldg plates. Occas spotting or browning. Contemp calf, rebacked. Wing C.6707. Anon.

(P and P Books) **£325 [≈ $579]**

Coxe, William

- Memoirs of the Life and Administration of Sir Robert Walpole, Earl of Orford ... London: Cadell & Davies, 1798. 3 vols. 4to. Frontis & table vol 1. 4 pp facs vol 2. Contemp polished calf, rebacked, v sl wear to crnrs. *(Waterfield's)* **£350 [≈ $623]**

Cradock, Samuel

- The Harmony of the Four Evangelists, and their Text Methodiz'd ... London: for Samuel Thompson, 1668. 1st edn. Folio. [xxxviii], 287, [1],[1 errata] pp. Rec calf. Wing C.6748.
(Young's) **£75 [≈ $134]**

The Craftsman Extraordinary ...

- See Bolingbroke, Henry St. John, Viscount

Craig, Sir Thomas

- Scotland's Soveraignty Asserted ... London: for Andrew Bell ... Thomas Brown ... Edinburgh, 1695. 1st edn. 8vo. Errata leaf. Contemp gilt panelled mor, a.e.g., rebacked. Wing C.6804. *(Georges)* **£150 [≈ $267]**

Crawford, John

- Cursus Medicinae; or a Complete Theory of Physic; in Five Parts ... Done, principally, from those admirable Institutions of H. Boerhaave. London: 1724. 1st edn. 8vo. 382 pp. Lib stamp on title. Contemp panelled calf, sl worn. *(Robertshaw)* **£68 [≈ $121]**

Crawfurd, George & Semple, William

- The History of the Shire of Renfrew ... Paisley: Alex Weir & the author, 1782. 1st edn. 4to. viii,vi,108, 334,6 pp. Occas spotting. Contemp half russia gilt.
(Finch) **£210 [≈ $374]**

Crazy Tales ...

- See Hall-Stevenson, John

Crevecoeur, Michel Guillaume St. Jean

- Letters from an American Farmer ... conveying Some Idea of the Late and Present Interior Circumstances of the British Colonies in North America ... London: 1783. 2nd London edn. [14],326,[2] pp. Half-title. 2 fldg maps. Occas foxing. Later calf. Anon.
(Reese) **$1,250 [≈ £702]**

Criticisms on the Rolliad ...

- Criticisms on the Rolliad. Part the First: Corrected and Enlarged. London: for James Ridgway, 1785. 8vo. Frontis. Contemp half calf. *(Waterfield's)* **£50 [≈ $89]**

Croke, Sir George

- The Second Part of the Reports of Sir George Croke Kt. ... Revised ... By Sir Harebotle Grimston ... Third Impression ... London: 1683. Folio. [xxvi],700,[701-722] pp. Port frontis. Contemp calf, spine worn, bds detached. Wing C.7018.
(Vanbrugh) **£165 [≈ $294]**

- The Third Part (though First Publish't) of the Reports ... Collected ... by Sir Harbottle Grimston ... Third Impression ... London: 1683. Folio. [xxx],610,[611-676] pp. Licence page. Mantissa page. Port frontis. Contemp calf, spine worn. Wing C.7020.
(Vanbrugh) **£165 [≈ $294]**

Croker, Richard

- Travels through Several Provinces of Spain and Portugal &c. London: for the author, 1799. 8vo. Minor spotting. Mod half calf. *(Waterfield's)* **£135 [≈ $240]**

Cromwell, Oliver

- Declaration ... for a Day of Solemn Fasting and Humiliation in the Three Nations. London: Hills & Field, 1656. Folio. Commonwealth arms on title. Stitched. Wing C.7069. *(Rostenberg & Stern)* **$125 [≈ £70]**
- His Highness Speech to the Parliament in the Painted Chamber ... Monday the 22d of January 1654 [1655]. London: Henry Hills, 1654. 1st edn. 4to. [ii],36 pp. Browned, occas staining. Disbound. Wing C.7171.
(Clark) **£100 [≈ $178]**

Cromwell, Richard

- The Speech of His Highness the Lord Protector made to both Houses of Parliament ... 27th of January 1658 ... London: Hills & Field, 1659. 1st edn. 4to. [ii],9,[iii],28 pp. Sep title to Fienne's speech. Some marking. Disbound, stitching broken. Wing C.7191 & F.881. *(Clark)* **£85 [≈ $151]**

Cross, Walter

- The Taghmical Art: or the Art of Expounding Scripture by the Points, usually called Accents ... London: S. Bridge for the author, 1698. 1st edn. Occas v sl spotting. Endpapers browned. Mottled calf, gilt dec spine, crnrs sl worn. Wing C.7265.
(P and P Books) **£160 [≈ $285]**

Crosthwaite, P.

- Seven Engraved Maps of the Lakes. Keswick: Peter Crosthwaite, 1788. 2nd edn. 8vo. 1 dble-page & 6 fldg maps. Contemp half calf, vellum tips.   *(Spelman)* **£350 [≃ $623]**

Crouch, Nathaniel

- See Burton, Robert

Crowe, William

- Lewesdon Hill. A Poem. Oxford: Clarendon Press, for Prince, Cooke ..., 1788. 2nd edn. 4to. 29 pp. Disbound.
        (Hartfield) **$165 [≃ £93]**

Crowne, William

- A True Relation of all the Remarkable Places and Passages Observed in the Travels of the Right Honourable Thomas Lord Howard, Earle of Arundell. London: for Henry Seile, 1637. 1st edn. Sm 4to. [4],70 pp. Lacks final blank. Occas browning. Later bds.
        (Spelman) **£400 [≃ $712]**

Croxall, S.

- An Original Canto of Spencer: Design'd as Part of his Fairy Queen, but never Printed. Now made Publick by Nestor Ironside, Esq. London: 1714. 1st edn. 4to. 30 pp. Occas sm marg damp stain. Lacks final blank. Mod wraps. Anon.   *(Robertshaw)* **£25 [≃ $45]**
- An Original Canto of Spencer: Design'd as Part of his Fairy Queen, but never Printed. Now made Publick by Nestor Ironside, Esq. London: 1714. 2nd edn. 4to. 30 pp. Lacks final blank. Mod wraps. Anon.
        (Robertshaw) **£15 [≃ $27]**

Cruden, Alexander

- A Complete Concordance to the Holy Scriptures of the Old and New Testament ... Fourth Edition ... London: Buckland, Rivington ..., 1785. 4to. [510] ff. Port & title mtd. Last 2 ff guarded. 19th c half calf gilt, sl rubbed.   *(Blackwell's)* **£65 [≃ $116]**
- A Complete Concordance to the Holy Scriptures of the Old and New Testament ... Fifth Edition. London: Owen, Longman ..., 1794. 4to. [514] ff. Port (offset onto title). Contemp mottled calf, jnts weak, crnrs worn.
        (Blackwell's) **£100 [≃ $178]**

Cruikshank, William Cumberland

- The Anatomy of the Absorbing Vessels of the Human Body. The Second Edition, considerably enlarged ... London: Nicol, 1790. 4to. viii,208, 207*-214*, 209-414 pp. 5 plates (ptd in cold inks). 1 plate marg reprd. Contemp calf gilt.   *(Gaskell)* **£550 [≃ $979]**

Crumpe, S.

- An Inquiry into the Nature and Properties of Opium ... London: 1793. x,304 pp. Title sl foxed & dusty. Three qtr leather antique.
        (Whitehart) **£150 [≃ $267]**

Cullen, William

- First Lines of the Practice of Physic. New York: 1793. 2 vols. xxxiv,442; xxi,410 pp. Frontis port. Water stains on endpapers, foxing on endpapers and titles & occas in text. Contemp tree calf, rebacked.
        (Whitehart) **£200 [≃ $356]**
- A Treatise of the Materia Medica. Dublin: Luke White, 1789. 1st Dublin edn. 2 vols. 8vo. Calf.   *(Goodrich)* **$150 [≃ £84]**

Cumberland, Richard

- Calvary; or the Death of Christ. A Poem in Eight Books. London: for C. Dilly, 1792. 1st edn. 4to. [2],291 pp. Lacks half-title. Contemp mottled calf gilt, upper hinge partly cracked.   *(Claude Cox)* **£75 [≃ $134]**
- The Fashionable Lover; a Comedy ... Dublin: for A. Leathley, 1772. 1st edn. 12mo. [8],64 pp. Rec wraps.   *(Fenning)* **£16.50 [≃ $30]**
- Henry; in Four Volumes. By the Author of Arundel. London: Dilly, 1795. 1st edn. 4 vols. 12mo. Contemp half calf, rebacked. Anon.   *(Hannas)* **£350 [≃ $623]**
- A Letter to Richard [Watson] Lord Bishop of Llandaff, on the subject of his Lordship's Letter to the late Archbishop of Canterbury [Frederick Cornwallis]. London: for Charles Dilly & J. Walter, 1783. 8vo. Mod qtr calf.
        (Waterfield's) **£140 [≃ $249]**
- The Observer: Being a Collection of Moral, Literary, and Familiar Essays. London: for C. Dilly, 1791-88. 4th edn vols 1-3, 1st edn vol 4, 2nd edn vol 5. 5 vols. 8vo. Contemp half calf, crnrs worn, rebacked.
        (Young's) **£65 [≃ $116]**
- Odes. London: for J. Robson, 1776. 1st edn. 4to. 27 pp. Long tears in title & last leaf, no loss. Disbound.   *(Hannas)* **£45 [≃ $80]**

Cunningham, T.

- A New Treatise on the Laws concerning Tithes ... London: J. Johnson ..., 1777. 4th edn, enlgd. Half-title. Contemp calf, rear jnt cracked, v sl rubbed.
        (P and P Books) **£195 [≃ $347]**

Cunningham, Timothy

- A Critical Review of the Liberties of British Subjects. With a Comparative View of the Proceedings of the House of Commons of Ireland ... London: R. Watkins, 1750. 8vo in

4s. 119 pp. Mod qtr calf over 18th c bds. Anon. *(Meyer Boswell)* **$250 [≈£140]**

Curio, Caelius
- The Visions of Pasquin, or, A Character of the Roman Court, Religion and Practices ... Translated out of the Italian ... London: Richard Baldwin, 1689. 1st edn in English. 4to. viii,64 pp. Disbound. Wing C.7622A.
(Young's) **£120 [≈$214]**

Curiosities of Literature ...
- See D'Israeli, Isaac

Curry, John
- An Historical and Critical Review of the Civil Wars in Ireland ... Extracted from Parliamentary Records, State Acts, and other authentic Materials. By J.C. Dublin: Hoey, 1775. 1st edn. 4to. xxiv,454 pp. Contemp half vellum, rebacked. *(de Burca)* **£270 [≈$481]**

Curtius Rufus, Quintus
- The History of the Life and Death of Alexander the Great ... render'd into English by several gentlemen of the University of Oxford ... London: for E.C., 1687. 12mo. [x], 386 pp. Frontis. Sl soiling. Contemp calf, sl worn. Wing C.7695. *(Clark)* **£225 [≈$401]**

Customs and Privileges ...
- Customs and Privileges of the Manors of Stepney and Hackney ... London: Nutt & Gosling, for Worrall ..., 1736. 1st edn (?). 12mo. [iv],128 pp. Pencil underlining. Lib stamp on title. Binder's cloth.
(Burmester) **£65 [≈$116]**

Cyprian, Saint
- The Genuine Works ... Done into English, from the Oxford Edition ... By Nath. Marshall ... London: W. Bowyer for W. Taylor ..., 1718. Folio. Contemp calf, rebacked, front endpaper renewed.
(Frew Mackenzie) **£90 [≈$160]**

Cyrano de Bergerac, Savinien
- The Comical History of the States and Empires of the Worlds of the Moon and Sun ... newly Englished by A. Lovell. London: 1687. 1st complete edn in English. 8vo. [viii],140, [ii],206,[ii] pp. Lacks frontis. Contemp sheep, sometime reprd, sl worn. Wing C.7717. *(Sotheran's)* **£350 [≈$623]**
- A Voyage to the Moon: with some Account of the Solar World. A Comical Romance. Done from the French ... by Mr. Derrick. Dublin: R. James, 1754. 1st Irish edn. 12mo. 2 advt ff. Contemp calf backed bds, spine worn.

(Hannas) **£750 [≈$1,335]**

D., T.
- The Progress of Honesty ... see D'Urfey, Thomas

Dacier, Andre
- The Life of Pythagoras, with his Symbols and Golden Verses ... Now done into English ... London: Tonson, 1707. 1st edn. 8vo. [ii], xxxiv,164, xi,[i],165-389,[15] pp. browned. Lge blot on pastedown. Contemp calf, extrs sl worn, jnts cracked but secure.
(Clark) **£150 [≈$267]**

Da Costa, Emmanuel Mendes
- Elements of Conchology: or, an Introduction to the Knowledge of Shells ... London: for Benjamin White, 1776. 1st edn. 8vo. viii,vi,318,[2 errata & advt] pp. 7 fldg plates, 2 fldg charts. Contemp tree calf.
(Claude Cox) **£110 [≈$196]**

Dagge, Henry
- Considerations on Criminal Law. London: T. Cadell, 1772. 1st edn. 8vo. Half-title. Orig (?) cloth backed bds, sl worn. Anon.
(Meyer Boswell) **$650 [≈£365]**

Daille, Jean
- A Treatise concerning the Right Use of the Fathers, in the Decision of the Controversies that are at this day in Religion. London: for John Martin, 1651. 4to. Red & black title. Contemp sheep, recased, extrs sl worn, hd of spine defective. Wing D.118.
(Waterfield's) **£70 [≈$125]**

Dallas, Robert
- Considerations upon the American Enquiry. London: 1779. 55 pp. Half-title. Sm lib stamp. Occas sl foxing. Mod cloth. Anon.
(Reese) **$250 [≈£140]**

Dallington, Sir Robert
- Aphorismes Civil and Militarie ... London: M. Flesher for R. Allot, 1629. 2nd edn. Sm folio. [6],339,[1 blank],61 pp. Foredges of prelims frayed. Contemp calf, rebacked & reprd. STC 6198. *(O'Neal)* **$300 [≈£169]**

Dalrymple, George
- The Practice of Modern Cookery ... Edinburgh: for the author ..., 1781. Only edn. 8vo. vi,475,[i errata] pp. Half-title. Contemp calf, jnts reprd, later label, rear bd scratched. *(Gough)* **£675 [≈$1,202]**

Dalrymple, John
- The Address of the People of Great Britain to the Inhabitants of America. London: 1775. 60 pp. Some staining & foxing. Later cloth. Anon.   *(Reese)* **$200 [≃ £112]**
- The Rights of Great Britain Asserted against the Claims of America ... London: 1776. 92 pp. Fldg table. Few sm reprs. Sl soiling. Half cloth, leather label. Anon.
                    (Reese) **$250 [≃ £140]**

Dalrymple, William
- Solomon's Ethics, or the Book of Proverbs Made Easy; a School Book, and Seasonal Present for the Youth of both Sexes ... Air: J. & P. Wilson, 1799. 8vo. viii,291 pp, inc half-title. Sl foxing. Uncut, sl nick in spine.
                    (Rankin) **£65 [≃ $116]**

Dalton, John
- An Epistle to a Young Nobleman, from his Praeceptor. London: for Lawton Gilliver, & Robert Dodsley, 1736. 1st edn. Folio. [2],17 pp, inc half-title. Mod bds. Anon.
                    (Hannas) **£110 [≃ $196]**

Dalton, Michael
- The Country Justice ... In the Savoy: sold by J. Knapton, 1727. 1st edn. Folio. [xxii], 679, [670-822] pp. Half-title. Early 19th c half calf, spine damaged, bds detached.
                    (Vanbrugh) **£195 [≃ $347]**

Dalzel, Archibald
- The History of Dahomy, an Inland Kingdom of Africa ... London: for the author, 1793. 1st edn. 4to. xxxvi,xxvi,230 pp. Fldg map, 6 plates. Occas sm marg water stain, some spotting. Rebound in speckled calf, vellum tips, uncut. *(Frew Mackenzie)* **£400 [≃ $712]**

Danett, Thomas
- A Continuation of the Historie of France, from the Death of Charles the Eight where Comines endeth ... London: Thomas East for Thomas Charde, 1600. 1st edn. Sm 4to. [viii], 148 pp. Errata. W'cut title border. V sl marg worm. Contemp sheep gilt. STC 6234. Kimbolton copy. *(Vanbrugh)* **£275 [≃ $490]**

Daniel, Gabriel
- A Voyage to the World of Cartesius. Written originally in French, and now translated into English. London: Thomas Bennet, 1692. 1st edn in English. 8vo. [xvi], 298,[6] pp. Text diags. Contemp calf, jnts reprd. Wing D.201. Anon.   *(Gaskell)* **£480 [≃ $854]**

Daniel, Samuel
- The Collection of the History of England; by S.D. [N. Oakes]. London: for Simon Waterson, 1626. Folio. [8],222 pp. Contemp calf. STC 6251.   *(Karmiole)* **$500 [≃ £281]**

Danois, The Countess of
- The Lady's Travels into Spain ... see Aulnoy, Marie Catherine, Comtesse d'

Darby, Charles
- Bacchanalia: or a Description of a Drunken Club. A Poem. London: Robert Boulter, 1680. 1st edn. Folio. [ii],14 pp. Sl used at ends. Rec qtr calf. Wing D.243. Anon.
                    (Clark) **£200 [≃ $356]**

D'Arnay, M.
- The Private Life of the Romans. Edinburgh: Donaldson & Reid, 1764. 2nd edn. 8vo. v,306 pp. Contemp calf, sl rubbed.
                    (Young's) **£40 [≃ $71]**

Darrell, John
- A Detection of that Sinnful, Shamful, Lying and Ridiculous Discours, of Samuel Harshnet, entituled: A Discoverie of the Fraudulent Practises of John Darrell ... N.p. [London?]: 1600. 1st edn. 4to. 208,[3] pp. Later calf, rebacked.
                    (Robertshaw) **£275 [≃ $490]**

Dart, John
- Westmonasterium or the History and Antiquities of the Abbey Church of St. Peters Westminster. London: James Cole ..., [1723]. 1st edn. 2 vols. 135 plates. Occas sl foxing. Sm reprs to titles. Contemp leather bds, rebacked.   *(Hermitage)* **$1,200 [≃ £674]**

Darwin, Erasmus
- A Plan for the Conduct of Female Education, in Boarding Schools. Derby: by J. Drewry, for J. Johnson, London, 1797. 1st edn. 4to. Frontis (margs foxed, offset on title). Lacks half-title. Last 2 ff reprd & mtd. Early half calf, Signet Library arms, worn.
                    (Hannas) **£650 [≃ $1,157]**

D'Assigny, Marius
- The Art of Memory. Second Edition. London: Andr. Bell, 1699. Lge 12mo. 16,80 pp. Frontis. Old MS notes. Contemp calf, rebacked, Signet Library stamp on bds. Wing D.281.   *(Spelman)* **£360 [≃ $641]**

Daubeny, Charles
- The Fall of Papal Rome: Recommended to the Consideration of England: In a Discourse

on Isaiah xlvi.9, 10 ... London: Cadell, 1798.
1st edn. 8vo. 45 pp. Half-title. Disbound.
(Young's) **£28 [≈ $50]**

Davenant, Charles

- Essays ... London: Knapton, 1701. 1st edn.
8vo. [iv],101,[i], 127-237,[iii], 233-288, [iv],
1-125,[3] pp. Half-title, blank leaf after 3rd
essay, final advt leaf. Sl marg damp stain at
ends. Rec half calf. Anon.
(Clark) **£450 [≈ $801]**

Davenant, Sir William

- The Works ... London: T.N. for Henry
Herringman, 1673. 1st coll edn. One vol
bound in 2. Folio. [viii],402, [iv],486, 111,[i]
pp. Lacks port frontis. Later half calf, worn.
Wing D.320.   *(Clark)* **£65 [≈ $116]**
- The Works ... London: T.N. for Henry
herringman, 1673. 1st coll edn. Folio. [viii],
402, [iv],486,111 pp. Port frontis. Contemp
calf, rebacked, new endpapers, used but
sound. Wing D.320.
(Sotheran's) **£425 [≈ $757]**

Davies, John

- The Civil Warres of Great Britain and
Ireland, Containing an Exact History of their
Occasion, Originall, Progress and Happy
End. By an Impartial Pen. London: Phillip
Chetwind, 1661. 1st edn. 4to. 384 pp. Rear
blank fly ff excised. Orig calf. Anon.
(Chapel Hill) **£600 [≈ $337]**

Davies, Sir John

- A Discoverie of the True Causes why Ireland
was never entirely Subdued, nor brought
under Obedience of the Crowne of England,
untill the Beginning of His Majesties happie
Raigne. London: Millar, 1747. 12mo. 283 pp.
Rec buckram.   *(de Burca)* **£90 [≈ $160]**

Davies, Thomas

- The Laws relating to Bankrupts ... In the
Savoy: Henry Lintot ..., 1744. 1st edn. Folio.
xii,470, [xxviii],515-522, [ii], 515-550.
Contemp calf, rebacked.
(Vanbrugh) **£255 [≈ $454]**
- Memoirs of the Life of David Garrick, Esq. ...
London: for the author, 1780. 1st edn. 2 vols.
8vo. Port. Sl foxing at start of each vol. Early
half calf, v worn.   *(Hannas)* **£85 [≈ $151]**
- Memoirs of the Life of David Garrick ...
Dublin: Joseph Hill, 1780. 1st Dublin edn. 2
vols. 8vo. [xvi],270; [xii],311 pp. Inserts
present as called for. Port frontis. Sm tear on
1st blank. Contemp calf, jnts sl worn, lacks
labels.   *(Blackwell's)* **£145 [≈ $258]**
- Memoirs of the Life of David Garrick ...

Fourth Edition, to which is added an accurate
Index. London: for the author, 1784. 2 vols.
8vo. Half-title vol 2. Port (sl foxed). Contemp
calf, gilt spines (1 relaid). Cator b'plates.
(Hannas) **£240 [≈ $427]**
- Memoirs of the Life of David Garrick ...
London: for the author, 1784. 4th edn. 2 vols.
8vo. [xvi],368; [xiv],471 pp. Occas spotting.
Calf, rebacked, 1 bd replaced.
(Young's) **£50 [≈ $89]**

Davila, Henrico Caterino

- The Historie oe [sic] the Civill Warres of
France ... Translated out of the Original.
London: R. Raworth, to be sold by W. Lee ...,
1647. 1st English edn. Lge folio. [iv],1478 pp.
Privilege leaf sl worn. Contemp calf, front
hinge cracked. Wing D.413.
(Vanbrugh) **£425 [≈ $757]**

Davys, John

- An Essay on the Art of Decyphering. In
which is inserted a Discourse of Dr. Wallis.
Now first published from his Original
Manuscript. London: for Gilliver & Clarke,
1737. 1st edn. 4to. [ii],iii,[i],58 pp. Half-title.
Disbound.   *(Burmester)* **£380 [≈ $676]**

Deane, William

- The Description of the Copernican System ...
London: 1738. Imprint without advt beneath.
8vo. vi,106 pp. Fldg frontis (sl water stained),
7 fldg plates. New qtr calf.
(Weiner) **£350 [≈ $623]**

Debes, Lucas Jacobson

- Faeroae, & Faeroa Reserata: That is a
Description of the Islands & Inhabitants of
Foeroe: being Seventeen Islands subject to the
King of Denmark ... London: for William
Isles, 1676. 1st English edn. 12mo. 2 fldg
maps. Mod calf gilt by Bayntun. Wing D.511.
(Hannas) **£900 [≈ $1,602]**

De Blancourt, Francois Haudicquer

- The Art of Glass. Shewing, how to make all
Sorts of Glass, Crystal and Enamel ... Now
first Translated into English. With an
Appendix ... London: for Dan. Brown, 1699.
8vo. [14],355,[13] pp. Half-title. 9 plates.
Occas sl browning. Rec half calf. Wing
H.1150.   *(Spelman)* **£850 [≈ $1,513]**
- See also Haudicquer de Blancourt, Francois
or Jean

De Chassepol, Francois

- A Treatise of the Revenue and False Money
of the Romans ... annexed, A Dissertation
upon the manner of distinguishing Antique

Medals from Counterfeit Ones. London: Knapton, 1741. 1st edn in English. 8vo. [viii], xxxii, 227,[i] pp. Sl soiling. Lib buckram. Anon.   *(Clark)* **£45 [≈ $80]**

Declaration ...

- A Declaration and Protestation of the Lords and Commons in Parliament ... October 22, 1642. London: Blackmore, 1642. 4to. W'cut title border. Wraps. Wing E.1309.
  (Rostenberg & Stern) **$85 [≈ £48]**

- A Declaration of the General Council of the Officers of the Army: Agreed upon at Wallingford-house, 27th Octob. 1659 ... London: Henry Hills, 1659. Only edn. 4to. 19 pp. Sm hole affecting occas letter. Half mor.   *(Young's)* **£68 [≈ $121]**

- A Declaration of the just causes of his Maiesties proceeding against those Ministers, who are now lying in Prison attainted of High Treason ... London: 1606. 4to. 45 pp. Mod bds. STC 21961. Sometime attributed to Thomas Hamilton, Earl of Haddington.
  (Robertshaw) **£95 [≈ $169]**

- A Declaration of the Lords and Commons in Parliament, in Answer to the Kings declaration concerning Hull ... 25 Maii 1642 ... London: for Ioseph Hunscot ..., May 26, 1642. 1st edn. Sm 4to. 8,[9]-20 pp. Sl cropped. Mod wraps. Wing E.1443.
  (Blackwell's) **£45 [≈ $80]**

- A Declaration of the Lords and Commons ... Concerning the Papers of The Scots Commissioners, Entituled, The Answer of the Commissioner of the Kingdom of Scotland ... upon the New Propositions of Peace. London: Husband, 1647 [8]. 4to. Stitched. Wing E.1392.
  (Rostenberg & Stern) **$140 [≈ £79]**

- A Declaration of the Variance betweene the Pope, and the Seignory of Venice. N.p.: 1606. 4to. Right marg of title trimmed. Stitched. STC 19482.
  (Rostenberg & Stern) **$200 [≈ £112]**

Decree ...

- A Decree of Starre-Chamber. Concerning Inmates, and Divided Tenements, in London or Three Miles About: Made the Fourteenth of February Last Past, 1636. London: Barker, 1636. Sm 4to. [6],39 pp. Half-title. Colophon. Some stains. Disbound. STC 7756.
  (O'Neal) **$200 [≈ £112]**

Defence ...

- A Defence of the Dissertation on the Validity of the English Ordination ... see Le Courayer, P.F.

Defoe, Daniel

- An Argument Proving that the Design of Employing and Enobling Foreigners, is a Treasonable Conspiracy against the Constitution ... London: for the booksellers, 1717. 1st edn. 8vo. 102 pp. Title reprd. Disbound. Anon.   *(Young's)* **£250 [≈ $445]**

- Conjugal Lewdness; or Matrimonial Whoredom. London: for T. Warner, 1727. 1st edn, 1st issue. vi,[2],406 pp. Red & black title. 1 repr without loss of text. Contemp calf, spine & jnts sl rubbed, lacks label. Anon.   *(C.R. Johnson)* **£1,150 [≈ $2,047]**

- Conjugal Lewdness; or Matrimonial Whoredom. London: for T. Warner, 1728. 1st edn. 1st issue, un-retitled. 8vo. vi,[ii],406 pp. Red & black title with sm marg repr. Contemp panelled calf, sl rubbed, lacks label. Anon.   *(Burmester)* **£1,150 [≈ $2,047]**

- An Elegy on the Author of the True-Born-English-Man. With an Essay on the Late Storm ... London: Printed [by H. Hills] in the Year 1708. 8vo. Later half calf. Anon.
  (Hannas) **£45 [≈ $80]**

- A General History of the Robberies and Murders of the most Notorious Pyrates ... by Captain Charles Johnson. London: Rivington, Lacy, Stone, 1724. 1st edn. 8vo. 3 plates (1 fldg). Sl browned at end. Contemp panelled calf. A 2nd vol was published in 1728.   *(Hannas)* **£550 [≈ $979]**

- The History and Remarkable Life of the truely honourable Colonel Jaque, vulgarly call'd, Colonel Jack ... The Third Edition. London: J. Brotherton, 1724. [viii],399 pp. Red & black title. Rebound. Anon.
  (C.R. Johnson) **£450 [≈ $801]**

- The History of Madamoiselle de Veleau; or, the New Roxana, the Fortunate Mistress ... Published by Mr. Daniel De Foe ... London: for the editor, & Noble, Lowndes, 1775. 1st edn thus. 12mo. [ii],288 pp, inc advt pp. Frontis. Half calf gilt, a.e.g., by Riviere, jnts rprd.   *(Burmester)* **£225 [≈ $401]**

- The History of the Union between England and Scotland ... With an Appendix ... Life of the Celebrated Author ... London: Stockdale, 1786. 4to. Frontis. Few sm lib stamps. Binder's cloth. *(Waterfield's)* **£125 [≈ $223]**

- An Impartial History of the Life and Actions of Peter Alexowitz, the present Czar of Muscov ... Written by a British Officer in the Service of the Czar. London: Chetwood ..., 1723. 1st edn. 8vo. [ii],1-207, 202-420, [ii advt] pp. Contemp calf, sl worn. Anon.
  (Clark) **£260 [≈ $463]**

- Jure Divino. A Satyr. In Twelve Books. By the Author of The True-Born-Englishman.

London: Printed in the Year, 1706. 1st edn. Folio. Port. Foxed. Contemp mottled calf, rebacked. Anon. *(Hannas)* £220 [≈ $392]

- Legion's New Paper: Being a Second Memorial to the Gentlemen of a late House of Commons. With Legion's Humble Address to His Majesty. London Printed. Re-printed by John Reid, 1702. 4to. 20 pp. Rec half calf, elab gilt spine, by Riviere. Anon. *(C.R. Johnson)* £380 [≈ $676]

- A Letter from a Member of the House of Commons to his Friend in the Country, relating to the Bill of Commerce ... London: J. Baker, 1713. 1st edn. Issue with comma after 'printed' on title. 8vo. [ii],46 pp. BM duplicate. Later bds. Anon.
  (Clark) £100 [≈ $178]

- Memoirs of a Cavalier ... London: for A. Bell ..., [1720]. 1st edn. 8vo. [viii],338 pp. Sl foxing. Mod qtr calf, mor label. Anon.
  (D & D Galleries) £180 [≈ £101]

- Memoirs of a Cavalier ... London: for A. Bell ..., [1720]. 1st edn. 8vo. [viii],338 pp. Lacks final blank. Title soiled & old repr at hd. Few sm closed tears reprd, some damp staining & thumbing. 19th c half calf, rubbed. Anon.
  (Sotheran's) £350 [≈ $623]

- Memoirs of a Cavalier ... London: Bell, Osborn, Taylor, Warner, [1720]. 1st edn. 8vo. Contemp panelled calf, rebacked by Riviere. Anon. *(Hannas)* £220 [≈ $392]

- The Memoirs of Capt. George Carleton, an English Officer, who served in the last two wars against France and Spain. London: for Tho. Astley, 1743. 8vo. Sl soiled. Early 20th c red half calf. Anon.
  (Waterfield's) £100 [≈ $178]

- Minutes of the Negotiations of Monsr. Mesnager at the Court of England ... Written by Himself. Done out of French. London: for S. Baker, 1717. 1st edn. 8vo. D2 a cancel with catch-word 'done'. Browned. Contemp calf, crnrs sl worn, jnts starting to split. Anon.
  (Hannas) £200 [≈ $356]

- Minutes of the Negotiations of Monsr. Mesnager at the Court of England ... Written by Himself ... The Second Edition. London: for J. Roberts, 1736. 8vo. Contemp calf, rebacked. Anon. *(Waterfield's)* £90 [≈ $160]

- More Short Ways with Dissenters. London: Printed in the Year, 1704. 1st edn. Half-title,[4],24 pp. Rebound in half calf, elab gilt spine, by Riviere. Anon.
  (C.R. Johnson) £280 [≈ $498]

- The Life and Most Surprising Adventures of Robinson Crusoe ... Second Edition. Revised by M. D***. Paris: J.G.A. Stoupe, sold by Barrois, 1783. 12mo. Half-title (sl soiled).

Possibly lacks final errata leaf. Contemp half calf, worn. Anon. *(Hannas)* £55 [≈ $98]

- The Scotch Medal Decipher'd, and the New Hereditary Right Men Display'd ... London: for S. Popping, 1711. 1st edn. 12mo. 24 pp. Rec bds. Anon. *(Burmester)* £450 [≈ $801]

- The Secret History of the White-Staff ... London: for J. Baker, 1714. 1st edn. 2 parts. 8vo. 71,72 pp. Titles & edges dust soiled. Amateur bds, uncut. Anon. A 3rd part was published the next year.
  (Hannas) £90 [≈ $160]

- The Secrets of the Invisible World Disclos'd or, an Universal History of Apparitions ... By Andrew Moreton ... London: for J. Clarke ..., 1738. 3rd edn. 8vo. xii, 395 pp. Title a cancel. Frontis, 5 plates. Half calf, sl worn.
  (Hartfield) $395 [≈ £222]

- The Storm: or a Collection of the most Remarkable Casualties and Disasters which happen'd in the Late Dreadful Tempest, both by Sea and Land. London: for G. Sawbridge, sold by J. Nutt, 1704. 1st edn. 8vo. Fldg plate. Occas sl water stain. Contemp calf, worn. Anon *(Hannas)* £180 [≈ $320]

- A Tour thro' the Whole Island of Great Britain ... giving a Particular and Diverting Account of Whatever is Curious and worth Observation ... London: G. Strahan, 1724. 8vo. viii,127,[i] pp. Occas spotting & sl creasing. Mod calf gilt. Anon.
  (Hollett) £150 [≈ $267]

- The Trade with France, Italy, Spain, and Portugal considered: with some Observations on the Treaty of Commerce between Great Britain and France. Fourth Edition. London: 1713. 8vo. 23 pp. Disbound. Anon.
  (Robertshaw) £65 [≈ $116]

- A True Collection of the Writings of the Author of the True Born English-Man. Corrected by himself. London: sold by most Booksellers in London & Westminster, 1703. 1st authorized edn. 8vo. Port. Contemp calf, rebacked. Anon. *(Hannas)* £180 [≈ $320]

- The True-Born English-Man. A Satyr. London: Printed [by H. Hills] in the Year, 1708. 8vo. 37 pp. Disbound. Anon.
  (Hannas) £40 [≈ $71]

- The Villainy of Stock-Jobbers Detected, and the Causes of the Late Run upon the Bank and Bankers discovered and considered. London: 1701. 1st edn. Sm 4to. [ii],26 pp. Sm marg tear. Disbound. Anon.
  (Burmester) £1,500 [≈ $2,670]

- See also The Universal Spectator.

Defoe, Daniel, attributed author
- An Essay upon Loans ... London: 1710. 1st

edn. 8vo. 27 pp. Disbound. Anon.
(Robertshaw) **£45 [≃ $80]**

Delamayne, Thomas Hallie
- The Senators: Or, A Candid Examination into the Merits of the Principal Performers of St. Stephen's Chapel. London: for G. Kearsly, 1772. 1st edn. 4to. Title vignette. Lacks half-title. Title & last leaf sl dusty. New bds. Anon.   *(Young's)* **£50 [≃ $89]**

De Lolme, Jean Louis
- The Constitution of England ... Fourth Edition, Corrected by the Author. Dublin: for W. Wilson, 1776. 8vo. ix,257,[1 advt] pp, inc half-title. V sm marg worm 1st 8 ff. Rec bds.
(Fenning) **£65 [≃ $116]**
- The Constitution of England ... A New Edition, Corrected. London: Robinson & Murray, 1793. 8vo. [viii],xvi,522,[xviii] pp. Period calf, gilt spine, sl scuffed.
(Rankin) **£85 [≃ $151]**

d'Emillianne, Gabriel (pseudonym)
- See Gavin, Antonio

De Moivre, Abraham
- Annuities upon Lives. London: by W.P. & sold by Francis Fayram, 1725. 1st edn. Post 8vo. [ii],4,viii, 108,[ii] pp. Errata slip. Lacks intl blank. Sl marg stains. Contemp calf, rebacked.   *(Ash)* **£1,250 [≃ $2,225]**

Denham, Sir John
- Poems and Translations, with the Sophy. London: for H. Herringman, 1668. 1st coll edn. 8vo. Errata leaf. 'Table' leaf. Some browning. A few head-lines cut into. 19th c half mor. Wing D.1005.
(Hannas) **£210 [≃ $374]**

Dennis, John
- Julius Caesar Acquitted, and his Murderers Condemn'd. In a Letter to a Friend ... added, A Second Letter ... London: for J. Mackuen, 1722. Only edn. 8vo. viii,39 pp. Title sl browned. Disbound. *(Young's)* **£240 [≃ $427]**
- Julius Caesar Acquitted, and his Murderers Condemn'd. In a Letter to a Friend ... added, a Second Letter ... London: for J. Mack-Euen; sold by J. Roberts, 1722. 1st edn. 8vo. [viii],39 pp. Disbound.
(Burmester) **£175 [≃ $312]**
- The Select Works ... London: John Darby, 1718. 1st coll edn. 2 vols. Fine Paper copy, with Strasbourg bend water-mark. 8vo. Errata leaf. 19th c calf antique, red edges.
(Hannas) **£450 [≃ $801]**

- The Usefulness of the Stage, to the Happiness of Mankind ... London: for Rich. Parker, 1698. 1st edn. 8vo. Errata on final page. Some foxing at ends. Lib cloth. Wing D.1045.   *(Hannas)* **£250 [≃ $445]**

Derham, William
- The Artificial Clock-Maker. A Treatise of Watch, and Clock-Work ... By W.D. London: for James Knapton, 1696. 1st edn. 8vo. [xii],132 pp. Fldg table, few text ills. 1 marg tear. Contemp speckled calf, later label. Wing D.1099. *(Vanbrugh)* **£2,955 [≃ $5,260]**
- The Artificial Clock-Maker; A Treatise of Watch and Clock-Work ... Third Edition. London: for James Knapton, 1714. Sm 8vo. [xvi], 140 pp. W'engvd fldg plate, 4 fldg tables, sev w'cut text ills. Outer margs 3 ff sl frayed. Contemp tree calf, rebacked. Anon.
(Gough) **£350 [≃ $623]**

D'Ermenonville, Rene Louis Gerardin, Viscount
- An Essay on Landscape: or, the means of improving and embellishing the Country round our Habitations. London: Dodsley, 1783. 1st edn in English. 8vo. [ii],lv, [i],160 pp. Lacks errata slip & plate. Lib stamps on title. Contemp calf, rebacked.
(Clark) **£40 [≃ $71]**

De Sade, Jacques Francois Paul Alonce
- The Life of Petrarch. Collected from Memoires pour la Vie de Petrarch. London: James Buckland, 1775. 1st edn. 2 vols. 8vo. [iii]-xxii,544; [ii],560 pp. Pasted-on errata slip vol 1. Frontis vol 1. Contemp calf, extrs sl worn. Anon. Translated by Susannah Dobson.   *(Clark)* **£120 [≃ $214]**

Desaguliers, John T.
- A Course of Experimental Philosophy. The Third Edition Corrected. London: A. Millar ..., 1763. 2 vols. 4to. 46 fldg plates. Contemp calf, gilt spines, red & green mor labels, v sl reprs. John Cator copy.
(Frew Mackenzie) **£480 [≃ $854]**

Description ...
- A Description of Holland: or, the Present State of the United Provinces ... London: Knapton, 1743. 1st edn. 8vo. xxiv,411,[1] pp. Last line of imprint partly cropped. Contemp calf, spine sl worn, upper jnt cracked but firm.   *(Burmester)* **£90 [≃ $160]**
- A Description of Millenium Hall ... see Montagu, Lady Barbara & Scott, Sarah
- A Description of South Carolina ... see Glen, James

- A Description of the Four Last Things ... see Bond, William

Des Fontaines, Pierre Francois Guyot de
- The History of the Revolutions of Poland, from the Foundation of that Monarchy, to the Death of Augustus II. Translated from the Original French. London: Woodward & Davis, 1736. 1st edn in English. 8vo. [iv],428 pp. Contemp sheep, extrs sl worn, sm splits in jnts. *(Clark)* £125 [≈ $223]

Desjardins, Marie Catherine Hortense
- The Exiles of the Court of Augustus Caesar ... Translated from the French of Mademoiselle Villedieu. London: for D. brown, 1726. 1st English edn. 8vo. [ii],235 pp. Prelims sl fingered. Period calf, sl worn. *(Rankin)* £85 [≈ $151]

Desmaizeaux, Pierre
- An Historical and Critical Account of the Life and Writings of W. Chillingworth, Chancellor of the Church of Sarum. London: Woodward & Peele, 1725. 1st edn. 8vo. [xii], 372, [x-viii sic],[ii] pp. Contemp calf, 'Cambridge' panelled, jnts cracked but firm, extrs sl rubbed. Anon. *(Blackwell's)* £65 [≈ $116]

The Detector Detected ...
- The Detector Detected: or, the Danger to which our Constitution now lies exposed, set in a True and Manifest Light. London: for M. Cooper, 1743. 1st edn. 8vo. 62 pp. Disbound. *(Hannas)* £75 [≈ $134]

Dewell, T.
- The Philosophy of Physic, founded on one General and Immutable Law of Nature ... Marlborough: ptd by E. Harold ..., 1785. 2nd edn, "revised & corrected". Sm 8vo. vii, [iii], xliii,[i],84 pp. Half-title. Sl damp staining. Contemp calf, jnt cracked, lacks label. *(Burmester)* £125 [≈ $223]

The Diaboliad ...
- See Combe, William

Dialogue(s) ...
- A Dialogue at Oxford between a Tutor and a Gentleman, Formerly his Pupil, Concerning Government. London: for Richard Janaway, 1681. 1st edn. 4to. [ii],21,[i] pp. Sl marg browning. Some offsetting on title. Disbound. Wing D.1290. *(Finch)* £90 [≈ $160]
- A Dialogue between Two Oxford Schollars. [Colophon] London: for H.H. & T.J.,

[1690?]. 1st edn. 4to. [2],10 pp. Disbound. Wing D.1343. *(Hannas)* £40 [≈ $71]
- Dialogues on ... Children ... see Forrester, James.
- A Dialogue which lately pass'd between the Knight and his Man John. London: ptd by W. Lloyd, n.d. [ie Edinburgh: 1739]. 16 pp. Disbound. *(C.R. Johnson)* £135 [≈ $240]

Dibdin, Charles, the elder
- Rose and Colin, a Comic Opera ... London: For G. Kearsly, 1778. 1st edn. 8vo. 28 pp, inc half-title. Rec wraps. *(Fenning)* £38.50 [≈ $69]
- The Wives Revenged; a Comic Opera ... London: for G. Kearsly, 1778. 1st edn. 8vo. 36 pp, inc half-title. Rec wraps. *(Fenning)* £38.50 [≈ $69]

Dickinson, John
- Letters from a Farmer in Pennsylvania, to the Inhabitants of the British Colonies. London: for J. Almon, 1768. 1st British edn. [4], 118 pp. Edges of ff sl stained. Self-wraps. Anon. *(Reese)* $350 [≈ £197]
- Letters from a Farmer in Pennsylvania, to the Inhabitants of the British Colonies. Philadelphia, Printed. London: reprinted, 1774. 136 pp. Half-title. Foxing. Mod cloth, leather label. Anon. *(Reese)* $400 [≈ £225]
- A New Essay [by The Pennsylvania Farmer] on the Constitutional Power of Great-Britain over the Colonies in America ... London: J. Almon, 1774. vii,126,[2] pp. Half-title. Occas fox marks. Mod cloth, leather label. Anon. *(Reese)* $500 [≈ £281]

Dickinson, Jonathan
- Familiar Letters to a Gentleman upon a Variety of Seasonable and Important Subjects in Religion ... Dundee: printed in the Year 1722. 8vo. [vi],314 pp. Contemp calf, jnts reprd. *(Young's)* £95 [≈ $169]

Dickson, A.
- A Treatise of Agriculture. A New Edition. London: 1770. 2 vols. 8vo. [vii],lxv,487; [vii], 564 pp. 2 fldg plates. Contemp calf, jnts & crnrs worn. *(Henly)* £125 [≈ $223]

Dickson, Sarah
- Poems on Several Occasions. Canterbury: J. Abree, 1790. 8vo in 4s. xxvi subscribers, [vi], 203 pp. Title browned. Mod half calf gilt. Anon. *(Hollett)* £160 [≈ $285]

Dictionary ...
- A Dictionary of the English Language ...

Second Edition, with Additions and Improvements. London: W. Peacock, 1788. 16mo in 4s. Some browning of page edges. Contemp sheep, extrs sl worn, jnts cracked but firm, lacks label.   *(Clark)* **£55 [≈ $98]**

Digby, Sir Kenelm

- Of Bodies, and of Mans Soul ... With Two Discourses. Of the Powder of Sympathy, and of the Vegetation of Plants. London: for John Williams, 1669. 4to in 8s. [56],439,[1], [10], 231,[1] pp. W'cut diags. Sl marks. Contemp calf, rebacked, some rubbing, endpaper renewed.   *(Goodrich)* **$600 [≈ £337]**
- Two Treatises: in the one of which, The Nature of Bodies; In the other The Nature of Mans Soul, Is Looked Into. London: Williams, 1658. 4to. Text diags. Panelled calf. Wing D.1450.
    (Rostenberg & Stern) **$675 [≈ £379]**

Digges, Dudley

- An Answer to a Printed Book, Intituled Observations vpon some of His Majesties Late Answers and Expresses. Oxford: Leonard Litchfield, 1642. 1st edn. 4to. 53 pp. Bds. Wing D.1455. Anon.
    (Young's) **£85 [≈ $151]**

Dilworth, W.H.

- The Adventures of Gil Blas de Santilane. Published for the Improvement, and Entertainment of the British Youth of Both Sexes. Glasgow: for the booksellers, 1785. 97 pp. Contemp calf.
    (C.R. Johnson) **£125 [≈ $223]**
- The History of Italy. London: for G. Wright, 1760. 1st edn. Cr 12mo. [iv],236 pp. Half-title. Sl spotted & thumbed. Contemp sheep backed bds, sl worn.
    (Ash) **£200 [≈ $356]**
- The Life and Heroic Actions of Frederick III King of Prussia ... Published for the Entertainment ... Youth of Both Sexes. London: for G. Wright, 1758. 168 pp. Port frontis. Contemp sheep, 2 sm splits hd of spine.   *(C.R. Johnson)* **£95 [≈ $169]**

Direction ...

- A Direction or Preparative to the Study of the Law ... see Fulbecke, William

Dirom, Alexander

- A Narrative of the Campaign in India which terminated with the War with Tippoo Sultan in 1792. London: 1793. 296 pp. 9 maps, plates, plans. Orig bds, crnrs sl bumped, new gilt spine.
    (Trophy Room Books) **$450 [≈ £253]**

- Plans for the Defence of Great Britain and Ireland. Edinburgh: 1797. 8vo. Qtr calf.
    (de Burca) **£135 [≈ $240]**

Discourse ...

- A Discourse Concerning a Guide in Matters of Faith ... see Tenison, Thomas
- A Discourse concerning Puritans ... see Ley, John
- A Discourse of the Sacrifice of the Mass ... see Payne, William

Discussion ...

- A Discussion of Lord Camden's Opinion and Decrees in Allen and the Duke of Newcastle. London: J. Wilkie, 1774. 4to. [4],46,[2] pp. Orig wraps, sl worn.
    (Meyer Boswell) **$350 [≈ £197]**

A Dispassionate Remonstrance ...

- A Dispassionate Remonstrance of the Nature and Tendency of the Law now in Force for the Reduction of Interest ... London: for J. Robinson, 1751. 1st edn. 8vo. [4],70 pp, inc half-title. Disbound.   *(Hannas)* **£50 [≈ $89]**

The Dispensary. A Poem ...

- See Garth, Samuel

D'Israeli, Isaac

- Curiosities of Literature ... London: for John Murray, 1791. 1st edn. 8vo. Orig bds, paper label sl rubbed, jnts sl worn. Anon.
    (Ximenes) **$750 [≈ £421]**
- Curiosities of Literature ... London: for J. Murray, 1793. 3rd edn, enlgd, of vol 1, 2nd edn of vol 2. 2 vols. 8vo. Fldg plate. Contemp calf, gilt spines, contrasting labels, minor rubbing. Anon.   *(Ximenes)* **$250 [≈ £140]**
- Curiosities of Literature ... London: for Murray & Highley, 1797. 4th edn, crrctd. 2 vols. 8vo. Fldg plate. Contemp mottled calf gilt, contrasting labels, upper jnts sl cracked. Anon.   *(Ximenes)* **$175 [≈ £98]**
- A Dissertation on Anecdotes. London: for C. & G. Kearsley, & J. Murray, 1793. 1st edn. 8vo. Contemp mottled calf gilt, fine. Anon.
    (Ximenes) **$600 [≈ £337]**
- Domestic Anecdotes of the French Nation, during the last Thirty Years ... London: Kearsley, 1794. 1st edn. 8vo. Contemp tree calf, gilt spine, jnts reprd. Anon.
    (Ximenes) **$400 [≈ £225]**
- An Essay on the Manners and Genius of the Literary Character. London: Cadell & Davies, 1795. 1st edn. 8vo. Advt leaf at end. 16 pp Cadell & Davies ctlg. Half calf, gilt spine, uncut. Anon.   *(Ximenes)* **$325 [≈ £183]**

- Miscellanies; or, Literary Recreations. London: for Cadell & Davies, 1796. 1st edn. 8vo. Errata leaf at end. 19th c half calf, gilt spine sl rubbed. *(Ximenes)* **$350 [≈ £197]**
- Romances. London: for Cadell & Davies ..., 1799. 1st edn. 8vo. Frontis. Lacks final advt leaf. Early 19th c straight grained mor gilt, gilt spine, a.e.g., spine trifle rubbed.
  (Ximenes) **£400 [≈ £225]**
- Vaurien: or, Sketches of the Times ... London: for Cadell & Davies ..., 1797. 1st edn. 2 vols. 12mo. Early 19th c tree calf gilt, contrasting labels, spines sl rubbed. Anon.
  (Ximenes) **$1,250 [≈ £702]**

Dodd, James Solas
- An Essay towards a Natural History of the Herring. London: for T. Vincent, 1752. 1st edn. 8vo. [8],178 pp, 12 contents ff, inc half-title. Final Proposal page. Lacks fldg plate. Disbound. *(Hannas)* **£70 [≈ $125]**

Dodd, William
- The Beauties of Shakespear ... With a General Index ... Notes ... Second Edition, with Additions. London: for T. Walker, 1757. 2 vols. 12mo. xxiv,268,[viii]; [iv],276,[8] pp. Contemp calf gilt, 1 jnt cracking at ft, sides rubbed.
  (Finch) **£75 [≈ $134]**
- The Rules and Regulations of the Magdalen Charity with Instructions to the Women who are admitted and Prayers for their use. The Fourth Edition. London: W. Faden, 1769. 8vo. frontis. Contemp sheep, red label.
  (Waterfield's) **£125 [≈ $223]**
- The Sisters; or, the History of Lucy and Caroline Sanson, entrusted to a False Friend. A Narrative ... New Edition. London: T. Wilkins, for T. Jones, 1791. 3 vols. 12mo. Half-titles. Contemp tree calf, spines sl worn.
  (Burmester) **£250 [≈ $445]**
- The Sisters; or, the History of Lucy and Caroline Sanson, entrusted to a False Friend. In Two Volumes. London: Harrison, 1791. 2 vols in one. Sm 4to. vi,169 pp. Double columns. 4 engvs by Stothard. Rec three qtr mor. *(Hartfield)* **$225 [≈ £126]**
- Thoughts in Prison ... added, his Last Prayer ... and other Miscellaneous Pieces. Dublin: Price, Sleater ..., 1778. 1st Dublin edn. 12mo. 251 pp. Contemp sheep, upper cvr wormed with loss of some leather, used but sound.
  (Sotheran's) **£300 [≈ $534]**
- Thoughts in Prison: in Five Parts ... London: Dilly, Kearsly, 1777. 1st edn. 8vo. [ii],iv,206, [ii],207-232,[2 advt] pp. Some spotting & browning. Contemp sprinkled calf, backstrip relaid, extrs rubbed. *(Finch)* **£275 [≈ $490]**

Doddridge, Sir John
- A History of the Ancient and Modern Estate of the Principality of Wales, Dutchy of Cornewall, and Earldome of Chester. London: Tho. Harper, for Edmondson & Alchorne, 1630. 1st edn. 4to. Lacks final blank. Title browned. Mod half mor. STC 6982. *(Hannas)* **£210 [≈ $374]**
- Honors Pedigree. or The Several Fountains of Gentry ... London: for William Sheares, 1652. 1st edn under this title (previously The Magazine of Honour). Sm 8vo. [vi],1-114, 139-170, 105-158 pp. Printer's device frontis. Rec half calf. Wing D.1793.
  (Vanbrugh) **£225 [≈ $401]**
- Honors Pedigree ... see also Bird, William.

Doddridge, Philip
- Christian Candour and Unanimity stated, illustrated and urged: a Sermon ... January 12, 1749-50. London: J. Waugh, 1750. 8vo. Disbound. *(Waterfield's)* **£40 [≈ $71]**
- A Course of Lectures on the Principal Subjects in Pneumatology, Ethics and Divinity ... Second Edition, Corrected. London: for J. Buckland ..., 1776. 4to. Contemp calf, rubbed but sound.
  (Waterfield's) **£120 [≈ $214]**
- The Rise and Progress of Religion in the Soul ... The Tenth Edition. Boston: Daniel Kneeland, 1772. Rebound in calf, gilt label.
  (D & D Galleries) **$125 [≈ £70]**
- Some Remarkable Passages in the Life of ... Col. James Gardiner, who was slain at the Battle of Preston-Pans ... London: Buckland & Waugh, 1747. 1st edn. 8vo in 4s. [xvi],260 pp. Errata leaf. Port frontis. Contemp calf, scuffed, extrs sl worn, jnts cracked.
  (Clark) **£65 [≈ $116]**
- Some Remarkable Passages in the Life of the Honourable Col. James Gardiner, who was slain at the Battle of Preston-Pans ... With an Appendix ... Wigan: W. Bancks, 1782. 8vo. [x], 263 pp. Half-title. Port. Rec half calf.
  (Young's) **£60 [≈ $107]**

Doderidge, John
- A Compleat Parson or, A Description of Advowsons, or Church-Living. Wherein is set forth, the interests of the Parson, Patron, and Ordinarie ... London: for John Grove ..., 1630. 1st edn. Sl dusty. Lacks A1 blank but for sgntr. Mod cloth backed bds. STC 6980.
  (Meyer Boswell) **$350 [≈ £197]**

Dodington, George Bubb
- The Diary of the late George Bubb Dodington ... With an Appendix ... A New Edition by Henry Penruddocke Wyndham.

Salisbury: E. Easton, 1784. 1st edn (despite wording of title). 8vo. xv,506,[1 advt] pp. Rebound in qtr leather.
(Bates & Hindmarch) **£65 [≈ $116]**

- The Diary of the late George Bubb Dodington ... With an Appendix ... by Henry Penruddocke Wyndham. Dublin: William Porter ..., 1784. 1st Dublin edn. 12mo. xiv,346 pp. Half-title bound at end. Old calf, sl worn. *(Young's)* **£45 [≈ $80]**

Dodoens, Rembert

Dodsley, Robert

- A Collection of Poems in Six Volumes by Several Hands. London: J. Hughes for J. Dodsley, 1766. 6 vols. 8vo. Contemp speckled calf, red mor labels.
(Waterfield's) **£235 [≈ $418]**

- The Oeconomy of Human Life. Translated from an Indian Manuscript, written by an Ancient Bramin. Seventh Edition. London: 1751. 12mo. 96 pp. Frontis. Contemp sprinkled calf. Anon.
(Robertshaw) **£28 [≈ $50]**

- Public Virtue: a Poem. In Three Books ... London: for R. & J. Dodsley, 1753. 1st edn. 4to. vi,[ii],88, [4],[4 advt] pp. Disbound.
(Burmester) **£500 [≈ $890]**

Dodsley, Robert (editor and publisher)

- A Select Collection of Old Plays. London: for R. Dodsley, 1744 [-45]. 1st edn. 12 vols. 12mo. Subscribers vol 1. Contemp calf, rebacked, crnrs sl rubbed.
(Blackwell's) **£565 [≈ $1,006]**

Dodwell, William

- The Sick Man's Companion: Or, the Clergyman's Assistant in Visiting the Sick. With a Preliminary Dissertation on Prayer ... London: for B. White, 1768. 2nd edn. 8vo. xlvii, 48-260 pp. Old sheep, jnts partly cracked. *(Young's)* **£65 [≈ $116]**

Dolce, Ludovico

- Aretin: A Dialogue on Painting. London: for P. Elmsley, 1770. 1st English edn. 8vo. [6], xviii,[2], 262 pp. Half-title, intl & final blanks. Contemp calf, gilt spine & label, speckled edges. *(Spelman)* **£320 [≈ $570]**

Donne, John

- Letters to Severall Persons of Honour ... London: J. Flesher, sold by John Sweeting, 1654. 1st edn, 2nd issue. 4to. [vi],318 pp. Lib marks on title (stained inner marg, frayed, margs reprd). No port, no intl blank. Old calf, rebacked. Wing D.1865.

(Clark) **£280 [≈ $498]**

- Poems ... with Elegies on the Authors Death. London: M.F. for John Marriot, 1639. 3rd coll edn. 8vo. [viii],300, [iv],301-388, [xxxii] pp. Lacks port. Some ff v sl soiled. Rec polished calf, by Bayntun. STC 7047.
(Clark) **£380 [≈ $676]**

Dorney, John

- A Briefe and Exact relation of the most materiall and remarkeable Passages that hapned in the late ... Seige laid before the City of Glocester ... London: 1643. 1st edn. Sm 4to. [ii],17 pp. Port frontis. Browned, cut close at ft. Mod wraps. Wing D.1931.
(Blackwell's) **£120 [≈ $214]**

Dornford, Josiah

- The Motives and Consequences of the Present War impartially considered. London: for J. Pridden, 1792. 8vo. Mod qtr calf. Inscrbd 'From the Author'. Anon.
(Waterfield's) **£60 [≈ $107]**

Dorrington, Theophilus

- Observations concerning the Present State of Religion in the Romish Church. with some Reflections upon them; made in a Journey through some Provinces of Germany ... London: 1699. 1st edn. 8vo. [xiv],396,[12] pp. half-title. Some marks. Contemp calf, sl worn Wing D.1944.
(Frew Mackenzie) **£125 [≈ $223]**

- The Regulations of Play propos'd and recommended in a Sermon Preached at the Chapel of Tunbridge Wells, August the 19th, 1706. London: M. Jenour, for John Wyat, 1706. 1st edn. 8vo. 16 pp. Disbound.
(Burmester) **£20 [≈ $36]**

Dossie, R.

- The Elaboratory Laid Open, or, the Secrets of Modern Chemistry and Pharmacy Revealed ... London: J. Nourse, 1758. 1st edn. Some soiling to edges of endpapers. Calf gilt, gilt dec spine, crnrs sl bumped. Anon.
(P and P Books) **£275 [≈ $490]**

Douglas, Robert

- A Phenix, Or the Solemn League and Covenant, of the Three Kingdoms of Scotland, England and Ireland; for Reformation and Defence of Religion ... [Edinburgh]: re-printed in the Year, 1707. 1st edn thus. 8vo. 8 pp. Last page soiled. Disbound. Anon. *(Young's)* **£125 [≈ $223]**

Douglass, William

- A Summary, Historical and Political, of the

First Planting, Progressive Improvements, and Present State of the British Settlements in North-America. London: Dodsley, 1760. 2nd English edn. 2 vols. 8vo. Fldg map. Contemp calf gilt, spines rubbed but sound.
(Ximenes) **$900 [≈ £506]**

Dovar, Thomas

- The Ancient Physician's Legacy to his Country. London: R. Bradly, 1733. Pirated edn. 12mo. 216,[4] pp. Some foxing, tear in title reprd. Later mor.
(Bookpress) **$300 [≈ £169]**

Downe, John

- Certain Treatises ... Oxford: for John Lichfield, 1633. 4to. [vi],57,185, 26,34, 24,26, 51,125,68 pp. Engvd title. Sl wear & reprs. Rebound in calf with contemp bds & spine laid down.
(Francis Edwards) **£125 [≈ $223]**

Downes, Samuel

- The Lives of the Compilers of the Liturgy ... Second Edition, Corrected and Improved. London: Rivington, 1722. 8vo. Frontis (sm repr outer marg). Lacks rear f.e.p. Contemp calf, lacks label. *(Waterfield's)* **£65 [≈ $116]**

Downing, Clement

- A Compendious History of the Indian Wars; with An Account of ... Angria the Pyrate ... London: for T. Cooper, 1737. 1st edn. 12mo. iv, 238 pp. Contemp sprinkled calf gilt, mor label, jnts just cracked. *(Finch)* **£275 [≈ $490]**

Drake, Francis

- Eboracum: or the History and Antiquities of the City of York ... London: W. Bowyer for the author, 1736. Folio. [xxvi],627, cx, [xxxiii] pp. 60 plates, plans, &c. Occas sl marks. Old calf gilt, worn & scratched, reprd & recased. *(Hollett)* **£345 [≈ $614]**

- Eboracum: or the History and Antiquities of the City of York ... London: W. Bowyer for the author, 1736. 1st edn. Folio. [xxviii], 627, cx,[i], [xxxiii] pp. 60 plates, 53 text engvs. Occas sl foxing. Early calf, later rebacking.
(Spelman) **£400 [≈ $712]**

Drake, Francis, abridgement

- An Accurate Description and History of the Cathedral and Metropolitical Church of St. Peter, York ... York: A. Ward, 1770. Issue without a vol number on title. 12mo. 14 fldg plates (sev clean tears). Contemp calf, gilt spine sl chipped at ft. Anon.
(Spelman) **£80 [≈ $142]**

- An Accurate Description and History of the

Cathedral and Metropolitical Church of St. Peter, York ... York: G. Peacock, 1790. 3rd edn of vol 1. Fcap 8vo. [4],145,[i] pp. 14 fldg plates. 1 plate reprd on verso. Contemp calf, front bd detached. *(Spelman)* **£30 [≈ $53]**

- An Accurate Description and History of the Cathedral and Metropolitical Church of St. Peter, York ... York: G. Peacock, 1790; A. Ward, 1770. 3rd edn vol 1, 1st edn vol 2. 2 vols. Fcap 8vo. [4],145,[i]; [8],274 pp. 14 fldg plates. Rec mrbld bds.
(Spelman) **£80 [≈ $142]**

- Eboracum: or, the History and Antiquities of the City of York ... York: Wilson & Spence, 1788. 2 vols. 8vo. [4],418; [2],382 pp. Fldg map, 16 plates. Contemp tree calf, spines rubbed, jnts reprd. Anon.
(Spelman) **£120 [≈ $214]**

- The History and Antiquities of the City of York ... York: A. Ward, 1785. 3 vols. Fcap 8vo. [4],400; [4],402; [2],292 pp. Fldg map, fldg plan, 20 plates (8 fldg). Occas foxing. 19th c cloth backed bds. Anon.
(Spelman) **£120 [≈ $214]**

- The History and Antiquities of the City of York ... York: A. Ward, 1785. 3 vols. Fcap 8vo. [4],400; [4],402; [2],292 pp. Fldg plan, 20 plates (8 fldg). Lacks the map in vol 3. 19th c cloth backed bds, some wear hd of spines. Anon. *(Spelman)* **£60 [≈ $107]**

Drake, James

- Historia Anglo-Scotica: or an Impartial History of all that happen'd between the Kings and Kingdoms of England and Scotland ... London: John Hartley, 1703. 1st edn. 8vo. Contemp calf, rebacked.
(Appelfeld) **$275 [≈ £154]**

Drexel, Jeremias [Hieremias Drexelius]

- The Considerations of Drexelius upon Eternity. London: J.R. for Richard Chiswell, & sold by Samuel Tidmarsh, 1684. 12mo. Addtnl engvd title, 4 plates. Occas sl marg water stains. Contemp sheep, sl reprd. Wing D.2178. *(Ximenes)* **$225 [≈ £126]**

Dring, Thomas

- A Catalogue of the Lords, Knights and Gentlemen that have compounded for their Estates. London: 1655. 1st edn. 8vo. Contemp sheep, upper cvr sl rubbed. Wing D.2187. Anon. *(Robertshaw)* **£55 [≈ $98]**

Drummond, William

- The Poems of William Drummond, of Hawthornden. London: for J. Jeffrey, 1790. Sm 8vo. viii,326 pp. Later diced calf, rebacked. *(Rankin)* **£50 [≈ $89]**

Dryden, John
- Britannia Rediviva: a Poem on the Birth of the Prince. London: for J. Tonson, 1688. 1st edn. Folio. [2],14 pp. Lacks intl blank. Stains in inner marg last 2 ff. Disbound. Wing D.2251.   *(Hannas)* **£250 [≈ $445]**
- The Comedies, Tragedies and Operas. Now first collected ... London: 1701. 2 vols. Folio. Title,iv,618; title,558 pp. Lacks fldg port frontis. Calf, sl worn, jnts cracked.
          (Francis Edwards) **£350 [≈ $623]**
- Eleonora: A Panegyrical Poem: dedicated to the Memory of the Late Countess of Abingdon. London: for Jacob Tonson, 1692. 1st edn. 4to. [8],24 pp. Disbound. Wing D.2270.   *(Hannas)* **£75 [≈ $134]**
- The Fables ... London: Bensley, 1798. Folio. 9 full-page engvs & 14 vignettes by Lady Diana Beauclerc. Three qtr mottled calf, rebacked.   *(Appelfeld)* **$450 [≈ £253]**
- The Hind and the Panther. A Poem in Three Parts. London: Tonson, 1687. 3rd edn. 4to. 145 pp. Half-title. Period style calf gilt.
          (Hartfield) **$395 [≈ £222]**
- The Hind and the Panther. A Poem in Three Parts. London: Tonson, 1687. 4to. [8],145 pp, inc half-title. Disbound. Wing D.2285. Anon.   *(Hannas)* **£80 [≈ $142]**
- Love Triumphant; or, Nature will Prevail. A Tragi-Comedy ... London: Tonson, 1694. 1st edn. 4to. [x],82,[2] pp. Marg wormhole in upper outer crnr throughout. Sm repr last leaf. Occas sl spotting. Crushed mor, by Sangorski & Sutcliffe. Wing D.2302.
          (Finch) **£150 [≈ $267]**
- The Miscellaneous Works ... London: Tonson, 1760. 4 vols. 8vo. Port frontis. Occas sl foxing. Contemp calf, old reback, extrs worn, sev jnts cracked & weak.
          (Clark) **£45 [≈ $80]**
- A Poem upon the Death of his late Highness Oliver, Lord Protector of England, Scotland, & Ireland. London: for William Wilson, 1659 [ie ca 1691]. 4to. 12 pp. Disbound. Wing D.2330.   *(Hannas)* **£130 [≈ $231]**
- Poems and Fables ... prefix'd an Account of his Life and Writings. Dublin: A reilly for William Smith, 1753. 2 vols. 8vo. Engvd title & port frontis vol 1. Contemp calf, spine ends sl defective, lacks labels, some splitting backstrip vol 2.   *(Waterfield's)* **£40 [≈ $71]**
- Religio Laici or a Laymans Faith. A Poem. London: Tonson, 1683. 4to. [xvi],28 pp. Browned, edges dusty & sl dogeared. Rec wraps. Wing D.2345.   *(Clark)* **£30 [≈ $53]**
- The Spanish Fryar, or, the Double Discovery. London: for Richard Tonson & Jacob Tonson, 1681. 1st edn. Sm 4to. Foxed.

Few sm marg worm holes. Disbound. Wing D.2368.   *(Ximenes)* **$350 [≈ £197]**
- Threnodia Augustalis: A Funeral-Pindarique Poem Sacred to the Happy Memory of King Charles II. Second Edition. London: 1685. 4to. 25 pp. Title sl dusty. Mod wraps. Wing D.2384.   *(Robertshaw)* **£25 [≈ $45]**
- Threnodia Augustalis: A Funeral-Pindarique Poem Sacred to the Happy Memory of King Charles II. The Second Edition. London: Tonson, 1685. 1st edn, 2nd issue. 4to. Title dust soiled & sl frayed. Stitched, uncut. Wing D.2384.   *(Hannas)* **£65 [≈ $116]**

Dryden, John, & others
- Three Poems Upon the Death of the late Usurper Oliver Cromwel. Written by Mr. Jo. Dryden, Mr. Sprat, of Oxford, Mr. Edm. Waller ... London: Baldwin, 1682. Issue with Sprat's poem's title amended. 4to. [ii],26,[2] pp. Final blank leaf. Disbound. Wing D.2382.   *(Clark)* **£50 [≈ $89]**

Du Bocage or Du Boccage, Marie-Anne Fiquet
- Letters concerning England, Holland and Italy ... Written during her Travels in those Countries. Translated from the French. London: Dilly, 1770. 1st English edn. 2 vols. 8vo. xii,185,[1 advt]; 213,[1 advt] pp. Port frontis. Contemp calf, tiny defect to each spine.   *(Young's)* **£130 [≈ $231]**
- Letters concerning England, Holland, and Italy ... Written during her Travels in those Countries. London: Dilly, 1770. 1st edn in English. 2 vols. Sm 8vo. Advt leaf vol 1. Port. Contemp tree calf gilt, sl worn, 1 jnt tender.   *(Ximenes)* **$275 [≈ £154]**
- Letters concerning England, Holland, and Italy ... Written during her Travels in those Countries. Dublin: P. & W. Wilson, 1771. 2 vols. 12mo. xi,203; 216 pp. Port frontis. Contemp calf.
          (Frew Mackenzie) **£145 [≈ $258]**

Dubreuil, Jean
- Perspective Practical ... Set forth in English by Robert Pricke for Lovers of Art. London: for Robert Pricke, 1698. 4to. Collates: [unsigned 2], a4,b2,A4-Z4, Aa4-Qq4, Rr2. Frontis, engvd head-piece to dedic, 150 full-page engvs. 3 sm marg reprs. Rec calf.
          (Spelman) **£300 [≈ $534]**
- Practical Perspective ... London: Bowles & Carver, [ca 1780]. 7th edn. 4to. xxx,[i],150 pp. 150 plates. Later half roan, cloth bds, hinges & tips rubbed. Anon.
          (Bookpress) **$350 [≈ £197]**
- The Practice of Perspective ... London: for

Tho. & John Bowles, 1749. Translated by Ephraim Chambers. 4to. xiii,[v], 150,[ii numbered 150] pp. 2 fldg plates, num plates in text. Occas minor browning. Contemp calf, rebacked. *(Vanbrugh)* **£325 [≈ $579]**

- The Practice of Perspective ... [translated] by E. Chambers. The Third Edition. London: Bowles, 1743. 4to. xviii,150 pp. 2 fldg & 150 full-page plates. Text pasted to Aa1v & Aa3v. Period calf gilt, sl worn, lacks label. Anon. *(Rankin)* **£225 [≈ $401]**

Duck, Stephen
- Poems on Several Occasions. London: for W. Bickerton, 1736. 8vo. Contemp calf, extrs worn, rebacked. *(Hannas)* **£180 [≈ $320]**

Dudley, Robert
- Secret Memoirs of Robert Dudley, Earl of Leicester, Prime Minister and Favorite of Queen Elizabeth ... London: Briscoe & Bragg, 1706. 8vo. [32],118 pp. Contemp calf, gilt spine, hinges cracked but firm.
  (O'Neal) **$110 [≈ £62]**

Du Fresnoy, Charles Alphonse
- The Art of Painting ... with Remarks. Translated into English, with an Original Preface ... by Mr Dryden. The Second Edition, Corrected, and Enlarg'd. London: 1716. Fcap 8vo. [16],lxviii, [4],397,[7] pp. Frontis. Contemp calf, sm crack in jnt.
  (Spelman) **£120 [≈ $214]**
- The Art of Painting ... Translated into English Verse by William Mason ... Annotations by Sir Joshua Reynolds. York: J. Dodsley ..., 1783. 1st edn of this translation. 4to. xix,[iii],213,[2] pp. Later qtr calf.
  (Bookpress) **$125 [≈ £70]**

Dugdale, Sir William
- The History of St. Paul's Cathedral in London ... London: Bowyer, 1716. 2nd edn. Sm folio. [ii],xxviii,210, 75,[1],88,[20] pp. Frontis, 12 dble-page plates, 29 text engvs. Occas sl foxing. Contemp calf, rebacked, new endpapers. *(Bookpress)* **$1,000 [≈ £562]**

Duhamel du Monceau, Henri Louis
- A Practical Treatise of Husbandry: wherein are contained, many Useful and Valuable Experiments and Observations in the New Husbandry ... Translated by John Mills. London: 1759. Sm 4to. xxiv,492,[7],[1 advt] pp. Fldg table, 6 plates. Later half leather.
  (Hortulus) **$380 [≈ £213]**

Du Jon, Francois
- The Painting of the Ancients, in Three

Bookes ... Written first in Latin by Franciscus Junius, F.F. And now by him Englished ... London: sold by Daniel Frere, 1638. Only edn in English. 4to. [viii], 355, [i] pp. Minor marg worm & browning. Rec half calf. STC 7302 *(Clark)* **£300 [≈ $534]**

Dummer, Jeremiah
- A Defence of the New-England Charters. London: W. Wilkins ..., 1721. 1st edn. 80 pp. W'cut decs & letters. Title & next 2 ff damp stained. Occas sl foxing. Mod mor.
  (Reese) **$1,250 [≈ £702]**
- A Defence of the New England Charters. London: [1765]. 3rd London edn. 88 pp. Later bds, mor label. *(Reese)* **$200 [≈ £112]**

Du Moulin, Pierre, the younger
- A Letter of a French Protestant to a Scottishman of the Covenant. Wherein one of their chiefe pretences is removed, which is their conformitie with the French Churches in points of Discipline and Obedience. London: 1640. 4to. Mod mor, gilt dec spine. STC 7345. Anon.
  (D & D Galleries) **$150 [≈ £84]**

Dumourier, Charles Francois
- Memoirs ... Written by himself. Translated by John Fenwick. London: Kearsley, 1794. 1st edn in English 2 vols in one. 8vo in 4s. Half-title & final blank vol 1. Later maroon half calf, spine sl chipped at hd.
  (Clark) **£65 [≈ $116]**

Duncan, A.
- Heads of Lectures on the Theory and Practice of Medicine. Edinburgh: 1790. 4th edn. xvi,300 pp. Lib marks on title & endpapers. Some discoloration of page edges. Contemp bds, crnrs sl worn. *(Whitehart)* **£180 [≈ $320]**

Duncan, William
- The Elements of Logic. In Four Books. London: Dodsley, 1748. 1st edn. 8vo. Contemp vellum backed bds.
  (Waterfield's) **£225 [≈ $401]**

Dundonald, Archibald Cochrane, 9th Earl of
- A Treatise, shewing the intimate connection that subsists between Agriculture and Chemistry ... London: Murray & Highley, 1795. 1st edn. 4to. vii,[i],252 pp. Few sm lib marks. Orig bds, untrimmed, rebacked, marked, crnrs sl worn. *(Clark)* **£170 [≈ $303]**

Dunton, John
- The Conventicle: or, a Narrative of the

Dissenters New Plot against the Present Constitution in Church and State ... By One of the Conspirators. London: for the author, 1714. 1st edn. 8vo. 100 pp. Occas sl browning. Later qtr roan. Anon.
(Robertshaw) **£85 [≈ $151]**

Dunton, John (editor)

- The Phoenix: or, A Revival of Scarce and Valuable Pieces from the Remotest Antiquity down to the Present Time ... By a Gentleman [Vol 1]. London: J. Morphew, 1707. 8vo. vi,570 pp. V sl browning. Later half calf. Anon.   *(O'Neal)* **$150 [≈ £84]**

Dupaty, Charles Marguerite Jean Baptiste

- Travels through Italy, in a Series of letters; written in the Year 1785 ... Translated from the French by an English Gentleman. London: Robinson, 1788. 1st edn in English. 8vo. Half-title. Contemp tree calf, gilt spine.
(Ximenes) **$600 [≈ £337]**

Durel, John

- A View of the Government and Publick Worship of God in the Reformed Churches beyond the Seas ... [bound with his] The Liturgy of the Church of England Asserted ... London: R. Royston, 1662. 1st edns. 2 vols in one. 4to. Addtnl engvd title. Mod cloth. Wing D.2695/92.   *(Clark)* **£85 [≈ $151]**

Du Retz, Cardinal

- Memoirs of the Cardinal Du Retz ... Containing all the Great Events during the Minority of Lewis XIV, and Administration of Cardinal Mazarin ... London: for J. Brotherton, 1723. 8vo. viii,[iv],332 pp. Contemp half calf, gilt spine (sl rubbed).
(Young's) **£30 [≈ $53]**

D'Urfey, Thomas

- Butler's Ghost: or, Hudibras. The Fourth Part. With Reflections upon these Times. London: Joseph Hindmarsh, 1682. 1st edn. 8vo. [viii], 188,[iv] pp. Prelims sl spotted. Later calf gilt. Wing D.2703. Anon.
(Clark) **£160 [≈ $285]**

- Butler's Ghost: or, Hudibras. The Fourth Part. With Reflections upon these Times. London: for Joseph Hindmarsh, 1682. 1st edn. 8vo. 2 advt ff at end. Contemp sheep. Wing D.2703. Anon.
(Hannas) **£100 [≈ $178]**

- The Malecontent; a Satyr: Being the Sequel of the Progress of Honesty, or a View of Court and City. London: for Joseph Hindmarsh, 1684. 1st edn. Folio. [8],30 pp. Disbound. Wing D.2748. Anon. *(Hannas)* **£160 [≈ $285]**

- New Opera's, with Comical Stories and Poems, on Several Occasions. Never Before printed. London: William Chetwood, 1721. 1st edn. 8vo. [x],88,[ii], 89-349, 348-382 pp. Sep titles to the 8 plays. Some browning. Contemp calf, extrs sl worn, jnts cracked.
(Clark) **£160 [≈ $285]**

- New Opera's, with Comical Stories, and Poems, on Several Occasions. Never Before printed ... London: William Chetwood, 1721. 1st edn. 8vo. x,88,[iv],89-349, 348-382 pp. Sep titles to the 8 plays. Some water staining at ends. Mod bds. *(Blackwell's)* **£100 [≈ $178]**

- The Progress of Honesty: or, a View of a Court and City. A Pindarick Poem. By T.D. London: for Joseph Hindmarsh, 1681. 1st edn. Folio. [2],23 pp. Possibly lacks an intl blank leaf. Disbound. Wing D.2764.
(Hannas) **£180 [≈ $320]**

Durham, James

- Clavis Cantici; or an Exposition of the Song of Solomon. Glasgow: John Bryce, 1767. 8vo. Contemp sheep, worn, jnts cracked.
(Waterfield's) **£60 [≈ $107]**

The Dutch Barrier Our's ...

- The Dutch Barrier Our's: or, the Interest of England and Holland Inseparable. With Reflections ... London: A. Baldwin, 1712. 8vo. [ii],37 pp. Stitched as issued, untrimmed. Sometimes attributed to Swift, also to John Oldmixon.
(Blackwell's) **£185 [≈ $329]**

Dyche, Thomas

- A New General English Dictionary ... Grammar ... Supplement, now finish'd by William Pardon. The Eighth Edition ... London: Richard Ware, 1754. Thick 8vo. Occas browning. Contemp mottled calf, new label.   *(Spelman)* **£65 [≈ $116]**

- A New General English Dictionary ... The Eighteenth Edition ... London: Toplis & Bunney, & J. Mozley, 1781. 8vo. Occas soil & stain. Old rough mor.   *(Clark)* **£45 [≈ $80]**

Dyer, Jaques

- Les reports des Divers select Matters & Resolutions des Reverend Judges & Sages del Ley ... London: W. Rawlins ..., 1688. Port. Mod half calf. Wing D.2927.
(Meyer Boswell) **$550 [≈ £309]**

Dyer, John

- The Ruins of Rome. A Poem. London: for Lawton Gilliver, 1740. 1st edn. 4to. [4],28 pp. Engv on title. Sl stains on title. Disbound. Anon.   *(Hannas)* **£110 [≈ $196]**

Eadon, John
- The Arithmetician's Guide: being a New, Improved, and Compendious System of Practical Arithmetic ... Sheffield: for W. Ward ..., 1766. 1st edn. 8vo. [iv],iv,[ii], v,333 pp. Few diags. Tear in last leaf (no loss). Contemp sheep. *(Burmester)* £150 [≈ $267]

Eastcott, Richard
- Sketches of the Origin, Progress and Effects of Music, with an Account of the Ancient Bards and Minstrels ... Bath: S. Hazard, 1793. Orig bds, uncut. Sgnd by the author on title. *(C.R. Johnson)* £160 [≈ $285]
- Sketches of the Origin, Progress and Effects of Music, with an Account of the Ancient Bards and Minstrels ... Bath: S. Hazard, 1793. 1st edn. 8vo. vii,[iii],viii, iv,[ii], 277,[i] pp. 5 pp subscribers. Rec half calf, untrimmed. *(Clark)* £100 [≈ $178]

Easton, James
- Human Longevity: Recording the Name, Age, Place of Residence, and Year, of the Decease of 1712 Persons, who attained a Century and Upwards, from A.D. 66 to 1799 ... Salisbury: James Easton, 1799. 1st edn. 8vo. xxxii, [lx],292 pp. Half-title. 19th c qtr calf. *(Young's)* £190 [≈ $338]

Eboracum ...
- Eboracum: or, the History and Antiquities of the City of York ... see Drake, Francis, abridgement.

Echard, Laurence
- An Abridgment of Sir Walter Raleigh's History of the World ... see under Raleigh, Sir Walter.
- The Gazetteer's, or, Newsman's Interpreter. Being a Geographical Index of ... Europe ... Asia, Africa and America ... London: for S. Ballard ..., 1741. 15th & 8th edns. 2 parts in one. 8vo. Old calf. *(Young's)* £46 [≈ $82]
- The History of England ... London: Tonson, 1718. 2nd edn vol 1, 1st edn vols 2 & 3. 3 vols. Folio. Port, 3 frontis. Contemp elab blind tooled calf, rebacked, 2 jnts sl cracked but firm. *(O'Neal)* $375 [≈ £211]

Ecton, John
- Liber Valorum & Decimarum; Being an Account of the Valuations and Yearly Tenths of all such Benefices in England and Wales, as now stand Chargable with the Payment of First-Fruits and Tenths. London: for Is. Harrison, 1711. 1st edn. [viii],396,[9] pp. Contemp calf, sl rubbed. *(Young's)* £67 [≈ $119]
- Liber Valorum & Decimum. Being an Account of Such Ecclesiastical Benefices in England and Wales, as now stand Charged with ... Payment of First-Fruits and Tenths. London: R. Gosling, 1728. 3rd edn. 8vo. [xliv], 475, [2] pp. Sm marg hole. Contemp calf, rebacked. *(Young's)* £35 [≈ $62]
- Thesaurus Rerum Ecclesiasticarum; being an Account of the Valuations of all the Ecclesiastical Benefices in ... England and Wales ... London: Browne, Millar ..., 1742. 1st edn. xl,784,8 pp. Contemp calf, v worn, bds held by cords, new label. *(Jermy & Westerman)* £75 [≈ $134]
- Thesaurus Rerum Ecclesiasticarum. Being an Account of all the Ecclesiastical Benefices in the several Dioceses in England and Wales ... London: Knapton ..., 1754. 2nd edn. 4to. xl, 704 pp. Old calf, jnts worn, cords holding. *(Young's)* £60 [≈ $107]
- Thesaurus Rerum Ecclesiasticarum; being an Account of the Valuations of all the Ecclesiastical benefices in ... England and Wales ... Second Edition ... Revised ... London: Knapton, 1754. 4to. xl,704 pp. Contemp calf, rebacked, crnrs worn. *(Blackwell's)* £125 [≈ $223]

Eden, Adam (pseudonym)
- A Vindication of the Reformation on foot among the Ladies, to abolish Modesty and Chastity, and restore the Native Simplicity of Going Naked ... London: for R. Griffiths, 1755. 2nd edn. 8vo. 55 pp. Contemp style calf gilt. *(Burmester)* £550 [≈ $979]

Eden, William, Baron Auckland
- Some Remarks on the Apparent Circumstances of the War in the Fourth Week of October 1795. London: for J. Walter, 1795. 1st edn. 8vo. 68 pp. Mod bds. Anon. *(Hannas)* £40 [≈ $71]

Edwards, Bryan
- An Historical Survey of the French Colony in the Island of St. Domingo ... London: for John Stockdale, 1797. 1st edn. 4to. xxiv,247 pp. Fldg map. Contemp tree calf, gilt ruled spine. Gunton Park copy. *(Gough)* £300 [≈ $534]
- An Historical Survey of the French Colony in the Island of St. Domingo ... London: for John Stockdale, 1797. 1st edn. 4to. xxiv,247 pp. Fldg map. Contemp tree calf, gilt spine. *(Gough)* £225 [≈ $401]

Edwards, Jonathan
- A Dissertation concerning Liberty and Necessity ... Worcester, MA: Leonard

Worcester, 1797. 1st edn. 8vo. 234,[2] pp. Lib b'plate. Sl browned. Contemp calf, front bd detached, spine tips worn.
(Gach) **$185 [≈ £104]**

Edwin and Emma ...
- See Mallet, David

Effusions ...
- The Effusions of Friendship and Fancy ... see Langhorne, John

The Elaboratory Laid Open ...
- The Elaboratory Laid Open, or the Secrets of Modern Chemistry and Pharmacy Revealed ... London: J. Nourse, 1758. xiv,375,index pp. Trifle soiled. Lacks endpapers. Contemp calf, red label, front bd almost detached, worn.   *(Jermy & Westerman)* **£75 [≈ $134]**
- See also Dossie, R.

Elliot, John
- An Account of the Nature and Medicinal Virtues of the Principal Mineral Waters of Great Britain and Ireland, and those most in repute on the Continent. London: 1781. 236 pp. Fldg frontis, ills. Contemp calf, gilt spine, sl stained & worn. *(Whitehart)* **£200 [≈ $356]**
- An Account of the Nature and Medicinal Virtues of the Principal Mineral Waters of Great Britain and Ireland ... Second Edition, Corrected and Enlarged. London: for J. Johnson, 1789. 8vo. Fldg plate. Contemp half calf, gilt spine. *(Waterfield's)* **£200 [≈ $356]**
- The Medical Pocket-Book. Containing a Short but Plain Account of the Symptoms, Causes, and Methods of Cure of the Diseases incident to the Human Body ... Fourth Edition ... London: for J. Johnson, 1794. 12mo. 183, [1 blank],[4] pp. Browning. Contemp calf, spine & crnrs reprd.
(Spelman) **£40 [≈ $71]**

Ellis, Clement
- The Gentile Sinner, or England's Brave Gentleman Character'd in a Letter to a Friend ... The Sixt Edition. London: Henry Hall, for Ric. Davis & Ed. Forrest, 1679. 12mo. Hole in D2 with sm loss. Some worm. Contemp calf, sl worn, rebacked. Wing E.561.
(Hannas) **£80 [≈ $142]**

Ellis, George (editor)
- Specimens of the Early English Poets. London: for Edwards, 1790. 1st edn. 8vo. [ii],v, [iii],323 pp. Contemp straight grain red mor gilt, gilt dentelles & edges, jnts rubbed at hd. Anon.   *(Finch)* **£150 [≈ $267]**

Ellis, Henry
- A Voyage to Hudson's-Bay, by the Dobbs Galley and California, in the Years 1746 and 1747, for Discovering a North-West Passage ... London: H. Whitridge, 1748. xxviii,1-96, 89-336 pp. 10 plates & maps. Old calf, rebacked. Ducal b'plate.
(High Latitude) **$1,400 [≈ £787]**
- Voyage to Hudson's-Bay. By the Dobbs Galley and California, in the Years 1746 and 1747. For Discovering a North West Passage ... London: Whitridge, 1748. 1st edn. Sm 8vo. xxviii, 336 pp. Trimmed. Fldg map, 9 plates. Sm marg reprs, sl stains. Rec mor gilt.
(Terramedia) **$1,500 [≈ £843]**

Ellis, William
- Chiltern and Vale Farming Explained, according to the latest Improvements ... London: for Weaver Bickerton, [1733]. 1st edn. 8vo. Frontis. Contemp calf, gilt spine, minor rubbing.   *(Ximenes)* **$650 [≈ £365]**
- The London and Country Brewer. Containing the Whole Art of Brewing all Sorts of Malt-Liquors ... Fifth Edition. London: Thomas Astley, 1744. 8vo. [2],[6],332,[4] pp. General title & 4 sectional title-pages. Contemp calf, jnts cracked.
(Spelman) **£180 [≈ $320]**
- The Practical Farmer. London: for Weaver Bickerton ..., 1732. 1st edn. 8vo. iv,[164], [ii] pp. Contemp calf, rebacked.
(Ash) **£250 [≈ $445]**

Elsum, John
- Epigrams upon the Paintings of the Most Eminent Masters, Antient and Modern. London: 1700. 8vo. Some browning. Clean tear in title. Contemp calf, rebacked. Wing E.643. Anon. *(D & D Galleries)* **$150 [≈ £84]**

Elsynge, Henry
- The Ancient Manner of Holding Parliaments in England ... London: for S.S., sold by Tho. Dring, 1675. 3rd edn. 12mo. [xii],371 pp. Last leaf reprd, affecting text. Early 19th c tree calf, rebacked. Wing E.645A.
(Vanbrugh) **£155 [≈ $276]**
- The Ancient Manner of Holding Parliaments in England ... The Third Edition enlarged. London: for S.S., sold by Tho. Dring, 1675. 371 pp. Rebound in qtr sheep. Wing E.645A.
(C.R. Johnson) **£125 [≈ $223]**
- The Ancient Method and Manner of Holding Parliaments in England. The Fourth Edition Enlarged. London: Thomas Dring, 1679. 12mo. [xii],371,[i] pp. Contemp sheep, sl rubbed, spine ends sl chipped. Wing E.646.
(Clark) **£110 [≈ $196]**

Emerson, William
- A System of Astronomy ... London: 1769. 8vo. x,ii,368,[4] pp. 16 fldg plates. Old calf, v worn, front bd & title detached.
  (Weiner) **£40 [≈ $71]**

Enfield, William
- Exercises in Elocution; selected from Various Authors ... intended as a Sequel to ... The Speaker. Warrington: W. Eyres, for J. Johnson, 1780. 1st edn. 12mo. vii,424 pp. Contemp sheep, extrs sl worn, jnts cracked but firm, lacks label.   *(Clark)* **£48 [≈ $85]**
- Institutes of Natural Philosophy, Theoretical and Experimental ... added an Introduction to the First Principles of Chemistry. London: J. Johnson, 1799. 2nd edn. 4to. xvi,428 pp. 13 plates. Minor spotting. Orig bds, rebacked, crnrs sl worn.   *(Clark)* **£160 [≈ $285]**
- The Speaker; or, Miscellaneous Pieces ... Fifth Edition, Corrected. London: Joseph Johnson, 1780. 8vo. xxxiv,405 pp. Contemp calf, gilt label, spine ends worn.
  (Spelman) **£45 [≈ $80]**

The English Pleader ...
- The English Pleader. Being a Select Collection of Various Precedents of Declarations on Actions brought in the Courts of King's Bench and Common Pleas ... By a Gentleman of Lincoln's Inn. Dublin: Peter Hoey, 1783. 8vo. 388,[16] pp. Contemp calf, jnt cracked but firm.
  (Burmester) **£75 [≈ $134]**

English, Harriet
- Conversations and Amusing Tales. Offered to the Publick for the Youth of Great Britain. London: for the author ..., 1799. 1st edn. 4to. xi,[iii],385,[7] pp. Frontis, 12 tinted aquatints. 2 engvd ff music. Lacks half-title. Few sl marks. Contemp calf, backstrip relaid. Anon.   *(Burmester)* **£275 [≈ $490]**

The Entertaining Instructor ...
- See Lockman, John

Entick, John
- Entick's New Spelling Dictionary ... Revised ... by William Crakelt. London: Charles Dilly, 1791. Oblong 8vo. xvi,373,[3] pp. Contemp tree calf, rebacked.
  (C.R. Johnson) **£135 [≈ $240]**

Epictetus
- Epictetus His Morals, With Simplicius His Comment. Made English from the Greek by George Stanhope ... London: Richard Sare, 1700. 2nd edn, crrctd. 8vo. [16],xli,[7],

432,[8] pp.. Top outer crnrs worn. Contemp calf, rebacked. Wing E.3154.
  (O'Neal) **£140 [≈ $79]**

Epictetus: a Poem ...
- Epictetus: a Poem, containing the Maxims of that celebrated Philosopher ... Done from the Original Greek of Arrian, with Notes ... added, The Table of Cebes. London: B. Bragge, 1709. 8vo. [xxiv],147 pp. Contemp sheep, some wear, rebacked.
  (Burmester) **£175 [≈ $312]**

Erasmus, Desiderius
- Twenty Two Select Colloquies out of Erasmus Roterodamus ... The second Impression Corrected and Amended ... By R. L'Estrange, Kt. London: Bentley & Sare, 1689. 8vo. [viii], 293,[3] pp. Intl & final blanks. Port. Contemp calf, gilt spine, jnts rubbed. Wing E.3213. *(Clark)* **£125 [≈ $223]**

Erskine, The Hon. Thomas
- A View of the Causes and Consequences of the Present War with France. London: for J. Debrett, 1797. 15th edn. 8vo. [iv],138,[2 advt] pp. Half-title. Brown paper wraps.
  (Young's) **£18 [≈ $32]**

Espiard de la Borde, Francois Ignace
- The Spirit of Nations. Translated from the French. London: Lockyer Davis, & R. Baldwin, 1753. 1st edn in English. 8vo. xvi,406,[2 advt] pp. Occas sl marg foxing. Contemp calf, rebacked & reprd, some rubbing, hinges strengthened. Anon.
  (Blackwell's) **£140 [≈ $249]**

Essay(s) ...
- An Essay for the Construction of Roads on Mechanical and Physical Principles. London: T. Davies, 1774. Half-title, iv,48 pp. Fldg plate. 2 sm old lib stamps. Rebound in cloth bds.   *(C.R. Johnson)* **£225 [≈ $401]**
- An Essay in Defence of the Female Sex ... see Astell, Mary
- An Essay on Laughter, wherein are Displayed, its Natural and Moral Causes, with the Art of exciting it. London: for T. Davies & L. Davis, 1769. 1st edn in English. 12mo. xii, 140 pp. Early 19th c bds, uncut, backstrip worn but sound.
  (Burmester) **£250 [≈ $445]**
- Essay on Political Lying. London: sold by S. Hooper, 1757. 2nd edn. 8vo. 28 pp. Disbound.   *(Young's)* **£90 [≈ $160]**
- An Essay on Punctuation ... see Robertson, Joseph

- An Essay on Reason ... see Harte, Walter
- An Essay on Satire ... see Brown, John
- An Essay on the Church ... see Jones, William

- An Essay on the Different Natural Situations of Gardens ... see Parkyns, G.I.
- An Essay on the Manners and Genius of the Literary Character ... see D'Israeli, Isaac.
- An Essay on the Natural History of Guiana ... see Bancroft, Edward
- An Essay on the Nature, Design, and Origin, of Sacrifices ... see Sykes, Arthur Ashley.
- An Essay on the Writings and Genius of Shakespear ... see Montagu, Elizabeth
- An Essay upon Loans ... see Defoe, Daniel, attributed author
- An Essay upon the Harmony of Language ... see Mitford, William
- Essays on Hunting ... see Blane, William
- Essays on Husbandry ... see Harte, Walter

Est or Este, William
- The Scourge of Securitie, or the Expulsion and Returne of the Uncleane Spirit. London: T.C. for Thomas Downe, & Ephraim Dauson, 1609. 1st edn. Sm 8vo. Sl browning. Disbound. STC 10537.
 (Ximenes) **$400 [≈ £225]**

Este, C.
- A Journey in the Year 1793, through Flanders, Brabant, and Germany, to Switzerland. London: for J. Debrett, 1795. 1st edn. 8vo. [iv],381,10 pp. Contemp calf, rebacked. *(Young's)* **£70 [≈ $125]**

Estimate ...
- An Estimate of the Manners and Principles of the Times ... see Brown, John, "Estimate".

Estwick, Samuel
- A Letter to the Reverend Josiah Tucker ... in which the Present War against America is shewn to be the Effect ... of a Fixed Plan of Administration ... London: 1776. 125,[3] pp. Mod cloth, leather label.
 (Reese) **$375 [≈ £211]**

Etherege, Sir George
- The Man of Mode; or, Sir Fopling Flutter. A Comedy ... London: T. Warren, for Henry Herringman ..., 1693. 4to. Disbound. Wing E.3376. *(Hannas)* **£120 [≈ $214]**
- Three Plays: The Comical Revenge ... She Would if She Could ... The Man of Mode ... Also Five Poems ... London: Tonson, 1723.

12mo. 276 pp. Frontis. Rebound in mor, gilt spine. *(Hartfield)* **$295 [≈ £166]**
- The Works ... London: for H.H., Tonson, Bennet, 1704. 1st coll edn. 8vo. Contemp calf gilt, jnts cracking. *(Hannas)* **£200 [≈ $356]**

Evans, Abel
- The Apparition. A Poem ... London: Printed in the Year, 1710. 1st edn. 8vo. 38 pp. Mrbld wraps. Anon. *(Young's)* **£75 [≈ $134]**

Evans, Evan
- Some Specimens of the Poetry of the Antient Welsh Bards. Translated into English, with Explanatory Notes ... London: Dodsley, 1764. 1st edn. 4to. A few ff water stained in upper marg. Mod half mor. *(Hannas)* **£130 [≈ $231]**

Evans, J. (publisher)
- A New Drawing Book. London: J. Evans, October 8th, 1796. Oblong 8vo. 4 plates, each plate comprising 3 states of the engraving. 2 of the outline plates partly cold. Orig wraps, some creasing to crnrs. *(Spelman)* **£95 [≈ $169]**

Evans, John
- The Case of Kneeling at the Holy Sacrament Stated and Resolved. London: for T. Basset, D. Took, F. Gardiner, 1683. 2 parts. 4to. Disbound. Wing E.3445, 3448. Anon. *(Waterfield's)* **£45 [≈ $80]**

Evelina ...
- See Burney, Frances

Evelyn, John
- An Essay on the First Book of T. Lucretius Carus de Rerum Natura. Interpreted and made English Verse ... London: 1656. 1st edn. 8vo. [xvi], "185" [ie 169],[7] pp. Errata & advts at end. Frontis. Old calf, rebacked, crnrs sl worn. Wing E.3446.
 (Clark) **£300 [≈ $534]**
- Kalendarium Hortense: or, the Gardener's Almanac ... London: for R. Chiswell, 1691. 8th edn. 8vo. [xx],175,[15] pp. Red & black title. Frontis, 1 plate. Contemp speckled sheep, sl rubbed. Wing E.3498.
 (Young's) **£165 [≈ $294]**
- Sculptura, or the History and Art of Chalcography, and Engraving in Copper. London: Payne, 1755. Enlgd edn. Lge 8vo. Port. Calf. *(Rostenberg & Stern)* **$475 [≈ £267]**
- Sculptura, or the History and Art of Chalcography, and Engraving in Copper. London: J. Payne, 1755. 2nd edn. Sm 8vo.

[iv],xxxvi,140 pp. Frontis, 2 plates (1 fldg mezzotint). Frontis foxed. Later calf backed mrbld bds.   *(Bookpress)* **$350 [≈£197]**
- Sylva, or a Discourse of Forest-Trees ... Pomono ... Kalendarium Hortense ... London: Martyn & Allestry, 1664. 1st edn. Folio. Errata leaf. Some browning. Contemp calf, backstrip relaid, new label, crnrs reprd. Wing E.3516.   *(Spelman)* **£550 [≈$979]**
- Sylva, Or A Discourse of Forest-Trees ... Pomona ... Kalendarium Hortense ... London: 1664. 1st edn. Folio. [xiv],120,[ii], 20, animadversion leaf, 21-83,[i errata] pp. Contemp calf, rebacked, new endpapers, sl surface damage to lower bd. Wing E.3516,   *(Finch)* **£750 [≈$1,335]**

Everard, Edmund
- Discourse on the Present State of the Protestant Princes of Europe ... London: Dorman Newman, 1679. Folio. [iv],44 pp. Page edges sl dusty. Disbound. Wing E.3528.   *(Clark)* **£35 [≈$62]**

Every Man His own Lawyer ...
- See Jacob, Giles.

Examination ...
- The Examination of Edw. Fitzharris, relating to the Popish Plot. London: for Thomas Fox, 1681. 1st edn. Folio. 18 pp, inc licence leaf, plus final blank leaf. Disbound. Wing E.3717.   *(Hannas)* **£20 [≈$36]**

Exempla Moralia ...
- Exempla Moralia or Third Book of New English Examples to be rendered into Latin ... New Edition, revised. Eton: T. Pote, 1789. 8vo. Lacks rear f.e.p. Contemp sheep.   *(Waterfield's)* **£45 [≈$80]**

Exercises ...
- Exercises, Instructive and Entertaining, in false English; written with a View to perfect Youth in their Mother Tongue ... The Sixth Edition. Leeds: for John Binns, 1797. viii,111,[1] pp. Contemp sheep, sl rubbed, jnt cracked.   *(C.R. Johnson)* **£110 [≈$196]**

Expediency ...
- The Expediency and Necessity of revising and improving the Publick Liturgy humbly represented, being the Substance of an Essay for a Review of the Book of Common Prayer ... London: for R. Griffiths, 1749. 8vo. Disbound.   *(Waterfield's)* **£60 [≈$107]**

The Expedition of Humphry Clinker ...
- See Smollett, Tobias

Fabricius, Friedrich Ernst Von
- The Genuine Letters of Baron Fabricius ... to Charles XII of Sweden ... Residence in Turkey ... London: Becket & De Hondt, 1761. 1st English edn. 8vo. Contemp mottled calf, fine. Colquhoun of Luss copy.   *(Hannas)* **£130 [≈$231]**

Faction Detected ...
- See Perceval, John, 2nd Earl of Egmont

Faction Display'd ...
- See Shippen, William

Fairfax, Thomas
- An Humble Representation ... Concerning ... the putting of the Souldiery into constant Pay. London: Clowes for Whittington, 1647 4to. Typographical title-border. Stitched. Wing F.169.   *(Rostenberg & Stern)* **$125 [≈£70]**

Fairfax, Thomas
- The Complete Sportsman. London: for J. Cooke, [1760?]. 12mo. 240 pp. Few sl marks. Later half calf gilt.   *(Ash)* **£200 [≈$356]**

Faithfull ...
- A Faithfull and Impartial Relation of What Passed Between His Majesty and the Commissioners from the two Houses. N.p.: [1648]. Folio broadside. Sm stain. Wing F.268.   *(Rostenberg & Stern)* **$85 [≈£48]**

Falconer, Richard
- The Voyages ... see Chetwood, William Rufus

Falconer, William
- A Dissertation on the Influence of the Passions upon Disorders of the Body; being the Essay to which the Fothergillian Medal was adjudged. London: 1788. 1st edn. 8vo. xix, 105,[3] pp. New calf.   *(Weiner)* **£200 [≈$356]**
- Observations on Dr. Cadogan's Dissertation on the Gout and all Chronic Diseases. Second Edition with Corrections and Additions. Bath: R. Cruttwell, 1772. 8vo. 115 pp. Title browned. Last leaf cut no loss of text. Mod qtr mor.   *(Robertshaw)* **£48 [≈$85]**
- Observations respecting the Pulse ... London: Cadell & Davies, 1796. 8vo. [ii],158 pp. Lacks half-title. 2 sm marg tears. Rec bds.   *(Burmester)* **£175 [≈$312]**

Falkland, Henry Cary, 1st Viscount
- The History of the most unfortunate Prince

King Edward II ... London: sold by John
Playford, 1680. 1st edn. 8vo. 3 advt pp at end.
Sl browning. Early 19th c calf, gilt backstrip
laid down. Wing F.314.
(Georges) **£150** [≈ **$267**]

**Familiar Letters from a Gentleman at
Damascus ...**
- Familiar Letters from a Gentleman at
Damascus to his Sister in London ... By a
Gentleman of Oxford. London: E. Duncomb
..., 1750. Only edn. 8vo. [ii],286,[2] pp. 6
plates. 19th c half calf, sl rubbed.
(Clark) **£380** [≈ **$676**]

The Family Guide to Health ...
- The Family Guide to Health; or, a General
Practice of Physic ... Methods ... from the
Writings and Practice of the most Eminent
Physicians ... London: for J. Fletcher; & B.
Collins, Salisbury, 1767. 1st edn. 8vo. xvi, v-
xix, [i], 331,[1] pp. Errata leaf. Contemp calf,
rebacked.   *(Burmester)* **£240** [≈ **$427**]

Farmer ...
- The Farmer's Guide in Hiring and Stocking
Farms ... see Young, Arthur
- The Farmer's Letters to the People of
England ... see Young, Arthur

Farmer, Hugh
- A Dissertation on Miracles that they are
Arguments of a Divine Interposition ...
London: for T. Cadell ..., 1771. 8vo.
Contemp calf, rebacked.
(Waterfield's) **£55** [≈ **$98**]

Farmer, Richard
- An Essay on the Learning of Shakespeare:
addressed to Joseph Cradock. Cambridge: J.
Archdeacon, for W. Thorlbourn & J.
Woodyer ..., 1767. 1st edn. 8vo. [2],50 pp.
Lacks half-title & final announcement leaf.
Mod pigskin.   *(Hannas)* **£75** [≈ **$134**]
- An Essay on the Learning of Shakespeare:
addressed to Joseph Cradock, Esq.
Cambridge: J. Archdeacon, 1767. 50 pp. Rec
qtr calf.   *(C.R. Johnson)* **£145** [≈ **$258**]
- An Essay on the Learning of Shakespeare ...
Third Edition. London: Longman;
Cambridge: Merrill, 1789. 8vo. Contemp half
calf, rubbed.   *(Waterfield's)* **£50** [≈ **$89**]

Farquhar, George
- The Works ... The Eighth Edition. London:
for J. & J. Knapton, Strahan ..., 1742. 2 vols.
12mo. Contemp mottled calf, lacks label vol
2.   *(Waterfield's)* **£50** [≈ **$89**]

- The Works ... The Ninth Edition. Corrected
... added some Memoirs of the Author, never
before Publish'd. London: for J. Clarke ...,
1760. 2 vols. 12mo. Final blank leaf vol 1, 3
advt pp vol 2. Contemp calf, gilt spines.
(Hannas) **£35** [≈ **$62**]

The Favorites Chronicle ...
- See Langlois, Francois

Fawcett, Benjamin
- Murther Lamented and Improved. A Sermon
Preached at Kidderminster June 16 1771 ...
Shrewsbury: J. Eddowes, 1771. Half-title, 35
pp. New bds.   *(C.R. Johnson)* **£30** [≈ **$53**]
- Observations on the Nature, Causes and Cure
of Melancholy; especially of that which is
called Religious Melancholy. Shrewsbury: J.
Eddowes, 1780. [80] pp. Contemp qtr sheep,
mrbld bds, rebacked.
(C.R. Johnson) **£225** [≈ **$401**]

Fawcett, John, D.D.
- An Essay on Anger. Leeds: Thomas Wright,
for the author ..., 1788. 2nd edn. 12mo.
Contemp sheep, upper jnt sl cracked.
(Ximenes) **$350** [≈ **£197**]

**Fawcett, John, of Magdalen College,
Cambridge**
- An Essay on the Propagation of the Christian
Religion. Cambridge: J. Archdeacon, 1791.
4to. Half-title. Mod mrbld bds.
(Waterfield's) **£45** [≈ **$80**]

Fawkes, Francis
- A Description of May, from Gawin Douglas,
Bishop of Dunkeld. London: Whiston &
White, 1752. 4to. xii,29,[3] pp. Some
browning. Rec wraps.
(Burmester) **£35** [≈ **$62**]
- Original Poems and Translations. London:
for the author, sold by Dodsley ..., 1761. 1st
edn. 8vo. Subscribers. Lacks errata slip. Tiny
marg worm holes throughout. Contemp
mottled calf gilt.   *(Hannas)* **£130** [≈ **$231**]

**The Fears and Sentiments of all True
Britains ...**
- See Hoadly, Benjamin.

Fell, John
- The Life of that Reverend Divine, and
Learned Historian, Dr. Thomas Fuller.
London: 1661. 1st edn. Sm 8vo. 106,[5 ctlg]
pp. Sm hole in title without loss. Sl damp
stain at beginning. Contemp calf. Wing
F.616. Anon.   *(Robertshaw)* **£38** [≈ **$68**]

Felton, Henry

- A Dissertation on Reading the Classics, and forming a Just Style. Written in the Year 1709 ... London: Jonah Bowyer, 1713. 1st edn. Lge 12mo. [2],xx,[12],[2 errata & blank],228 pp. Contemp calf, 19th c label.
(Spelman) £180 [≈ $320]

Female ...
The Female Faction ...

- The Female Faction: or, the Gay Subscribers. A Poem. London: for J. Roberts, 1729. Folio. 8 pp. 2 sm marg tears.
(C.R. Johnson) £485 [≈ $863]
- The Female Faction: or, the Gay Subscribers, a Poem. London: for J. Roberts, 1729. 1st edn. Folio. 2 tears in one leaf, no loss. Disbound. *(Ximenes)* $600 [≈ £337]
- The Female Mentor: or, Select Conversations. Dublin: R. Napper, 1793. viii, 279 pp. Contemp tree calf, red label.
(C.R. Johnson) £110 [≈ $196]

Fenelon, Francois de Salignac de la Mothe

- The Archbishop of Cambray's Pastoral Letter concerning The Love of God. London: Rivington& James, 1715-14. 2 parts in 1 vol. 8vo. Calf. *(Rostenberg & Stern)* $60 [≈ £34]
- Instructions for the Education of a Daughter. By the Author of Telemachus ... added, a Small Tract of Instructions for the Conduct of Young Ladies ... London: Bowyer, 1707. 1st English edn. 12mo. Frontis. Contemp calf, jnts weak. *(Hannas)* £120 [≈ $214]

Fenner, Dudley

- The Whole Doctrine of the Sacraments, Plainlie and Fullie set downe and declared out of the word of God. Middleburgh: Richard Schilders, 1588. 1st edn. 8vo. Trimmed a bit close at ft. Disbound. STC 10778.
(Ximenes) $750 [≈ £421]

Fenning, Daniel

- A New Grammar of the English Language ... London: S. Crowder, 1771. 1st edn. xii,204 pp. Contemp calf, rubbed & worn.
(Jermy & Westerman) £35 [≈ $62]
- The Young Measurer's Complete Guide ... London: S. Crowder, 1772. 1st edn. 12mo. xii, liv,322 pp. Text diags. Contemp sheep, extrs sl worn, jnts cracked but firm.
(Clark) £75 [≈ $134]

Fenton, Elijah

- Poems on Several Occasions. London: for Bernard Lintot, 1717. 8vo. Advts (sheet Q) present. Frontis. Minute marg wormhole

some ff. Contemp calf, mor label, minor splits in jnts. *(Waterfield's)* £180 [≈ $320]

Fenton, Elijah (editor)

- Oxford and Cambridge Miscellany Poems. London: for Bernard Lintott, [1708]. 1st edn. 8vo. Frontis. Rather browned. Contemp panelled calf, gilt spine, jnts cracking.
(Hannas) £150 [≈ $267]

Ferguson, James

- The Art of Drawing in Perspective made easy to those who have no previous knowledge of the Mathematics. London: for W. Strahan, 1775. 1st edn. 8vo. xii,123,[2] pp. 9 fldg plates. Lacks half-title. Sl browning. 1 sm repr. Rec bds. *(Fenning)* £125 [≈ $223]
- Astronomy Explained upon Sir Isaac Newton's Principles ... The Sixth Edition, Corrected. London: Strahan ..., 1778. 8vo. [viii], 501,[15] pp. Fldg frontis, 17 fldg plates. Contemp calf. *(Hartfield)* $295 [≈ £166]
- Astronomy explained upon Sir Isaac's Principles. Eighth Edition. London: 1790. 8vo. 503,index pp. 17 fldg plates. Mod cloth.
(Robertshaw) £50 [≈ $89]
- Astronomy Explained upon Sir Isaac Newton's Principles. London: Rivington ..., 1790. 8th edn. 8vo. [8],503,[16] pp. 18 plates. Some tears. Occas stains & foxing. Contemp calf, sl worn. *(D & D Galleries)* $150 [≈ £84]
- An Introduction to Electricity. In Six Sections. London: Strahan & Cadell, 1770. 1st edn. 8vo. iv,140 pp. 3 fldg plates. Contemp calf, crnrs & spine ends worn, lacks free endpapers. *(Gaskell)* £450 [≈ $801]
- Lectures on Select Subjects in Mechanics, Hydrostatics, Pneumatics and Optics, with the Use of the Globes, the Art of Dialling ... London: 1764. 4to. viii,252,[4] pp. 23 fldg plates. Sm lib stamp title. Contemp calf, sl worn & marked. *(Weiner)* £250 [≈ $445]
- Lectures on Select Subjects in Mechanics, Hydrostatics, Pneumatics and Optics, with the Use of the Globes, the Art of Dialing ... Ninth Edition. London: 1799. 8vo. [xiv],396, [6],48 pp. 36 fldg plates. Contemp tree sheep, mor label. *(Weiner)* £150 [≈ $267]

Ferguson, Robert

- An Enquiry into, and Detection of the Barbarous Murther of the Late Earl of Essex ... [Holland?]: Anno 1684. 1st edn. 4to. [iv], 76 pp. Disbound. Anon.
(Young's) £110 [≈ $196]
- The Late Proceedings and Votes of the Parliament of Scotland; contained in an Address delivered to the King. Glasgow:

Andrew Hepburn, 1689. 1st edn. 4to. 63 pp.
A1 blank. Sm hole in last leaf with loss of 2
letters. Disbound. Wing F.746. Anon.
(Robertshaw) £22 [≈ $39]

Ferne, Henry
- Conscience Satisfied. That there is no
warrant for the Armes now taken up by the
Subjects ... Oxford: Leonard Lichfield [vere
London], 1643. Sm 4to. [vii],85,[i] pp. Sl
shaved at hd. Occas faint marg water stain.
Disbound. Wing F.791.
(Blackwell's) £45 [≈ $80]

Field, Richard
- Of the Church, Five Books. The Third
Edition. Oxford: William Turner, 1635.
Folio. [xvi],906 pp. Occas marks & marg
worming. Lacks free endpapers. Contemp
calf, crnrs worn, jnt ends split. STC 10859.
(Clark) £90 [≈ $160]

Fielding, Henry
- A Clear State of the Case of Elizabeth
Canning ... London: for A. Millar, 1753. 2nd
edn. 8vo. 62 pp. Disbound.
(Young's) £75 [≈ $134]
- A Clear State of the Case of Elizabeth
Canning ... Dublin: for George Faulkner ...,
1753. 1st Dublin edn. 8vo. 48 pp. Disbound.
(Young's) £270 [≈ $481]
- A Compleat and Authentick History of the
Rise, Progress, and Extinction of the Late
Rebellion ... London: for M. Cooper, 1747.
1st edn. 8vo. "155" [ie 163] pp. Lacks half-
title & fldg plan. Disbound. Anon.
(Young's) £200 [≈ $356]
- An Enquiry into the Causes of the Late
Increase of Robbers, &c. ... Second Edition.
London: for A. Millar, 1751. 12mo. Half-title.
Faint water stains at front. Contemp mrbld
bds, calf spine. (Hannas) £240 [≈ $427]
- The Historical Register, for the Year 1736.
As it is acted at the New Theatre in the Hay-
Market ... Euridice Hiss'd ... London: J.
Roberts, [1737]. 8vo. [16],48 pp. Disbound.
Anon. (Young's) £220 [≈ $392]
- The History of Tom Jones, a Foundling.
London: A. Millar, 1749. 1st edn. With errata
leaf C8 vol 1, uncorrected text, & all cancels
as in Rothschild. 6 vols. 12mo. Occas sl
browning. Contemp calf, backstrips relaid,
extrs sl rubbed. 2 slipcases.
(Heritage) $5,000 [≈ £2,809]
- The History of the Adventures of Joseph
Andrews ... London: for A. Millar, 1742. 1st
edn. 2 vols. 12mo. Lacks advt ff. Few sm
marg tears. Late 19th c mottled calf gilt.
Anon. (Hannas) £580 [≈ $1,032]

- The History of the Adventures of Joseph
Andrews ... Fifth Edition, Revised and
Corrected. London: for A. Millar, 1751. 2
vols. 8vo. 12 plates. Somewhat used &
browned. Contemp calf, rubbed, 1 jnt
cracked. (Waterfield's) £75 [≈ $134]
- The Adventures of Joseph Andrews, and his
Friend Mr. Abraham Adams. With Prints by
T. Rowlandson. London & Edinburgh: J.
Murray, J. Sibbald, 1792. 8 plates by Thomas
Rowlandson. Contemp calf, rebacked.
(C.R. Johnson) £250 [≈ $445]
- The Journal of a Voyage to Lisbon. London:
A. Millar, 1755. 1st edn, 1st issue. "228" [ie
276] pp. Half-title. Contemp calf, rebacked.
(C.R. Johnson) £220 [≈ $392]
- Love in Several Masques. A Comedy ...
London: John Watts, 1728. 1st edn. 8vo.
[viii], 82,[i Epilogue] pp. Sl browning. Rec
qtr mor. (Blackwell's) £235 [≈ $418]
- The Miser. A Comedy. Taken from Plautus
and Moliere ... London: for J. Watts, 1732.
1st edn. 8vo. Mod cloth backed bds.
(Hannas) £100 [≈ $178]
- A True State of the Case of Bosavern Penlez,
who suffered on Account of the late Riot in
the Strand ... London: for A. Millar, 1749. 1st
edn. 8vo. 54 pp. Sm stain on 1st 2 ff.
Disbound. (Young's) £275 [≈ $490]
- The Works ... with the Life of the Author.
London: A. Millar, 1762. 1st coll edn. 4 vols.
4to. Port frontis. Occas sl foxing. Contemp
calf, rebacked, paper labels, rubbed, crnrs sl
worn, some inner jnts cracked.
(Clark) £280 [≈ $498]

Fielding, Sir John
- The Universal Mentor; containing Essays on
the most important Subjects in Life ...
London: A. Millar, 1763. [12],vii, [1],254 pp.
Contemp calf, red label, sm repr ft of spine.
(C.R. Johnson) £185 [≈ $329]

Fielding, Sarah
- Xenophon's Memoirs of Socrates. With the
Defence of Socrates before his Judges.
Translated from the Original Greek: C.
Pope, 1762. Title, errata, vi,8 subscribers,
339, 21 pp. Contemp calf, rubbed, lacks label.
(Jermy & Westerman) £125 [≈ $223]

Finch, Heneage, Earl of Nottingham
- An Exact and most Impartial Account of the
Indictment, Arraignment, Trial, and
Judgment (according to Law) of Twenty Nine
Regicides ... London: R. Scot ..., 1679. 8vo.
[iv],329, [i] pp. Imprimatur leaf. Browning.
Contemp calf, spine rubbed, jnts cracked but
firm. Wing N.1404. Anon. (Clark) £48 [≈ $85]

- The Indictment, Arraignment, Tryal, and Judgment, at large, of Twenty-Nine Regicides, the Murtherers of ... King Charles the 1st. London & Dublin: Fairbrother, 1730. 8vo. Frontis port. Three qtr calf. Anon. *(Rostenberg & Stern)* **$250 [≈£140]**

Finett, Sir John
- Finetti Philoxenis: Some Choice Observations of Sir John Finett, Knight ... Touching the Reception ... of Forren Ambassadors in England. London: for Twyford & Bedell, 1656. 1st edn. 8vo. [14],250,[10] pp. Sl browning. 19th c half calf, hinge cracked. Wing F.947. *(O'Neal)* **$250 [≈£140]**
- Finetti Philoxensis: Some Choice Observations touching the Reception ... of Forren Ambassadors in England. London: 1656. 1st edn. 8vo. 250,index pp. Later calf backed bds. Wing F.947. *(Robertshaw)* **£110 [≈$196]**

The First of April ...
- See Combe, William

Fisher, Ann
- A Practical New Grammar, with Exercises of Bad English ... Appendix ... New Edition, enlarged ... London: A. Millar, E. Law, & R. Cater, & for Wilson & Spence, York, 1789. xii, 192 pp. Red & black title. Contemp sheep, sl worn. *(C.R. Johnson)* **£95 [≈$169]**

Fisher, Edward
- The Marrow of Modern Divinity ... Second Edition, Corrected, Amended and much Enlarged by the Author. London: 1646. Sm 8vo. 255 pp. Some underlining. Lower marg occas cut close. Later half calf. Wing F.997. Anon. *(Robertshaw)* **£36 [≈$64]**

Fisher, George
- The Instructor; or, The Young Man's Best Companion. London: for C. Hitch & L. Hawes, H. Woodfall ..., 1760. 16th edn. Post 12mo. xii,384 pp. Frontis, fldg plate. Thumbed & soiled, sl nicks & chips. Contemp sheep. *(Ash)* **£75 [≈$134]**

Fitzgerald, Thomas
- Poems on Several Occasions. The Second Edition. London: J. Watts, 1736. 8vo. Contemp calf gilt, spine a little worn. Anon. *(Hannas)* **£150 [≈$267]**

Fitzosborne, Sir Thomas
- The Letters of Sir Thomas Fitzosborne, On Several Subjects ... London: Dodsley, 1758.

5th edn. 8vo. xii,452 pp. Contemp speckled calf, spine trifle worn, hinges cracked but firm, lacks label. *(Vanbrugh)* **£95 [≈$169]**

Flavel, John
- Navigation Spiritualiz'd: or, a New Compass for Seamen ... Fourth Edition. London: for Tho. Parkhurst, 1698. 8vo. [xxii],118, [ii],80 pp. Frontis. Contemp panelled calf, hd of spine & jnts worn. Wing F.1173A. *(Sotheran's)* **£375 [≈$668]**

Fleetwood, William
- Chronicon Preciosum: or, an Account of English Gold and Silver Money, The Price of Corn and other Commodities ... London: for T. Osborne, 1745. 8vo. [x],147,[iii], 30,[30 ctlg], [ii] pp. 12 plates. Sl foxing. Contemp calf, rebacked. *(Sotheran's)* **£175 [≈$312]**
- Chronicon Preciosum: or, an Account of English Gold and Silver Money, The Price of Corn and other Commodities ... London: T. Osborne, 1745. 2nd edn. 8vo. [x],147,[iii], [30],[ii advt] pp. 12 plates. Title soiled. Rec half calf. *(Blackwell's)* **£200 [≈$356]**
- The Relative Duties of Parents and Children, Husbands and Wives, Masters and Servants ... London: for Charles Harper ..., 1705. 8vo. [xii],495,[1 advt] pp. Occas sl browning. Panelled calf, sl worn. *(Francis Edwards)* **£100 [≈$178]**
- A Sermon Preach'd before the Right Honourable The Lord Mayor and Court of Aldermen, At St. Mary Le Bow, on Friday the 11th of April, 1692 ... London: for Thomas Newborough, 1692. Only edn. 4to. 30 pp. Disbound. Wing F.1253. *(Young's)* **£32 [≈$57]**

Fletcher, Phineas
- Piscatory Eclogues, with other Poetical Miscellanies. Illustrated with Notes ... Edinburgh: Kincaid & Creech, 1771. 2nd edn. 8vo. viii,151,[4] pp. Half-title. Title vignette. Contemp style half calf. *(Young's)* **£90 [≈$160]**
- The Purple Island, or The Isle of Man: Together with Piscatorie Eclogs and Other Poeticall Miscellanies. By P.F. Cambridge: 1633. 1st edn. 2 parts in one vol. Sm 4to. Lacks 2R4 at end (blank). Few sl marks. Rec half calf. STC 11082. *(Vanbrugh)* **£295 [≈$525]**

Florian, Jean Pierre Claris de
- The Adventures of Numa Pompilius, Second King of Rome. Translated from the French ... London: for C. Dilly, 1787. 1st edn of this translation. 2 vols. 8vo. [4],iv,267; [2], iii,

290 pp. Contemp half calf, sl wear hd of spines.   *(Fenning)* **£85 [≈ $151]**

- Gonzalva of Cordova; or, Grenada Reconquered. Now first translated from the French. London: for J. Johnson, 1793. 1st London edn. 3 vols in one. 12mo. Possibly lacks a half-title. Contemp calf gilt, rebacked.
        (Hannas) **£250 [≈ $445]**

Florus, Lucius Annaeus
- The Roman Histories ... Translated into English [by Edmund Bolton]. London: William Stansby for Tho: Dewe, [1621?]. 1st English edn. 2nd issue, with 'Dewe' in imprint. 12mo. Final blank. Engvd title. Sl water stain at end. Contemp calf, early repr. STC 11104.   *(Hannas)* **£55 [≈ $98]**

The Flower-Piece ...
- The Flower-Piece: a Collection of Miscellany Poems. By Several hands. London: for J. Walthoe, & H. Walthoe, 1731. 1st edn. 12mo. Contemp panelled calf, upper jnt broken. John Cator's b'plate. Edited by Matthew Concanen.   *(Hannas)* **£450 [≈ $801]**

Floyer, Sir John
- [Title in greek, Psychrolousia] ... or, the History of Cold-Bathing ... in two Parts ... The Second ... by Dr Edward Baynard. London: for Benj. Walford, 1709. 3rd edn. 8vo. [xxii],426,[32] pp. 2 advt pp. Contemp panelled calf, sl worn. *(Clark)* **£185 [≈ $329]**
- [Title in greek] ... or, the History of Cold-Bathing, both Ancient and Modern. To which is added, an Appendix, by Dr Edward Baynard. The Fifth Edition. London: Innys, 1722. 8vo. [22],491, [30],[1 advt] pp. Contemp calf, gilt spine reprd at ends, new label.   *(Spelman)* **£160 [≈ $285]**

Fontenelle, Bernard le Bovier
- The History of Oracles and Cheats of the Pagan Priests. In Two Parts. Made English [by Aphra Behn]. London: Printed in the Year, 1688. 8vo. Contemp sheep, sl rubbed. Wing F.1413. Anon.
        (Waterfield's) **£175 [≈ $312]**

Foote, Samuel
- The Cozeners, a Comedy ... London: for John Wheble, 1778. 1st edn. 8vo. [4],79 pp. Rec wraps. Anon.   *(Fenning)* **£35 [≈ $62]**
- The Dramatic Works ... Prefixed A Life of the Author. London: A. Millar, 1797. 2nd coll edn (19 pieces). 2 vols. 12mo. 366; 434 pp. Vignettes (some after Bewick). Few sm lib blind stamps. Contemp sheep, sl worn.
        (Clark) **£75 [≈ $134]**

- The Dramatic Works, to which is prefixed a Life of the Author. London: Lowndes & Bladon, [1797?]. 19 sep paginated plays in 2 vols. 8vo. Calf gilt, rebacked.
        (Hartfield) **$295 [≈ £166]**

Fordyce, James
- Addresses to Young Men. London: Cadell, 1777. 1st edn. 2 vols. Sm 8vo. [iv],viii, 329,[3]; [iv],368 pp. Final advt leaf vol 1. Some offsetting. 19th c calf, jnts sl rubbed.
        (Clark) **£85 [≈ $151]**

Fordyce, W.
- A New Enquiry into the Causes, Symptoms and Cure of Putrid and Inflammatory Fevers. With an Appendix on the Hectic Fever, and on the Ulcerated and Malignant Sore Throat. London: 1777. 4th edn. xvi,228 pp. Contemp calf, rebacked.   *(Whitehart)* **£120 [≈ $214]**

The Foreigner's Guide ...
- The Foreigner's Guide: or, a necessary and instructive Companion both for the Foreigner and Native in their Tour through the Cities of London and Westminster ... London: H. Kent ..., 1763. Sm 8vo. vii,[vi],[2 advt],227,[i advt] pp. Occas sl foxing. Calf, jnts cracking.   *(Francis Edwards)* **£85 [≈ $151]**

Forrester, James
- Dialogues on the Passions, Habits, and Affections peculiar to Children ... Designed for the Use of Parents ... London: for R. Griffiths, at the Dunciad, 1748. 1st edn. 8vo. xii,59 pp. Title sl soiled. Contemp style qtr calf. Anon.   *(Burmester)* **£300 [≈ $534]**
- The Polite Philosopher or, an Essay on that Art which makes a Man Happy in himself and agreeable to to others. Edinburgh: Robert Freebairn, 1734. 1st edn. 8vo. Inner gutter of title sl defective. Disbound. Anon.
        (Waterfield's) **£45 [≈ $80]**
- The Polite Philosopher: or, an Essay on that Art which makes a Man Happy in Himself and Agreeable to Others. Dublin: S. Powell for P. Crampton, 1734. 1st edn. Lge 12mo. 56 pp. Sl soiling, few headlines touched. Rec wraps. Anon.   *(Fenning)* **£55 [≈ $98]**

Forster, John Reinhold
- History of the Voyages and Discoveries made in the North. Dublin: for Luke White, 1786. 1st Dublin edn. 8vo. 489,[30] pp. Fldg frontis map. Sm blind stamps on map & title. Orig calf, rebacked, edges sl rubbed.
        (Chapel Hill) **$250 [≈ £140]**
- Observations made during a Voyage round the World ... London: G. Robinson, 1778. 1st

edn. 4to. Title,dedic, [i]-iii,[i]-iv, [9]-649, errata, subscribers pp. Fldg map, fldg chart of languages. Rebound in calf, uncut.
(Frew Mackenzie) **£1,500 [≈ $2,670]**

Fortescue, John, Lord
- Reports of Select Cases in all the Courts of Westminster-Hall ... In the Savoy: Henry Lintot ..., 1748. 1st edn. Folio. 2 preface ff supplied in 19th c MS. Contemp calf, front bd detached.   *(Vanbrugh)* **£125 [≈ $223]**

Foster, James
- An Account of the Behaviour of the late Earl of Kilmarnock, after his Sentence, and on the Day of his Execution. London: 1746. 1st edn. 8vo. 51 pp. Mod wraps.
(Robertshaw) **£20 [≈ $36]**

Fothergill, Anthony
- Wicked Christians Practical Atheists: or Free Thoughts of a Plain Man on ... Religion in General and ... Christianity in Particular ... London: J. Payne, 1755. Only edn. 8vo. xviii, 225,[i] pp. Contemp calf, v sl worm to upper cvr.   *(Blackwell's)* **£55 [≈ $98]**

Foulis, Henry
- The History of Romish Treasons & Usurpations ... London: J.C. for Tho. Basset, 1671. 1st edn. Folio. [xliv], "726" [ie 688], [viii] pp. Half-title sl soiled. Occas marg water stain. 18th c calf, rebacked. Wing F.1640.
(Blackwell's) **£140 [≈ $249]**
- The History of the Wicked Plots and Conspiracies of our Pretended Saints ... London: E. Cotes for A. Seile, 1662. 1st edn. Sm folio. [xvi],247 pp. Occas sl spotting. Contemp sheep, some rubbing, hinges cracked but firm. Wing F.1642.
(Blackwell's) **£135 [≈ $240]**

Foulkes, Robert
- An Alarme for Sinners: Containing the Confession, Prayers, Letters, and Last Words of Robert Foulkes ... London: for Langley Curtis, 1679. 1st edn. Sm 4to. [4],39 pp. Later half calf. Wing F.1644.
(O'Neal) **$100 [≈ £56]**

Fowler, Edward
- An Answer to the Paper delivered by Mr. Ashton at his Execution to Sir Francis Child, Sheriff of London etc. Together with the Paper itself. London: 1690. 1st edn. 4to. 31 pp. Disbound. Wing F.1695. Anon.
(Robertshaw) **£25 [≈ $45]**

Fox, Charles James
- A Letter ... to the Worthy and Independent Electors of the City and Liberty of Westminster ... London: for J. Debrett, 1793. 3rd edn. 8vo. [iv],43,[4 advt] pp. Disbound.
(Young's) **£15 [≈ $27]**
- The Speech ... July 17, 1792 ... London: Debrett, 1792. New edn. 8vo. 38,[2 advt] pp. Disbound.   *(Young's)* **£16 [≈ $28]**
- The Speech ... Dec. 4th, 1792 ... London: James Ridgway, (1793). 1st edn. 8vo. 15 pp. Disbound.   *(Young's)* **£34 [≈ $61]**

Fox, George
- Gospel-Truth Demonstrated, in a Collection of Doctrinal Books, given forth by ... George Fox ... London: T. Sowle, 1706. 1st edn. Folio. [14],1090,[6] pp. Clean tear in 2 ff without loss. Contemp calf, crnrs worn.
(Fenning) **£185 [≈ $329]**
- The Great Mistery of the Great Whore Unfolded: and Antichrists Kingdom revealed unto destruction. London: for Tho: Simmons, 1659. 1st edn. Folio. Occas browning, 4 ff at end washed. Early 19th c calf, rebacked. Wing F.1832.
(Hannas) **£240 [≈ $427]**
- A Journal or Historical Account of the Life, Travels, Sufferings, Christian Experiences, and Labour of Love ... of George Fox. The Third Edition, Corrected. London: sold by Luke Hinde, 1765. Folio. [ii], lix, [i], 679,[xxix] pp. Contemp calf, backstrip relaid, crnrs reprd.   *(Clark)* **£75 [≈ $134]**

Foxton, Joseph
- Serino: or, The Character of a Fine Gentleman ... prefixed An Account of ... Joseph Addison. London: sold by T. Tonson [ie Curll], [1725]. 12mo. Port frontis. Last few margs wormed. Contemp sheep, worn, jnts breaking.   *(Sanders)* **£50 [≈ $89]**

A Fragment on Government ...
- See Bentham, Jeremy

Francis, of Sales, Saint
- A Treatise of the Love of God. Written in French by B. Francis de Sales ... Translated ... by Miles Car [ie Miles Pinkney] ... Doway: Gerard Pinchon, 1630. 1st edn in English. 8vo. Errata leaf. Engvd title, port. Contemp calf, rebacked, some rubbing. STC 11323.
(Ximenes) **$750 [≈ £421]**

Francklin, Thomas
- The Epistles of Phalaris. Translated from the Greek. To which are added, Some Select

Epistles of the most eminent Greek Writers ...
London: R. Francklin, 1749. 1st edn. 8vo.
[xiv], xxiii,224 pp. Half-title. Subscribers.
Frontis. Calf, rebacked.
                          (Young's) £38 [≈ $68]
- Sermons on Various Subjects, and preached
on Several Occasions. London: for T. Cadell,
1785-87. 2nd edn vols 1 & 2, 1st edn vol 3. 3
vols. 8vo. Contemp calf.
                    (Burmester) £600 [≈ $1,068]

Frankland, Thomas
- The Annals of King James and King Charles
the First ... London: for Clavel, 1681. Only
edn. Folio. [x],113,[i] pp, 114-129 ff [ie 14
pp], 121-568 pp, 569-604 ff [ie 72 pp],
605-913, [15] pp. Some wear & tear. Contemp
calf, old reback. Wing F.2078. Anon.
                       (Clark) £160 [≈ $285]

Franklin, Benjamin
- Experiments and Observations on Electricity,
made at Philadelphia in America ... Fifth
Edition. London: for F. Newbery, 1774. 4th.
[viii],514,[16] pp. Half-title. 7 plates. Sl
browning & foxing. Contemp tree calf,
rebacked, crnrs worn.
                     (Gaskell) £1,500 [≈ $2,670]

Franks, David
- The New-York Directory ... New York:
Shepard Kollock, 1786. 16mo. 82 pp. Each
leaf encased in mylar, browned, some margs
trimmed. Later mor gilt. Cloth slipcase.
                      (Reese) $7,500 [≈ £4,213]

Freart, Roland
- An Idea of the Perfection of Painting ...
Rendred English by J.E. [John Evelyn] ...
London: Henry Herringman, 1668. 1st (only)
English edn. 8vo. [40],136 pp. Intl & final
blanks. Rebound in calf, gilt ruled spine &
label. Wing F.1922. *(Spelman)* £350 [≈ $623]

Frederick II, King of Prussia
- Anti-Machiavel: or, an Examination of
Machiavel's Prince. With Notes Historical
and Political. Published by Mr. de Voltaire.
Translated from the French. London: for T.
Woodward, 1741. 1st English edn. 8vo. 2
advt ff. Early calf, rebacked. Anon.
                       (Hannas) £420 [≈ $748]
- Military Instructions from the late King of
Prussia to his Generals ... Particular
Instruction ... Translated from the French by
Major Foster ... Third Edition. Sherborne:
Cruttwell, [1797]. 8vo. Half-title. 13 fldg
plates. Contemp half calf, rubbed.
                     (Blackwell's) £175 [≈ $312]

Free ...
- A Free Conference touching the Present State
of England both at Home and Abroad: In
order to the Designs of France. London: E.T.
for R. Royston, 1668. 1st edn. 8vo. [viii],72
pp. Imprimatur leaf. Contemp sheep,
rebacked, crnrs sl worn. Wing F.2112.
                        (Clark) £90 [≈ $160]

The Freeholders Choice ...
- The Free Holders Choice: or, a Letter of
Advice concerning Elections. [London:
1679]. 1st edn. Folio. Drop-head title. 4 pp.
Disbound.   *(Hannas)* £25 [≈ $45]

Freeman, Samuel
- The Massachusetts Justice: Being a
Collection of the Laws of the Commonwealth
of Massachusetts, relative to the Power and
Duty of Justices of the Peace. Boston: Isaiah
Thomas & Ebenezer T. Andrews, 1795. 1st
edn. 8vo. Sl foxing & browning. Orig sheep,
v worn, rebacked.
                   (Meyer Boswell) $350 [≈ £197]

Freind, John
- Emmenologia. London: T. Cox, 1729. 1st
edn in English. 8vo. [xvi],222, [2],[16] pp.
Contemp calf, rebacked.
                      (Bookpress) $275 [≈ £154]

Frejus, Roland
- The Relation of a Voyage made into
Mauritania, in Africk ... in the Year 1666 ...
English'd out of French. London: Godbid &
Pitt, 1671. 1st edn in English. 2 parts in 1 vol.
Sm 8vo. [viii],119,[1]; [ii],71,[1] pp. 3 advt ff
at end. Contemp sheep, rebacked. Wing
F.2161.   *(Burmester)* £850 [≈ $1,513]

The French Spy ...
- See Courtilz de Sandras, Gatien de

Frith, John
- A boke made by John Fryth prysoner in the
tower of London ... Newly corrected ...
London: Richard Jugge, [1548]. 3rd edn. 108
ff. Sl cropped, sl marked. 18th c calf, gilt
spine, jnts cracked but firm, crnrs sl worn.
Cloth box. STC 11383.
                       (Clark) £750 [≈ $1,335]

Frowde, Neville
- The Life, Extraordinary Adventures,
Voyages, and Surprising Escapes ... see
Kimber, Edward.

Fryer, John
- A New Account of East India and Persia ...

Nine Years' Travels ... London: for Ri. Chiswell, 1698. 1st edn. Folio. [ix],427,xxiv pp. 3 maps, port (half-title on verso), 5 plates, text ills. Contemp style dark calf.
(Gough) **£750 [≈ $1,335]**

Fugitive Pieces ...

- Fugitive Pieces, on Various Subjects. By Various Authors. The Third Edition. London: Dodsley, 1771. Contemp calf, red labels. *(C.R. Johnson)* **£55 [≈ $98]**

Fulbecke, William

- A Direction or Preparative to the Study of the Law ... London: for the Company of Stationers, 1620. Browned. Vellum, worn & loose. STC 11411. Anon.
(Meyer Boswell) **$950 [≈ £534]**

Fulke, William

- A Retentive to stay good Christians, in true faith and religion, against the motives of Richard Bristow ... London: Thomas Vautrollier for George Bishop, 1580. 1st edn. Sm 8vo. [viii],316,[2] pp. Sl marks & marg worm. Contemp limp vellum, sl worn. STC 11449. *(Clark)* **£480 [≈ $854]**

Fuller, Samuel

- A Serious Reply to the Twelve Sections of Abusive Inquiries proposed to the Consideration of the People called Quakers ... Dublin: the author, 1728. 1st edn. 8vo. 146, [2],index pp. Calf, rebacked.
(Hartfield) **$245 [≈ £138]**

Fuller, Thomas, 1608-1661

- The Church-History of Britain; from the Birth of Jesus Christ, until the Year 1648. London: Williams, 1655. 1st edn. Folio. [viii], 1-171,[ix], 1-200,(153)-427,[ix], 1-235, [ix], 1-114,[vi],117-238, [x], 1-172, 22, [xx] Fldg plan, 4 plates. Rec half mor. Wing F.2416. *(Clark)* **£260 [≈ $463]**
- A Happy Handful, or Green Hopes in the Blade ... London: for John Williams, 1660. 1st edn. Sm 4to. Mod calf. Wing F.2437. Anon. *(Ximenes)* **$650 [≈ £365]**
- The History of the Worthies of England. London: 1662. 1st edn. Folio. [viii],300, 317-368, 354,232,60 pp. Intl blank. Frontis port (creased). Sep title to 'Wales'. Sl wear & tear. Contemp calf, rebacked, some rubbing. Wing F.2440. *(Blackwell's)* **£225 [≈ $401]**
- The History of the Worthies of England. London: ptd by J.G.W.L. & W.G., 1662. 1st edn. Folio. Port. 12-page 1737 index bound at end. Lacks intl blank. Elab gilt citron mor, a.e.g., by Riviere, trivial rubbing. Wing

F.2440. *(Georges)* **£600 [≈ $1,068]**
- The Holy State. Cambridge: Roger Daniel ..., 1642. 1st edn. Sm folio. [viii],441 pp. 20 ports. Some wear & tear. Lacks engvd title. Old calf, rebacked, somewhat worn, some loss of leather. Wing F.2443.
(Bow Windows) **£105 [≈ $187]**
- Introductio ad Prudentiam: or Directions, Counsels and Cautions, tending to Prudent Management of Affairs in Common Life ... London: for Wyat & Austin, 1726-27. 2nd edn & 1st edn. 2 parts in one vol. 8vo. vii,217,[5 advt]; viii,242,[2 advt] pp. Early calf. *(Young's)* **£190 [≈ $338]**

Fuller, Thomas, 1654-1734

- Pharmacopoeia Extemporanea: or, A Body of Medicines, containing a Thousand Select Prescripts ... Fourth Edition. London: 1730. 8vo. Port. Blind stamp on title. Contemp calf, rebacked. *(Robertshaw)* **£75 [≈ $134]**

Fuller, William

- A Plain Proof of the True Father and Mother of the Pretended Prince of Wales, by Several Letters written by the late Queen in France ... London: for the author, 1700. 1st edn. 8vo. 16 pp. Some page numerals cropped. Rec qtr calf. Wing F.2485. *(Young's)* **£60 [≈ $107]**
- The Whole Life of Mr. William Fuller ... Impartially writ, by Himself, during his Confinement to the Queen's-Bench. London: most booksellers in London & Westminster, 1703. 1st edn. 8vo. Port. Browned. Contemp calf, rebacked, Signet Library arms.
(Hannas) **£150 [≈ $267]**
- The Whole Life of Mr. William Fuller ... Impartially writ, by Himself ... London: 1703. 1st edn. 8vo. [viii],142 pp. Port (sl frayed, rehinged). Browned. BM duplicate. Old calf, rebacked, rubbed, crnrs sl worn. *(Clark)* **£160 [≈ $285]**

Fullwood, Francis

- Obedience due to the Present King, Notwithstanding our Oaths to the Former. Written by a Divine of the Church of England. London: for Awnsham Churchill, 1689. 1st edn. 4to. 8 pp. Disbound. Wing F.2511. Anon. *(Young's)* **£85 [≈ $151]**

Furber, J.

- A Short Introduction to Gardening: or, a Guide to Gentlemen and Ladies, in furnishing their Gardens. Being several useful Catalogues of Fruits and Flowers. London: 1733. 8vo. [xviii],68,[1] pp. 2 plates. Half calf, trifle rubbed.
(Wheldon & Wesley) **£500 [≈ $890]**

Furley, J. Dennis

- Choheleth, or The Royal Preacher, A Poem. Most humbly inscribed to the King. London: for the author, & sold by W. Johnston, 1765. 1st edn. 4to. [ii],xxv,[i errata],141,[3 blank] pp. 19th c half roan, front jnt weak, spine ends worn, extrs rubbed. Anon.
(Finch) **£125 [≈ $223]**

Gage, Thomas

- A New Survey of the West-Indies: or, The English American his Travel by Sea and Land ... London: 1677. 3rd edn. 8vo. "577" [ie 477], [18] pp. V sl foxing at end. Lacks map. Early 20th c mor gilt, a.e.g., gilt dentelles.
(Chapel Hill) **$750 [≈ £421]**

Galba. A Dialogue on the Navy ...

- See Moncreiff, John

Gale, Thomas

- An Antidotarie conteyning Hidde and Secrete Medicines Simple and Compounde: as also all suche as are required in Chirurgerie. London: Thomas Gale, 1563. 1st edn. Sm 8vo. [3],90 ff. 19th c calf, rebacked.
(Bookpress) **$750 [≈ £421]**

Galen of Pergamon

- Galen's Method of Physick ... Commentary ... by its translator, Peter English. Edinburgh: A.A. for Svintoun & Glen, 1656. 12mo. [4],344 pp. Some gatherings loose. Calf, rebacked.
(Goodrich) **$1,750 [≈ £983]**

Galloway, Joseph

- A Candid Examination of the Mutual Claims of Great-Britain and the Colonies ... New York: James Rivington, 1775. State without errata on title verso. [2],62 pp. Later three qtr mor. Anon.
(Reese) **$1,000 [≈ £562]**

Gambado, Geoffrey

- An Academy for Grown Horsemen ... see Bunbury, Henry W.

Garat, D.

- Memoirs of the Revolution; or, An Apology for my Conduct, in the Public Employments which I have held ... Edinburgh: for G. Mudie & Son, 1797. 1st edn. 8vo. iii,281 pp. Half calf, edges sl rubbed.
(Young's) **£40 [≈ $71]**

Gardiner, Ralph

- Englands Grievance Discovered, in relation to the Coal Trade, with the Map of the River Tine, and Situation of the Town and Corporation of Newcastle. Newcastle: D.

Akenhead, 1796. 2nd edn. 8vo. viii,216 pp. Fldg map, 3 plates, 17 ports. 19th c calf, rubbed.
(Young's) **£100 [≈ $178]**

Garencieres, Theophilus

- General Instructions, Divine, Moral, Historical, Figurative, &c. shewing the Progress of Religion from the Creation to this time ... York: J. White for the author, 1728. 8vo. Lacks front f.e.p. 2 gatherings sl loose. Contemp sheep, worn but sound.
(Waterfield's) **£45 [≈ $80]**

Garrick, David

- The Fribbleriad. London: for J. Coote, 1761. 1st edn. 4to. Frontis (offset). Mod qtr mor, vellum crnrs. Anon.
(Hannas) **£850 [≈ $1,513]**

- Lethe. A Dramatic Satire ... as it is performed at the Theatre-Royal in Drury-Lane ... London: Paul Vaillant, 1749. 1st authorized edn. 8vo. Half-title (marg torn, dust soiled). Mod half calf. *(Hannas)* **£110 [≈ $196]**

Garth, Samuel

- The Dispensary. A Poem. London: Tonson, 1714. 7th edn. 8vo. [22],84 pp. 7 plates. Sl browning. Contemp calf, rebacked. Anon.
(O'Neal) **$95 [≈ £53]**

- The Dispensary. A Poem ... With severall Descriptions and Episodes never before Printed. London: for J.T., 1726. 9th edn. 8vo. [xx],84 pp. 7 plates. Edges browned. New bds. Anon. *(Young's)* **£55 [≈ $98]**

- The Poetical Works ... Glasgow: Foulis, 1771. 16mo. [8],158,[2] pp. Contemp calf, rebacked. *(Goodrich)* **$95 [≈ £53]**

Garthwait, Henry

- [Greek title, then] The Evangelicall Harmonie, reducing the foure Evangelists into one Continued Context ... Cambridge: Buck & Daniel, 1634. 1st edn. 4to. [xxii],262,[ii] pp. Lacks intl blank. Contemp half calf, worn. STC 11633.
(Clark) **£110 [≈ $196]**

Garvey, Gideon

- The Vanities of Philosophy and Physick: Together with Directions and Medicines easily prepared ... London: 1700. 2nd edn, enlgd. 143 pp. Old calf, rebacked, new endpapers, hd of spine chipped.
(King) **$250 [≈ £140]**

Gastrell, Francis

- The Religious Education of Poor Children recommended, in a Sermon ... London: Joseph Downing, for Bowyer & Clement,

1707. 1st edn. 8vo. 16 pp. Disbound.
(Burmester) **£25** [≈ **$45**]

Gataker, Thomas
- Of the Nature and Use of Lots: a Treatise Historicall and Theologicall. London: Edward Griffin, sold by William Bladen, 1619. 8vo. Contemp vellum, jnts sl strained. STC 11670. *(Waterfield's)* **£225** [≈ **$401**]
- Of the Nature and Use of Lots. A Treatise Historicall and Theologicall. The Second Edition ... enlarged ... London: John Haviland, 1627. Sm 4to. [xvi],416,[4] pp. Minute wormholes through bottom of central text. Period calf, sl worn. STC 11671.
(Rankin) **£160** [≈ **$285**]

Gauger, Nicholas
- Fires Improv'd; being a New Method of Building Chimneys, so as to prevent their smoaking ... made English and improved by J.T. Desaguliers ... London: 1715. 1st edn. Sm 8vo. [vi],161,[9],[2 ctlg] pp. 9 fldg plates. Contemp polished calf.
(Weiner) **£300** [≈ **$534**]

Gavin, Antonio
- A Short History of Monastical Orders, in which the Primitive Institution of Monks, Their Tempers, Habits, Rules ... are Treated of. By Gabriel d'Emillianne [pseudonym]. London: 1693. 1st English edn. 8vo. 312 pp. Contemp calf, rebacked. Wing G.394.
(Robertshaw) **£48** [≈ **$85**]

Gay, John
- Achilles. An Opera ... With the Musick ... London: for J. Watts, 1733. 1st edn. 8vo. half-title (dust soiled). 2 advt ff. Disbound.
(Hannas) **£85** [≈ **$151**]
- Achilles. An Opera. London: for J. Watts, 1733. 1st edn. 8vo. 2 advt ff. Lacks half-title. Red straight grained mor, t.e.g., by Sangorski & Sutcliffe. *(Ximenes)* **$350** [≈ **£197**]
- Achilles. An Opera. With the Musick prefix'd to each Song. London: J. Watts, 1733. 1st edn. 8vo. [6],68,[5] pp. Lacks half-title. Rec cloth backed mrbld bds.
(Hartfield) **$295** [≈ **£166**]
- The Distress'd Wife. London: for Thomas Astley, 1743. 1st edn. 8vo. 88 pp. Lacks half-title. Title dust soiled, tear in 1 leaf (no loss). Early wraps, uncut. *(Hannas)* **£40** [≈ **$71**]
- Fables of Mr. John Gay, with an Italian Translation by Gian Francesco Giorgetti. London: for T. Davies, 1773. 1st edn thus. 8vo. Contemp calf, backstrip laid down.
(Ximenes) **$350** [≈ **£197**]

- Poems on Several Occasions. London: Tonson & Lintot, 1720. 1st coll edn. 2 vols. 4to. Subscribers. Frontis, 2 plates. Contemp calf, worn, jnts reprd.
(Hannas) **£120** [≈ **$214**]
- Poems on Several Occasions. London: for H. Lintot, & J. & R. Tonson, 1737. 3rd coll edn. 2 vols. 12mo. Frontis vol 1, 2 plates. Contemp mottled calf gilt, trifle rubbed.
(Ximenes) **$150** [≈ **£84**]
- The Shepherd's Week. In Six Pastorals. London: sold by Ferd. Burleigh, 1714. 1st edn. 8vo. frontis, 6 plates. Calf gilt, backstrip relaid. *(Ximenes)* **$450** [≈ **£253**]
- The Shepherd's Week. In Six Pastorals. London: Tonson, 1721. 8vo. 7 plates in collation. Sl traces of use. Disbound, loose.
(Hannas) **£70** [≈ **$125**]
- Trivia: or, the Art of Walking the Streets of London. London: for Bernard Lintot, [1716]. 1st edn. Fine Paper issue, with engvd headpieces. Early 20th c green half mor, gilt spine.
(Hannas) **£380** [≈ **$676**]
- Trivia ... The Second Edition. London: for Bernard Lintot, [1716]. 8vo. [4],65,[10] pp. Title vignette. Disbound.
(Hannas) **£200** [≈ **$356**]
- Two Epistles; one, to the Right Honourable Richard Earl of Burlington; the Other, to a Lady. London: for Bernard Lintot, [1717]. 1st edn. 8vo. Sep title to 2nd poem marked 'fifth edition'. Half-title. 2 advt ff. Rec wraps.
(Ximenes) **$850** [≈ **£478**]

Gaynam, John
- Marlborough Still Conquers: or, Union has got the Day. A Poem, upon the late Victory ... London: H. Hills, 1708. 8vo. 16 pp. Disbound. *(Hannas)* **£70** [≈ **$125**]

Gayton, Edmund
- Pleasant Notes upon Don Quixot. London: William Hunt, 1654. 1st edn. Sm folio. [xiv], "290" [ie 288] pp. Possibly lacks an intl leaf. Some browning & marg worming. Mod calf, sl rubbed. Wing G.415.
(Blackwell's) **£800** [≈ **$1,424**]

Gedde, John
- The English Apiary: or, the Compleat Bee-Master ... London: Curll, Mears, Corbet, 1721-22. 12mo. xxii,82,87-108 pp. Frontis (outer marg sl trimmed). Lacks the blank leaf between the 2 parts. Contemp sheep, rebacked. *(Blackwell's)* **£210** [≈ **$374**]

Geddes, Alexander
- L'Avocat du Diable: The Devil's Advocate;

or, Satan Versus Pictor. Tried before the
Court of Uncommon Pleas ... London:
Johnson & Faulder, 1792. 4to. 19 pp. Sl dusty
& browned. Mod qtr calf. Anon.
                    (Meyer Boswell) **$750 [≈ £421]**

Geddes, Michael
- The Church-History of Ethiopia ... London:
for Ri. Chiswell, 1696. 1st edn. 8vo. [xxiv],
488 pp. Occas marg worm hole. Rec contemp
style calf. Wing G.4444.
                    (Young's) **£145 [≈ $258]**

Gee, Joshua
- The Trade and Navigation of Great-Britain
Considered. Second Edition. London: 1730.
8vo. 147 pp. Disbound. Anon.
                    (Robertshaw) **£75 [≈ $134]**

Gellert, C.E.
- Metallurgic Chymistry. Being a System of
Mineralogy in General, and of all the Arts
arising from this Science ... London: T.
Becket, 1776. Half-title. 4 fldg plates. Fldg
table supplied in facsimile. Later sheep, gilt
spine.   (P and P Books) **£325 [≈ $579]**

General ...
- A General Index to The Spectators, Tatlers
and Guardians. London: W. Owen, 1757. 1st
edn. Sm 8vo. Contemp calf, hinges sl cracked.
                    (Black Sun) **$350 [≈ £197]**

**Genlis, Felicite Ducrest de Saint-Aubin,
Comtesse de**
- The Knights of the Swan; or, the Court of
Charlemagne: an Historical and Moral Tale
... Dublin: for P. Wogan ..., 1797. 1st Irish
edn. 2 vols. 12mo. Sev sections browned.
Contemp half calf, gilt spines, minor rubbing.
                    (Ximenes) **$250 [≈ £140]**
- Tales of the Castle ... Translated into English
by Thomas Holcroft. London: Robinson,
1785. 1st edn. 5 vols. Lge 12mo. Half-titles.
V sl worming (no loss). Contemp calf gilt, sl
rubbed.   (Blackwell's) **£325 [≈ $579]**
- Theatre of Education. Translated from the
French. London: for T. Cadell ..., 1781. 1st
edn in English. 4 vols. 8vo. Half-titles. No
port. 19th c half cloth.
                    (Claude Cox) **£45 [≈ $80]**

Gent, Thomas
- Annales Regioduni Hullini; or, The History
of the Royal and Beautiful Town of Kingston-
upon-Hull. York: sold by Ward & Chandler
..., 1735. 1st edn. 8vo. Subscribers. W'cut
map, fldg view, 4 plates, some w'cut text ills.
Diced calf, mor reback.

                    (Hannas) **£160 [≈ $285]**
- The Antient and Modern History of the
Famous City of York ... York: for Thomas
Hammond, 1730. 1st edn. 1st imp, with
crown p 84. Fcap 8vo. viii,256,[8] pp. Fldg
plan, fldg view, 6 w'cut ills & decs. Inserted
w'cut p 171. Contemp calf, rebacked.
                    (Spelman) **£180 [≈ $320]**
- The Antient and Modern History of the
Famous City of York ... By T.G. [Thomas
Gent]. York & London: Thomas Hammond &
A. Bettesworth, 1730. 12mo. viii,256,[8] pp.
Fldg map (sm repr), 2 ills. Old calf, rebacked,
sl worn.   (D & D Galleries) **$150 [≈ £84]**
- The Antient and Modern History of the
Famous City of York ... York: for Thomas
Hammond, 1730. 1st edn. 1st imp, with
crown p 84. Fcap 8vo. viii,256,[8] pp. Fldg
plan, fldg view, 6 w'cut ills & decs. Without
the inserted w'cut p 171. Contemp calf,
rebacked.   (Spelman) **£160 [≈ $285]**
- The Antient and Modern History of the
Famous City of York ... York: for Thomas
Hammond, 1730. 1st edn, 2nd imp. Fcap
8vo. viii,256,[8] pp. Fldg plan, fldg view, 6
w'cut ills & decs. Without the inserted w'cut
p 171. 19th c half calf, backstrip relaid.
                    (Spelman) **£140 [≈ $249]**
- The Antient and Modern History of the
Loyal Town of Rippon ... York: 1733. 8vo.
xvi, [170], 73,[2 advt],[2 list of carriers], [2
subscribers] pp. 76 w'cuts inc fldg frontis
(reprd). Rebound in qtr calf.
                    (Francis Edwards) **£150 [≈ $267]**
- The Antient and Modern History of the
Loyal Town of Ripon ... York: at the Printing
Office ..., 1733. 1st edn. 7 advt pp at
end. Subscribers. Fldg map & view of
Rippon, num w'cut text ills. Citron mor gilt,
a.e.g., by S. Wright, fine.
                    (Hannas) **£280 [≈ $498]**

Gentleman ...
- The Gentleman and Lady's Key to Polite
Literature; or, a Compendious Dictionary of
Fabulous History ... London: T. Carnan & F.
Newbery, 1776. 12mo. [126] ff. Engvd title &
frontis. Contemp calf, backstrip relaid.
                    (Spelman) **£80 [≈ $142]**
- The Gentleman's Calling ... see Allestree,
Richard
- The Gentleman's Recreation ... see Cox, N.

Geography ...
- Geography for Children or A Short and Easy
Method of Teaching and Learning
Geography. London: J. Johnson & E.
Newbery, [ca 1787]. 15th edn. 10,141,10,[5

advt] pp. 2 fldg frontis. Orig calf bds, rather stained, ft of spine worn.
(James) **£110 [≈ $196]**

- Geography Reformed. A New System of General Geography, according to an Accurate Analysis of the Science ... The Second Edition. London: E. Cave, 1749. 315,2 advt pp. Contemp qtr calf, mrbld bds, hinges weakening. *(C.R. Johnson)* **£125 [≈ $223]**

Georgirenes, Joseph
- A Description of the Present State of Samos, Nicaria, Patmos, and Mount Athos. Translated by One that knew the Author in Constantinople. London: W.G. & sold by Moses Pitt, 1678. 12 pp. Contemp sheep, sl rubbed. Wing G.536.
(C.R. Johnson) **£650 [≈ $1,157]**

Gersaint, Edme Francois
- A Catalogue and Description of the Etchings of Rembrandt Van-Rhyn, with Some Account of his Life ... Translated from the French. London: T. Jeffreys, 1752. 8vo. [8], 184 pp. Frontis. Contemp calf, rebacked.
(Ars Libri) **$450 [≈ £253]**

Gessner, Salomon
- Idyls, or Pastoral Poems; to which is annexed, a Letter to M. Fuesslin, on Landscape Painting. Translated from the German ... Edinburgh: for Mudie & Constable, 1798. 1st edn of this translation. 12mo. xviii, 140 pp. Half-title. 2 plates. Contemp calf.
(Burmester) **£75 [≈ $134]**
- New Idylles. Translated by W. Hooper M.D. With a Letter to M. Fuslin, on Landscape Painting, and the Two Friends of Bourbon, a Moral Tale, by M. Diderot. London: 1776. Sm 4to. Illust title, 22 engvs. Calf gilt, sl worn. *(Francis Edwards)* **£175 [≈ $312]**

Gibbon, Edward
- The History of the Decline and Fall of the Roman Empire. London: Strahan & Cadell, 1782-88. Vols 1-3 "New Edition", vols 4-6 1st edn. 6 vols. 4to. Port frontis, fldg map. Orig mrbld bds, rebacked in brown calf, orig leather labels.
(Frew Mackenzie) **£950 [≈ $1,691]**
- Miscellaneous Works ... Notes ... by John Lord Sheffield. London: Strahan ..., 1796. 1st edn. 2 vols. 4to. Cancels as usual. Frontis silhouette port vol 1. Contemp calf, rebacked to style, yellow edges, crnrs sl worn. A 3rd 4to vol was published in 1815.
(Blackwell's) **£295 [≈ $525]**
- Miscellaneous Works ... With Memoirs of his Life and Writings composed by himself:

Illustrated from his Letters with Occasional Notes and Narrative by John Lord Sheffield. Dublin: P. Wogan ..., [1796]. 3 vols. Silhouette frontis. Contemp qtr russia, fine.
(C.R. Johnson) **£180 [≈ $320]**

Gibbons, Thomas
- Memoirs of the Rev. Isaac Watts. London: James Buckland & Thomas Gibbons, 1780. 1st edn. 8vo. [xii],491,[ix] pp. 8 advt pp. Port frontis. Rec half calf. *(Clark)* **£110 [≈ $196]**
- Rhetoric; or a View of its Principal Tropes and Figures ... London: J. & W. Oliver, 1767. [16],478,[2 advt] pp. Frontis. Contemp calf, rebacked. *(C.R. Johnson)* **£185 [≈ $329]**
- Rhetoric; or, a View of its Principal Tropes and Figures ... London: J. & W. Oliver, 1767. 1st edn. 8vo. [16],478 pp. Frontis. Occas foxing & browning. Contemp calf, jnts & crnrs reprd, new label.
(Spelman) **£220 [≈ $392]**

Gibbs, James
- Bibliotheca Radcliviana: or, a Short Description of the Radcliffe Library, at Oxford ... London: for the author, 1747. Only edn. Lge folio. 12 pp. Port of Gibbs by Hogarth, port of Radcliffe by Kneller, 21 plates. Contemp style half calf.
(Vanbrugh) **£655 [≈ $1,166]**
- Rules for Drawing the Several Parts of Architecture ... London: Innys ..., 1753. 3rd edn. Folio. viii,28 pp. 63 (of 64, lacks plate 61) plates. Contemp qtr calf, worn.
(Bookpress) **$300 [≈ £169]**

Gibson, Edmund
- The Causes of the Discontents in relation to the Plague, and the Provisions against it fairly stated and consider'd. London: for J. Roberts, 1721. 4to. 14 pp. Rebound in bds, uncut. Anon. *(C.R. Johnson)* **£165 [≈ $294]**
- Synodus Anglicana: Or, the Constitution and proceedings of the English Convocation ... London: Churchill, 1702. 1st edn. 8vo. [ii],xii, [x-xiv], 222, "306" [ie 266],[x] pp. Contemp calf, mor label, spine & crnrs worn. *(Blackwell's)* **£60 [≈ $107]**

Gibson, James
- A Journal of the Late Siege by the Troops from North America, against the French at Cape Breton ... London: J. Newbery, 1747. viii, 9-46 pp. Lacks map. Occas foxing. 19th c polished calf. *(Reese)* **$1,000 [≈ £562]**

Gibson, Thomas
- The Birth of Christ, an Irregular Ode. Cambridge: Fletcher & Hodson ..., 1765. 1st

edn. 4to. 18 pp. Last leaf soiled, sl marg damp staining. Disbound.
(Burmester) **£250 [≈ $445]**

Gilbert, Sir Geoffrey

- The Law of Devises, Revocations, and Last Wills. To which is added, choice Precedents of Wills. London: henry Lintot, for T. Waller, 1756. 1st edn. 8vo. viii,[12], 254, [38] pp. Sl browned, 1st few ff sl dog-eared. Contemp style qtr calf.
(Burmester) **£150 [≈ $267]**

- The Law of Evidence. Fourth Edition, corrected; with many additions ... London: His Majesty's Law Printers ..., 1777. 8vo. [iv], 286,[76] pp, advt leaf. Few ff sl water stained at ft. Contemp calf.
(Burmester) **£75 [≈ $134]**

- Reports of Cases in Equity ... in the Courts of Chancery and Exchequer, chiefly in the Reign of King George I ... In the Savoy: 1734. 1st edn. Folio. [viii],275,[276-296] pp. Contemp calf, hinges cracked but firm.
(Vanbrugh) **£145 [≈ $258]**

Gilbert, S.

- The Florist's Vade-Mecum, being a Choice Compendium ... the Rarest Flowers and Plants that our Climate and Skill ... will perswade to live with us. London: 1682. 12mo. [xxii], 1-120, 131-252, [22], [almanack 36] pp, correct. Port. Contemp calf, rebacked, edges reprd.
(Wheldon & Wesley) **£120 [≈ $214]**

Gilbert, Thomas

- A View of the Town: in an Epistle to a Friend in the Country. A Satire. London: R. Penny, for the author, sold by A. Dodd [probably an Edinburgh piracy], 1735. 1st 8vo edn. [6],20 pp, final blank leaf. Disbound. Anon.
(Hannas) **£120 [≈ $214]**

Gilchrist, Ebenezer

- The Use of Sea Voyages in Medicine; and particularly in a Consumption: with Observations on that Disease. London: for T. Cadell, 1771. 3rd edn, enlgd. 8vo. xiii, [iii], 308,[12] pp. Half-title. Sl marg stain few ff. Single worm hole. Contemp calf, sl worn.
(Burmester) **£150 [≈ $267]**

Gillett, Charles Ripley Gillett

- See under McAlpin Collection

Gillies, John

- The History of Ancient Greece. Its Colonies and Conquests. London: 1792-93. 3rd edn. 4 vols. 8vo. Engvd frontis, 2 fldg maps.

Contemp calf, hinges tender.
(Worldwide) **$75 [≈ £42]**

- A View of the Reign of Frederick II of Prussia; with a Parallel between that Prince and Philip II of Macedon. London: Strahan & Cadell, 1789. 8vo. [iii],503,[i advt] pp. Lacks half-title. Contemp mrbld calf, elab gilt flat spine, sl rubbed.
(Blackwell's) **£55 [≈ $98]**

Gilpin, William

- An Essay upon Prints. The Second Edition. London: G. Scott, 1768. Fcap 8vo. xii,[2], 246, [12] pp. Occas sl foxing, v sm stamp on pastedown. Contemp half calf, rebacked.
(Spelman) **£90 [≈ $160]**

- An Exposition of the New Testament ... Second Edition. London: R. Blamire, 1793. 2 vols. 8vo. lx,iv,408; v,[1],458,ctlg pp. Contemp continental stained calf, spine ends sl chipped, some rubbing.
(Spelman) **£45 [≈ $80]**

- Observations relative chiefly to Picturesque Beauty ... particularly the Mountains and Lakes of Cumberland, and Westmorland. London: Blamire, 1786. 1st edn. 2 vols. 8vo. [2],xxxi,[i],xvi,230; [2],268, xvi pp. 28 plates. Contemp calf, a.e.g., spines rubbed, new labels
(Spelman) **£160 [≈ $285]**

- Observations Relative Chiefly to Picturesque Beauty ... particularly the High-Lands of Scotland. London: Blamire, 1789. 1st edn. 2 vols. 8vo. xi,221; [2],196, xx,[i] pp. 40 plates (inc 5 maps & 1 plan). Contemp calf, rebacked.
(Spelman) **£200 [≈ $356]**

- Observations Relative Chiefly to Picturesque Beauty ... particularly the High-Lands of Scotland. Second Edition. London: Blamire, 1792. 2 vols. 8vo. xi,[i], 221; [2],195,[i],xvi pp. 40 plates (inc 5 maps & 1 plan). Contemp tree calf, elab gilt, fine.
(Spelman) **£350 [≈ $623]**

- Observations Relative Chiefly to Picturesque Beauty ... particularly the Highlands of Scotland. London: Blamire, 1792. 2nd edn. 2 vols in one. 8vo. xvi,221; 195 pp. 40 plates. Old half calf gilt, v rubbed.
(Hollett) **£130 [≈ $231]**

- Observations on the Western Parts of England, relative chiefly to Picturesque Beauty ... added, a Few Remarks on the Picturesque Beauties of the Isle of Wight. London: 1798. 8vo. xvi,359,advt pp. 18 plates (v sl offset). Mod qtr mor.
(Francis Edwards) **£140 [≈ $249]**

- Observations on the Western Parts of England, relative chiefly to Picturesque Beauty ... London: Cadell & Davies, 1798. 1st edn. 8vo. xvi,359,[1] pp. 18 plates. Orig bds, uncut, backstrip chipped.
(Spelman) **£280 [≈ $498]**

- Observations on the River Wye, and several Parts of South Wales, &c. relative chiefly to Picturesque Beauty ... London: for R. Blamire ..., 1782. 1st edn. 8vo. [iv],vii,[v],99 pp. Half-title. 16 hand-tinted aquatint plates. Contemp tree calf, gilt spine sl rubbed.
  (Burmester) £150 [≈ $267]
- Observations on the River Wye, and several Parts of South Wales, &c. relative chiefly to Picturesque Beauty ... Second Edition. London: Blamire, 1789. 8vo. xvi,152 pp. 17 oval aquatint plates. Contemp tree calf, rebacked. *(Spelman)* £140 [≈ $249]
- Observations on the River Wye, and several Parts of South Wales, &c. relative chiefly to Picturesque Beauty ... Third Edition. London: Blamire, 1792. 8vo. xvi,152 pp, advt leaf. 17 oval aquatint plates. Contemp tree calf, elab gilt spine. *(Spelman)* £220 [≈ $392]
- Remarks on Forest Scenery ... Illustrated by the Scenes of New-Forest in Hampshire. London: Blamire, 1791. 1st edn. 2 vols. 8vo. [4],vii,[i], 328,iv,7; [2],308,iii, [i],xx pp. Map, 31 plates. Contemp half calf, gilt spines.
  (Spelman) £180 [≈ $320]
- Remarks on Forest Scenery ... Illustrated by the Scenes of New-Forest in Hampshire. London: Blamire, 1794. 2nd edn. 2 vols. 8vo. vii,[i], 340,iv,; [4],310,[2 ctlg],iv errata, iv, 30,xx pp. Map, 31 plates. Contemp tree calf gilt, elab gilt spines, yellow edges.
  (Spelman) £350 [≈ $623]
- Sermons Preached to a Country Congregation: to which are added, a Few Hints for Sermons. Lymington: 1799-1805. 1st edn. 4 vols. 8vo. Contemp sprinkled calf, spines sl rubbed. *(Spelman)* £85 [≈ $151]
- Three Dialogues on the Amusements of Clergymen. London: B. & J. White, 1796. Half-title, 224 pp. Contemp half calf, rebacked. Anon.
  (C.R. Johnson) £125 [≈ $223]
- Three Essays: on Picturesque Beauty; on Picturesque Travel; and on Sketching Landscape. London: for Blamire, 1792. 1st edn. Half-title, vii dedic,88 pp. 7 aquatint plates (1 hand cold). Contemp tree calf gilt, rebacked, crnrs sl worn (1 reprd).
  (Europa) £100 [≈ $178]
- Three Essays ... London: Blamire, 1792. 1st edn. 8vo. [iv],viii,88, v,[iii],44,iii pp. 7 aquatint plates. Contemp qtr sheep, uncut, hinges cracked, cvrs rubbed.
  (Bookpress) $450 [≈ £253]
- Three Essays: on Picturesque Beauty; on Picturesque Travel; and on Sketching Landscape ... Second Edition. London: Blamire, 1794. 8vo. [2],viii,143, [i],[iii], [i ctlg] pp, errata leaf. Half-title. 7 plates (1

cold, 5 tinted). Contemp tree calf, elab gilt spine. *(Spelman)* £280 [≈ $498]
- Three Essays ... London: Blamire, 1794. 2nd edn. 8vo. viii,143,[1],5 7 plates. Orig cloth backed bds, uncut, minor rubbing.
  (Bookpress) $275 [≈ £154]
- See also the companion IRBP volume Voyages, Travel and Exploration.

Gisbert, Blaise
- Christian Eloquence in Theory and Practice. Made English from the French Original, by Samuel D'Oyley. London: H. Clements, 1718. 8vo. [32],435,[1 errata] pp. Single marg worm hole in 1st 60 pp. Contemp panelled calf, label sl chipped, sm crack hd of spine.
  (Spelman) £75 [≈ $134]

Gisborne, Thomas
- An Enquiry into the Duties of Men in the Higher and Middle Classes of Society in Great Britain ... London: Davis for White, 1794. 1st edn. 4to. [8],648 pp. Browning to margs of 1st & last ff. Contemp calf, rebacked. *(O'Neal)* $300 [≈ £169]
- An Enquiry into the Duties of the Female Sex. The Fourth Edition, Corrected. London: 1799. 8vo. viii,448 pp. Old calf, rebacked.
  (Bow Windows) £75 [≈ $134]
- The Principles of Moral Philosophy Investigated, and briefly applied to the Constitution of Civil Society ... The Third Edition, corrected ... London: B. & J. White, 1795. Half-title,367 pp. Orig bds, uncut, hinges cracked.
  (C.R. Johnson) £110 [≈ $196]
- Walks in a Forest: or, Poems Descriptive of Scenery and Incidents Characteristic of a Forest ... Second Edition, Corrected and Enlarged. London: Davis for White, 1796. 8vo. [xii],123 pp. Contemp polished calf, mor label, front jnt sl tender. *(Finch)* £90 [≈ $160]

Glanvill, Joseph
- Lux Orientalis, or an Enquiry into the Opinion of the Eastern Sages ... London: 1662. 1st edn. 8vo. [xl],192 pp. Few old lib stamps, sl damp staining. Contemp calf, hd of spine sl defective, jnts cracked but firm. Wing G.814. Anon. *(Clark)* £250 [≈ $445]
- Saducismus Triumphatus: or, Full and Plaine Evidence concerning Witches and Apparitions. London: Newcomb, 1682; Lownds, 1681-2. 2nd edn. 5 parts in one. 8vo. [16], [52], [10],162,[4],78, [9],273,67, 45,[14], 24, [1] pp. Sl scraped & soiled. Mod period style calf. Wing G.823.
  (D & D Galleries) $475 [≈ £267]

- Sadducismus Triumphatus: or, a Full and Plain Evidence, concerning Witches and Apparitions ... Fourth Edition, with Additions. London: Bettesworth & Batley, 1726. 8vo. Frontis, engvd title at 2nd part, 1 plate. Contemp tree calf, backstrip relaid, some rubbing. *(Blackwell's)* **£300 [≃ $534]**
- Scepsis Scientifica: or, Confest Ignorance, the way to Science; In an Essay of The Vanity of Dogmatizing ... London: 1665. Sm 4to. [32],92,[4] pp. Imprimatur & errata ff. Longitudinal title. Sep title to Reply. Few sl marks. Contemp calf, rebacked, sl wear. Wing G.827/828. *(D & D Galleries)* **$500 [≃ £281]**
- The Zealous, and Impartial Protestant, shewing Some great, but less heeded Dangers of Popery ... London: M.C. for Henry Brome, 1681. 1st edn. Sm 4to. [ii],60,[4] pp. Disbound. Wing G.837. Anon. *(Finch)* **£120 [≃ $214]**

Glass, Samuel

- An Essay on Magnesia Alba. Wherein its History is attempted, its Virtues Pointed Out, and the Use of it Recommended ... Oxford: Davis & Fletcher, 1764. 1st edn. 8vo. 6,38 pp. Rec wraps. *(Fenning)* **£245 [≃ $436]**

Glasse, Hannah

- The Art of Cookery, Made Plain and Easy ... Eighth Edition. London: for A. Millar ..., 1763. 8vo. vi,[xxiv], 384,[24] pp. Hannah Glasse's printed signature at Chapter One. Contemp calf gilt, sm reprs. *(Gough)* **£295 [≃ $525]**
- The Art of Cookery, made Plain and Easy ... By a Lady. New Edition. London: 1767. 8vo. vi,xxiv, 384,[xxiv] pp. MS notes on endpapers. Contemp calf, jnts sometime reprd, upper jnt cracked, sl worn. Anon. *(Frew Mackenzie)* **£200 [≃ $356]**
- The Art of Cookery, Made Plain and Easy ... Edinburgh: for Alexander Donaldson ..., 1774. vi,[xviii], 440,[24] pp. Few sm stains. Lacks final blanks. Contemp calf, lower bd v sl split at hd. *(Gough)* **£275 [≃ $490]**
- The Art of Cookery, made Plain and Easy ... By a Lady. A New Edition, with all the Modern Improvements ... London: for Strahan, Rivington ..., 1778. 8vo. [ii],vi,[xx], 397, [25] pp. Lge fldg table (clean tear at fold). Contemp sheep, rebacked. Anon. *(Burmester)* **£225 [≃ $401]**

Glasse, Samuel

- The Magistrates Assistant; or, a Summary of those Laws which immediately respect the Conduct of a Justice of the Peace ... The Third Edition. By a County Magistrate.

Glocester: R. Raikes, 1794. xvi,550, lxv,[1], xxii pp. Contemp calf, red label, spine ends reprd. *(C.R. Johnson)* **£125 [≃ $223]**

The Gleaner ...

- The Gleaner: A Selection from Modern Writers, in Prose and Verse. Perth: R. Morison Junior, for R. Morison & Son, & Vernor & Hood, London, 1796. 1st edn. 12mo. iv,252 pp. Frontis. Orig bds, sl soiled, upper jnt tender. *(Burmester)* **£125 [≃ $223]**

Glover, Richard

- Admiral Hosier's Ghost. To the Tune of, Come and Listen to my Ditty. London: for Mr. Webb, 1740. Folio. 7,[1] pp. Disbound. Anon. *(C.R. Johnson)* **£450 [≃ $801]**
- Leonidas, a Poem. London: for R. Dodsley, 1737. 1st edn. 4to. Intl blank leaf. Contemp calf, rebacked. Anon. *(Hannas)* **£30 [≃ $53]**
- London: or, The Progress of Commerce. A Poem. The Second Edition. London: for T. Cooper, 1739. 4to. [1],30 pp. Argument leaf. Lacks final blank leaf. 2 footnotes cut into. Disbound. *(Hannas)* **£45 [≃ $80]**
- Medea, a Tragedy. London: H. Woodfall, sold by J. Morgan, 1761. 1st edn. 4to. Mod wraps. Anon. *(Waterfield's)* **£65 [≃ $116]**

Glynn, Robert

- The Day of Judgement: a Poetical Essay. The Third Edition. Cambridge: J. Bentham, 1758. 4to. Sm blot on title. Disbound. *(Waterfield's)* **£40 [≃ $71]**

Godwin, Francis

- A Catalogue of the Bishops of England ... London: [Eliot's Court Press, for] Thomas Adams, 1615. 4to in 8s. [xii],699,[i] pp. Black Letter. Few sl marks. Rec calf. STC 11938. *(Clark)* **£280 [≃ $498]**
- The Strange Voyage and Adventures of Domingo Gonsales, to the World in the Moon ... Second Edition. London: John Lever, 1768. 1st edn under this title. 8vo. Frontis. 49, [1], [4 advt] pp. New qtr mor, mor label. *(Chapel Hill)* **$400 [≃ £225]**

Godwin or Godwyn, Thomas

- Romanae Historiae ... An English Exposition of the Roman Antiquities ... For the Use of Abingdon School. London: R.W. for Peter Parker, 1661. 4to. 270,[18] pp. Some edge browning. Rec contemp style calf. *(Young's)* **£40 [≃ $71]**
- Romanae Historiae Anthologia Recognita et Aucta. An English Exposition of the Roman Antiquities ... London: M. White, for R.

Chiswel & J. Wright, 1680. Sm 4to. [6],270, [20] pp. Some marks, 1 sm tear. Three qtr calf old style. Wing G.995. Anon.
(O'Neal) $250 [≈ £140]

Godwin, William

- The Enquirer. Reflections on Education, Manners and Literature in a Series of Essays. Dublin: for J. Moore, 1798. 8vo. Sm repr to title. Later half calf, rebacked.
(Waterfield's) £300 [≈ $534]
- An Enquiry concerning Political Justice, and its Influence on General Virtue and Happiness ... London: Robinson, 1793. 1st edn. 2 vols. 4to. [iii]-xiii, [xxiii],378; [xxvi], [379]-895 pp. Mod antique style half calf.
(Finch) £2,800 [≈ $4,984]
- Inquiry concerning Political Justice and its Influence on Morals and Happiness ... Second Edition Corrected. London: Robinson, 1796. 2 vols. 8vo. Sm lib stamp on titles. Minor marg reprs. Mod qtr calf, vellum tips.
(Waterfield's) £750 [≈ $1,335]
- Things As They Are; or, The Adventures of Caleb Williams. The Second Edition Corrected. London: Robinson, 1796. 3 vols. 12mo. Half-titles. Contemp calf, spines worn.
(Hannas) £420 [≈ $748]

Goethe, Johann Wolfgang von

- The Sorrows of Werter: a German Story. New Edition. London: for J. Dodsley, 1784. 2 vols in one. 12mo. Early 19th c half calf, gilt spines, sides sl rubbed. Anon.
(Burmester) £75 [≈ $134]
- The Sorrows of Werter; A German Story. A New Edition. London: for J. Dodsley, 1784. 2 vols. Sm 8vo. Half-titles. Contemp calf. Anon.
(Hannas) £160 [≈ $285]
- The Sorrows of Werther; a German Story. Dublin: for C. Jackson, 1780. 1st Irish edn. 2 vols in one, consecutively paginated. 12mo. Half-titles. Contemp calf. Anon.
(Hannas) £220 [≈ $392]

Goldsmith, Oliver

- The Citizen of the World ... London: for J. Newbery, 1762. 1st coll edn. 2 vols. 8vo. Contemp sheep, rebacked.
(Waterfield's) £350 [≈ $623]
- The Citizen of the World ... London: for J. Newbery, 1762. 1st edn. 2 vols. 12mo. Dark brown crushed levant gilt, a.e.g., by Riviere. Cloth case. Anon. *(Ximenes)* $1,250 [≈ £702]
- The Citizen of the World ... Third Edition. London: Carnan & Newbery ..., 1774. 2 vols. 12mo. vii,259; [iv],217,[xvi] pp. Intl blank vol 2. Sl foxing, marg paper flaw in C6 vol 2.

Contemp tree calf, mor labels, lemon edges. Anon. *(Sotheran's)* £150 [≈ $267]
- Essays. London: for W. Griffin, 1765. 1st edn. True 1st edn, with engvd title. 12mo. Final advt leaf. Engvd title (sl water stained, 2 names). Lacks final blank leaf. 19th c calf, jnts cracked. *(Hannas)* £65 [≈ $116]
- Essays. London: for W. Griffin, 1765. 1st edn. 12mo. 236,[2 advt] pp. Engvd title vignette. Contemp calf, crnrs bumped, jnts sl worn. *(Chapel Hill)* £650 [≈ $365]
- The Grecian History ... Dublin: for James Williams, 1774. 1st Dublin edn. 2 vols. 12mo. [ii],282; [ii],203,[lxix] pp. Half-titles not called for. Occas browning. Contemp sheep, mor labels.
(Blackwell's) £200 [≈ $356]
- An History of England, in a Series of Letters from a Nobleman to his Son. London: Carnan & Newbery, 1772. 2 vols. 12mo. 4 advt ff. Contemp calf. Anon. *(Hannas)* £45 [≈ $80]
- An History of the Earth and Animated Nature. Phila: for Mathew Carey, May 12, 1795. 4 vols. 8vo. 55 plates. Some offsetting. Rebound in cloth. *(Key Books)* $150 [≈ £84]
- The Life of Richard Nash. London: 1762. 1st edn. 8vo. 4 advt pp. Port frontis. Mod mor gilt, a.e.g., by Lloyd. Anon.
(D & D Galleries) $475 [≈ £267]
- Dr. Goldsmith's Roman History Abridged by Himself for the Use of Schools. London: for S. Baker & G. Leigh ..., 1772. 1st edn. 12mo. [iv],viii,311 pp. Title re-attached at inner marg. Lib stamp on title. Mod half calf.
(Finch) £50 [≈ $89]
- Dr. Goldsmith's Roman History, abridged by himself for the Use of Schools. London: for S. Baker & G. Leigh; T. Davies; & L. Davis, 1782. 2nd abridged edn (?). 8vo. xii,311 pp. Sl spotted. Contemp sheep, sl worn but sound. *(Burmester)* £45 [≈ $80]
- The Traveller, or, a Prospect of Society. A Poem ... London: for J. Newbery, 1765. 1st edn. 4to. [ii],iv,22 pp. Lacks half-title & final advt leaf. Marg repr to last leaf. Early 20th c red mor gilt, a.e.g., by Riviere.
(Sotheran's) £498 [≈ $886]
- The Traveller; a Poem. London: Carnan & Newbery, 1770. 4to. Engvd vignette title. Sl crease in text. Half-title & title sl stained on lower margs. Half calf gilt, uncut.
(Blackwell's) £160 [≈ $285]
- The Vicar of Wakefield: a Tale ... The Second Edition. London: for F. Newbery, 1766. 2 vols. 12mo. [viii],214,[ii]; [vi],223 pp. Final blank leaf vol 1. Contemp calf, mor labels, sl worn. Anon.
(Sotheran's) £500 [≈ $890]

- The Vicar of Wakefield; a Tale. Supposed to be written by Himself. The Second Edition. London: for F. Newbery, 1766. 2 vols. 12mo. Final blank leaf vol 2, intl blank vol 1. Contemp calf, gilt spines (rubbed, lack labels). Anon.   *(Hannas)* **£350 [≈ $623]**
- The Vicar of Wakefield; a Tale. London: Carnan & Newbery, 1773. 5th edn. 2 vols. 12mo. Contemp calf, gilt spines, jnts cracked, 1 jnt reprd. Anon.   *(Burmester)* **£50 [≈ $89]**
- The Vicar of Wakefield. A Tale ... London: for J. Murray, 1774. 2 vols in one. 12mo. iv, 111; 110 pp. Sl soiling & foxing. Contemp calf, sometime rebacked & recrnrd. Anon.
                        (Sotheran's) **£85 [≈ $151]**
- The Vicar of Wakefield. Glasgow: J. & M. Robertson, 1790. 2 vols. Half calf, gilt labels, top edge cut, others uncut, sl scuffed.
          (D & D Galleries) **$100 [≈ £56]**
- The Vicar of Wakefield: a Tale. Supposed to be written by himself. London: Grant, 1791. 2 vols in one. 8vo. Later half calf.
                  (de Burca) **£85 [≈ $151]**

Goldsmith, Oliver & Parnell, Thomas
- Poems. London: Bulmer & Co., Shakespeare Printing Office, 1795. 1st edn on Large Paper. 4to. xx,76 pp. 5 w'engvd plates & 8 vignettes by Thomas & John Bewick. Contemp calf gilt, rebacked to style, crnrs worn.   *(Blackwell's)* **£250 [≈ $445]**

Goldsmith, Oliver (editor)
- Poems for Young Ladies. In Three Parts. Devotional, Moral, and Entertaining ... London: for J. Payne, 1767. 1st edn. 8vo. Sl crease 1st 2 ff. Contemp calf, gilt spine, minor wear. Anon.   *(Ximenes)* **$750 [≈ £421]**

Gonsales, Domingo
- The Strange Voyage and Adventures ... see Godwin, Francis

Gooch, Elizabeth Sarah
- The Life of Mrs. Gooch. Written by Herself. Dedicated to the Public. London: for the authoress, sold by C. & G. Kearsley, 1792. 3 vols in one. 192; 160; 141 pp. Rebound in qtr calf.   *(C.R. Johnson)* **£450 [≈ $801]**

Goodwin, John
- A Candle to see the Sunne ... [Colophon] London: M.S. for H. Overton, 1647. 4to. [4] pp. Drop-title. Rec wraps. Wing G.1154. Anon.   *(Fenning)* **£75 [≈ $134]**
- Hagiomastix, or the Scourge of Saints Displayed in his Colours of Ignorance & Blood ... London: Matthew Simmons, for

Henry Overton, 1646. 1st edn. 4to. [32],134 pp. Rec wraps. Wing G.1169.
                  (Fenning) **£85 [≈ $151]**
- A Post-script, or Appendix to ... Hagio-Mastix ... London: for H. Overton, [1646]. 1st edn. 4to. [10],28,[2 blank] pp. Rec wraps. Wing G.1191.   *(Fenning)* **£75 [≈ $134]**
- Right and Might well met. Or, a briefe and unpartiall enquiry into the late and present proceedings of the Army under the Command of His Excellency Lord Fairfax ... London: 1648. 1st edn. Sm 4to. [iv],44 pp. Sl browned, 2 lower margs ragged. Disbound. Wing G.1200   *(Blackwell's)* **£65 [≈ $116]**
- Sion-Colledg Visited. Or, some briefe Animadversions upon a Pamphlet lately published, under the title of, A Testimonie to the Truth of Jesus Christ ... London: M.S. for Henry Overton, 1648. 1st edn. 4to. [2], 29, [1 errata] pp. Rec wraps. Wing G.1202.
                  (Fenning) **£75 [≈ $134]**
- Some Modest and Humble Queries concerning a Printed Paper, intituled, An Ordinance presented to the ... Commons ... London: Matthew Simmons for Henry Overton, 1646. 1st edn. 4to. [2],6,9-12 pp, complete. Rec wraps. Wing G.1204. Anon.
                  (Fenning) **£75 [≈ $134]**

Goodwin, Thomas
- The History of the Reign of Henry the Fifth, King of England ... London: J.D. for S. & J. Sprint ..., 1704. 1st edn. Folio. viii,344, [ii],347-362 pp. Port frontis supplied from another, later, work. Title & sl page sl dust soiled. Contemp calf, rebacked. Anon.
                  (Vanbrugh) **£235 [≈ $418]**
- The History of the Reign of Henry the Fifth, King of England ... London: J.D. for S. & J. Sprint ..., 1704. 1st edn. Folio. viii,362 pp. Port frontis. Few lib blind stamps. Contemp calf, rebacked, sl worn. Anon.
                  (Clark) **£85 [≈ $151]**

Gordon, Thomas
- An Appeal to the Unprejudiced, concerning the Present Discontents occasioned by the late Convention with Spain. London: for T. Cooper, 1739. 1st edn. 8vo. 32 pp. Uncut, stitched as issued. Anon.
                  (Burmester) **£70 [≈ $125]**
- An Appeal to the Unprejudiced, concerning the present Discontents occasioned by the late Convention with Spain. London: for T. Cooper, 1739. 1st edn. Issue with catch-word 'had' on page 5. 8vo. 32 pp. Disbound. Anon.
                  (Hannas) **£75 [≈ $134]**
- The Conspirators; or, The Case of Catiline [Part 1] ... London: for J. Roberts ..., 1721.

1st edn. 8vo. xiv,57 pp. Some page numbers & catchwords cropped. Disbound. Anon.
(Young's) £80 [≈ $142]

- The Humourist: being Essays upon Several Subjects ... The Third Edition. London: for D. Browne, W. Mears ..., 1724. Presumed 2nd edn. 12mo. xxx,[vi], 240,[xii] pp. 2 sm marg tears. Contemp calf, spine rubbed & worn at ends, jnt cracked, crnrs worn. Anon.
(Finch) £110 [≈ $196]

Gosling, Mrs
- Moral Essays and Reflections. Sheffield: ptd by W. Ward; sold by G.G.J. & J. Robinson, 1789. 1st edn. 8vo. [xvi],127 pp. Subscribers. Rec qtr calf, uncut.
(Burmester) £120 [≈ $214]

Gostling, William
- A Walk in and about the City of Canterbury ... Canterbury: Simmons & Kirkby, 1796. 4th edn. 12mo. Frontis, fldg map, 3 plates. Orig ptd wraps, paper side label.
(Ximenes) $250 [≈ £140]

Gough, William
- Londinium Triumphans, or an Historical Account of the City of London. London: for the author, sold by Thomas Simmons, 1682. 1st edn. 2nd issue, with the cancel title "The Antiquity ... of this Famous City". Cr 8vo. [xii],374 pp. Few sl marks. Contemp calf, rebacked.
(Ash) £400 [≈ $712]

Goulard, Thomas
- A Treatise on the Effects and Various Preparation of Lead ... for different Chirurgical Disorders. Third Edition. London: 1772. 8vo. Damp marks on last few ff. Contemp sheep, hd of spine worn.
(Robertshaw) £45 [≈ $80]

- A Treatise on the Effects and Various Preparations of Lead ... for different Chirurgical Disorders. Translated from the French. New Edition, with Remarks by G. Arnaud. London: Elmsly, 1773. Lge 12mo. [8], 232 pp. Contemp calf, rebacked.
(Spelman) £85 [≈ $151]

- A Treatise on the Effects and Various Preparations of Lead ... for different Chirurgical Disorders. Translated from the French. The Sixth Edition, with Remarks by G. Arnaud. Dublin: 1777. Lge 12mo. [8],231,[1] pp. Contemp calf, new label.
(Spelman) £90 [≈ $160]

Gould, Robert
- Poems Chiefly consisting of Satyrs and Satyrical Episodes ... London: sold by most

Booksellers, 1689. 1st edn. 8vo. [xxx],65, [vii],67-310 pp. Lacks intl & final blanks. 1st ff browned, occas spotting. Disbound. Wing G.1431.
(Finch) £150 [≈ $267]

Gracian, Baltasar
- The Compleat Gentleman: or a Description of the several qualifications ... that are necessary to form a great man ... Translated into English by T. Saldkeld. London: for T. Osborne, 1730. 2nd edn. 8vo. [xii],236 pp. Contemp calf, spine sl worn, upper jnt broken.
(Burmester) £90 [≈ $160]

Grainger, James
- The Sugar-Cane: A Poem in Four Books: With Notes. London: 1766. 16mo. ix,180 pp. Frontis. Rec qtr bndg.
(McBlain) $125 [≈ £70]

- The Sugar-Cane: a Poem. In Four Books: with Notes ... London: the Booksellers, 1766. 8vo. ix,[i],180,[ii] pp. Half-title. Frontis. Contemp calf, mor label (chipped), some surface insect damage. *(Finch)* £68 [≈ $121]

Grainger, Lydia
- Modern Amours: or, a Secret History of the Adventures of some Persons of the First Rank. Faithfully related from the Author's Own Knowledge of each Transaction ... London: 1733. 1st edn. 12mo. [ii],166 pp, all published. Lacks final advt leaf. Contemp calf, rebacked. Anon.
(Burmester) £750 [≈ $1,335]

Granger, James
- A Biographical History of England ... Second Edition, with large Additions and Improvements. London: T. Davies ..., 1775. 4 vols. 8vo. Frontis port vol 1. Minor crnr worm in 4 ff, occas faint spotting. Contemp calf, sl worn, spines darkened.
(Blackwell's) £100 [≈ $178]

Grant, Archibald, attributed author
- A Dissertation on the Chief Obstacles to the Improvement of Land, and introducing better Methods of Agriculture throughout Scotland. Aberdeen: Francis Douglas ..., 1760. 1st edn. 8vo. [ii],94 pp. Disbound. Anon.
(Burmester) £225 [≈ $401]

Grant, John & Leslie, William
- A Survey of the Province of Moray; Historical, Geographical, and Political. Aberdeen: for Isaac Forsyth, 1798. 1st edn. 8vo. vii,353 pp. Fldg map, frontis. Mod half mor gilt. Anon. *(Hollett)* £150 [≈ $267]

Grant, William

- An Enquiry into the Nature, Rise and Progress of the the Fevers most common in London ... for the last twenty years ... London: 1771. 1st edn. 8vo. 463 pp. V sl marg worm at end. Lib stamp on title & at end. Contemp calf. *(Robertshaw)* **£125 [≈ $223]**

Granville, George, Baron Lansdowne

- Three Plays, viz. The She-Gallants ... Heroick-Love ... The Jew of Venice ... London: Tooke, Lintott, 1713. 1st coll edn. 8vo. Contemp calf, rebacked.
(Hannas) **£180 [≈ $320]**

Gratton, John

- A Journal of the Life of that ancient Servant of Christ, John Gratton ... London: J. Sowle, 1720. 1st edn. 8vo. 432 pp. Calf, wear to spine ends, new label.
(Hartfield) **$195 [≈ £110]**

Graves, Richard

- Columella; or, the Distressed Anchoret. A Colloquial Tale. London: for J. Dodsley, 1779. 1st edn. 2 vols. 12mo. iv,240; [ii],248 pp. Frontises. Contemp tree calf, gilt spines, jnts reprd, new labels. Anon.
(Burmester) **£300 [≈ $534]**
- Euphrosyne: or, Amusements on the Road of Life by the Author of the Spiritual Quixote. London: Dodsley, 1776. 1st edn. 8vo. Frontis. Blank strip cut from hd of title. Contemp calf, jnts cracked, lacks label, crnrs worn. Anon. *(Waterfield's)* **£130 [≈ $231]**

The Gray's-Inn Journal ...

- See Murphy, Arthur.

Gray, Robert

- Letters during the Course of a Tour through Germany, Switzerland and Italy, in the years M.DCC.XCI, and M.DCC.XCII ... London: Rivington, 1794. 1st edn. 8vo. ix, [v], 468 pp. Tear in 1 leaf reprd, few sm marg tears. Contemp style qtr calf.
(Burmester) **£120 [≈ $214]**

Gray, Thomas

- Designs by Mr. R. Bentley, for Six Poems by Mr. T. Gray. London: for R. Dodsley, 1753. 1st edn. 1st issue, with half-title reading 'Drawings &c.'. 4to. [iv],36 ff inc half-title. 6 plates. 2 marg reprs. Rec red half mor.
(Rankin) **£325 [≈ $579]**
- Poems. London: for J. Dodsley, 1768. 1st coll edn. 8vo. Lacks half-title & final blank. Contemp half calf, rebacked.
(Hannas) **£35 [≈ $62]**

- Poems by Mr. Gray. Glasgow: Robert & Andrew Foulis, 1768. Fine Paper issue. 4to. [4],64 pp. Sl spotting. Mod bds, paper label, sl soiled. *(Claude Cox)* **£85 [≈ $151]**
- Poems. Dublin: William Sleater, 1775-76. 2 parts in one vol. 12mo. 185,[6], 180-211,[1]; (189)-211,[1] pp. Engvd frontis, engvd & w'cut ills. Blank crnr torn from 1 leaf. Contemp calf, spine sl worn, upper jnt cracked. *(Burmester)* **£75 [≈ $134]**
- Poems. A New Edition. London: Murray, 1776. 8vo. xviii,[3],22-146 pp. Frontis, title vignette. Contemp calf, jnts cracked but firm, crnrs bumped. *(Spelman)* **£25 [≈ $45]**
- The Poems ... To which are added Memoirs of his Life and Writings, by W. Mason, M.A. York: A. Ward, 1778. 1st 8vo edn. 4 vols. Port frontis. Lacks 1 endpaper. Period qtr calf, jnts weakening. *(Young's)* **£68 [≈ $121]**

The Great Bastard ...

- The Great Bastard, Protector of the Little One. Cologne [London: Baldwin] 1689. 4to. Wraps. Wing G.1663.
(Rostenberg & Stern) **$130 [≈ £73]**

Greatheed, Bertie

- The Regent: A Tragedy ... Dublin: for Burnet ..., 1788. 1st Dublin edn. 8vo. [iv], 67,[5] pp. Disbound. *(Young's)* **£25 [≈ $45]**

Greaves, J.

- Pyramidographia: or, a Description of the Pyramids in Aegypt ... London: Brindley, 1736. 8vo. ix,164 pp. 4 fldg plates. Mod half mor. *(Terramedia)* **$250 [≈ £140]**

Greco, Gioachino

- The Royal Game of Chesse-Play ... Being the Study of Biochimo the famous Italian. London: for Henry Heringman, 1656. 1st edn. Sm 8vo. [xviii],120,[ii] pp. Errata. 1 w'cut ill. Lacks port as usual. Date in imprint sl shaved. Early 19th c tree calf, gilt spine. Wing G.1810. *(Vanbrugh)* **£455 [≈ $810]**

Green, George Smith

- Oliver Cromwell: an Historical Play ... London: J. Watts, 1752. 1st edn. 8vo. 134 pp, final blank leaf. Port. Red & black title. Disbound. *(Hannas)* **£35 [≈ $62]**

Green, Valentine

- A Survey of the City of Worcester ... Worcester: J. Butler for S. Gamidge, 1764. 1st edn. 8vo. [iv],vii,[i],252 pp. 16 plates. Contemp half calf, sl rubbed, spine chipped at hd. *(Clark)* **£110 [≈ $196]**

Green, William
- Poetical Parts of the Old Testament ... and other Poetical Pieces ... With Notes ... Cambridge: J. Archdeacon, for J. Dodsley, 1781. 1st edn. 4to. Errata slip pasted to p xii. Contemp half calf, rebacked.
(Hannas) £95 [≈ $169]

Greene, Edward Burnaby
- The Satires of Juvenal Paraphrastically Imitated, and adapted to the Times. With a Preface. London: for J. Ridley, 1763. 1st edn. 8vo. xxiv,229,[i blank],[i errata] pp. Contemp sprinkled calf, mor label, red edges, tiny nick hd of spine. Anon. *(Finch)* £185 [≈ $329]

Gregory, George
- The Life of Thomas Chatterton, with Criticisms of his Genius and Writings, and a Concise View of the Controversy surrounding Rowley's Poems. London: Kearsley, 1789. 1st edn. 8vo. vi,[ii],263 pp. Engvd facs. Sl marg water stains. Early 19th c half calf, sl wear hd of spine. *(Burmester)* £85 [≈ $151]

Gregory, John
- A Comparative View of the State and Faculties of Man with those of the Animal World. A New Edition. London: Dodsley, 1785. 8vo. [4],xx,286,[9] pp. Half-title. Lacks a blank flyleaf. Contemp calf, gilt ruled spine.
(Fenning) £45 [≈ $80]

Greville, Sir Fulke, Baron Brooke
- The Life of the Renowned Sir Philip Sidney. London: Henry Seile, 1652. 1st edn. 12mo. [vi],247 pp. Frontis. Speckled calf, rebacked. Wing B.4899. *(Bookpress)* $850 [≈ £478]
- The Remains of Sir Fulk Grevill Lord Brooke: being Poems of Monarchy and Religion: Never before Printed. London: T.N. for Henry Herringman, 1670. 1st edn. 8vo. Licence leaf, final blank. Contemp sheep, sl worn. Wing B.4900.
(Hannas) £280 [≈ $498]

Grew, Nehemiah
- The Anatomy of Plants ... London: W. Rawlins, 1682. 1st edn. Sm folio. 304,[19] pp. 83 plates. Unobtrusive blind stamps on title & plates, plates sl damp stained. Mod half mor. *(Chapel Hill)* $1,200 [≈ £674]
- Musaeum Regalis Societatis. or a Catalogue of the Natural and Artificial Rarities belonging to the Royal Society ... London: W. Rawlins, 1681. 1st edn. Folio. [xii],386, [vi], 43, [i] pp. Port frontis, 31 plates. Few lib marks. Rec calf. Wing G.1952.
(Clark) £350 [≈ $623]

- Museum Regalis Societatis. Or a Catalogue and Description of the Natural and Artificial rarities belonging to the Royal Society ... London: 1694. Folio. [xii],386,[ii], [iv],43 pp. 31 plates. Sl stain & v sl marg worm. Contemp calf, rebacked & recrnrd.
(Frew Mackenzie) £225 [≈ $401]

Grey, Richard
- Memoria Technica: or, a New Method of Artificial Memory. The Fourth Edition, Corrected and Improv'd. London: Henry Lintot, 1756. Fcap 8vo. [4],xvi,[8], 159,[i],[14], [11],[i advt] pp. Contemp calf, upper jnt sl cracked, some damage rear bd.
(Spelman) £60 [≈ $107]
- Memoria Technica, or A New Method of Artificial Memory, applied to and exemplified in Chronology, History, Geography, Astronomy ... London: 1799. 12mo. 165 pp. Contemp sheep.
(Robertshaw) £35 [≈ $62]

Griffith, John
- A Journal of the Life, Travel, and Labours in the Work of the Ministry ... London: James Phillips, 1779. 1st edn. 8vo. iv,427 pp. Contemp calf, sl rubbed, jnts partly cracked.
(Young's) £40 [≈ $71]
- A Journal of the Life, Travels and Gospel Labours in the Work and of the Ministry of John Griffith ... London: James Phillips, 1779. 1st edn. 8vo. Lacks front f.e.p. Contemp speckled calf.
(Waterfield's) £50 [≈ $89]

Grimston, Sir Harbottle
- Mr. Grimston's Speech, in the High Court of Parliament. London: Thomas Walkely, 1641. 1st edn. Sm 4to. [i],1-12, 14-16 pp, as issued. Lacks A1 (blank?). 19th c qtr roan gilt, sl rubbed. Wing G.2038.
(Blackwell's) £60 [≈ $107]

The Groans of Germany ...
- The Groans of Germany. London: 1741. 8vo. Stitched. *(Rostenberg & Stern)* $85 [≈ £48]

Groome, Samuel
- A Glass for the People of New-England, in which they may see themselves ... [London]: 1676. Sm 4to. 43 pp. Crnrs rounded, sm marg repr to title, occas sm reprs affecting some letters. Mod mor, gilt dentelles. Wing G.2065. Anon. *(Reese)* $8,500 [≈ £4,775]

Grose, Francis
- The Antiquities of Scotland. London: for S. Hooper ..., 1789. 2 vols. Sm 4to. xxiii, iii, [2

advt],iv,308 pp. 2 frontis, illust titles, num plates. Occas mainly marginal browning. Contemp crushed mor gilt, a.e.g., vol 1 front bd detached, extrs sl rubbed.
(Francis Edwards) **£160 [≈ $285]**

- A Classical Dictionary of the Vulgar Tongue. [Bound with his] A Provincial Glossary ... London: for S. Hooper, 1785-87. 1st edns. 2 vols in one. [ii],viii,[204]; viii,284,75 pp. Sl marg foxing. Period russia gilt, sl worn. Anon.   *(Rankin)* **£550 [≈ $979]**

- A Classical Dictionary of the Vulgar Tongue. The Second Edition, Corrected and Enlarged. London: for S. Hooper, 1788. 8vo. xv,[248] pp. Occas sl foxing. Period half calf, hinges cracked but firm. Anon.
(Rankin) **£165 [≈ $294]**

- A Classical Dictionary of the Vulgar Tongue. The Third Edition corrected and enlarged. London: for Hooper & Co, 1796. 8vo. xvi,[238] pp. Some browning & foxing. Name cut from title & reprd. 19th c half calf, sm splits in jnts, some wear spine ends. Anon.
(Rankin) **£110 [≈ $196]**

- A Classical Dictionary of the Vulgar Tongue. London: for S. Hooper, 1785. 1st edn. 8vo. [2],(viii),[204] pp. Sl browned. Contemp half calf, sl rubbed. Anon.   *(Ash)* **£200 [≈ $356]**

- Military Antiquities respecting a History of the English Army. London: 1786-88. 1st edn. 2 vols. 4to. vi,434; [ii],352,vi,[x], 40,40 pp. Title vignettes, 78 plates. Sl foxing. Contemp calf gilt, upper bds detached.
(Francis Edwards) **£250 [≈ $445]**

- The Olio: being a Collection of Essays, Dialogues, Letters, Biographical Sketches, Anecdotes ... Chiefly Original. London: for S. Hooper, 1792. 1st edn. 8vo. 3 advt pp. Possibly lacks half-title. Few minor stains. Contemp calf gilt.   *(Hannas)* **£180 [≈ $320]**

- A Provincial Glossary; with a Collection of Local Proverbs, and Popular Superstitions. London: for S. Hooper, 1790. 2nd edn, enlgd. 8vo. 19th c red half mor gilt, fine.
(Ximenes) **$200 [≈ £112]**

Grose, John Henry
- A Voyage to the East Indies ... Mogul Government ... Trade of India ... A New Edition ... added a Journey from Aleppo ... by Mr. Carmichael. London: 1772. 2 vols. 8vo. 9 plates & plans. Minor marg worm. Contemp polished calf, elab gilt spines sl rubbed, jnts cracked but firm.
(Frew Mackenzie) **£350 [≈ $623]**

Grosvenor, Benjamin
- Health: an Essay on its Nature, Value, Uncertainty,   Preservation   and   best

Improvement ... Second Edition. London: for H. Piers, sold by R. Hett, 1748. 12mo. Minor damage to half-title. Contemp sheep, worn but sound, front jnt cracked.
(Waterfield's) **£40 [≈ $71]**

Grubb, Sarah
- Some Account of the Life and Religious Labours of Sarah Grubb. With an Appendix ... and Extracts from Many of her Letters. Trenton: Isaac Collins, 1795. 1st Amer edn. 12mo. vi,418 pp. Orig calf, red label. Edited by Lindley Murray. *(Karmiole)* **$150 [≈ £84]**

- Some Account of the Life and Religious Labours of Sarah Grubb. With an Appendix, Containing an Account of the Schools at Ackworth and York ... Trenton: Isaac Collins, 1795. Foxed. Calf, gilt label.
(D & D Galleries) **$125 [≈ £70]**

- Some Account of the Life and Religious Labours of Sarah Grubb. London: Phillips, 1796. 3rd edn. 8vo. Calf. Edited by Lindley Murray.   *(Rostenberg & Stern)* **$85 [≈ £48]**

Gualdi, Abbot
- The Life of Donna Olimpia Maldachini ... see Leti, Gregorio.

The Guardian's Instruction ...
- See Penton, Stephen

Gueullette, Thomas Simon
- Tartarian Tales ... Written in French ... The whole now for the first time translated into English, by Thomas Flloyd. London: for J. & R. Tonson, 1759. 1st edn in English. 12mo. xii,369 pp. Frontis. Contemp speckled calf, gilt spine rubbed & lacks label.
(Burmester) **£175 [≈ $312]**

Guibert, Jacques Antoine Hippolyte, Comte de
- Observations on the Establishment and Discipline of His Majesty the King of Prussia; with an Account of the Private Life of that celebrated Monarch ... London: Fielding & Walker, 1780. 1st English edn. 8vo. [iv],101,[3 advt] pp. Disbound. Anon.
(Young's) **£95 [≈ $169]**

Guide ...
- A Guide to the Lakes, in Cumberland, Westmorland, and Lancashire ... see West, Thomas

Guillet de Saint Georges, Georges
- An Account of a late Voyage to Athens, containing the Estate both Ancient and Modern of that Famous City ... Now

Englished. London: J.M. for Henry Herringman, 1676. 8vo. 422 pp. Endpapers trifle wormed. Old calf gilt, spine wormholed. Wing G.2218. *(Hollett)* **£200 [≈$356]**

- The Gentleman's Dictionary. In Three Parts ... The Art of Riding the Great Horse ... The Military Art ... The Art of Navigation ... London: 1705. 1st edn in English. 8vo. [370] pp. 3 fldg plates. Contemp calf, spine sl worn, crnrs rubbed, hd of front jnt cracking.
(Finch) **£300 [≈$534]**

Guillim, John

- A Display of Heraldrie ... Corrected and much enlarged ... London: Thomas Cotes for Jacob Blome, 1638. 3rd edn. Folio. [xvi],433 pp, some mispagination. Num text w'cuts, some full-page. Contemp calf, gilt spine, hinges cracked but firm. STC 12503.
(Vanbrugh) **£355 [≈$632]**

- A Display of Heraldry. The Sixth Edition ... with large additions ... [with] A Treatise on Honour Military and Civil ... London: 1724. Folio. 64 ports & plates, num w'cuts in text. Occas sl browning. Rec qtr mor.
(Fenning) **£375 [≈$668]**

Gulliveriana ...

- See Smedley, Jonathan

Gumble, Thomas

- The Life of General Monck, Duke of Albemarle, &c. with Remarks upon his Actions. London: J.S. for Thomas Basset, 1671. 1st edn. 8vo. [xxii],486 pp. Port frontis. Some browning & sl spotting. Rec qtr calf. Wing G.2230. *(Clark)* **£90 [≈$160]**

Gunning, Mrs.

- A Letter from Mrs. Gunning. Addressed to His Grace the Duke of Argyll. London: for the author; & sold by Mr. Ridgway, 1791. 3rd edn. 8vo. [iv],147,[1 errata] pp. Half-title. Orig wraps, uncut. *(Young's)* **£44 [≈$78]**

Gurdon, Brampton

- The Pretended Difficulties in Natural or Reveal'd Religion no Excuse for Infidelity. Sixteen Sermons ... London: 1723. 1st edn. 8vo. 503 pp. Contemp calf, upper cvr loose.
(Robertshaw) **£45 [≈$80]**

Gurdon, Thornagh

- The History of the High Court of Parliament ... and the History of Court Baron and Court Leet. London: Knaplock & Tonson, 1731. 2 vols. 8vo. Contemp calf, rubbed, jnts cracked but sound. Lacks 1 label. Anon.
(Waterfield's) **£80 [≈$142]**

Guthry, Henry

- The Memoirs ... Wherein the Conspiracies and Rebellion against King Charles I ... are briefly and faithfully narrated. Glasgow: A. Stalker, 1748. 12mo. [viii],xii,[iv], 304, [xxxvi] pp. Contemp calf, gilt spine, sl rubbed. *(Clark)* **£65 [≈$116]**

Gwynn, John

- An Essay on Design, including Proposals for Erecting a Public Academy ... for Educating the British Youth in Drawing ... London: J. Brindley, 1749. 8vo. [2],vi,92 pp. Frontis, engvd title. Rec calf, gilt label.
(Spelman) **£680 [≈$1,210]**

- London and Westminster Improved, Illustrated by Plans ... with Observations on the State of Arts and Artists in this Kingdom ... London: for the author ..., 1766. 1st edn. 4to. xv,[i errata],132 pp. 4 fldg hand cold plans. Occas spotting. Contemp style qtr calf.
(Finch) **£750 [≈$1,335]**

H., J.

- The History of Sr. Thomas More ... see Hoddesdon, John; Three Treatises ... see Harris, James.

Habington, William

- The History of Edward the Fourth, King of England. London: Tho. Cotes, for William Cooke, 1640. 1st edn. Sm folio. [iv],232 pp. Port frontis (sm faint marg damp stain). Contemp sheep, rebacked. STC 12586.
(Vanbrugh) **£225 [≈$401]**

Hacket, John

- Scrinia Reserata: a Memorial Offer'd to the Great Deservings of John Williams, D.D. ... London: Edw. Jones for Samuel Lowndes, 1693. 1st edn. Sm folio. [ii],228, 230 pp, errata & advt ff. Port (discold). Some fox & dust marks. Contemp calf, jnts cracked, extrs worn. Wing H.171.
(Blackwell's) **£100 [≈$178]**

Hackett, John

- Select and Remarkable Epitaphs on Illustrious and Other Persons ... London: Osborne & Shipton, 1757. 1st edn. 2 vols. Lge 12mo. [iv],288; [iv],245,[xxi] pp. Contemp calf, rubbed. *(Blackwell's)* **£65 [≈$116]**

Hadley, George

- Introductory Grammatical Remarks on the Persian Language. With a Vocabulary ... Bath: R. Cruttwell, for the author; sold by T. Cadell, London, 1776. 1st edn. 4to. [iv], 9-216 pp. Sm marg title repr. Contemp tree calf, rebacked.   *(Burmester)* **£350 [≈ $623]**

Haigh, James
- The Dyer's Assistant in the Art of Dying Wool and Woollen Goods ... With Additions and Practical Experiments. York: Crask & Lund ..., 1787. 3rd edn. 12mo. xvi,[iv], 17-256 pp. Some soil & use. Contemp calf backed bds, worn but sound.
(Burmester) **£300 [≈ $534]**

Hailes, Sir David Dalrymple, Lord (editor)
- The Secret Correspondence of Sir Robert Cecil with James VI. King of Scotland. Now first published. Edinburgh: A. Millar, 1766. 1st edn. 12mo. xi,235 pp. Contemp speckled calf gilt, spine ends sl worn.
(Blackwell's) **£85 [≈ $151]**

Hakewill, William
- The Manner How Statutes are enacted in Parliament by Passing of Bills ... London: T.H. for John Benson, 1641. 1st edn. 12mo. [xx],148 pp. Blank leaf before title. Contemp sheep, rubbed, backstrip sl defective. Wing H.211.   *(Clark)* **£125 [≈ $223]**
- Modus Tenendi Parliamentum: or, the Old Manner of holding Parliaments in England. Extracted out of Ancient Records ... Second Edition. London: Abel Roper, 1671. 12mo. [6], 220 pp. Title sl close shaved with sl loss of border. Rec half calf. STC 217.
(Spelman) **£85 [≈ $151]**
- The Order and Course of Passing Bills in Parliament ... London: for I. Benson, 1641. Only edn. 4to. Title, "47" [ie 43] pp. Sl browned. Sm lib stamp at end. Self wraps. Wing H.218. Anon.
(Meyer Boswell) **$250 [≈ £140]**

Hale, Sir Matthew
- The History and Analysis of the Common Law of England. London: J. Nutt ..., 1713. 1st edn. 8vo. Foxing & browning. Mod calf, gilt spine. Anon.
(Meyer Boswell) **$750 [≈ £421]**

Halhed, N.B. (editor)
- A Code of Gentoo Laws, or Ordinations of the Pundits. From a Persian Translation, Made from the Original, Written in the Shanscrit Language. London: 1777. 2nd edn. 8 plates. Some browning. Contemp calf, rebacked.   *(Meyer Boswell)* **$450 [≈ £253]**

Halifax, George Savile, Marquis of
- Miscellanies ... I. Advice to a Daughter ... VII. Maxims of State, &c. London: for W. Rogers ..., 1704. 2nd edn. 8vo. With the

funeral poem by Settle. Lacks intl blank leaf. Contemp calf, rebacked.
(Hannas) **£75 [≈ $134]**
- Observations upon a Late Libel, called A Letter from a Person of Quality to his Friend, concerning the Kings declaration, &c. (London: for C.M., 1681). 1st edn. Folio. 8 pp. Drop-head title. Disbound. Wing H.316. Anon.   *(Hannas)* **£55 [≈ $98]**

Halket, Lady Anna (nee Murray)
- Meditations on the Twenty-Fifth Psalm ... prefixed, an Account of her Life. Edinburgh: Bayne & Menons, 1778. 8vo. [iv],268 pp. Minor browning. 19th c half calf, edges rubbed.   *(Clark)* **£100 [≈ $178]**

Hall, Joseph
- Meditations and Vowes, Divine and Morall ... Newly enlarged ... London: Humfrey Lownes, for Henry Fetherston, 1616. 12mo. [viii], 341, [vii],409-618, [xvi],637-837, [vii], 845-946, [x],957-979 pp. A1 blank (edges worn). Contemp vellum. STC 12683.
(Vanbrugh) **£255 [≈ $454]**
- Resolutions and Decisions of divers Practicall Cases of Conscience ... The Second Edition, with some Additionalls. London: for N.B., sold by R. Royston, 1650. 12mo. Final blank leaf. Port (laid down). Sl worm at end reprd. 19th c calf antique. Wing H.407.
(Hannas) **£40 [≈ $71]**

Hall, Richard
- The Life & Death of that renowned John Fisher, Bishop of Rochester ... Carefully selected from severall ancient Records, by Tho: Baily. London: 1655. 1st edn. Sm 8vo. Port. Minor water stains. Contemp sheep, reprd. Wing B.1513. Anon.
(Hannas) **£75 [≈ $134]**

Hall-Stevenson, John
- Crazy Tales. London: 1762. 1st edn. 4to. viii,116 pp. Frontis. Contents page reprd in margin. Sl spotting. Orig front wrapper (soiled), rear wrapper renewed. Cloth box. Anon.   *(Frew Mackenzie)* **£380 [≈ $676]**

Hallett, Joseph
- The Immorality of the Moral Philosopher: being an Answer to a Book lately published, intitled The Moral Philosopher. London: for John Noon, 1737. 8vo. Some soiling verso last leaf. Sewn as issued, uncut & unopened. Anon.   *(Waterfield's)* **£125 [≈ $223]**

Hallifax, and its Gibbet-Law ...
- See Midgley, Samuel

Hamilton, Count Anthony

- Memoirs of the Count Grammont ... A New Translation, with Notes and Illustrations ... London: for S. & E. Harding, (1793). 8vo. iii, 363, lxxxix,6 pp. 76 engvd ports. 19th c calf, a.e.g., sometime rebacked.
(Young's) **£80 [≈$142]**

Hamilton, William, Archdeacon of Armagh

- The Exemplary Life and Character of James Bonnell, late Accomptant General of Ireland. London: Downing, 1707. 8vo. xxiii,278 pp. Fldg port frontis. Ex-lib. Contemp qtr calf.
(de Burca) **£60 [≈$107]**
- The Exemplary Life and Character of James Bonnell, Esq; late Accomptant General of Ireland. The Fourth Edition, corrected. London: Joseph Downing, 1718. 8vo. xxiv, 280,[viii] pp. 19th c half calf, sl rubbed.
(Blackwell's) **£45 [≈$80]**
- Observations on Mount Vesuvius, Mount Etna, and Other Volcanos: in a Series of Letters, addressed to the Royal Society ... Second Edition. London: Cadell, 1773. 8vo. iv, 179,1 advt] pp. 5 plates inc fldg map. Sm marg water stain. Contemp sheep, mor label.
(Gaskell) **£250 [≈$445]**
- Observations on Mount Vesuvius, Mount Etna, and Other Volcanos: in a Series of Letters to the Royal Society ... Second Edition. London: 1773. 8vo. iv,179 pp. Fldg map, 5 plates. Sm lib stamp title verso. Half calf.
(Weiner) **£160 [≈$285]**

Hammond, Henry

- The Christians Obligation to Peace and Charity. Delivered in an Advent Sermon ... Now published with IX. Sermons more. London: Royston, 1649. 1st edn. 4to. [viii],263,[i] pp. Contemp sheep, later reback, sl rubbed. Wing H.520. *(Clark)* **£75 [≈$134]**
- A Collection of severall Replies and Vindications Published of late, most of them in Defence of the Church of England ... In Three Volumes. London: R. Royston, 1657. Vol 1 only. 4to. Contemp calf, extrs worn, jnts tender. Wing H.523, containing H.618, 514, 599, 529 524 *(Clark)* **£85 [≈$151]**
- A Paraphrase and Annotations upon all the Books of the New Testament ... Second Edition Corrected and Enlarged. London: J. Flesher for R. Royston, 1659. Folio. [viii],xii, 949, [xxiii] pp. Half-title, final advt leaf. Contemp half calf, worn. Wing H.573A.
(Clark) **£55 [≈$98]**
- A View of some exceptions which have beene made by a Romanist to the Lord Viscount Falkland's Discourse of the Infallibilitie of the Church of Rome. Oxford: 1646. 1st edn. 4to.

204 pp. Mod qtr mor. Wing H.609. Anon. *(Robertshaw)* **£36 [≈$64]**
- A View of the New Directory and a Vindication of the Ancient Liturgy of the Church of England ... The Third Edition. Oxford: Henry Hall [but London], 1646. 8vo. Mod qtr calf. Anon. Wing H.614.
(Waterfield's) **£85 [≈$151]**

Hammond, James

- Love Elegies ... Written in the Year 1732. With a Preface by the Earl of C[hesterfield] ... London: for G. Hawkins & T. Cooper [Edinburgh: Ruddiman], 1743. 8vo. iv,23,[i] pp. Mod bds. *(Finch)* **£68 [≈$121]**

Hancocke, John

- Febrifugum Magnum; or, Common Water the Best Cure for Fevers, and probably for the Plague. Third Edition. London: 1723. 8vo. 108 pp. One leaf torn without loss. Disbound, stained. *(Weiner)* **£40 [≈$71]**

Hanger, George, later Lord Coleraine

- Military Reflections on the Attack and Defence of London; proved by the Author to have been the most vulnerable Part of Consequence in the Whole Island ... London: Debrett, 1795. Rebound in qtr calf.
(C.R. Johnson) **£55 [≈$98]**

Hanway, Jonas

- Advice from Farmer Trueman, to his Daughter Mary, upon her going to Service ... London: ptd in the year, 1792. 1st sep edn. 12mo. viii,232 pp. Early 19th c half calf, ft of jnt cracked. Anon. *(Burmester)* **£75 [≈$134]**

Hardres, Sir Thomas

- Reports of Cases adjudged in the Court of Exchequer, in the Years 1655 ... 1660 ... London: assigns of Atkins ..., 1693. 1st edn. Folio. [xii],512,[513-532], pp. Licence leaf. Contemp calf, front hinge cracked, label damaged. Wing H.703.
(Vanbrugh) **£145 [≈$258]**

Hardwicke, Philip Yorke, 2nd Earl

- Miscellaneous State Papers. London: Strahan & Cadell, 1778. 1st edn. 2 vols. 4to. [xx],(588); [xii],(648) pp. Contemp red half mor, elab gilt spines, v sl rubbed, few faint marks. *(Ash)* **£300 [≈$534]**

Hare, Francis

- The Management of the War. In a Second Letter to A Tory-Member ... London: for A. Baldwin, 1711. 2nd edn. 8vo. 42 pp. Disbound. Anon. *(Young's)* **£38 [≈$68]**

- The Management of the War. In a Letter to A Tory-Member. London: for A. Baldwin, 1711. 3rd edn. 8vo. 39 pp. Half-title. Disbound. Anon. *(Young's)* **£42 [≃ $75]**
- The Negociations for a Treaty of Peace, in 1709. Consider'd in a Third Letter to A Tory-Member. Part the First ... London: for A. Baldwin, 1711. 1st edn. 8vo. 50 pp. Wraps. Anon. *(Young's)* **£35 [≃ $62]**

Harmer, Thomas

- The Outline of a New Commentary of Solomon's Song drawn by the Help of Instructions from the East ... by the Author of Observations in divers Passages of Scripture. London: J. Buckland, 1768. 8vo. Index sheet Cc8. Title vignette. Sm lib stamp. 19th c calf. Anon *(Waterfield's)* **£50 [≃ $89]**

Harrington, James

- The Censure of the Rota upon Mr. Milton's Book, entitled, The Ready and Easie Way to Establish a Free Common-Wealth. London: Paul Giddy, 1660. 4to. 16 pp. Disbound. Wing H.808. *(C.R. Johnson)* **£950 [≃ $1,691]**
- The Commonwealth of Oceana. London: for D. Pakeman, 1656. 2nd issue, with cancel title. Folio. [xii],1-239, [i],255-286, 189-210,[ii] pp. Sl browned, occas sl marg wear. Contemp sheep, recased, new endpapers, spine rubbed, crnrs sl worn. Wing H.809A. *(Clark)* **£480 [≃ $854]**
- The Oceana ... and his other Works ... booksellers, 1700. Folio. [ii],x,xiii-xliv, 546,[ii] pp. Frontis, port, 1 plate. Sm lib stamp on title verso (creased). Rec half calf. Wing H.816. *(Clark)* **£260 [≃ $463]**

Harris, James

- Hermes or A Philosophical Inquiry Concerning Universal Grammar ... London: for John Nourse, 1765. 2nd edn, rvsd. 8vo. xix, 442, 29 pp. Old calf, worn, rebacked. *(Young's)* **£70 [≃ $125]**
- Three Treatises. The First Concerning Art. The Second Concerning Music, painting and Poetry. The Third concerning Happiness ... By J.H. London: H. Woodfall ..., 1744. 1st edn. 8vo. [iv],357,[i blank] pp. Contemp calf gilt, jnts cracking at ft. *(Finch)* **£225 [≃ $401]**
- Three Treatises: the First Concerning Art, the Second Music, Painting and Poetry, the Third concerning Happiness. By J.H. London: H. Woodfall ..., 1744. 1st edn. 8vo. K3 & S4 cancelled. Frontis from a later edn inserted. Contemp calf, backstrip relaid. Anon. *(Waterfield's)* **£135 [≃ $240]**
- Three Treatises. The First Concerning Art.

The Second Concerning Music, painting, and Poetry. The Third Concerning Happiness. London: for J. Nourse, 1765. 2nd edn. 377 pp. Frontis. Sl marg loss in index. Later calf. *(Europa)* **£65 [≃ $116]**

Harris, John

- The Description and Use of the Globes and the Orrery. To which is prefixed by way of Introduction a brief Account of the Solar System. London: 1745. 6th edn. viii,190 pp. 6 plates (1 v sl cropped). Few sl stains. Contemp leather, rebacked. *(Whitehart)* **£60 [≃ $107]**
- Lexicon Technicum: or an Universal English Dictionary of Arts and Sciences ... London: 1704-10. 1st edn. 2 vols. folio. [xx,906; xxiv, 758] pp. Port, 7 + 7 plates. Occas sl browning. Contemp panelled calf, sl worn. *(Gaskell)* **£6,000 [≃ $10,680]**
- Lexicon Technicum: or, an Universal English Dictionary of Arts and Sciences [Volume I only] ... London: 1704. 1st edn. Folio. [xii],[vi],[894] pp. Port frontis, 7 plates (2 in facs). 1 sm repr, sm marg water stain at front. Contemp leather, rebacked & recrnrd. *(Whitehart)* **£350 [≃ $623]**

Harris, W.

- A Discourse Concerning Transubstantiation ... London: for R. Ford, 1735. 2nd edn. 8vo. 43,6 pp. half-title. Disbound. *(Young's)* **£18 [≃ $32]**

Harris, Walter

- The History and Antiquities of the City of Dublin ... Dublin: Flinn, 1766. 8vo. 509 pp. 2 plans, ills. Contemp calf, rebacked. *(de Burca)* **£160 [≃ $285]**
- The History of the Life and Reign of William-Henry, Prince of Nassau and Orange ... With an Appendix ... Dublin: 1749. 1st edn. Folio. 502,xcii pp. 4 plates of medals, 7 plates of Irish town plans. Contemp calf, sl rubbed. *(Robertshaw)* **£230 [≃ $409]**

Harris, Walter (editor)

- Hibernica: or, Some Antient Pieces relating to Ireland ... Dublin: for William Williamson, 1757. Folio. [iv],150 pp. Sl soiling. Contemp pale tan calf backed mrbld bds, vellum crnrs. Anon. The Colquhoun copy. *(Finch)* **£340 [≃ $605]**

Harris, William

- An Historical and Critical Account of the Life of Oliver Cromwell ... Appendix ... London: for A. Millar, 1762. 1st edn. 8vo. [viii], 543 pp. Sl spotting & browning. 19th c half

vellum, mor label, t.e.g.
(Blackwell's) **£85 [≈ $151]**

Harrison, Sarah
- The House-Keeper's Pocket-Book, and Compleat Family Cook ... Seventh Edition, Revised and Corrected ... by Mary Morris. London: for C. & R. Ware, 1760. [iv],216, [xxiv], 36,[viii] pp. 20 w'engvd plates. Later half calf. *(Gough)* **£295 [≈ $525]**

Harrod, William
- Sevenoke. A Poem. Humbly inscribed to His Grace the Duke of Dorset. London: for J. Fuller; & Bryan Holland, Sevenoke, 1753. 1st edn. 4to. [ii],21 pp. Half-title. Sl used. Stitched as issued, uncut.
(Burmester) **£350 [≈ $623]**

Hartcliffe, John
- A Compleat Treatise of Moral and Intellectual Virtues ... The Second Edition, Corrected. London: for J. Hooke, 1721. 8vo. Mod qtr calf. *(Waterfield's)* **£100 [≈ $178]**
- A Treatise of Moral and Intellectual Virtue ... London: for C. Harper, 1691. 1st edn. 8vo. Thick paper. Imprimatur leaf. Errata slip on b8r. Final advt leaf. Occas sl spotting & staining. Contemp gilt panelled black mor, a.e.g. Wing H.971. *(Hannas)* **£250 [≈ $445]**

Harte, Walter
- An Essay on Reason. London: J. Wright for Lawton Gilliver, 1735. 1st edn. Folio. [iv], 30, [2] pp. Final advt leaf. Sl stain on title. Sl creased. Disbound. Anon.
(Clark) **£150 [≈ $267]**
- An Essay on Reason. London: J. Wright, for Lawton Gilliver, 1735. 1st edn. Folio. [4],30 pp, advt leaf. Tall, only sl trimmed. Mod cloth. Anon. *(Hannas)* **£100 [≈ $178]**
- Essays on Husbandry ... London: for W. Frederick in Bath, & sold by J. Hinton ..., 1764. 1st edn. 8vo. 5 plates, w'cuts in text. Contemp calf, gilt spine. Anon.
(Georges) **£200 [≈ $356]**
- Poems on Several Occasions. London: for Bernard Lintot, 1727. 1st edn. 8vo. A3 (dedic) not cancelled. Subscribers list. 2 advt ff at end. Frontis. Intl ff water stained. Contemp calf, extrs worn, rebacked.
(Hannas) **£180 [≈ $320]**
- Poems on Several Occasions. London: Lintot, 1727. 8vo. Subscribers. A3 cancelled as usual. Some staining on prelims. Mod calf.
(Waterfield's) **£145 [≈ $258]**

Hartley, David
- Observations on Man, his Frame, his Duty, and his Expectations. In Two Parts. London: S. Richardson; for Leake & Frederick, Bath, 1749. Contemp calf, sl rubbed, lacks 1 label.
(C.R. Johnson) **£1,200 [≈ $2,136]**

Hartlib, Samuel
- Samuel Hartlib; His Legacy of Husbandry ... London: J.M. for Richard Wodnothe, 1655. 3rd edn. 8vo. 303 pp. Some old MS notes. Mod calf, mor label.
(Chapel Hill) **$450 [≈ £253]**

Hartliffe, John
- A Sermon Preached before the Honourable House of Commons ... Thirtieth of January, 1694/5. London: for Charles Harper, 1695. 1st edn. 4to. 27 pp. Half-title. Disbound. Wing H.970. *(Young's)* **£28 [≈ $50]**

Hartson, Hall
- Youth. A Poem. London: for W. Griffin, 1773. 1st edn. 4to. [4],24 pp, inc half-title. Title vignette. Orig wraps, backstrip frayed.
(Hannas) **£180 [≈ $320]**

Harvey, Gideon
- The Family Physician, and the House Apothecary ... London: for T.R[ooks]., 1676. 1st edn. 12mo. [24],165,[1] pp, errata leaf. 18th c half calf, 19th c endpapers, jnts & crnrs reprd, new label. Wing H.1064.
(Spelman) **£680 [≈ $1,210]**

Harvey, James
- A Collection of English Precedents relating to the Office of a Justice of the Peace ... The Third Edition. London: In the Savoy, ptd by henry Lintot, 1751. [vi],371, [29] pp. Contemp calf. *(C.R. Johnson)* **£110 [≈ $196]**
- Praesagium Medicum, or, the Prognostick Sings of Acute Diseases; Established by Ancient Observations, and Explain'd by the Best Modern Discoveries. London: Strahan, 1706. 1st edn. 8vo. xxix,216 pp. Panelled calf. *(Goodrich)* **$395 [≈ £222]**

Harwood, Edward
- A View of the Various Editions of the Greek and Roman Classics, with Remarks. Third Edition, Corrected and Enlarged. London: 1782. 12mo. 269,index pp. Contemp calf, rubbed. *(Robertshaw)* **£40 [≈ $71]**

Hastings, Thomas
- The Regal Rambler; or Eccentrical Adventures of the Devil in London ... Translated from the Syriack MS. of Rabbi

Solomon ... London: for H.D. Symonds, Owen, 1793. 1st edn. 8vo. 103,[1] pp. Plate. Sl water stain. Disbound. Anon.
(Burmester) £250 [≃ $445]

Hatton, Edward
- Comes Commercii, or, the Trader's-Companion. The Ninth Edition, with large Additions. Accurately Revised ... by W. Hume. [With] A Supplement to Comes Commercii ... London: Innys, Richardson, 1754. Tall narrow 8vo. [8],318,[2], 90,[2] pp. Contemp calf, spine ends reprd.
(Spelman) £85 [≃ $151]
- A Mathematical Manual: or, Delightful Associate ... The whole very useful and pleasant ... London: for S. Illidge, 1728. 1st edn. 8vo. viii,246,[10 advt] pp. Contemp calf, jnts trifle cracked but firm.
(Burmester) £150 [≃ $267]

Haudicquer de Blancourt, Francois or Jean
- The Art of Glass. Shewing to make all Sorts of Glass, Crystal and Enamel ... Now first Translated into English. With an Appendix ... London: for Dan. Brown ..., 1699. 1st English edn. 8vo. Half-title. 9 plates. Few marg tears. Contemp calf, rebacked. Wing H.1150. *(Hannas)* £680 [≃ $1,210]

Hawkesworth, John (editor)
- The Adventurer. A New Edition. London: for Strahan, Rivington ..., 1770. 4 vols. Contemp calf gilt, rubbed, hd of spines worn, some jnts cracking & weak.
(Jermy & Westerman) £50 [≃ $89]
- The Adventurer. New Edition. London: for Strahan, Dodsley, Newbery ..., 1778. 4 vols. 12mo. Port. Sl water stain vol 1. Contemp calf, spines sl rubbed. Samuel Johnson contributed 29 of the 140 papers. Anon.
(Burmester) £75 [≃ $134]

Hawkins, William
- An Abridgement of the First Part of my Lord Coke's Institutes; with Some Additions ... The Fifth Edition ... added ... Index. London: Nutt & Gosling, for Osborne, 1736. 12mo. vi,501,[xcix] pp. Final advt leaf. Contemp calf, extrs worn, jnts cracked but firm.
(Clark) £32 [≃ $57]
- The Thimble, an Heroi-Comical Poem, in Four Cantos ... By a Gentleman of Oxford. London: for J. Shuckburgh, sold by M. Cooper, 1744. 1st complete edn. 4to. viii,27 pp. Disbound. Anon.
(Burmester) £250 [≃ $445]

Hawles, Sir John
- The Englishman's Right: A Dialogue, Between a Barrister at Law and a Juryman ... London: Re-printed by the London Corresponding Society ..., 1793. 8vo. iv,[2], 41 pp. Some browning, some marks to title. New qtr calf. *(Meyer Boswell)* $350 [≃ £197]

Hayes, Richard
- Interest at One View calculated to a Farthing ... The Seventh Edition, with Additions. London: for W. Meadows, 1747. 16mo. Contemp calf, rebacked, crnrs reprd.
(Waterfield's) £75 [≃ $134]
- Interest at One View, calculated to a Farthing ... The Eighteenth Edition, corrected. London: for Johnson & Robinson, 1789. 12mo. 384 pp. Orig sheep, jnts broken but cords holding. *(Claude Cox)* £25 [≃ $45]
- The Negociator's Magazine. London: for John Noon, 1740. 7th edn. 8vo. [xvi],(480) pp. Fldg table. Sl thumbed & soiled. Rec calf.
(Ash) £200 [≃ $356]
- The Negociator's Magazine: or the most Authentic Account of the Monies, Weights, and Measures, of the Principal Places of Trade in the Known World ... Eleventh Edition, revised ... by Benjamin Webb ... London: 1777. [xvi], 466 pp. Tables (2 fldg). Contemp roan, rebacked.
(C.R. Johnson) £250 [≃ $445]

Hayley, William
- Epistle to a Friend on the Death of John Thornton Esq. ... The Second Edition, Corrected. London: Dodsley, 1780. 4to. With addenda leaf D1. Mod half calf.
(Waterfield's) £75 [≃ $134]
- Plays of Three Acts; written for a Private Theatre ... London: for T. Cadell, 1784. 1st edn. 4to. [iii]-xv,[i],430 pp. Lacks half-title. Old style half calf, mor label.
(Finch) £95 [≃ $169]
- Plays of Three Acts; written for a Private Theatre. Dublin: Price ..., 1784. 8vo. xii, 276 pp. Rec qtr leather.
(Bates & Hindmarch) £48 [≃ $85]
- A Poetical Epistle to an Eminent Painter. London: for T. Payne & Son, 1778. 4to. Disbound. Anon. *(Waterfield's)* £40 [≃ $71]
- The Triumphs of Temper. A Poem in Six Cantos. London: for J. Dodsley, 1781. 4to. xii, 164 pp. Few sm ink notes. Sl spotting. Mod half calf. *(Francis Edwards)* £35 [≃ $62]
- Two Dialogues; containing a Comparative View of the Lives, Characters, and Writings, of Philip, the late Earl of Chesterfield, and Dr. Samuel Johnson. London: for T. Cadell,

1787. 1st edn. 8vo. xxiv,240 pp. Contemp tree calf, jnts reprd, spine sl rubbed. Anon. *(Burmester)* **£275 [≈ $490]**

Haynes, James

- Travels in several Parts of Turkey, Egypt, and the Holy Land ... London: for the author, 1774. Only edn. 8vo. xii,167 pp. 1 plate (of 2?, probably lacks frontis). Old calf.
(Young's) **£180 [≈ $320]**

Hayward, Thomas

- The British Muse, or a Collection of Thoughts Moral, Natural and Sublime, of our English Poets ... London: Cogan & Nourse, 1738. 1st edn. 3 vols. 12mo. Red & black titles. Contemp calf, jnts reprd.
(Hannas) **£320 [≈ $570]**

Haywood, Eliza

- Memoirs of a Certain Island adjacent to the Kingdom of Utopia ... London: [Henry Woodfall] sold by the booksellers of London & Westminster, 1725-26. 1st edn. 2 vols. Half-titles, final blank ff. 2 pp of 'Key' vol 1. Contemp calf, jnts worn. Anon.
(Hannas) **£680 [≈ $1,210]**
- A New Present for a Servant-Maid: Containing Rules for the Moral Conduct ... The Whole Art of Cookery ... London: for G. Pearch, 1771. 1st edn. Lge 12mo. xiv,272 pp. Frontis. Few marks. Contemp mottled sheep, rebacked, crnrs reprd. *(Gough)* **£395 [≈ $703]**
- A Present for a Servant-Maid; or, the Sure Means of Gaining Love and Esteem ... Directions for Going to Market ... Washing ... London: T. Gardner, 1743. 1st edn. 8vo. [iv],76 pp. Sl marg water stain. Marg worm hole reprd. Rec qtr calf. Anon.
(Burmester) **£850 [≈ $1,513]**

Head, Richard

- The English Rogue Described, in the Life of Merion Latroon ... London: for Francis Kirkman, 1672. 6th issue of Part 1. 8vo. [iv, 383] pp, pagination v erratic. Frontis in facs. Rec qtr calf. Wing H.1248B. Anon.
(Vanbrugh) **£195 [≈ $347]**
- Proteus Redivivus: or the Art of Wheedling, or Insinuation ... London: printed by W.D., 1675. 1st edn. 8vo. Some gatherings browned. Lacks port (as most copies do). Sm hole in 1 leaf. Contemp calf, rebacked. Wing H.1272. Anon. *(Hannas)* **£320 [≈ $570]**
- Proteus Redivivus: or the Art of Wheedling, or Insinuation ... London: printed by W.D., 1675. 1st edn. 8vo. [xvi],352 pp. Sl browned. Contemp calf. Rebacked. Wing H.1272. Anon. *(Vanbrugh)* **£755 [≈ $1,344]**

- Proteus Redivivus ... now reprinted with Additions in every Chapter ... By the same Author. London: for Tho. Passinger, 1684. 12mo. Frontis. Contemp calf, sl worn. Wing H.1274A. Anon. *(Hannas)* **£250 [≈ $445]**

Headley, Henry

- Poems and Other Pieces. London: J. Robson, 1786. viii,9-52 pp. Rec wraps.
(C.R. Johnson) **£185 [≈ $329]**

Healde, Thomas

- The New Pharmacopoeia of the Royal College of Physicians of London. Translated into English. With Notes ... Third Edition, Corrected. London: Galabin for Longman, 1788. 8vo. xvi,368 pp. Intl approbation leaf. Contemp calf, green edges.
(Finch) **£120 [≈ $214]**

Hearn, Thomas

- A Short View of the Rise and Progress of Freedom in Modern Europe, as connected with the Causes which led to the French Revolution ... answer to the Calumnies of Thomas Paine ... London: for W. Richardson, 1793. 1st edn. 8vo. iv,132 pp. Half-title sl worn. Stitched as issued.
(Young's) **£110 [≈ $196]**

Hearne, Thomas (editor)

- A Collection of Curious Discourses, Written by Eminent Antiquaries upon several Heads in our English Antiquities. Oxford: at the theater, 1720. 1st edn. 8vo. cxliv, 327, [i] pp. 10 pp subscribers. Final advt leaf. 2 plates. Mod qtr calf. *(Clark)* **£85 [≈ $151]**

Heath, Benjamin

- A Revisal of Shakespeare's Text, wherein the Alterations introduced into it by the more modern Editors and Critics, are particularly considered. London: W. Johnston, 1765. 1st edn. 8vo. xiv,[iv], 573,[i],[16 later ctlg] pp. Old bds, lacks backstrip. Anon.
(Clark) **£100 [≈ $178]**

Heathcote, Ralph

- Sylva; or, the Wood: being a Collection of Anecdotes, Dissertations, Characters ... By a Society of the Learned. London: for T. Payne & Son, 1786. 1st edn. 8vo. xix,[i],315 pp. Contemp half calf, upper jnt tender. Anon.
(Burmester) **£85 [≈ $151]**

Helsham, Richard

- A Course of Lectures in Natural Philosophy ... Published by Bryan Robinson, M.D. London: 1739. 1st edn. 8vo. viii,404,[3] pp.

11 fldg plates. Title sl soiled, name cut from blank crnr. New qtr calf.
(Weiner) **£150 [≈ $267]**

- A Course of Lectures in Natural Philosophy. Published by Bryan Robinson, M.D. The Second Edition. London: J. Nourse, 1743. 404 pp. Advt leaf. Fldg plates. Contemp calf, rebacked.   *(C.R. Johnson)* **£95 [≈ $169]**

Henderson, John

- Letters and Poems ... With Anecdotes of his Life, by John Ireland. London: for J. Johnson, 1786. 1st edn. 8vo. Half-title & errata leaf. B6 cancelled. B1 slit for cancellation & crudely reprd. Contemp sheep, rebacked & recrnrd. *(Hannas)* **£170 [≈ $303]**

Henderson, William Augustus

- The Housekeeper's Instructor; or, Universal Family Cook ... Seventh Edition. London: W. & J. Stratford ..., [ca 1798]. 8vo. 440,[xvi index],[4 subscribers] pp. Frontis, 11 plates (2 fldg). Contemp sheep, sl worn.
(Gough) **£500 [≈ $890]**

Henry, David

- The Complete English Farmer. London: for F. Newbery, 1771. 1st edn. Demy 8vo. [xxviii], 432,2 pp. 2 plates. Occas sl foxing. Mod half calf gilt. Anon. *(Ash)* **£200 [≈ $356]**

Hentzner, Paul

- A Journey into England ... In the Year M.D.XC.VIII. Strawberry-Hill: 1757. One of 220. 8vo. Title vignette. With the 9 of p 39 present. Red mor. Cased.
(Rostenberg & Stern) **£375 [≈ £211]**

The Heraldry of Nature ...

- The Heraldry of Nature; or, Instructions for the King at Arms ... London: for M. Smith, 1785. 1st edn. Sm 8vo. Frontis, 4 plates. 19th c red mor gilt, a.e.g. *(Hannas)* **£210 [≈ $374]**

Hermippus Redivivus ...

- See Cohausen, Johann Heinrich

Hermsprong; or, Man as he is not ...

- See Bage, Robert

Herodotus

- The History of Herodotus: translated from the Greek. By Isaac Littlebury. Third Edition. London: D. Midwinter, 1737. 2 vols. 8vo. xv,[1],447, [1],[15]; [2],430,[18] pp. Lacks one f.e.p. Occas foxing. Contemp calf, rubbed.   *(Spelman)* **£65 [≈ $116]**
- The History of Herodotus. Translated from

the Greek, with Notes, by the Rev. William Beloe. London: Leigh & Sotheby, 1791. 1st edn of this translation. 4 vols. Contemp vellum, Etruscan style, gilt, a.e.g., silk markers, fine.   *(O'Neal)* **$375 [≈ £211]**

Heron, Robert

- Observations made in a Journey through the Western Counties of Scotland; in the Autumn of MDCCXCII ... Perth: 1793. 2 vols. 8vo. iv, [ii],387; [i],513,[i] pp. Occas sl foxing. Orig bds, uncut, soiled, rebacked with tape.
(Francis Edwards) **£85 [≈ $151]**
- Observations made in a Journey through the Western Counties of Scotland; in the Autumn of MDCCXCII ... Perth: R. Morison junior ..., 1793. 2 vols. 8vo. vi,387,[i]; [ii],513,[i] pp. 23 mezzotint plates. Contemp tree calf gilt, rebacked, contrasting labels.
(Hollett) **£285 [≈ $507]**

Herrera, Antonio de

- The General History of the Vast Continent and Islands of America, Commonly called the West Indies ... London: Jer. Batley, 1725. 1st English edn. 6 vols. 8vo. 3 maps, 15 plates. Later three qtr calf.
(Appelfeld) **$2,500 [≈ £1,404]**

Hervey, Christopher

- Letters from Portugal, Spain, Italy and Germany, in the Years 1759, 1760 and 1761. London: J. Davis ... for R. Faulder, 1785. 1st edn. 3 vols. 8vo. Contemp tree calf, gilt spines (worn, new labels).
(Frew Mackenzie) **£250 [≈ $445]**

Hervieux de Chanteloup, J.C.

- A New Treatise of Canary-Birds. Containing the Manner of Breeding and Coupling Them ... Translated into English. London: for Bernard Lintot ..., 1718. 1st edn in English. 12mo. [viii], 163,[5 blank & advt] pp. 2 w'cut plates. Lacks half-title. Contemp sheep, worn.
(Burmester) **£350 [≈ $623]**

Heskyns, Thomas

- The Parliament of Chryste avouching and declaring the enacted and received truthe of the ... blessed Sacrament ... Antwerp: William Sylvius, 1566. 1st edn. Folio. [xii], cccc,[vii] ff. Privilege leaf. Final blank. Title reprd. 17th c calf, rebacked. STC.13250.
(Blackwell's) **£725 [≈ $1,291]**

Hetley, Sir Thomas

- Reports and Cases taken in the Third ... Seventh Years of the late King Charles ... Now Englished ... London: for Matthew

Walbanke ..., 1657. 1st edn in English. Folio. [xii],177,[178-182]   pp.   Licence   page. Contemp calf, bds detached. Wing H.1627.
(Vanbrugh) **£175 [≈ $312]**

Heton, Thomas
- Some Account of Mines, and the Advantages of them to this Kingdom. With an Appendix relating to the Mine-Adventures in Wales. London: W.B. for John Wyat, 1707. 1st edn. Sl marg worming at end. Contemp calf, sometime rebacked, split in front jnt. Anon.
(P and P Books) **£650 [≈ $1,157]**

Hewat, Alexander
- Historical Account of the Rise and Progress of the Colonies of South Carolina and Georgia. London: for Alexander Donaldson, 1779. 1st edn. 2 vols. 8vo. 347; 309 pp. 19th c half calf & mrbld bds, sl shelfwear. Anon.
(Chapel Hill) **$3,000 [≈ £1,685]**

Heylin, Peter
- Examen Historicum; or a Discovery and Examination of the Mistakes, falsities, and Defects in some Modern Histories ... London: Seile & Royston, 1659. 1st edn. 8vo. [xxxii], 294,[x], 208,[22] pp. Sep title to 2nd part. Outer ff dusty. Disbound. Wing H.1706.   *(Clark)* **£85 [≈ $151]**

Heylyn, Peter
- Bibliotheca Regia, or the Royal Library, containing a Collection of such Papers of his late Majesty King Charls ... as have escaped the Wrack and Ruines of these Times ... London: Seile, 1659. 2 parts in one vol. Engvd title, frontis port. Contemp calf, sl worn. Wing H.2151. *(Stewart)* **£85 [≈ $151]**
- Cyprianus Anglicus: or, the History of the Life and Death of the most reverend and renowned Prelate William [Laud] ... London: 1668. 1st edn. Folio. [iv],547 pp. General title, 2 part titles. 2 'Elegie' ff at end. Occas sl staining. Early calf gilt, sl rubbed. Wing H.1699.   *(Young's)* **£180 [≈ $320]**
- A Help to English History ... continued to this present Year 1680. With the Coats of Arms of the Nobility, Blazon'd. London: Basset & Wilkinson, 1680. 12mo. Final advt leaf. Num sm w'cut ills. Contemp calf, worn, rebacked. Wing H.1720.
(Hannas) **£55 [≈ $98]**
- A Help to English History ... continued to this present Year, 1680 ... London: Basset, Wilkinson, 1680. 12mo. 634,[ii] pp. Final advt leaf. W'cut arms. Sev sm lib stamps, sl soiling. Rec antique style sheep. Wing H.1720.   *(Clark)* **£90 [≈ $160]**

- A Help to English History. London: for T. Basset, & C. Wilkinson, 1680. 12mo. Num w'cut coats-of-arms in text. Contemp panelled calf, sl rubbed. Wing H.1720.
(Ximenes) **$125 [≈ £70]**
- The Historie of that Famous Saint and Souldier ... St. George of Cappadocia ... London: for Henry Seile, 1631. 1st edn. Sm 4to. [xx],351 pp. Errata. Frontis. Few sl damp stains. Contemp calf, gilt spine, sl rubbed, sl worn. STC 13272. *(Vanbrugh)* **£295 [≈ $525]**

Heywood, Thomas
- The Hierarchie of the Blessed Angells. Their Names, orders and Offices ... London: Adam Islip, 1635. 1st edn. Folio. Imprimatur leaf. Final blank leaf. Engvd title, 9 full-page engvs. Minor marg worm. Contemp calf, rebacked. STC 13327.
(Hannas) **£650 [≈ $1,157]**
- The Life of Merlin, Sirnamed Ambrosius. His Prophesies, and Predictions Interpreted ... By T.H. London: J. Okes, sold by Jasper Emery, 1641. 1st edn. Sm 4to. [lxvi],376 pp. Port frontis (sm tear & loss). Some marg worm, wear & tear. Victorian calf, rebacked. Wing H.1786.   *(Vanbrugh)* **£195 [≈ $347]**

Hibernica ...
- See Harris, Walter (ed.)

Hickeringill, Edmund
- Scandalum Magnatum: or, the Great Trial at Chelmnesford Assizes, held March 6, for the County of Essex ... faithfully related. London: 1682. 1st edn. Folio. 108 pp, irregular but complete. Occas soiling. Mod cloth backed bds. Wing H.1825. Anon.
(Robertshaw) **£48 [≈ $85]**

Higden, Henry
- A Modern Essay on the Tenth Satyr of Juvenal. London: ptd by T.M., sold by Randal Taylor, 1687. 1st edn. Sm 4to. Sidenotes on sev ff v sl shaved. Disbound.
(Ximenes) **$450 [≈ £253]**

Higgins, Bryan
- Experiments and Observations made with a View of improving the Art of composing and applying Calcareous Cements and of preparing Quick-lime ... London: Cadell, 1780. Sm 8vo. xi,233 pp. Half-title. Rec half calf.   *(Blackwell's)* **£550 [≈ $979]**

Hildrop, John
- A Letter to a Member of Parliament, containing a Proposal for bringing in a Bill to Revise, Amend or repeal Certain Obsolete

Statutes, commonly called the Ten Commandments. London: for R. Minors, 1738. 38 pp. 8vo. Disbound. Anon.
(Ximenes) **$125 [≈ £70]**

- A Modest Apology for the Ancient and Honourable Family of the Wrongheads. In a Letter to the Right Honourable the E. of C----. London: for M. Cooper, 1744. 1st edn. 8vo. Lacks half-title. Disbound. Anon.
(Ximenes) **$225 [≈ £126]**

- A Modest Apology for the Ancient and Honourable Family of the Wrongheads. In a Letter to the Right Honourable the E. of C---. London: M. Cooper, 1744. 1st edn. 8vo. [iv],67,[i] pp. Half-title. Minor stains. Disbound. Anon.   *(Clark)* **£85 [≈ $151]**

Hill, Aaron
- The Northern-Star. A Poem Sacred to the Name and Memory, of the Immortal Czar of Russia. The Third Edition. London: for W. Mears, 1725. 8vo. [8],23 pp. Disbound.
(Hannas) **£65 [≈ $116]**

Hill, J.
- The Exact Dealer Refined: Being a Useful Companion for all Traders. In Three Parts ... Fourth Edition, enlarged. London: 1698. 12mo. 164,index,advt pp. Lacks F12. Contemp calf, some wear. Wing H.1991A. Anon.   *(Robertshaw)* **£40 [≈ $71]**

Hill, John, fl. 1712
- The Young Secretary's Guide: or, a Speedy Help to Learning. In Two Parts ... The One and Twentieth Edition. London: for J. Rhodes, 1724. 12mo. [xii],15-48, 51-74, 73-167,[1] pp. W'cut frontis. Contemp sheep, rebacked.   *(Burmester)* **£80 [≈ $142]**

Hill, "Sir" John
- The British Herbal ... London: Osborne, Shipton ..., 1756. 1st edn. Lge folio. [iii], 533,[3] pp. Frontis, title vignette, 75 plates. Sm marg repr. Contemp calf, rebacked.
(Vanbrugh) **£475 [≈ $846]**

- The Construction of Timber, from its Early Growth; explained by the Microscope ... London: for the author ..., 1770. 1st edn. 8vo. 170,[8],[2] pp. 43 plates (inc plate 14 in 2 states, plain & cold). Contemp calf, sm reprs.
(Gaskell) **£550 [≈ $979]**

- Essays in Natural History and Philosophy containing a Series of Discoveries by the Assistance of Microscopes. London: 1752. 8vo. [viii],415 pp. Title foxed. Mod bds.
(Wheldon & Wesley) **£125 [≈ $223]**

- A General Natural History or New and Accurate Descriptions of the Animals,

Vegetables, and Minerals of the Different Parts of the World ... Vol. 1 The History of Fossils. London: for Thomas Osborne, 1748. 1st edn. Folio. 12 plates, fldg table. Some foxing. Cloth   *(Key Books)* **$325 [≈ £183]**

- A History of Fossils. London: for Thomas Osborne, 1748. Folio. [2],vi,654,vi pp. Fldg table, 12 plates. Leather, rebacked. Vol 1 of "A General Natural History".
(Gemmary) **$1,000 [≈ £562]**

- Theophrastus's History of Stones. London: for C. Davis, 1746. 1st edn. 8vo. xxiii, 211, [1],21 pp. Subscribers. Calf, rebacked.
(Gemmary) **$1,350 [≈ £758]**

- [Greek title, then] Theophrastus's History of Stones, with an English version, and Critical and Philosophical Notes ... London: for C. Davis, 1746. 1st edn. 8vo. xxiii,[i], 211,[1] pp. Subscribers. Contemp speckled calf, jnts sl cracked.   *(Burmester)* **£500 [≈ $890]**

Hill, Wills, Marquis of Downshire
- A Proposal for Uniting the Kingdoms of Great Britain and Ireland. London: for A. Millar, 1751. 1st edn. 8vo. 60 pp. Disbound. Anon.   *(Hannas)* **£140 [≈ $249]**

The Hind and the Panther ...
- See Dryden, John

The Hind and the Panther Transvers'd ...
- See Prior, Matthew

Hindmarsh, Robert
- Letters to Dr. Priestley: containing Proofs of the ... Divinity of Jesus Christ ... Divine Mission of Emanuel Swedenborg ... London: R. Hindmarsh, 1792. 1st edn. 8vo. xvi, 395 pp. Some foxing. 19th c cloth, mor label, spine ends sl frayed.
(Burmester) **£60 [≈ $107]**

Historical ...
- Historical Account of the Rise and Progress of the Colonies of South Carolina and Georgia ... see Hewat, Alexander
- An Historical and Critical Account of the Life and Writings of W. Chillingworth ... see Desmaiseaux, Pierre
- An Historical and Descriptive Guide to Scarborough and its Environs. York: W. Blanchard, [1787]. 8vo. viii,192 pp. Inner top marg of title sl reprd. Contemp mrbld bds, vellum crnrs, rec calf spine.
(Spelman) **£120 [≈ $214]**

- Historical Applications and Occasional Meditations... see Berkeley, George Berkeley, Earl of

- The Historical Register ... see Fielding, Henry
- Historical Remarks and Anecdotes on the Castle of the Bastille ... see Howard, John (editor)

Historie ...
- The Historie of the Councel of Trent ... see Sarpi, Paolo.

History ...
- The History and Analysis of the Common Law of England ... see Hale, Sir Matthew
- The History and Antiquities of Gloucester ... see Rudder, S.
- The History and Antiquities of the City of York ... see Drake, Francis, abridgement.
- A History and Description of the Royal Abbaye of Saint Denis, with an Account of the Tombs of the Kings and Queens of France, and other distinguished Persons, interred there ... London: for J.S. Jordan, 1795. 1st edn. 8vo. iv,96 pp. Disbound.
  (Burmester) £45 [≈ $80]
- The History and Present State of Virginia ... see Beverley, Robert
- An History of England, in a Series of Letters ... see Goldsmith, Oliver
- The History of Female Favourites ... see La Roche-Guilhem, Anne de
- The History of Man (1704) ... see Wanley, Nathaniel
- The History of Marcus Attilius Regulus; collected from Polybius, Appian ... London: for Jacob Robinson, 1744. 1st edn. 8vo. 30 pp. Disbound. *(Young's)* £58 [≈ $103]
- The History of Nourjahad ... see Sheridan, Frances.
- The History of Oracles ... see Fontenelle, Bernard le Bovier
- The History of Pompey the Little ... see Coventry, Francis
- The History of the famous Town of Hallifax ... with a true Account of their Antient Old Customary Gibbet-Law. London: E. Tracy, 1712. 12mo. [6],174 pp. Frontis. Browning, leading edge of title worn. Contemp calf, rebacked. Wm. Ormerod's b'plate.
  (Spelman) £80 [≈ $142]
- The History of the High Court of Parliament ... see Gurdon, Thornagh
- The History of the Life and Actions of St. Athanasius ... see Bacon, Nathaniel
- The History of the Life and Death of Sr. Thomas More ... see Hoddesdon, John
- The History of the Life and Reign of the late

Czar Peter the Great ... see Banks, John
- The History of the Life and Reign of William III ... see Banks, John [≈ $80]
- The History of the Original and Progress of Ecclesiastical Revenues ... see Simon, Richard *(Waterfield's)* £75 [≈ $134]
- The History of the Reign of Henry the Fifth ... see Goodwin, Thomas
- The History of the Stage. In which is included, the Theatrical Characters of the most Celebrated Actors who have adorn'd the Theatre ... London: J. Miller, 1742. [4],144, 147-230 [ie 228] pp. Rec wraps.
  (C.R. Johnson) £120 [≈ $214]
- The History of the Voyages of Christopher Columbus, in order to discover America and the West-Indies. London: D. Midwinter ..., 1777. 190 pp. Contemp sheep, rebacked. *(C.R. Johnson)* £110 [≈ $196]
- The History of Virginia ... see Beverley, Robert

Hitt, Thomas
- The Modern Gardener. London: for Hawes, Clarke & Collins ..., 1771. 1st edn. Post 12mo. 8, "530" [ie 532] pp. Plates. Sl discold. 1 leaf torn with sl loss. Contemp sheep, rebacked. *(Ash)* £200 [≈ $356]

Hoadly, Benjamin
- An Enquiry into the Reasons of the Conduct of Great Britain, with Relation to the Present State of Affairs in Europe. London: James Roberts, 1727. 1st edn. 8vo. Disbound. Anon. *(Waterfield's)* £40 [≈ $71]
- An Enquiry into the Reasons of the Conduct of Great Britain, with Relation to the Present State of Affairs in Europe. London: James Roberts, 1727. 1st edn. 8vo. 112 pp. Title sl dust soiled. Disbound. Anon.
  (Hannas) £45 [≈ $80]
- The Fears and Sentiments of all True Britains with respect to National Credit, Interest, Religion. London: Baldwin, 1710. 8vo. Stitched. Anon.
  (Rostenberg & Stern) $75 [≈ £42]

Hobart, Sir Henry
- The Reports ... the Fifth Edition. Review'd and Corrected ... In the Savoy: for R. Gosling ..., 1724. Folio. [xii], 350, [351-412] pp. Contemp calf, sl worn.
  (Vanbrugh) £155 [≈ $276]

Hobbes, Thomas
- The Art of Rhetoric, with a Discourse of the Laws of England. London: for William Crooke, 1681. 2 parts in one vol. 8vo. [viii],

168; 208 pp. Port. Marg worm hole 1st 28 ff.
Contemp calf, rebacked. Wing H.2212.
(Burmester) **£750 [≈ $1,335]**
- Considerations upon the Reputation,
Loyalty, Manners & Religion, of Thomas
Hobbes of Malmesbury. Written by himself
... London: for William Crooke, 1680. 2nd
edn. 8vo. [vi], 63, [1],[10 advt] pp. Sm marg
worm hole in 2 final advt ff. Rec calf. Wing
H.2218.   *(Burmester)* **£550 [≈ $979]**
- De Mirabilibus Pecci: being the Wonders of
the Peak in Darby-Shire ... In English and
Latine ... The English by a Person of Quality.
London: Crook, 1678. 1st edn in English.
8vo. [ii],83,[vii] pp. Lacks final blank. 19th c
half calf, worn, rebacked. Wing H.2224.
(Blackwell's) **£250 [≈ $445]**
- Tracts of Mr. Thomas Hobbes ... London:
for W. Crooke, 1682. 8vo. Port, fldg plate.
Contemp calf, surface sl eroded. Wing
H.2265.   *(Burmester)* **£500 [≈ $890]**

Hodder, James
- Hodder's Arithmetick. Or that necessary Art
made easie ... The Twelfth Edition, revised ...
by Henry Mose ... London: T.H. for Ric.
Chiswell, 1678. [10],216 pp. Frontis port.
Contemp sheep, crnrs sl worn. Wing
H.2286A.   *(C.R. Johnson)* **£225 [≈ $401]**

Hoddesdon, John
- The History of the Life and Death of Sr.
Thomas More. London: Eversden, 1662.
12mo. Red & black title. Calf, rebacked.
Wing H.2293. Anon.
(Rostenberg & Stern) **$400 [≈ £225]**
- Tho. Mori Vita & Exitus: or, The History of
Sr. Thomas More, Sometime Lord High
Chancellor of England. Collected out of
severall Authors by J.H. Gent. London: Cotes
for Eversden, 1652. 1st edn. 8vo. Fldg frontis
port. Lacks last blank. Calf, rebacked. Wing
H.2296. *(Rostenberg & Stern)* **$475 [≈ £267]**

Hodges, William
- Travels in India during the Years 1780, 1781,
1782, and 1783. London: for the author,
1794. 2nd edn, crrctd. 4to. vii,154,[2] pp. Lge
fldg map, 14 plates. Contemp calf, rebacked,
crnrs worn.
(Bates & Hindmarch) **£250 [≈ $445]**

Hody, Humphrey
- A History of English Councils and
Convocations. And of the Clergy's sitting in
Parliament ... London: Clavell, 1701. 1st edn.
8vo. [xvi],431,[i], 288,[iv] pp. Some marg
worm & fraying. Contemp calf, spine wormed
at ft.   *(Blackwell's)* **£95 [≈ $169]**

Hoffman, F. & Ramazzini, B.
- A Dissertation on Endemical Diseases ... with
a Treatise on the Diseases of Tradesmen ...
Translated by Dr. James. London: 1746. xv,
432,4 advt pp. Sl foxing & discoloration of
page edges. Leather, sl worn, rebacked.
(Whitehart) **£180 [≈ $320]**

Hogarth, William
- The Analysis of Beauty. London: Reeves, for
the author, 1753. 1st edn. xxii, errata,153 pp.
Title vignette, 2 fldg plates (linen backed).
Tiny worm hole in final blanks. Contemp
calf, hinges & ft of spine worn.
(Europa) **£250 [≈ $445]**
- Hogarth Moralized ... see Trusler, John

Holberg, Ludvig, Baron
- An Introduction to Universal History.
Translated from the Latin ... With Notes ...
by Gregory Sharpe. London: for L. Davis,
1787. 3rd edn. 8vo. xxv,[ii],354 pp. Old calf,
sl worn.   *(Young's)* **£40 [≈ $71]**
- A Journey to the World Under-Ground. By
Nicholas Klimius. Translated from the
Original. London: Astley & Collins, 1742. 1st
English edn. 12mo. 12 advt ff. Mod old style
panelled calf. Anon. *(Hannas)* **£380 [≈ $676]**

Holdsworth, William & Aldridge, William
- Natural Short-Hand, Wherein the Nature of
Speech and the manner of Pronunciation are
briefly explained ... London: for the authors
..., [1770?]. 1st edn. 8vo. viii,78 pp. Engvd
title, 28 plates (1 reprd without loss). Occas sl
spotting. Rec half calf. *(Clark)* **£120 [≈ $214]**

Hole, Richard
- Remarks on the Arabian Nights'
Entertainments ... London: Cadell & Davies,
1797. 8vo. iv,258 pp, errata leaf. Period
mottled calf, rebacked, inner marg of upper
cvr sl wormed, sl scratched.
(Rankin) **£145 [≈ $258]**
- Remarks on the Arabian Nights' Entertainments; in which the Origin of Sindbad's
Voyages, and other Oriental Fictions, is
particularly considered. London: Cadell &
Davies, 1797. 1st edn. 8vo. iv,258, [2 errata]
pp. Few sm lib blind stamps. Sl browned. Rec
qtr calf.   *(Burmester)* **£50 [≈ $89]**

Holles, Denzil Holles, Baron
- Lord Hollis his Remains: being a Second
Letter to a Friend, concerning the Judicature
of the Bishops in Parliament. London: for R.
Janeway, 1682. 8vo. Contemp mottled calf,
rubbed, sl loose. Wing H.2466.
(Waterfield's) **£70 [≈ $125]**

- Memoirs of Denzil Lord Holles, Baron of Ifield in Sussex, from the Year 1641 to 1648. London: 1699. 1st edn. 8vo. Port. Contemp calf, jnts cracked. Wing H.2464.
(Robertshaw) **£60 [≈ $107]**
- Memoirs of Denzil Lord Holles, Baron of Ifield in Sussex, from the Year 1641, to 1648. London: for Tim. Goodwin, 1699. 1st edn. 8vo. Port. Heavy worming in lower blank marg in front. Contemp calf. Wing H.2464.
(Hannas) **£30 [≈ $53]**

Holmes, G.

- Sketches of some of the Southern Counties of Ireland, collected during a Tour in the Autumn, 1797. In a Series of Letters ... London: Longman, 1801. 8vo. Orig bds, rebacked. *(de Burca)* **£135 [≈ $240]**

Holmes, John

- The Art of Rhetoric made Easy: or, the Elements of Oratory. The third impression, corrected and improved. London: L. Hawes, 1766. 8vo. [18],96, 71,[7] pp. Sm marg stain. Rec half leather. *(Spelman)* **£80 [≈ $142]**

Holt, Richard

- A Short Treatise of Artificial Stone, as 'tis now made, and converted into all manner of Curious Embellishments, and Proper Ornaments ... London: for Stephen Austin, & John Brindley, 1730. 1st edn. 8vo. viii,55 pp. Sl soiled. Qtr mor, sl marked.
(Burmester) **£450 [≈ $801]**

Holwell, William

- A Mythological, Etymological, and Historical Dictionary; Extracted from the Analysis of Ancient Mythology. London: for C. Dilly, 1793. xix,449,index pp. Occas v sl spotting. Gilt dec tree calf, crnrs sl rubbed.
(Francis Edwards) **£75 [≈ $134]**

Home, Francis

- Clinical Experiments, Histories, and Dissections. Edinburgh: 1780. 1st edn. 8vo. xvi,458 pp, errata leaf. Lib stamp on dedic leaf. Contemp calf, rebacked, orig label, crnrs reprd. *(Spelman)* **£180 [≈ $320]**
- Principia Medicinae. Third Edition. Edinburgh: 1770. 8vo. xii,340,16 advt pp. Contemp calf, jnts & spine ends reprd.
(Spelman) **£85 [≈ $151]**

Home, Robert

- Select Views in Mysore, the Country of Tippoo Sultan; from Drawings taken on the Spot ... With Historical Descriptions. London: R. Bowyer, 1794. 1st edn. Lge 4to.

45 pp. Fldg map, 3 fldg plans, 29 plates. Some foxing, mainly to text. Mod half calf.
(Frew Mackenzie) **£320 [≈ $570]**

Homer

- The Iliad ... Translated by Alexander Pope. Glasgow: Robert & Andrew Foulis, 1771. 4 vols. 12mo. Fldg map vol 1. Contemp calf, lacks all but 1 label.
(Waterfield's) **£125 [≈ $223]**
- The Iliad ... Translated by Alexander Pope. Glasgow: Foulis, 1771. 4 vols. 12mo in 6s. Half-titles. Fldg map in vol 1. Crnr torn from 1 leaf affecting 3 letters. Contemp calf gilt, mor labels, 1 jnt sl rubbed.
(Blackwell's) **£150 [≈ $267]**
- The Iliad and Odyssey of Homer, translated into English Blank Verse by William Cowper. London: J. Johnson, 1791. 1st edn. 2 vols. 4to. Subscribers. Vol 1 title creased & sl frayed. Contemp tree calf, rebacked, sl scuffed. *(Burmester)* **£300 [≈ $534]**

Hoofnail, John

- New Practical Improvements and Observations on some of the Experiments and Considerations touching Colours, of the Honourable and Judicious Robert Boyle, Esq; ... Painting in Water Colours ... London: Gosling, 1738. 1st edn. 8vo. vi,[2],64 pp. Sl marked. Later bds. *(Spelman)* **£420 [≈ $748]**

Hooke, Andrew

- An Essay on the National Debt and National Capital ... Second Edition, with Additions. London: for T. Owen, 1751. 8vo. [2],vi,xii,67 pp, inc half-title. Disbound. Sgnd by the author on verso of half-title. *(Hannas)* **£85 [≈ $151]**

Hooke, Nathaniel

- An Account of the Conduct of the Dowager Duchess of Marlborough, from her first Coming to Court to the Year 1710. London: Hawkins, 1742. 8vo. Calf. Anon.
(Rostenberg & Stern) **$150 [≈ £84]**

Hooke, Robert

- An Attempt to Prove the Motion of the Earth from Observations ... London: for John Martyn, 1674. 1st edn. 8vo. [viii],28 pp. Fldg plate. 1st word of title & sev headlines shaved, title sl dusty, fold marks at ft. Contemp style mor. Wing H.2613.
(Gaskell) **£2,250 [≈ $4,005]**
- A Description of Helioscopes, and some other Instruments made by Robert Hooke. London: for John Martyn, 1676. 1st edn. 4to. [ii],32 pp. 3 fldg plates on 2 ff. Rec mor. Wing H.2614. *(Gaskell)* **£1,250 [≈ $2,225]**

Hooker, Richard
- Of the Laws of Ecclesiastical Politie. The Sixth Edition. London: William Stansbye, 1632-31. Sm folio. [2],27,1, 583,8 ff. Engvd general title, 6 sectional titles included in pagination. Sm repr general title. Contemp calf, rebacked.   *(Spelman)* £120 [≈ $214]
- Of the Lawes of Ecclesiastical Politie. Eight Books. London: Richard Bishop, sold by George Lathum, [1639]. Sm folio. [lx],'583" [ie 579],[xv] pp. Engvd title. Lacks intl blank. Sl water stain. Contemp calf, lacks label, piece missing hd of spine. STC 13720.
(Blackwell's) £80 [≈ $142]
- Of the Lawes of Ecclesiastical Politie. London: Richard Bishop for George Lathum, [1639]. Folio. [lx],453, [iii],453-583,17 pp. Engvd title. Contemp calf, extrs worn, ft of spine defective. STC 13720.
(Clark) £65 [≈ $116]
- The Works ... in Eight Books of Ecclesiastical Polity ... With an Account of his Holy Life ... London: J. Best for Andrew Crook, 1662. Folio. Engvd title, port. V sl marks. Contemp calf, jnts cracked, sm piece missing ft of spine. Wing H.2630.   *(Blackwell's)* £250 [≈ $445]

Hoole, Samuel
- Modern Manners; or, the Country Cousins in a Series of Poetical Epistles ... The Second Edition, Corrected and Enlarged. London: Dodsley, 1782. 8vo. Frontis. Few pen trials on title. Contemp sheep, worn, jnts cracked.
(Waterfield's) £65 [≈ $116]

Hooson, William
- The Miners Dictionary ... Wrexham: the author & T. Payne, 1747. 8vo. [vi],224] pp. Subscribers. Browned. Marg worm in 1st 10 gatherings. Rec calf gilt. The Kenny copy.
(Blackwell's) £500 [≈ $890]

Hope, John
- Occasional Attempts at Sentimental Poetry, by a Man in Business: with some Miscellaneous Compositions of his Friends. London: for T. Durham, 1769. 1st edn. Sm 8vo. half-title. Sl worming in inner marg. Contemp calf gilt, upper jnt cracking. Anon.
(Hannas) £180 [≈ $320]

Hopkins, Charles
- Boadicea Queen of Britain. A Tragedy ... London: Tonson, 1696. 1st edn. 4to. 1st & last few gatherings browned. Disbound. Wing H.2719.   *(Hannas)* £110 [≈ $196]

Hopkins, Thomas
- Two Godly and Profitable Sermons ... against

the Sinnes of this Citie of London. London: [John Legat] for George Hodges, 1623. Sm 4to. [viii],72 pp. Title reprd. 1 tear without loss. Mod half calf. STC 13773.
(Blackwell's) £75 [≈ $134]

Horace
- The Poems ... rendred in English Verse by Several Persons. London: E. Cotes for Henry Brome, 1666. 1st edn of this translation. 8vo. Licence leaf. Port, addtnl engvd title. 19th c half calf. Wing H.7281.
(Hannas) £500 [≈ $890]
- The Poems ... Rendred in English and Paraphrased by Several Persons. The Second Edition with alterations. London: A.C. for H. brome, 1671. 8vo. [xxxi],400 pp. Licence leaf. Port. Sl marg worm at end. Contemp calf, backstrip sometime relaid, worn. Wing H.2783A.   *(Blackwell's)* £50 [≈ $89]
- The Poems ... Rendred into English and Paraphrased by Several Persons. The Third Edition with Alterations. London: M.C. for H. brome, 1680. 8vo. Licence leaf. 2 ports. Paper fault in 1 crnr affecting catchword. Contemp sheep. Wing H.2784.
(Hannas) £300 [≈ $534]

Horne, George
- A Commentary on the Book of Psalms. In which their Literal or Historical Sense, as they relate to King David, and the People of Israel, is Illustrated ... Oxford: Clarendon Press, 1778. 2nd edn. 2 vols. 8vo. Old qtr calf, sometime rebacked.
(Young's) £50 [≈ $89]
- A Picture of the Female Character, As It Ought to Appear when formed. London: Nicholson, 1795. 12mo. Stitched.
(Rostenberg & Stern) $75 [≈ £42]

Horne afterwards Horne Tooke, John
- A Letter to a Friend on the Reported Marriage of his Royal Highness the Prince of Wales ... The Second Edition. London: for J. Johnson, 1787. 8vo. Half-title. Disbound.
(Waterfield's) £50 [≈ $89]

Horneck, Anthony
- The Glories of the Other World: a Sermon preached ... on Easter Day, March 27, 1687. London: Joseph Downing, 1708. 8vo. 15,[1] pp. Disbound.   *(Burmester)* £20 [≈ $36]

Horsley, John
- A Short and General Account of the most necessary and fundamental Principles of Natural Philosophy ... Revised, corrected and adapted ... by John Booth. Glasgow: Andrew

Stanton, 1743. Sm 8vo. iv,100 pp. 4 fldg plates. Sl affected by damp. Contemp calf, sl worn.   *(Burmester)* £120 [≈ $214]

Horsley, Samuel

- Tracts in Controversy with Dr. Priestley upon the Principal Question of the Belief of the First Ages in Our Lord's Divinity ... Revised and Augmented ... Glocester: R. Raikes, 1789. 8vo. Orig bds, front bd detached.   *(Waterfield's)* £125 [≈ $223]

Horsley, William

- A Treatise on Maritime Affairs: or a Comparison between the Commerce and Naval Power of England and France. London: for R. Wellington, 1744. 1st edn. 8vo. [2],94 pp. Disbound.
                             (Hannas) £75 [≈ $134]

Horsman, Gilbert

- Precedents in Conveyancing ... In the Savoy: Lintot for Knapton, 1744. 1st edn. 3 vols. Folio. Erratum. Marg worm hole in a few ff. Contemp calf, 2 bds detached, other hinges cracked & weak.   *(Vanbrugh)* £275 [≈ $490]

Hotoman, Francis

- Franco-Gallia: or, an Account of the Ancient Free State of France, and Most other Parts of Europe, before the Loss of their Liberties ... London: 1711. 8vo. vi,[vi],10, vi,144 pp. Half-title. Minor browning. Speckled calf gilt, jnts cracking.
                    (Francis Edwards) £75 [≈ $134]

Houghton, John

- Husbandry and Trade Improv'd ... Revised, Corrected, and Published ... by Richard Bradley ... London: Woodman & Lyon, 1727. 1st edn in book form. 3 vols. 8vo. Contemp mottled calf gilt, spine ends sl chipped, crnrs bumped. A 4th vol was published in 1728.
                  (Frew Mackenzie) £150 [≈ $267]

How, Charles

- Devout Meditations ... Edinburgh: Hamilton, Balfour, & Neill, 1752. 2nd edn, enlgd. 12mo. [ii],viii,187 pp. Contemp reversed calf, a.e.g., upper jnt sl worn but sound.   *(Burmester)* £75 [≈ $134]

Howard, John

- An Account of the Principal Lazarettos in Europe ... Warrington: William Eyres, 1789. 1st edn. Lge 4to. (v)-viii,259,(13) pp. 21 plates (20 fldg), fldg table. Occas v sl foxing. Contemp sprinkled calf, front hinge cracking.
                     (Bookpress) $750 [≈ £421]

Howard, John (editor)

- Historical Remarks and Anecdotes on the Castle of the Bastille. Translated from the French published in 1774. London: for Cadell & Conant, 1780. 1st edn in English. 8vo. [vi], 29 pp. Fldg plan (caption just shaved). Disbound. Anon.
                       (Burmester) £60 [≈ $107]

Howard, Sir Robert

- The Duell of the Stags: a Poem. In the Savoy: for Henry Herringman, 1668. 1st edn. 4to. [4],14 pp. Lacks final blank. Foredge uncut & sl frayed. Qtr mor. Wing H.2991.
                       (Hannas) £130 [≈ $231]

- The Duel of the Stags, A Poem ... Together with an Epistle to the Author, by Mr. John Dryden. London: H. Hills, 1709. 1st edn printed by Hills. 8vo. 16 pp. Sl staining. Disbound.   *(Young's)* £45 [≈ $80]

- Five New Plays ... The Second Edition Corrected. London: for Henry Herringman, sold by Francis Saunders, 1692. 4to. [x],252,[2] pp. Divisional titles. Port frontis. Browned, some wear & tear & reprs. 19th c calf, rebacked, new endpapers. Wing H.299A.   *(Sotheran's)* £150 [≈ $267]

- The Great Favourite, or, The Duke of Lerma. As it was Acted at the Theatre-Royal ... In the Savoy: for Henry Herringman, 1668. 1st edn. 4to. Title v dust soiled. Disbound. Wing H.2996.
                       (Hannas) £220 [≈ $392]

- The Life and Reign of King Richard the Second. By a Person of Quality. London: sold by Langly Curtis, 1681. 1st edn. 8vo. [viii],240 pp. Contemp sheep, gilt spine. Wing H.3001. Anon.
                      (Vanbrugh) £225 [≈ $401]

- Poems, viz. 1. A Panegyrick to the King ... 6. A Panegyrick to General Monck. London: for Henry Herringman, 1660. 1st edn, 1st issues. 8vo. Sl spotted & browned, few headline shaved. Mod mor by Sangorski & Sutcliffe. Wing H.3003.   *(Hannas)* £280 [≈ $498]

Howard, Sylvanus

- Every Tradesman his Own Lawyer; or, a Digest of the Law concerning Trade, Commerce, and Manufactures ... London: for W. & J. Stratford, [1794]. 1st edn. 8vo. 167,[2] pp. Some foxing. Contemp half calf, sl worn, upper jnt tender.
                    (Burmester) £200 [≈ $356]

Howell, James

- The Ancient and Present State of England, being a Compendious History of all its Monarchs from the Time of Julius Caesar

Eleventh Edition. London: 1750. 8vo.
Frontis, 12 plates. Contemp calf, sl rubbed,
upper jnt cracked. *(Robertshaw)* **£34 [≈ $61]**
- Epistolae Ho-Elianae. Familiar Letters,
Domestic and Forren ... London: for Thomas
Guy, 1678. 5th edn. 8vo. [xiv],510,[21] pp.
Frontis. calf, sometime rebacked.
(Young's) **£50 [≈ $89]**
- Instructions for Forreine Travell ... London:
T.B. for Humphrey Moseley, 1642. 1st edn.
12mo. [8],236 pp. Port frontis (cut close with
sl loss to border). Lacks final blank. Sl marg
worm, occas marg stain. 19th c half calf.
Wing H.3082.   *(Spelman)* **£350 [≈ $623]**
- A Survay of the Signorie of Venice ...
London: for Richard Lowndes, 1651. 1st edn.
Folio. [viii],210, [211-218] pp. Port frontis, 1
other plate. V sl occas foxing. Victorian half
calf, gilt spine, front hinge cracked but firm.
Wing H.3112.   *(Vanbrugh)* **£375 [≈ $668]**
- A Survay of the Signorie of Venice ...
London: Richard Lowndes, 1651. 1st edn.
Sm folio. Irregular pagination but complete.
Frontis with explanatory leaf, port. Occas
stains. Contemp sheep, extrs worn, jnts
cracked. Wing H.3112.
(Clark) **£220 [≈ $392]**

Hoyle, Edmond
- Hoyle's Games Improved. Revised by Charles
Jones. London: for R. Baldwin, B. Law, C.
Dilly ..., 1796. Cr 12mo. viii,304 pp. Fldg
plate. Few faint marks. Contemp sheep,
rebacked, lemon edges. *(Ash)* **£200 [≈ $356]**
- Mr. Hoyle's Games of Whist, Quadrille,
Piquet, Chess, and Back-Gammon Complete
... The Fifteenth Edition ... London: [ca
1770?]. 12mo. xii,216 pp. Hoyle's sgntr
reproduced from a wood block. Sm worm
hole in a few ff. Old sheep, rebacked & reprd.
(Bow Windows) **£75 [≈ $134]**
- A Short Treatise on the Game of Whist ... By
a Gentleman. London: Bath printed and
London reprinted for W. Webster, 1743. 8vo.
8,[iv],86 pp. Half-title. Sev ff weak, frayed or
torn at foredge, marg worm in crnr
throughout. Contemp calf, label chipped,
rubbed, stained.   *(Finch)* **£55 [≈ $98]**
- A Short Treatise on the Game of
Backgammon. London: for T. Osborne ...,
1745. 2nd edn. Cr 12mo. [ii],(62) pp. Hoyle's
authenticating signature. Mod half mor gilt.
(Ash) **£500 [≈ $890]**

Huckell, John
- Avon. A Poem in Three Parts. Birmingham:
by John Baskerville, sold by R. & J. Dodsley,
London, 1758. 1st edn. Issue with K2 crrctly
sgnd. 4to. Intl blank leaf. Sl foxing at ends.

Half roan, uncut. Anon.
(Hannas) **£180 [≈ $320]**

Huddesford, William
- The Lives of those eminent Antiquaries John
Leland, Thomas Hearne and Anthony a
Wood ... London: 1772. Large Paper. 2 vols.
8vo. 11 plates. Contemp calf. Anon.
(Robertshaw) **£75 [≈ $134]**

Hudibras ...
- See Butler, Samuel

Hudibras Redivivus ...
- See Ward, Edward

Hudson, J.
- The Florist's Companion, containing the
Culture and Properties of the Auricula,
Polyanthus, Hyacinth, etc. Newcastle upon
Tyne, [1794]. 12mo. xii,84 pp. Tailpieces by
T. Bewick. Contemp calf, rebacked.
(Wheldon & Wesley) **£75 [≈ $134]**

Hughes, John
- Poems on Several Occasions. With Some
Essays in Prose. London: Tonson & Watts,
1735. 1st coll edn. 2 vols. 12mo. Subscribers.
Port (tear outer marg), 5 plates. Contemp calf,
rebacked, new endpapers. Subscriber's
b'plate.   *(Hannas)* **£140 [≈ $249]**

Huie, James
- An Abridgment of All the Statutes now in
Force, relative to the Revenue of Excise ...
Edinburgh: for the author, 1797. 1st edn.
Some browning. Early qtr sheep & mrbld bds,
front jnt cracking.
(Meyer Boswell) **$350 [≈ £197]**

Hull, T.
- Richard Plantagenet. A Legendary Tale.
London: [1774]. 1st edn. Sm sq folio. 30 pp.
Vignette title. Lacks half-title. Mod wraps.
(Francis Edwards) **£60 [≈ $107]**

Humble ...
- The Humble Address of the Lords Spiritual
and Temporal, in Parliament Assembled ...
presented to Her Majesty on Monday the
First Day of March, 1707 ... London: 1707.
Folio. 40 pp. Mod qtr mor.
(Robertshaw) **£55 [≈ $98]**
- The Humble Petition and Remonstrance of
Divers Citizens and other Inhabitants of the
City of London ... who lately presented their
Humble Presentation to the Houses of
Parliament. London: Maynwaring, 1642. 4to.
Title border. Stitched. Wing H.3436.

(Rostenberg & Stern) **$75** [≃ **£42**]
- The Humble Petition of both Houses of Parliament: Presented to His Majesty on the 14th of November. Oxford: Litchfield, 1642. 4to. Typographical title border. Stitched. Wing E.1570.
(Rostenberg & Stern) **$75** [≃ **£42**]
- The Humble Petition of Many Thousands of Young Men, and Apprentices of the City of London, to ... the ... Parliament Assembled ... 13 of July, 1647. London: 1647. 4to. Title within typographical border. Stitched. Wing H.3477. *(Rostenberg & Stern)* **$75** [≃ **£42**]
- The Humble Representation of the Committee, Gentry ... in the County of Leicester: to ... Thomas Lord Fairfax ... In reference to the Agreement of the People. London: Hood, 1648. 4to. Title border. Stitched. Wing H.3641.
(Rostenberg & Stern) **$125** [≃ **£70**]

Hume, David
- Dialogues concerning Natural Religion ... Second Edition. London: 1779. 8vo. Later name on title. Contemp tree calf, rebacked, new endpapers. *(Waterfield's)* **£350** [≃ **$623**]
- Essays, Moral and Political. The Third Edition, Corrected, with Additions. London: for A. Millar, & A. Kincaid, 1748. 12mo. Contemp calf. *(Hannas)* **£800** [≃ **$1,424**]
- Essays and Treatises on Several Subjects. A New Edition. London: for A. Millar, & A. Kinkaid & A. Donaldson, Edinburgh, 1758. 4to. viii,539,[1] pp. Contemp calf, brown label. *(C.R. Johnson)* **£1,350** [≃ **$2,403**]
- Essays and Treatises on Several Subjects. A New Edition. Dublin: J. Williams, 1779. 2 vols. Contemp tree calf, rebacked.
(C.R. Johnson) **£245** [≃ **$436**]
- Essays and Treatises on Several Subjects ... A New Edition. London: for T. Cadell, 1788. Contemp calf, black labels, fine.
(C.R. Johnson) **£350** [≃ **$623**]
- Essays and Treatises on Several Subjects ... Edinburgh: for T. Cadell ..., 1793. 2 vols. 8vo. iv,17-526, [errata leaf]; vii, 17-642 pp. Titles sl fingered with lib marks. Occas foxing. New qtr calf. *(Rankin)* **£135** [≃ **$240**]
- The History of England under the House of Tudor. London: for A. Millar, 1759. 1st edn. 2 vols. 4to. Half-titles. Sl marg worming. Contemp calf, gilt spines, contrasting morr labels. *(Ximenes)* **£375** [≃ **£211**]
- The History of England ... New Edition, with the Author's last Corrections and Improvements ... Life, written by himself. London: Cadell, 1778. 8 vols. 8vo. Frontis port vol 1. Half-titles where called for. Occas

sl marks. 19th c half calf, extrs sl worn.
(Blackwell's) **£175** [≃ **$312**]
- Political Discourses. The Second Edition. Edinburgh: R. Fleming, for A. Kincaid & A. Donaldson, 1752. 12mo. Intl advt leaf. Minor marg tears in 2 ff. 1 gathering foxed. Contemp calf. *(Hannas)* **£850** [≃ **$1,513**]

Hume, Hugh, Earl of Marchmont
- The Present Interest of the People of Great Britain, at Home and Abroad, consider'd: In a Letter to a Member of Parliament. London: for T. Cooper, [1758?]. 1st edn. 8vo. [2],54 pp, inc half-title. Disbound. Anon.
(Hannas) **£55** [≃ **$98**]
- A State of the Rise and Progress of Our Disputes with Spain, and of the Conduct of our Ministers relating thereto. London: for T. Cooper, MDCCXXIXX [1739]. 1st edn. 8vo. [4],76 pp, inc half-title. Disbound. Anon.
(Hannas) **£85** [≃ **$151**]

The Humourist ...
- See Gordon, Thomas

Humphreys, Samuel (translator & editor)
- Tales and Novels in Verse. From the French ... By Several Hands. Published and Compleated by Samuel Humphreys, Esq. London: printed in the year 1735. 1st edn. All published. 8vo. [ii],xii,vii, [i],252 pp. Frontis, 8 engvs. Sl wear. 19th c half calf.
(Burmester) **£175** [≃ **$312**]

Hunt, Thomas
- A Defence of the Charter, and Municipal Rights of the City of London. And the Rights of other Municipal Cities and Towns of England. Directed to the Citizens of London. London: Baldwin, [1682]. 1st edn. Sm 4to. [ii],46 pp. Cloth backed bds. Wing H.3750.
(Frew Mackenzie) **£60** [≃ **$107**]
- A Defence of the Charter and Municipal Rights of the City of London. London: Richard Baldwin, [1683]. 1st edn. 4to. [2],46 pp. Minute holes in 2 ff. Disbound. Wing H.3750. *(Hannas)* **£65** [≃ **$116**]
- The Great and Weighty Considerations, relating to the Duke of York ... London: Printed in the Year, 1680. 1st edn (?). Folio. [2],37 pp. Disbound. Wing H.3752. Anon.
(Hannas) **£35** [≃ **$62**]

Hunter, John
- A Treatise on the Blood, Inflammation, and Gun-Shot Wounds. To which is prefixed a Short Account of the Author's Life ... London: Nicol, 1794. 1st edn. 4to. lxvii,575 pp. Port, 9 plates. Orig bds, uncut, sm tear in

headband.   *(Gaskell)* **£1,850 [≈ $3,293]**
- A Treatise on the Venereal Disease. London:
1788. 2nd edn. 4to. [xii],398,index pp. 7
plates. Lib stamps on pastedowns & title.
Lacks free endpapers. Some spotting. Bds,
rebacked, crnrs sl worn, hinges reprd.
          (Francis Edwards) **£300 [≈ $534]**

Huntington, William
- A Divine Poem on the Shunamite. Addressed
to a Friend. London: sold by G. Terry ...,
1787. 1st edn. 8vo. Half-title. Advt leaf.
Disbound.   *(Ximenes)* **$375 [≈ £211]**

Hurtley, Thomas
- A Concise Account of Some Natural
Curiosities, in the Environs of Malham, in
Craven, Yorkshire. London: J. Walter, at the
Logographic Press, 1786. 1st edn. 8vo.
lxviii,200 pp. 3 plates (1 fldg). Rec half calf
gilt.   *(Hollett)* **£185 [≈ $329]**

Hutcheson, Francis
- An Essay on the Nature and Conduct of the
Passions and Affections with Illustrations on
the Moral Sense. London: for James & John
Knapton ..., 1730. 1st edn, 2nd issue. 8vo.
Contemp panelled calf Cambridge style,
rebacked.   *(Waterfield's)* **£675 [≈ $1,202]**
- An Inquiry into the Original of Our Ideas of
Beauty and Virtue; in Two Treatises ... The
Second Edition, Corrected and Enlarg'd.
London: for J. Darby ..., 1726. 8vo. Contemp
calf, rebacked.
          (Waterfield's) **£350 [≈ $623]**
- An Inquiry into the Original of our Ideas of
Beauty and Virtue; In Two Treatises ... The
Second Edition, Corrected and Enlarg'd.
London: for J. Darby, 1726. 8vo. xxvi, [ii],
304 pp. Contemp calf, mor label, red
sprinkled edges, rubbed, jnts cracked but
firm, sl worn. Anon. *(Finch)* **£300 [≈ $534]**
- An Inquiry into the Original of our Ideas of
Beauty and Virtue; in Two Treatises. The
Third Edition, corrected. London: Knapton,
1729. 8vo. xxii,[2],304 pp. Occas spotting.
Contemp calf, rebacked.
          (Spelman) **£280 [≈ $498]**
- A Short Introduction to Moral Philosophy, in
Three Books ... Translated from the Latin.
Glasgow: Foulis, 1764. 3rd English edn. 2
vols in one. 12mo. ix,[xv],186; [iii], 190-373,
[3] pp. Contemp continental mrbld bds, gilt
spine, mor label. *(Burmester)* **£250 [≈ $445]**

Hutchinson, Thomas
- The History of the Colony of Massachuset's
[sic] Bay ... Second Edition. London: M.
Richardson, 1765. Issue with corrected date.

8vo. iv,566 pp. 1 gathering springing.
Contemp speckled calf gilt, rebacked, crnrs sl
bumped.   *(Frew Mackenzie)* **£140 [≈ $249]**

Hutchinson, William
- An Excursion to the Lakes in Westmorland
and Cumberland ... London: Wilkie &
Charnley, 1776. 1st edn. 382,[4] pp. 19 plates
inc port frontis, vignette on p 1. Few sl spots.
Old tree calf gilt, gilt extra spine, hinges just
cracking.   *(Hollett)* **£220 [≈ $392]**

Hutchison, William
- The Spirit of Masonry, in Moral and
Elucidatory Lectures. Carlisle: for F. Jollie,
1795. 2nd edn. 8vo. [viii],362 pp.
Subscribers. Occas spotting. 19th c calf,
uncut, front jnt cracked.
          (Young's) **£140 [≈ $249]**

Huxham, John
- An Essay on Fevers. To which is now added,
a Dissertation on the Malignant, Ulcerous
Sore-Throat. Third Edition. London: 1757.
8vo. 356 pp. Contemp calf, sl worn.
          (Robertshaw) **£90 [≈ $160]**
- Medical and Chemical Observations upon
Antimony. London: 1756. 1st edn. 78 pp.
Half-title. Disbound.
          (Robertshaw) **£65 [≈ $116]**

The Idler ...
- See Johnson, Samuel

Imison, John
- The School of Arts. The Second Edition,
with very considerable additions. London: for
the author, by John Murray, [ca 1790]. 8vo.
xv, [i], errata leaf,319, [i],[2],advt leaf,
[4],errata leaf,176 pp. 24 plates. Rebound in
qtr calf gilt.   *(Spelman)* **£140 [≈ $249]**
- A Treatise of the Mechanical Powers. I. Of
the Lever ... VI. The Inclined Plane ...
London: for the author, sold by J. Murray,
[1787]. 1st edn. 8vo. [iv],39 pp. 2 fldg plates
inc frontis. Sm tear in 2nd plate, no loss. Mod
qtr calf.   *(Finch)* **£225 [≈ $401]**

Imitations ...
- Imitations of the Characters of Theophrastus.
London: for S. Leacroft, 1774. 1st edn. 8vo.
[vi],xxx,[ii],112 pp. Half-title. Contemp black
mor backed mrbld bds.
          (Burmester) **£125 [≈ $223]**

Imlay, Gilbert
- A Topographical Description of the Western
Territory of North America ... By George
[sic] Imlay. London: for J. Debrett, 1793. 2nd

edn. 8vo. "171" [ie 433],[19],[1],[2 advt] pp. 2
fldg maps, fldg plan, fldg table. Contemp tree
calf, gilt spine, sl worn.
                    (Chapel Hill) **$1,250 [≈ £702]**

Impartial ...
- An Impartial History of the French
Revolution, from its Commencement. Perth:
R. Morison Junior, for R. Morison & Sons,
1795. 2 vols. 8vo. Fldg map, 3 ports. Orig
bds, 1 jnt cracked, vol 2 backstrip defective.
                    (Waterfield's) **£80 [≈ $142]**

Impeachment ...
- The Impeachment of the Duke and Dutchess
of Lauderdale, with their brother My Lord
Hatton. Presented to His Majesty by the City
of Edenbrough. [London: 1679]. Drop-head title. 4 pp. Disbound.
Wing I.99.   *(Hannas)* **£35 [≈ $62]**

Inchbald, Elizabeth
- A Simple Story. In Four Volumes. London:
Robinson, 1791. 1st edn. 8vo. Lacks half-title
& 4 advt ff. Contemp half calf, sl worn.
                    (Hannas) **£280 [≈ $498]**
- A Simple Story. London: for G.G.J. & J.
Robinson, 1791. 1st edn. 4 vols. Sm 8vo.
Half-titles. 2 ff sprung. Contemp tree calf, gilt
spines, contrasting labels, trifle rubbed, 1
hinge sl cracked.   *(Ximenes)* **$600 [≈ £337]**

Ingen-Housz, John
- Experiments upon Vegetables, discovering
their great Power of Purifying the Common
Air in the Sun-shine ... London: for P.
Elmsly, 1779. 1st edn. 8vo. lxviii,302,[18] pp.
Title sl dusty & sm marg tear. Contemp calf,
rebacked, crnrs worn.
                    (Gaskell) **£1,800 [≈ $3,204]**

Inquiry ...
- An Inquiry into the Revenue, Credit, and
Commerce of France ... see Turner, G.

The Intelligencer ...
- See Swift, Jonathan & Sheridan, Thomas

Ireland, William Henry
- An Authentic Account of the Shakesperian
Manuscripts, &c. London: Debrett, 1796. 1st
edn. 8vo. [2],43 pp. Title ornament.
Disbound.   *(Hannas)* **£200 [≈ $356]**

Ironside, Nestor
- An Original Canto of Spencer ... see Croxall, S.

Irwin, Eyles
- A Series of Adventures in the Course of a

Voyage up the Red Sea, on the Coasts of
Arabia and Egypt ... Second Edition. London:
Dodsley, 1780. 4to. xvi,400 pp. Half-title. 3
fldg maps, 5 engvd plates on 3 pp. V occas sl
spotting. Contemp calf, backstrip relaid.
                    (Gough) **£350 [≈ $623]**

Ives, John
- Remarks upon the Garianonum of the
Romans: The Site and Remains Fixed and
Described. London: for S. Hooper ..., 1774.
Sm thin 8vo. Half-title,title, dedic, contents,
54 pp. Fldg map, 6 fldg plates. Contemp calf,
crnrs rubbed with sl loss, mod mor reback.
                    (Francis Edwards) **£135 [≈ $240]**

Izacke, Richard
- Remarkable Antiquities of the City of Exeter
... The Second Edition. Now very much
Enlarged ... by Samuel Izacke ... London:
Score, March, Birt, 1724. 8vo. Frontis, fldg
map, fldg plate. Contemp mor gilt, a.e.g.,
rebacked, rubbed, extrs worn.
                    (Clark) **£85 [≈ $151]**

**Jackson, Thomas, of Corpus Christi
College, Oxford**
- The Works ... With the Authors Life ...
London: Clark, for Martyn, Chiswell, Clark,
1673. 3 vols. Folio. [l],1043,[i]; [vi], 1096, [i];
[i],980,[xxxviii],[i] pp. Contemp calf,
rebacked, new endpapers. Wing J.90.
                    (Blackwell's) **£175 [≈ $312]**

Jackson, William
- Thirty Letters on Various Subjects. Third
Edition with considerable additions. London:
1795. 8vo. 236 pp. Lacks half-title. Contemp
tree calf.   *(Robertshaw)* **£60 [≈ $107]**

Jacob, Giles
- The Complete Court-Keeper: Or, Land-
Steward's Assistant ... London: His Majesty's
Law Printers, 1764. 6th edn. 8vo. viii, 534,25
pp. Minor marg worm. Old calf.
                    (Young's) **£75 [≈ $134]**
- A New Law-Dictionary ... The Third
Edition, with very large Additions ... London:
1736. Folio. Lib labels on endpapers, lib
stamp on final leaf. Contemp calf, worn, jnts
cracked but secure, lacks label.
                    (Clark) **£85 [≈ $151]**
- A New Law-Dictionary ... Tenth Edition.
London: Strahan & Woodfall ..., 1782. Lge
folio. [vi],[iv],[989] pp. Unpaginated.
Contemp calf, bds detached.
                    (Vanbrugh) **£285 [≈ $507]**
- The Poetical Register: or, the Lives and
Characters of all the English Poets ...

London: A. Bettesworth ..., 1723. 2 vols. 8vo.
xxvi,[vi], 328,[xxviii]; vii,[i blank], [xi], [i
blank],444 pp. 2 port frontis, 12 ports. Sl
marks. Contemp calf, spine ends worn. Anon.
(Finch) **£300 [≈ $534]**

- The Rape of the Smock. An Heroi-Comical
Poem. In Two Books. London: for R.
Burleigh, 1717. 1st edn. 8vo. [6],39 pp.
Frontis. Disbound. Anon.
(Hannas) **£280 [≈ $498]**

Jacob, Giles, possible author
- The Complete Parish-Officer ... Second
Edition, with additions. London: Eliz. Nutt &
R. Gosling ..., 1720. 12mo. [iv],138,[10] pp.
Clean tear in 1 leaf. Contemp sheep. Anon.
(Burmester) **£100 [≈ $178]**

- Every Man His own Lawyer: or, a Summary
of the Laws of England in a New and
Instructive Method ... Third Edition, with
additions. London: E. & R. Nutt ..., 1740.
8vo. vi,456, [14] pp. Contemp reversed calf,
minor traces of wear. Anon.
(Burmester) **£160 [≈ $285]**

Jacob, Hildebrand
- Chiron to Achilles; a Poem. London: for
H.R. [ie Edinburgh: Ruddiman], 1732. 1st
8vo edn. 15 pp. Disbound. Anon.
(Hannas) **£55 [≈ $98]**

Jacob, J.
- Observations on the Structure and Draught of
Wheel-Carriages. London: E. & C. Dilly,
1773. 1st edn. 4to. 14 fldg plates. Contemp
calf, rebacked, orig label.
(Spelman) **£550 [≈ $979]**

Jago, Richard
- Poems Moral and Descriptive ... To which is
added, Some Account of the Life and
Writings of Mr. Jago. London: Dodsley,
1784. 1st edn. 8vo. [iii],vi-xxxi, [i],269 pp. 5
plates. Presumably lacks half-title. Rec qtr
calf. *(Burmester)* **£90 [≈ $160]**

James I, King of England
- At the fourth Session of Parliament begun
and holden by Prorogation at Westminster ...
in the seventh yeere of the Reigne of our most
Gracious Sovereigne Lord James ... London:
Robert Barker, 1610. Some browning. Mod
bds. STC 9506.5.
(Meyer Boswell) **$200 [≈ £112]**

- At the Parliament begun and holden at
Westminster by Prorogation, the 18. day of
November, in the fourth yeere of the Raigne
of our most Gracious Souveraigne Lord James
... London: Robert Barker, 1607. Some

browning. Mod three qtr calf. STC 9505.
(Meyer Boswell) **$350 [≈ £197]**

- The Kings Majesties Declaration to his
Subjects, concerning lawfull Sports to be
used. London: Bonham Norton, 1618. 4to.
[iv], 9,[iii] pp. Intl blank with w'cut 'A', final
blank. Disbound. STC 8566.
(Clark) **£300 [≈ $534]**

- The Kings Majesties Speech to the Lords and
Commons ... at Whitehall, on Wednesday the
xxi. of March ... London: Robert Barker,
[1609]. One of 3 issues. 4to. [68] pp. Some
staining, marg worm hole. Disbound. STC
14396.3. *(Clark)* **£75 [≈ $134]**

- The True Law of Free Monarchies. Or The
Reciprock and mutuall dutie betwix a free
King, and his naturall Subjects. London:
T.C. according to the copie printed at
Edenburgh, 1603. 8vo. Some wear, cut close.
New calf. STC 14410.5.
(Meyer Boswell) **$450 [≈ £253]**

Jardine, Alexander
- Letters from Barbary, France, Spain,
Portugal, &c. by an English Officer. London:
1788. 1st edn. 2 vols. xv,496; vii,528 pp. Tree
calf, gilt spines & dentelles, red & green
labels. Anon. *(Petrilla)* **$250 [≈ £140]**

Jefferies, David
- A Plain Narrative of a Journey from London
to Rome, etc. Liverpool: J. Sadler, [1750]. [4],
5-143 pp. Early 19th c half calf, mrbld bds.
(C.R. Johnson) **£265 [≈ $472]**

Jeffries, David
- A Treatise on Diamonds and Pearls ...
London: W.L. Molyneux, 1771. 4th edn,
crrctd. 8vo. xxiv,96 pp. 30 litho plates &
tables. Orig cloth, faded.
(Burmester) **£70 [≈ $125]**

Jenkins, David
- Eight Centuries of Reports: or, Eight
Hundred Cases solemnly adjudged in the
Exchequer Chamber ... The Second Edition
Corrected ... In the Savoy: for John Worall,
1734. Folio. Contemp calf.
(Vanbrugh) **£135 [≈ $240]**

Jenyns, Soame
- Poems. By *****. London: for R. Dodsley,
1752. 1st edn. 8vo. Final blank leaf. H5 & H6
are cancels. Contemp mottled calf, gilt spine.
Anon. *(Hannas)* **£140 [≈ $249]**

- A View of the Internal Evidence of the
Christian Religion. Boston: I. Thomas &
E.T. Andrews, 1793. Lge 12mo. 162 pp.
Foxed. Some fraying prelims. Rec wraps.

(Hartfield) **$165 [≃ £93]**
- The Works ... prefixed, Short Sketches of the Author's Family, and also of his Life; by Charles Nalson Cole. London: Cadell, 1790. 1st coll edn. 4 vols. 8vo. Port. Contemp tree calf, spines rubbed, lacks labels.
(Burmester) **£50 [≃ $89]**

Jerningham, Edward
- The Ancient English Wake. A Poem. London: William Richardson for James Robson, 1779. 4to. Engv inserted to face title. 19th c half mor, rubbed.
(Waterfield's) **£50 [≃ $89]**
- The Fall of Mexico, a Poem. London: Scott for Robson, 1775. 1st edn. 4to. [4],59 pp. Disbound. *(Hannas)* **£85 [≃ $151]**
- The Funeral of Arabert, Monk of La Trappe: a Poem. A New Edition. London: for J. Robson, 1771. 2nd edn. 4to. 24 pp. New bds.
(Claude Cox) **£18 [≃ $32]**
- Poems. London: Scott for J. Robson, 1774. 8vo. 126 pp. Contemp half leather, v worn.
(Bates & Hindmarch) **£35 [≃ $62]**
- Poems. London: Scott for Robson, 1774. 1st coll edn. Thick Paper. 8vo. [6],126 pp. Mod half calf, uncut. *(Hannas)* **£120 [≃ $214]**

Johnson, Charles
- The Wife's Relief: or, the Husband's Cure. A Comedy ... London: Tonson, 1712. 1st edn. 4to. Lib number on title verso. Early 20th c half mor. *(Hannas)* **£160 [≃ $285]**

Johnson, Charles, Captain
- A General History of the Robberies and Murders of the most Notorious Pyrates ... see Defoe, Daniel.

Johnson, Richard
- Choice Scraps, Historical and Geographical, consisting of Pleasing Stories and Diverting Anecdotes ... London: E. Newbery, [1790]. 178,2 advt pp. 4 engvs. Pink bds, worn, spine taped. *(James)* **£325 [≃ $579]**

Johnson, Samuel, 1649-1703
- A Confutation of a late Pamphlet Intituled, A Letter Ballancing the Necessity of keeping a Land-Force in Times of Peace. London: A. Baldwin, 1698. 4to. Disbound. Wing J.824. Anon. *(Rostenberg & Stern)* **£125 [≃ £70]**
- Julian's Arts to undermine and extirpate Christianity. Together with Answers to Constantius the Apostate, and Jovian. London: J.D. for the author ..., 1689. 1st edn. 8vo. Half-title. Errata leaf. Contemp mottled calf, gilt spine (trifle rubbed). Wing J.832.

(Ximenes) **$150 [≃ £84]**
Johnson, Samuel
- A Dictionary of the English Language ... London: W. Strahan for J. & P. Knapton ..., 1755. 1st edn. 2 vols. Folio. Vol 1 title sl creased, few sm marg tears, 1 sm marg repr, v sl worm at end of vol 2. Calf, mid-19th c reback. *(Gough)* **£5,750 [≃ $10,235]**
- A Dictionary of the English Language ... Abstracted from the Folio Edition, by the Author ... Second Edition, Corrected. London: for J. Knapton ..., 1760. 2 vols. 8vo. Abrasion of vol 1 title. Marg stain vol 1. Contemp calf, rebacked.
(Burmester) **£350 [≃ $623]**
- A Dictionary of the English Language ... abstracted from the Folio Edition. The Fourth Edition, Corrected. London: Strahan, 1770. 2 vols. 8vo. Occas sl browning. Contemp calf, gilt spines, jnts, spine ends & crnrs reprd. *(Spelman)* **£120 [≃ $214]**
- A Dictionary of the English Language ... Abstracted from the Folio Edition, by the Author ... Fourth Edition, corrected ... London: for W. Strahan ..., 1770. 2 vols. 8vo. Contemp calf, gilt spines, contrasting labels, jnts reprd. *(Burmester)* **£250 [≃ $445]**
- A Dictionary of the English Language ... Fifth Edition. London: Strahan ..., 1773. 2 vols in one. 8vo. Sl spotting. Contemp calf, rebacked to style. *(Blackwell's)* **£250 [≃ $445]**
- A Dictionary of the English Language ... Abstracted from the Folio Edition, by the Author ... Fifth Edition, Corrected. London: for W. Strahan ..., 1773. 2 vols in one. 8vo. Contemp calf, spine ends reprd.
(Burmester) **£250 [≃ $445]**
- A Dictionary of the English Language ... The Fifth Edition. London: Strahan ..., 1784. 2 vols. Folio. Sm marg worm hole in 1st few gatherings vol 1. Contemp tree calf, gilt spine, red labels, jnts & extrs reprd.
(Frew Mackenzie) **£1,300 [≃ $2,314]**
- A Dictionary of the English Language ... Fifth Edition. London: Strahan, 1784. 2 vols. Folio. Port frontis dated 1786 mtd. Rec period style polished calf gilt.
(Hartfield) **$4,500 [≃ £2,528]**
- A Dictionary of the English Language ... London: John Jarvis, 1786. 2 vols. 4to. Port frontis. Half-title vol 1. Occas foxing & dusting. Contemp calf, mor labels, sl scuffed, spine ends sl worn. *(Clark)* **£450 [≃ $801]**
- A Dictionary of the English Language ... English Grammar ... Account of the Author's Life ... Dublin: Marchbank, 1798. 2 vols. 8vo. Port. Rec cloth. *(de Burca)* **£340 [≃ $605]**

- The False Alarm. The Second Edition. London: Cadell, 1770. Half-title, 53 pp. V sl occas traces of damp. Rebound in qtr calf, mrbld bds. *(C.R. Johnson)* **£245 [≈ $436]**
- The False Alarm. The Second Edition. London: T. Cadell, 1770. 8vo. [2],53 pp. Half-title. Mod qtr leather. Anon. *(O'Neal)* **$550 [≈ £309]**
- The Idler. Third Edition. London: T. Davies, J. Newbery ..., 1767. 2 vols. 294; 330 pp. Contemp tree calf gilt, sl rubbed, hd of spines worn. Anon. *(Jermy & Westerman)* **£50 [≈ $89]**
- A Journey to the Western Islands of Scotland. London: Strahan & Cadell, 1775. 1st edn. 8vo. [iv],384 pp. 6-line errata. Usual cancels D8 & U4. Closed tears to title reprd. Some foxing. Contemp calf, rebacked. Anon. *(Sotheran's)* **£200 [≈ $356]**
- A Journey to the Western Islands of Scotland. London: Strahan & Cadell, 1775. 1st edn. 6-line errata. 8vo. [ii],[ii errata],384 pp. Contemp qtr calf, jnts worn & splitting at hd, extrs rubbed, label worn. Anon. *(Finch)* **£200 [≈ $356]**
- A Journey to the Western Islands of Scotland. Dublin: for J. Williams, 1775. 12mo. Few clean tears, occas sl stains. Early Amer lib label. Contemp sheep backed mrbld bds, uncut, spine worn. *(Ximenes)* **$250 [≈ £140]**
- A Journey to the Western Islands of Scotland. New Edition. London: Strahan & Cadell, 1791. 3rd edn. 8vo. [ii],384 pp. Half calf gilt, rubbed, jnts just cracking. *(Hollett)* **£95 [≈ $169]**
- Letters to and from the late Samuel Johnson, LL.D. to which are added some Poems never before printed. Published ... by Hester Lynch Piozzi. London: Strahan & Cadell, 1788. 1st edn. 2 vols. 8vo. Some marg damp stain. Contemp qtr calf, rebacked, crnrs worn. *(Clark)* **£185 [≈ $329]**
- The Lives of the most Eminent English Poets ... London: for C. Bathurst ..., 1781. 4 vols. 8vo. Occas sm lib stamps. Sl later calf gilt, 1 jnr cracked, crack in lower section of 1 spine. *(Rankin)* **£150 [≈ $267]**
- The Poetical Works ... Now first collected in One Volume. London: for the editor, & sold by G. Kearsley, 1785. 1st coll edn. Sm 8vo. viii, 196,[4 advt] pp. Usual cancels A2, N2, N3, N4. Contemp sheep, rebacked. *(Sotheran's)* **£450 [≈ $801]**
- The Poetical Works ... Complete in One Volume. A New Edition. London: W. Osborne & T. Griffin ... & J. Mosley, Gainsborough, 1785. 2nd authorised edn. 8vo. viii,152 pp. Contemp sheep, sl worn.

(Clark) **£70 [≈ $125]**
- The Poetical Works. A New Edition. London: W. Osborne & T. Griffin ..., 1785. Contemp calf. *(C.R. Johnson)* **£85 [≈ $151]**
- The Poetical Works ... Complete in One Volume. A New Edition. London: W. Osborne & T. Griffin ..., & J. Mozley, Gainsborough, 1785. Half-title. Contemp calf, lacks label. *(C.R. Johnson)* **£85 [≈ $151]**
- The Poetical Works. A New Edition considerable enlarged. London: George Kearsley, 1789. Half-title, 212,12 advt pp. Rebound in qtr calf. *(C.R. Johnson)* **£85 [≈ $151]**
- Political Tracts. Containing, The False Alarm ... Dublin: for W. Whitestone ...; 1777. 1st Irish edn. 12mo. Contemp mottled calf, gilt spine, upper jnt sl cracked. Anon. *(Ximenes)* **$650 [≈ £365]**
- The Prince of Abissinia. A Tale ... The Fourth Edition. London: for W. Strahan ..., 1766. 2 vols. 12mo. Contemp calf, rebacked, dble mor labels. Anon. *(Waterfield's)* **£165 [≈ $294]**
- The Prince of Abissinia. A Tale. The Fifth Edition. London: Strahan, Dodsley, Johnston, 1775. 12mo. viii,304 pp. Contemp calf gilt, rubbed. *(Blackwell's)* **£65 [≈ $116]**
- The Rambler. Eighth Edition. London: W. Bowyer, W. Strahan ..., 1771. 4 vols. Contemp calf gilt, labels sl chipped, some jnts cracking. Anon. *(Jermy & Westerman)* **£60 [≈ $107]**
- The Rambler. The Eleventh Edition. London: Rivington ..., 1789. 4 vols. 12mo. Frontises (sl offset). Few ff sl foxed. Contemp calf gilt, gilt dec flat spines, mor labels, spines sl rubbed. Anon. *(Blackwell's)* **£135 [≈ $240]**
- The Works of the English Poets. With Prefaces, Biographical and Critical, by Samuel Johnson. London: H. Hughes ..., 1779-81. 1st edn. 67 (of 68) vols. 12mo. 29 port frontises. Sep titles to the 10 vols of "Prefaces ...". Orig calf, 19th c rebacking, sl worn. *(Chapel Hill)* **$2,800 [≈ £1,573]**
- The Works. Together with his Life, and Notes on his Lives of the Poets by Sir John Hawkins. London: J. Buckland ..., 1787. 1st coll edn. 13 vols. 8vo. Port. Occas spotting. Contemp calf, rebacked, red & black labels, some wear to crnrs. *(Appelfeld)* **$2,250 [≈ £1,264]**

Johnston, Nathaniel
- The Assurance of Abby and Other Church Lands in England to the Possessors, Cleared from the Doubts and Arguments Raised about the Danger of Resumption ... London: Henry

Hills, 1687. 1st edn. 8vo. [8],206,errata pp. Sl marks. Old calf, rebacked, worn. Wing J.872.
(D & D Galleries) **$200 [≃£112]**
- The Excellency of Monarchical Government, Especially of the English Monarchy ... London: for Robert Clavel, 1686. Large Paper. Folio. [x],480,[8] pp. Few sl lib marks. Sl soiling. Contemp calf, rebacked in mor, rubbed. Wing J.877.. *(Clark)* **£400 [≃$712]**

Johnston, Thomas
- General View of the Agriculture of the County of Tweedale with Observations ... London: Bulmer, 1794. 1st edn. 4to. 42,[2 blank] pp. Half-title. Disbound.
(Claude Cox) **£30 [≃$53]**
- General View of the Agriculture of the County of Selkirk, with Observations ... London: Bulmer, 1794. 1st edn. 4to. 50,[2 blank] pp. Half-title. Disbound.
(Claude Cox) **£30 [≃$53]**

Johnstone, Charles
- Chrysal: or, the Adventures of a Guinea ... By an Adept. The Second Edition greatly inlarged and corrected. London: for T. Becket, 1761. 2 vols. 12mo. Occas sl stains. Contemp sheep, rebacked. Anon.
(Hannas) **£40 [≃$71]**

Johnstone, James
- The Norwegian's Account of Haco's Expedition against Scotland; A.D. 1263. Now first published ... London: for the author, 1782. 1st edn. 8vo. xv,143,[14] pp. Lacks half-title & dedic leaf. Title frayed & mtd. Sl crnr stains. Rec qtr calf, uncut.
(Claude Cox) **£25 [≃$45]**

Jones, A.
- The Art of Playing at Skittles: or, the Laws of Nine-Pins Displayed ... London: for the author, & sold by J. Wilkie, 1773. 1st edn. 8vo. 56,[4 advt] pp. Rec calf, uncut.
(Burmester) **£850 [≃$1,513]**

Jones, David, Captain of the Horse Guards
- A Compleat History of Europe ... from ... 1676, to ... 1699. The Second Edition, Corrected and very much Enlarged ... London: Mead for Nicholson ..., 1699. 8vo. Contemp calf, later label. Wing J.928. Anon.
(Hannas) **£95 [≃$169]**
- The Secret History of Whitehall, from the Restoration .. to the Abdication of the late K. James [with: A Continuation of the Secret History ... to 1696]. London: 1697. 1st edn. 2 vols. 8vo. Lacks intl & final blank ff. Contemp calf, sl worn. Wing J.934,929,

934B. Anon. *(Hannas)* **£120 [≃$214]**
- The Secret History of White-Hall, from the Restoration of Charles II down to the Abdication of the late K. James. London: R. Baldwin, 1697. 1st edn. 8vo. Contemp sheep, rebacked in calf, crnrs rubbed. Wing J.934.
(Ximenes) **$175 [≃£98]**

Jones, Edward
- Musical and Poetical Relicks of the Welsh Bards ... London: for the author, [1794]. New edn, enlgd. 4to. 183,viii pp. 8 pp subscribers. Frontis (foxed), 1 plate. Calf gilt, minor wear spine ends, jnts splitting.
(Francis Edwards) **£200 [≃$356]**
- Musical and Poetical Relicks of the Welsh Bards ... New Edition, doubly augmented ... London: for the author ..., 1794. Sm folio. [ii],viii,123 pp. Frontis, engvd dedic, 30 dble-sided engvd ff of music (pp 124-183). Sl marg wear, browned. Mod buckram.
(Blackwell's) **£150 [≃$267]**

Jones, Henry
- The Heroine of the Cave. A Tragedy ... Dublin: W. Spotswood, 1775. 1st Dublin edn. 8vo. 60 pp. Disbound.
(Young's) **£25 [≃$45]**

Jones, John, Brecon
- Judges Judged out of their Own Mouthes: or, the Question resolved by Magna Carta ... London: W. Bently, 1650. 1st edn. 32mo. [4],117,[115] pp. Trimmed, no loss. 18th c calf, hd of spine chipped.
(Hermitage) **£200 [≃£112]**

Jones, R.
- An Inquiry into the State of Medicine, on the Principles of Inductive Philosophy. With an Appendix ... Edinburgh: 1781. xvi,376 pp. Some discoloration page edges. Contemp tree calf, backstrip relaid on cloth reback.
(Whitehart) **£140 [≃$249]**

Jones, Stephen
- Rudiments of Reason; or, The Young Experimental Philosopher ... London: E. Newbery, 1793. 1st edn. 3 vols in one. xv, 163; 186; 204,20 pp. Lacks front f.e.p. Reversed calf, rubbed.
(Jermy & Westerman) **£150 [≃$267]**

Jones, Sir William
- A Grammar of the Persian Language. London: J. Richardson, 1775. 2nd edn. 8vo. xix,191 pp. 2 lib stamps. Rec qtr leather gilt.
(Bates & Hindmarch) **£60 [≃$107]**

Jones, William, of Nayland
- An Essay on the Church ... Glocester: R. Raikes, 1787. 1st edn. 8vo. xv,[3],143 pp. Blank part of last leaf torn away. Disbound, uncut. Anon.   *(Young's)* **£70 [≈ $125]**
- An Essay on the First Principles of Natural Philosophy ... in Four Books. Oxford: Ptd at the Clarendon printing House ... London ... Dublin, 1762. 1st edn. 4to. [vi], 281 pp. 3 fldg plates. Contemp half mor, rather scuffed.
  (Burmester) **£150 [≈ $267]**
- The Religious Use of Botanical Philosophy. A Sermon. London: G. Robinson, 1784. 1st edn. 4to. [iv],iv,18 pp. Disbound.
  (Bookpress) **$85 [≈ £48]**

Jonson, Ben
- The Workes. London: Richard Bishop, sold by Andrew Crooke, 1640. 2nd folio edn. Sm folio. Port, engvd title. Contemp calf, rebacked, v sl surface damage. STC 14753.
  (Georges) **£400 [≈ $712]**
- The Works ... With Additions ... London: Thomas Hodgkin for H. Herringman ..., 1692. 3rd coll edn. Folio. Port. Occas browning, marg repr last leaf. Contemp calf, later reprs, scuffed, upper crnrs sl worn. Wing J.1006.   *(Clark)* **£380 [≈ $676]**

Jortin, John
- Discourses concerning the Truth of the Christian Religion. The Second Edition. London: for John Whiston, 1747. 8vo. Red & black title. 1 sm repr. Contemp calf, jnts cracked but sound, lacks label. Anon.
  (Waterfield's) **£45 [≈ $80]**
- The Life of Erasmus. London: J. Whiston & B. White, 1758. 1st edn. 4to. vi,[ii], 630, [ii] pp. Final advt leaf. Fldg port frontis, 2 pp facss at end. Few lib stamps. Rec half calf.
  (Clark) **£100 [≈ $178]**

Josephus, Flavius
- The Famous and Admirable Workes ... Faithfully Translated out of the Latine, and French, by Tho. Lodge ... London: Thomas Adams, 1620. 3rd edn of Lodge's version. Folio. [x],554,[iv], (555)-811,[29] pp. Sl marked. Contemp calf, later reback, crnrs sl worn. STC 14811.   *(Clark)* **£135 [≈ $240]**
- The Works ... Translated into English by Sir Roger L'Estrange ... London: Richard Sare, 1702. Folio. Title, [ii],1130 pp. Frontis, fldg map, fldg plan, 2 plates. Contemp calf, gilt spine, extrs sl worn, sm splits jnt ends.
  (Frew Mackenzie) **£320 [≈ $570]**

Journal ...
- The Journal of the Lds Commissioners of

Both Nations in the Treaty of Union. Edinburgh: Bell, 1706. 4to. Stitched.
  (Rostenberg & Stern) **$60 [≈ £34]**

Judgment on Alexander and Caesar ...
- See Saint-Evremond, C.M. de St. D.

Junius
- The Letters of Junius. London: for J. Wheble, 1770. 1st Wheble edn. 8vo. [iv],232 pp. Cap of liberty vignette on title with Wheble imprint below. [iv],232 pp. Old calf, rebacked.   *(Young's)* **£55 [≈ $98]**
- Stat Nominis Umbra. Letters of Junius. London: for Henry Sampson Woodfall, 1772. 2 vols. [2],xxxii,208; [2],356 pp. Fcap 8vo. Sl marg worm hole vol 1. Contemp qtr polished calf, gilt spines, vellum crnrs.
  (Spelman) **£38 [≈ $68]**
- Junius Stat Nominis Umbra. London: 1796. 2 vols. xv,[4],325; 366 pp. Engvd titles, 16 plates. Titles sl spotted. Rec half calf.
  (Francis Edwards) **£125 [≈ $223]**

Junius, Franciscus
- The Painting of the Ancients ... see Du Jon, Francois

Jura Coronae ...
- See Brydall, John

Juvenal de Carlencas, Felix de
- The History of the Belles Lettres, and of Arts and Sciences, from their Origin down to the Present Times ... Translated from the French. London: for James Hodges, 1741. 1st edn, 2nd issue. 8vo. Half-title. Contemp calf gilt, sl rubbed.   *(Ximenes)* **$450 [≈ £253]**

Kalm, Peter
- Travels into North America ... Translated ... by John Reinhold Foster. London: T. Lowndes, 1777. 2nd English edn. 2 vols. 8vo. 414,423 pp. Fldg map, 6 plates. 20th c three qtr mor, t.e.g., by Bradstreet.
  (Chapel Hill) **$1,800 [≈ £1,011]**

Kames, Henry Home, Lord
- Sketches of the History of Man. Considerably enlarged by the last additions and corrections of the Author. Edinburgh: for Strahan & Cadell, London, & Creech, Edinburgh, 1788. 4 vols. Japanese paper over bds. Anon.
  (Wreden) **$250 [≈ £140]**

Keate, George
- The Alps. A Poem. London: for R. & J. Dodsley, 1763. 1st edn. 4to. [viii],27 pp. Title vignette. Disbound. *(Burmester)* **£45 [≈ $80]**

- An Epistle from Lady Jane Gray to Lord Guilford Dudley supposed to have been written in the Tower a few days before they suffered. London: Dodsley, 1762. 4to. Mod wraps. Anon. *(Waterfield's)* £135 [≈ $240]

Keating, Geoffrey

- The General History of Ireland ... London: B. Creake, 1732. 2nd edn. Folio. [10],563,[1 blank], [2],[12], [2],xvi pp. Frontis, 2 fldg maps, 40 plates. Old style calf.
  (O'Neal) $625 [≈ £351]

Keay, Isaac

- The Practical Measurer his Pocket Companion ... The Third Edition ... With an Appendix ... London: T. Wood, for J. Knapton ..., 1724. Narrow 8vo. [iv],3,[xiii], 143, [1], 15,[3],10 pp. Tables. Contemp sheep, fine. *(Burmester)* £150 [≈ $267]

Keill, John

- An Introduction to the True Astronomy ... London: 1760. 5th edn. 8vo. xvii,396 pp. 25 plates. Calf, spine worn.
  (Key Books) $600 [≈ £337]

Keith, George

- George Keith's Fourth Narrative of his Proceedings at Turners-Hall ... London: Brabazon Aylmer, 1700. 1st edn. 4to. [viii], 116,[4] pp. Half-title. Disbound.
  (Clark) £35 [≈ $62]
- A Third Narrative of the Proceedings at Turners Hall, The Twenty First Day of April 1698 ... London: C. Brome, 1698. 1st edn. 4to. [iv],68 pp. Some browning, tear in last 2 ff. Disbound. Wing K.218.
  (Clark) £30 [≈ $53]

Keith, William, Sir

- A Collection of Papers and other Tracts, Written occasionally on Various Subjects ... London: J. Mechell, 1740. 1st edn. 8vo. (iii)-xxiv,228 pp. 2 lib stamps. 1 sm repr. Lib buckram. *(Clark)* £85 [≈ $151]

Kellison, Matthew

- The Right and Ivrisdiction of the Prelate, and the Prince. Or, a Treatise of Ecclesiasticall, and Regall Authoritie ... [Douai: P. Auroi] Anno Dom: 1621. 2nd edn, enlgd. Sm 8vo. 412,[4] pp. Sl damp stains. 18th c calf, new label, jnt ends split. STC 14911.
  (Sotheran's) £125 [≈ $223]

Kelly, Hugh

- Thespis: or, a Critical Examination into the Merits of all the Principal Performers

belonging to Drury-Lane Theatre. London: for G. Kearsly, 1766. 1st edn. 4to. half-title. Errata slip on final blank. 1st & last pp dust stained. Mod qtr mor, vellum crnrs. Anon.
  (Hannas) £400 [≈ $712]

Kelly, James

- A Complete Collection of Scottish Proverbs. Explained and Made Intelligible to the English Reader. London: William & John Innys, 1721. 1st edn. 8vo. [14],400,[18] pp. Later bds, spine sl worn.
  (Karmiole) $175 [≈ £98]

Kelynge, William

- A Report of Cases in Chancery, the King's Bench, &c. In the Fourth ... Eighth Years of his late Majesty King George the Second ... London: in Bell-Yard, 1764. 2 parts in one vol. Folio. Contemp calf, front bd detached.
  (Vanbrugh) £125 [≈ $223]

Kennedy, John

- A Treatise upon Planting, Gardening, and the Management of the Hot-House ... Dublin: for W. Wilson, 1784. 1st Dublin edn. 8vo. xiii, [iii], 462,[2 advt] pp. Tiny marg worm, occas sl spot. Contemp tree calf, smooth spine, mor label, spine worn, sides rubbed.
  (Finch) £75 [≈ $134]
- A Treatise upon Planting, Gardening, and the Management of the Hot-House ... Dublin: W. Wilson, 1784. 1st Irish edn. 462,2 advt pp. Contemp calf, red label.
  (C.R. Johnson) £175 [≈ $312]

Kennet, White

- A Sermon preach'd at the Funeral of the Right Noble William Duke of Devonshire ... With some Memoirs of the Family of Cavendish. London: 1708. 1st edn. 8vo. 208 pp. Contemp calf. *(Robertshaw)* £38 [≈ $68]

Kennett, Basil

- A Brief Exposition of the Apostles Creed, According to Bishop Pearson, In a New Method ... London: Churchill, 1705. 1st edn. 8vo. xxiv,191 pp. Sm rust hole in 1 leaf. Contemp panelled calf. *(Young's)* £55 [≈ $98]
- An Essay towards a Paraphrase of the Psalms, in English Verse. To which is added a Paraphrase of the Third Chapter of the Revelations. London: B.H. for B. Aylmer, 1706. 1st edn. 8vo. Contemp panelled calf.
  (Ximenes) $275 [≈ £154]
- Romae Antiquae Notitia: Or, the Antiquities of Rome ... London: T. Child & R. Knaplock, 1699. 2nd edn, enlgd. 8vo. [38], 376, [22] pp. 11 plates. Contemp calf. Wing K.299.

(O'Neal) **$300 [≈ £169]**

- Romae Antiquae Notitia: or, the Antiquities of Rome ... Tenth Edition. London: Knapton, 1737. 4to. [16],xxx,375,[23] pp. Port frontis, 13 plates. Contemp calf gilt (rubbed, worn).   *(Ars Libri)* **$175 [≈ £98]**
- Romae Antiquae Notitia: or, the Antiquities of Rome ... Fifteenth Edition. London: C. Bathurst, 1776. [xvi],xxx,375, [1], [24] pp. Plates. Contemp calf, worn, front hinge cracked, tips worn. *(Bookpress)* **$100 [≈ £56]**
- Romae Antiquae Notitia: or, the Antiquities of Rome ... Sixteenth Edition. London: C. Bathurst ..., 1785. 8vo. [xvi], xxx, 375,[27] pp. Port frontis, 14 plates. Contemp sheep, inelegantly rebacked, crnrs sl worn.
(Clark) **£24 [≈ $43]**

Kent, Nathaniel
- General View of the Agriculture of the County of Norfolk ... Norwich: the Norfolk Press ..., 1794. 2nd edn. 8vo. Errata leaf. Fldg map, 3 plates (1 fldg). Contemp red half mor, grey bds sides sl marked.
(Georges) **£200 [≈ $356]**
- General View of the Agriculture of the County of Norfolk. London: Richard Phillips, 1796. 8vo. xvi,236,[2] pp. Fldg hand cold map, 3 plates. Orig bds, paper label.
(Spelman) **£170 [≈ $303]**
- Hints to Gentlemen of Landed Property ... London: Dodsley, 1775. 1st edn. 8vo. vii,[i], 268 pp. 10 fldg plates, tables in text. Contemp calf, mor label, gilt spine, hd of spine chipped, crnrs worn, jnts cracked.
(Finch) **£165 [≈ $294]**
- Hints to Gentlemen of Landed Property ... London: Dodsley, 1775. 1st edn. 8vo. vii,[i], 268 pp. 10 fldg plates, tables in text. Contemp calf, mor label, gilt spine, hd of spine chipped, crnrs worn, jnts cracked.
(Finch) **£165 [≈ $294]**
- Hints to Gentlemen of Landed Property ... London: Dodsley, 1776. 2nd edn. 8vo. vii,282 pp. 9 fldg plates. Sm worm hole occas touching a letter. Rec half calf.
(Young's) **£120 [≈ $214]**
- Hints to Gentlemen of Landed Property. To which are now first added, Supplementary Hints. London: Dodsley, 1793. New edn. 8vo. vii,286 pp. 10 plates (6 fldg). Rebound in half calf.   *(Francis Edwards)* **£140 [≈ $249]**

Kersey, John
- The Elements of that Mathematical Art commonly called Algebra ... London: Godbin for Passenger & Hurlock, 1673-74. 1st edn. 2 vols in one. Folio. [x],323,[i]; [iv],416 pp. 2

errata pp. Occas sl foxing. Contemp calf, gilt spine, hinges cracked but firm. Wing K.352.
(Vanbrugh) **£495 [≈ $881]**
- The Elements of that Mathematical Art commonly called Algebra, expounded in Four Books. London: William Godbid for Thomas Passinger and Benjamin Hurlock, 1673-74. 1st edn. 2 vols in one. [x],323; [iv],323 pp. Intl blank. Port. Contemp calf, sl worn. Wing K.352.   *(Gaskell)* **£850 [≈ $1,513]**

Keys, J.
- The Antient Bee-Master's Farewell; or, Full and Plain Directions for the Management of Bees. London: 1796. 1st edn. 8vo. xvi,273 pp. 2 plates. Trifle foxed. Calf, reprd.
(Wheldon & Wesley) **£175 [≈ $312]**

Keysler, John George
- Travels through Germany, Bohemia, Hungary, Switzerland, Italy, and Lorraine ... London: for G. Keith ..., 1760. 3rd edn. 4 vols. 8vo. 9 plates, fldg list. Speckled calf gilt, gilt dentelles, gilt spines, minor rubbing to extrs.   *(Francis Edwards)* **£350 [≈ $623]**

Kidgell, John
- The Card. London: for the maker, sold by J. Newbery, 1755. 1st edn. 2 vols. 12mo. Cold frontis & plate. Early notes on 1st title. Contemp calf, spine sl worn. Anon.
(Hannas) **£480 [≈ $854]**

Kilburn, Richard
- Choice Presidents upon all Acts of Parliament, relating to the Office and Duty of a Justice of Peace ... The Seventh Edition, very much enlarged ... London: for Jacob Tonson, 1703. 497,table pp. Contemp calf, jnts cracking. *(C.R. Johnson)* **£145 [≈ $258]**

Killigrew, Henry
- The Conspiracy. A Tragedy ... London: John Norton, for Andrew crooke, 1638. 1st edn. 4to. Final blank N4. Leaf E3 crrctly signed. Sm hole in 1 leaf. Disbound. STC 14958.
(Hannas) **£380 [≈ $676]**

Killigrew, Thomas
- Comedies and Tragedies. London: for Henry Herringman, 1664. 1st coll edn. Folio. 576,80 pp. 8 sep title-pages. Lacks port frontis. Occas spotting & browning to prelims. Sm repr last leaf. Few marg blind stamps. Mod half calf gilt. Wing K.450.   *(Hollett)* **£250 [≈ $445]**

Kilner, Dorothy
- Father's Advice to his Son. Written chiefly for the Perusal of Young Gentlemen. London:

John Marshall, [1790?]. [2],153,[3] pp. Advts. Contemp mrbld bds, sheep spine (sl chipped in 2 places). Anon.
(C.R. Johnson) **£350 [≈ $623]**

Kimber, Edward

- The Life, Extraordinary Adventures, Voyages, and Surprising Escapes of Capt. Neville Frowde, of Cork. In Four Parts. Written by himself. Berwick: for W. Phorson ..., 1792. 12mo. iv,[vi],218,[2 advt] pp. Soiled. Contemp sheep, rebacked. Fiction.
(Burmester) **£185 [≈ $329]**

Kimber, Isaac

- The Life of Oliver Cromwell ... Fourth Edition. London: J. Brotherton, 1741. 8vo. vi,[2 advt],vii-xxii,408 pp. Port. Sl wear to title. Contemp calf, sl rubbed, sl worm to rear pastedown. Anon. *(Blackwell's)* **£85 [≈ $151]**
- The Life of Oliver Cromwell. Fifth Edition. Birmingham: C. Earl, 1778. 373 pp. Occas lib stamps, foxing. Lib cloth.
(Jermy & Westerman) **£20 [≈ $36]**

King, Edward

- Morsels of Criticism tending to illustrate some few Passages in the Holy Scriptures upon Philosophical principles and an Enlarged View of Things. London: J. Nichols, 1788. 4to. Contemp half calf, reprd. Anon. *(Waterfield's)* **£85 [≈ $151]**

King, William

- The Art of Love: in Imitation of Ovid De Arte Amandi ... London: for Bernard Lintott, sold by William Taylor & Henry Clements, [1708]. 1st edn. 8vo. xl,194,[4 advt] pp. Frontis. Sl water stain. Contemp panelled sheep, rebacked. *(Fenning)* **£85 [≈ $151]**
- The Art of Love: In Imitation of Ovid De Arte Amandi, with a Preface containing the Life of Ovid. London: [1709]. 1st edn. 8vo. 195,[4 advt] pp. Frontis. Crnr of title torn without loss. Contemp calf, rebacked.
(Robertshaw) **£60 [≈ $107]**
- The State of the Protestants in Ireland under the late King James's Government ... London: Robert Clavell, 1691. 4to. [xxviii], 1-336, 341-372,365-396, 387-408,[2] pp. Imprimatur leaf, final advt leaf. Occas sl spotting. Contemp calf, later reback. Wing K.538 Anon. *(Clark)* **£220 [≈ $392]**

King-Killing ...

- The King-Killing Doctrine of the Jesuites: Delivered in a Plain and Sincere Discourse to the French King, Concerning the Re-establishment of the Jesuites in his

Dominions. London: Crooke & Dring, 1679. 4to. Stitched. Wing K.560A.
(Rostenberg & Stern) **$150 [≈ £84]**

The Kingdom of Sweden restored ...

- See Cerdan, Jean Paul, Comte de

Kingston, R.

- A True History of the Several Designs and Conspiracies against His Majesties Sacred Person and Government ... London: for the author, sold by Abel Roper, 1698. 8vo. [xii], 312, [6 advt] pp. MS index. 2 faint marg blind stamps. Mod half calf gilt. Wing K.615.
(Hollett) **£65 [≈ $116]**

Kingston, Richard

- A True History of the Several Designs and Conspiracies, against his Majesties Sacred Person and Government ... By R.K. London: for the author, 1698. 8vo. [iv],311 pp. Possibly lacks half-title. Period mottled calf, sl worn. Wing K.615. *(Rankin)* **£125 [≈ $223]**

Kippis, Andrew

- The Life of Captain James Cook. Dublin: Chamberlaine, Colles ..., 1788. 527 pp. Half-title. Contemp calf, red label.
(C.R. Johnson) **£550 [≈ $979]**

Kirby, John

- The Suffolk Traveller: or, a Journey through Suffolk ... By John Kirby who took an Actual Survey of the whole County .... Ipswich: John Bagnall, 1735. 1st edn. 12mo. title, [ii],206,[i errata] pp. Sl later calf, spine rubbed. Inscrbd by author's son.
(Frew Mackenzie) **£180 [≈ $320]**

Kirby, Joshua

- Dr. Brook Taylor's Method of Perspective Made Easy, both in Theory and Practice. Ipswich: 1755. 2nd edn. xvi,78,84 pp. Frontis by Hogarth, 22 + 27 plates. Sl spotting. Contemp half calf. *(Europa)* **£260 [≈ $463]**

Kirkland, Thomas

- A Commentary on Apoplectic and Paralytic Affections and on Diseases connected with the Subject. London: Wm. Dawson, 1797. 8vo. vii, 191, index,[1 advt] pp. Contemp calf, later gilt spine.
(Bates & Hindmarch) **£325 [≈ $579]**

Knatchbull, Sir Norton

- Annotations upon Some Difficult Texts in all the Books of the New Testament. Cambridge: J. Hayes for W. Graves, 1693. 1st edn in English. 8vo. [xvi],320 pp. Imprimatur leaf.

Contemp calf, rubbed, crnrs sl worn. Wing K.672. *(Clark)* **£45 [≈ $80]**

Knight, Ellis Cornelia
- Dinarbas; a Tale: being a Continuation of Rasselas. Prince of Abissinia. London: for C. Dilly, 1779. 1st edn. 12mo. Contemp roan, rebacked. Anon. *(Hannas)* **£320 [≈ $570]**
- Dinarbas, a Tale, being a Continuation of Rasselas, Prince of Abissinia. London: for C. Dilly, 1790. 8vo. Contemp calf, mor label. Anon. *(Waterfield's)* **£125 [≈ $223]**

Knight, Richard Payne
- The Landscape, a Didactic Poem ... The Second Edition. London: W. Bulmer, 1795. 2nd edn, enlgd. 4to. xv,[1],104 pp. 3 plates. Orig bds, uncut, rebacked, crnrs bumped, 2-inch split in upper jnt.
(Spelman) **£280 [≈ $498]**

Knox, John
- A Tour through the Highlands of Scotland, and the Hebride Isles, in MDCCLXXXVI. London: for J. Walter ..., 1787. 1st edn. 8vo. clxxii, 274, [ii],104,[4] pp. Endpapers spotted or browned. Contemp tree calf gilt, rebacked. *(Hollett)* **£250 [≈ $445]**

Knox, Vicesimus
- Essays Moral and Literary. London: for Charles Dilly, 1782. 3rd edn. 2 vols. 12mo. Engvd frontis & vignette to each vol. Contemp sprinkled calf, spines worn, 1 jnt weak. *(Young's)* **£29 [≈ $52]**

The Koran
- The Alcoran of Mahomet Translated ... into French by the Sieur du Ryer ... newly Englished [by Alexander Ross]. London: 1649. 1st English edn & translation. 408 pp. Crnrs of title reprd, ink stain. Old leather, rebacked, new endpapers, hd of spine chipped. *(King)* **$450 [≈ £253]**
- The Alcoran of Mahomet. Translated ... into French by the Sieur du Ryer ... newly Englished ... London: Printed, 1649. 1st English translation. 4to. [xxiv],407,[xiv] pp. Final blank. V sl damp staining. Mod qtr calf. Wing K.747. *(Blackwell's)* **£285 [≈ $507]**
- The Alcoran of Mahomet. Translated ... into French by the Sieur du Ryer ... newly Englished ... London: Printed, 1649. 8vo. [xx], 405,[xv] pp. Some marg ink marks throughout. Mod half calf. Wing K.747A. *(Blackwell's)* **£200 [≈ $356]**

Kytchin, John
- Le Court Leete, et Court Baron. London:

Tottel, 1580. 1st sep edn. Contemp calf, worn but sound. STC 15017 (& Addenda). *(Meyer Boswell)* **$1,750 [≈ £983]**

L., B.
- A True and Faithful Coppy of a Real Letter, written by a Friend in Utrecht, to a Friend in London. Giving an Account of some remarkable Passages, relating to his Grace James, Duke of Monmouth. [London: 1679?]. 1st edn. Folio. 4 pp. Disbound. Wing L.8. *(Hannas)* **£45 [≈ $80]**

Labelye, Charles
- A Short Account of the Methods made use of in Laying the Foundation of the Piers of Westminster-Bridge ... London: A. Parker, 1739. 1st edn. 8vo. [iv],vi,82 pp. Some water staining throughout. Later bds.
(Bookpress) **$450 [≈ £253]**

La Calprenede, Gaultier de Coste, Seigneur de
- Cassandra: The Fam'd Romance ... Rendered into English by Sir Charles Cotterell ... London: for A. Moseley, 1664. 4th English edn. Folio. [xii],358, [iv],363-858,[i] pp. Addtnl engvd title. Occas sl damp stains. Contemp sheep, Victorian reback. Wing L.108. Anon. *(Vanbrugh)* **£255 [≈ $454]**
- The Famous History of Cassandra ... Written originally in French, and newly translated into English, by several hands. London: Isaac Cleave ..., 1703. 8vo. iv,286; 208; 127 pp. Frontis (laid down on endpaper). Sl marks. Some sm marg worm holes. Contemp calf, rebacked *(Burmester)* **£200 [≈ $356]**

La Condamine, Charles Marie de
- Journal of a Tour to Italy ... London: Lewis, Kearsley, 1763. 1st edn. 12mo. xxii,[ii], 253,errata,[4 advt] pp. Contemp calf gilt.
(Frew Mackenzie) **£200 [≈ $356]**

Ladies ...
- The Ladies Calling ... see Allestree, Richard
- The Ladies Visiting-Day ... see Burnaby, William

Lady ...
- The Lady's Rhetorick: containing Rules for Speaking and Writing Elegantly ... Done from the French, with some improvements. London: for J. Taylor & A. Bell, 1707. [4],138,[2] pp. Contemp sheep, rebacked. *(C.R. Johnson)* **£385 [≈ $685]**
- The Lady's Rhetorick: containing Rules for Speaking and Writing Elegantly ... Done from the French, with some Improvements.

London: for J. Taylor, 1707. Sm 8vo. [4],138 pp, contents leaf. Some browning. Contemp calf, rebacked.   *(Spelman)* **£220 [≈ $392]**

La Fare, Charles Augustus de, Marquis
- Memoirs and Reflections upon the Principal Passages of the Reign of Louis the XIVth ... by Monsieur L.M.D.F. Translated from the French. London: for Mary Kettilby ..., 1719. 8vo. Contemp calf, rubbed, sm chip hd of spine. Anon.   *(Waterfield's)* **£75 [≈ $134]**

La Fontaine, Jean de
- Fables and Tales from La Fontaine. In French and English. Now first Translated ... Prefix'd, The Author's Life. London: for A. Bettesworth, & C. Hitch & C. Davis, 1743. 8vo. [14],xxvi,293,[1 advt] pp. Sl damp stain prelims. Contemp calf, rebacked.   *(O'Neal)* **$275 [≈ £154]**

La Martiniere, Pierre Martin de
- A New Voyage into the Northern Countries, describing ... the Norwegians, Laponians, Kilops ... London: for John Starkey, 1674. 1st English edn. 12mo. Cancel title. Lacks A1 (as always, presumably blank). Mod calf. Wing L.204.   *(Hannas)* **£1,500 [≈ $2,670]**

Lamb, Patrick
- Royal Cookery: or, The Compleat Court Cook ... Second Edition ... London: for Nutt & Roper ..., 1716. 2nd edn, enlgd. viii,302, [iii], [v],[i] pp. 40 plates. V occas sl damp stains. Some plates sl torn at hinges. Contemp calf, sometime rebacked.   *(Gough)* **£600 [≈ $1,068]**

Lambard, William
- Eirenarcha, or of the Office of the Justices of Peace, in foure bookes ... [Bound with] The Duties of Constables ... London: Company of Stationers, 1614. [ii],634,[80], 94 pp. Contemp calf, backstrip relaid. Some wear & worm. STC 15173, 15159.   *(Meyer Boswell)* **$650 [≈ £365]**
- Eirenarcha, or Of the Office of the Justices of the Peace, in foure bookes: Revised, corrected, and enlarged ... London: 1619. Occas damp staining & sl browning. Closely trimmed & sl marg worm without loss. Contemp style sheep. STC 15174.   *(P and P Books)* **£325 [≈ $579]**

Lambard, William, probable author
- The Orders, Proceedings, Punishments, and Priviledges of the Commons House of Parliament in England. [London?]: 1641. Browned. Mod three qtr calf. Wing E.2675.

Anon.   *(Meyer Boswell)* **$350 [≈ £197]**

Lambe, Robert
- An Exact and Circumstantial History of the Battle of Floddon. In Verse ... With Notes. Berwick upon Tweed: R. Taylor, 1774. 1st edn. 8vo. 126,[1 erratum],156 pp. Frontis. 1 sm repr. New contemp style half calf, uncut.   *(Young's)* **£110 [≈ $196]**

Lambert de Saumery, Pierre
- The Devil turn'd Hermit: or, the Adventures of Ashtaroth banish'd from Hell. A Satirical Romance. London: J. Hodges ..., 1741. 1st edn in English. 12mo. Frontis. Contemp calf gilt, rebacked. Anon.   *(Ximenes)* **$475 [≈ £267]**

Lamy, Bernard
- The Art of Speaking: written in French by Messieurs du Port Royal ... rendred into English. London: W. Godbid, sold by M. Pitt, 1676. 1st edn in English. 8vo. 3 advt ff. Mod half calf. Wing L.307A.   *(Ximenes)* **$275 [≈ £154]**

Lancelot, Claude (editor & translator)
- A New Method of Learning the Italian Tongue. Translated from the French of Messieurs de Port Royal ... London: for J. Nourse, 1750. 1st edn in English. 8vo. [xvi], 366,[2 advt] pp. Half-title. Contemp calf, section missing from hd of spine. Anon.   *(Burmester)* **£110 [≈ $196]**

Langbaine, Gerard
- The Foundation of the University of Oxford, with a Catalogue of the Principall Founders and Speciall Benefactors of all the Colleges ... London: for Thomas Jenner, 1651. 1st edn. 4to. [ii],17 pp. Rec half calf. Wing L.370. Anon.   *(Gaskell)* **£200 [≈ $356]**

Langhorn, Richard
- The Speech ... at his Execution July 14, 1679 ... [London: 1679]. 1st edn. Folio. 4 pp. Drop-head title. Disbound. Wing L.399.   *(Hannas)* **£25 [≈ $45]**

Langhorne, John
- The Effusions of Friendship and Fancy. In Several Letters to an from Select Friends ... London: Becket & De Hondt, 1763. 1st edn. 2 vols. Sm 8vo. [iv],180; [iv],157, [i],[xxx] pp. Contemp mottled calf gilt, mor labels, spine ends worn, jnts splitting but firm. Anon.   *(Finch)* **£180 [≈ $320]**
- The Letters that passed between Theodosius and Constantia ... Second Edition. London: Becket & De Hondt, 1764. Sm 8vo.

xxvii,185,[2 advt] pp. Half-title. Frontis. Early polished calf gilt, gilt spine, jnts cracked but strong.   *(Fenning)* **£75 [≈$134]**

- Owen of Carron: a Poem. London: Edward & Charles Dilly, 1778. 8vo. Title vignette. Minor marg reprs at end. Disbound.
        (Waterfield's) **£125 [≈$223]**

- The Poetical Works ... London: Becket & De Hondt, 1766. 1st coll edn. 2 vols. Sm 8vo. Final advt leaf. frontis. Contemp roan, rebacked.   *(Hannas)* **£250 [≈$445]**

Langley, Batty

- The Builder's Director, or Bench-Mate: being a Pocket Treasury of the Grecian, Roman and Gothic Orders of Architecture ... London: A. Webley, 1763. 12mo. xxiv pp. 184 engvd plates on 92 ff. Contemp calf, rebacked.
        (Sotheran's) **£250 [≈$445]**

- The Builders Complete Assistant ... London: Richard Ware, [1738]. 1st edn. 2 vols (text & plates). Roy 8vo in 4s. [viii],200 pp; 77 dble-page plates. Subscribers. Contemp calf gilt, spine of plate vol v worn.
        (Vanbrugh) **£855 [≈$1,522]**

- Practical Geometry applied to the Useful Arts of Building, Surveying, Gardening and Mensuration ... London: for R. & J. Innys ..., 1726. 1st edn. Folio. [iv],viii, [viii], 136 pp. 40 fldg plates. Red & black title, w'cut decs. Contemp calf, jnts cracked but sound.
        (Gaskell) **£1,250 [≈$2,225]**

- Practical Geometry Applied to the Useful Arts of Building, Surveying, Gardening and Mensuration ... London: Innys ..., 1726. 1st edn. Folio. 40 fldg plates. Contemp panelled calf, label chipped, jnts cracked.
        (Georges) **£450 [≈$801]**

Langley, Batty & T.

- The Builder's Jewel: or, The Youth's Instructor and Workman's Remembrancer ... London: for R. Ware, 1757. 4th edn. 8vo. 34 pp. 99 engvd plates, plus 2 duplicates. Contemp calf, front jnt weak.
        (Young's) **£220 [≈$392]**

- The Builder's Jewel ... New Edition. London: T. Longman, 1794. 14th edn. Sm 8vo. [1],45,[1] pp. Frontis, 99 plates. Mod calf.
        (Sotheran's) **£320 [≈$570]**

Langley, Thomas

- The History and Antiquities of the Hundred of Desborough, and Deanery of Wycombe, in Buckinghamshire ... London: 1797. Only edn. 4to. xiv,[ii],482 pp, errata leaf. Fldg frontis map, 3 fldg plates, 2 fldg pedigrees. Lacks half-title. Contemp half calf, sl worn & rubbed.   *(Blackwell's)* **£180 [≈$320]**

Langlois, Francois

- The Favorites Chronicle. London: 1621. 1st English edn. Sm 4to. [ii],41 pp. Tiny hole at hd of title. Rec half calf, new endpapers. STC 15203 (edn with 'began' on line 2 of B2v). Anon.   *(Sotheran's)* **£248 [≈$441]**

La Roche-Guilhem, Anne de

- The History of Female Favourites. London: Parker, 1772. 8vo. Calf, front bd detached. Anon.   *(Rostenberg & Stern)* **$225 [≈£126]**

La Rochefoucault, Francois de

- Maxims and Moral Reflections. London: T. Pridden, 1775. 12mo. [ix],14-160 pp. Contemp sheep, gilt spine, sl rubbed.
        (Clark) **£40 [≈$71]**

- Moral Maxims: by the Duke de la Roche Foucault. Translated from the French. With Notes. London: for A. Millar, 1749. 1st edn of this translation. 12mo. half-title. Contemp calf, worn, upper jnt cracked.
        (Hannas) **£65 [≈$116]**

Last ...

- The Last Years Transactions Vindicated from the Aspersions Cast upon them in a Late Pamphlet. London: Baldwin, 1690. 4to. Wraps. Wing L.536. *(Rostenberg & Stern)* **$85 [≈£48]**

Latrobe, Benjamin Henry

- Characteristic Anecdotes, and Miscellaneous Authentic Papers, tending to Illustrate the Character of Frederic II, late King of Prussia ... London: Stockdale, 1788. 1st edn. 8vo. xxiii,[i]. 342,[2 errata] pp. Contemp calf, gilt spine. hd of spine reprd.
        (Burmester) **£150 [≈$267]**

Laud, William

- A relation of the Conference between William Laud ... and Mr. Fisher the Jesuit ... The Fourth Edition revised ... London: for Thomas Basset ..., 1686. Folio. [xiv], 253, [xiii] pp. Minor marks. Contemp sheep, rubbed, 1 crnr sl worn. Wing L.595.
        (Clark) **£50 [≈$89]**

- A Summarie of Devotions ... Now published according to the Copy written with his own hand ... Oxford: William Hall, 1667. 1st Oxford edn. 8vo. [iv], "333" [ie 331],[i] pp. Some spotting. Contemp calf, gilt spine, extrs worn, jnts tender. Wing L.600.
        (Clark) **£48 [≈$85]**

Laughing Philosopher ...

- The Laughing Philosopher. Dublin: for James Williams, 1777. 244 pp. Rebound in calf.   *(C.R. Johnson)* **£75 [≈$134]**

Laurence, John

- The Fruit-Garden Kalendar: or, A Summary of the Art of Managing the Fruit-Garden. London: 1718. 1st edn. 8vo. [ii],vi,v, [i], 149, [3] pp. Fldg plate, text ills. Lacks half-title. Later sprinkled calf, jnt weak.
(Henly) **£100 [≈ $178]**

- A New System of Agriculture. Being a Complete Body of Husbandry and Gardening ... London: for Tho. Woodward, 1726. 1st edn. Folio. [xxiv],456 pp. Frontis, 2 plates, w'cut ornaments. Contemp calf, few scrapes. Earl of Hadington b'plate.
(Sotheran's) **£598 [≈ $1,064]**

Lavardin, Jacques de

- The Historie of George Castriot, surnamed Scanderberg, King of Albanie ... London: for William Ponsonby, 1596. 1st English edn. Folio. [xiv],498,[18] pp. Final leaf laid down. Lacks 1st blank. Occas soil. 20th c calf gilt. STC 15318.
(Hollett) **£250 [≈ $445]**

Lavater, Jean-Caspar

- Essays on Physiognomy; for the Promotion of the Knowledge and Love of Mankind. London: for Robinson, 1789. 3 vols. 8vo. vi,240; 324; 314,index pp. 360 plates. Contemp calf gilt, rebacked, vol 2 jnts weak.
(Europa) **£295 [≈ $525]**

- Essays on Physiognomy ... Translated from the last Paris Edition by the Rev. C. Moore ... London: 1797. 4 vols. 243; 186; 288; 334 pp. Num engvd plates (inc 3 by William Blake). Later leather.
(Fye) **$500 [≈ £281]**

- Letter to the French Directory. London: Hatchard, 1799. 8vo. Advts at end. Stitched.
(Rostenberg & Stern) **$100 [≈ £56]**

- Secret Journal of a Self-Observer; or, Confessions and Familiar Letters ... Translated from the German Original, by the Rev. Peter Will. London: Cadell & Davies, [1795]. 1st edn in English. 2 vols. 8vo. viii, 280; xxxv,[i],372 pp. Contemp half calf, rubbed.
(Burmester) **£160 [≈ $285]**

Law is a Bottomless-Pit ...

- See Arbuthnot, John

Law, William

- A Serious Call to a Devout and Holy Life ... London: William Innys, 1729. 1st edn. 8vo. [ii],vi,499,[5 advt] pp. Mod buckram.
(Blackwell's) **£250 [≈ $445]**

Lawson, John

- The History of Carolina ... London: for W. Taylor & J. Baker, 1714. 1st edn, 2nd issue.

Sm 4to. [6],258,[1] pp. Fldg map (sl foxed), 1 plate. Contemp calf, rebacked, crnrs rubbed.
(Chapel Hill) **$8,500 [≈ £4,775]**

- Lectures Concerning Oratory. Delivered in Trinity College, Dublin. Dublin: George Faulkner, 1759. 1st edn. 8vo. xxviii,454,[2 advt] pp. 3 ff sl soiled. Contemp mottled calf, gilt label.
(Spelman) **£180 [≈ $320]**

Lawson, William & Markham, Gervase

- A New Orchard and Garden ... With [Gervase Markham's] The Country Housewifes Garden ... London: Okes for Harrison, 1631. 4th edn. Sm 4to. [viii],74, [ii],77-134 pp. Colophon at end. Num w'cuts. Sm worm in gutter. 19th c bds, rebacked. STC 17396.
(Vanbrugh) **£275 [≈ $490]**

The Lay-Man's Answer ...

- The Lay-Man's Answer to the Lay-Man's Opinion. In a Letter to a Friend. London: Printed in the Year, 1687. 1st edn. 4to. 12 pp. Blank foredge of title torn off. Disbound. Wing L.747.
(Hannas) **£35 [≈ $62]**

Leake, Stephen Martin

- An Historical Account of English Money ... Third Edition, with Additions. London: for R. Faulder ..., 1793. 8vo. viii,428, [xx],[6 appendix] pp. 14 plates (occas sl spotting). Period calf, gilt spine, hinges cracked but firm.
(Rankin) **£85 [≈ $151]**

Le Clerc, Daniel

- The Compleat Surgeon. Second Part ... Containing an Exact and Complete Treatise of Osteology ... London: 1710. x,348 pp. Contemp calf, rebacked.
(Whitehart) **£120 [≈ $214]**

- The Compleat Surgeon. or, The Whole Art of Surgery explain'd in a most familiar Method. London: 1727. 6th edn. Occas sl foxing. Tear in last page. Contemp Cambridge calf, sl worn, new label. *(Whitehart)* **£350 [≈ $623]**

Le Clerc, Sebastien

- Practical Geometry: Or, A New and Easy Method of Treating that Art ... London: for T. Bowles, print and Map-Seller ..., 1727. 3rd edn. 8vo. 195,[6] pp. 80 engvd letterpress plates. Occas sl soiling. Contemp panelled calf, front jnt cracking.
(Young's) **£260 [≈ $463]**

- A Treatise of Architecture, with remarks and Observations ... engraven ... by John Sturt. Translated by mr. Chambers. London: Richard Ware, 1732. 8vo. [6 engvd],[8],v,[1], 143,[3] pp. Frontis, 181 plates on 91 ff. Rec half calf. *(Sotheran's)* **£375 [≈ $668]**

Le Comte, Louis Daniel

- Memoirs and Observations ... Made in a Late Journey Through the Empire of China ... London: Tooke ..., 1697. 1st English edn. 8vo. Port, 3 plates (2 fldg, 1 full-page), fldg table, 1 text engv. Contemp sprinkled calf, fine. Wing L.831.
  (Georges) £1,250 [≈ $2,225]
- Memoirs and Observations ... Made in a Late Journey Through the Empire of China. London: Tooke, 1697. 1st English edn. 8vo. Advts at end. Frontis, 3 plates (2 fldg, 1 full-page), half-page plate & chart. Calf, rebacked, somewhat loose in bndg. Wing L.831.
  (Rostenberg & Stern) $425 [≈ £239]

Le Courayer, Pierre Francois

- A Defence of the Dissertation on the Validity of the English Ordination. Against the Several Answers made to it ... London: William & John Innys, 1728. 1st edn. 2 vols. 8vo. xx,520,[4 advt]; [vi,[2 advt],584 pp. Contemp panelled calf, spine hds nicked. Anon.
  (Young's) £100 [≈ $178]

Lediard, Thomas

- The Naval History of England, in all its Branches; from the Norman Conquest in 1066, to the Conclusion of 1734. London: 1735. 1st edn. 2 vols in one. Folio. Frontis vol 1. Inner marg of 1st few ff strengthened. Contemp calf, rebacked.
  (Robertshaw) £150 [≈ $267]

Lee, Nathaniel

- The Dramatick Works. London: W. Feales ..., 1734. 3 vols. 12mo. 13 plates. Contemp calf, gilt spines, extrs sl worn, jnts cracked, 2 labels defective. *(Clark)* £38 [≈ $68]
- Gloriana, or the Court of Augustus Caesar ... London: for J. Magnes & R. Bentley, 1676. 1st edn. 4to. Lacks intl blank leaf. Prelims sl browned. Disbound. Wing L.849.
  (Hannas) £220 [≈ $392]
- Lucius Junius Brutus; Father of his Country. A Tragedy. London: for Richard & Jacob Tonson, 1681. 1st edn. Sm 4to. Epilogue leaf. Mor, inner dentelles gilt, upper jnt cracked. Wing L.853. *(Ximenes)* $350 [≈ £197]
- Lucius Junius Brutus; Father of his Country. A Tragedy ... London: Richard Tonson & Jacob Tonson, 1681. 1st edn. 4to. Sm marg reprs. Some stains. Half calf, spine sl worn. Wing L.852. *(Hannas)* £180 [≈ $320]
- Sophonisba, or Hannibal's Overthrow. A Tragedy. London: for R. Magnes & R. Bentley, 1676. 1st edn. Sm 4to. Straight grained mor gilt, spine rubbed, front cvr detached. Wing L.870.

(Ximenes) $475 [≈ £267]
- The Tragedy of Nero, Emperour of Rome ... London: for Magnes & Bentley, 1675. 1st edn. 4to. Epilogue leaf. Title sl dust soiled. Disbound. Wing L.883.
  (Hannas) £160 [≈ $285]

Lee, Sophia

- The Chapter of Accidents: a Comedy ... Dublin: J. & R. Byrn, 1781. 1st Irish edn. Lge 12mo. xi,[1],71 pp. Rec wraps.
  (Fenning) £35 [≈ $62]

Le Gendre, Louis

- The History of the Reign of Lewis the Great, till the General Peace Concluded at Reswick, In the Year 1697. Made English from the third Edition of the French. London: 1699. Only English edn. [xl],310,[ii errata] pp. Minor stains. Rec half calf. Wing L.944.
  (Clark) £125 [≈ $223]

Le Grand, Anthony

- Entire Body of Philosophy, according to the Principles of the Famous Renate Des Cartes, in Three Books ... Now Carefully Translated ... London: 1694. 1st edn in English. [xxviii],403, [2],[264] pp. 102 engvs (1 fldg). Contemp leather, bds loose.
  (Gach) $650 [≈ £365]

Leigh, Charles

- The Natural History of Lancashire, Cheshire and the Peak in Derbyshire ... Oxford: 1700. Folio. [xviii],190,[4], 97,[1], 109,[33] pp. Port, engvd title, imprimatur, dble page map, 24 plates. Occas offsetting. Half calf, rebacked, crnrs reprd. *(Henly)* £315 [≈ $561]
- The Natural History of Lancashire, Cheshire and the Peak, in Derbyshire ... Oxford: for the author, 1700. Folio. [xx],[4 subscribers],[2 advt],112,[36 index] pp. Port, dble page map, 24 plates. Contemp polished calf gilt, edges worn, jnts cracked but sound.
  (Hollett) £280 [≈ $498]

Leigh, Edward

- Critica Sacra: or Philologicall and Theological Observations upon all the Greek Words of the New Testament ... The second Edition corrected, and much enlarged ... London: 1646. 4to. [xvi],456,[xxviii] pp. Contemp calf, sl worn. Wing L.990.
  (Clark) £48 [≈ $85]
- A Philologicall Commentary: or, an Illustration of the most obvious and useful words in the Law ... London: for Charles Adams, 1658. 2nd edn, enlgd. Sm 8vo. [xvi], 245, [11] pp, inc A1 blank & final advt leaf.

Name removed from hd of title. Contemp calf, rebacked. WIng L.999.

(Burmester) **£300 [≈ $534]**

Leigh, Edward & Leigh, Henry

- Select and Choyce Observations, Containing All the Romane Emperours ... London: R. Daniel for J. Williams, 1657. 8vo. [12],277 pp. 19th c half leather, spine gilt extra. Wing L.1003.

(O'Neal) **$225 [≈ £126]**

Leighton, Francis

- The Muse's Blossoms: or, Juvenile Poems. London: printed by W. Frederick, at Bath ..., 1769. [8],58 pp. Disbound. Anon.

(C.R. Johnson) **£320 [≈ $570]**

Leland, John

- The Itinerary ... Collated, and Improved from the Original MS [by Thomas Hearne]. Oxford: at the Theater, 1744-45. 2nd Hearne edn. 9 vols. 8vo. 3 plates. Calf.

(D & D Galleries) **$475 [≈ £267]**
- The Itinerary ... Third Edition. Printed from Mr. Hearne's corrected Copy in the Bodleian Library. Oxford: 1770. 9 vols in 4. 8vo. Title vignettes, 3 plates, 23 ills. Lacks list of subscribers vol 1. Faint offsetting. Contemp calf gilt, sl worn but firm.

(Blackwell's) **£175 [≈ $312]**

Leland, Thomas

- The History of Ireland from the Invasion of Henry II ... Dublin: R, Marchbank for R. Moncrieffe, 1773. 1st edn. 3 vols. 4to. Half-titles. Occas faint foxing. Contemp calf gilt, red & green labels, some sl wear.

(Blackwell's) **£375 [≈ $668]**
- The History of the Life and Reign of Philip King of Macedon; the Father of Alexander. The Second Edition. London: E. Johnston, 1775. 2 vols in one. 8vo. lxxv, [1], 319, [1],[2],476 pp. Half-titles. Fldg map, fldg plate. 19th c half calf gilt.

(Spelman) **£50 [≈ $89]**

Le Maire, Henri

- The French Gil Blas; or, Adventures of Henry Lanson. London: C. & G. Kearsley, 1793. 1st English edn. Contemp polished calf, black labels.

(C.R. Johnson) **£650 [≈ $1,157]**

Lemery, Louis

- A Treatise of all Sorts of Foods, Both Animal and Vegetable: also of Drinkables ... Translated by D. Hay, M.D. ... Third Edition ... London: for T. Osborne, 1745. Lge 12mo. xii,372,[xxiv] pp. Approbation

leaf before title. V sl marg worm. Contemp calf, spine ends sl chipped.

(Gough) **£350 [≈ $623]**

Lemery, Nicolas

- A Course of Chymistry, containing an easie Method of Preparing those Chymical Medicins which are used in Physick ... London: R.N. for Kettilby, 1698. 3rd edn. 7 plates & Explication. New calf, orig bds laid down. Wing L.1040.

(P and P Books) **£280 [≈ $498]**

Lempriere, William

- A Tour from Gibraltar to Tangier, Sallee, Mogodore, Santa Cruz, Tarudant ... to Morocco ... London: for the author, 1791. 1st edn. 8vo. xl,464 pp. Fldg map (laid down). Contemp tree calf, rebacked.

(Gough) **£145 [≈ $258]**

Le Neve, John

- Monumenta Anglicana: Being Inscriptions on the Monuments of Several Eminent Persons Deceased in or since the Year 1680, to the end of the Year 1699 ... London: 1718. 8vo. Half-title, title, [i advt],[ii],[i errata], 210,[iv],[vi] pp. Occas browning. Contemp calf, rebacked.

(Francis Edwards) **£75 [≈ $134]**

Lenthall, William

- A Letter sent from the Speaker of both Houses of Parliament to his Majestie on the Isle of Wight ... the 25th of August 1648. London: M.B., 1648. 4to. Royal arms on title. Stitched. Wing L.1075. Anon.

(Rostenberg & Stern) **$85 [≈ £48]**

Leonardo Da Vinci

- See Da Vinci, Leonardo

Le Poivre, M.

- Travels of a Philosopher: Or Observations on the Manners and Arts of Various Nations in Africa and Asia ... Dublin: for P. & W. Wilson ..., 1770. 1st Dublin edn. 12mo. vi, [ii], 183 pp. Contemp calf.

(Young's) **£230 [≈ $409]**

Le Sage, Alain Rene

- The Bachelor of Salamanca, or Memoirs of Don Cherubim de la Ronda. In Three Parts. Translated by Mr. Lockman. Dublin: George Faulkner, 1737. 1st Dublin edn. 12mo. [8], 259, [1] pp. 3 plates. Contemp calf, hinges rubbed & starting to crack.

(Karmiole) **$100 [≈ £56]**

Leslie, Charles
- The Best Answer Ever was Made. And to which no Answer Ever will be Made ... London: J. Morphew, 1709. 1st edn. 8vo. [iv],28 pp. Sl browned. Some page numerals cropped. Rec wraps. Anon.
 (Young's) £45 [≈ $80]
- Mr. Lesley to the Lord Bishop of Sarum. [London: 1715]. 4to. Caption title. Stitched.
 (Rostenberg & Stern) $40 [≈ £22]
- A New History of Jamaica ... Second Edition. London: for J. Hodges, 1740. 8vo. 2 fldg maps. Sl browning. Contemp calf, red label, crnrs bumped, jnts starting but firm. Anon.
 (Georges) £450 [≈ $801]
- Satan Disrob'd from his Disguise of Light: or, The Quakers Last Shift to Cover their Monstrous Heresies ... Second Edition, with some Improvements ... London: C. Brome ..., 1698. 4to. [xii],100 pp. Some browning, outer ff sl soiled. Disbound. Wing L.1151. Anon.
 (Clark) £28 [≈ $50]

Leslie, Charles & Dodwell, Henry
- A Sermon Preached at Chester, against Marriages in Different Communions ... London: W.B. for Brome & Strahan, 1702. 1st edn. 8vo. [xvi],63, [ix],254,[i] pp. Final blank. Sl marked. Contemp calf, later rebacked, crnrs sl worn. *(Clark)* £85 [≈ $151]

L'Estrange, Hamon
- The Alliance of Divine Offices, Exhibiting all the Liturgies of the Church of England since the Reformation; as also the late Scotch Service-Book ... Second Edition. London: 1690. Folio. [xvi], "339" [ie 330], [i] pp. Contemp calf, rebacked, sl worn & used. Wing. L.1184.
 (Clark) £110 [≈ $196]

L'Estrange, Sir Roger
- Fables of Aesop and other Eminent Mythologists: With Morals and Reflections. London: 1738. 8th edn, crrctd. [x],548 pp. Port frontis, 1 plate. Contemp speckled calf, edges rubbed, spine ends sl chipped, jnts sl tender. *(Francis Edwards)* £48 [≈ $85]
- Remarks on the Growth and Progress of Non-Conformity. London: Walter Kettilby, 1682. 1st edn. 4to. [ii],51,[i] pp. Disbound. Anon. Wing L.1296. *(Clark)* £45 [≈ $80]

Leti, Gregorio
- The Life of Donna Olimpia Maldachini ... Written in Italian by Abbot Gualdi: and faithfully rendred into English. London: sold by Richard Littlebury, 1667. Sm 8vo. Lacks final blank. Title laid down, some foredges strengthened. Mod calf. Wing L.1334A.

Anon.   *(Hannas)* £55 [≈ $98]

Letter(s) ...
- A Letter concerning the Disabling Clauses lately offered to the House of Commons, for regulating Corporations. London: Randal Taylor, 1690. 1st edn. Sm 4to. 22 pp. Final blank (C4) present. Rec qtr cloth, unpressed & untrimmed. Wing L.1351.
 (Blackwell's) £50 [≈ $89]
- A Letter from a Gentleman in Town to his Friend in the Country, recommending the Necessity of Frugality. London: for W. Webb ..., 1751. 3rd edn. 8vo. 24 pp. Marg hole in last leaf. 1 blank crnr torn.
 (Young's) £20 [≈ $36]
- Letter from a Member of the States-General in Holland to a Member of Parliament in England; by which the Saddle is put upon the Right Horse ... London: J. Robinson, 1743. 1st edn. 8vo. [iv],54 pp. Half-title. Cropped. Disbound. *(Young's)* £50 [≈ $89]
- A Letter from an English Traveller to his Friend at London relating to the Difference betwixt the Courts of Prussia and Hanover ... London: 1730. 8vo. 57,[3 advt] pp. Disbound. *(Robertshaw)* £20 [≈ $36]
- A Letter from the Devil to the Pope and his Prelates, written at the beginning of the Reformation, and now published for the Confirmation of Protestants ... [London?: 1670]. 1st edn. Folio. 4 pp. Drop-head title. 2-inch stain on both ff. Wing L.1517.
 (Hannas) £25 [≈ $45]
- A Letter of a French Protestant to a Scottishman of the Covenant ... see Du Moilin, Pierre, the younger
- A Letter sent from the Inhabitants of Hull to the Right Worshipfull the high Sheriffe, and the rest of the Gentry in the County of Yorke ... London: F.B., 164[2]. Sm 4to. [i],5 pp. Faint crnr water stain. Mod wraps, untrimmed. Wing L.1609/1609A, variant.
 (Blackwell's) £65 [≈ $116]
- A Letter sent from the Speaker of both Houses of Parliament to his Majestie on the Isle of Wight ... see Lenthall, William
- A Letter to a Member of Parliament, concerning the Four Regiments commonly called Mariners. London: for A. Baldwin, 1699. 1st edn. 4to. 14 pp, blank leaf. Disbound. Wing L.1670.
 (Hannas) £60 [≈ $107]
- A Letter to a Member of Parliament concerning the four Regiments commonly called Marines. London: A. Baldwin, 1699. 1st edn. Sm 4to. 14 pp. Final 3 blanks present. Sl stained. New qtr calf. Wing

L.1670. *(Blackwell's)* £100 [≈$178]
- A Letter to a Member of Parliament. Concerning the Present State of Affairs at Home and Abroad. By a True Lover of the People. London: for T. Cooper, 1740. 1st edn. 8vo. [iv],60 pp. Half-title. Sl dusty at ends. Disbound. *(Young's)* £45 [≈$80]
- Letter to a Proprietor of the East-India Company. London: for T. Osborne, 1750. 1st edn. 8vo. 123 pp. Lacks half-title. Disbound. *(Hannas)* £180 [≈$320]
- A Letter to a Right Honourable Member of Parliament, demonstrating the absolute Necessity of Great Britain's assisting the House of Austria ... By an Impartial Hand. London: for T. Cooper, 1742. 1st edn. 8vo. iv, 55,[4] pp. Disbound.
(Hannas) £95 [≈$169]
- A Letter to David Garrick, Esq. concerning a Glossary to the Plays of Shakespeare ... see Warner, Richard
- A Letter to His Royal Highness the Duke of York, touching his Revolt from, or Return to the Protestant Religion. By an Old Cavalier. [Colophon] London: for William Inghall, 1681]. 1st edn. Folio. 8 pp. Disbound. Wing L.1707. Signed: Philanax Verax.
(Hannas) £40 [≈$71]
- A Letter to Lord B----. With an Address to the Town. [London]: for W. Flexney, Holborn, 1768. Only edn. 8vo. [ii],28 pp. No half-title. Disbound. *(Young's)* £150 [≈$267]
- A Letter to Mr. S. a Romish Priest concerning the Impossibility of the Publick Establishment of Popery here in England. [London: 1672]. 1st edn. Folio. 4 pp. Drophead title. Marg water stains. Disbound. Wing L.1718. *(Hannas)* £20 [≈$36]
- A Letter to the Author of the History and Mystery of Good-Friday. By A Layman ... Cambridge: Francis Hodson, 1782. Only edn. 8vo. viii,31 pp. Disbound.
(Young's) £80 [≈$142]
- A Letter to the Late Recorder of N[ewcastle] from an Old Friend. London: for W. Webb ..., [1754?]. 1st edn. 8vo. xxiv,87 pp. Inner margs frail with sl loss on last leaf. Disbound. *(Young's)* £50 [≈$89]
- A Letter to the Prince of Wales, on a Second Application to Parliament, to discharge Debt wantonly contracted since May, 1787 ... London: for J. Owen, 1795. 11th edn. 8vo. xxiv,87 pp. Disbound. *(Young's)* £20 [≈$36]
- A Letter to the Right Honourable William Pulteney Esq occasion'd by a Bill depending in the House of Commons for raising One Hundred Thousand Pounds upon the Roman-Catholicks ... London: for J. Roberts,

1723. Folio. Marg tear to title. Sewn as issued. *(Waterfield's)* £225 [≈$401]
- A Letter to the Right Honourable Charles Townshend ... London: for W. Nicoll ..., 1764. 1st edn. 8vo. 43 pp. Disbound.
(Young's) £65 [≈$116]
- A Letter to the Right Honourable J--- P---, Speaker of the House of Commons in Ireland. London: for J. Wilkie, 1767. 1st edn. 8vo. 44 pp. Some spotting at end. Disbound.
(Young's) £45 [≈$80]
- Letters and Tracts on the Choice of Company and other Subjects ... see Bolton, Robert.
- Letters from a Farmer in Pennsylvania ... see Dickinson, John.
- Letters from an American Farmer ... see Crevecoeur, M.G.St.J.
- Letters from an Officer in the Guards to his Friends in England ... see Ayscough, George Edward
- Letters from Barbary ... see Jardine, Alexander
- Letters from Paris, during the Summer of 1791 ... see Weston, Stephen
- The Letters of Simkin the Second ... see Broome, Ralph
- Letters to a Young Nobleman ... see Bolton, Robert
- Letters, in the Original, with Translations and Messages, that passed between the King, Queen, Prince, and Princess of Wales; on Occasion of the Birth of the Young Princess. London: 1737. 1st edn. Sm 4to. 30 pp. Sl staining at beginning. Mod wraps.
(Robertshaw) £18 [≈$32]

Lettsom, J.C.
- Memoirs of John Fothergill, M.D. London: 1786. 4th edn. 8vo. viii,280,[8] pp. Engvd title, 5 ports. Mod buckram.
(Wheldon & Wesley) £70 [≈$125]

Lewis, David (editor)
- Miscellaneous Poems by Several Hands. London: J. Watts, 1726. 1st edn. 8vo. [xvi], 320 pp. Occas sl foxing, few page edges dusty. Rec qtr calf. *(Clark)* £150 [≈$267]

Lewis, John
- A Complete History of the several Translations of the Holy Bible, and New Testament, in English ... The Second Edition, with large Additions. London: H. Woodfall, for Joseph Pote, Eton, 1739. 8vo. xx,48, 65-376, [iv] pp. Fldg plate. Contemp calf, sl worn. *(Clark)* £75 [≈$134]
- The History of Great-Britain, From the First

Inhabitants ... 'Till the Death of Cadwalader
... London: F. Gyles ..., 1729. 1st edn. Folio.
[6],251,[1 blank],[18], 52, [38] pp. Sep title to
Lloyd's Breviary of Britayne. Vignette. Few sl
marks. Contemp calf, rebacked.
                              (O'Neal) $225 [≈£126]
- The History of the Life and Sufferings of the
Reverend and Learned John Wicliffe ...
London: Knaplock & Wilkin, 1720. 1st edn.
8vo. xxvi,405,[i] pp. Contemp calf, extrs
worn, lacks label, upper jnt cracked.
                              (Clark) £35 [≈ $62]

Lewis, Matthew Gregory
- Ambrosio, or The Monk ... The Fourth
Edition, with considerable Additions and
Alterations. London: for J. Bell, 1798. 1st
expurgated edn. 8vo. 2 sm marg tears. Orig
mrbld bds, yellow paper spines, unpressed &
uncut, backstrips worn but stitching firm.
                       (Blackwell's) £600 [≈ $1,068]
- The Monk: a Romance. London: for J. Bell,
1797. 3rd edn. 3 vols. 12mo. Contemp green
half mor, gilt spines, crnrs & spine tips sl
worn.   *(Burmester)* £275 [≈ $490]

Lewis, William
- Commercium Philosopho-Technicum; or,
the Philosophical Commerce of Arts ...
London: 1763. 4to. xviii,x, 646,[14] pp. Dble-
page frontis, 5 plates. Lacks licence &
privilege leaf. Polished calf, worn, front jnt
cracked.   *(Weiner)* £275 [≈ $490]
- The New Dispensatory: containing I. The
Theory and Practice of Pharmacy ... V. A
Collection of Cheap Remedies for the Use of
the Poor ... London: J. Nourse, 1753. 1st edn.
8vo. Contemp calf, trivial wear, jnts cracked
but firm. Anon.   *(Georges)* £125 [≈ $223]
- The New Dispensatory containing I. The
Theory and Practice of Pharmacy ... V. A
Collection of Cheap Remedies for the Use of
the Poor ... London: Nourse, 1753. 1st edn.
8vo. xii,664 pp. Contemp calf, backstrip
relaid. Anon. *(David White)* £180 [≈ $320]

Lex Londinensis ...
- Lex Londinensis; or, The City Law. Shewing
the Powers, Customs and Practice of all the
several Courts belonging to the Famous City
of London ... London: S. Roycroft for Henry
Twyford ..., 1680. 1st edn. Browned.
Contemp sheep, worn but sound. Wing
L.1858.   *(Meyer Boswell)* $3503 [≈£197]

Ley, John
- A Discourse concerning Puritans. A
Vindication of those, who unjustly suffer by
the mistake, abuse, and misapplication of that

Name ... N.p.: for Robert Bostock, 1641. 1st
edn. 4to. 58 pp. Few lower margs cropped.
Mod cloth. Anon. *(Robertshaw)* £35 [≈ $62]

Leybourn, William
- An Introduction to Astronomy and
Geography ... London: for Morden & Berry,
1675. 1st edn. 8vo. [viii],234 pp. 5 plates.
Running title trimmed close in parts.
Contemp calf, rebacked. Wing L.1915.
                            (Vanbrugh) £275 [≈ $490]
- An Introduction to Astronomy and
Geography: being a Plain and Easie Treatise
of the Globes. In VII Parts. London: J.C. for
Robert Morden & William Berry, 1675. 8vo.
Fldg plate at end. Occas headline shaved.
Contemp calf, rebacked. Wing L.1915.
                          (Waterfield's) £125 [≈ $223]
- Leybourn's Dialling, Improv'd. Or, the
Whole Art Perform'd. I. Geometrically ...
Concluding with Tables ... by Henry Wilson.
London: Wilford & Jauncy, 1721. 12mo. [12],
276 pp. 12 fldg plates. Orig calf, rebacked,
crnrs rubbed.   *(Karmiole)* $200 [≈£112]

Leycesters Common-Wealth ...
- See Parsons, Robert

Life ...
- The Life and Reign of King Richard the
Second ... see Howard, Sir Robert
- The Life of Ernestus the Pious, first Duke of
Sax-Gotha ... see Philipps, J.T.
- Life of George-Frederick Handel. London:
for J. Dixwell, 1784. Half-title, 26 pp.
Disbound.   *(C.R. Johnson)* £350 [≈ $623]
- The Life of James, late Duke of Ormonde ...
London: M. Cooper, 1747. 1st edn. 8vo.
vi,544,[iv] pp. Port frontis. Contemp calf,
extrs worn, label defective, jnts tender.
                               (Clark) £40 [≈ $71]
- The Life of John Buncle ... see Amory,
Thomas
- The Life of Mr. Rich. Hooker ... see Walton,
Izaak
- The Life of Oliver Cromwell ... see Kimber,
Isaac
- The Life of Petrarch ... see De Sade, J.F.P.A.
- The Life of Richard Nash ... see Goldsmith,
Oliver
- The Life of the Famous John Baptist Colbert
... see Courtilz de Sandras, Gatien de
- The Life of the Learned Sir Thomas Smith ...
see Strype, John
- The Life of the Most Learned Father Paul ...
see Micanzio, Fulgenzio

- The Life of Theodore Agrippa d'Aubigne ...
see Scott, Sarah

Light, Edward
- Introduction to the Art of Playing on the
Harp-Lute & Apollo-Lyre ... London: for the
author, 8 Foley Place, [1798?]. 1st edn. 8vo.
28 pp. Stitched as issued but without the
wraps.   *(Young's)* **£300 [≈ $534]**

Lightfoot, John
- Erubhin or Miscellanies Christian and
Judaicall, and Others. Penned for Recreation
at Vacant Hours. London: 1629. 1st edn. Sm
8vo. Some damp staining. Contemp calf,
rebacked. STC 15593.
                          (Robertshaw) **£85 [≈ $151]**

Lillingston, Luke
- Reflections on Mr Burchet's Memoirs. Or,
Remarks on his Account of Captain Wilmot's
Expedition to the West-Indies ... London &
Westminster: the booksellers, 1704. 1st edn.
Issue with catchword "Eight" p 87. 8vo.
Contemp sheep, red label, rubbed.
                          (Georges) **£450 [≈ $801]**

Lillo, George
- Elmerick: or, Justice Triumphant. A Tragedy
... London: for John Gray, 1740. 1st edn. 8vo.
Errata slip pasted on A5. Disbound.
                          (Hannas) **£45 [≈ $80]**
- The Works ... with some Account of his Life.
London: for T. Davies, 1775. 1st coll edn. 2
vols. Sm 8vo. Final advt leaf. Contemp mrbld
paper bds, calf spines (v worn), uncut.
                          (Hannas) **£45 [≈ $80]**

Lilly, John
- The Practical Conveyancer: In Two Parts ...
Third Edition ... In the Savoy: Lintot for
Osborne, 1742. Lge folio. [lxxx], 812,
[813-842] pp. Contemp calf, spine v worn.
                          (Vanbrugh) **£225 [≈ $401]**

Lilly, William
- Mr. William Lilley's True History of King
James the First, and King Charles the First ...
London: 1715. 12mo. 108 pp. Text diags.
Contemp calf, worn.
                          (Robertshaw) **£85 [≈ $151]**

**Limojon de Saint-Didier, Alexandre
Toussaint**
- The City and Republick of Venice. London:
Brome, 1699. 3 parts in one vol. 8vo. Few
blank margs reprd. Calf. Inscrbd by the
translator Fra. Terne. Wing L.2306.
                          (Rostenberg & Stern) **$475 [≈ £267]**

Lind, J.
- A Treatise on the Scurvy in Three Parts ...
London: 1772. 3rd edn. xvi,554 pp. Some
foxing. Some marg worm, affecting text
minimally. Contemp calf, some worm.
                          (Whitehart) **£180 [≈ $320]**

Linden, D.W.
- A Treatise on the Three Medicinal Waters at
Llandrindod ... London: Everingham &
Reynolds, 1756. Half-title. Frontis. Occas sl
spotting. Contemp calf, rebacked.
                          (P and P Books) **£250 [≈ $445]**

Linden, Diederick Wessel
- Three Letters on Mining ... added, a Fourth
Letter; setting forth, a Discovery of an Easy
method to secure Ships Bottoms from
Worms. London: George Keith, 1750. 96 pp.
Rec wraps.   *(C.R. Johnson)* **£225 [≈ $401]**

Lindesay, Patrick
- The Interest of Scotland considered, with
Regard to its Policy in imploying of the Poor,
its Agriculture, Its Trade, Its Manufactures,
and Fisheries. Edinburgh: R. Fleming, 1733.
1st edn. 8vo. Few lib stamps. Contemp calf,
rebacked, rubbed, crnrs worn. Anon
                          (Clark) **£220 [≈ $392]**

Lindsay, Sir David
- The Works ... with several new Additions by
the same Author ... never before published.
Edinburgh: Williamson & Elliot, 1776. 8vo.
151,84 pp. Sl foxing. Later half calf.
                          (Rankin) **£65 [≈ $116]**

Ling, Nicholas
- Politeuphia, Wits Common-Wealth. Newly
corrected and amended. London: M. Flesher,
sold by George Badger, 1647. 12mo. [vi], 322,
[8] pp. Occas sl dusty. Rec half calf. Wing
L.2336A. Anon.   *(Clark)* **£140 [≈ $249]**

Lingua: or the Combat of the Tongue ...
- See Tomkis, Thomas

Linnaeus, C.
- Voyages and Travels in the Levant 1749-52.
Containing Observations in Natural History,
etc. ... London: 1766. 1st edn in English. 8vo.
[viii],viii,1-268, 273-307,380-456 pp. Fldg
map. Sl water stained at ends. Contemp calf,
rebacked. *(Wheldon & Wesley)* **£300 [≈ $534]**

Lipsius, Justus
- A Discourse of Constancy in Two Books ...
Translated into English by Nathaniel
Wanley. London: Redmayne for Allestry,

1670. Sm 8vo. [xvi],288,[xvi] pp. Some browning & foxing, few pen trials. Late 18th c sheep, rebacked, crnrs reprd. Wing L.2360.
(Blackwell's) **£55 [≈ $98]**

Lisle, Edward
- Observations in Husbandry. London: J. Hughs, for C. Hitch & L. Hawes ..., 1757. 1st edn. Lge 4to. xvi,450,[4] pp. Port frontis. Contemp calf, rebacked.
(Karmiole) **$450 [≈ £253]**

The Literary Miscellany ...
- The Literary Miscellany; or, Elegant Selections of the most admired Fugitive Pieces, and Extracts ... With Originals; in Prose and Verse. Manchester: ptd by Nicholson & Co ..., 1794. 19 works in 1 vol, preceded by general title. Contemp half calf, sl used.   *(Burmester)* **£125 [≈ $223]**

Littelton, Adam
- Linguae Latinae Liber Dictionarius Quadripartitus. A Latine Dictionary in Four Parts ... London: T. Basset ..., 1684. 4to. [x], A1-8D4 pp. Frontis, 2 maps. Occas soiling. Contemp calf, extrs worn, some loss hd of spine. Wing L.2564.   *(Clark)* **£100 [≈ $178]**

Little, Janet
- The Poetical Works of Janet Little, the Scotch Milkmaid. Air: John & Peter Wilson, 1792. 1st edn. 8vo. Subscribers. Contemp half calf, worn.   *(Hannas)* **£280 [≈ $498]**

Littleton, Adam
- Linguae Latinae liber dictionarius Quadripartibus. A Latine dictionary in four parts ... London: for Basset, Wright ..., 1678. 1st edn. 4 parts in one. Thick 4to. 2 maps. Lacks frontis (called for?). Rec qtr calf. Wing L.2563.   *(Fenning)* **£195 [≈ $347]**

Littleton, Sir Thomas
- Tenures in Englishe. London: [colophon] Rychard Tottel ..., 1574. Contemp calf, rebacked, some wear. STC 15770. Anon.
(Meyer Boswell) **$1,500 [≈ £843]**

Lloyd, Charles
- The Anatomy of a late Negociation earnestly addressed to the Serious Consideration of the People of Great-Britain. London: J. Wilkie, 1763. 4to. Half-title. Disbound. Anon.
(Waterfield's) **£65 [≈ $116]**
- The Anatomy of Negociation. Earnestly Addresses to the Serious Consideration of the People of Great Britain. London: for J. Wilkie, 1763. 2nd edn. 4to. 28 pp. New bds.

Anon.   *(Young's)* **£30 [≈ $53]**
- Poems on Various Subjects. Carlisle: F. Jollie, for J. Richardson, Penrith, & sold by C. Law, London, T. Pearson, Birmingham, 1795. 3,[5], 7-104,[2] pp. Errata. Sm lib stamp on title. Rebound in half calf, uncut.
(C.R. Johnson) **£1,200 [≈ $2,136]**

Lloyd, David
- Memoires of the Lives ... of those Noble ... Personages that suffered by Death, Sequestration, Decimation ... for the Protestant Religion ... from the Year 1637 to ... 1666 ... London: 1668. 1st edn. Folio. Frontis. Black bordered contents leaf. Calf. Wing L.2642.
(Rostenberg & Stern) **$250 [≈ £140]**

Lloyd, Robert
- The Poetical Works ... prefixed an Account of the Life and Writings of the Author. By W. Kenrick. London: for T. Evans, 1774. 2 vols. 8vo. Half-titles. Contemp calf, rebacked.
(Burmester) **£85 [≈ $151]**
- The Poetical Works ... prefixed an Account of the Life and Writings of the Author. By W. Kenrick. London: for T. Evans, 1774. 1st coll edn. 2 vols in one. Half-titles. Vignette port on titles. Later panelled calf, rebacked.
(Hannas) **£140 [≈ $249]**
- Shakespeare: an Epistle to Mr. Garrick; with an Ode to Genius. London: for T. Davies ..., 1760. 1st edn. Folio. [2],8 pp. Lacks half-title. Mod half mor. Anon.
(Hannas) **£280 [≈ $498]**

Lloyd, William
- The Pretences of the French Invasion Examined. For the Information of the People of England. London: for R. Clavel, 1692. 1st edn. 4to. [4],16 pp, inc licence leaf. Mod half sheep. Wing L.2690. Once thought to be by Defoe. Anon.   *(Hannas)* **£65 [≈ $116]**

Lobb, T.
- A Practical Treatise of Painful Distempers, with some Effectual Methods of Curing them, exemplified in a great Variety of suitable Histories. London: 1739. xxx,[2], 320,[14] pp. Contemp calf, rebacked, edges & crnrs worn.   *(Whitehart)* **£120 [≈ $214]**

Lobo, Jerome
- A Voyage to Abyssinia ... With a Continuation ... By Mr. Le Grand from the French ... [translated by Samuel Johnson]. London: Bettesworth & Hitch, 1735. 1st edn in English. 8vo. xii,396,[8] pp. Sl wear & tear. Early sheep, worn & soiled.
(D & D Galleries) **$950 [≈ £534]**

Lochee, Lewis

- An Essay on Military Discipline. London: for the author, 1776. 2nd edn. 8vo. 106 pp. Text ends on p 106 in mid-sentence with catchword, but verso is blank. Disbound.
(Young's) £50 [≈ $89]

Locke, John

- An Abridgment of Mr. Locke's Essay concerning Human Understanding. Boston: Manning & Loring, 1794. 8vo. Calf, damaged. *(Rostenberg & Stern)* $150 [≈ £84]
- An Essay Concerning Humane Understanding. London: Churchill, Manship, 1694. 2nd edn. Folio. [xxxx],408,[12] pp. Port from the 3rd edn (1695) tipped in. Contemp calf gilt, sl worn, hinges cracked. *(Bookpress)* $600 [≈ £337]
- An Essay concerning Humane Understanding ... the Third Edition. London: for Awnsham & John Churchill & Samuel Manship, 1695. Folio. Frontis. Contemp calf, front jnt cracked, minor loss at hd of jnts. Wing L.2741. *(Waterfield's)* £635 [≈ $1,130]
- An Essay Concerning Humane Understanding ... Third Edition. London: Awnsham & John Churchill, Samuel Manship, 1695. Folio. Frontis port. Mod calf. Wing L.2741.
(Waterfield's) £550 [≈ $979]
- An Essay Concerning Humane Understanding ... The Third Edition. London: 1695. Folio. Title, [xix],407,[xii] pp. Frontis port (sl cropped). Contemp calf, sometime rebacked, crnrs reprd. Wing L.2741. *(Frew Mackenzie)* £425 [≈ $757]
- An Essay Concerning Human Understanding. London: for J. Churchill, Samuel Manship, 1716. 2 vols. Cr 8vo. Port. 1 sm repr, minor flaws, sl browning. Contemp sprinkled calf, rebacked to style.
(Ash) £200 [≈ $356]
- An Essay concerning Human Understanding ... The Ninth Edition, with large Additions. London: T.W. (vol 2 M.J.) for Churchill & Parker, 1726. 2 vols. 8vo. Port. Contemp panelled calf, tiny hole in 1 spine.
(Hannas) £130 [≈ $231]
- Some Thoughts Concerning Education. London: for A. & J. Churchill, 1693. 1st edn. With the reading "patronnge" A3v (no priority). 8vo. [viii],262,[2] pp. Contemp calf, rebacked in paler calf. Wing L.2762. Anon.
(Burmester) £1,350 [≈ $2,403]
- Some Thoughts concerning Education. The Sixth Edition enlarged. London: A. & J. Churchill, 1709. 392 pp. Contemp panelled calf, rebacked. *(C.R. Johnson)* £145 [≈ $258]

Lockhart, George

- The Case of Mr. Greenshields, Fully Stated and Discuss'd, in a Letter from a Commoner of North Britain, to an English Peer. [Edinburgh?]: Printed in the Year 1711. 1st edn. 4to. 22 pp. Disbound. Anon.
(Young's) £180 [≈ $320]

Lockman, John

- The Entertaining Instructor: in French and English ... By the Author of The History of England by Question and Answer ... for the use of Schools. London: A. Millar, 1765. Only edn. [2],xx,287,[1] pp. Half-title. Contemp sheep, hd of spine chipped.
(C.R. Johnson) £120 [≈ $214]

Logan, John, Revd

- Poems. The Second Edition. London: T. Cadell, 1782. 8vo. vii,[i],118 pp. Contemp qtr sheep, mrbld bds, sl rubbed.
(Clark) £25 [≈ $45]

Logic; or, the Art of Thinking ...

- See Arnauld, Antoine & Nicole, Pierre

London ...

- The London and Country Brewer, containing the Whole Art of Brewing all sorts of Malt-Liquors ... Seventh Edition. London: (1758)-59. 4 parts in one vol. 8vo. 4 ff, 332,[4] pp. Sep title to each part. Old calf, worn, backstrip relaid. *(Weiner)* £200 [≈ $356]

The Londoners Last Warning ...

- The Londoners Last Warning. [London]: 1659. 4to. caption title. Stitched. Wing L.2919. *(Rostenberg & Stern)* $85 [≈ £48]

Long, Kien

- The Imperial Epistle from Kien Long, Emperor of China. To George the Third, King of Great Britain ... London: for T. Becket, 1798. 4th edn. 8vo. 40 pp. Disbound.
(Young's) £18 [≈ $32]

Long, Roger

- The Music Speech, spoken at the Public Commencement in Cambridge, July the 6th, 1714. London: J. Morphew, & C. Crownfield, Cambridge, 1714. 1st edn. 8vo. Half-title, final blank. Some foxing. Disbound. *(Ximenes)* £400 [≈ $225]

Longinus, Dionysius

- On the Sublime: translated from the Greek, with Notes ... By William Smith. London: J. Watts, 1739. 1st edn of this translation. 8vo. [16],xxxiv,187 pp. Frontis. Contemp calf,

backstrip relaid, new label.
(Spelman) **£85 [≈ $151]**
- The Works of Dionysius Longinus, on the
Sublime ... Translated ... with some Remarks
on the English Poets by Mr Welsted. London:
1712. 1st edn. 8vo. 192 pp. Later ink
inscrptns. Some foxing. Later half calf,
rubbed.   *(King)* **$200 [≈ £112]**
- The Works of Dionysius Longinus, on the
Sublime ... Translated ... with some Remarks
on the English Poets. By Mr Welsted.
London: for Sam Briscoe, 1712. 1st edn thus.
8vo. xiv, [10],192 pp. Some browning. 19th c
half calf.   *(Spelman)* **£140 [≈ $249]**

Lord, Henry
- A Discoverie of the Sect of the Banians.
Containing their History, Law, Liturgie,
Casts, Customes, and Ceremonies ... The
Religion of the Persees. London: 1630. 1st
edn. 2 parts in one vol. 4to. Lacks engvd title.
Few marg stains. Mod cloth. Anon. STC
16825.   *(Robertshaw)* **£50 [≈ $89]**

Loskiel, George Henry
- History of the Mission of the United
Brethren among the Indians in North
America. London: for the Brethren;s Society
..., 1794. 1st edn in English. 3 parts in 1 vol.
8vo. 159; 234; 233,[22] pp. Fldg map frontis.
Orig sheep, rebacked.
(Chapel Hill) **$275 [≈ £154]**

Louis XIV, King of France
- The French King's Appeal from the
Proceedings of the Pope to a General Council,
September 28, 1688. London: Baldwin, 1688.
4to. Stitched. Wing L.3100.
(Rostenberg & Stern) **$90 [≈ £51]**

Lovat, Simon Fraser, Lord
- Memoirs of the Life of Lord Lovat. London:
for M. Cooper, 1746. 1st edn. 8vo. [iv],123
pp. Half-title. Title marg & final leaf reprd
without loss.   *(Young's)* **£45 [≈ $80]**

Love of Fame ...
- See Young, Edward

Love, John
- Geodaesia: or The Art of Surveying and
Measuring of Land Made Easy ... Also, How
to Lay Out New Lands in America, or
Elsewhere ... The Fourth Edition. London:
Bettesworth & Hitch, 1731. 8vo. [20],196,
[16],4,[26] pp. Diags & tables. Rec calf.
(Karmiole) **$150 [≈ £84]**

Loveday, Robert
- Loveday's Letters Domestick and Forrein. To
Several Persons ... London: J.G. for Nath.
Brook, 1659. 1st edn. 8vo. [xiv],280,[x] pp. 10
pp ctlg at end. Port frontis (cropped & mtd).
Lacks A1 (blank?). Later calf, rebacked, crnrs
worn. Wing L.3225. *(Clark)* **£200 [≈ $356]**

Lovelass, Peter
- The Law's Disposal of a Person's Estate who
dies without Will or Testament ... London:
for the author, 1792. 8vo. xix, 302, [303-316]
pp. Erratum. Contemp calf, rebacked.
(Vanbrugh) **£95 [≈ $169]**

Lovibond, Edward
- Poems on Several Occasions. London: for J.
Dodsley, 1785. 1st coll edn. Sm 8vo. Half-
title. 1 gathering misbound. Mod polished
calf.   *(Hannas)* **£120 [≈ $214]**

Lowe, John
- A Treatise on the Solar Creation and
Universal Deluge of the Earth ... By a Native
of Manchester. London: for the author, [ca
1790]. 1st edn. 8vo. [2],viii,viii subscribers,
361 pp. Sl browned & foxed. Contemp calf,
worn.   *(D & D Galleries)* **$150 [≈ £84]**

Lowe, Robert
- General View of the Agriculture of the
County of Nottingham. London: Richard
Phillips, 1798. 8vo. xii,192,[16 advt] pp. Fldg
hand cold map. Orig bds, paper label, uncut,
crnrs sl bumped, spine ends reprd.
(Spelman) **£80 [≈ $142]**

Lowman, Moses
- Three Tracts. I. Remarks ... Appearances of
the true God ... III. Texts of Scripture
relating to the Logos, considered. London: for
J. Noon, 1756. 8vo. Contemp calf, rebacked.
(Waterfield's) **£135 [≈ $240]**

Lowth, Robert
- The Life of William of Wykeham, Bishop of
Winchester ... London: for A. Millar & R. &
J. Dodsley, 1758. 8vo. Frontis, title vignette,
fldg table. Contemp calf, rubbed.
(Waterfield's) **£40 [≈ $71]**
- A Short Introduction to English Grammar:
with Critical Notes. A New Edition,
corrected. London: for J. Dodsley, 1772. 221,
[2 advt] pp. Contemp calf, hinges weakening,
spine dried. Anon.
(C.R. Johnson) **£125 [≈ $223]**
- A Short Introduction to English Grammar;
with Critical Notes. New Edition. London:
for J. Dodsley, 1783. 8vo. 221 pp. Early 19th

c qtr calf. Anon. *(Burmester)* **£110 [≈$196]**
- A Short Introduction to English Grammar: with Critical Notes. A New Edition, corrected. London: J. Dodsley & T. Cadell, 1789. 184 pp. Contemp calf, red label. Anon. *(C.R. Johnson)* **£95 [≈$169]**

Lipsius, Justus
- A Discourse of Constancy, in Two Books ... Translated into English by Nathaniel Wanley, M.A. London: J. Redmayne, for James Allestry, 1670. 1st edn. 12mo. [xvi],288,[16] pp. 19th c calf, gilt spine. Wing L.2360.   *(Burmester)* **£150 [≈$267]**

Lucan
- Lucan's Pharsalia, Translated into English verse by Nicholas Rowe. London: Tonson, 1718. 1st edn. 4to. xxv,[5 subscribers],446,55 pp. Fldg map frontis, vignettes. Sl foxing. Orig panelled calf, rebacked to style, wear to cvrs.   *(Hartfield)* **$895 [≈£503]**
- Pharsalia. Translated into English Verse by Nicholas Rowe. London: for Jacob Tonson, 1718. 1st edn thus. Lge folio. [6],xxv,[3 subscribers [only, lacks 2 pp]], 446,55,[1 errata] pp. Frontis, fldg maps, text vignettes. Contemp calf backed bds, sl rubbed.   *(O'Neal)* **$350 [≈£197]**

Lucas, Charles
- The Old Serpentine Temple of the Druids, at Avebury, in North Wiltshire, a Poem. Marlborough: ptd by E. Harold, & sold by W. Meyler, Bath, 1795. 1st edn. Sm 4to. 31 pp. 2 fldg plates (1 backed). Half-title damaged. Contemp qtr calf, spine worn. Anon.   *(Burmester)* **£225 [≈$401]**

Lucas, Richard
- An Inquiry after Happiness. In Three Parts ... Edinburgh: William Gray, 1754. 8th edn. 2 vols. 8vo. xi,371; iv,345 pp. Contemp calf.   *(Young's)* **£120 [≈$214]**
- Practical Christianity: or, an Account of the Holinesse which the Gospel Enjoyns ... London: for R. Pawlet, 1677. 1st edn. Orig calf, elab gilt spine, lacks label. Anon. Wing L.3408.   *(P and P Books)* **£65 [≈$116]**

Lucas, William
- A Five Weeks Tour to Paris, Versailles, Marli, &c. ... Fourth Edition. London: T. Waller, 1765. 8vo. 44 pp. Mod wraps.   *(Blackwell's)* **£45 [≈$80]**

Lucian
- Dialogues of Lucian from the Greek [translated by John Carr]. London: ptd in the year, 1773. xxiv,297,[1] pp. Subscribers. Engvd title. Contemp tree calf, sm section of spine defective.   *(C.R. Johnson)* **£225 [≈$401]**

Luckombe, P.
- A Concise History of the Origin and Progress of Printing ... London: Adlard & Browne, 1770. 1st edn. 8vo. Three qtr mor, sm split hd of 1 jnt.   *(Book Block)* **$695 [≈£390]**

Ludlow, Edmund
- Memoirs ... Vevay, Switzerland: 1698-99. 1st edn. 3 vols. 8vo. Port. Lacks final blank in vols 1 & 2. Some foxing throughout. Late 18th c mottled calf, backstrips sometime relaid, sl rubbed. *(Blackwell's)* **£150 [≈$267]**
- Memoirs. Switzerland. Printed at Vivay in the Canton of Bern: 1698-99 (3rd Part, 2nd edn, for W. Mears & F. Clay, 1720). 3 vols. 8vo. Frontis vol 1. Few sm worm holes. Contemp calf, spines rubbed, jnts cracked. Wing L.3460.   *(Waterfield's)* **£210 [≈$374]**

Luffman, John
- The Charters of London Complete; also Magna Charta, and the Bill of Rights. With Explanatory Notes and Remarks. London: for John Luffman, & T. Evans, 1793. 1st edn thus. 8vo. [vi],ii,431 pp. Half-title. Orig bds, minor wear to spine.   *(Burmester)* **£150 [≈$267]**

Lumisden, Andrew
- Remarks on the Antiquities of Rome and its Environs ... London: W. Bulmer & Co, 1797. 1st edn. 4to. iv,478,[12 index] pp. Port frontis, fldg map, fldg plan, 10 plates. 19th c half calf, jnts rubbed, hd of spine reprd.   *(Spelman)* **£120 [≈$214]**
- Remarks on the Antiquities of Rome and its Environs: Being a Classical and Topographical Survey of the Ruins of that Celebrated City. London: Bulmer, 1797. 1st edn. 4to. 478 pp. Port frontis, 12 plates inc a map. Minimal marg worm. Contemp bds, uncut, rebacked in calf.   *(Europa)* **£120 [≈$214]**

Lupton, Donald
- The Glory of their Times, or, the Lives of ye primitive Fathers ... London: J. Okes, 1640. 1st edn. 4to. Engvd title, num engvd ports. 19th c roan, sl rubbed. STC 16943. Anon.   *(Hannas)* **£85 [≈$151]**

Luther, Martin
- A Commentary upon the Fifteen Psalmes, called Psalmi Graduum, that is, Psalmes of

Degrees ... Translated ... by Henry Bull. London: Richard Field, 1615. 3rd edn of Bull's version. 8vo. [x],318 pp. Later calf, a.e.g., backstrip sometime relaid, sl worn. STC 16976   *(Clark)* £150 [≈ $267]

Lux Orientalis ...
- See Glanvill, Joseph

Lyly, John
- Euphues, or Anatomie of Wit ... [bound with] Euphues and his England ... London: John Haviland, 1636. Black Letter. 1st title laid down & sl defective. Sl browned. Occas marg defects. 19th c half calf, worn cvrs detached. STC 17067.
        (Jermy & Westerman) £290 [≈ $516]

Lynch, Bernard
- A Guide to Health ... London: for the author, & Mrs. Cooper ..., 1744. 1st edn. 8vo. xxxii,480 pp. Subscribers. Errata page. Contemp calf gilt, front hinge cracked but firm.   *(Vanbrugh)* £375 [≈ $668]

Lyon, John
- Experiments and Observations made with a View to Point Out the Errors of the Present Received Theory of Electricity ... London: 1780. 4to. xxiv,280,[8] pp. 2 fldg plates. Orig bds, uncut, unopened, worn, spine defective, front bd sl loose. *(Weiner)* £600 [≈ $1,068]

Lysons, Daniel
- Practical Essays upon Intermitting Fevers, Dropsies, Diseases of the Liver ... Bath: 1772. 1st edn. 8vo. xxiv,214,[2] pp. Some browning at ends. Contemp calf, gilt spine.
        (Spelman) £180 [≈ $320]

Lyttelton, George, Lord Lyttelton
- Considerations upon the Present State of our Affairs, at Home and Abroad. In a Letter to a Member of Parliament from a Friend in the Country. London: for T. Cooper, 1729. 2nd edn. 8vo. [ii],67,[2] pp. Disbound. Anon.
        (Young's) £30 [≈ $53]
- Considerations upon the Present State of Affairs at Home and Abroad. In a Letter to a Member of Parliament from a Friend in the Country. The Second Edition. London: for T. Cooper, 1739. 8vo. [2],67,[68-69] pp. Disbound. Anon.   *(Hannas)* £85 [≈ $151]
- The Court-Secret: A Melancholy Truth. Now first translated from the Original Arabic. By an Adept in Oriental Tongues. London: for T. Cooper, 1741. 1st edn. 8vo. [2],50 pp. Disbound. Anon. Also attributed to David Mallet.   *(Hannas)* £280 [≈ $498]

- The Court-Secret ... The Second Edition. London: for T. Cooper, 1742. 8vo. 47 pp. Disbound. Anon.   *(Hannas)* £180 [≈ $320]
- Dialogues of the Dead. [Bound with] New Dialogues of the Dead. London: W. Sandby, R. & J. Dodsley, 1760-62. 1st edns. 2 vols in one. xii,320; xx,206 pp. Contemp calf, sl rubbed, hinges cracked but firm.
        (Bookpress) $450 [≈ £253]
- Dialogues of the Dead. London: for W. Sandby, 1760. 2nd edn. 8vo. xii,320,[1 erratum] pp. Contemp qtr calf, jnts starting to crack. Dialogues 26-28 were written by Elizabeth Montague. *(Young's)* £48 [≈ $85]
- The History of the Life of King Henry the Second, and of the Age in which he Lived ... London: for Sandby & Dodsley, 1761-71. 1st edn. 4 vols. 4to. Title vignettes. Contemp speckled calf, rebacked.
        (O'Neal) $450 [≈ £253]
- Letters ... Dublin: for Messrs. Price ..., 1780. 8vo. vii,190 pp. Sm rust spot on 2 ff. Irish mottled calf, red label. Often attributed to William Combe.   *(Young's)* £95 [≈ $169]
- Letters of the Late Lord Lyttelton. London: for J. Bew, 1780. 8vo. Contemp half calf, sl rubbed. Commonly attributed to William Combe.   *(Waterfield's)* £50 [≈ $89]
- To the Memory of a Lady lately Deceased. A Monody. London: for A. Millar, sold by M. Cooper, 1747. Folio. [2],15 pp. Lacks half-title. Title a little stained. Stitched, uncut, as issued, edges frayed. Anon.
        (Hannas) £65 [≈ $116]
- The Works ... Published by George Edward Ayscough ... Third Edition ... added a general Index. London: Dodsley, 1776. 3 vols. 8vo. Half-titles. Blank leaf vol 1, errata leaf vol 3. Port. Contemp calf, gilt spines, spine sl cracking, sl torn at foot. John Cator b'plates.
        (Hannas) £150 [≈ $267]

M., A.
- The Reformed Gentleman: or, the Old English Morals rescued from the Immoralities of the Present Age ... London: for T. Salusbury, 1693. 1st edn. 8vo. Frontis (marg sl frayed). Water stain 1st few ff. Contemp sheep, rebacked.
        (Burmester) £200 [≈ $356]

McAlpin Collection
- Catalogue of the McAlpin Collection of British History and Theology, 1500-1700. Compiled and Edited by Charles Ripley Gillett. New York: Union Theological Seminary, 1927-30. 5 vols (inc index). Med 8vo. Orig buckram.
        (Blackwell's) £250 [≈ $445]

McArthur, John
- The Army and Navy Gentleman's Companion; or a New and Complete Treatise ... of Fencing. London: for J. Murray, 1784. 2nd edn. 4to. (xxvi),162 pp. Engvd frontis & title, 19 plates. Few creases & marks, 1 plate reprd. Rec red half mor retaining orig bds.
(Ash) **£850 [≈ $1,513]**

Macarty, Captain
- An Appeal to the Candour and Justice of the People of England, in behalf of the West India Merchants and Planters ... London: J. Debrett, 1792. xvi,118 pp. Disbound.
(C.R. Johnson) **£225 [≈ $401]**

Macaulay, Aulay, Vicar of Rothley
- The History and Antiquities of Claybrook, in the County of Leicester ... London: for the author ... Leicester ... Loughborough ... Hinckley ... Northampton, 1791. 1st edn. 8vo. viii,137,[5] pp. Early 19th c half mor, sl rubbed.
(Burmester) **£120 [≈ $214]**

Macbean, Alexander
- A Dictionary of Ancient Geography ... Designed for the Use of Schools. London: Robinson, Cadell, 1773. 1st edn. 8vo. Contemp calf, rebacked.
(Ximenes) **$1,250 [≈ £702]**

MacBride, David
- Methodical Introduction to the Theory and Practice of Physic. London: Strahan, Cadell ..., 1772. 1st edn. 4to. [iv],xvi,660 pp. Orig bds, uncut, crnrs & spine worn.
(Gaskell) **£225 [≈ $401]**

Macdonald, John
- Travels, in Various Parts of Europe, Asia, and Africa, during a Series of Thirty Years and Upwards ... Dublin: for P. Byrne ..., 1791. 1st Irish edn. 12mo. vi,282 pp. Contemp tree calf, sm splits in jnts.
(Burmester) **£175 [≈ $312]**

Macfarlan, Robert, & others
- The History of the Reign of George the Third ... To which is prefixed, a Review of the late War. London: for the author, & sold by T. Evans, 1770-96. 1st edn. 4 vols. 8vo. Half-titles in vols 1 & 2. Clean tear in 1 marg. Contemp sheep, sl wear to jnts.
(Burmester) **£150 [≈ $267]**

Machiavelli, Niccolo
- Discourses upon the First Decade of T. Livius ... To which is added his Prince. London: Harper & Amery, 1674-73. 2nd edn

of this translation by Edward Dacres. 2 works in one. 8vo. Frontis port. Qtr calf. Wing M.135A. *(Rostenberg & Stern)* **$675 [≈ £379]**
- Political Reflections upon the Government of the Turks. The King of Sweden's Descent into Germany ... Martin Luther Vindicated. London: 1656. 12mo. Lacks front free endpaper. Contemp calf, cracked, rubbed, spine chipped with loss.
(Francis Edwards) **£150 [≈ $267]**

Mackenzie, Sir George
- A Discourse wherein the Author endeavours to prove, that Point of Honour ... obliges Men to be Vertuous ... Edinburgh: for Robert Broun [sic], 1667. 1st edn. Sm 8vo. [ii],136 pp. Title border. Occas sl spotting. Mid 19th c blue calf, rebacked. Wing M.175.
(Vanbrugh) **£275 [≈ $490]**
- The Institutions of the Law of Scotland ... Fourth Edition, Revised, Corrected and Augmented ... Appendix ... Edinburgh: James Watson for John Vallange sic, 1706. Sm 8vo. [viii],253,[3] pp. Contemp calf, spine worn.
(Vanbrugh) **£75 [≈ $134]**
- A Moral Paradox: Maintaining, That it is much easier to be Vertuous than Vitious ... Edinburgh: for Robert Broun, 1667. 1st edn. 8vo. 87,[i], Consolation against Calamities 30 pp. Title border. Rec qtr calf. Wing M.181.
(Vanbrugh) **£255 [≈ $454]**
- Reason. An Essay. London: Joseph Hindmarsh & Richard Sare, 1695. 2nd edn. 12mo. [x], 3-158 pp. Sm repr to title marg, minor browning & soiling. Contemp calf, old reback, rubbed, crnrs worn. Wing M.194.
(Clark) **£85 [≈ $151]**
- A Vindication of the Government in Scotland. During the Reign of King Charles II ... London: for J. Hindmarsh, 1691. 1st edn. Sm 4to. 66 pp. Title sl dust soiled. Disbound. Wing M.213.
(Vanbrugh) **£175 [≈ $312]**

Mackenzie, George, Earl of Cromarty
- An Historical Account of the Conspiracies by the Earls of Gowry and Robert Logan of Restalrig ... Edinburgh: James Watson, 1713. 8vo. Half-title. 19th c bds, uncut.
(Rankin) **£75 [≈ $134]**
- A Vindication of Robert III, King of Scotland, from the Imputation of Bastardy ... Edinburgh: Heirs and Successors of Andrew Anderson ..., 1695. Only edn. 4to. 47 pp. Disbound. Wing C.7027.
(Young's) **£90 [≈ $160]**

Mackenzie, Henry
- The Man of the World. London: for W.

Strahan & T. Cadell, 1773. 1st edn. 2 vols.
8vo. Contemp calf, rebacked, orig labels.
Anon.   *(Waterfield's)* **£265 [≈ $472]**
- The Man of the World. In Two Parts.
London: for W. Strahan, & T. Cadell, 1773.
2nd edn. 2 vols. 12mo. Half-titles. Contemp
calf, gilt spines sl worn. Anon.
                        (Ximenes) **$150 [≈ £84]**
- Prince of Tunis. A Tragedy ... Edinburgh:
for A. Kincaid & W. Creech, 1773. 1st edn.
8vo. Final errata leaf. Title soiled. Disbound.
Anon.   *(Hannas)* **£30 [≈ $53]**

Mackenzie, J.
- The History of Health and the Art of
Preserving It ... Edinburgh: 1758. xii,464 pp.
Lib stamp on title verso & front endpaper.
Occas foxing. Half leather & mrbld bds.
                        (Whitehart) **£130 [≈ $231]**

Mackintosh, James
- Vindiciae Gallicae. Defence of the French
Revolution and its English Admirers against
the Accusations of the Right Hon. Edmund
Burke ... London: Robinson, 1791. 1st edn.
8vo. 351 pp. Rec half calf.
                        (Young's) **£130 [≈ $231]**
- Vindiciae Gallicae. Defence of the French
Revolution and its English Admirers, against
the Accusations of the Right Hon. Edmund
Burke ... London: Robinson, 1791. 3rd edn.
8vo. [iv],202, 203-205, 203-342 pp. Occas sl
marks. Early tree calf, backstrip laid down.
                (Meyer Boswell) **$350 [≈ £197]**

Macklin, Charles
- The Man of the World. A Comedy. Love a la
Mode. A Farce. London: J. Bell, 1793. 1st
authorised edn. 4to. [xvii],vi,vii,[i], 68, [iv],
32,[vi] pp. Half-title. Subscribers. 5 advt pp.
Port frontis. Minor spots & stains. Contemp
half calf, gilt spine, sl rubbed.
                        (Clark) **£85 [≈ $151]**

Macky, John
- A Journey through the Austrian Netherlands
... London: for J. Pemberton, & J. Hooke,
1725. 1st edn. 8vo. xxx,[ii],(27) pp. Half-title.
Advt leaf. Lacks inserted errata leaf. Contemp
sheep, spine worn but sound.
                        (Burmester) **£120 [≈ $214]**

Macleod, Allan
- The Bishop of Llandaff's "Apology for the
Bible" examined. In a Series of Letters ...
London: for B. crosby, 1796. 1st edn. 8vo.
[iv], 288 pp. Half-title. Contemp sheep.
                        (Burmester) **£75 [≈ $134]**

M'Nicol, Samuel
- Remarks on Dr. Samuel Johnson's Journey to
the Hebrides ... London: Cadell, 1779. Half-
title. Contemp calf, backstrip sometime
relaid.   *(C.R. Johnson)* **£225 [≈ $401]**

M'Pherson, I.
- The Christian going to posses the Heavenly
Canaan. A Sermon. Huddersfield: Printed by
J. Brook, Bookseller, 1796. 1st edn. 8vo. 28
pp. Sl soiled. Disbound.
                        (Young's) **£39 [≈ $69]**

Macpherson, James
- The History of Great Britain from the
Restoration, to the Accession of the House of
Hanover. London: for W. Strahan, & T.
Cadell, 1775. 1st edn. 2 vols. 4to. Contemp
calf.   *(Hannas)* **£110 [≈ $196]**
- The Poems of Ossian ... Translated by James
Macpherson ... prefixed, Dissertations on the
Era and Poems of Ossian. Glasgow: Chapman
& Lang, for J. Imray, 1799. 2 vols in one.
12mo. Addtnl engvd titles. Early 19th c green
half calf, rubbed. *(Burmester)* **£60 [≈ $107]**

McReady, William
- The Irishman in London; or, the Happy
African. A Farce, in two Acts ... New Edition.
London: Longman, 1796. 8vo. 45,[2 advt] pp.
Spotted. Early qtr leather.
                (Bates & Hindmarch) **£18 [≈ $32]**

Madan, Spencer
- A Letter to Doctor Priestley in consequence
of his 'Familiar Letters addresses to the
Inhabitants of the Town of Birmingham,
&c.'. Birmingham: E. Piercy, [1790]. 8vo.
Disbound.   *(Waterfield's)* **£110 [≈ $196]**

Madden, Samuel
- A Proposal for the General Encouragement of
Learning in Dublin-College ... Second
Edition. Dublin: George Faulkner, 1732. 24
pp. Disbound. Anon.
                   (C.R. Johnson) **£165 [≈ $294]**

Madox, Thomas
- Baronia Anglica. An History of Land-Honors
and Baronies and of Tenure in Capite verified
by Records. London: for Francis Gosling,
1741. Folio. Publisher's (?) bds, uncut.
                     (Waterfield's) **£135 [≈ $240]**
- Baronia Anglica. An History of Land-Honors
and Baronies, and of Tenure in Capite ...
London: for Francis Gosling, 1741. Folio.
[ii], 292,[xxviii] pp. Title vignette, head- &
tail-pieces. Contemp calf, rebacked.
                     (Sotheran's) **£198 [≈ $352]**

- The History and Antiquities of the Exchequer of the Kings of England ... London: for William Owen, 1769. 2nd edn, with index. 2 vols. 4to. 2 engvs. Occas sl spotting. Rebound in qtr calf.
(Francis Edwards) **£250** [≈ **$445**]

The Magistrates Assistant ...
- See Glasse, Samuel

The Maid of the Oaks ...
- See Burgoyne, John

Maillet, Benoit de
- Telliamed: or, Discourses between an Indian Philosopher and a French Missionary, on the Dimunition of the Sea, the Formation of the Earth, the Origin of Men and Animals ... London: 1750. 8vo. lii,284 pp. Contemp calf, worn, rebacked. *(Weiner)* **£200** [≈ **$356**]

Maimbourg, Louis
- The History of the League ... Translated ... by Mr. Dryden. London: M. Flesher, for Jacob Tonson, 1684. 1st English edn. 8vo. Frontis. Contemp calf, sl worn. Wing M.292.
(Hannas) **£55** [≈ **$98**]
- The History of the League ... Translated into English ... by Mr. Dryden. London: M. Flesher for Jacob Tonson, 1684. 8vo. Frontis. Mod qtr calf. Wing M.292.
(Waterfield's) **£85** [≈ **$151**]
- The History of the League ... Translated ... by Mr. Dryden. London: M. Flesher, for Jacob Tonson, 1684. 1st edn in English. Cr 8vo. [lx],524, 731-966, [50],[xlii] pp. Frontis. Few sl marks. Contemp calf, rebacked.
(Ash) **£250** [≈ **$445**]

Mainwaring, Sir Thomas
- A Defence of Amicia, Daughter of Hugh Cyveliok, Earl of Chester ... London: for Sam. Lowndes, 1673. 1st edn. Sm 8vo. red & black title. [10],80,[3] pp. Old style calf. Wing M.300. *(Hannas)* **£120** [≈ **$214**]
- A Reply to an Answer to the Defence of Amicia ... London: for S. Lowndes, 1673. Sm 8vo. [2],105 pp. Red & black title. Old style calf. Wing M.303. *(Hannas)* **£110** [≈ **$196**]
- A Reply to an Answer to the Defence of Amicia ... London: for S. Lowndes, 1673. 1st edn. Sm 8vo. [ii],105 pp. Red & black title. Rec calf. Wing M.303.
(Burmester) **£90** [≈ **$160**]

Maitland, William
- The History of Edinburgh ... In Nine Books. Edinburgh: Hamilton, Balfour & Neill, 1753.

Folio. viii,518 pp. Fldg plan, 19 plates. Occas spotting & browning. Contemp calf, rebacked, crnrs reprd. *(Frew Mackenzie)* **£350** [≈ **$623**]

Mall, Thomas
- A Cloud of Witnesses; or, The Sufferers Mirrour ... London: for the author, 1665. 1st edn. 8vo. [xii],258, [vi],318, [xiv],214, [ii], [viii],132 pp. 3 red & black titles. Few early notes. Old calf, sometime rebacked, recased, new label. Wing M.329.
(Hollett) **£120** [≈ **$214**]

Mallet, David
- Edwin and Emma. Birmingham: John Baskerville, for A. Millar, 1760. 1st edn. 4to. 15 pp. Three qtr crushed green mor, uncut. Anon. *(Hannas)* **£160** [≈ **$285**]
- The Life of Francis Bacon ... London: for A. Millar, 1740. 1st edn. 8vo. viii,197,[i] pp. Engvd title vignette. Lacks half-title. Contemp calf, rebacked.
(Vanbrugh) **£175** [≈ **$312**]
- Poems on Several Occasions. London: for A. Millar, 1762. 1st edn. 8vo. Contemp name stamp on title. Mod half calf.
(Hannas) **£130** [≈ **$231**]

Mallory, John
- Observations humbly offer'd against passing the Bill, intitled, A Bill for the more easy and speedy recovery of Small Debts, into Law. London: J. Roberts, 1730. [2],61, [1] pp. Sm marg tear title. Rec wraps.
(C.R. Johnson) **£85** [≈ **$151**]

Malone, Edmund
- An Inquiry into the Authenticity of Certain Miscellaneous Papers and Legal Instruments ... attributed to Shakespeare, Queen Elizabeth, and Henry, Earl of Southampton ... London: 1796. 1st edn. 8vo. viii,424,[4] pp. Half-title. 3 plates (sl foxed). Contemp calf, rebacked. *(Burmester)* **£160** [≈ **$285**]

Malton, James
- An Essay on British Cottage Architecture. London: Hookham & Carpenter, 1798. 1st edn. 4to. [4],27,[1] pp. 21 aquatint plates ptd in bistre. Rec half calf.
(Sotheran's) **£725** [≈ **$1,291**]

Malvezzi, Virgilio, Marquis
- Discourses upon Cornelius Tacitus ... Translated into English by Sir Richard Baker. London: E.G. for R. Whitaker & Tho. Whitaker, 1642. 1st English edn. Folio. W'cut title border. Mod half sheep. Wing M.359. *(Waterfield's)* **£125** [≈ **$223**]

The Man of Honour ...
- The Man of Honour. London [ie Edinburgh]: 1737. 1st 8vo edn. 12 pp. Disbound.
(Hannas) **£75 [≃ $134]**

The Man of the World ...
- See Mackenzie, Henry

Mandeville, Sir John
- The Voiage and Travaile ... Now publish'd Entire from an Original Ms in the Cotton Library ... London: Woodman & Lyon, 1725. Index,xvi,[8], 384,[5] pp. Later old leather, worn. *(McBlain)* **£450 [≃ £253]**

Manley, Mary De La Riviere
- John Bull Still in his Senses ... see Arbuthnot, John
- Memoirs of Europe, towards the Close of the Eighth Century. Written by Eginardus ... and done into English by the Translator of the New Atlantis. London: for John Morphew, 1710. 1st edn. 8vo. Contemp panelled calf. Anon. *(Hannas)* **£280 [≃ $498]**
- The Power of Love: in Seven Novels ... London: for C. Davis, 1741. 1st edn, 2nd issue. 8vo. Sm marg repr to dedic. Contemp calf gilt, rebacked, sl worn.
(Ximenes) **$750 [≃ £421]**
- The Royal Mischief. A Tragedy. London: for R. Bentley, 1696. 1st edn. 4to. Browned. Qtr mor. Wing M.436. *(Ximenes)* **$850 [≃ £478]**

Manners, Catherine Rebecca, Lady
- Review of Poetry, Ancient and Modern. A Poem. By Lady M******. London: for J. Booth, 1799. 1st edn. 4to. [4],30 pp, inc half-title. Stitched, uncut, as issued. Anon.
(Hannas) **£55 [≃ $98]**

Manning, Owen
- Considerations on the State of Subscription to the Articles and Liturgy of the Church of England, towards the close of the year 1773 ... by a Consistent Protestant. London: for J. Wilkie, 1774. 8vo. Disbound. Anon.
(Waterfield's) **£45 [≃ $80]**

Manning, Robert
- England's Conversion and Reformation Compared ... "Antwerp" [ie London]: for R.C. & C.F., 1725. 1st edn. Issue with p 325 crrctly numbered. 8vo. lv,[vii],330 pp. 1 marg lib stamp. Contemp sheep, rebacked, crnrs worn. Anon. *(Clark)* **£75 [≃ $134]**

Manstein, Baron de
- Memoirs of Russia. From the Year 1727 to

the Year 1744. Translated from the Original Manuscript ... Second Edition ... Improved. London: 1773. 4to. xxvi,416,index pp. 10 fldg maps & plans. Rec qtr mor.
(Terramedia) **$750 [≃ £421]**

Manwood, John
- A Treatise and Discovrse of the Lawes of the Forrest ... London: Thomas Wight & Bonham Norton, 1598. 1st published edn. 4to. 14,167 ff. Sl dusty at ends. Later half calf. STC 17291.
(Meyer Boswell) **$2,250 [≃ £1,264]**
- A Treatise of the Laws of the Forest ... also a Treatise of the Pourallee ... The Third Edition, Corrected and Much Enlarged. London: Company of Stationers, 1655. 4to. [32], 552 pp. Orig calf, rebacked, worn. Wing M.554. *(Karmiole)* **$250 [≃ £140]**
- A Treatise of the Laws of the Forest ... Third Edition Corrected, and much Inlarged. London: for the Company of Stationers, 1665. 8vo. [xxx],552 pp. Minor browning & soiling. Rebound in half calf. Wing M.354.
(Clark) **£350 [≃ $623]**

Mar, John Erskine, Earl of
- A Journal of the Earl of Mar's Proceedings, from his First Arrival in Scotland ... London: Reprinted, & sold by J. Baker, (1716). 1st English edn. 8vo. xvi,32 pp. Disbound. Introduction by Defoe.
(Young's) **£180 [≃ $320]**

Marcellinus, Ammianus
- The Roman Historie ... Now Translated Newly into English ... By Philemon Holland ... London: Adam Islip, 1609. 1st edn in English. Sm folio. [4],432,[75] pp. Title remargined. Some damp stains. Last few ff worn in margs. Rec half calf. STC 17311.
(O'Neal) **$250 [≃ £140]**

Markham, Francis
- Five Decades of Epistles of Warre. London: Augustine Matthews, 1622. 1st edn. Folio. [x], 200 pp. No intl blank or free endpapers. Title sl soiled, sl marg hole. 17th c calf, extrs sl worn, upper jnt cracked but firm. STC 17332. *(Clark)* **£350 [≃ $623]**

Markham, Gervase
- Cheape and Good Husbandry ... The fift Edition. London: Okes for Harrison, 1631. Sm 4to. [xxvi],188 pp. Lacks A1 (blank). Sm worm hole through centre of text touching some letters. Lge w'cut of garden. Rec half calf. STC 17339. *(Vanbrugh)* **£275 [≃ $490]**
- The English House-Wife ... Now the Fourth

Time much augmented ... By G.M. London: Nicholas Oakes for John Harrison, 1631. Sm 4to. [x],252 pp. Lacks blank A1. Rec half calf. STC 17353. *(Vanbrugh)* £455 [≈ $810]

- Markhams Farewell to Husbandry ... London: E. Brewster & George Sawbridge, 1656. 6th edn. [vi],126,[4] pp. Later half calf. Wing M.650. *(Bookpress)* $285 [≈ £160]

Markland, George

- Pteryplegia: or, the Art of Shooting-Flying. A Poem. London: for Stephen Austen, 1727. 8vo. iv,32 pp, inc intl advt leaf. 4 ff ctlg at end. Disbound. *(Hannas)* £250 [≈ $445]

Marmion, Shakerley

- The Antiquary. A Comedy ... London: F.K. for I.W. & F.E., 1641. 1st edn. Sm 4to. Lacks intl blank. Straight grained mor gilt, front cvr detached, lower jnt rubbed. Cloth slipcase. Wing M.703. *(Ximenes)* $900 [≈ £506]

Marmontel, Jean Francois

- The Incas: or, the Destruction of the Empire of Peru. London: for J. Nourse ..., 1777. 1st English edn. 2 vols. 12mo. Half-titles. Contemp calf, worn, rebacked. Bibliotheca Lindesiana b'plate. *(Hannas)* £320 [≈ $570]
- Moral Tales. London: for T. Becket, 1766. 2nd English edn. 3 vols. Sm 8vo. Three qtr polished calf, gilt spines, red & green labels. *(Appelfeld)* $150 [≈ £84]

Marnix Van Sant Aldegonde, Philips van

- The Bee Hive of the Romish Church. A Worke of all good Catholikes to be read, and most necessary to be understood ... London: 1636. 8vo. 365 pp. Later half calf. STC 17448.5. Anon. *(Robertshaw)* £55 [≈ $98]

Marriott, James

- The Case of the Dutch Ships Considered. London: T. Harrison, 1778. 4th edn. 8vo. [vi], 137 pp. Half-title. New bds. *(Young's)* £40 [≈ $71]

Marriott, Sir James

- Poems Written chiefly at the University of Cambridge; together with a Latin Oration upon ... the Roman and Canon Laws. [London]: James Bettenham, 1760. 1st edn. 8vo. Frontis, vignettes. Lacks half-title. Lib stamp on frontis verso & title. Lib cloth. Anon. *(Hannas)* £75 [≈ $134]

Marsh, Charles

- The Winter's Tale, a Play. Alter'd from Shakespear. Second Edition. London: for

Charles Marsh, 1756. 8vo. 19th c half mor gilt, sl rubbed. *(Ximenes)* $275 [≈ £154]

Marsh, Henry

- A New Survey of the Turkish Empire and Government ... London: for Henry Marsh, 1663. 2 vols. 24mo. [12],76,108, [8],172 pp. Frontises. Old leather, worn. *(McBlain)* $375 [≈ £211]

Marshall, Nathaniel

- A Defence of our Constitution in Church and State: or, an Answer to the Late Charge of the Non-Jurors, Accusing us of Heresy and Schism ... London: H. Parker for William Taylor, 1717. 1st edn. 8vo. 191,[51] pp. New half calf. *(Young's)* £80 [≈ $142]

Marshall, Stephen

- A Sacred Record to be made of Gods Mercie to Zion ... London: Rich. Cotes for Stephen Bowtell, [16--]. Only edn. 4to. [iv],36 pp. Disbound. Wing M.773. *(Young's)* £45 [≈ $80]

Marshall, William

- Planting and Rural Ornament. Being a Second Edition with large additions of Planting and Ornamental Gardening, a Practical Treatise. London: 1796. 2 vols. 8vo. xxxii,408,[8]; xx,454,[6] pp. Contemp tree calf, part of 1 label missing. *(Henly)* £152 [≈ $271]
- Planting and Rural Ornament: being a Second Edition, with large additions of Planting and Ornamental Gardening, a Practical Treatise. London: G. Nichol, 1796. 2 vols. 8vo. xxxii,408,[8]; xx,454,[4] pp. Contemp half calf, raised gilt bands, gilt spine & labels. *(Spelman)* £200 [≈ $356]
- The Rural Economy of the West of England. London: for G. Nicol ..., 1796. 1st edn. 2 vols. 8vo. 2 advt ff vol 1. Fldg map. Vol 1 title sl spotted. Mod calf, uncut. *(Claude Cox)* £140 [≈ $249]

Martial, Marcus Valerius

- Select Epigrams of Martial Englished [by Henry Killigrew]. London: Edward Jones, for Samuel Lowndes, 1689. 1st edition of this translation. 8vo. Frontis (sl shaved). Contemp calf, gilt spine. Wing M.833. *(Hannas)* £140 [≈ $249]
- Select Epigrams of Martial. Translated and Imitated by William Hay, Esq; with an Appendix of some by Cowley, and other Hands. London: Dodsley, 1755. 8vo. [10],[2 advt], 239, [i], [20],[4 advt] pp. 2 title-pages, parallel text. Contemp calf, backstrip relaid, sl rubbed. *(Spelman)* £45 [≈ $80]

Martin, Benjamin
- The Philosophical Grammar; Being a View of the Present State of Experimental Physiology, or Natural Philosophy. In Four Parts ... London: John Noon, 1748. 3rd edn. 2 tables, 26 fldg plates. Occas foxing & sl browning. Contemp calf, rebacked.
(P and P Books) **£145 [≈ $258]**

Martin, Martin
- A Description of the Western Islands of Scotland ... London: Andrew Bell, 1703. 1st edn. 8vo. [xxxii],392 pp. Fldg map, fldg plate. Few sm tears, occas sl damp stain. Contemp calf, sl rubbed, 1 crnr worn, upper jnt cracked but firm. *(Clark)* **£325 [≈ $579]**

Martin, T.
- Mary Magdalen's Tears Wip't Off, or the Voyce of Peace to an Unquiet Conscience. Written by Way of Letter to a Person of Quality. London: for T. Garthwaite, 1659. 1st edn. Sm 8vo. Frontis (frayed at foredge with sl loss). Advt leaf. Used. Contemp calf, worn. Wing M.850. Anon.
(Hannas) **£35 [≈ $62]**

Martine, George
- Reliquiae Divi Andreae, or the State of the Venerable and Primital See of St. Andrews ... St. Andrews: James Morison, 1797. 1st edn. 4to. viii,[2],256 pp. 3 plates (browned). Old qtr calf, rebacked. *(Young's)* **£100 [≈ $178]**

Martyn, Thomas
- The English Entomologist exhibiting all the Coleopterous Insects found in England. London: 1792. Roy 4to. [v],33,[vi], 41,[4] pp. 2 engvd titles, 2 plates of medals, 42 hand cold plates. Contemp half russia, rebacked, crnrs reprd.
(Wheldon & Wesley) **£750 [≈ $1,335]**
- Thirty-Eight Plates, with Explanations; intended to Illustrate Linnaeus's System of Vegetables. London: B. White, 1788. 1st edn. 8vo. [vi],72,2 pp. 38 plates. Orig bds, uncut, sl worn, jnts weak. *(Bookpress)* **$275 [≈ £154]**

Marvell, Andrew
- The Works ... With a New Life of the Author, by Capt. Edward Thompson. London: for the editor, by Henry Baldwin ..., 1776. 1st edn. 3 vols. 4to. Subscribers. Frontis port vol 1. Contemp tree calf gilt, rebacked. *(Ximenes)* **$450 [≈ £253]**

Maseres, Francis
- Considerations on the Bill now depending in the House of Commons, for enabling Parishes

to Grant Life-Annuities to Poor Persons. London: for B. White, 1773. 1st edn. 8vo. 59 pp. Lib stamps at end. Disbound. Anon.
(Hannas) **£65 [≈ $116]**
- An Enquiry into the Extent of the Power of Juries ... Dublin: Lynch, Byrne ..., 1792. 1st sep Irish edn. 8vo. Disbound. Anon.
(Ximenes) **$200 [≈ £112]**
- An Enquiry into the Extent of the Power of Juries ... Dublin: Lynch, Byrne ..., 1792. [2], 32, 33-40, 33-40 pp. Rec wraps. Anon.
(C.R. Johnson) **£220 [≈ $392]**

Mason, Charlotte
- The Ladies' Assistant for Regulating and Supplying the Table ... Sixth Edition, Enlarged, Corrected and Improved ... London: for J. Walter, 1787. 8vo. [xviii],484, [xix, [i advt] pp. Half-title. Contemp tree calf, sometime rebacked. *(Gough)* **£275 [≈ $490]**

Mason, Francis
- A Vindication of the Church of England and of the Lawful Ministry thereof ... Translated ... by John Lindsay. London: for the translator, 1728. Folio. [vi],cxxvi,[xiv], 623, [ii],lii, [xi,i] pp. Lib stamp on title, some dust & fox marks. Contemp calf, jnts weak.
(Blackwell's) **£140 [≈ $249]**

Mason, George
- An Essay on Design in Gardening. First Published in 1768, now Greatly Augmented. London: C. Roworth, 1795. 1st edn thus. xii, 215 pp. Contemp gilt panelled calf, backstrip relaid. *(Gough)* **£150 [≈ $267]**

Mason, John
- Spiritual Songs: or, Songs of Praise, with Penitential Cries to Almighty God ... Bocking: ptd & sold by Fenno & Shearcroft; sold also by Fenno, Colchester, [1795]. 8vo. iv, 164 pp. Contemp qtr calf, worn but sound. Anon. *(Burmester)* **£90 [≈ $160]**

Mason, William
- The English Garden: a Poem ... A New Edition, Corrected ... York: ptd by A. Ward; sold by J. Dodsley, T. Cadell ..., 1783. 1st complete edn. 8vo. ix,[i],243 pp. Early 19th c half sheep, spine sl worn. Non-authorial inscrptn "From the Author".
(Burmester) **£75 [≈ $134]**
- The English Garden: a Poem. In Four Books. A New Edition, Corrected. To which is added a Commentary and Notes by W. Burgh. York: A. Ward ..., 1783. 1st edn of Commentary & Notes. 8vo. Contemp sheep, v rubbed. *(Hannas)* **£30 [≈ $53]**

- Isis. An Elegy. London: for R. Dodsley, sold by M. Cooper, 1749. 1st edn. 4to. 16 pp. Lacks half-title. Disbound.
(Hannas) £60 [≈ $107]
- Odes. Cambridge: by J. Bentham, sold by William Thurlbourn, & R. & J. Dolsley [sic, not crrctd in ink as most copies], 1756. 1st edn, 2nd issue. 4to. 32 pp. Wraps.
(Hannas) £45 [≈ $80]
- Odes. Cambridge: by J. Bentham, sold by William Thurlbourn, & R. & J. Dodsley [Dolsley crrctd in ink as usual], 1756. 1st edn, "second" issue, with cancellans title-page. Some staining title. reprd along former fold. Mod mrbld bds. *(Waterfield's)* £125 [≈ $223]
- Poems. London: for Robert Horsfield & sold by J. Dodsley, 1764. 1st coll edn. 8vo. Title vignette. S5 cancelled as usual. Sl staining last few ff. Insignificant marg worm hole in sheet N. Contemp calf, rebacked, orig label.
(Waterfield's) £105 [≈ $187]
- Poems. The Fourth Edition. York: A. Ward, & sold by Robert Horsfield, 1774. 8vo. [4], 294 pp, contents leaf. V sl marg worm. Contemp calf, rebacked.
(Spelman) £50 [≈ $89]

Massey, William
- The Origin and Progress of Letters. An Essay, in Two Parts ... London: for J. Johnson, 1763. 1st edn. 8vo. Frontis, 6 plates (1 plate shaved at ft). Old half calf, rebacked, minor rubbing. *(Ximenes)* $475 [≈ £267]

Massinger, Philip
- The Duke of Millaine. A Tragedy ... London: John Raworth for Edward Blackmore, 1638. 2nd edn. 4to. Mod qtr calf. STC 17635.
(Hannas) £220 [≈ $392]

Mastin, John
- The History and Antiquities of Naseby, in the County of Northampton. Cambridge: 1792. 8vo. 31,206 pp. Half-title. 27 pp subscribers. Half calf, t.e.g., some wear hd of jnts, spine chipped with sl loss.
(Francis Edwards) £100 [≈ $178]
- The History and Antiquities of Naseby in the County of Northampton. Cambridge: 1792. 8vo. iv,5-206 pp. Half-title. Fldg frontis (reprd on verso). Sl dusty. Rec half calf, uncut. *(Spelman)* £60 [≈ $107]

Mather, Samuel
- An Abridgement of the Life of the late reverend and learned Dr. Cotton Mather, of Boston, in New England ... London: for Oswald & Blackstone, 1744. 1st edn of this abridgement, with a preface by Isaac Watts.

12mo. xii,[iv],143 pp. Contemp calf, sl worn, lacks fly ff. *(Burmester)* £90 [≈ $160]

Mathias, Thomas James
- The Pursuits of Literature. A Satirical Poem, in Four Dialogues. With Notes ... Dublin: for J. Milliken, 1798. 8th edn. 8vo. xxxi, 380 pp. Light tan mor. Anon. *(Young's)* £50 [≈ $89]

Maundrell, Henry
- A Journey from Aleppo to Jerusalem at Easter A.D. 1697. Oxford: at the Theater, 1703. 1st edn. 12mo. [15],142,[7] pp. 9 plates. Old leather, rebacked. *(McBlain)* $450 [≈ £253]

Maurice, Henry
- Remarks from the Country upon the Two Letters relating to the Convocation and Alterations in the Liturgy. London: sold by most booksellers, 1689/90. 8vo. Disbound. Wing M.1369. Anon.
(Waterfield's) £45 [≈ $80]

Mavor, William Fordyce
- The Juvenile Olio; or Mental Medley: containing Original Essays ... Written by a Father chiefly for the Use of his Children. London: for E. Newborn, 1796. 266,2 advt pp. Frontis. Contemp calf, red label.
(C.R. Johnson) £55 [≈ $98]

Mawe, Thomas (& Abercrombie, John)
- Every Man his own Gardener ... London: 1767. 1st edn. 12mo. [iv],1-72, 73*-84*, 73-422 pp. Lacks frontis. Red mor gilt.
(Wheldon & Wesley) £100 [≈ $178]
- Every Man his own Gardener ... Dublin: for P. Byrne, 1798. 14th edn. 8vo. [iv],626,[19] pp. Old sheep, rubbed. *(Young's)* £42 [≈ $75]

Maxims ...
- Maxims for Playing the Game of Whist ... see Payne, William

Maxwell, Robert
- The Practical Husbandman ... Edinburgh: 1757. 1st edn. 432, index pp. Sl staining. Sgnd by the author on title verso. Old calf, v worn & spotted. *(King)* $95 [≈ £53]
- The Practical Husbandman: being a Collection of Miscellaneous Papers on Husbandry. Edinburgh: C. Wright for the author, 1757. xii,432,[6] pp. Fldg plate. Contemp calf, red label.
(C.R. Johnson) £350 [≈ $623]

May, Thomas
- A Discourse concerning the Successe of Former Parliaments. London: 1642. 1st edn.

4to. 12 pp. Disbound. Wing M.1404. Anon.
(Robertshaw) £45 [≈ $80]
- A Discovrse Concerning The Svccesse of
Former Parliaments. London: 1642. 4to.
Stitched. Anon. Wing M.404.
(Rostenberg & Stern) $125 [≈ £70]

Mayo, Charles
- A Chronological History of the European
States ... from the Treaty of Nimeguen in
1678 to the Close of the Year 1792 ... Bath:
S. Hazard, 1793. 1st edn. Folio. [viii], [cxviii],
87,[viii] pp. Half-title. Orig bds, vellum crnrs,
sl worn.   *(Blackwell's)* £60 [≈ $107]

**Mazarin, Hortense de la Porte, Duchesse
de**
- The Memoirs of the Dutchess Mazarine.
Written in French by her Own Hand, and
done into English by P. Porter. London:
William Cademan, 1676. 1st English edn. Sm
8vo. Licence leaf, final errata leaf. Minor
marg staining. Old style sheep. Wing S.355.
(Hannas) £220 [≈ $392]

Mead, Richard
- A Mechanical Account of Poisons in Several
Essays. London: J.R. for Ralph South, 1702.
1st edn. 8vo. [viii],175,[1] pp. Fldg plate.
Contemp calf, rebacked, ft of spine & 1 crnr
worn.   *(Burmester)* £275 [≈ $490]
- A Mechanical Account of Poisons in Several
Essays. Fourth Edition. Dublin: 1736. 8vo.
[8], 109,[3] pp. Fldg plate. Contemp calf,
spine reprd, new label.
(Spelman) £120 [≈ $214]
- The Medical Works ... London: Hitch,
Hawes ..., 1762. 4to. xxiv,xxvi-662, [48] pp.
Sl foxing. Contemp calf, backstrip relaid.
(Goodrich) $895 [≈ £503]
- A Treatise concerning the Influence of the
Sun and Moon upon Human Bodies and the
Diseases thereby produced. Translated from
the Latin by Thomas Stack. London:
Brindley, 1748. 2 vols in one. 8vo. 130,204
pp. Title dusty & chipped at foredge. New old
style bds.   *(Goodrich)* $145 [≈ £81]

Meadows, Sir Philip
- A Narrative of the Principal Actions
occurring in the Wars between Sueden and
Denmark ... London: A.C. for H. Brome,
1677. 1st edn. 12mo. Minor stains. Contemp
calf, rather worn. Wing M.1566.
(Hannas) £150 [≈ $267]
- Observations concerning the Dominion and
Sovereignty of the Seas ... London: Edw.
Jones, sold by Lowndes & Jones, 1689. 4to.
xiv, 47 pp. Lacks licence leaf. Sl spotting &

browning. 19th c mor elab gilt, spine flaked,
recased. Wing M.1567.
(Hollett) £240 [≈ $427]

Meadows, Samuel
- A Warning to the Sluggard; or, A Picture of
a Slothful Man Void of Understanding ...
London: for the author, 1768. 1st edn. 8vo.
39 pp. Disbound.   *(Young's)* £35 [≈ $62]

Meager, L.
- The English Gardner: or a Sure Guide to
Young Planters. London: 1688. Sm 4to. viii,
144 pp. 24 plates. Half calf.
(Wheldon & Wesley) £220 [≈ $392]

Meagher, Andrew
- The Popish Mass celebrated by Heathen
Priests, for the Living and the Dead, for
several Ages before the Birth of Christ ...
annexed, a Dissertation of the Conformity of
Popery and Paganism ... Limerick: T. Welsh,
1771. 8vo. Contemp sheep, worn but sound.
(Waterfield's) £65 [≈ $116]

Mede, Joseph
- Churches, that is, Appropriate Places for
Christian Worship; both in, and ever since
the Apostles Time. London: 1637. 1st edn.
4to. 74 pp. Mod wraps. STC 17765.
(Robertshaw) £25 [≈ $45]
- The Name Altar ... anciently given to the
Holy   Table.   A   Common-place,   or
Theologicall Discourse ... London: 1637. 4to.
39 pp. Mod wraps. STC 17768.5.
(Robertshaw) £20 [≈ $36]
- The Reverence of Gods House. A Sermon
preached at St. Maries in Cambridge.
London: 1638. 1st edn. 4to. Mod wraps. STC
17769.   *(Robertshaw)* £25 [≈ $45]
- The Reverence of Gods House. A Sermon
Preached at St. Maries in Cambridge ... on St.
Matthies Day, Anno 1635/6 ... London: M.F.
for John Clark, 1638. 1st edn. 4to. 71 pp. Sm
repr to title & 2nd leaf. Stained. Disbound.
STC 17769.   *(Young's)* £35 [≈ $62]

Meilan, Mark Anthony
- Holy   Writ   Familiarized   to   Juvenile
Conceptions. In a Series of Pathetic Stories,
and Affecting Dialogues ... London: W.
Wilson, 1791. 4 vols. 404; 424; 460; 436,443,
[8] pp. 4 frontis. Contemp speckled calf,
green labels, fine.
(C.R. Johnson) £125 [≈ $223]

Meilhan, Gabriel Denac de
- Considerations upon Wit and Morals.
Translated from the French. London: for

G.G.J. & J. Robinson, 1788. 8vo. Sm lib stamp title verso. Contemp qtr calf, leather renewed. Anon. *(Waterfield's)* **£80 [≈ $142]**

Meldrum, Sir John
- The Copy of a Letter sent to the King. London: for Joseph Hunscott, Octob. 18, 1642. Only edn. 4to. 8 pp. Imprint & border just cropped. Num contemp MS corrections. Disbound. *(Young's)* **£130 [≈ $231]**

Melmoth, William
- The Letters of Pliny the Consul: With Occasional Remarks ... London: for J. Dodsley, 1777. New edn. 2 vols. 8vo. [x],692, 4 pp. Half-titles. Contemp calf, new labels. *(Young's)* **£65 [≈ $116]**

Melville, Sir James
- The Memoires of Sir James Melvil, of Hal-Hill ... Now Published from the Original Manuscript. London: E.H. for Robert Boulter, 1683. 1st edn. Sm folio. [16],204,[24] pp. Contemp calf, rebacked, crnrs worn. Wing M.1654. *(O'Neal)* **£225 [≈ £126]**
- The Memoirs ... containing an Impartial Account of the most Remarkable Affairs of State during the Sixteenth Century ... Published from the Original Manuscript by George Scott ... Third Edition, Corrected. Glasgow: Robert Urie, 1751. 8vo. Contemp sheep, sl worn. *(Waterfield's)* **£55 [≈ $98]**

Memoirs ...
- Memoirs concerning the Life and Manners of Captain Mackheath. London: for A. Moore, 1728. 1st edn. 8vo. Half-title. Mod bds. *(Ximenes)* **£650 [≈ $365]**
- Memoirs of a Cavalier ... see Defoe, Daniel.
- Memoirs of a certain Island adjacent to the Kingdom of Utopia ... see Haywood, Eliza
- Memoirs of Europe ... see Manley, Mary De La Riviere
- The Memoirs of the Marquess de Langallerie ... see Courtilz de Sandras, Gatien de

Memorial ...
- The Memorial to the Church of England, Humbly Offer'd to the Consideration of all true Lovers of our Church and Constitution, Seriously Consider'd Paragraph by Paragraph. London: printed in the year 1705. 1st edn. 4to. 58 pp. Disbound. *(Young's)* **£90 [≈ $160]**

Memorialls ...
- Memorialls for the Government of the Royal-Burghs in Scotland ... see Skene, Alexander.

Memorials ...
- Memorials of the English Affairs ... see Whitelocke, Sir Bulstrode

Mengs, Anthony Raphael
- The Works ... Translated from the Italian. Published by the Chevr. Don Joseph Nicholas d'Azara, Spanish Minister at Rome. London: Faulder, Robinson, 1796. 3 vols in 2. Sm 4to. [2],5,[1], iv,225,[4], 153,162,[4] pp. 2 engvd titles. Contemp calf, front bds detached. *(Ars Libri)* **$375 [≈ £211]**

Menon, L.F.H. de, Marquis de Turbilly
- A Discourse on the Cultivation of Waste and Barren Lands. Translated from the French ... Part I [all published]. London: Dodsley, 1762. 1st edn in English. 8vo. [iv],xv,[i], 111 pp. W'cut frontis. Old wraps. *(Burmester)* **£150 [≈ $267]**

Mental Amusement ...
- See Sael, George (editor)

Meredith, William
- The Question Stated, Whether the Freeholders of Middlesex Lost Their Right, by Voting for Mr. Wilkes at the Last Election? Second Edition. London: for G. Woodfall ..., 1769. Mod qtr calf. Anon. *(Meyer Boswell)* **$300 [≈ £169]**

The Merry and Facetious Companion ...
- The Merry and Facetious Companion, in French and English: being a Collection of the most Entertaining Stories, Witty Sayings ... Third Edition. London: sold by Duncombe & Peisley, 1746. 8vo. 112,97-175, 179-195 pp, complete. Contemp sheep, rebacked. *(Burmester)* **£350 [≈ $623]**

Mervin, or Mervyn, Sir Audley
- Captaine Audley Mervin's Speech delivered in the Upper House to the Lords in Parliament, May 24, 1641 ... London: for R. Royston, 1641. 1st edn. Sm 4to. [i],17 pp. Faint marg browning. Mod wraps. Wing M.1887. *(Blackwell's)* **£65 [≈ $116]**
- A Speech Made By Captain Audley Mervin to the Vpper House of Parliament in Ireland, March 4, 1640. Together with certaine Articles (of high Treason) against Sir Richard Bolton. [London]: Perry, 1641. 4to. Stitched. Wing M.1889. *(Rostenberg & Stern)* **$100 [≈ £56]**

Mesnager, Monsr.
- Minutes of the Negotiations ... see Defoe, Daniel

Method ...

- The Method of the Proceedings in the House
of Lords and Commons in Cases of
Impeachments for High Treason, with
Presidents Ancient and Modern ... London:
1715. 1st edn. 8vo. 67 pp. Some damp
staining, few pp numbers cropped. Later qtr
mor.   *(Robertshaw)* **£20 [≈ $36]**

Mexia, Pedro

- The Imperiall Historie: or the Lives of the
Emperors, from Ivlivs Caesar ... Translated
into English by W. T. [Trahern] ... continued
... by Edvvard Grimeston. London: 1623.
Folio. [viii],867 pp. Engvd title. Lacks A1
(blank). Contemp calf, rebacked. STC 17852.
            (Sotheran's) **£375 [≈ $668]**

Mezeray, Francois

- A General Chronological History of France ...
London: T.N. for Thomas Basset ..., 1683.
1st edn in English. folio. [8],968,[39] pp.
Addtnl engvd title. Old panelled calf,
rebacked, rubbed. Wing M.1958.
            (O'Neal) **$250 [≈ £140]**
- A General Chronologicall History of France
... By the Sieur de Mezeray ... London: for
Thomas Basset ..., 1683. 1st English edn. 3
vols in one. Thick folio. Frontis (laid down).
Offset to title. Contemp calf, spine ends
worn, front hinge cracked.
            (Vanbrugh) **£375 [≈ $668]**

Micanzio, Fulgenzio

- The Life of the Most Learned Father Paul
[Paolo Sarpi] ... Councellour of State to the
Most Serene Republick of Venice ...
Translated out of Italian ... London: Moseley,
Marriot, 1651. 1st edn in English. 8vo.
[8],204 pp. Contemp calf, front hinge
cracked. Wing M.1959. Anon
            (O'Neal) **$150 [≈ £84]**

Michell, John

- A Treatise of Artificial Magnets ... Mariner's
Needle ... The Second Edition corrected and
improved. Cambridge: Joseph Bentham,
1751. 78 pp. Fldg plate. Cloth bds.
            (C.R. Johnson) **£160 [≈ $285]**

Middleton, Conyers

- The History of the Life of Marcus Tullius
Cicero. Dublin: for John Smith & Abraham
Bradley, 1741. 2 vols. 8vo. Contemp speckled
calf, green labels, some wear spine ends &
crnrs, jnts cracking.
            (Waterfield's) **£50 [≈ $89]**

Midgley, Samuel

- Hallifax, and its Gibbet-Law Placed in a True
Light. Together with a Description of the
Town ... London: J. How, for William
Bently, Halifax, 1708. 1st edn. 12mo. Frontis
(foredge shaved). Contemp black mor gilt,
a.e.g. & gauffered, backstrip relaid. Anon.
            (Hannas) **£140 [≈ $249]**

Miege, Guy

- A Relation of Three Embassies from His
Sacred Majestie Charles II to the Great Duke
of Moscovie, the King of Sweden, and King
of Denmark ... London: Starkey, 1669. 1st
edn. 8vo. 3 advt ff. 2 ports (frontis laid down).
Contemp calf, rebacked. Wing M.2025.
Anon.   *(Hannas)* **£150 [≈ $267]**

Milbourne, Luke

- The Christian Pattern Paraphras'd: or, the
Book of the Imitation of Christ, commonly
ascribed to Thomas A Kempis. By Luke
Milbourne. London: for Abel Roper, & Roger
Clavel, 1697. 1st edn. 8vo. Frontis. Contemp
panelled calf, rebacked. Wing T.945.
            (Ximenes) **$500 [≈ £281]**
- Tom of Bedlam's Answer to his Brother Ben
Hoadly, St. Peter's-Poor Parson, near the
Exchange of Principles. London: sold by B.
Bragge, 1709. 1st edn. 8vo. 16 pp. Half-title.
Sl browned. Disbound. Anon.
            (Young's) **£95 [≈ $169]**

Military ...

- A Military Dictionary. Explaining all
difficult Terms in Martial Discipline,
Fortification, and Gunnery ... By an Officer
... London: for J. Nutt, 1704. 2nd edn, "with
additions". 12mo. Unpaginated. Fldg plate,
text diags. 19th c calf, rebacked.
            (Burmester) **£200 [≈ $356]**
- Military Orders and Instructions for the
Wiltshire Battalion of Militia; beginning XIV
August, MDCCLVIII, and ending XX
October, MDCCLXX. Chelsea: Printed by J:
R: W., 1772. 1st edn. 8vo. [ii],534 pp.
Contemp tree calf, gilt spine.
            (Burmester) **£300 [≈ $534]**

Mill, Job

- The Present Practice of Conveyancing ... In
the Savoy: Lintot, Hawkins, 1746. 1st edn.
Lge folio. [iv],686,[687-700] pp. Contemp
calf.   *(Vanbrugh)* **£225 [≈ $401]**

Miller, James

- The Humours of Oxford. A Comedy ... By a
Gentleman of Wadham-College. London: for
J. Watts, 1730. 1st edn. 8vo. Tear in 1 leaf,

no loss. Mod bds. Anon.
(Hannas) £50 [≈ $89]

Miller, Joe
- Joe Miller's Jests ... see Mottley, John

Miller, Philip
- The Gardener's and Botanist's Dictionary. Ninth Edition, edited by T. Martyn. London: 1797-1807. 2 vols in 4. Folio. 18 (of 20) plates. Dedic mtd. Mod half leather.
(Wheldon & Wesley) £275 [≈ $490]
- The Gardener's Dictionary ... London: for the author, & sold by C. Rivington, 1731. 1st edn. Folio. xvi,[iv] pp, B1-8D2, a1-zz2 in 2s. Frontis, 4 fldg plates. Occas stains, sm marg worm, sm hole 1 leaf. Contemp calf, rebacked, crnrs reprd. *(Clark)* £280 [≈ $498]
- The Gardeners Kalendar ... London: 1732. 1st edn. 8vo. xv,252 pp. Frontis. New half calf, antique style.
(Wheldon & Wesley) £120 [≈ $214]
- The Gardeners Kalendar. London: for John Rivington ..., 1757. Post 8vo. xviii, 352, [xii] pp. Frontis. Some ff discold. Contemp (orig?) calf, sl worn. *(Ash)* £125 [≈ $223]
- The Gardener's Kalendar ... Thirteenth Edition, adapted to the New Style ... London: for the author, 1762. 8vo. xv,47,369,[1] pp. Frontis, 5 fldg plates. Sl browning & soiling. Contemp calf, extrs worn, lower jnt cracked.
(Claude Cox) £75 [≈ $134]
- The Gardiners Kalendar ... The Fourteenth Edition. With a List of the Medicinal Plants ... London: for the author, 1765. 8vo. xvi, 50, 376,[22] pp. Frontis, 5 fldg plates. Contemp calf, sl rubbed, sm chip hd of spine.
(Karmiole) £150 [≈ $84]
- The Gardeners Kalendar ... The Fifteenth Edition. London: Rivington, 1769. 8vo. lxvi, [2 blank],282,[22] pp. Frontis, 5 fldg plates. Contemp calf, gilt backstrip relaid.
(Spelman) £90 [≈ $160]

Millot, Claude Francois Xavier
- Elements of the History of France. London: for J. Dodsley, & T. cadell, 1771. 1st edn in English. 3 vols. 12mo. Contemp calf gilt, trifle rubbed. *(Ximenes)* $200 [≈ £112]
- Elements of the History of France, translated from the Abbe Millot ... By a Lady [Miss R. Roberts]. London: for J. Dodsley, & T. Cadell, 1771. 1st edn in English. 3 vols. 12mo. Contemp calf, traces of rubbing.
(Burmester) £90 [≈ $160]

Milns, William
- The Well-Bred Scholar, or Practical Essays

on ... assisting the Exertions of Youth in their Literary Pursuits. London: ptd by S. Gosnell; sold by Rivingtons ... & the author, 1794. 1st edn. 8vo. 16,559 pp. Half-title, intl advt leaf. Orig bds, cvrs worn.
(Burmester) £250 [≈ $445]

Milton, John
- Comus, a Mask ... L'Allegro and Il Penseroso, and Mr. Warton's Account of the Origin of Comus. London: T. Bensley, for Harding, West, 1799. 1st edn thus. 12mo. [iv], 124 pp. Half-title. frontis, 3 plates. Contemp calf, spine rubbed, lacks label, upper jnt cracked. *(Burmester)* £50 [≈ $89]
- The History of Britain, That Part especially now call'd England ... London: J.M. for John Martyn, 1677. 1st 8vo edn. 8vo. 357,[59] pp. With blank A1. Minor browning. Contemp calf, rebacked & recrnrd. Wing M.2121.
(Clark) £280 [≈ $498]
- Milton's Italian Poems Translated and Addressed to a Gentleman of Italy. By Dr. Langhorne. London: for T. Becket, 1776. 1st edn. 4to. Disbound, stitching loose.
(Ximenes) $350 [≈ £197]
- Paradise Lost ... Thirteenth Edition. London: Tonson, 1727. 8vo. (iii)-xxv,[xi], 524,[34] pp. Frontis, port vignette, 12 plates. Minor staining & browning. Contemp sheep, gilt spine, crnrs sl worn, upper jnt cracked & tender. *(Clark)* £32 [≈ $57]
- Paradise Lost. [With] Paradise Regained. Birmingham: John Baskerville for J. & R. Tonson, 1758. 1st Baskerville edns. 2 vols. 8vo. [3],[18], [6],416; lxix,390 pp. 1 title sl foxed. Three qtr red mor gilt, g.e., extrs sl scuffed. *(Wreden)* $600 [≈ £337]
- Paradise Regain'd ... Samson Agonistes; and Poems upon Several Occasions. With a Tractate of Education ... London: Tonson, 1727. 7th edn. 8vo. [vi],97,[i], [viii], 108-189, [i], [ii],193-484, [ii],487-504 pp. Frontis. Contemp calf gilt, sl worn.
(Vanbrugh) £115 [≈ $205]
- The Works. London: Printed in the Year, 1697. Folio. Contemp panelled calf, rebacked, orig label retained. Wing M.2086.
(Waterfield's) £400 [≈ $712]

Minsheu, John
- Minshaei Emendatio ... The Guide into Tongues ... The second Edition. London: John Haviland, 1627. Folio. pp, 760 columns [ie 380 pp]. Later half russia, sl worn. STC 17947. *(Clark)* £420 [≈ $748]

Missionary Society of Connecticut
- A Missionary Voyage to the Southern Pacific

Ocean, Performed in the Years 1796, 1797, 1798, in the Ship Duff, Commanded by Capt. James Wilson ... London: T. Chapman, 1799. 1st edn. 4to. c,395,[7 subscribers] pp. Fldg frontis, 6 plates, 6 charts, sl marks. Rec calf.
(Francis Edwards) **£425 [≈ $757]**

Mitchell, Joseph

- The Highland Fair; or, Union of the Clans. An Opera ... With the Musick ... London: for J. Watts, 1731. 1st edn. 8vo. [xvi],78 pp. 2 advt ff in prelims. Engvd frontis by Hogarth. Half calf.   *(Burmester)* **£275 [≈ $490]**

Mitford, William

- An Essay upon the Harmony of Language, intended principally to illustrate that of the English Language. London: Scott, 1774. iv,288 pp. Contemp calf, red label, fine. Anon.   *(C.R. Johnson)* **£350 [≈ $623]**

Modern ...

- Modern Ballads. Preston: ptd & sold by W. Stuart, & Z. Stuart, London, [ca 1780]. 12mo. Contemp sheep, rebacked.
(C.R. Johnson) **£220 [≈ $392]**
- The Modern Practice of the London Hospitals ... A New Edition. With an useful Index of Diseases, and their Remedies. London: for G. Lister, [1785]. 121 pp. Frontis. Rec bds.
(C.R. Johnson) **£180 [≈ $320]**

Modest Enquiry ...

- A Modest Enquiry concerning the Election of the Sheriffs of London. London: 1682. 1st edn. 4to. 46 pp. Mod bds, leather label. Wing M.2365.   *(Robertshaw)* **£45 [≈ $80]**

Moffet, Thomas

- Health's Improvement; or Rules Comprizing and Discovering the Nature, Method and Manner of Preparing all sorts of Food ... Enlarged by Christopher Bennet ... London: 1746. 2nd edn. 8vo. xxxii,398 pp. Sl used. Contemp sheep, spine ends reprd, crnrs trifle rubbe   *(Gough)* **£450 [≈ $801]**

Molesworth, Robert, Viscount

- An Account of Denmark, As it was in the Year 1692. Sixth Edition. Glasgow: R. Urie, 1752. xxxii,188 pp. Contemp calf, red label, jnts cracked, held by cords.
(Jermy & Westerman) **£35 [≈ $62]**

Moliere, Jean Baptiste Poquelin

- The Works of Moliere, French and English. In Ten Volumes. London: John Watts, 1739. 1st edn to include all 31 pieces. 10 vols. 8vo.

Port frontis, 30 plates. Contemp calf, gilt dec spines, labels, sl worn & used.
(Clark) **£400 [≈ $712]**
- The Works. A New Translation. Berwick: for R. Taylor, 1771. 6 vols. 8vo. Browned, sl foxing, reprs. Mod half calf.
(D & D Galleries) **$325 [≈ £183]**

Monck, George, later Duke of Albemarle

- The Lord General Monck His Speech Delivered by Him in the Parliament on Monday, Feb. 6. 1659. 1st edn. 8vo. [ii],5,[i] pp. Occas stains. Disbound. Wing A.869.
(Clark) **£100 [≈ $178]**
- Observations upon Military and Political Affairs. London: R. White, 1796. 8vo. lxiii,[i],224 pp. 3 fldg plates. Later bds, paper label, untrimmed, sm snag ft of spine.
(Clark) **£125 [≈ $223]**
- The Speech and Declaration of his Excellency the Lord Generall Monck Delivered at Whitehall upon Tuesday the 21 of february 1659 ... London: S. Griffin, for John Playford, 1659. 1st edn. 8vo. [ii],6 pp. Browned. Disbound. Wing A.867.   *(Clark)* **£100 [≈ $178]**

Moncreiff, John

- Camillus. A Dialogue on the Navy ... By the Author of Galba. London: for J. Roberts, 1748. 1st edn. 8vo. [2],66 pp. Disbound. Anon.   *(Hannas)* **£95 [≈ $169]**
- Galba. A Dialogue on the Navy. London: for J. Roberts, 1748. 1st edn. 8vo. [2],65 pp. Disbound. Anon.   *(Hannas)* **£110 [≈ $196]**

Monro, A.

- The Structure and Physiology of Fishes explained, and compared with those of Man and Other Animals. Edinburgh: 1785. Large Paper. Folio (455 x 285 mm). 50 engvd plates on 44 ff. Occas minor foxing. 2 sm marg reprs. Contemp bds, rebacked in calf..
(Wheldon & Wesley) **£400 [≈ $712]**

Monro, D.

- A Treatise on Mineral Waters. London: 1770. 2 vols. xxiv,476; viii,420 pp. Old calf, v worn, water stains on rear cvr of vol 1.
(Whitehart) **£180 [≈ $320]**

Monro, Robert

- The Scotch Military Discipline learnd from the valiant Swede, and collected for the use of all worthy Commanders ... London: for William Ley, 1644. 1st edn under this title. Folio. Title soiled. Contemp sheep, v rubbed. Wing M.2454A.   *(Hannas)* **£500 [≈ $890]**

Monro, Thomas

- Essays on Various Subjects. London: J. Nichols, 1790. 228 pp. Half-title. Orig blue bds, paper spine, uncut.
(C.R. Johnson) **£145 [≈ $258]**

Monro, Thomas, & others

- The Olla Podrida, a Periodical Work, Complete in Forty-Four Numbers ... London: J. Nichols ..., 1788. 1st edn thus. 8vo. 443 pp. Half calf, red label. Anon.
(Young's) **£80 [≈ $142]**

Monroe, James

- A View of the Conduct of the Executive in the Foreign Affairs of the United States, as connected with the Mission to the French Republic ... Philadelphia, Printed. London: reprinted for James Ridgway, 1798. 1st English edn. 8vo. viii,117,[1],[2 advt] pp. Dsbnd
(Burmester) **£75 [≈ $134]**

Montagu, Lady Barbara & Scott, Sarah

- A Description of Millenium Hall, and the Country Adjacent ... By a Gentleman on his Travels. The Second Edition Corrected. London: for J. Newbery, 1764. 12mo. [4],264 pp. Frontis. Orig calf, rubbed, spine & crnrs chipped. Anon. *(Karmiole)* **$100 [≈ £56]**

Montagu, Edward Wortley

- Reflections of the Rise and Fall of the Antient Republicks. London: for A. Millar, 1759. 1st edn. Post 8vo. [viii],384 pp. Prelims faintly damp marked. Contemp calf gilt.
(Ash) **£125 [≈ $223]**

Montagu, Elizabeth

- An Essay on the Writings and Genius of Shakespear sic ... Second Edition. London: J. & H. Hughs, sold by Dodsley ..., 1770. 8vo. Lib stamps on title. Lib half mor, sl defective. Anon. *(Hannas)* **£35 [≈ $62]**
- An Essay on the Writings and Genius of Shakespeare ... Withsome Remarks on the Misrepresentations of Mons. de Voltaire. London: 1770. 2nd edn. 8vo. [iv],288 pp. Contemp calf, gilt spine, upper jnt cracked but firm. *(Burmester)* **£60 [≈ $107]**
- An Essay on the Writings ... of Shakespear sic ... Fourth Edition. To which are now first added, Three Dialogues of the Dead. London: Dilly, 1777. 8vo. Contemp calf, gilt spine (worn). *(Hannas)* **£55 [≈ $98]**
- An Essay on the Writings and genius of Shakespear. London: Hughs, 1770. 2nd edn. 8vo. Inscrptn on title. Three qtr calf. Anon.
(Rostenberg & Stern) **$135 [≈ £76]**

Montague, Lady Mary Wortley

- Letters ... written during her Travels in Europe, Asia and Africa ... Second Edition. London: Becket & De Hondt, 1763. 3 vols. Sm 8vo. xii (for x),[iv],165; [ii],167; [ii],134 pp. Lacks half-titles. Early 19th c half calf, mor labels. *(Blackwell's)* **£160 [≈ $285]**
- Letters ... written during her Travels in Europe, Asia and Africa ... London: for T. Becket ..., 1763-67. 3rd edn vols 1-3, 1st edn vol 4. 4 vols. 8vo. half-titles vols 1-3. Contemp speckled calf, gilt, sl rubbed.
(Young's) **£140 [≈ $249]**
- The Poetical Works of the Right honourable Lady M-- W--y M--e. London: for J. Williams, 1767. 1st coll edn. Sm 8vo. Mod half calf. *(Hannas)* **£120 [≈ $214]**

Montaigne, Michel

- Montaigne's Essays In three Books. Translated by Charles Cotton ... The sixth Edition. London: B. & B. Barker ..., 1743. 3 vols. 8vo. Contemp calf, rubbed, extrs worn, some jnts cracked but firm.
(Clark) **£32 [≈ $57]**

Montaigne, Michel de

- Essays ... done into English ... by John Florio. London: Bradwood for Blount & Barret, 1613. Folio. [10],630 pp. Port, decs. 1 sm marg repr, 1 sm tear (no loss). Sl marks. Lacks final blank. Contemp calf, backstrip sometime laid down, jnts sl cracked.
(Spelman) **£550 [≈ $979]**

Montesquieu, Charles de Secondat, Baron de

- Miscellaneous Pieces ... Translated from the New Edition of his Works printed at Paris. London: for D. Wilson, 1759. 8vo. Lacks a blank part of half-title. Conjugate B4.5 sl springing. Contemp calf, jnts cracked but sound, amateur repr top jnt.
(Waterfield's) **£425 [≈ $757]**
- Reflexions on the Causes of the Rise and Fall of the Roman Empire. Translated from the French ... The Third Edition, Improved and Corrected ... London: for R. Manby ..., 1759. 8vo. Mod qtr calf.
(Waterfield's) **£225 [≈ $401]**
- The Spirit of Laws ... With Corrections and Additions communicated by the Author. London: Nourse & Vaillant, 1750. 1st English edn. 2 vols. 8vo. viii,[xx], 452,[ii]; [ii],xvi, 483,[xlvi],[ii] pp. Some browning & occas spotting. Contemp calf, rebacked.
(Sotheran's) **£985 [≈ $1,753]**
- The Spirit of Laws. Translated from the French ... With Corrections and Additions

communicated by the Author. London: Nourse & Vaillant, 1750. 1st English edn. 2 vols. 8vo. Contemp tree calf, orig elab gilt backstrips relaid.
(Waterfield's) **£2,750 [≈ $4,895]**

- The Spirit of Laws Translated from the French ... by Mr. Nugent ... the Second Edition, Corrected and Considerably Improved. London: Nourse & Vaillant, 1752. 2nd English edn. 2 vols. 8vo. Contemp calf, new labels.   *(Waterfield's)* **£400 [≈ $712]**

Montfaucon, Bernard de

- Antiquity Explained and represented in Sculptures ... Cambridge: Tonson & Watts, 1721-25. 1st edn in English. 7 vols. Folio. Num plates. Contemp calf, sl worn, few bds loose.   *(Bookpress)* **$1,200 [≈ £674]**

Montgomery, James

- Prison Amusements, and Other Trifles: principally written during Nine Months Confinement in the Castle of York. By Paul Positive. London: for J. Johnson, 1797. viii,200 pp. Contemp tree calf, hinges cracking. Anon. *(C.R. Johnson)* **£350 [≈ $623]**

Moody, Christopher Lake (editor)

- A Sketch of Modern France. In a Series of Letters to a Lady of Fashion. Written in the Years 1796 and 1797, during a Tour through France. By a Lady. London: Cadell & Davies, 1798. 1st edn. 8vo. viii,518,[2 advt] pp. Contemp calf, lacks label, jnts cracked.
(Burmester) **£150 [≈ $267]**

Moore, Edward

- Gil Blas. A Comedy ... London: for R. Francklin, 1751. 1st edn. 8vo. Lib number on 1 page. Half calf, a.e.g. *(Hannas)* **£25 [≈ $45]**

Moore, Francis

- Travels into the Inland Parts of Africa ... Second Edition. London: Henry & Cave, [1738]. 8vo. xi,xiii,229, 84,iii,[i],25 pp. Fldg map, 10 plates (1 fldg). Occas foxing, marg stain in middle of book. Contemp gilt panelled calf, later rebacking.
(Gough) **£195 [≈ $347]**

Moore, Sir Francis

- Cases Collect & Report ... London: R. Norton for Robert Pawlet, 1663. 1st edn. Folio. Errata, licence leaf. Port frontis. Contemp sheep, bds detached. Wing M.2535.
(Vanbrugh) **£195 [≈ $347]**

Moore, J. Hamilton

- Young Gentleman and Lady's Monitor, and

English Teacher's Assistant ... The Latest Edition. New York: 1792. Fcap 8vo. vi,406,[6],[2 advt] pp. Browned. Rec half calf.
(Spelman) **£60 [≈ $107]**

Moore, John

- A View of Society, and Manners in France, Switzerland, and Germany ... London: for A. Strahan, 1786. 6th edn, crrctd. 2 vols. 8vo. xvi,420; xii,420 pp. Old calf, rebacked.
(Young's) **£55 [≈ $98]**

Moore, W.

- A Ramble through Holland, France, and Italy. Second Edition. London: Cadell, 1793-94. 2 vols. Lge 12mo. xxiv,287,[1]; [2],278 pp. Subscribers. Lacks vol 1 half-title. Contemp polished calf, gilt spine. Anon.
(Spelman) **£300 [≈ $534]**

Moral and Instructive Tales ...

- Moral and Instructive Tales for the Improvement of Young Ladies: calculated to Amuse the Mind, and form the Heart to Virtue. London: John Marshall & Co., [1786]. Half-title, [6],5-92 pp. Orig qtr calf, mrbld bds.   *(C.R. Johnson)* **£265 [≈ $472]**

Mordecai, Benjamin Ben

- The Apology of Benjamin ben Mordecai ... see Taylor, Henry

More, Cresacre

- The Life of Sir Thomas More, Kt. ... by his Great Grandson, Thomas [sic] More. London: Woodman & Lyon, 1726. 8vo. Publisher's list at end. Port frontis. Red & black title. Calf, rebacked. Long erroneously attributed to the author's brother Thomas. Anon.   *(Rostenberg & Stern)* **$375 [≈ £211]**

More, Hannah

- Essays on Various Subjects, principally designed for Young Ladies. The Second Edition. London: for J. Wilkie, 1778. [6],214,[2] pp. Half-title. Contemp calf, spine rubbed, hinges weak. Anon.
(C.R. Johnson) **£85 [≈ $151]**

- Sir Eldred of the Bower, and the Bleeding Rock. Two legendary Tales. London: for T. Cadell, 1776. 1st edn. 4to. [6],49 pp. Sm tear in inner marg. Disbound.
(Hannas) **£85 [≈ $151]**

- Strictures on the Modern System of Female Education ... London: Cadell & Davies, 1799. 5th edn. 2 vols. 8vo. xx,302; viii,338 pp. Half-title in vol 1 as called for. Contemp tree calf, gilt spines, sl rubbed, hd of spines trifle worn.   *(Burmester)* **£75 [≈ $134]**

More, Henry

- Discourses on Several Texts of Scripture. London: J.R., sold by Brabazon Aylmer, 1692. 1st edn. 8vo. [xiv],485,[iii] pp. Blank crnr torn from 1 leaf. Mod qtr calf gilt.
  (Blackwell's) £65 [≈ $116]
- An Explanation of the Grand Mystery of Godliness ... London: J. Flesher, for W. Morden, Cambridge, 1660. 1st edn. Folio. Contemp calf, rebacked, crnrs reprd, new endpapers. Wing M.2658.
  (Waterfield's) £225 [≈ $401]
- An Explanation of the Grand Mystery of Godliness ... London: J. Flesher for W. Morden, 1660. Folio. Contemp panelled calf, most of backstrip relaid. Wing M.2658.
  (Waterfield's) £275 [≈ $490]
- Philosophicall Poems. Cambridge: Roger Daniel, 1647. 8vo. Publisher's device on title. Contemp calf, jnts & extrs rubbed. Wing M.2670.
  (Waterfield's) £650 [≈ $1,157]
- The Theological Works ... London: Joseph Downing, 1708. 1st coll edn in English. Folio. [iv],xiv, 383,[iii], 389-856 pp. Port frontis. Occas browning. Contemp calf, spine ends reprd, jnts cracked but firm.
  (Clark) £200 [≈ $356]

More, Sir Thomas

- Vtopia. London: Alsop, 1624. 1st edn of Alsop's correction of Robinson's translation. Sm 4to. Qtr calf & bds. STC 18097.
  (Rostenberg & Stern) £750 [≈ £421]

Moreton, Andrew

- The Secrets of the Invisible World Disclos'd ... see Moreton, Andrew

Morgan, J.

- A Complete History of Algiers. To which is prefixed An Epitome of the General History of Barbary ... London: for the author by J. Bettenham, 1728-29. 1st edn. 2 vols. 4to. vi,[vi],xxix, [vii],352; xxvii,[iii],[i], 16,353-680,[24] pp. Contemp calf, jnts split, sl worn
  (Gough) £180 [≈ $320]

Morgan, T.

- The Mechanical Practice of Physick. In which the Specifick method is Examin'd and Exploded; and the Bellinian Hypothesis of Animal Secretion amd Muscular Motion, Consider'd and refuted. London: 1735. xvi,362 pp. Contemp calf, sl marked.
  (Whitehart) £375 [≈ $668]
- The Mechanical Practice of Physick: in which the Specifick Method is Examin'd and Exploded ... London: 1735. 362 pp. New calf

gilt.
  (Goodrich) $265 [≈ £149]

Mornay Du Plessis, Philippe

- A Worke Concerning the Trunesse of Christian Religion, written in French ... Begunne to be translated into English by ... Sir Philip Sidney ... finished by Arthur Golding. London: Potter, 1604. 4to. Few stains. Mottled calf, rebacked. STC 18151.
  (Rostenberg & Stern) £450 [≈ £253]

Morrice, Matthias

- Social religion Exemplified, In an Account of the First Settlement of Christianity in the City of Caerludd ... Revised ... by Edward Williams. Shrewsbury: J. Eddowes ..., 1786. 4th edn. 12mo. xxiii,[i], 422,[xvi],[i] pp. Calf, sl worn. *(Francis Edwards)* £60 [≈ $107]

Morris, Corbyn

- A Letter to the Reverend Mr. Thomas Carte, Author of the Full Answer to the Letter from a Bystander. By a gentleman of Cambridge. London: for Jacob Robinson, 1743. 1st edn. 8vo. [4],114 pp, inc half-title. Disbound. Anon. *(Hannas)* £100 [≈ $178]

Morris, Valentine

- A Narrative of the Official Conduct of Valentine Morris, Late Captain General, Governor-in-Chief, &c., of the Island of St. Vincent ... London: J. Walter, 1787. 1st edn. xvii,[ii],[i],467 pp. Half-title. Engvd title vignette. Contemp calf, spine trifle rubbed. *(Gough)* £300 [≈ $534]

Morse, Jedidiah

- New and Corrected Edition of The American geography ... Edinburgh: for R. Morison & Son ... & Vernor & Hood, 1795. 5th edn. 8vo. 531 pp. 7 fldg maps (linen backed). Lib blindstamp. Contemp half calf, front jnt cracked but holding. *(Chapel Hill)* $650 [≈ £365]

Morsels of Criticism ...

- See King, Edward

Moseley, Walter Michael

- An Essay on Archery: Describing the Practice of that Art in all Ages and Nations. Worcester: I. & I. Holl, 1792. 1st edn. 8vo. x,348 pp. Errata. Frontis, engvd title, 4 plates (foxed). Some offsetting. Mod qtr calf. *(D & D Galleries)* $225 [≈ £126]

Moser, Joseph

- The Adventures of Timothy Twig, Esq. in a Series of Poetical Epistles. London: for E. &

T. Williams, 1794. 1st edn. 2 vols in one. 8vo. Contemp half calf, v worn.
(Hannas) **£240 [≈ $427]**

Moss, Thomas
- A Treatise of Gauging. Containing not only what is common ... but likewise a great variety of New and Interesting Improvements ... London: for the author ..., also by W. Owen ..., 1765. 1st edn. 8vo. [xii],268 pp. Fldg plate. Single marg wormhole. Contempcalf.
(Burmester) **£250 [≈ $445]**

Motte, Andrew
- A Treatise of the Mechanical Powers, wherein the Laws of Motion, and the Properties of those Powers are explained ... London: for Benjamin Motte, 1727. 1st edn. 8vo. [viii],222,[1 errata],[1 advt] pp. 3 plates. Contemp calf gilt, rubbed, jnts cracked but sound.
(Gaskell) **£650 [≈ $1,157]**

Motteux, Peter Anthony [Pierre Antoine]
- Love's a Jest. London: for Peter Buck ..., 1696. 1st edn. Sm 4to. Straight grained mor gilt, by Sangorski & Sutcliffe, jnts trifle rubbed. Wing M.2953.
(Ximenes) **$600 [≈ £337]**

Mottley, John (compiler)
- Joe Miller's Jests: or, the Wits Vade-Mecum ... Now set forth and published by his lamentable friend and former companion, Elijah Jenkins ... London: T. Read, 1739. 1st edn. 8vo. Crushed levant gilt, a.e.g., by Riviere. Anon. *(Ximenes)* **$5,000 [≈ £2,809]**
- Joe Miller's Jests: or the Wits Vade-Mecum ... Twelfth Edition, with large additions. London: for J. Hodges & W. Reeves, [ca 1750]. 12mo. [iv],192 pp. Frontis, Contemp half calf, rubbed, upper jnt tender.
(Burmester) **£150 [≈ $267]**
- Joe Miller's Jests: or, the Wits Vade-Mecum ... London: for John Lever, [175-?]. 12mo. Ptd on blue laid paper. 84 pp. Port frontis. Disbound. Anon. *(Finch)* **£260 [≈ $463]**
- Joe Miller's Jests, or, Wit's Merry Companion ... New Edition. London: T. Sabine & Son, [ca 1790]. 12mo. [iii],6-76 pp, apparently complete. Sm hole in title affecting 2 letters. Rec cloth.
(Burmester) **£150 [≈ $267]**

Mountfort, William
- Greenwich-Park: a Comedy. London: for J. Hindmarsh ..., 1691. 1st edn. Sm 4to. Straight grained mor gilt, spine chipped, front bd detached. Wing M.2973.
(Ximenes) **$600 [≈ £337]**

- Six Plays ... prefix'd some Memoirs of his Life ... London: Tonson ..., 1720. Only coll edn. 12mo. Sep title for each play, irregular pagination, 3 advt pp at end. Occas sl marks. Contemp calf, gilt dec spines.
(Clark) **£240 [≈ $427]**

Mowbray, geoffrey
- Remarks on the Conduct of the Opposition during the Present Parliament ... London: for J. Wright, 1798. 1st edn. 8vo. 117 pp. Stiff wraps. *(Young's)* **£25 [≈ $45]**

Moxon, Elizabeth
- English Housewifery. Exemplified in above Four Hundred and Fifty receipts ... with an Appendix ... Introduction ... Leeds: Griffith Wright ..., 1775. 11th edn. Lge 12mo. viii,203, 33,[vii],[vii] pp. Fldg table, 8 plates on 5 ff. Sm reprs. Csheep, rebacked
(Gough) **£275 [≈ $490]**

Muentz, J.H.
- Encaustic: or, Count Caylus's Method of Painting in the Manner of the Ancients. To which is added a sure and easy Method for Fixing of Crayons. London: for the author, & A. Webley, 1760. 1st edn. Fcap 8vo. viii,139,advt,[3] pp. Half-title. 1 plate. Contemp calf,slwrn *(Spelman)* **£450 [≈ $801]**

Muffett, Thomas
- Healths Improvement: or, Rules comprizing and discovering the Nature, Method, and Manner of Preparing all Sorts of Food used in this Nation ... Enlarged by Christopher Bennet ... London: 1655. 4to. Imprimaturf, 8,296 pp. Csheep, smsplitsin jnts. Wing M.2382. *(C.R. Johnson)* **£2,200 [≈ $3,916]**

Muller, John
- The Attack and Defence of Fortified Places. In Three Parts ... The Fourth Edition; Corrected, and very much Enlarged, by Isaac Landmann ... London: Egerton, 1791. 8vo. xv,[i],222,[2 blank],32 pp, advtf. 29 plates (1-XXV, V bis, 1-3). Contemp calf, gilt label.
(Spelman) **£260 [≈ $463]**
- A Treatise of Artillery ... London: 1780. 3rd edn, enlgd. 8vo. [viii],xl,214,[2 advt] pp. Frontis, 28 fldg plates. V sl marg browning at ends. Contemp calf, jnts splitting, spine chipped. *(Francis Edwards)* **£400 [≈ $712]**

Murphy, Arthur
- An Essay on the Life and Genius of Samuel Johnson, LL.D. London: Longman ..., 1793. 2nd sep edn. 8vo. [iv],187,[i] pp. Half-title. Port pasted to title verso. Few sm lib stamps.

Contemp calf, rebacked in mor, sl worn.
(Clark) **£45 [≈ $80]**
- The Gray's Inn Journal. London: 1756. 2 vols. 12mo. Later qtr mor. Anon.
(Robertshaw) **£60 [≈ $107]**
- The Gray's-Inn Journal. London: W. Faden, for P. Vaillant, 1756. 1st coll edn. 2 vols. 12mo. [xii],328; [iv],338 pp. Red qtr mor, by Kelly & Sons. *(Burmester)* **£300 [≈ $534]**
- The Works. London: Cadell, 1786. 7 vols. 8vo. Port frontis. Few lib marks. Later lib buckram. *(Clark)* **£160 [≈ $285]**

Murray, Lord George
- A Particular Account of the Battle of Culloden, April 16, 1746. In a Letter from an Officer of the Highland Army, to his Friend in London ... London: for T. Warner, 1749. 1st edn. 8vo. 25 pp. Half-title. Disbound. Anon. *(Young's)* **£70 [≈ $125]**

Murray, Lindley
- English Exercises, adapted to the Grammar lately published ... The Fourth Edition, Corrected. London: T.N. Longman ..., 1799. 182 pp. Contemp sheep, spine sl cracked.
(C.R. Johnson) **£35 [≈ $62]**
- See Grubb, Sarah

Museum Rusticum et Commerciale ...
- Museum Rusticum et Commerciale: or, Select papers on Agriculture, Commerce, Arts, and Manufactures ... Volume the First. London: 1764. viii,488 pp. Frontis. Leather spine v worn, hinges cracked, spine ends defective. *(Whitehart)* **£40 [≈ $71]**

Musgrave, Samuel
- Dr. Musgrave's Reply to a Letter Published in the News-Papers by the Chevalier D'Eon. Plymouth: R. Weathersley, 1769. 1st edn. 8vo. Disbound. *(Ximenes)* **$175 [≈ £98]**

The Musical Miscellany ...
- The Musical Miscellany: being a Collection of Choice Songs, set to the Violin and Flute, by the most Eminent Masters. London: John Watts, 1729-31. 1st edn. 6 vols. Sm 8vo. Frontises. Musical notation throughout. Contemp green half mor, gilt spines.
(Hannas) **£750 [≈ $1,335]**

Myles, William
- A Chronological History of the People called Methodists ... Liverpool: ptd for the author by J. Nuttall ..., [1799]. 4th edn. 12mo. Title sl soiled. Contemp calf.
(Burmester) **£60 [≈ $107]**

The Mysterious Mother ...
- See Walpole, Horace

Nabbes, Thomas
- Hannibal and Scipio. An Historical Tragedy. Acted in the year 1635 ... London: Richard Oulton for Charles Greene, 1637. 1st edn. 4to. [78] pp. Some wear & tear, lacks final blank. Rec half calf. STC 18341.
(Clark) **£325 [≈ $579]**
- Microcosmus. A Morall Maske, presented ... at the Private House in Salisbury Court ... London: Richard Oulton for Charles Greene, 1637. 1st edn. 4to. Lacks intl blank. Sl browned. 3 sm marg reprs. Half mor gilt by Winstanley, Manchester. STC 18342.
(Hannas) **£360 [≈ $641]**

Naismith, John
- Thoughts on Various Objects of Industry pursued in Scotland, with a View to Enquire by what means the Labour of the People may be directed to promote the Public Prosperity. Edinburgh: fortheauthor 1790. Thick 8vo. xii,656,24 pp. 1 p soiled. Mod half calf.
(Weiner) **£350 [≈ $623]**

Nalson, John
- The Countermine: or, A Short but true Discovery of the Dangerous Principles, and secret Practices of the Dissenting Party, especially the Presbyterians ... Second Edition. London: 1677. 8vo. 317 pp. Contemp calf, sm splits at jnt ends. Wing N.97. Anon. *(Robertshaw)* **£38 [≈ $68]**

National Oeconomy Recommended ...
- National Oeconomy Recommended, as the only Means of retrieving our Trade and securing our Liberties ... London: for M. Cooper, 1746. 1st edn. 8vo. [4],51 pp, inc half-title. Disbound. *(Hannas)* **£95 [≈ $169]**

The Nations Agrievance ...
- The Nations Agrievance, (By way of Address from Loyal Subjects) presented to his Majesty ... [London: 1679]. 1st edn. Folio. Drop-head title. 4 pp. Sl water stained. Disbound. Wing N.236. *(Hannas)* **£25 [≈ $45]**

Naunton, Sir Robert
- Fragmenta Regalia or Observations on the late Queen Elizabeth ... London: 1642. 3rd edn. 4to. 40 pp. Interleaved. Some wear & tear. Port inserted from another work. Later half mor, gilt spine, rubbed. Wing N.251. *(Clark)* **£48 [≈ $85]**
- Fragmenta Regalia: or, Observations on the late Queen Elizabeth Her Times and

Favourites. London: G. Dawson, 1653. 12mo. [ii], "87" [ie 89] pp. Lacks A1 (blank). Cut close at hd, shaving a few headlines. Disbound. Wing N.253.
(Blackwell's) £60 [≈ $107]

Neal, Daniel
- The History of the Puritans or Protestant Non-Conformists ... Second Edition. London: Richard hett, 1732-38. 4 vols. 8vo. Contemp calf gilt, 19th c labels chipped, sm piece missing from hd of 1 spine, knts cracked & sl rubbed. *(Blackwell's)* £225 [≈ $401]

Neale, Mary
- Some Account of the Life and Religious Exercises of Mary Neale, formerly Mary Peisley. Principally compiled from her Writings. Edited ... by Samuel Neale. Dublin: John Gough, 1795. 1st edn. 12mo. 120 pp. Half mor. *(Black Sun)* $325 [≈ £183]

Neau, Elias
- An Account of the Sufferings of the French Protestants, Slaves on board the French Kings Galleys ... London: for Richard Parker, sold by A. Baldwin, 1699. 1st edn. 4to. [ii],22 pp. Few sm marg reprs. 19th c half calf. Wing N.363. *(Burmester)* £200 [≈ $356]

Necker, Jacques
- Historical Review of the Administration of Mr. Necker. Written by himself. Translated from the French. London: 1791. 8vo. 423 pp. Inner marg of title strengthened. Some stains at end. Mod calf backed bds.
(Robertshaw) £40 [≈ $71]
- Of the Importance of Religious Opinions. Boston: Hall, 1796. 2nd Amer edn. 8vo. Foxed. Orig calf, rebacked, reprd. Translated by Mary Wollstonecraft.
(Rostenberg & Stern) $250 [≈ £140]
- On the French Revolution ... Translated from the French. London: for T. Cadell, 1797. 2 vols. 8vo. Date seemingly erased from vol 1 title. Contemp mottled calf, spines rubbed, jnts cracked. *(Waterfield's)* £295 [≈ $525]

Nedham, Marchamont sic
- The Case of the Common-Wealth of England, Stated ... London: for E. Blackmore, & R. Lowndes, (1650). 1st edn. 4to. [viii],24 pp. Lower crnr sl stained, not affecting text. Disbound. Wing N.376.
(Young's) £115 [≈ $205]

The Negotiations of Thomas Wolsey ...
- See Cavendish, George

Nelson, James
- An Essay on the Government of Children, under Three General Heads, Viz Health, Manners, and Education. The Third Edition. London: Dodsley, 1763. 373,errata pp. Contemp calf, hinges weakening, spine dried.
(C.R. Johnson) £165 [≈ $294]

Nelson, Robert
- The Life of Dr. George Bull, late Lord Bishop of St. David's ... London: Richard Smith, 1713. Large Paper. 8vo. xvi,542,[2] pp. Final blank. Port frontis. Contemp calf gilt, extrs sl worn, jnts cracked but firm. Inscrbd 'ex dono Authoris'.
(Clark) £65 [≈ $116]

Nelson, William
- The Office and Authority of a Justice of the Peace ... In the Savoy: Nutt, Gosling ...; 1721. 8vo. [viii],162 pp. Half-title. Some marg worm, affecting text. Contemp calf, rebacked. *(Vanbrugh)* £75 [≈ $134]

Neve, Timothy
- Animadversions upon Mr. Phillips's History of the Life of Cardinal Pole ... Oxford: Clarendon Press, 1766. 1st edn. 8vo. [xiv],562,[6] pp. Sm stain on title & last leaf. Closed tear in title. Rec qtr calf.
(Young's) £75 [≈ $134]

Neville, Henry
- Plato Redevivus sic: or a Dialogue concerning Government ... London: for S.I., 1681. 8vo. Contemp calf, rebacked. Wing N.513.
(Waterfield's) £250 [≈ $445]
- Plato Redevivus: or a Dialogue concerning Government ... London: for S.I., 1681. 8vo. Contemp calf, sm snag at hd of spine, sl shaken. Wing N.513.
(Waterfield's) £185 [≈ $329]

Neville, Thomas
- Imitations of Horace. London: 1758. 1st edn. 8vo. 163 pp. Red & black title. Orig wraps.
(Robertshaw) £95 [≈ $169]

New ...
- The New Bath Guide ... see Anstey, Christopher
- The New Brighton Guide ... see Williams, John ('Anthony Pasquin')
- The New Children's Friend: or, Pleasing Incitements to Wisdom and Virtue ... Translated chiefly from the German. London: for Vernor & Hood; & E. Newbery, 1797. 1st edn. 12mo. viii,171 pp. Frontis (sl

marg water stain). Contemp sheep, rebacked, new endpapers. *(Burmester)* £200 [≈ $356]
- A New Collection of Enigmas, Charades, Transpositions, &c. London: for Hookham & Carpenter, 1791. 1st edn. 2 vols in one. 12mo. xv,[i],96; [iv],116 pp. Subscribers. Contemp calf, rebacked. *(Burmester)* £200 [≈ $356]
- The New Dispensatory ... see Lewis, William
- A New History of Jamaica ... see Leslie, Charles
- A New Method of Learning the Italian Tongue ... see Lancelot, Claude.
- A New Theory of Acute and Slow Continu'd Fevers ... see Cheyne, George
- The New Universal Parish Officer. Containing all the Laws now in force, relating to Parish Business ... The Second Edition ... London: S. crowder, 1767. [4],332 pp. Contemp sheep.
(C.R. Johnson) £125 [≈ $223]
- A New Voyage to Georgia ... see Tailfer, Patrick

Newcomb, Thomas
- A Miscellaneous Collection of original Poems ... Written chiefly on Political and Moral Subjects. London: J. Wilson, 1740. 1st edn. (?) Large Paper, with watermark GM/T. 4to. Half-title. Early polished calf, spine a little worn. Anon. *(Hannas)* £210 [≈ $374]

Newcome, Peter
- The History of the Ancient and Royal Foundation called the Abbey of St. Alban ... London: J. Nichols for the author, 1795. xiii,547 pp. Fldg plan, map, 1 engvd view. Mod half calf, uncut. *(Europa)* £85 [≈ $151]

Newte, Thomas
- Prospects and Observations on a Tour in England and Scotland ... London: Robinson, 1791. 4to. viii,440 pp. Fldg map, 23 steel engvd plates. Old calf, edges sl scraped, rebacked. *(Hollett)* £320 [≈ $570]

Newton, Sir Isaac
- Observations upon the Prophecies of Daniel, and the Apocalypse of St. John. In Two Parts. London: J. Darby ..., 1733. 1st edn. 4to. vi,323 pp. Contemp half calf, worn, jnts cracked but sound. *(Gaskell)* £600 [≈ $1,068]
- The System of the World Demonstrated in an Easy and Popular Manner ... Second Edition, Corrected and Improved. London: for J. Robinson, 1740. Reissue of 1st edn of 1731, the title-page is a a cancel. 8vo. 2 plates. Contemp calf, front jnt cracked, lacks label. *(Waterfield's)* £400 [≈ $712]

- A Treatise of the Method of Fluxions and Infinite Series ... Translated from the Latin edition not yet published ... London: for Woodman & Millan, 1737. 1st edn. 2nd issue, with errata on 2B3v. 8vo. 4 fldg tables. Contemp calf, rubbed, jnts cracked but sound. *(Gaskell)* £850 [≈ $1,513]

Nichols, J. (editor)
- Antiquities in Kent and Sussex; being the first volume of the Bibliotheca Topographica Britannica. London: J. Nichols, 1790. 4to. 55 pp of plates (inc 2 aquatint plates), 2 fldg pedigrees, others in text. Occas sl spotting. Mod half mor gilt. *(Hollett)* £120 [≈ $214]
- Antiquities in Leicestershire; being the eighth volume of the Bibliotheca Topographica Britannica. London: J. Nichols, 1790. 4to. 40 pp of plates (inc a map frontis & 2 fldg panoramas), sev ills in text. Occas sl spotting. Mod half mor gilt. *(Hollett)* £125 [≈ $223]
- Antiquities in Lincolnshire; being the third volume of the Bibliotheca Topographica Britannica. London: J. Nichols, 1790. 4to. 16 pp of plates, fldg pedigree, other ills in text. Occas sl spotting. Mod half mor gilt. *(Hollett)* £95 [≈ $169]
- Antiquities in Middlesex and Surrey; being the second volume of the Bibliotheca Topographica Britannica. London: J. Nichols, 1790. 4to. 66 pp of plates (9 more than called for, & inc a fldg map), fldg pedigree, other ills in text. Occcslsptng. Mod1/2mor gilt. *(Hollett)* £140 [≈ $249]

Nichols, John & Steevens, George
- Biographical Anecdotes of William Hogarth, with a Catalogue of his Works ... Second Edition. London: J. Nichols, 1782. 8vo. iv,474 pp. Sl foxing. Contemp calf gilt, rebacked, some wear.
(Hartfield) $285 [≈ £160]

Nichols, T.
- Observations on the Propagation and Management of Oak Trees in general; but more immediately applying to His Majesty's New-Forest in Hampshire ... Southampton: [ca 1791]. 8vo. 42,[i table] pp. Minor browning. Disbound.
(Francis Edwards) £75 [≈ $134]

Nicholson, J. & Burn, R.
- The History and Antiquities of the Counties of Westmorland and Cumberland. London: Strahan & Cadell, 1777. 1st edn. 2 vols. 4to. cxxxiv,630; 615,[8] pp. 2 lge fldg maps. Qtr calf gilt, rubbed, bds worn, hinges cracked. *(Hollett)* £350 [≈ $623]

Nicholson, Peter
- The Student's Instructor in Drawing and Working the Five Orders of Architecture. London: 1795. 1st edn. Sm 4to. iv,29 pp. 33 plates (2 dble-page, 1 fldg). Few plates sl water stained. Endpapers sl soiled. Contemp calf, reprd & rebacked.
(Quest Books) **£95 [≈ $169]**

Nicolson, William
- The English Historical Library, in Three Parts ... Second Edition, Corrected and Augmented. London: for Timothy Childe, 1714. Folio. xviii,272 pp. Title sl dusty. Period panelled calf, upper jnt holding on 1 cord, spine ends chipped.
(Rankin) **£75 [≈ $134]**
- The English, Scotch and Irish Historical Libraries ... London: Strahan ..., 1736. 3rd (1st complete) edn. Folio. xviii,273,18, xx, 148, xvi,118 pp. Contemp calf, rebacked.
(O'Neal) **£325 [≈ £183]**

Nimmo, William
- A General History of Stirlingshire ... with the Natural History of the Shire. Edinburgh: William Creech, 1777. 1st edn. 8vo. viii,527 pp. Fldg map. Contemp qtr calf, mrbld bds, lower jnt sl split.
(Gough) **£225 [≈ $401]**

Nisbet, Alexander
- An Essay on the Ancient and Modern Use of Armories ... Edinburgh: William Adams for James MackEven, 1718. 4to. viii,[vi], 224, [xvi] pp. 7 plates. Sl wear & tear. Period calf, sl worn.
(Rankin) **£135 [≈ $240]**

Nisbet, Charles
- An Address to the Students of Dickinson College, Carlisle. On his Re-election to the Office of Principal of said College. Edinburgh: W. Martin, 1786. 12 pp. Rec wraps.
(C.R. Johnson) **£95 [≈ $169]**

Noble, Edward
- The Elements of Linear Perspective demonstrated by Geometrical Principles ... London: for T. Davies, 1771. 1st edn. 8vo. [iv],cxvi,298 pp. 52 plates. Contemp calf, gilt spine, jnts reprd. *(Burmester)* **£180 [≈ $320]**

Noorthouck, John
- A New History of London. London: for R. Baldwin, 1773. 1st edn. 4to. [4],(xii), 902, [xlii] pp. 42 plates & maps. Occas sl spotting & offsetting. Rec half calf gilt.
(Ash) **£750 [≈ $1,335]**

Norden, Frederick Lewis
- Travels in Egypt and Nubia: Enlarged by Dr. Templeman. London: Davis & Reymers, 1757. 1st 8vo. 2 vols in one. xl,154; 232,[6 advt] pp. 7 fldg plates. Fldg map in facs. Contemp calf, later rebacked, crnrs rubbed. *(Gough)* **£120 [≈ $214]**
- Travels in Egypt and Nubia. London: Lockyer Davis, 1757. 2 vols in one. Fldg map, 6 fldg plates. Sev lib stamps inc on plates. Occas sl foxing. Lib cloth.
(P and P Books) **£115 [≈ $205]**
- Travels in Egypt and Nubia. London: Lockey Davis & Charles Reymers, 1757. 1st edn in English. 2 vols. Folio. xxiv,124; viii,155 pp. Frontises, 162 plates & maps. Pencilled captions. Mod half leather.
(McBlain) **$1,750 [≈ £983]**

Norden, John
- Speculum Britanniae; an Historical and Chorographical Description of Middlesex and Hartfordshire. London: for Daniel Browne Senior and Junior, 1723. Cr 4to. [iv],24, [viii], (54),[vi],(32) pp. Engvd titles, maps. Contemp calf, rebacked to style.
(Ash) **£600 [≈ $1,068]**

Norris, John
- An Account of Reason and Faith in relation to the Mysteries of Christianity. London: for S. Manship, 1697. 8vo. Contemp calf, rebacked, new endpapers. Wing N.1243.
(Waterfield's) **£125 [≈ $223]**
- An Account of the Reason of Faith: in Relation to the Mysteries of Christianity. London: S. Manship, 1697. 1st edn. 8vo. [xiv], 346,[vi] pp. Contemp calf. Wing N.1243. *(Blackwell's)* **£140 [≈ $249]**
- A Collection of Miscellanies: consisting of Poems, Essays, Discourses & Letters ... Second Edition, Corrected. London: for J. crisley & Samuel Manship, 1692. 8vo. Contemp calf, rebacked. Wing N.1249.
(Waterfield's) **£135 [≈ $240]**
- A Collection of Miscellanies: Consisting of Poems, Essays, Discourses & Letters ... London: for J. Crosley, 1692. 2nd edn, crrctd. 8vo. [xvi],467, [1],[4] pp. Rec calf. Wing N.1249. *(Young's)* **£120 [≈ $214]**

A North Briton Extraordinary ...
- See Boswell, James

North, R.
- The History of Esculent Fish, with Plates ... by E. Albin: and an Essay on the Breeding of Fish, and the Construction of Fish-Ponds.

London: 1794. 4to. 80 pp. 18 hand cold plates (sl offset onto text). 1 fig sl trimmed. Contemp straight grain blue mor.
(Wheldon & Wesley) **£750 [≈ $1,335]**

Northleigh, John
- Parliamentum Pacificum: or, the Happy Union of Kings and People in a Healing Parliament ... London: M. Turner, 1688. 1st edn. 4to. [ii],75,[i] pp. Imprimatur leaf. Outer ff dusty. Disbound, untrimmed. Anon. Wing N.1302.
(Clark) **£35 [≈ $62]**

Norton, John
- Directions for Taking the Drops. London: [ca 1780]. Lge folio. Single sheet, ptd on both sides. Sm piece torn from crnr just touching text.
(Burmester) **£200 [≈ $356]**

Nott, John
- The Cooks and Confectioners Dictionary: or, the Accomplish'd Housewives Companion ... Third Edition, Revised and Recommended. London: H.P. for Charles Rivington, 1726. 8vo. [viii],[620] pp. Frontis, w'engvd 'Model of a Dessert'. Contemp calf gilt, sl worn.
(Gough) **£550 [≈ $979]**

Nottingham, Heneage Finch, Earl of
- See Finch, Heneage, Earl of Nottingham

Noy, William
- The Grounds and Maxims of the English Law. Fifth Edition. London: Henry Lintot ..., 1757. 12mo. [16],[172], [2],[4 advt] pp. Some foxing. repr to title. Mod qtr calf, gilt spine. *(Meyer Boswell)* **$350 [≈ £197]**

Nugent, Robert Craggs, Lord Nugent
- Considerations upon a Reduction of the Land-Tax. London: for R. Griffiths, 1749. 1st edn. Issue with errata on p 67. 8vo. [4], viii, 67 pp, inc half-title. Lge fldg table. Disbound. Anon. *(Hannas)* **£95 [≈ $169]**

Nye, Nathaniel
- The Art of Gunnery. London: William Leak, 1648. 1st edn. Sm 8vo. [xxii],88,102 pp. Frontis, 5 tables, 7 engvs (3 fldg), 7 w'cut ills. Sl marg stains. Polished calf gilt, a.e.g.
(Bookpress) **$3,250 [≈ £1,826]**

O'Flaherty, Roderic
- The Ogygia Vindicated: Against the Objections of Sir George MacKenzie ... Dublin: Faulkner, 1775. 8vo. lxxxiv,299 pp. Contemp calf, upper jnt split but firm. Anon.
(de Burca) **£400 [≈ $712]**
- Ogygia, or, A Chronological Account of Irish

Events: Collected from very ancient Documents ... Now translated by the Rev. James Hely. Dublin: M'Kenzie, 1793. 2 vols in one. 8vo. [i],lxxiii,292; [2],2,419 pp. Contemp half mor. *(de Burca)* **£400 [≈ $712]**

Oates, Titus
- A True Narrative of the Horrid Plot and Conspiracy of the Popish Party against the Life of His Sacred Majesty ... London: Thomas Parkhurst & Thomas Cockerill, 1679. Folio. [xii], 68 pp. Imprimatur leaf creased & sl soiled. Disbound. Wing O.59.
(Clark) **£50 [≈ $89]**

Observations ...
- Observations made during a Tour through Parts of England, Scotland, and Wales ... see Sullivan, R.J.
- Observations on Poetry ... see Pemberton, Henry
- Observations on the Conduct of Great-Britain, with regard to the Negociations and other Transactions Abroad. London: Roberts, 1729. 8vo. Stitched.
(Rostenberg & Stern) **$85 [≈ £48]**
- Observations on the Conduct of Great britain, with regard to the Negociations and other Transactions Abroad. London: J. Roberts, 1729. 1st edn. 8vo. 61 pp. Title sl browned. Rec wraps.
(Blackwell's) **£75 [≈ $134]**
- Observations on the Conduct of Great-Britain, with regard to the Negociations and other Transactions abroad. London: J. Roberts, 1729. 1st edn. 8vo. 61, [3] pp, inc final blank leaf. Sm stains on title. Mod bds.
(Hannas) **£55 [≈ $98]**
- Observations on the Correspondence between Poetry and Music ... see Webb, Daniel
- Observations on the late Famous Tryal of Sir G.W. Father Corker, &c. [London?: 1679]. 1st edn. Folio. 4 pp. Drop-head title. Marg water stains. Disbound. Wing O.104A.
(Hannas) **£20 [≈ $36]**
- Observations on the Present Convention with Spain ... see Robins, Benjamin
- Observations upon some of his Majesties late Answers and Expresses ... see Parker, Henry
- Observations upon the Manifesto of His Catholick Majesty; with an Answer to his Reasons for not Paying the Ninety-Five Thousand Pounds ... The Second Edition. London: for T. Cooper ..., 1739. 8vo. [2],42 pp. Disbound. *(Hannas)* **£45 [≈ $80]**

Ockley, Simon
- The Conquest of Syria, Persia, and Aegypt,

by the Saracens ... London: R. Knaplock ...,
1708. 1st edn. 8vo. xxiv,[iv], 391,[19] pp.
Occas spotting & marg browning. Contemp
style panelled calf. Vol 1 of his History of the
Saracens. Vol 2 was published in 1718.
(Frew Mackenzie) **£200 [≈ $356]**

Oeconomy ...
- The Oeconomy of Love ... see Armstrong,
John

Of the Torments of Hell ...
- See Richardson, Samuel, Baptist minister

The Officer's Manual ...
- The Officer's Manual in the Field; or, a Series
of Military Plans, representing the Principal
Operations of a Campaign. Translated from
the German. London: Bensley ..., 1798. Sq
8vo. [viii],70 pp. 61 plates (some sl offset).
Rec qtr calf. *(Rankin)* **£80 [≈ $142]**

Oldfield, T.H.B.
- History of the Original Constitution of
Parliaments from the Time of the Britons to
the Present Day. London: 1797. 8vo. Mod
cloth backed bds. *(Waterfield's)* **£40 [≈ $71]**

Oldham, John
- Poems and Translations. London: for Jos.
Hindmarsh, 1683. 1st edn. 8vo. Sl browning.
Mod panelled calf. Wing O.237.
(Hannas) **£180 [≈ $320]**
- Some New Pieces Never Before Published ...
London: M.C. for Jo. Hindmarsh, 1684. 2nd
edn. 8vo. [x],134 pp. A1 blank present at end
of prelims. Some browning, occas stain. Rec
wraps. Wing O.249. Anon.
(Clark) **£40 [≈ $71]**
- The Works ... together with his Remains.
London: Nathaniel Rolls, 1695. 8vo. [vi],148,
[x], 134,[viii], 215,[xxix],132 pp. 1 sm marg
tear. Contemp calf, extrs worn, minor defects.
Wing O.230. *(Clark)* **£55 [≈ $98]**

Oldmixon, John
- Reflections on Dr. Swift's Letter to the Earl
of Oxford, about the English Tongue.
London: A. Baldwin, [1712]. 1st edn. 8vo.
[iv], 35 pp. Disbound. Anon.
(Burmester) **£400 [≈ $712]**

Oldys, Francis (pseudonym)
- See Chalmers, George.

Oldys, William
- The British Librarian ... London: T. osborne,
1738. 8vo. [ii],vii, [v],402,[ii] pp. Occas minor

browning & spotting. Contemp calf, gilt
spine, extrs worn, jnts cracked, lacks label.
Anon. *(Clark)* **£150 [≈ $267]**

Olive-Branch, Simon (pseudonym)
- The Looker-On ... see Roberts, William.

The Olla Podrida ...
- See Monro, Thomas, et al.

Oosten, H. van
- The Dutch Gardener: or, the Compleat
Florist ... Written in Dutch. Translated into
English. London: 1711. 2nd edn. 8vo. [vi],
249, [i],11,[1] pp. Frontis, 2 plates. Contemp
panelled calf, trifle used.
(Wheldon & Wesley) **£260 [≈ $463]**

Ord, Craven
- Vain Boastings of Frenchmen. The Same in
1386 as in 1798. Being an Account of the
Threatened Invasion of England by the
French. London: Fridden ..., 1798. 8vo.
Stitched. Anon.
(Rostenberg & Stern) **$125 [≈ £70]**

Orders ...
- The Orders Proceedings, Punishments and
Priviledges of the Commons House of
Parliament in England. [London]: 1641. 4to.
Title device. Stitched. Wing E.2675.
(Rostenberg & Stern) **$85 [≈ £48]**

Ordinance ...
- An Ordinance ... In Parliament, for the
Preservation and Keeping Together ... such
Books, Evidences ... sequestred ... as are fit to
be so Preserved. London: Husbands, 1643.
4to. Title border. Stitched. Wing E.1780.
(Rostenberg & Stern) **$575 [≈ £323]**
- An Ordinance of the Lords and Commons
Assembled in Parliament. After Advice had
with the Assembly of Divines, for the
Ordination of Ministers pro Tempore ... 2.
Octob. 1644. London: Smith, 1644. 4to. Title
border. Stitched. Wing E.1801.
(Rostenberg & Stern) **$85 [≈ £48]**
- An Ordinance ... in Parliament. Declaring the
Causes, whereof after the Refusall of many
Remonstrances ... had and sent by the
Kingdome of Scotland, unto His Majesty ...
London: Wright, 1643. 4to. Title border.
Stitched. Wing E.1835.
(Rostenberg & Stern) **$75 [≈ £42]**
- An Ordinance ... in Parliament ... For the
selling of the Lands of all Bishops in the
Kingdome of England. London: Bellamie,
1646. 4to. Title border. Stitched. Wing
E.2038A. *(Rostenberg & Stern)* **$90 [≈ £51]**

- An Ordinance of the Lords and Commons ... For the true payment of Tythes ... 8. Novemb. 1644. London: Wright, 1644. 4to. Typographical title border. Stitched. Wing E.2065 (9 November).
(Rostenberg & Stern) $85 [≃ £48]
- An Ordinance of ... Parliament assembled for the better observation of the Monthly Fast. London: Blaiklock, 1642. 4to. Title border. Crnr of title torn affecting sm part of border. Stitched. Wing O.1943.
(Rostenberg & Stern) $100 [≃ £56]

Orem, William
- A Description of the Chanonry in Old Aberdeen in the Years 1724 and 1725. (Bibliotheca Topographica Britannica No. III). London: J. Nichols, 1782. 4to. Fldg map. Mod half calf.
(Waterfield's) £95 [≃ $169]

The Origin of Printing ...
- See Bowyer, William & Nichols, John (editors)

Orrery, John Boyle, Earl of
- See Boyle, John, Earl of Orrery

The Orthodox Trinitarian ...
- The Orthodox Trinitarian: or an Explication and Assertion of the Doctrine of the Holy Trinity & Unity, According to Scripture, and the Late Act of Parliament. By a Lover of Truth and Peace. London: M. Fabian, 1701. Only edn. 4to. 36 pp. Disbound.
(Young's) £150 [≃ $267]

Orton, Job
- Memoirs of the Life, Character and Writings of the late Reverend Philip Doddridge, D.D. of Northampton. Salop: J. Cotton & J. Eddowes, 1766. 1st edn. 8vo. xvi, 361,[iii] pp. Port frontis. Contemp calf gilt, extrs sl worn.
(Clark) £50 [≃ $89]

Osbeck, Peter
- A Voyage to China and the East Indies ... Translated from the German ... London: for Benjamin White, 1771. 1st English edn. 2 vols. 8vo. xx,396; [2],[368],[32] pp. 13 plates. Contemp calf, rebacked, sl used.
(Heritage) $1,000 [≃ £562]

Osborne, F.
- Advice to a Son; or, Directions for your better Conduct, through the Various Important Encounters of this Life. Second Edition. London: H. Hall, 1656. Sm 8vo. [8],136 pp. Intl blank laid down. Occas sl soiling. Early

19th c calf. Wing O.509.
(Spelman) £260 [≃ $463]

Otway, Thomas
- The Atheist: or, The Second Part of The Souldiers Fortune. Acted at the Duke's Theatre. London: for Bentley & Tonson, 1684. 1st edn. 4to. No signature F, correct. Page 74 mispaginated 72. No pp 33-40. Qtr roan. Wing O.548. *(Hannas)* £170 [≃ $303]
- The Orphan: or, The Unhappy Marriage. A Tragedy. London: for C. Hitch, 1749. 12mo. 83,[1] pp. Frontis. Rec wraps.
(Fenning) £24.50 [≃ $45]
- Plays ... London: Strahan ..., [ca 1755]. 2 vols. 12mo. Sep plays dated 1733-54, with general title. 8 frontis. Contemp calf, gilt spines, extrs sl worn, lacks labels.
(Clark) £25 [≃ $45]
- Venice Preserv'd: or, a Plot Discover'd. A Tragedy. London: Strahan & Bathurst, 1748. 12mo. 84 pp. Rec wraps.
(Fenning) £24.50 [≃ $45]

Ovalle, Alonso de
- An Historical Relation of the Kingdom of Chile ... London: for A. & J. Churchill, 1703. 1st edn in English. Folio. [viii],154 pp. Map in text. 19th c buckram.
(Gough) £350 [≃ $623]

Overbury, Sir Thomas
- His Observations on his Travailes upon the State of the xvii Provinces as they stood Anno Dom. 1609 ... [London]: 1626. 1st edn. 4to. [2],28 pp. Minute hole in 1 leaf. Mod half calf. STC 18903. *(Hannas)* £230 [≃ $409]

Ovid
- Ovid's Epistles; with his Amours. Translated into English Verse, by the Most Eminent Hands. London: Tonson, 1748. 12mo. Frontis, plate. Contemp calf, rebacked.
(Hannas) £55 [≃ $98]
- Ovid's Metamorphoses in Fifteen Books. Translated by the most Eminent Hands. Adorn'd with Sculptures. London: Tonson, 1717. 1st edn thus. Folio. [vi],xx,[iv],548 pp. Frontis, port, 16 plates. Sl tired. Contemp calf, rebacked. *(Sotheran's)* £450 [≃ $801]
- Metamorphoses In fifteen Books. Translated by the most Eminent Hands. London: Tonson, 1717. 1st edn of this coll. Folio. [vi],xx, [iv],548 pp. Frontis, port, 16 plates. Browned. Contemp calf, gilt dec spine, sl worn, sm reprs. *(Clark)* £160 [≃ $285]
- Ovid's Metamorphoses Epitomized in an English Poetical Style. For the Use and

Entertainment of the Ladies of Great Britain. London: for Robert Horsfield, 1760. 1st edn thus. Sm 8vo. xv,236,[3 advt] pp. Some foxing & soiling. Contemp calf, jnts cracked but firm.   *(Sotheran's)* **£150 [≈$267]**

- Ovid's Metamorphosis Englished by G.S. [George Sandys]. London: (William Stansby), 1626. Sm folio. [20],326,[6] pp. Engvd title (with expl leaf), full page engv of Ovid. Last 2 ff from a smaller copy. Old calf, spinne ends worn. STC 18964.   *(O'Neal)* **$350 [≈£197]**
- Phaetons Folly, or The Downfall of Pride: being a Translation of the Second Book of Ovids Metamorphosis ... London: for George Calvert, 1655. Only edn. 8vo. [xxiv],151 pp. Sm marg worm hole. Rec calf backed bds. Wing O.692.   *(Vanbrugh)* **£175 [≈$312]**

Owen, Charles

- An Essay towards a Natural History of Serpents. London: 1742. 4to. xxiii,240,[12] pp. 7 plates. V sl marg staining. Mod half calf antique style.
          (Wheldon & Wesley) **£300 [≈$534]**
- An Essay towards a Natural History of Serpents ... London: John Gray, 1742. 1st edn. Sm 4to. xxiii,240,[12] pp. 7 plates. 1st 23 pp browned in outer marg. Later calf, sl rubbed.   *(Bromer)* **$750 [≈£421]**

Owen, Charles, D.D.

- The Danger of the Church and State from Foreigners ... Third Edition, with large Additions. London: for J. Robinson, R. Dodsley, J. Sheepy, 1750. 8vo. 127 pp. Contemp sheep backed bds, crnrs bumped, spine rubbed & defective at ft.
          (Finch) **£165 [≈$294]**

Owen, Revd Henry

- Sixteen Sermons on Various Subjects. London: for J. Nichols, 1797. 1st edn. 8vo. viii, 351, [46 subscribers] pp. Spotted. Cloth (stained).   *(Young's)* **£20 [≈$36]**

Oxford ...

- Oxford and Cambridge Miscellany Poems ... see Fenton, Elijah (ed.)
- The Oxford Sausage ... see Warton, Thomas, & others.

P., H.

- The Grandeur of the Law ... see Philipps, Henry

P., J.

- A Letter to a Friend in the Country: being a Vindication of the Parliaments whole

proceedings this last Session. With the State of the Plot, and Manner of its Discovery. [London: 1681]. 1st edn (?). Folio. 4 pp. Disbound. Wing P.55. *(Hannas)* **£30 [≈$53]**

P., K.

- Poems ... see Philips, Katherine

Page, John

- Receipts for Preparing and Compounding the Principal Medicines Made Use of by the late Mr. Ward ... London: Henry Whitridge, 1763. 1st edn. 8vo. [2],33 pp. Disbound.
          (Young's) **£200 [≈$356]**

Paget, Thomas Catesby, Lord

- Some Reflections upon the Administration of Government ... London: Dodsley, 1740. 1st edn. 8vo. [iv],104 pp. Half-title. red & black title. Marg hole not affecting text. Disbound. Anon.   *(Young's)* **£55 [≈$98]**

Pain, William

- The Practical Builder, or Workman's General Assistant ... London: Taylor, 1776. 4to. [16] pp. 83 plates (sl soiled). Contemp calf, rebacked.   *(Sotheran's)* **£310 [≈$552]**

Paine, James

- Plans, Elevations, and Sections, of Noblemen and Gentlemen's Houses ... London: for the author, 1783. 2nd edn. 2 vols. Lge folio. 19 + 34 dble-page & 37 + 33 single-page plates (numbered 1-175, 1-101). Contemp half calf, untrimmed, jnts sl cracked.
          (Sotheran's) **£4,000 [≈$7,120]**
- Plans, Elevations, Sections and other Ornaments of the Mansion-House belonging to the Corporation of Doncaster. London: for the author, 1751. Only edn. Folio. [4],3,42 pp. Title vignette, 17 plates (4 dble-page with dble numbering). Few sm reprs. Rec half mor.   *(Sotheran's)* **£1,900 [≈$3,382]**

Paine, Thomas

- Dissertation on First Principles of Government. Paris: ptd at the English Press, [1795]. 1st Paris edn. 8vo. 40 pp. Sl browned. Disbound, uncut & partly unopened.
          (Burmester) **£175 [≈$312]**
- Dissertation on the First Principles of Government. Paris: ptd at the English Press, Third Year of the French Republic [1795]. 1st edn. 1st issue, with "stands" p 25. 8vo. Sl foxing. Disbound. *(Black Sun)* **$850 [≈£478]**

Painting Illustrated ...

- See Aglionby, William

Paley, William

- The Principles of Moral and Political Philosophy. The Second Edition, corrected. London: J. Davies, 1786. 4to. Half-title, 657 pp. Contemp tree calf.
(C.R. Johnson) **£145 [≈ $258]**

Palladio, Andrea

- The Architecture of A. Palladio; in Four Books. London: the author, 1721. 2nd edn of Leoni's edn. 2 vols. Folio. [xii],93; [ii], 90, [4] pp. 2 frontis, 61 + "104" [ie 91] plates. Contemp calf, rebacked, minor wear.
(Bookpress) **$950 [≈ £534]**
- The First Book of Architecture ... London: for Bettesworth, Hitch ..., 1733. Sm 4to. [4], 206,[2 advt] pp. Addtnl engvd frontis, fldg plate, 70 plates. Sl aged. Contemp panelled calf, sl scuffed, crnrs bumped, rebacked.
(O'Neal) **$500 [≈ £281]**
- The Four Books of Andrea Palladio's Architecture ... London: Isaac Ware, 1738. 1st edn thus. Folio. [xii],110 pp. 4 engvd titles, 212 plates, sev text ills. Few v sm marg tears. 4 plates sl browned at crnrs. Contemp gilt panelled calf, rebacked.
(Gough) **£1,100 [≈ $1,958]**

Palliser, Sir Hugh

- The Defence of Vice-Admiral Sir Hugh Palliser, Bart. At the Court Martial lately held upon him with the Court's Defence. London: Cadell, 1789. [iv],71 pp. Rec mrbld wraps. *(C.R. Johnson)* **£35 [≈ $62]**

Panton, Edward, Captain

- Speculum Juventutis: or, a True Mirror; where Errors in Breeding Noble and Generous Youth ... are clearly made manifest ... London: for Charles Smith & Thomas Burrell, 1671. 1st edn. 8vo. Imprimatur leaf. 2 advt ff. Contemp calf, sl rubbed, jnts sl cracked. Wing P277 *(Hannas)* **£250 [≈ $445]**

A Paradox against Liberty ...

- A Paradox against Liberty. Written by the Lords during their Imprisonment in the Tower. A Poem. Londn [sic]: Printed in the Year, 1679. 1st edn. Folio. [2],2 pp. Disbound. Wing P.330.
(Hannas) **£95 [≈ $169]**

Pare, Ambroise

- The Workes of that famous Chirurgion Ambrose Parey. Translated out of Latine and compared with the French by Jh. Johnson. London: Th. Cotes, 1634, reprinted New York: Milford House, 1968. Folio. Ills. Slipcase. *(Goodrich)* **$175 [≈ £98]**

Park, Mungo

- Travels in the Interior Districts of Africa ... With an Appendix ... Second Edition. London: 1799. 4to. xxviii,372, xcii, [ii] pp. 2 fldg maps, fldg chart, port, 3 engvd views, 2 fldg plates of plants, 2 engvd pp music. Plate margs spotted. Contemp calf, rebacked.
(Gough) **£250 [≈ $445]**

Parker, Benjamin

- Philosophical Meditations with Divine Inferences. London: for the author, 1734. 8vo. Disbound. *(Waterfield's)* **£90 [≈ $160]**

Parker, George

- Life's Painter of Variegated Characters in Public and Private Life. By George Parker, Librarian to the College of Wit, Mirth, and Humour ... London: for James Ridgway, 1789. 1st edn. 8vo. 90,239,[1] pp. Subscrs. Port. Some marg water stains. Contemp style qtr calf. *(Burmester)* **£400 [≈ $712]**

Parker, Henry

- Observations upon some of his Majesties late Answers and Expresses. [London: 1642]. 1st edn (?). Sm 4to. 47 pp. Drop-title. Faint marg browning. Mod qtr calf. Wing P.412. Anon. Sometimes attributed to John Milton.
(Blackwell's) **£45 [≈ $80]**

Parker, Samuel

- A Free and Impartial Censure of the Platonick Philosophie ... Second Edition. Oxford: Henry Hall, 1667. 8vo. Both title-pages present. Contemp calf, recased & resewn. Wing P.464.
(Waterfield's) **£225 [≈ $401]**

Parker, Thomas

- Reports of Cases concerning the Revenue, argued and determined in the Court of Exchequer, from Easter Term 1743 to ... 1767 ... London: Strahan & Woodfall ..., 1776. 1st edn. Folio. Errata. Contemp calf, fine. *(Vanbrugh)* **£145 [≈ $258]**

Parkinson, A.

- Collectanea Anglo-Minoritica, or, a Collection of the Antiquities of the English Franciscans, or Friers Minor, commonly called Gray Friars. In Two Parts. With an Appendix ... London: 1726. 1st edn. 4to. 4 plates. Occas sl foxing. Contemp calf, worn, jnts cracked.Anon *(Robertshaw)* **£50 [≈ $89]**

Parkinson, James

- The Soldier's Tale, Extracted from the Village Association: With Two or Three

Words of Advice, by Old Hubert. [London: ca 1793]. 1st edn. 8vo. 8 pp. Drop-title. Disbound. Anon.   *(Young's)* **£120 [≈ $214]**

Parkinson, John

- Theatrum Botanicum ... An Herball of Large Extent ... London: Thos. Cotes, 1640. 1st edn. Folio. xviii,1738 pp, errata leaf. W'cuts. Ptd title, errata leaf & 1st 7 ff laid down with loss. Lacks engvd title & last 2 ff of Table at end. 19th c calf, upper jnts sl split.
(Gough) **£495 [≈ $881]**

Parkyns, George Isham

- An Essay on the Different Natural Situations of Gardens. London: Dodsley, 1774. 1st edn. 4to. [iv],27,[1] pp. Half-title. Rec wraps. Anon.   *(Burmester)* **£225 [≈ $401]**

Parkyns, Thomas

- The Inn-Play: or, Cornish-Hugg Wrestler ... Third edition corrected, with large additions. London: Tho. Weekes, 1727. Sm 4to. [8], xviii, 9-64, [11] pp. Port, 10 figs & 2 other w'cut ills (1 full-page). Some browning. Contemp red half calf, gilt spine rubbed.
(Spelman) **£350 [≈ $623]**

The Parliaments Answer ...

- The Parliaments Answer to the Two Petitions of the Countie of Buckingham. [London]: 1641. 4to. W'cut of royal arms at end. Stitched. Wing E.2129.
(Rostenberg & Stern) **$90 [≈ £51]**

Parnell, Thomas

- Poems on Several Occasions ... Published by Mr. Pope. London: for B. Lintott, 1722. 1st edn. 8vo. Red & black title. Contemp panelled calf, jnts cracked.
(Hannas) **£150 [≈ $267]**
- Poems on Several Occasions ... A New Edition. To which is prefixed the Life of Dr. Parnell, written by Dr. Goldsmith. London: for T. Davies, 1770. 1st edn thus. 8vo. Intl commendatory leaf, final contents leaf. 2 plates. Contemp half calf, rebacked.
(Hannas) **£55 [≈ $98]**
- The Poetical Works. Glasgow: Andrew Foulis, 1786. Folio. [2],xii,388 pp. Without the 2 ff subscribers. Sl spotting on title & a few ff. Sm marg snag 4 ff. Later half leather, uncut, upper hinge splitting but secure.
(Claude Cox) **£70 [≈ $125]**

Parr, Samuel

- A Free Translation of the Preface to Bellendenus; Containing Animated Strictures on the Great Political Characters of the

Present Time. London: Stafford & Davenport, 1788. 1st edn. 8vo. xii,159 pp. New bds. Anon.   *(Young's)* **£40 [≈ $71]**
- A Free Translation of the Preface to Bellendenus; containing Animated Strictures on the Great Political Characters of the Present Time ... London: for Payne, Davies, Debrett, 1788. 1st English edn. 8vo. xii,159,[i] pp. Contemp half calf, mor label, sl worn. Anon   *(Finch)* **£40 [≈ $71]**
- A Sequel to the Printed Paper lately circulated in Warwickshire by the Rev. Charles Curtis ... London: for Charles Dilly, 1792. 8vo. Binder's cloth. Anon.
(Waterfield's) **£120 [≈ $214]**

Parsons, Robert, supposed author

- Leycesters Common-Wealth ... [London]: Printed, 1641. 2nd edn under this title. 8vo. [viii], 183 pp. Title border. Sl wear. Early ink notes. Early 19th c diced calf, gilt spine. Wing L.969A. Anon.
(Vanbrugh) **£175 [≈ $312]**

Parsons, William

- A Poetical Tour, in the Years 1784, 1785, and 1786. By a Member of the Arcadian Society at Rome. London: Logographic Press, 1787. [4],[4], 208,[2] pp. Orig mrbld wraps, uncut, paper spine largely missing. Author's pres inscrptn. Anon.
(C.R. Johnson) **£260 [≈ $463]**

Pascal, Blaise

- Thoughts on Religion and Other Subjects. Translated from the French. London: W.B. for A. & J. Churchill, 1704. Sm 8vo. [2],lviii, [12], 392 pp. Contemp panelled calf, mod mor label, hinges sl rubbed.
(Karmiole) **$375 [≈ £211]**

Pasquin, Anthony

- The New Brighton Guide ... see Williams, John ('Anthony Pasquin')

The Pastor, a Poem ...

- The Pastor, a Poem: or, a Caution against Error and Delusion ... Recommended to ... the Methodists in particular ... London: for G. Pearch, W. Tilley, & T. Street, [ca 1765]. 1st edn. 4to. 3-30 pp. Presumably lacks half-title. Sl browned & spotted. Disbound.
(Burmester) **£375 [≈ $668]**

Paterson, Daniel

- A New and Accurate Description of all the Direct and Principal Cross Roads in Great Britain ... The Twelfth Edition: including the Roads of Scotland. London: for the

proprietor, 1799. 8vo. 2 dble page maps. Contemp calf, most of backstrip relaid.
(Waterfield's) £110 [≈ $196]

Paterson, Samuel
- Speculation upon Law and Lawyers; applicable to the Manifest Hardships, Uncertainty, and Abusive Practices of the Common Law. London: Robson & Clarke ..., 1788. 1st edn. 8vo. Early 19th c diced half russia, spine chipped. Anon.
(Ximenes) $900 [≈ £506]

Patoun, Archibald
- A Complete Treatise of Practical Navigation, demonstrated from it's First Principles ... London: for W. Mount, 1770. 8th edn. xii,525 pp. Qtr mor, uncut.
(Young's) £90 [≈ $160]

Patrick, Simon
- Angliae Speculum: A Glass that flatters not; Presented to a Country Congregation at the Solemn Fast, April 24, 1678 ... London: for Richard Royston, 1678. 1st edn. 4to. 38 pp. Some staining. Disbound. Wing P.744. Anon.
(Young's) £75 [≈ $134]
- A Friendly Debate between a Conformist and a Non-Conformist. London: Richard Royston, 1669. 8vo. [vi],240,[vi] pp. Minor soil. Contemp black mor gilt, a.e.g., worn, front bd almost detached. Wing P.798A. Anon.
(Clark) £30 [≈ $53]
- A Treatise of Repentance and of Fasting. Especially of the Lent-Fast. London: R. Royston, 1686. 1st edn. 12mo. [xxiv],214 pp. Imprimatur leaf. Contemp calf, rubbed, minor loss hd of spine. Wing P.857. Anon.
(Clark) £48 [≈ $85]
- The Witnesses to Christianity; or, The Certainty of our Faith and Hope ... L; R. Royston, 1675. 1st edn. 8vo. [xx],662 pp. Half-title. Errata leaf. Frontis. 2nd title 'Jesus and the Resurrection'. Contemp speckled calf, extrs sl worn. Wing P.864 (inc P.816).
(Clark) £48 [≈ $85]

Patrick, Simon
- The Parable of the Pilgrim: Written to a Friend. London: Robert White for Francis Tyton, 1667. 2nd edn. 4to. [xvi],527,[i] pp. Imprimatur leaf. Some marg worm, occas sl browning. Contemp calf, a.e.g., rebacked, rubbed, extrs sl worn. Wing P.827.
(Clark) £50 [≈ $89]
- The Parable of the Pilgrim: Written to a Friend. The Sixth Edition Corrected. London: Richard Chiswell, 1787 sic. Sm 4to. [14],527 pp. Frontis. Contemp panelled calf,

later reprs, 1 crnr worn.
(Spelman) £90 [≈ $160]
- A Sermon preached upon St. Peter's Day ... By a Divine of the Church of England. London: for Ric. Chiswell, 1687. 8vo. Imprimatur leaf. Mod buckram. Anon. Wing P.845.
(Waterfield's) £40 [≈ $71]

Patten, Robert
- The History of the Rebellion in the Year 1715. With Original Papers ... The Fourth Edition. London: James Roberts, 1745. 8vo. [x], 245,[i] pp. Contemp speckled calf, gilt dec spine, extrs sl worn, jnts cracked but firm.
(Clark) £40 [≈ $71]

Patten, Thomas
- King David Vindicated from a Late Misrepresentation of his Character. In a Letter to His Grace the Archbishop of Canterbury ... Oxford: Clarendon Press, 1762. 1st edn. 8vo. [iv],131 pp. Disbound.
(Young's) £30 [≈ $53]

Paul, Sir George Onesiphorus
- Considerations on the Defects of Prisons, and their Present System of Regulation, submitted to the Attention of the Gentlemen of the County of Gloster ... London: Cadell, 1784. Half-title, title, viii,88 pp. Rec wraps. Author's pres inscrptn.
(C.R. Johnson) £225 [≈ $401]

Payne, John
- A New and Complete System of Universal Geography ... describing Asia, Africa, Europe and America ... New York: John Low, 1798-1800. 1st edn. 4 vols. 8vo. 60 maps & plates (some foxing, 1 torn). Sm blind stamps on titles & plates. Contemp calf, mor labels.
(Chapel Hill) $1,300 [≈ £730]

Payne, William
- A Discourse of the Sacrifice of the Mass. London: Brabazon Aylmer, 1688. 1st edn. 4to. [iv], 96 pp. Disbound, outer ff sl soiled. Wing P.901. Anon.
(Clark) £18 [≈ $32]
- Maxims for Playing the Game of Whist; with all necessary calculations, and Laws of the Game. London: sold by T. Payne, 1773. 1st edn. Sm 8vo. Mod bds. Anon.
(Ximenes) $350 [≈ £197]

Peacham, Henry
- The Compleat Gentleman ... inlarged ... by a very good hand. London: E. Tyler, for Richard Thrale, 1661. 3rd edn. Sm 4to. [x], 304, [viii], 304-455 pp. Addtnl engvd title. Num text w'cuts. Late 19th c calf elab gilt.

Wing P.403.   *(Vanbrugh)* **£625 [≈ $1,113]**

Pearce, Zachary
- The Miracles of Jesus Vindicated ... London: for J. Roberts, 1729. 2nd edn of Parts 1-3, 1st edn part 4. 4 parts. 8vo. 31, 31, 32, 39 pp. Disbound. Anon.   *(Young's)* **£80 [≈ $142]**

Pearsall, Richard
- Early Seeking after God opened, and recommended to Young Ones. In a Sermon preached in Taunton ... London: for J. Buckland, 1758. 1st edn. 8vo. vi,43 pp. Disbound.   *(Young's)* **£20 [≈ $36]**

Pearson, Anthony
- The Great Case of Tithes truly stated, clearly open'd, and fully resolv'd ... with an Appendix. London: assigns of J. Sowle, 1732. 8vo. 8 advt pp. Orig wraps.
    (Waterfield's) **£50 [≈ $89]**

Pearson, John
- An Exposition of the Creed. London: J.M. for John Williams, 1676. 4th edn, enlgd. Folio. Port frontis. Sl marg wear to title. Contemp calf, rubbed, split in front jnt. Wing P.998.
    (P and P Books) **£45 [≈ $80]**
- An Exposition of the Creed ... The Fourth Edition, Revised and now more Enlarged. London: J.M. for John Williams, 1676. Folio. [viii], 398, [ii] pp. Final blank leaf. Port frontis. Red-ruled title. Mod binders cloth. Wing P.998.   *(Clark)* **£28 [≈ $50]**
- Pearson's Political Dictionary ... London: for J.S. Jordan, 1792. 1st edn. 8vo. 59 pp. Lacks half-title. Old wraps.
    (Burmester) **£150 [≈ $267]**

Pechey, John
- Collections of Acute Diseases, in Five Parts ... London: sold by Henry Bonwicke, 1691 [-88]. 2nd edn. Sm 8vo. [viii],101, [ix], [2 blank],8,[iii], 100,[vii],[ii],94, [iv],[iv], 107,[v] pp. Divisional titles, licence leaf. Some marg worm. New calf. Wing P.1020.
    (Blackwell's) **£600 [≈ $1,068]**

Pegge, Samuel
- The Forme of Cury, A Roll of Ancient English Cookery, Compiled, about A.D. 1390 ... London: J. Nichols ..., 1780. 1st edn. iv,xxxvi,188 pp. Port of Pegge (dated 1785), 1 plate. Contemp mottled calf, gilt dec spine, jnts cracked but sound, hd of spine reprd.
    (Gough) **£675 [≈ $1,202]**

Peirce, Sir Edmund
- The Petition of the Gentry, Ministers and

Commonalty of the County of kent. London: 1642. 4to. Stitched. Wing P.1064. Anon.
    (Rostenberg & Stern) **$90 [≈ £51]**

Pelling, Edward
- A Practical Discourse Concerning the Redeeming of Time ... London: for John Everingham, 1695. 1st edn. 8vo. 104,[5],[3 advt] pp. Old sheep, rebacked. Wing P.1085.
    (Young's) **£165 [≈ $294]**

Pellow, Thomas
- The History of the Long Captivity and Adventures of Thomas Pellow, in South-Barbary ... London: for R. Goadby, & sold by W. Owen, [1739]. 1st edn. 8vo. [iv],388 pp inc intl advt leaf. Marg worm, minor soil. Contemp sheep, rebacked, crnrs worn.
    (Clark) **£260 [≈ $463]**
- The History of the Long Captivity and Adventures of Thomas Pellow, in South-Barbary ... [Sherborne?]: Printed for R. Goadby, & sold by W. Owen, London, [1751?]. 2nd edn. 8vo. [iv],388 pp inc intl advt leaf. Contemp calf, jnts cracked but firm, lacks label.   *(Burmester)* **£300 [≈ $534]**

Pemberton, Henry
- The Dispensatory of the Royal College of Physicians, London, Translated into English with Remarks ... London: for Longman ..., 1746. 1st edn. 8vo. Contemp calf, gilt spine, fine.   *(Georges)* **£350 [≈ $623]**
- The Dispensatory of the Royal College of Physicians, London. Translated into English with Remarks ... London: 1746. x,420 pp. Contemp calf, early reback, crnrs reprd.
    (Whitehart) **£180 [≈ $320]**
- The Dispensatory of the Royal College of Physicians, London. Translated into English with Remarks ... London: 1748. 2nd edn. x,414 pp. Contemp calf gilt, mor label, crnr edges worn.   *(Whitehart)* **£135 [≈ $240]**
- The Dispensatory of the Royal College of Physicians, London. Translated into English with Remarks, &c. Fourth Edition. London: J. Nourse, 1760. 8vo. x,414 pp. Contemp calf, orig paper label, sm surface damage rear bd.   *(Spelman)* **£140 [≈ $249]**
- Observations on Poetry, especially the Epic: occasioned by the late Poem upon Leonidas. London: H. Woodfall, sold by J. Brotherton ..., 1738. 1st edn. Sm 8vo. Half-title. Errata leaf. Contemp calf gilt, some wear. Anon.
    (Ximenes) **$425 [≈ £239]**
- Observations on Poetry, Especially the Epic: Occasioned by the late Poem upon Leonidas. London: H. Woodfall, sold by J. Brotherton ..., 1738. Only edn. 8vo. xii, [ii], 167 pp.

Half-title. Contemp calf gilt, lacks label, extrs worn, rubbed, upper jnt cracked.Anon
(Finch) **£165 [≈ $294]**

- A View of Sir Isaac Newton's Philosophy. London: S. Palmer, 1728. 1st edn. 4to. Title, [xlviii],407 pp. 12 fldg plates. Repr to title verso, tiny hole p 203. Contemp calf, sometime rebacked. Anon.
(Frew Mackenzie) **£350 [≈ $623]**

- A View of Sir Isaac Newton's Philosophy. London: S. Palmer, 1728. 1st edn. 4to. [50], 407 pp. 12 plates, engvd decs. Contemp calf, rebacked. *(O'Neal)* **$325 [≈ £183]**

- A View of Sir Isaac Newton's Philosophy. London: S. Palmer, 1728. 4to. Subscribers. 12 plates, num decs by Pine. Few sm marg worm holes. Contemp calf, rebacked. Anon.
(Waterfield's) **£450 [≈ $801]**

- A View of Sir Isaac Newton's Philosophy. Dublin: re-printed by and for John Hyde, 1728. 44,333 pp. 12 fldg plates. Contemp calf. *(C.R. Johnson)* **£350 [≈ $623]**

Pemble, William
- The Workes ... The third Edition. London: T. Cotes for E.F. [Edward Forrest, Oxford], 1635. Folio. [xxvii],'590" [ie 592],48, 28, [iv], 50 pp. Text within ruled borders. 1st 2 ff reprd. Some damp stains, lower margs wormed with v sl loss. Contemp calf, extrs worn. STC 19570.5
(Blackwell's) **£85 [≈ $151]**

Pembroke, Henry Herbert, 10th Earl of
- A Method of Breaking Horses, and Teaching Soldiers to Ride, Designed for the Use of the Army. London: J. Hughs, 1761. 1st edn. Sm 8vo. [xii],112 pp. 2 fldg plates. Red half mor, rebacked. *(Burmester)* **£150 [≈ $267]**

Penn, James
- A Latin Grammar for the Use of Christ's Hospital. The Second Edition. London: 1771. 261, [5] pp. Engvd frontis & title. Contemp sheep, sl rubbed. Anon.
(C.R. Johnson) **£125 [≈ $223]**

Penn, William
- An Account of William Penn's Travels in Holland and Germany, Anno M.DC.LXXVII. For the Service of the Gospel of Christ; By Way of Journal ... Third Impression, corrected ... London: F. Sowle, 1714. 12mo. [10],240,56 pp. Sl marked. Later polished calf, sl worn.
(D & D Galleries) **£235 [≈ £132]**

- England's Present Interest Considered, with Honour to the Prince. And Safety to the People ... Fourth Edition. London: T. Sowle,

1698. 12mo. [xii],168 pp. Contemp calf, sl rubbed, couple of sm holes in calf. Wing P.1282. *(Clark)* **£160 [≈ $285]**

- England's Present Interest Considered, with Honour to the Prince and Safety of the People. London: T. Sowle, 1698. 12mo. 6 inserted advt ff at end. Sl foxing & worm in upper marg. Contemp calf, new label. Wing P.1282. Anon. *(Hannas)* **£65 [≈ $116]**

- Englands Great Interest in the Choice of this New Parliament. [London: 1679]. 1st edn. Folio. 4 pp. Drophead title. Sl water stained. Disbound. Wing P.1278. Anon.
(Hannas) **£85 [≈ $151]**

Penn, William; Barclay, Robert; Pike, Joseph
- Three Treatises, in which the Fundamental Principle, Doctrines, Worship, Ministry and Discipline of the People called Quakers, are Plainly Declared ... Wilmington: James Adams, 1783. Inscrptn. Contemp calf, hinges starting. *(D & D Galleries)* **$125 [≈ £70]**

Pennant, Thomas
- British Zoology Illustrated by Plates and Brief Explanations. London: 1770. 8vo. iv, 96, [iv] pp. 103 plates. Contemp calf. Anon.
(Wheldon & Wesley) **£120 [≈ $214]**

- The Journey from Chester to London. London: B. White, 1782. 1st edn. 4to. iv, 452, [vi] pp. Engvd title with vignette, 22 plates (some sl offset). Contemp tree calf, rebacked, crnrs sl worn.
(Clark) **£160 [≈ $285]**

- The Journey from Chester to London. Dublin: 1783. Title,ii, 468,[6 index] pp. Marg soiling. Sl water staining to 1st 64 pp. Rebound in half calf.
(Francis Edwards) **£75 [≈ $134]**

- A Tour in Scotland MDCCLXIX. Chester: 1771. 1st edn. 8vo. viii,316 pp. 18 plates. Contemp half calf, worn. Anon.
(Spelman) **£70 [≈ $125]**

- A Tour in Scotland MDCCLXIX. London: for B. White, 1772. 2nd edn. viii,331,[i] pp. 18 plates. Contemp calf, edges sl worn, rebacked in calf gilt extra.
(Hollett) **£130 [≈ $231]**

- A Tour in Scotland, and A Voyage to the Hebrides. London: Benj. White, 1776. 2nd edn. 3 vols. 4to. 400; 439; 481,34 pp. 133 ills. Speckled calf, rebacked, some wear.
(Hartfield) **$985 [≈ £553]**

Pennecuik, Alexander, d.1730
- An Historical Account of the Blue Blanket: or, Crafts Mens Banner ... Edinburgh: John Mosman & Co, 1722. 1st edn. 8vo. [x],x,140

pp. Some marg damp stain, some fingering. Contemp sheep, scuffed, later label, crnrs worn.   *(Rankin)* **£130** [≃ **$231**]

Penny, Anne

- Poems, with a Dramatic Entertainment. By **★★★★ ★★★★★**. London: for the authour, sold by Dodsley ..., [1771]. 1st edn. 4to. Intl blank leaf, errata leaf. 5 vignettes. Contemp mottled calf, rebacked. Anon. *(Hannas)* **£260** [≃ **$463**]

Penrose, Thomas

- Address to the Genius of Great Britain. London: S. Crowder; Newbury: J. Willis, [1775]. 1st edn. 4to. Half-title trifle soiled. Disbound.   *(Ximenes)* **$650** [≃ **£365**]
- Flights of Fancy. London: J. Walter; Newbury: J. Willis, 1775. 1st edn. 4to. Couple of page numbers shaved. Rec wraps.
              (Ximenes) **$450** [≃ **£253**]

Penton, Stephen

- The Guardian's Instruction, or, The Gentleman's Romance: Written for the Diversion and Service of the Gentry ... London: for the author, 1688. Only edn. 12mo. [xvi], 92 pp. Some sm reprs with v sl loss. Rec contemp style calf. Wing P.1429. Anon.   *(Young's)* **£245** [≃ **$436**]

Perceval, John, 2nd Earl of Egmont

- Faction Detected, by the Evidence of Facts, containing an Impartial View of Parties at Home and Affairs Abroad ... Second Edition. London: for J. Roberts, 1743. 8vo. Contemp calf backed bds. Anon.
              (Waterfield's) **£60** [≃ **$107**]
- Faction Detected by the Evidence of Facts. Containing an Impartial View of Parties at Home and Affairs Abroad. Second Edition. London: 1743. 8vo. 175 pp. Sm hole in title & H3 with sl loss. Mod qtr mor. Anon.
              (Robertshaw) **£30** [≃ **$53**]

Percy, Thomas

- The Hermit of Warkworth. A Northumberland Ballad. In Three Fits or Cantos. London: for T. Davies, & S. Leacroft, 1771. 1st edn. 4to. viii, 52 pp, inc half-title. Title engv. Disbound, wraps.
              (Hannas) **£75** [≃ **$134**]

Percy, Thomas (editor)

- The Regulations and Establishment of Henry Percy, Fifth Earl of Northumberland ... Begun A.D. MDXII. London: 1770. 8vo. xxvi,[2 advt], x, 464, 3,[i] pp. Half-title. Occas sl browning. 19th c calf gilt, elab gilt spine.
              (Gough) **£375** [≃ **$668**]

Perefixe, Hardouin de Beaumont

- The History of Henry IV surnamed the Great, King of France and Navarre ... made English by J.D. London: for John Martyn, & Henry Herringman, 1672. 2nd edn in English. 8vo. Contemp calf, rebacked. Wing P.1465A.   *(Ximenes)* **$175** [≃ **£98**]

The Perfect Painter ...

- See Bell, Henry

Perkins, John

- A Profitable Booke of Master John Perkins, fellowe of the Inner Temple, Treating of the Lawes of Englande. London: Richarde Tottel ..., 1586. Sl dusty. Contemp calf, rebacked. STC 19638. *(Meyer Boswell)* **$1,500** [≃ **£843**]
- A Profitable Booke of Master John Perkins, Fellow of the Inner Temple, Treating of the Lawes of England. London: Thomas Wight, 1601. Contemp calf, jnts sl cracked. STC 19641.   *(Meyer Boswell)* **$750** [≃ **£421**]

Pernetti, Jacques

- Philosophical Letters upon Physiognomies. To which are added, Dissertations ... London: for R. Griffiths ..., 1751. 1st edn in English. 8vo. xxiv,259,[1 blank],[4 advt] pp. Old wraps, uncut. Anon.
              (Burmester) **£140** [≃ **$249**]

Perrault, Claude

- A Treatise of the Five Orders of Columns in Architecture ... Made English by John James. London: for Benj. Motte, 1708. Folio. Addtnl engvd title, engvd title with vignette, dedic, 2 pp subscrs, 6 plates. V sl soil. Contemp speckled calf.   *(Europa)* **£325** [≃ **$579**]

Perry, Charles

- A View of the Levant; particularly of Constantinople, Syria, Egypt, and Greece ... London: T. Woodward ..., 1743. 1st edn. Folio. xviii,[viii], 1-440, 449-524,[iv] pp, complete. 33 engvd ills on 20 pp (7 fldg). Sl browning. Contemp calf backed bds, uncut, sl worn. *(Frew Mackenzie)* **£1,250** [≃ **$2,225**]

Perry, John

- An Account of the Stopping of Daggenham Breach. London: for Benjamin Tooke, 1721. 1st edn. Post 8vo. (132) pp. Errata slip on title verso. Fldg map. Some browning. Mod calf.   *(Ash)* **£250** [≃ **$445**]
- The State of Russia under the present Czar ... London: for Benjamin Tooke, 1716. 8vo. Fldg map. Without the errata slip sometimes found. Contemp calf, rubbed, jnts cracked, lacks label.   *(Waterfield's)* **£300** [≃ **$534**]

- The State of Russia under the present Czar ... London: Benjamin Tooke, 1716. 1st edn. 8vo. [x],280 pp. Fldg map. Contemp panelled calf, sl stain upper cvr, hd of spine sl worn.
(Frew Mackenzie) **£200 [≈ $356]**

Person, David
- Varieties: or, a Surveigh of Rare and Excellent Matters, necessary and delectable for all sorts of Persons ... London: for Thomas Alchorn, 1635. 1st edn. 4to. Sep title to each part. 2 sm paper flaws. Contemp calf, backstrip laid down, crnrs worn. STC 19781.
(Gaskell) **£600 [≈ $1,068]**

Petavius, Dionysus (Denis Petau)
- The History of the World ... Compiled by the late Dionisius Petavius ... with a Geographical Description of Europe, Asia, Africa, and America. London: 1659. 1st edn in English. Folio. [10],610,[34], [2],154,[5] pp. Port. Lacks map. Contemp calf. W.1677B.
(O'Neal) **£425 [≈ £239]**
- The History of the World ... with a Geographicall Description of Europe, Asia, Africa, and America ... London: 1659. 1st edn in English. Folio. [x],610,[36], 154,[vi] pp. Port. Lacks map. Some wear & tear. Contemp calf, sl stained. W.1677D.
(Clark) **£140 [≈ $249]**

Petition ...
- The Petition of Both Houses of Parliament Presented to His Majestie at York, March 26, 1642. London: Barker & Bill, 1642. 4to. Title border. Stitched. Wing E.2164.
(Rostenberg & Stern) **$90 [≈ £51]**
- The Petition of the Lords and Commons in Parliament, Together VVith His Majesties Answer. London: Barker & Bill, 1642. 4to. Title border. Stitched. Wing E.2174.
(Rostenberg & Stern) **$125 [≈ £70]**
- A Petition of the Mayor, Aldermen, and Common Councell of the City of London, to His Majestie. N.p.: 1641. 4to. Title border. Stitched. Wing P.1819.
(Rostenberg & Stern) **$90 [≈ £51]**
- The Petition of the Six Counties of South-Wales, and the County of Monmouth, Presented to the Parliament of the Common-wealth of England. For a supply of Ministers, in lieu of those who have been ejected. N.p.: 1652. 4to. Stitched. Wing P.1836.
(Rostenberg & Stern) **$80 [≈ £45]**

Petrarch, Francesco
- Sonnets and Odes translated from the Italian [by John Nott] ... With the Original Text and some Account of his Life. London: for T.

Davies, 1777. 8vo. Contemp qtr sheep, hd of spine defective. *(Waterfield's)* **£50 [≈ $89]**

Pettus, Sir John
- Fleta Minor. The Laws of Art and Nature, in ... Metals. In Two Parts ... London: Stephen Bateman, 1686. 1st edn. 3rd issue, with the sep titled dictionary of terms dated 1683. Folio. Errata. Port frontis, num text engvs. Contemp calf, rebacked. Wing P.1907.
(Vanbrugh) **£1,855 [≈ $3,302]**
- Volatiles from the History of Adam and Eve: containing, many unquestioned Truths, and allowable Notions, of several Natures. London: for T. Bassett, 1674. 1st edn. 8vo. Errata leaf. Lacks final blank leaf. Contemp sheep, rebacked. Wing P.1912.
(Hannas) **£160 [≈ $285]**

Petyt, William
- Miscellanea Parliamentaria; containing Presidents 1. Of Freedom from Arrests ... London: N. Thompson ..., 1681. 8vo. [xxxii], 220, [lxiv] pp. Blank before title. Contemp calf, crnrs sl worn, jnts rubbed. Wing P.1949.
(Clark) **£120 [≈ $214]**

Phalaris
- The Epistles ... translated from the Greek. To which are added, some Select Epistles of the most eminent Greek Writers. By Thomas Francklin. London: R. Francklin, 1749. 8vo. [14],224 pp. Half-title. Frontis (imprint cropped). Some browning. Contemp panelled calf.
(Spelman) **£65 [≈ $116]**

Phalaris ...
- The Epistles of Phalaris ... see Francklin, Thomas.

Philipot, John
- A Perfect Collection or Catalogue of all Knights Batchelaurs made by King James since his coming to the Crown of England. London: 1660. 1st edn. 8vo. 94,[32 ctlg] pp. 19th c half calf. Wing P.1988. Anon.
(Robertshaw) **£40 [≈ $71]**

Philipps, Henry
- The Grandeur of the Law ... By H.P. London: for Arthur Jones ..., 1684. 1st edn. 1 blank defective. Sheep, rebacked. Wing P.2022. *(Meyer Boswell)* **$450 [≈ £253]**

Philipps, Jenkin Thomas
- The Life of Ernestus the Pious, first Duke of Sax-Gotha. The great grandfather of the present Princess of Wales ... Now republish'd ... London: Francis Bishop, 1750. [6],49,[1]

pp. Disbound. Anon.
(*C.R. Johnson*) **£45** [≈ **$80**]

Philips, Ambrose
- The Distrest Mother. A Tragedy ... London: for S. Buckley, & J. Tonson, 1712. 1st edn. 4to. Lacks half-title. browned. Mod half calf.
(*Hannas*) **£130** [≈ **$231**]

Philips, Edward
- Certain Godly and Learned Sermons ... London: Richard Field for Cuthbert Burbie, 1605. 1st edn. Sm 4to. [xxii],462,[i] pp. Occas sl foxing. Contemp vellum, sl soiled, front inner hinge gone. STC 19853.
(*Finch*) **£100** [≈ **$178**]

Philips, John
- Cyder. A Poem. In Two Books. London: Tonson, 1708. 1st edn. Ordinary paper (ie 1st) issue. 8vo. Fly-title following title. frontis (shaved at lower edge). Contemp sheep, rebacked. (*Hannas*) **£140** [≈ **$249**]
- Cyder. A Poem in Two Books. With the Splendid Shilling; Paradise Lost and Two Songs. London: 1709. 8vo. 48 pp. Sm stain on 2 pp. Mod bds. Anon.
(*Robertshaw*) **£15** [≈ **$27**]
- The Whole Works ... To which is prefixed his Life, by Mr Sewell. London: Tonson, 1720. 1st edn. 8vo. [2],xxxix,[4], 30-60, half-title, 89,[1], half-title, [3],4-13 pp. Port frontis, plate before Cyder. Contemp calf, upper jnt cracked but firm. (*Spelman*) **£50** [≈ **$89**]

Philips, Katherine
- Poems. By the Incomparable, Mrs. K.P. London: J.G. for Rich. Marriott, 1664. 1st, unauthorised, edn. 8vo. [xvi],236, [iv], 237-242 pp. Errata leaf. Blank leaf Q8. Lacks A1 (imprimatur leaf). 19th c elab gilt mor. Wing P.2032. (*Vanbrugh*) **£855** [≈ **$1,522**]
- Poems ... To which is added Monsieur Corneille's Pompey & Horace ... London: J.M. for Henry Herringman, 1667. 1st authorised edn. Folio. [xxxiv],198, [viii],65,[i], [ii], 69-112 pp. Imprimatur. Frontis port. Contemp calf, elab gilt 19th c reback. (*Vanbrugh*) **£355** [≈ **$632**]
- Poems ... To which is added Monsieur Corneilles Pompey and Horace ... London: T.N. for Henry Herringman, 1678. 2nd (authorised) edn. Folio. [xxxiv],198, [viii],65,[i], [ii], 69-112 pp. Port frontis (sl marg wear). Sm marg worm. Contemp calf, rebacked. Wing P.2035.
(*Vanbrugh*) **£225** [≈ **$401**]

Phillips, Edward
- Theatrum Poetarum, or a Compleat Collection of the Poets, especially the most Eminent, of all Ages ... London: for Charles Smith, 1675. 1st edn. 12mo. 2 advt pp at end. Title sl stained & reprd in inner marg. Crushed red mor gilt, a.e.g., by Riviere. Wing P.2075. (*Hannas*) **£550** [≈ **$979**]

Phillips, Sarah
- The Ladies Handmaid: or, a Compleat System of Cookery ... London: for J. Coote, 1758. Only edn. 8vo. 472,[18] pp. Frontis incorporating a port of the author & 4 copperplates. Rec half calf over old mrbld bds. (*Sotheran's*) **£995** [≈ **$1,771**]

Philosophical ...
- A Philosophical Dialogue concerning Decency ... see Buckler, Benjamin.
- A Philosophical Enquiry into the Origin of our Ideas of the Sublime and Beautiful ... see Burke, Edmund.
- A Philosophical Essay towards an Eviction of the Being and Attributes of God ... see Ward, Seth
- Philosophical Letters upon Physiognomies ... see Pernetti, Jacques.
- A Philosophical Survey of the South of Ireland ... see Campbell, Thomas

Philosophicall ...
- A Philosophicall Essay for the Reunion of the Languages ... see Besnier, Pierre

Phipps, Constantine John
- A Voyage Towards the North Pole, Undertaken by His Majesty's Command, 1773. London: Bower & Nichols, 1774. 1st edn. Large Paper. 8vo. viii,253,1 pp. 15 fldg plates & charts, 11 fldg ptd tables. Contemp calf, rebacked. (*Terramedia*) **$1,500** [≈ **£843**]
- A Voyage Towards the North Pole undertaken by His Majesty's Command. London: Nourse, 1774. 1st edn. 4to. viii,253 pp. 3 charts, 12 engvs. [Bound with] Horsley, Samuel. Remarks on the Observations ... London: 1774. 15 pp. Crnr torn from last leaf. Contemp calf, rebacked.
(*Walcot*) **£450** [≈ **$801**]

Phipps, Constantine John & Ludwidge, Captain
- The Journal of a Voyage undertaken by Order of His Present Majesty, for making Discoveries towards the North Pole ... London: for F. Newbery, 1774. 1st edn. xxviii, 118 pp. 2 fldg maps, 1 plate. Contemp

gilt panelled calf, sm split in jnt.
(Gough) £295 [≈ $525]

Phipps, Joseph
- The Original and Present State of Man briefly considered ... by the People called Quakers. London Printed. Phila: Reprinted, 1783. 8vo. Browned. Contemp sheep, rubbed. *(Waterfield's)* £90 [≈ $160]

The Phoenix ...
- See Dunton, John (editor)

A Physical Vade Mecum ...
- See Poole, Robert

Picart, Bernard
- The Ceremonies and Religious Customs of the Various Nations of the Known World ... Vol. III, Containing the Ceremonies of the Idolatrous Nations ... London: William Jackson, 1734. Folio. [12],496,[26] pp. 45 plates. Rebound in half calf.
(Karmiole) $375 [≈ £211]

Pierce, Thomas
- A Decad of Caveats to the People of England ... London: for Richard Davis, Oxford, 1679. 1st edn. 4to. [xxvii], [i], 449, [i blank],[iv] pp. Sl water stain. Contemp calf, gilt spine, lacks label, some wear & rubbing. Wing P.2176.
(Finch) £95 [≈ $169]

Pigott, Charles
- A Political Dictionary ... Illustrated and Exemplified in the Lives, Morals, Character and Conduct of ... Illustrious Personages. London: for D.I. Eaton, 1795. 8vo. [ii],175 pp. Few crnrs damp stained. Orig bds, rebacked in cloth, sl worn.
(Rankin) £65 [≈ $116]
- A Political Dictionary: explaining the True Meaning of Words. Illustrated and Exemplified ... London: for D.I. Eaton, 1795. 8vo. Contemp half calf, rebacked.
(Waterfield's) £135 [≈ $240]

Pike, Nicholas
- A New and Complete System of Arithmetic, composed for the Use of the Citizens of the United States. Newbury-port: John Mycall, 1788. 1st edn. 8vo. Some wear & tear. Lacks half-title & 2 advt ff. Contemp calf, rebacked, worn. *(D & D Galleries)* $250 [≈ £140]

Piles, Roger de
- The Art of Painting, with the Lives and Characters of above 300 of the Most Eminent Painters ... Second Edition. London: for

Charles Marsh, 1744. 8vo. xviii,430 pp. Contemp gilt panelled calf, rebacked.
(Gough) £135 [≈ $240]

Pilkington, M.
- The Gentleman's and Connoisseur's Dictionary of Painters ... New Edition ... Supplement ... London: Spilsbury, 1798. Roy 4to. xii,840,xxiii pp. Sl spotting. Crnr of last 5 ff damp stained. Rebound in half calf.
(Francis Edwards) £100 [≈ $178]

Pilkington, Mary S.
- Edward Barnard; or, Merit Exalted; containing the History of the Edgerton Family. London: for E. Newbery, 1797. 167,[1] pp. Frontis. Contemp calf, hinges cracking. *(C.R. Johnson)* £185 [≈ $329]

Pilkington, Matthew
- Poems on Several Occasions. Dublin: George Faulkner, 1730. 1st edn. 8vo. Subscribers. 19th c half calf, rubbed, cvrs detached.
(Ximenes) $450 [≈ £253]
- Poems on Several Occasions ... With several Poems not in the Dublin Edition. Revised by the Reverend Dr. Swift. London: for T. Woodward ..., 1731. 1st London edn. 8vo. Lacks a flyleaf. Contemp calf, hd of jnts sl cracked. *(Ximenes)* $750 [≈ £421]
- Poems on Several Occasions ... With several Poems not in the Dublin Edition. Revised by the Rev. Dr. Swift. London: for T. Woodward ..., 1731. 1st London edn. 8vo. Frontis. Contemp calf, worn.
(Hannas) £320 [≈ $570]

Pinchard, Elizabeth
- The Blind Child, or Anecdotes of the Wyndham Family. Written for the Use of Young People. By a Lady. London: for E. Newbery, 1791. 1st edn. 8vo. 178,[2 advt] pp. Frontis. Contemp tree calf, flat spine relaid, mor label. Anon. *(Finch)* £110 [≈ $196]
- The Two Cousins, a Moral Story, for the Use of Young Persons ... By the Author of The Blind Child and Dramatic Dialogues. London: E. Newbery, 1794. viii,144,[4] pp. Advts. Frontis. Contemp sheep, hinges beginning to crack. Anon.
(C.R. Johnson) £135 [≈ $240]

Pindar, Peter
- See Wolcot, John

Pinelli, Maffei
- Bibliotheca Pinelliana. A Catalogue of the Magnificent and Celebrated Library .. Sold by Auction. [London]: Robson, Clarke &

Edwards, [1789]. Thick 8vo. Orig bds, rebacked. *(Rostenberg & Stern)* **$450 [≈ £253]**

Pinkerton, John
- Rimes. London: for Charles Dilly, 1781. 1st edn. 8vo. [viii],136 pp. Contemp floral bds, crnrs worn, rebacked in calf. Anon.
(Burmester) **£150 [≈ $267]**
- Rimes ... Second Edition. London: for Charles Dilly, 1782. 8vo. Frontis, tissue guard. Title vignette. Contemp tree calf, rebacked.   *(Waterfield's)* **£125 [≈ $223]**

Pinkerton, John (editor)
- Ancient Scottish Poems, never before in print. But now published from the MS. Collections of Sir Richard Maitland ... London: Dilly; Edinburgh: Creech, 1786. 1st edn. 2 vols. 8vo. cxliv,558 pp. 1 plate. Sl water stain. Contemp half calf, sl worn. Anon.   *(Claude Cox)* **£65 [≈ $116]**

Pinkney, Miles
- Sweete Thoughts of Jesus and Marie or Meditations for all the Feasts of our B. Saviour and his B. Mother ... By Thomas Carre ... Paris: Vincent du Moutier, 1665. 2 vols in one. 8vo. Contemp calf, rebacked, crnrs sl worn. Sl used. Wing P.2276. Anon.   *(Clark)* **£120 [≈ $214]**

Piozzi, Hester Lynch
- See Thrale (later Piozzi), Hester Lynch

Pitt, Christopher
- An Essay on Virgil's Aeneid. Being a Translation of the First Book. London: for A. Bettesworth; & W. Hinchcliffe, 1728. 1st edn. 8vo. 71 pp. Disbound. *(Hannas)* **£55 [≈ $98]**
- The Plague of Marseilles: a Poem. By a Person of Quality. London: for J. Bateman, & J. Nicks, 1721. 1st edn. 8vo. 30,[1] pp, inc half-title & advt leaf. Disbound. Anon.
(Hannas) **£75 [≈ $134]**

Pitt, Christopher (translator)
- Vida's Art of Poetry, translated into English Verse. London: Sam. Palmer, for A. Bettesworth, 1725. 1st edn of this translation. 12mo. Final advt leaf. Contemp elab gilt red mor, a.e.g., jnts cracked.
(Hannas) **£85 [≈ $151]**

Pitt, William
- An Authentic Copy of Mr. Pitt's Letter to his Royal Highness The Prince of Wales ... see Burke, Edmund.
- Political Debates. Paris: J.W., 1766. 8vo.

Lacks half-title. Wraps. Anon.
(Rostenberg & Stern) **$80 [≈ £45]**
- The Speech ... in the House of Commons, on Friday, February 21, 1783. London: Debrett, 1783. 8vo. Advts at end. Stitched.
(Rostenberg & Stern) **$125 [≈ £70]**

Pix, Mary
- The Deceiver Deceived: a Comedy ... London: for R. Basset, 1698. 1st edn. 4to. Title & last leaf dust soiled. Disbound. Wing P.2327. Anon.   *(Hannas)* **£150 [≈ $267]**

Plain Truth ...
- See Chalmers, James

Plante-Amour, Chevalier
- The Art of Knowing Women ... see Bruys, Francois

Platina, Bartolomeo
- The Lives of Bishops and the Popes ... Written Originally in Latin by Baptista Platina ... Edinburgh: 1688. 2nd edn, crrctd. 394,index pp. Port of Sir Paul Rycaut. Leather, worn, rebacked. Wing P.2404.
(D & D Galleries) **$325 [≈ £183]**
- The Lives of the Popes ... London: for C. Wilkinson, 1688. 2nd edn, crrctd. Folio. [xxxii], 394,[16] pp. Port of Rycaut (the translator). Occas sm lib stamps. Contemp calf, rebacked. Wing P.2404.
(Young's) **£60 [≈ $107]**

Plato
- The Banquet of Xenophon. Done from the Greek, with an Introductory Essay ... By James Welwood. London: John Barnes & Andrew Bell, 1710. 8vo. [2],168 pp. Contemp sheep.   *(O'Neal)* **$125 [≈ £70]**
- Plato His Apology of Socrates, and Phaedo or Dialogue concerning the Immortality of Mans Soul, and Manner of Socrates his Death ... London: for Magnes & Bentley, 1675. 1st English edn. 8vo. Intl blank, 2 terminal blanks. Contemp calf, headband worn. Wing P.2405.   *(Hannas)* **£150 [≈ $267]**

Platt, Sir Hugh
- The Garden of Eden. Or an accurate Description of all Flowers and Fruits now growing in England ... The fifth edition. London: William Leake, 1660. 1st edn of part 2. 2 parts in one vol. 12mo. 175,[i]; [16], 159, [i] pp. Some browning. Contemp calf, rebacked, crnrs reprd. Wing 2387A.
(Spelman) **£420 [≈ $748]**
- The Garden of Eden: or, an accurate

Description of all Flowers and Fruits now growing in England ... London: 1675. 6th edn. 2 parts in one vol. Sm 8vo. [xxviii],148, [xiv], 159 pp. Mod calf.
(Wheldon & Wesley) **£275 [≈ $490]**

Plattes, Gabriel

- A Discovery of Subterraneal Treasure: viz. Of all manner of Mines and Minerals, from Gold to the Coal ... London: for J.E., 1653. 60 pp. Sm marg tear title. Disbound. Wing P.2410. Anon.   *(C.R. Johnson)* **£750 [≈ $1,335]**

Pliny, the younger

- The Letters of Pliny the Consul: with Occasional Remarks. By William Melmoth, Esq. The Third Edition. London: Dodsley, 1748. 2 vols. 8vo. [x],368; [vi],371-692,[iv] pp. Half-titles. Red & black titles with vignettes. Contemp calf, rubbed, extrs sl worn.   *(Clark)* **£35 [≈ $62]**
- Pliny's Panegyrick upon the Emperor Trajan ... Rendered into English from the Original by George Smith ... London: the booksellers, 1702. 1st edn thus. 8vo. 176 pp. Contemp calf, rebacked.   *(O'Neal)* **$175 [≈ £98]**
- Pliny's Epistles and Panegyrick translated by several Hands with the Life of Pliny by Mr. Henley. London: W. Mears, 1724. 2 vols. 8vo. Contemp panelled calf, rebacked.   *(Waterfield's)* **£150 [≈ $267]**

Pliny, the elder

- The Historie of the World ... Translated into English by Philemon Holland ... London: Adam Islip, 1601. 1st edn. 2 vols in one. Lge folio. Errata & colophon leaf. Title with sm repr & laid down. Early 19th c elab gilt 2-tone calf, backstrip relaid. STC 20020.
(Vanbrugh) **£1,275 [≈ $2,270]**

Plot, Robert

- The Natural History of Oxfordshire ... Second Edition, with large Additions and Corrections ... Oxford: Leon. Lichfield ..., 1705. Folio. [xii],366,[x] pp. Fldg map (linen backed), 16 plates. Contemp calf, sometime rebacked, crnrs reprd, edges sl rubbed.
(Blackwell's) **£500 [≈ $890]**

Plowden, Francis

- An Investigation of the Native Rights of British Subjects. London: for the author & sold by R. Baldwin ..., 1784. 1st edn. 8vo. vii,[i errata],200 pp. Few ff faintly foxed. Rec half calf. Anon. A supplement was published the following year.
(Blackwell's) **£125 [≈ $223]**

Pluche, Noel-Antoine

- The History of the Heavens, considered according to the Notions of the Poets and Philosophers, compared with the Doctrines of Moses ... Second Edition. London: Osborn, 1743. 2nd English edn. 2 vols. 12mo. Frontis & 24 plates vol 1. Contemp calf, worn, jnts cracked but sound.   *(Gaskell)* **£140 [≈ $249]**
- Spectacle de la Nature: or Nature Display'd ... Translated from the Original French, by Mr. Humphreys. London: 1740-49. 5th edn, vol 4 3rd edn, 5-7 2nd edn. 7 vols. 12mo. 207 plates (of 208, lacks 2 plates but with 1 duplicate). Rec half calf. Anon.
(Frew Mackenzie) **£295 [≈ $525]**

Plumptre, James

- Observations on Hamlet ... being an Attempt to prove that he designed it as an Indirect Censure on Mary Queen of Scots. Cambridge: J. Burges ..., 1796. 1st edn. 8vo. [6],44 pp. Disbound, wraps.
(Hannas) **£100 [≈ $178]**

Plutarch

- The Lives of the Noble Grecians and Romaines ... Translated ... into English by Sir Thomas North ... London: Richard Field, 1612. 4th edn. Thick folio. Num medallion ports in text. Title sl used. 18th c calf backed bds.   *(Vanbrugh)* **£395 [≈ $703]**
- Plutarchs Lives. Translated from the Greek by several Hands. To which is prefixed the Life of Plutarch. London: for Jacob Tonson, 1700-1699. 5 vols. 8vo. 5 frontis, 49 ports. Browning. Contemp calf, rubbed, some wear extrs. Wing P.2635C, 2637A, 2638A, 2639B, 2641.   *(Clark)* **£100 [≈ $178]**
- Plutarch's Lives. In Eight Volumes. Translated from the Greek. With Notes ... from M. Dacier. London: Tonson, 1727. 8 vols. 8vo. 58 plates. Occas foxing. Contemp calf, pitted, extrs worn, some jnts cracked.
(Clark) **£45 [≈ $80]**

Pococke, Richard

- A Description of the East, and Some Other Countries. London: Bowyer, 1743. 3 parts in 2 vols. Folio. 310; 268; 308 pp. Dedic, map, 178 plates. Old leather, scuffed, rebacked, vol 2 spine chipped & worn.
(McBlain) **$1,400 [≈ £787]**

Poem ...

- A Poem in Memory of Robert Nelson Esquire. London: George James for Richard Smith, 1715. 1st edn. 8vo. 21,[3] pp. Disbound.   *(Burmester)* **£120 [≈ $214]**

Poems ...

- Poems for Young Ladies ... see Goldsmith, Oliver (editor)
- Poems on Several Occasions ... 1736 ... see Fitzgerald, Thomas
- Poems on Several Occasions ... Edinburgh 1754 ... see Blacklock, Thomas
- Poems upon Various Subjects, Latin and English ... see Browne, Isaac Hawkins

The Poetical Register ...

- See Jacob, Giles

Pointer, John

- A Rational Account of the Weather, shewing Signs of its Several Changes and Alterations, together with the Philosophical Reasons of them. Oxford: L.L. for S. Wilmot ..., 1723. 76 pp. Rebound in panelled calf.
  (C.R. Johnson) **£220 [≈ $392]**

Polano, Pietro Soave

- See Sarpi, Paolo

Polanus, Amandus

- The Substance of Christian Religion ... London: Arn. Hatfield for William Aspley, 1608. Sm 8vo. [16],571,[1] pp. Ends on Oo6, possibly lacks advts at end. Sl dusty at ends. Late 17th c calf. STC 20085.
  (Fenning) **£245 [≈ $436]**

Pole, Thomas

- The Anatomical Instructor; or, an Illustration of the Modern and most Approved Methods of preparing and preserving the different parts of the Human Body and of Quadrupeds ... London: 1790. 8vo. lxxx,[6], 304, [7] pp. 10 plates. calf, jnts split.
  (Goodrich) **$275 [≈ £154]**

Polesworth, Sir Humphry

- See Arbuthnot, John

Polite ...

- The Polite Gentleman ... see Barker, Henry, translator.
- The Polite Philosopher ... see Forrester, James

Politeuphia, Wits Common-Wealth ...

- See Ling, Nicholas

Political Catechism ...

- See Robinson, Robert

Pollexfen, Sir Henry

- The Arguments and Reports ... In Some Special Cases ... London: for R. Smith & John Reeve, 1702. Folio. [xii],662,[664-672] pp. Licence leaf. Contemp calf, spine worn.
  (Vanbrugh) **£155 [≈ $276]**

Polybius

- The General History ... Translated from the Greek by Mr Hampton. The Second Edition. London: J. Hughs, for R. & J. Dodsley, 1761. 2 vols in 4. 2 fldg maps. Occas foxing. Contemp calf, gilt spines, new labels, cracking to spines, crnrs bumped.
  (Spelman) **£40 [≈ $71]**
- The General History of Polybius, In Five Books. Translated from the Greek by Mr. [James] Hampton. The Third Edition. London: Dodsley, 1772. 2 vols. 4to. xxiv,[8],559; [16], 423,[16] pp. 2 fldg maps. Contemp diced calf gilt, backstrips laid down.
  (O'Neal) **$425 [≈ £239]**

Pomfret, John

- Miscellany Poems on Several Occasions. By the Author of the Choice. London: for John Place, 1702. 1st coll edn. 8vo. Intl advt leaf. Contemp panelled calf, later label, jnts cracking. Anon. *(Hannas)* **£200 [≈ $356]**
- Poems upon Several Occasions. The Tenth Edition, Corrected. With Some Account of his Life and Writings. To which are added his Remains. London: S. Birt, 1740. Fcap 8vo. xii, 132, vi,17 pp. Frontis. Occas foxing & soiling. Contemp calf, jnts cracked but firm.
  (Spelman) **£35 [≈ $62]**

Poole, Robert

- A Physical Vade Mecum or Fifth Gift of Theophilus Philanthropos. Wherein is Contain'd, the Dispensatory of St. Thomas's Hospital ... London: 1741. liv,324,[xii] pp. Frontis. Contemp leather, rebacked.
  (Whitehart) **£375 [≈ $668]**
- A Physical Vade Mecum: or Fifth Gift of Theophilus Philanthropos. Wherein is Contain'd, the Dispensatory of St. Thomas's Hospital ... London: E. Duncomb, 1741. 1st edn. 8vo. [ii],xviii, liv,324,[xii] pp. Contemp calf, some wear, sl used. Anon.
  (Sotheran's) **£350 [≈ $623]**

Pope, Alexander

- Additions to the Work of Alexander Pope ... London: H. Baldwin ..., 1776. 1st edn. 2 vols in one. 8vo. Half-titles. Sep titles in vol 2. Lib stamp on title versos, occas sl spotting. Later three qtr calf. *(Hartfield)* **$395 [≈ £222]**
- An Epistle from Mr Pope, to Dr Arbuthnot.

London: J. Wright for Lawton Gilliver, 1734.
1st edn. Folio. [4],30 pp. Stitched as issued,
uncut, fine. *(Spelman)* **£1,200 [≈ $2,136]**

- An Essay on Criticism. The Sixth Edition,
Corrected. London: for Bernard Lintot, 1719.
8vo. [2]-48 pp. Frontis. Disbound.
(Hannas) **£55 [≈ $98]**

- An Essay on Man ... Enlarged and Improved
by the Author. With Notes by William
Warberton [sic], M.A. London, printed.
Phila: re-printed, & sold by W. Dunlap, 1760.
2nd Amer edn. 8vo. Frontis. Some water
stains. Contemp wraps, lacks spine.
(Ximenes) **$750 [≈ £421]**

- Ode for Music on St. Cecilia's Day. The
Third Edition. London: for Bernard Lintot,
1719. 1st 8vo edn. 12 pp, advt leaf. Frontis.
(Hannas) **£100 [≈ $178]**

- The Poetical Works. Glasgow: Andrew
Foulis, 1785. 3 vols. Folio. Contemp tree calf
gilt, rebacked, some wear to cvrs & edges.
(Hartfield) **$1,250 [≈ £702]**

- The Rape of the Lock ... Fourth Edition,
Corrected. London: for Bernard Lintot, 1715.
8vo. Frontis, 5 plates. Sl soiling. Contemp
panelled calf, crnrs rubbed, spine worn.
(Ximenes) **$125 [≈ £70]**

- The Rape of the Lock ... London: T. Bensley;
for F.J. Du Roveray, Great St. Helens, 1798.
1st edn thus. 8vo. xxix, [i], 79, [i] pp. 6 plates
(1 designed by Fuseli). Occas foxing.
Contemp calf, rubbed, spine defective at ft.
(Clark) **£20 [≈ $36]**

- Temple of Fame: a Vision. The Second
Edition. London: for Bernard Lintot, 1715.
8vo. 52,[4] pp, inc half-title & 2 advt ff at end.
Frontis. *(Hannas)* **£85 [≈ $151]**

Pope, Alexander (editor)
- Miscellany Poems. The Sixth Edition.
London: for Bernard Lintot; sold by Henry
Lintot, 1732. 2 vols. 12mo. Half-titles. Port
on recto of 1st half-title. Contemp calf gilt.
(Hannas) **£75 [≈ $134]**

Popham, Sir John
- Reports and Cases ... Translated into English
... London: assigns of Richard & Edward
Atkins ..., 1682. 1st edn, 3rd issue. Folio.
[viii],212,[213-220] pp. Contemp calf, bds
detached. Wing P.2842B.
(Vanbrugh) **£175 [≈ $312]**

Pordage, Samuel
- The Siege of Babylon: as it is Acted at the
Dukes Theatre. London: Tonson, 1678. 1st
edn. 4to. A few catchwords & bottom line of
1 page cut into. Disbound. Wing P.2977.

(Hannas) **£120 [≈ $214]**

Portal, Abraham
- Poems. London: for the author, 1781. 1st
edn. 8vo. [iv],7,[i],295 pp. Subscribers. Occas
sl spotting & soiling. Contemp calf, rebacked,
crnrs sl worn. *(Burmester)* **£150 [≈ $267]**

Portal, Paul
- The Compleat Practice of Men and Woman
Midwives, or, the True Manner of Assisting
a Woman in Child-Bearing ... London: H.
Clark, for S. Crouch, 1705. 1st English edn.
8vo. [xvi], 245,[3 advt] pp. 2 plates. Sl stain
on title. Rec contemp style calf.
(Young's) **£450 [≈ $801]**

Porter, Thomas
- The Villain, a Tragedy. London: for H.
Herringman, 1670. 2nd edn. 4to. Early mrbld
wraps. Wing P.2996. *(Hannas)* **£120 [≈ $214]**

Positive, Paul (pseudonym)
- See Montgomery, James

Postlethwayt, Malachy
- Universal Dictionary of Trade and
Commerce, translated from the French of the
celebrated Monsieur Savary ... with Large
Additions and Improvements ... London:
1757. 2nd edn. 2 vols. Folio.
xxii,xiv,1917,[1]; [viii], 856 pp. Frontis, fldg
table. Lib cloth. *(Whitehart)* **£200 [≈ $356]**

Potter, Francis
- An Interpretation of the Number 666 ...
Oxford: Leonard Lichfield, 1642. 1st edn. Sm
4to. [18],214 pp. Title reprd. New qtr calf.
Wing P.3028. *(Chapel Hill)* **$500 [≈ £281]**

Potter, John
- Archaeologiae Graecae: or the Antiquities of
Greece. Oxford: Timothy Child, 1697-99. 1st
edn. 2 vols. 8vo. Title vignettes, 30 plates (11
fldg). Some foxing throughout. Sl marg worm
vol 2. Contemp calf, jnts cracked but firm,
later labels. Wing P.3030, 3032.
(Blackwell's) **£120 [≈ $214]**

- Archaeologia Graeca; or, the Antiquities of
Greece. London: 1744. 2 vols. 8vo. 30 plates.
1 gathering partly detached. Calf, raised
bands, leather labels.
(Francis Edwards) **£90 [≈ $160]**

Potter, Robert
- The Oracle concerning Babylon. And the
Song of Exultation ... London: Wilkie, 1785.
1st edn. 4to. [iv],iv,11,[1] pp. New bds.
(Claude Cox) **£45 [≈ $80]**

Povey, Charles

- An Enquiry into the Miscarriages of the Four Last Years Reign. London: 1714. 1st edn. 8vo. 32 pp. Few page numbers cropped. Disbound. Anon.   *(Robertshaw)* **£18 [≈$32]**
- The Virgin in Eden: or, The State of Innocency ... Progress from Sodom to Canaan. London: J. Roberts, 1714. 2nd edn. 8vo. 118 pp. W'cut arms on title. Few faint blind stamps. Occas sl soiling. Mod half calf gilt. Anon.   *(Hollett)* **£120 [≈$214]**

Practical ...

- Practical Perspective ... see Dubreuil, Jean
- Practical Treatise on Painting in Oil-Colours ... see Bardwell, Thomas

Prance, Miles

- A True Narrative and Discovery of several very remarkable Passages relating to the Horrid Popish Plot ... London: Dorman Newman, 1679. Folio. [viii],40 pp. Licence leaf. Port frontis. Minor soil. Disbound. Wing P.3177.   *(Clark)* **£45 [≈$80]**

Pratt, Samuel Jackson

- Gleanings through Wales, Holland and Westphalia, with Views of Peace and War at Home and Abroad ... London: for T.N. Longman ..., 1795. 1st edn. 3 vols. 8vo. Contemp calf, damp marked, affecting blanks.   *(Young's)* **£125 [≈$223]**
- The Tutor of Truth. By the Author of The Pupil of Pleasure, &c. &c. London: for Richardson & Urquhart, 1779. 2 vols. Sm 8vo. xiv, 225; 291 pp. Lower marg vol 2 wormed, not affecting text. Contemp calf, crnrs sl bumped, spine ends sl chipped. Anon.   *(Francis Edwards)* **£45 [≈$80]**

Present ...

- The Present Conduct of the War. London: for W. Webb, 1746. Only edn. 8vo. [ii],56 pp. Title dusty. Last leaf creased.   *(Young's)* **£70 [≈$125]**
- The Present Danger of Popery in England. London: How, 1710. 8vo. Browned, blank crnr chipped. Stitched.   *(Rostenberg & Stern)* **$65 [≈£37]**
- A Present for a Servant-Maid ... see Haywood, Eliza
- The Present State of Ireland Consider'd. Dublin Printed. London: reprinted for Weaver Bickerton, 1730. 8vo. 32 pp. Disbound.   *(Robertshaw)* **£55 [≈$98]**
- The Present State of the Protestants in France. London: Holford, 1681. 4to. Title reprd & laid down. Stitched. Wing F.3274.

(Rostenberg & Stern) **$125 [≈£70]**

- The Present State of Russia ... see Weber, Friedrich Christian

Prestwich, J.

- Prestwich's Respublica; or a Display of the Honors, Ceremonies & Ensigns of the Common-Wealth, under ... Oliver Cromwell ... London: Nichols, 1787. Only edn. All published. 4to. ix,[i],279,[i] pp. Engvd frontis & title. Sl spotting. Early 19th c half mor gilt.   *(Blackwell's)* **£200 [≈$356]**

Pretences ...

- The Pretences of the French Invasion Examined ... see Lloyd, William **[≈$116]**

Price, Richard

- Additional Observations on the Nature and Value of Civil Liberty, and the War with America ... The Second Edition. London: T. Cadell, 1776. 176 pp. Contemp mrbld bds, rebacked in mor.   *(C.R. Johnson)* **£145 [≈$258]**
- An Essay on the Population of England, From the Revolution to the Present Time. With an Appendix ... The Second Edition, with Corrections and Additions. London: for T. Cadell, 1780. 88 pp. Contemp calf, rebacked.   *(C.R. Johnson)* **£550 [≈$979]**
- Four Dissertations. I. On Providence ... IV. On the Importance of Christianity, the Nature of Historical Evidence, and Miracles. Fourth Edition, with Additions. London: 1777. 8vo. Contemp calf, rebacked.   *(Robertshaw)* **£65 [≈$116]**
- Observations on Reversionary Payments ... and on the National Debt ... Third Edition, much enlarged. London: for T. Cadell, 1773. 8vo. Old names on title. Contemp calf, crnrs reprd, spine faded.   *(Waterfield's)* **£235 [≈$418]**
- Observations on Reversionary Payments ... added Four Essays on different subjects ... The Fourth Edition, enlarged into Two Volumes. London: for T. Cadell, 1783. 2 vols. 8vo. Contemp tree calf, elab gilt spines, lacks 1 numbering roundel.   *(Waterfield's)* **£380 [≈$676]**
- Observations on the Nature of Civil Liberty, the Principles of Government, and the Justice and Policy of the War with America ... Third Edition. London: for T. Cadell, 1776. 1st edn, 3rd imp. 8vo. Lacks half-title. Mod qtr calf.   *(Waterfield's)* **£155 [≈$276]**
- A Review of the Principal Questions and Difficulties in Morals ... London: for A. Millar, 1758. 1st edn. 486,2 advt pp. Sm lib

stamp. Rebound in qtr calf, elab gilt spine.
(C.R. Johnson) **£2,750 [≈ $4,895]**
- A Review of the Principal Questions and
Difficulties in Morals. Particularly those
relating to the Original of our Ideas of Virtue
... London: for A. Millar, 1758. 8vo. Some
spotting endpapers. Title marg browned.
Contemp speckled calf, rubbed.
(Waterfield's) **£3,250 [≈ $5,785]**

Price, Uvedale
- An Essay on the Picturesque, as compared
with the Sublime and the Beautiful ...
London: J. Robson, 1794. 1st edn. 8vo. xv,
[1], 288 pp. 1 leaf torn at foredge. 19th c half
calf, gilt spine. *(Sotheran's)* **£500 [≈ $890]**
- An Essay on the Picturesque, as compared
with the Sublime and the Beautiful; and on
the Use of Studying Pictures for the Purpose
of Improving Real Landscape. London:
Robson, 1794. 1st edn. 8vo. xv,[i],288 pp. Sev
ff loose. Sm biro inscrptn on endpaper. Mod
mor gilt. *(Blackwell's)* **£140 [≈ $249]**
- A Letter to H. Repton, Esq. on the
Application of the Practice as well as the
Principles of Landscape-Painting to
Landscape-Gardening ... London: for J.
Robson, 1795. 1st edn. 8vo. xii,163,[i errata]
pp. Orig wraps, torn at edges, paper largely
gone from spine. *(Finch)* **£385 [≈ $685]**

Prideaux, Humphrey
- The True Nature of Imposture Fully
Display'd in the Life of Mahomet ... London:
for W. Rogers, 1697. 2nd edn, crrctd. 8vo.
xxvii, 162,180 pp. Addtnl title for the
Discourse. Contemp calf, rebacked. Wing
P.3417. *(O'Neal)* **£275 [≈ £154]**
- The True Nature of Imposture fully
displayed in the Life of Mahomet ... London:
for William Rogers, 1697. 1st edn. 8vo. iv,
xxiii, iv, 192,152 pp. Half-title. Contemp
calf, edges rubbed, spine ends strengthened
with cloth. *(Worldwide)* **£225 [≈ £126]**
- The True Nature of Imposture fully display'd
in the Life of Mahomet ... The Sixth Edition,
Corrected. London: for E. Curll, J. Hooke, T.
Caldecott, 1716. 8vo. Mod half calf.
(Waterfield's) **£45 [≈ $80]**
- The True Nature of Imposture Fully
Display'd in the Life of Mahomet ... London:
for E. Curll, 1723. 8th edn. 8vo. xvi, [iii], 260
pp. Rec half calf. *(Young's)* **£40 [≈ $71]**

Prideaux, Mathias
- An Easy and Compendious Inrtodvction [sic]
For Reading all sorts of Histories ... Sixth
Edition, Corrected and Augmented ...
Oxford: 1682. Sm 4to. [vi],156,[ii], [154]-392,

375-[382], [xxvii], 57,[iii] pp. Some marks &
marg worm. Mod old style calf. Wing P.3445.
(Finch) **£90 [≈ $160]**

Priestley, Joseph
- An Appeal to the Public, on the Subject of the
Riots in Birmingham. To which are added,
Strictures on a Pamphlet, intitled 'Thoughts
on the late Riot at Birmingham'.
Birmingham: 1792. 2nd edn. 2 vols. Sm 8vo.
Crnr vol 2 title clipped. New qtr leather.
(Whitehart) **£255 [≈ $454]**
- A Description of a Chart of Biography ... The
Seventh Edition, with Improvements.
London: for J. Johnson, 1778. 8vo. 2 fldg
tables (sm reprs). Mod qtr calf.
(Waterfield's) **£80 [≈ $142]**
- Disquisitions concerning Matter and Spirit.
London: for J. Johnson, 1777. 1st edn. 8vo.
Frontis. Q2, Q7 cancelled as usual. Contemp
sheep, mor label. *(Waterfield's)* **£300 [≈ $534]**
- Heads of Lectures on a Course of
Experimental Philosophy, particularly
including Chemistry, delivered at the New
College in Hackney. Dublin: 1794. 12mo.
208 pp. Contemp calf, lower cvr damaged.
(Robertshaw) **£55 [≈ $98]**
- Lectures on History and General Policy.
London: for J. Johnson, 1793. 2 vols. 8vo.
Fldg 'specimen of a chart' in vol 1. Contemp
half calf, leather renewed.
(Waterfield's) **£185 [≈ $329]**
- Lectures on History, and General Policy; to
which is prefixed, an Essay on a Course of
Liberal Education for Civil and Active Life.
London: 1793. 2 vols. xvi,408; vii,488 pp. 2
fldg frontis. Paper bndg with protective
plastic covering, uncut.
(Whitehart) **£350 [≈ $623]**
- A Letter to the Right Honourable William
Pitt ... on the Subjects of Toleration and
Church Establishment ... London: for J.
Johnson, 1787. 8vo. Disbound.
(Waterfield's) **£85 [≈ $151]**
- Letters to the Right Honourable Edmund
Burke, occasioned by his Reflections on the
French Revolution. Birmingham: Thomas
Pearson, 1791. 1st edn. 8vo. Few contemp
pencil marks. Mod qtr calf.
(Waterfield's) **£225 [≈ $401]**
- Letters to the Right Honourable Edmund
Burke, occasioned by his Reflections on the
Revolution in France, &c. Birmingham: ptd
by Thomas Pearson; sold by J. Johnson,
1791. 3rd edn, "corrected". 8vo. xii,[iii],
155,[1],[8 advt] pp. Contemp continental bds,
sl rubbed. *(Burmester)* **£150 [≈ $267]**

Primitive Christian Discipline ...
- Primitive Christian Discipline not to be slighted: or, Man, Look Home, and know thy Self. [London?]: 1658. 8vo. [xiv],269,[xli] pp. Few marg blind stamps. Few margs sl worn. Early notes. New calf gilt. Wing P.3469.
(Hollett) **£95 [≈$169]**

Prince ...
- The Prince of Abyssinia ... see Johnson, Samuel
- The Prince of Tunis ... see Mackenzie, Henry

Principles ...
- The Principles and Duties of Christianity ... see Wilson, Thomas

Pringle, J.
- Observations upon Diseases of the Army, in Camp and Garrison. The Second Edition, corrected with additions. London: 1753. xxvii, 403, 51 pp. Orig calf, jnts reprd.
(Whitehart) **£280 [≈$498]**

Prior, Matthew
- The Hind and Panther Transvers'd to the Story of the Country-Mouse and the City-Mouse. London: 1687. 1st edn. 4to. 28 pp. Ink notes on verso of A1 blank. Disbound. Wing P.3511. Anon.
(Robertshaw) **£25 [≈$45]**
- The Hind and the Panther Transvers'd to the Story of the Country Mouse and the City-Mouse. London: for W. Davis, 1687. 1st edn. 4to. [8],28 pp, inc intl blank leaf. Disbound. Wing P.3511. Anon. *(Hannas)* **£160 [≈$285]**
- Poems on Several Occasions. London: for Jacob Tonson, 1713. 12mo. Frontis. Endpapers stained. Contemp calf, a little worn, front jnt cracked. Anon.
(Waterfield's) **£40 [≈$71]**
- Poems on Several Occasions ... Glasgow: Robert & Andrew Foulis, 1751. 2 vols in one. 8vo. 219; 214,6,4 advt pp. Contemp calf, raised bands, gilt spine, red label, sl rubbed.
(Young's) **£40 [≈$71]**

Prior, Thomas
- An Authentic Narrative of the Success of Tar-Water in curing a Great Number and Variety of Distempers ... Dublin: R. Gunne, 1746. 1st edn. 8vo. [iv],248 pp. Some browning. Contemp calf, front hinge cracked.
(Bookpress) **$300 [≈£169]**

Private Worth ...
- Private Worth the Basis of Public Decency.

An Address to People of Rank and Fortune, dedicated to the Bishop of London. By a Member of Parliament. London: W. Richardson, 1789. 4to. 59 pp. Rec bds.
(C.R. Johnson) **£75 [≈$134]**

Proceedings ...
- The Proceedings of the Commissioners sent from the Parliament of Scotland: To the King. N.p.: [1640]. 4to. Caption title. Stitched. STC 21927.
(Rostenberg & Stern) **$90 [≈£51]**

Procopius, of Caesarea
- The History of the Warres of ... Justinian ... Englished by Henry Holcroft ... London: for Humphrey Moseley, 1653. Only edn. Folio. Addtnl engvd title. Browned. 19th c bds, rebacked. Wing P.3640.
(Vanbrugh) **£275 [≈$490]**

The Prophecy of Liberty ...
- The Prophecy of Liberty: a Poem. Humbly inscrib'd to the Right Hon. Robert Lord Romney. London: for G. Pearch, & S. Steare, 1768. 1st edn. 4to. 23,[1] pp. Half-title. Some marg damp stain. Disbound.
(Burmester) **£150 [≈$267]**

Proposal ...
- A Proposal for Humbling Spain. Written in 1711 by a Person of Distinction. And now first printed from the Manuscript ... London: for J. Roberts, [1739]. 1st edn. 8vo. viii,72 pp. Ink stains on title. Disbound.
(Hannas) **£100 [≈$178]**

The Provok'd Wife ...
- See Vanbrugh, Sir John

Pryce, William
- Archaeologia Cornu-Britannica; or, an Essay to Preserve the Ancient Cornish Language ... Sherborne: W. Cruttwell, 1790. 4to. Half-title. Sl browning. Half calf, uncut, spine v rubbed, jnts breaking.
(P and P Books) **£200 [≈$356]**

Prynne, William
- Brevia Parliamentaria in XIII Sections. London: Edward Thomas, 1662. Sm 4to. Errata leaf at end. Top edge cropped without loss. Contemp tree calf, rebacked. Wing P.3902. *(P and P Books)* **£165 [≈$294]**
- Demophilos, or the Assertor of the Peoples Liberty .. . London: for Francis Coles, 1658. 1st edn. 4to. [vi],64 pp. W'cut title border. Sl soiled or browned. Calf backed bds. Wing P.3943. *(Young's)* **£160 [≈$285]**

- The First & Second Part of the Signal Loyalty and Devotion of Gods true Saints and Pious Christians ... towards their Kings. London: Childe & Parry, 1660. 2 parts in one vol. 4to. Calf, gilt arms (rubbed). Wing P.3955.
  (Rostenberg & Stern) **£600 [≃ £337]**
- The First [to Fourth] Part[s] of a Brief Register, Kalendar and Survey of the several Kinds, Forms of all Parliamentary Writs ... London: for the author [& other imprints], 1659-64. 4 parts bound in 2 vols. Contemp calf, rebacked. Wing P.3956, 4071, 3902, 3961. *(Meyer Boswell)* **£850 [≃ £478]**
- The History of King John, King Henry III. And the most Illustrious King Edward the I. ... London: Tho. Ratcliff ..., 1670. Only edn. Large Paper. Folio. [xcii],1307,[i] pp. Contemp calf, sl worn. Wing P.3980.
  (Clark) **£250 [≃ $445]**
- An Humble Remonstrance against the Tax of Ship-Money lately imposed ... London: for Michael Sparke Senior, 1643. 1st (authorized) edn. 4to. [ii],34 pp. Mod wraps.
  (Gough) **£125 [≃ $223]**
- A New Discovery of the Prelates Tyranny. In their late Prosecution of Mr. William Prynn ... London: for M.S., 1641. 4to. 226 pp. Title soiled & reprd, errata slip pasted to verso. Occas sl marg staining. Mod calf gilt. Wing P.4108. *(Hollett)* **£75 [≃ $134]**
- A Plea for the Lords ... London: for Michael Spark, 1648. 4to. [iv],69 pp. Blind stamp on title & last leaf. A few spots. Old calf gilt, edges rubbed, rebacked. Wing P.4034.
  (Hollett) **£75 [≃ $134]**
- A Vindication of the Imprisoned and Secluded Members of the House of Commons, from the Aspersions ... in a Paper ... Intituled, An Humble Answer ... London: for Michael Spark, 1649. 1st edn. 4to. 28 pp. Disbound. Wing P.4128. Anon.
  (Young's) **£70 [≃ $125]**

Psalmanazar, George

- Memoirs of ****. Commonly known by the Name of George Psalmanazar; A Reputed Native of Formosa ... London: for R. Davis, 1765. 2nd edn. Port frontis. Old lib b'plate, minor browning. Calf gilt, extrs rubbed with some loss, sometime rebacked.
  (Francis Edwards) **£150 [≃ $267]**

The Publick Spirit of the Whigs ...

- See Swift, Jonathan

Puckle, James

- The Club; or, a Grey-Cap for a Green-Head ... The Fifth Edition, with Additions. London: for Edward Symon, 1733. 12mo.

Subscribers. Title a cancel. No frontis port. Contemp sheep, headband worn.
  (Hannas) **£75 [≃ $134]**
- England's Path to Wealth and Honour; in a Dialogue between an Englishman and a Dutchman ... Dutch Hering-Fishery [sic]. London: for F. Cogan, 1750. 8vo. [2],9-53 pp, seemingly complete. Disbound.
  (Hannas) **£55 [≃ $98]**

Pufendorf, Samuel

- An Introduction to the History of the Principal Kingdoms and States of Europe. Made English from the original ... Second Edition with Additions. London: 1697. 8vo. [vi], [vii], 515,[xi] pp. Repr to 1 crnr. Contemp calf, gilt spine chipped, sm split upper jnt. *(Francis Edwards)* **£75 [≃ $134]**
- An Introduction to the History of the principal Kingdoms and States of Europe. Begun by Baron Puffendorf [sic]. Enlarged, and continued ... by M. Martiniere ... London: Knapton, 1748. 2 vols. 8vo. Contemp calf, gilt spines, mor labels, somewhat rubbed.
  (Blackwell's) **£175 [≃ $312]**
- Of the Law of Nature and Nations. Oxford: L. Lichfield for A. & J. Churchill ..., 1703. 1st edn in English. Folio. [xxiv],400, 262,[2 errata] pp. Title foxed, few sm marg dust marks. Contemp calf, gilt spine, edges sl rubbed, spine varnished.
  (Gach) **$1,500 [≃ £843]**

Pulteney, Richard

- A General View of the Writings of Linnaeus. London: 1781. 1st edn. 8vo. iv,425, [1] pp. Mod half vellum.
  (Wheldon & Wesley) **£175 [≃ $312]**
- Historical and Biographical Sketches of the Progress of Botany in England ... London: Cadell, 1790. 1st edn. 2 vols. xx,360; viii, 352, index, 32,2 pp. Orig bds, untrimmed, vol 1 sl worn.
  (Jermy & Westerman) **£240 [≃ $427]**

Pulteney, William, Earl of Bath

- The Conduct of the Late and Present M---ry compared with an Impartial Review of Public Transactions since the Resignation of the Right Honourable Earl of Orford ... London: for T. Cooper, 1742. 1st edn. 8vo. [iv],52 pp. half-title. New bds. Anon.
  (Young's) **£35 [≃ $62]**
- The Politicks on Both Sides, with Regard to Foreign Affairs ... London: H. Haines, at Mr. Franklin's, 1734. 1st edn, with 'Erratum' on p 75. 8vo. 75 pp. Disbound. Anon.
  (Hannas) **£85 [≃ $151]**

- A Proper Answer to the By-Stander ... London: for T. Cooper, 1742. 1st edn. 8vo. [2], 78 pp. Disbound. Anon.
(Hannas) **£85 [≈ $151]**

- A Review of all that hath pass'd between the Courts of Great Britain and Spain, relating to Our Trade and Navigation from the Year 1721 ... London: for H. Goreham, 1739. 1st edn. 8vo. [4],60 pp, inc half-title. Disbound. Anon.
(Hannas) **£120 [≈ $214]**

- A Short View of the State of Affairs, with a Relation to Great Britain for Four Years Past ... London: 1730. 1st edn. 8vo. 36 pp. Disbound. Anon.
(Robertshaw) **£30 [≈ $53]**

- A State of the National Debt, as it stood December the 24th, 1716 ... London: for R. Francklin, 1727. 1st edn. 4to. Thick paper. [4],83,[29] pp, inc half-title (loose). Final leaf shaved at foredge. Disbound. Anon.
(Hannas) **£110 [≈ $196]**

Purchas, Samuel

- Purchas, His Pilgrimage, or Relations of the World and the Religions observed in All Ages and Places ... London: Henry Fetherstone, 1617. 3rd edn. Folio. [xl], "1102" [ie 1096], [40] pp. Few sm paper reprs. Later mor. STC 20507.
(Bookpress) **$1,500 [≈ £843]**

The Pursuits of Literature ...

- See Mathias, T.J.

Pye, Henry James

- Beauty, a Poetical Essay. In Three Parts. London: Becket & De Hondt, 1766. 1st edn. 4to. [2],26 pp. Disbound. Anon.
(Hannas) **£100 [≈ $178]**

Pym, John

- The Heads of a Conference delivered by Mr. Pymm, at a Committee of both Houses, Iunii 24. 1641. London: Printed in the yeare, 1641. 1st edn. Sm 4to. [i],6 pp. Sl marg browning. Mod bds. Wing P.4268.
(Blackwell's) **£60 [≈ $107]**

- The Heads of a Conference delivered by Mr. Pymm. At a Committee of both Houses, Junii 24, 1641. [London]: Printed in the Year, 1641. 1st edn. 4to. [2],6 pp. Mod wraps. Wing P.4268. Anon. *(Hannas)* **£45 [≈ $80]**

- The Speech or Declaration of John Pym, Esquire: after the Recapitulation or summing up of the Charge of High-Treason, against Thomas, Earle of Stratford, 12 April, 1641. London: Bartlet, 1641. 1st edn. Sm 4to. [i], 29 pp. Mod qtr calf. Wing P.4293.
(Blackwell's) **£130 [≈ $231]**

Quarles, Francis

- Argalus and Parthenia. London: J. Redmayne, 1677. Port frontis, addtnl engvd title (dated 1690), 29 plates. Occas sl soiling. Contemp calf, crnrs reprd, jnts tender. Wing Q.46.
(P and P Books) **£175 [≈ $312]**

- Divine Fancies, digested into Epigrams, Meditations, and Observations. The seventh Edition, Corrected. London: T.D. for John Williams, 1675. Sm 8vo. Mod mor. Wing Q.68.
(Hannas) **£85 [≈ $151]**

- Divine Poems ... Fifth Edition ... London: Jeremiah Batley, 1717. 12mo. [xii],431,[i] pp. Port frontis, addtnl engvd title, 5 plates (of 6). Sl cropped at hd, minor soiling. Later panelled calf, rubbed, sm split in 1 jnt.
(Clark) **£48 [≈ $85]**

Quarles, John

- Regale Lectum Miseriae: Or, A Kingly Bed of Miserie ... [London]: Printed in the Year, 1658. 3rd edn. Sm 8vo. [8],72 pp. Contemp calf, rebacked. Wing Q.138.
(O'Neal) **$225 [≈ £126]**

Querela Cantabrigiensis ...

- See Barwick, John

Quin, James

- The Life of Mr. James Quin, Comedian ... [Bound with his] Quin's Jests; or, the Facetious Man's Companion. London: 1766. 1st edns. 2 vols in one. 12mo. 1st title sl soiled. 19th c half calf, rubbed.
(Robertshaw) **£60 [≈ $107]**

Quincy, John

- The Dispensatory of the Royal College of Physicians in London ... London: for R. Knaplock ..., 1721. 1st edn. 8vo. [xvi], 362, [363-377] pp. Errata. Occas sl stains. Title marg sl worn. Contemp calf, crnrs bumped.
(Vanbrugh) **£255 [≈ $454]**

- Lexicon Physico-Medicum: or, a New Medical Dictionary ... The Fourth Edition, with new Improvements ... London: Osborn & Longman, 1730. 8vo. xvi,480 pp. Sm marg tear title. Contemp calf.
(Spelman) **£140 [≈ $249]**

- Pharmacopoeia Officinalis & Extemporanea: or a Complete English Dispensatory in Four Parts ... Fourth Edition, much enlarged ... London: E. Bell, 1722. 8vo. xvi,674,59 pp. Contemp panelled leather, worn but firm.
(Bates & Hindmarch) **£85 [≈ $151]**

- Pharmacopoeia Officinalis & Extemporanea: or, A Compleat English Dispensatory. The Twelfth Edition, much enlarged and

corrected. London: for Thomas Longman, 1742. 8vo. xvi, 700, ix pp. Sm reprs to title. Occas sl browning. Old calf, rebacked.
(David White) £38 [≈ $68]

- Pharmacopoeia Officinalis & Extemporanea: or, A Complete English Dispensatory, in Two Parts, Theoretic and Practical. London: 1761. 13th edn. xxiv,704,index pp. Endpapers detached & torn. Old leather, sl worn. *(Whitehart)* £120 [≈ $214]

Quincy, Samuel
- Twenty Sermons ... preached in the Parish of St. Philip, Charlestown, South Carolina. Boston, New England: John Draper, 1750. 8vo. Sm tear reprd. Contemp calf, rubbed, rebacked, crnrs reprd.
(Waterfield's) £80 [≈ $142]

Rabelais, Francois
- The Works ... formerly translated by Sir Thomas Urquart M.D. and explained by Mr Motteux ... revised ... by Mr Ozell. A New Edition, with Improvements ... London: 1750. 5 vols. 12mo. 28 plates (inc 5 frontis), 1 text engv. Contemp calf gilt, v sl worn.
(Spelman) £250 [≈ $445]
- Works ... With Explanatory Notes by M. Le Du Chat, and Others. London: for T. Evans, 1784. 4 vols. 12mo. 4 frontis, port vignette on 1st title. Contemp calf, rebacked.
(O'Neal) $175 [≈ £98]

Rackstrow, Benjamin
- An Explanation of the Figure of Anatomy, Wherein the Circulation of the Blood is made visible thro' Glass Veins and Arteries ... [London]: 1747. 2nd edn. 8vo. 15,[1] pp. Fldg plate. Unbound & uncut.
(Goodrich) $395 [≈ £222]

Radcliffe, Alexander
- The Ramble: An Anti-Heroick Poem. Together with some Terrestrial Hymns and Carnal Ejaculations. London: for the author, sold by Walter Davis, 1682. 1st edn. 8vo. Lacks intl blank. Sl used, occas scribbles. Contemp calf, rebacked. Wing R.129.
(Hannas) £280 [≈ $498]

Radcliffe, Ann
- The Italian, or the Confessional of the Black Penitents. London: Cadell & Davies, 1797. 1st edn. 3 vols in 2. 12mo. Frontises inserted in vols 1 & 2. Occas sl stains. Late 19th c half calf. *(Hannas)* £280 [≈ $498]
- The Italian, or the Confessional of the Black Penitents. A Romance. London: for Cadell & Davies, 1797. 2nd edn. 3 vols. 12mo. 19th c

polished calf, contrasting labels, 2 jnts reprd.
(Burmester) £90 [≈ $160]
- A Journey made in the Summer of 1794, through Holland and the Western Frontier of Germany ... London: Robinson, 1795. 4to. Lacks half-title. Sm marg worm hole in 2 prelims. Occas sl browning. Contemp half russia, sl worn. *(Rankin)* £160 [≈ $285]
- The Mysteries of Udolpho, a Romance ... Second Edition. London: Robinson, 1794. 4 vols. 12mo. Half-titles in vols 2-4 (lacking in vol 1). Occas minor marg tears. Contemp half calf, rebacked. *(Hannas)* £250 [≈ $445]
- A Sicilian Romance. By the Authoress of the Castles of Athlin and Dunbayne ... Second Edition. London: for Hookham & Carpenter, 1792. 2 vols. 12mo. [iv],239; [iv],216 pp. Half-titles. Sl wear & tear. Antique style qtr calf. Anon. *(Finch)* £140 [≈ $249]

Radcliffe, John
- Dr. Radcliffe's Life and Letters, with A True Copy of his Last Will and Testament ... London: for E. Curll, 1716. 3rd edn. 8vo. [iv], 100 pp. Edges browned. Early scribbles on title. New calf. *(Young's)* £85 [≈ $151]

Rae, Peter
- The History of the late Rebellion; Rais'd against His Majesty King George ... 'Drumfries': Robert Rae, 1716. 1st edn. xiv, 388,8 index pp. Pp 49-52 sl defective. Occas worm hole. Contemp calf, red label, rubbed.
(Jermy & Westerman) £90 [≈ $160]

Raffald, Elizabeth
- The Experienced English Housekeeper ... Ninth Edition ... London: for R. Baldwin, 1784. 8vo. viii,384,[13] pp. Port, 3 fldg plates. Raffald's signature printed across the heading of Chapter 1. Half mor, by Bayntun.
(Gough) £375 [≈ $668]

Raleigh, Sir Walter
- An Abridgement of Sir Walter Raleigh's History of the World ... added, His Premonition to Princes. London: Gillyflower, Bell, 1698. 1st edn of this version. 8vo. [liv], 415,[3] pp. Errata leaf A2 bound at end. Port. Browned. Contemp calf, sl marked. Wing R.151. *(Clark)* £160 [≈ $285]
- An Abridgment [by Laurence Echard] of Sir Walter Raleigh's History of the World ... added, His Premonition to Princes. London: Gillyflower, Bell, 1698. 1st edn of this version. 8vo. Errata leaf. Port. Contemp calf, rebacked. Wing R.151.
(Hannas) £65 [≈ $116]
- The Cabinet-Council: Containing the Cheif

[sic] Arts of Empire, and Mysteries of State ... Published by John Milton. London: Tho. Newcomb, 1658. 1st edn. Issue with p 123 correctly numbered. 12mo. [8],200 pp. Frontis port. Old calf, rebacked, rubbed. Mor case. Wing R.156. *(Karmiole)* **$750 [≃ £421]**

- The History of the World. London: 1614. 1st edn. Thick folio. Errata leaf. Colophon. Engvd title. Frontis poem, 7 (of 8) maps. Lacks ptd title & final blank. Old calf, sometime rebacked, jnts cracked.
  (Petrilla) **$1,100 [≃ £618]**

- The History of the World. London: 1614. 1st edn. Thick folio. Errata leaf. Colophon. Engvd title. Frontis poem, 7 (of 8) maps. Lacks ptd title & final blank. Old calf, sometime rebacked, jnts cracked.
  (Petrilla) **$1,100 [≃ £618]**

- The History of the World. London: for R. Best ..., 1652. 1st edn. Sm thick folio. 555, 669, [55] pp. 8 maps. 19th c mor gilt, a.e.g., by Manderson of Brighton, 1 crnr bumped.
  (Chapel Hill) **$900 [≃ £506]**

- The Works ... prefix'd, A new Account of his Life by Tho. Birch. London: Dodsley, 1751. 2 vols. 8vo. [ii],cxx,280,[ii]; [ii], 400 pp. Port frontis vol 1. Contemp calf, rather worn.
  (Finch) **£75 [≃ $134]**

Raleigh, Revd Walter
- Reliquiae Raleighianae, being Discourses and Sermons on several Subjects. London: Macock for Hindmarsh, 1679. Only coll edn. 4to. [xiv],404 pp. No imprimatur leaf. Some stains, sm tears. Contemp calf, rebacked, recrnrd. Wing R.192. *(Clark)* **£65 [≃ $116]**

Ralph, James
- The Muses' Address to the King: an Ode. London: for J. Meadows, 1728. 1st edn. 8vo. [1],v,[1],43 pp, inc half-title. Disbound.
  (Hannas) **£100 [≃ $178]**

The Rambler ...
- See Johnson, Samuel

Ramsay, Allan
- The Ever Green, being a Collection of Scots Poems, wrote by the Ingenious before 1600. Edinburgh: for Alexander Donaldson, 1761. 2nd edn. 2 vols. 12mo. Contemp calf, gilt spines, lacks 1 label. *(Hannas)* **£180 [≃ $320]**
- The Gentle Shepherd ... Edinburgh: ptd by Robert and Richard Wilson, for J. Wood and W. Darling, 1776. 8vo. Port frontis, 5 plates. Few sm reprs, occas minor browning. Rec calf backed bds. *(Vanbrugh)* **£75] [≃ $134]**
- The Gentle Shepherd. A Pastoral Comedy.

Glasgow: A. Foulis, sold by D. Allan ..., 1788. 4to. 18 pp music. Port, 12 plates. Contemp half calf, worn, rebacked.
  (Hannas) **£75 [≃ $134]**
- The Gentle Shepherd: a Scots Pastoral Comedy. Edinburgh: Geo. Reid & Co., 1798. 8vo. Later wraps. *(Waterfield's)* **£40 [≃ $71]**
- Poems. London: A. Millar & W. Johnston, 1751. 2 vols. 8vo. xiv,[ii],238; [iv], 307, [xxv] pp. Port frontis. Contemp calf, sl worn, lacks labels. *(Clark)* **£30 [≃ $53]**
- Poems. Glasgow: for Peter Tait, 1770. 8vo. Early 19th c diced calf, mrbld endpapers.
  (Waterfield's) **£125 [≃ $223]**
- The Tea-Table Miscellany: A Collection of Choice Songs, Scots and English. Edinburgh: J. Dickson, 1775. 2 vols in one. Sm 8vo. 252; 259, glossary pp. Calf, old reback, shelf wear.
  (Hartfield) **£165 [≃ £93]**
- The Tea-Table Miscellany; a Collection of Choice Songs, Scots and English. Edinburgh: for J. Dickson, 1775. 2 vols in one. 12mo. Some soiling. Contemp sheep, rubbed.
  (Claude Cox) **£28 [≃ $50]**

Ramsay, David
- The History of the American Revolution. Dublin: William Jones, 1795. 2 vols in one. Continuously paginated. Contemp tree calf, black label, ft of spine sl chipped, hinges weakening. *(C.R. Johnson)* **£145 [≃ $258]**

Ramsay, William Michael, 'The Chevalier'
- The Travels of Cyrus. To which is annex'd, A Discourse upon the Theology and Mythology of the Pagans. Dublin: Wm. Smith, 1763. 9th edn. 12mo. xxiv,311,[1 advt] pp. Early polished calf gilt, some wear to spine & jnts. *(Hartfield)* **$295 [≃ £166]**

Randall, John
- The Semi-Virgilian Husbandry, deduced from Various Experiments: or, an Essay towards a New Course of National Farming ... London: B. Law ..., 1764. 1st edn. 8vo. lxiii,[i], 356, 11, [i] pp. 3 plates. Contemp calf, gilt dec spine (ends chipped).
  (Clark) **£200 [≃ $356]**

Randolph, Thomas
- Poems: with the Muses looking glasse and Amyntas, whereunto is added The Jealous Lovers ... fifth edition, with several additions, corrected and amended. Oxford: for F. Bowman, sold by John Crosley, 1668. 8vo. 19th c calf, rebacked. Wing R.246.
  (Waterfield's) **£100 [≃ $178]**

The Rape of the Smock ...
- See Jacob, Giles

Rapin, Rene
- The Comparison of Plato and Aristotle. With the Opinions of the Fathers on their Doctrine ... London: T.R. & N.T. for Dorman Newman ..., 1673. 1st edn in English. 8vo. Intl licence leaf. Mod bds. Wing B.260.
(Ximenes) **$250 [≈£140]**
- The Modest Critick: or Remarks upon the most Eminent Historians, Antient and Modern ... By one of the Society of the Port-Royal. London: John Barnes, 1689. 8vo. [xxiv],151 pp. Licence leaf. 19th c calf, jnts cracking, sl rubbed. Wing R.264. Anon.
(Blackwell's) **£60 [≈$107]**
- Reflections upon the Eloquence of these Times; particularly of the Barr and Pulpit. London: Thomas Sawbridge, 1672. 1st English edn, variant issue. Sm 8vo. [16],160 pp. Licence leaf & final blank. Sl marks. Rec calf. Wing R.274A. *(Spelman)* **£95 [≈$169]**

Rawlet, John
- Poetick Miscellanies of Mr. John Rawlet, B.D. and late Lecturer of S. Nicholas Church in the Town and County of New-castle upon Tine. London: Tidmarsh, 1687. 1st edn. 8vo. [ii], ii,[ii], 143,[i] pp. Port. Sl used. Contemp sheep, rebacked. Wing R.358.
(Clark) **£125 [≈$223]**

Rawlinson, John
- Quadriga Salutis. Foure Quadragesimal, or Lent-Sermons, preached at White-Hall. Oxford: 1625. 1st edn. 4to. Orig wraps, uncut. STC 20774.
(Robertshaw) **£75 [≈$134]**

Rawlinson, Richard
- The English Topographer ... Alphabetically Digested ... London: for T. Jauncy, 1720. xliv, 275,[13] pp. 10 text engvs. Mod calf gilt. Anon. *(Hollett)* **£120 [≈$214]**
- The English Topographer ... London: T. Jauncy, 1720. 1st edn. 8vo. [viii],xliv, 275, [13] pp. Contemp calf, spine extrs sl chipped.
(Bookpress) **$550 [≈£309]**

Ray, John
- A Collection of English Proverbs ... Second Edition, Enlarged ... Cambridge: John Hayes for W. Morden, 1678. Sm 8vo. [viii],414 pp. Lacks final advt leaf. Some discoloration throughout. 18th c sheep, 19th c reback, spine worn & rubbed. Wing R.387.
(Blackwell's) **£160 [≈$285]**

- A Compleat Collection of English proverbs ... added A Collection of English Words not generally used. London: 1768. 4th edn. 8vo. xv,319, 350 pp. Contemp calf, 1 jnt cracked.
(Wheldon & Wesley) **£120 [≈$214]**
- Select Remains of the Learned John Ray. With his Life by William Derham. London: 1760. 8vo. vii,336 pp. Frontis port, 3 text engvs. Lacks errata slip. Contemp calf, rebacked, crnrs reprd.
(Weiner) **£180 [≈$320]**

Raymond, John
- An Itinerary contayning a Voyage made through Italy in the Yeare 1646, and 1647. London: 1648. 1st edn. 12mo. Errata & imprimatur ff. Addtnl engvd title, text engvs. Lacks last leaf, probably blank. Mod period style mor. Wing R.415.
(D & D Galleries) **$750 [≈£421]**

Raynal, Guillaume Thomas Francois
- The Revolution of America. London: for Lockyer Davis, 1781. 1st edn in English. 8vo. xvi,181,[i],[2 advt] pp. Occas spotting. Contemp sprinkled calf, gilt dec smooth spine, mor label, hd of spine sl worn.
(Finch) **£275 [≈$490]**

Rea [or Ray], John
- Flora: seu De Florum Cultura. Or a Complete Florilege ... With many Additions ... London: for George Marriott, 1676. 2nd edn. Folio. [xxiv],231, [232-239] pp. 'Mind of front' leaf. Frontis, 8 plates, 2 text engvs. Contemp calf, front hinge cracked, crnrs bumped. Wing R.422. *(Vanbrugh)* **£655 [≈$1,166]**
- Flora: seu, de Florum Cultura. or, a Complete Florilege furnished with all Requisites belonging to a Florist. London: 1676. 2nd edn. Folio. [xxvi],231,[9] pp. 'Mind of the Front' leaf. Frontis, 3 engvd headpieces, 8 plates of 16 plans. Contemp calf, worn, rebacked.
(Wheldon & Wesley) **£600 [≈$1,068]**

Read, Alexander
- The Workes of that famous Physitian [sic] Dr. Alexander Read ... Third Edition. London: E.T. for Richard Thrale, 1659. Sm 4to. [8], 524, [6] pp. Lacks Nn2-4. Lacks A1 (blank?). Title reprd. Some browning. Contemp calf, 19th c reback. Wing R.426.
(Spelman) **£200 [≈$356]**

Reasonableness ...
- The Reasonableness of Parliamentary Proceedings, by Attainders, Banishments, Pains and Penalties, in Cases of High

Treason, Shewn by Various Precedents ...
London: T. Payne, 1723. Only edn. 8vo. [iv],
48 pp. Half-title. Disbound.
(Young's) **£50 [≈ $89]**

Reasons ...

- Reasons for a War; From the Imminent
Danger with which Europe is threatened, by
the Exorbitant Power of the House of
Bourbon ... London: for W. Mears, 1734. 2nd
edn. 8vo. viii, 56 pp. Disbound.
(Young's) **£120 [≈ $214]**

- Reasons for Giving up Gibraltar ... With an
Appendix, containing Extracts of the
Addresses to the Throne ... regarding the
Importance of Gibraltar. London: for W.
Webb, 1749. 1st edn. 8vo. vi,74 pp. Fldg
plan. Disbound.   *(Hannas)* **£110 [≈ $196]**

- Reasons Why This Kingdome ought to
adhere to the Parliament. [London: 1642].
4to. Caption title. Typographical headpiece.
Stitched. Wing R.592.
(Rostenberg & Stern) **$125 [≈ £70]**

The Rebels Doom ...

- The Rebels Doom: or, an Historical Account
of the Most remarkable Rebellions from
Edward the Confessor's Reign to this Present
Wicked Rebellion of Monmouth ... London:
1685. 4to. 100, [4 ctlg] pp. Mod half calf.
Wing R.600.   *(Robertshaw)* **£60 [≈ $107]**

Record ...

- A Record of Some VVorthie Proceedings: in
the Honorable, Wise, and Faithfvll Hovse of
Commons in the Parliament holden in the
yeare, 1611 .. London: Printed in the Yeare,
1641. 1st edn. Sm 4to. [v],41 pp. Occas sl
browning. Mod qtr calf. Wing E.2698.
(Blackwell's) **£65 [≈ $116]**

Record, Robert

- Record's Arithmetick: or, The Ground of
Arts ... London: James Flesher, 1654. 8vo.
[xxiv], 629,[i] pp. Minor worming at end,
affecting a few letters. Occas sl staining. Few
headlines cropped. Contemp sheep, rubbed.
Wing R.644.   *(Clark)* **£280 [≈ $498]**

- The Urinall of Physicke. London: Thomas
Dawson, 1599. 8vo. Black Letter. 3 w'cuts.
Lacks last 2 ff (k7-8). Marg reprs to title.
Some soiling & staining. 19th c calf, rebacked.
STC 20819.   *(Goodrich)* **$1,650 [≈ £927]**

Rede, Leman Thomas

- Bibliotheca Americana; or, A Catalogue of
the most Curious and Interesting Books ...
upon the subject of North and South America
... London: Debrett, 1789. 4to. 271 pp.

Errata. Contemp tree calf, rebacked. Anon.
(C.R. Johnson) **£750 [≈ $1,335]**

Reeve, Clara

- The Old English Baron: A Gothic Story.
Fourth Edition. London: 1789. 12mo.
Frontis. Some offsetting on title. New calf.
Anon.   *(Robertshaw)* **£65 [≈ $116]**

Reeve, Joseph

- Ugbrooke Park: A Poem. London: for J.
Robson & Co., 1776. 1st edn. 4to. 29 pp.
Engv on title. Title dust soiled. Disbound.
Anon.   *(Hannas)* **£180 [≈ $320]**

Reflections ...

- Reflections and Considerations occasioned by
the Petition presented to the Honourable
House of Commons, for Taking off the
Drawback on Foreign Linens, &c. London:
for T. Cooper, 1738. 1st edn. 8vo. 28 pp.
Half-title. Disbound. *(Young's)* **£130 [≈ $231]**

- Reflections on a Late Speech by the Lord
Haversham, in so far as it relates to the Affairs
of Scotland ... In a Letter to a Friend.
London: B. Bragg, 1704. 1st edn. 4to. 32 pp.
Disbound. Anon. Attributed to Daniel Defoe
by Morgan.   *(Hannas)* **£50 [≈ $89]**

- Reflections on a Paper, Pretending to be an
Apology for the Failures charged on Mr.
Walker's Account of the Siege of London-
Derry. London: for Robert Clavel, 1689. 1st
edn. 4to. 20 pp. Sl browned. Wrappers. Wing
R.695.   *(Young's)* **£110 [≈ $196]**

- Reflections on Dr. Swift's Letter to the Earl
of Oxford ... see Oldmixon, John

- Reflections   upon   Naturalization,
Corporations, and Companies; supported by
the Authorities of both Ancient and Modern
Writers. By a Country Gentleman. London:
M. Cooper, 1753. [2],91,[1] pp. Half-title.
Rec qtr calf.   *(C.R. Johnson)* **£300 [≈ $534]**

- Reflections upon Tithes ... see Scrope, John

The Reformation. A Comedy ...

- See Arrowsmith, Joseph

Regnault, Noel

- Philosophical Conversations: or, a New
System of Physics, by Way of Dialogue.
Translated into English and illustrated with
Notes by Thomas Dale, M.D. London: for
W. Innys ..., 1731. 1st edn in English. 3 vols.
8vo. 89 plates. Contemp calf, spines rubbed,
sl wear at ends.   *(Burmester)* **£450 [≈ $801]**

Reid, Thomas

- Essays on the Intellectual Powers of Man.

Edinburgh: for Bell & Robinson, London, 1785. 1st edn. 4to. xii,766 pp. Sl browning. Mod buckram. *(Gach)* **$850 [≈ £478]**

Relation ...
- A Relation of the Defeating Card. Mazarine & Oliv. Cromwel's Design to have taken Ostend by Treachery, In the Year, 1658. Written in Spanish by a Person of Quality ... London: Herringman, 1666. Only edn. 12mo. [x],132 pp. Lacks intl blank. Contemp calf, sl worn. Wing R.821. *(Clark)* **£85 [≈ $151]**

The Religion of Nature Delineated ...
- See Wollaston, William

Remarks ...
- Remarks upon some Wrong Computations and Conclusions, contained in a late Tract entitled, Discourses on the Public Revenue, and on the Trade of England. London: 1698. 1st edn. 8vo. 47 pp. Disbound. Wing R.947. *(Robertshaw)* **£50 [≈ $89]**

Remond des Cours, Nicolas
- The True Conduct of Persons of Quality. Translated out of French. London: for Walter Kettilby, 1694. 1st edn in English. 8vo. Errata leaf at end. Title dusty, some foxing. Early 19th c calf gilt, a.e.g., rubbed, front jnt weak. Wing R.958A. Anon. *(Ximenes)* **$450 [≈ £253]**

Remonstrance ...
- A Remonstrance of the Lords and Commons Assembled in Parliament, or The Reply ... to ... His Majesties Answer to ... A Remonstrance. London: Wright, 1642. 4to. Stitched. Wing E.2220. *(Rostenberg & Stern)* **$150 [≈ £84]**
- A Remonstrance of the State of the Kingdom. London: Hunscott, 1641. 4to. Stitched. Wing E.2221A. *(Rostenberg & Stern)* **$200 [≈ £112]**
- The Remonstrance of the Commissioners of the Generall Assembly of Scotland to the Great Convention. London: Paine & Simmons, 1643. 4to. Stitched. *(Rostenberg & Stern)* **$100 [≈ £56]**

Renaudot, Eusebius
- Ancient Accounts of India and China, by Two Mohammedan Travellers. Who went to those parts in the 9th Century. Translated from the Arabic ... with Notes ... London: 1733. xxxviii, 100, 260,[xii] pp. Some marg damp staining. Early calf gilt, rebacked, rubbed. *(Hollett)* **£200 [≈ $356]**

Rennell, James
- Memoir of a Map of Hindoostan; or the Mogul Empire ... London: the author, 1792. 2nd edn. 4to. cxli,428 pp. 5 maps. Contemp tree calf, rebacked, new endpapers. *(Bates & Hindmarch)* **£230 [≈ $409]**

Repton, Humphry
- A Letter to Uvedale Price, Esq. London: 1794. 8vo. 20 pp. Cloth. *(Wheldon & Wesley)* **£85 [≈ $151]**

Reresby, Tamworth
- A Miscellany of Ingenious Thoughts and Reflections, In Verse and Prose ... London: H. Meere for the author, 1721. 1st edn. 4to. [viii],422,[2] pp. Occas spotting & staining. Calf gilt, rebacked in sheep, sides worn, crnrs bumped. *(Finch)* **£95 [≈ $169]**
- A Miscellany of Ingenious Thoughts and Reflections, In Verse and Prose ... London: H. Mears, 1721. 4to. Some sl marg spotting. Contemp qtr calf. *(Waterfield's)* **£225 [≈ $401]**

Resolutions ...
- The Resolutions of the Agitators of the Army concerning the Prosecution of their late Remonstrances against the sitting of the late Usurpers of Parliamentary Power ... London: Field, 1647. 4to. Stitched. Wing R.1143. *(Rostenberg & Stern)* **$85 [≈ £48]**

Reynolds, Edward
- A Treatise of the Passions and Faculties of the Soul of Man ... London: for Robert Bostock, 1647. 2nd edn. 4to. xviii,324, 391-553 pp. 2 lib stamps. Date altered in ink. Contemp sheep, headcap reprd. Wing R.1294. *(Gaskell)* **£550 [≈ $979]**

Reynolds, Henry Revell
- An Address to the Ladies from a Young Man. London: for J. Parsons, 1796. 1st edn. 8vo. Sl browning, writing on title. Disbound. Anon. *(Hannas)* **£180 [≈ $320]**

Reynolds, Sir Joshua
- Seven Discourses delivered in the Royal Academy by the President ... London: Cadell, 1778. 1st coll edn. 8vo. [vii],[i]-iv, 5-326, [ii] pp. Half-title & title faintly stained at hd, sm sl stains in lower gutter crnr throughout. Contemp calf, rebacked. *(Blackwell's)* **£175 [≈ $312]**

Rhodes, Benjamin
- A Concise English Grammar, rendered easy to every capacity ... Birmingham: J. Belcher,

1795. Fcap 8vo. vi,[i],8-204 pp. Contemp calf, rebacked.   *(Spelman)* £95 [≈ $169]

Riccoboni, Lewis
- An Historical and Critical Account of the Theatres in Europe ... London: for T. Waller, 1741. 1st English edn. 8vo. [xvi],333,[18] pp. Contemp calf, rebacked.
(Young's) £195 [≈ $347]

Rich, Henry, Earl of Holland
- A Declaration Made to the Kingdome. London: 1643. 4to. Wraps. Wing H.2419.
(Rostenberg & Stern) $85 [≈ £48]

Rich, Robert
- A Letter ... to the Right Honourable Lord Viscount Barrington, His Majesty's Secretary at War ... London: for P. Mitchell, 1775. 1st edn. 4to. [ii],63, xxv,[1 errata] pp. Appendix & table. Disbound.   *(Young's)* £70 [≈ $125]

Richard, John
- A Tour from London to Petersburgh, and from thence to Moscow. [Dublin]: 1781. 1st Dublin edn. 8vo. viii,[viii],220 pp. Frontis, engvd title vignette. 3 ff sl soiled. Rec qtr vellum.   *(Young's)* £245 [≈ $436]

Richardson, Gabriel
- Of the State of Europe, XIII Bookes. Containing the Historie, and Relation of the Many Provinces Hereof ... Oxford: H. Cripps, 1627. 1st edn. Sm folio. Some library use. Contemp calf, rebacked. STC 21020.
(O'Neal) $350 [≈ £197]

Richardson, John
- An Account of that Ancient Servant of Christ John Richardson ...in the Ministry in England, Ireland, America ... London: Mary Hinde, 1774. 3rd edn. 8vo. 242 pp. Sheep, new label.   *(Hartfield)* £195 [≈ £110]
- The Canon of the New Testament Vindicated: in Answer to the Objections of J.T. in his Amyntor. London: for Richard Sare, 1700. 1st edn. 8vo. Contemp mottled sheep, sl wear spine ends. Wing R.1384.
(Ximenes) $150 [≈ £84]

Richardson, Jonathan
- An Essay on the Theory of Painting. The Second Edition, Enlarg'd and Corrected. London: for A.C. & sold by A. Bettesworth, 1725. 8vo. viii,279 pp. Contemp calf, backstrip relaid.   *(Spelman)* £220 [≈ $392]
- The Works ... Theory of Painting ... Art of Criticism ... The Science of a Connoisseur ... Strawberry-Hill: 1792. 1st Strawberry-Hill

edn. 4to. [viii],(5)-287 pp. 12 ports (1 sepia washed on recto). Lacks half-title. Contemp calf, rebacked. Hazen 10.1 state a.
(Blackwell's) £160 [≈ $285]

Richardson, Samuel, Baptist minister
- Of the Torments of Hell. The Foundation and Pillars thereof Discovered, Searched, Shaken and Removed ... London: W. Boreham, [ca 1720]. 8vo in 4s. 56 pp. Marg worm, minor soil. Disbound. Anon.
(Clark) £35 [≈ $62]

Richardson, Samuel
- The History of Sir Charles Grandison. In a Series of Letters. London: Rivington ..., 1766. 5th edn. 7 vols in 4. 12mo. Intl advt leaf vol 7. Port vol 1. 19th c half calf, gilt spines, rubbed.   *(Ximenes)* $250 [≈ £140]
- The History of Sir Charles Grandison ... The Seventh Edition. London: for John Donaldson, sold by T. Wilson at York ..., 1774. Pirated edn. 8 vols. 12mo. Port. Contemp calf, some spines v sl affected by worm.   *(Hannas)* £140 [≈ $249]

Richardson, William
- Essays on Shakespeare's Dramatic Characters ... The Second Edition. London: for J. Murray, 1785. Sm 8vo. Contemp calf, worn.
(Hannas) £45 [≈ $80]
- Essays on some of Shakespeare's Characters. To which is added, and Essay on the Faults of Shakespeare. The Fifth Edition. London: Murray & Highley, 1797. 8vo. vi, [ii], 401,[i] pp. Port frontis. 19th c half mor, gilt spine.   *(Clark)* £60 [≈ $107]
- A Philosophical Analysis and Illustration of Some of Shakespeare's Remarkable Characters. The Third Edition, Corrected. London: for J. Murray, 1784. Sm 8vo. Title marked. Contemp calf. *(Hannas)* £30 [≈ $53]

Richers, Thomas
- The History of the Royal Genealogy of Spain ... Made English from the French Copy ... With several useful Notes ... London: James Round, 1724. 1st edn. 8vo. [viii],xxii, [2],437,[1] pp. 14 pp subscribers. Port. Contemp calf.   *(Young's)* £120 [≈ $214]

Ridley, Gloucester
- The Life of Dr. Nicholas Ridley, sometime Bishop of London ... London: J. Whiston & B. White, 1763. 1st edn. 4to. xxvi,689 pp. Port. Contemp speckled calf, elab gilt spine, mor label, front jnt weak, crnrs bumped.
(Blackwell's) £75 [≈ $134]
- A Review of Mr. Phillip's History of the Life

of Reginald Pole. London: Whiston, White, Dodsley, 1766. 8vo. viii,374 pp. Fldg pedigree. Sl discoloration. Contemp calf, jnts beginning to crack. *(Blackwell's)* **£45 [≈$80]**

Rimius, Henry

- A Candid Narrative of the Rise and Progress of the Herrnhuters, commonly called Moravians, or Unitas Fratrum ... Phila: William Bradford, 1753. 1st Amer edn. 12mo. [2], 5-112 pp. Title & last p sl damp stained. Orig ptd wraps, disbound.
(Chapel Hill) **$1,500 [≈£843]**

Ritson, Joseph

- Robin Hood: a Collection of all the Ancient Poems, Songs, and Ballads ... London: for Egerton & Johnson, 1795. 1st edn. 2 vols. 8vo. Vignettes by Bewick. Contemp tree calf, gilt spines, contrasting labels, some rubbing, 1 jnt tender, 1 label sl chipped. Anon.
(Ximenes) **£325 [≈£183]**

Riverius, Lazarus

- The Universal Body of Physick, In five Books ... Translated by William Carr. London: Henry Eversden, 1657. 1st edn. Sm folio. [xiv], 1-236, 257-417,[4] pp, inc 2 fldg tables (sl worn). Occas sl marks. Old calf, rebacked. Wing R.1567. *(David White)* **£435 [≈$774]**

Robbins, N.

- An Exact Abridgement of all the Irish Statutes, from ... Edward II to the End of the Eighth Year of the Reign of ... George II. Dublin: 1736. 1st edn. 4to. [6],770,[98] pp. Sl marks. Contemp calf, sl worn.
(Claude Cox) **£45 [≈$80]**

Roberts, Alexander

- An Exposition upon the hundred and thirtie Psalme gathered out of some of the Ancient Fathers and later writers. London: Iohn Winder for Robert Runckworth, 1610. 8vo. Few sidenotes in last gathering narrowly shaved. Later wraps. STC 21073.
(Waterfield's) **£40 [≈$71]**

Roberts, William

- The Looker-On: a Periodical Paper. By Simon Olive-Branch, A.M. [pseudonym]. London: Egerton, Murray, Richardson, 1792-93. 1st edn. Folio. Complete run of the 86 numbers. Contemp half russia, jnts sl cracked but sound.
(Burmester) **£240 [≈$427]**

Roberts, William Hayward

- Poems by Dr. Roberts of Eton College.

London: for J. Wilkie, T. Payne ..., 1774. 1st coll edn. 8vo. Contemp spanish calf gilt.
(Hannas) **£65 [≈$116]**

- A Poetical Epistle, to Christopher Anstey, Esq; on the English Poets, chiefly those who have written in Blank Verse. London: For Wilkie, Payne ..., 1773. 1st edn. 4to. [3]-18 pp. Lacks half-title & final advt leaf. Disbound. Anon. *(Hannas)* **£40 [≈$71]**

Robertson, Archibald

- A Topographical Survey of the Great Road from London to Bath and Bristol ... In Two Parts. London: for the author ..., 1792. Only edn. Half-title in vol 1 only, correctly. 11 maps, 65 aquatint views with grey wash. Straight grain red mor gilt extra by Zaehnsdorf. *(Blackwell's)* **£800 [≈$1,424]**

Robertson, John

- Rusticus ad Clericum or, the Plow-Man rebuking the Priest ... [Edinburgh: John Reid,] Printed in the Year, 1694. 8vo. "375" [ie 365],[iii] pp. Final errata leaf. Sm tear, sm paper flaw. Contemp sheep, extrs worn, no free endpapers. Wing R.1607.
(Clark) **£150 [≈$267]**

Robertson, Joseph

- An Essay on Punctuation. London: for J. Walter, 1785. 1st edn. 12mo. [xii],177 pp. Half-title. 19th c half calf. Anon.
(Burmester) **£175 [≈$312]**

- An Essay on Punctuation. London: for J. Walter, 1785. 177,[2 advt] pp. Half-title. Contemp calf, brown label. Anon.
(C.R. Johnson) **£225 [≈$401]**

Robertson, R.

- An Essay on Fevers ... and the Cure Established on Philosophical Induction. London: 1740. xvi,286 pp. Lib marks on title & endpaper. Sl foxing on endpapers & half-title. Contemp mrbld bds, sl marked, rebacked in cloth. *(Whitehart)* **£90 [≈$160]**

Robertson, William

- An Historical Disquisition concerning the Knowledge which the Ancients had of India ... London: for A. Strahan, 1791. 1st edn. 4to. xii, 364,[10] pp. 2 fldg maps. Contemp qtr calf, rebacked. *(Young's)* **£85 [≈$151]**

- The History of America. London: Strahan ..., 1792. 6th edn. 3 vols. 8vo. Fldg plate, 4 fldg maps. Contemp speckled calf, gilt ruled spines, red labels, green numbering pieces, trivial rubbing upper cvr vol 3.
(Frew Mackenzie) **£250 [≈$445]**

- The History of the Reign of the Emperor

Charles V ... London: Strahan, 1769. 1st edn.
3 vols. 4to. Half-titles. Vol 1 half-title sl soiled
on recto. Contemp pale speckled calf, elab gilt
spines & labels, vol 1 jnt ends splitting at
ends, extrs sl rubbed.
(Blackwell's) **£300 [≈ $534]**

- Phraseologia Generalis. A full, large, and
general Phrase Book ... Cambridge: John
Hayes, 1681. Thick 8vo. [6],1366 pp. Intl
advt leaf. End ff sl chipped & soiled. Rec qtr
calf, vellum crnrs. STC 1616.
(Spelman) **£260 [≈ $463]**

Robin Hood ...
- Robin Hood: a Collection of all the Ancient
Poems ... see Ritson, Joseph
- Robin Hood's Garland. Being a Complete
History of all the Notable and Merry Exploits
performed by him and his men ... added a
Preface ... Nottingham: 1794. 8vo. [2],62 pp.
W'cut ills. Some marks & v sl marg worm.
Later cloth, spine worn.
(Spelman) **£70 [≈ $125]**

Robins, Benjamin
- An Address to the Electors, and other Free
Subjects of Great Britain; occasion'd by the
Late Secession ... London: for H. Goreham,
1739. 1st edn. 8vo. iv,63 pp. Title sl dust
soiled. Disbound.   *(Hannas)* **£75 [≈ $134]**
- Observations on the Present Convention with
Spain. London: for T. Cooper, 1739. 1st edn.
8vo. [4],60 pp, inc half-title (bound after
title). Disbound. Anon.
(Hannas) **£65 [≈ $116]**

Robinson, Hugh
- Scholae Wintonensis Phrases Latinae. The
Latine Phrases of Winchester Schoole.
Corrected, and much augmented ... Fifth
Edition, with many additions ... London: for
Anne Mosely, 1667. 396 pp. Old ink notes.
Contemp calf. Wing R.1685.
(C.R. Johnson) **£75 [≈ $134]**

Robinson, John
- An Account of Sweden. London: Goodwin,
1694. 8vo. Calf, front cvr detached. Wing
R.1690. Anon.
(Rostenberg & Stern) **$250 [≈ £140]**

Robinson, Robert
- Political Catechism. London: for J. Buckland,
C. Dilly ..., 1782. 1st edn. 8vo. Mod qtr calf.
Anon.   *(Waterfield's)* **£75 [≈ $134]**

Robinson, Thomas
- The Anatomie of the English Nunnery at
Lisbon in Portugall. Second Edition.

[London]: 1628. 8vo. Title engv. Later half
calf, spine worn. STC 21124. Anon.
(Robertshaw) **£160 [≈ $285]**

Robison, John
- Proofs of a Conspiracy against all the
Religions and Governments of Europe,
carried on in the Secret Meetings of Free
Masons ... Third Edition, corrected. London:
Cadell & Davies ..., 1798. 8vo. Cancel leaf
*g4. Orig bds, sl worn.
(Blackwell's) **£75 [≈ $134]**

Rochester, John Wilmot, Earl of
- Poems, (&c.) On Several Occasions: with
Valentinian; a Tragedy ... London: Tonson,
1696. 8vo. [x],xxii,224 pp. Some browning &
staining. Contemp calf, new label, spine ends
worn, extrs rubbed.   *(Finch)* **£300 [≈ $534]**

Rochon, A.
- A Voyage to Madagascar, and the East Indies
translated from the French. Illustrated with
Accurate Map of the Island of Madagascar to
which is added a Memoir on the Chinese
Trade. London: 1792. 1st English edn. 475
pp. Fldg map. Contemp half leather, worn.
(Trophy Room Books) **$400 [≈ £225]**

Rogers, Henry
- The Protestant Church Existent. London:
1638. 1st edn. Sm 4to. [16],176 pp. Margs
trimmed, few headlines shaved. Mod leather-
backed wooden bds. STC 21778.
(D & D Galleries) **$175 [≈ £98]**

Rohault, Jacques
- System of Natural Philosophy illustrated with
Dr. Samuel Clarke's Notes, taken mostly out
of Sir Isaac Newton's Philosophy ... Second
Edition. London: 1729-28. 2 vols. 8vo. 27
fldg plates. Contemp polished calf, backstrips
relaid.   *(Weiner)* **£200 [≈ $356]**
- A Treatise of Mechanics: or, the Science of
the Effects of Power of Moving Forces, as
apply'd to Machines ... [translated] by
Thomas Watts. London: Symon, 1716. 1st
English edn. 8vo. xii,160,[2] pp. 4 fldg plates.
Contemp mor elab gilt, rather worn.
(Gaskell) **£550 [≈ $979]**

Rollin, Charles
- The History of the Arts and Sciences of the
Antients. Translated from the French.
London: for John & Paul Knapton, 1737-39.
4 vols. 8vo. 52 fldg plates. Few lib marks.
Contemp calf gilt, some jnts split.
(Key Books) **$160 [≈ £90]**
- The Method of Teaching and Studying the

Belles Lettres; or, an Introduction to Language, Poetry, Rhetoric ... London: Bettesworth & Hitch, 1734. 1st English edn. 4 vols. 8vo. 2 jnts cracked, 1 bd detached, spines worn. *(Spelman)* £60 [≈ $107]

- The Method of Teaching and Studying the Belles Lettres or, an Introduction to Language, Poetry, Rhetoric ... Translated from the French. The Fifth Edition. London: Hitch & Hawes, 1758. 4 vols. 12mo. Titles foxed. 2 ff torn, no loss. Contemp calf, sl worn. *(Hannas)* £45 [≈ $80]

Rolt, Richard

- Memoirs of the Life of the late Right Honourable John Lindesay, Earl of Craufurd and Lindesay ... London: Henry Kopp ..., 1735. 1st edn. 4to. [l],432,[xi],[ii] pp. 2 subscribers. Port frontis, 5 fldg plans, 2 headpieces. Contemp sheep, sl worn. *(Blackwell's)* £125 [≈ $223]

Romaine, William

- The Parable of the Dry Bones Interpreted in a Sermon ... October 24, 1756 ... London: for J. Worrall, 1756. 2nd edn. 8vo. 31 pp. Disbound. *(Young's)* £22 [≈ $39]

Roman Stations in Britain ...

- See Salmon, Nathaniel

Ronayne, Philip

- A treatise of Algebra in Two Books ... The Second Edition with Additions. London: Innys, 1727. 2nd edn. 8vo. [viii],v,[iii errata], 160; 177-461,[3 advt] pp. Contemp calf gilt, worn, upper jnt cracked.
  (Gaskell) £375 [≈ $668]

Ronsil, G.A.D.

- A Dissertation on Hernias, or Ruptures ... London: 1748. vii,[8],412 pp. Endpapers sl stained. Pp 413-439 (vocabulary of terms) never bound in. Orig leather, rubbed & worn, rebacked. *(Whitehart)* £65 [≈ $116]

Roscommon, Wentworth Dillon, Earl of

- Horace: or the Art of Poetry: A Poem. London: H. Hills, 1709. 8vo. 16 pp. Disbound. *(Hannas)* £30 [≈ $53]
- Poems by the Earl of Roscommon. To which is added, An Essay on Poetry, By the Earl of Mulgrave, now Duke of Buckingham. Together with Poems by Mr. Richard Duke. London: Tonson, 1717. 1st edn. 8vo. [xx],536 pp. Contemp calf, red label, crnrs v sl bumped. *(Finch)* £100 [≈ $178]
- Poems by the Earl of Roscommon. To which is added, an Essay on Poetry, By the ... Duke

of Buckingham. Together with Poems by Mr. Richard Duke. London: Tonson, 1717. 1st edn. 2 parts. 8vo. U6-U8 are cancels. Minor marg worm. Contemp calf, rebacked.
(Hannas) £160 [≈ $285]

Rose, John

- The English Vineyard Vindicated, with an address, where the best Plants are to be had at easie rates. London: 1672. Sm 8vo. 48 pp. Fldg plate. Lib stamps on title. Sl soiled. Later half calf, sl worn. Wing R.1937.
  (Weiner) £150 [≈ $267]

Ross, Alexander

- Panzebeia: Or, A View of all Religions in the World: with the several Church-Governments ... [London]: for John Williams ..., 1672. "4th" edn. 8vo. [xxx], 544, [8],[xx], 78,[2] pp. Frontis. 17 w'cut ports. Table ff shaved v close. Rec contemp style calf. Wing R.1975
  (Young's) £135 [≈ $240]

Ross, William

- The French Scholar's Guide; or a New and Compendious Grammar of the French Tongue. Glasgow: Daniel Reid for Morison & M'Allum, 1772. 1st edn. 12mo. viii,280 pp. 1st few ff v sl browned. Lacks fly leaves. Contemp sheep, rubbed.
  (Burmester) £110 [≈ $196]

Rous, George

- The Restoration of the King of Tanjore Considered. N.p.: Printed in the Year 1777. Only edn. Part 1 only. 4to. vi,123 pp. 1st 2 ff v sl stained. Orig wraps, uncut. Anon.
  (Young's) £285 [≈ $507]

Rousseau, J.J.

- Letters on the Elements of Botany. Addressed to a Lady ... System of Linnaeus. Translated by T. Martyn. London: 1787. xxv, 500, [28] pp. Fldg table. Contemp calf, rebacked.
  (Whitehart) £85 [≈ $151]

Rowe, Nicholas

- The Fair Penitent. A Tragedy. London: Tonson & Draper, 1747. 12mo. [14],[15]-82,[2] pp. Rec wraps.
  (Fenning) £21.50 [≈ $39]
- The Golden Verses of Pythagoras. Translated from the Greek. [Edinburgh]: Printed in the Year, 1740. 1st sep edn. 8vo. 12 pp. Disbound. *(Hannas)* £85 [≈ $151]
- The Royal Convert. A Tragedy ... London: Tonson, 1708. 1st edn. Sm 4to. [34] ff. Half-title. Sl browning. Rec half calf.
  (Blackwell's) £200 [≈ $356]

- Tamerlane. A Tragedy ... Second Edition. London: Tonson, sold by David, 1703. 4to. Half-title. Epilogue leaf (guarded). Browned, a few stains. Mod half roan.
(Hannas) **£40 [≃ $71]**
- Tamerlane, a Tragedy. London: Tonson, 1744. 12mo. [12],70,[2] pp. Frontis. Wraps.
(Fenning) **£21.50 [≃ $39]**
- The Tragedy of Jane Shore. Written in Imitation of Shakespear's Style. London: for W. Feales, 1735. 12mo. [10],13-66,[2] pp. Lacks intl blank. Title dusty. Rec wraps.
(Fenning) **£85£21. [≃ $151]**
- The Tragedy of the Lady Jane Gray ... London: for Bernard Lintot, 1715. 1st edn. 4to. Epilogue leaf. Qtr calf by Lloyd.
(Hannas) **£120 [≃ $214]**
- The Tragedy of the Lady Jane Gray ... London: Lintot, 1715. 4to. x,66,[ii] pp. Prologue leaf misbound. Last leaf sl stained. Mod qtr calf. *(Blackwell's)* **£175 [≃ $312]**

Rowlands or Verstegan, Richard

- A Restitution of Decayed Intelligence. Concerning the most noble and renovvmed [sic] English nation. By the study and trauaile of R.V. Antwerp: 1605. 1st edn. Sm 4to. [xxiv], 338,[14] pp. Title vignette, 10 text engvs, arms at end. 17th c calf, gilt spine. STC 21361. *(Sotheran's)* **£285 [≃ $507]**

Rowlandson, Thomas

- Hungarian & Highland Broad Sword ... Designed and Etched by T. Rowlandson, under the direction of Messrs. H. Angelo and Son ... London: H. Angelo, 1799. 1st edn. Oblong folio. [vii] pp. 23 hand cold aquatints inc title. Sl mor soil. Rec half mor, t.e.g., by Zaehnsdorf. *(Sotheran's)* **£5,850 [≃ $10,413]**

Rowley, Thomas

- Poems ... see Chatterton, Thomas

Royal ...

- The Royal Charter of Confirmation granted by King Charles II to the City of London. London: for Samuel Lee & Benjamin Alsop ..., 1680. Browned. Contemp sheep, rebacked. *(Meyer Boswell)* **$350 [≃ £197]**
- Royal Society for the Encouragement of Arts, Manufactures, and Commerce. Transactions ... with the Premiums offered ... London: Dodsley ..., 1789-1804. Vols 1-4 2nd edn, rest 1st edn. 22 vols. Num plates. Occas browning & staining. Contemp calf, gilt spines, some worn. *(Frew Mackenzie)* **£260 [≃ $463]**

Rudder, S.

- The History and Antiquities of Gloucester ...

Cirencester: 1781. xiii,[ii],[2 advt], 524, cxi pp. Fldg frontis. 7 pp of Preface supplied in MS. Minor browning & soiling. Rebound in half calf gilt. Anon.
(Francis Edwards) **£160 [≃ $285]**

Ruffhead, Owen

- The Life of Alexander Pope, Esq. ... London: C. Bathurst, H. Woodfall ..., 1769. 1st edn. 8vo. [4],578 pp. Frontis. Contemp polished calf, rebacked, signs of wear.
(Hartfield) **$245 [≃ £138]**

Rugeley, Rowland

- Miscellaneous Poems, and Translations from La Fontaine and Others. Cambridge: Fletcher & Hodson ..., 1763. 1st edn. 8vo. Half-title. Crnr faintly water stained. Contemp mottled calf, gilt spine. *(Hannas)* **£450 [≃ $801]**

Ruggle, George

- Ignoramus. Comedia. London: 1630. 2nd edn, rvsd. 12mo. Frontis. Stained. Calf, rubbed. STC 21446. Anon.
(Rostenberg & Stern) **$250 [≃ £140]**

Rush, Benjamin

- An Account of the Bilious Remitting Yellow Fever, as it appeared in the City of Philadelphia, in the Year 1793. Phila: 1794. 8vo. x,363 pp. Sm ink spots on title. Contemp qtr calf, new endpapers.
(Goodrich) **$550 [≃ £309]**

Russel, Richard

- A Dissertation on the Use of Sea-Water in the Diseases of the Glands. Particularly the Scurvy, Jaundice, Kings-Evil, Leprosy, and the Glandular Consumption. London: W. Owen, 1752. 1st edn. Fcap 8vo. xii,204 pp. Frontis. Contemp calf, jnt ends & hd of spine reprd. *(Spelman)* **£260 [≃ $463]**

Russell, R.

- A Dissertation Concerning the Use of Sea Water in Diseases of the Glands, &c. To which is added An Epistolary Dissertation to R. Frewin, M.D. Oxford: 1753. xv,398 pp. 7 engvs. Occas foxing. Contemp leather.
(Whitehart) **£180 [≃ $320]**

Russell, Rachel, Lady

- Letters from the Manuscript in the Library at Woburn Abbey. To which is prefixed, An Introduction ... London: for Edward & Charles Dilly, 1774. 3rd edn. 8vo. cxii,332 pp. Calf gilt, jnts splitting but firm. Anon.
(Young's) **£20 [≃ $36]**

Russell, Lord William
- A Vindication of Lord Russell's Speech and Innocence, in a Dialogue betwixt Whig & Tory: being the same that was promis'd to the Observator in a Penny-Post-Letter. London: for the author, 1683. 1st edn (?). 4to. [2], 22 pp. Disbound. Wing V.516,
(Hannas) **£40 [≈$71]**

Rust, George
- A Discourse of the Use of Reason in Matters of Religion ... Translated into English, with Annotations upon it by Hen. Hallywell. London: Hen. Hills Jun. for Walter Kettilby, 1683. 8vo. Disbound. Wing R.2361.
(Waterfield's) **£65 [≈$116]**

Rutter, J. & Carter, D.
- Modern Eden: or the Gardener's Universal Guide. London: 1769. 8vo. xiv,396 pp. Trifle foxed. Mod dec half mor.
(Wheldon & Wesley) **£75 [≈$134]**

Rutty, John
- Observations on the London and Edinburgh Dispensatories: with an Account of the Various Subjects of the Materia Medica, not contained in either of those Works. London: Dilly, 1776. 1st edn. 8vo. [ii],viii,208,[2] pp. Lacks half-title. Contemp sheep, jnts cracked.
(Burmester) **£120 [≈$214]**

Rycaut, Paul
- The Present State of the Ottoman Empire ... In three Books. London: John Starkey & Henry Brome, 1668. 4to. 218 pp. Frontis (torn), 2 plates, text ills. 2 ff torn. Old leather, worn. *(McBlain)* **$235 [≈£132]**
- The Present State of the Ottoman Empire ... London: John Starkey & Henry Brome, 1668. Sm folio. [xii],218 pp. Frontis, 2 plates, 19 vignettes (few with later hand colouring). Interesting later MS notes. 19th c half parchment, rubbed & marked. Wing R.2413.
(Clark) **£225 [≈$401]**

Rymer, Thomas
- A Short View of Tragedy: its Original, Excellency, and Corruption. With some Reflections on Shakespear ... London: Richard Baldwin, 1693. 1st edn. 8vo. Final advt leaf. Lacks intl blank leaf. 19th c half calf. Wing R.2429. *(Hannas)* **£550 [≈$979]**
- A Short View of Tragedy; its Original, Excellency, and Corruption. With Some Reflections on Shakespear, and other Practitioners for the Stage. London: Baldwin, 1693. 1st edn. 8vo. [xvi],182,[2] pp. Intl blank & final advt ff. Contemp calf, rebacked. Wing

R.2429. *(Burmester)* **£300 [≈$534]**

Sael, George (editor)
- Mental Amusement: consisting of Moral Essays, Allegories, and Tales ... Calculated for the Use of Private Families and Public Schools. London: for G. Sael, 1797. Frontis. Contemp sheep, ft of spine sl worn. Anon.
(C.R. Johnson) **£220 [≈$392]**

Safety ...
- The Safety of France to Monsieur the Dauphin ... Done into English from the Second Edition of the French Original printed in Holland. London: for Tho. Salusbury, 1690. Only edn in English. 12mo. [ii],154,[2] pp. Sl used. Contemp sheep, rubbed, extrs worn. Wing S.282D.
(Clark) **£250 [≈$445]**

Sage, John
- An Account of the late Establishment of Presbyterian Government by the Parliament of Scotland in Anno 1690 ... in a fifth Letter from a Gentleman at Edinburgh ... London: for Jos. Hindmarsh, 1693. 2nd edn. Sm 4to. [viii], 100 pp. Disbound. Wing S.284. Anon.
(Vanbrugh) **£95 [≈$169]**
- Presbytery, Untwisted from the Bottom. With the Rise and Growth of its in Scotland ... London: for Charles Brome, 1709. 1st edn thus. 8vo. cxciv,422 pp. Contemp panelled calf, sl worn. Anon. *(Young's)* **£75 [≈$134]**
- The Principles of the Cyprianic Age, with regard to Episcopal Power and Jurisdiction, Asserted and recommended ... By J.S. London: for Walter Ketilby, & sold by Richard Wilkin, 1742. 2nd edn. 8vo. 95,[1 advt] pp. Sm paper flaw in title. Disbound.
(Young's) **£55 [≈$98]**

Sainbel, Charles Vial de
- Elements of the Veterinary Art ... prefixed, a Short Account of his Life. London: for J. Wright, 1797. 3rd edn. 3 parts in 1 vol. 4to. Port, frontis to Lectures on Farriery, 7 plates. Orig bds, uncut, jnts reprd.
(Burmester) **£650 [≈$1,157]**
- Lectures on the Elements of Farriery ... London: for the author, 1793. 1st edn. 4to. xii,[iv],202 pp. Frontis, 2 plates. Orig bds, uncut, rebacked, new label.
(Burmester) **£400 [≈$712]**

Saint-Didier, A.T. Limojon de
- See Limojon de Saint-Didier, A.T.

Sainte-Marthe, Scevole de
- Paedotrophia; or, the Art of Nursing and

Rearing Children, a Poem ... Translated from the Latin ... Notes ... Life of the Author ... by H.W. Tytler. London: for the author, 1797. 8vo. cxci,224 pp. Subscribers. Name erased from title. Contemp half calf, sl worn.
(Weiner) **£150 [≈ $267]**

Saint-Evremond, Charles M. de Saint Denis

- Judgment on Alexander and Caesar; And also on Seneca, Plutarch, and Petronius. Translated out of the French. London: A. Maxwell, for Jonathan Edwin, 1672. 1st edn in English. 8vo. (3)-78,[ii] pp. Final blank. No A1 (blank?). Rec bds. Wing S.303A. Anon.
(Clark) **£45 [≈ $80]**

St. German, Christopher

- The Dialogue in English, betweene a Doctor of Divinitie and a Student in the Lawes of England. London: for the Company of Stationers, 1623. 8vo. [Blank],title, 176,4 ff, [blank]. Early calf, rubbed, backstrip laid down. STC 21581. Anon.
(Meyer Boswell) **$450 [≈ £253]**

St.-John, Oliver

- Mr. St.-John's Speech to the Lords in the Upper House of Parliament January 7. 1640. concerning Ship-Money. London: Printed Anno 1641. 4to. [ii],45,[2] pp. Occas minor soiling & staining. Disbound. Wing S.333.
(Clark) **£60 [≈ $107]**

- Mr. St.John's Speech, or Argument in Parliament; shewing whether a man may be a Judge, and a Witness in the same Cause. [London]: 1641. Only edn. 4to. [2],6 pp. Wing S.328. Anon.
(Meyer Boswell) **$250 [≈ £140]**

- The Speech and Declaration of ... Concerning Ship-Money. London: E.P. for Henry Seyle, 1641. 1st edn under this title. Issue with erratum on final page of text. 4to. [ii], 65,[i] pp. Some wear & tear. Disbound. Wing S.329.
(Clark) **£45 [≈ $80]**

Saint Jure, Jean Baptiste

- The Holy Life of Monsieur de Renty, a late Nobleman of France, and sometime Councellor to King Lewis the Thirteenth. London: 1684. 2nd edn in English. 8vo. 347 pp. Contemp calf, rebacked. Wing S.335.
(Robertshaw) **£36 [≈ $64]**

Salkeld, William

- Reports of Cases Adjudged in the Court of King's Bench ... Sixth Edition. Dublin: for James Moore, 1791. Only Irish edn. 3 vols. 8vo. Some browning. Contemp calf, rubbed,

some jnts cracked.
(Meyer Boswell) **$150 [≈ £84]**

Salmon, Nathanael

- The History of Hertfordshire. London: [Samuel Richardson], 1728. 1st edn. Folio. [viii], 368 pp. Fldg map (sm reprs). Sl browning. Contemp calf, sl worn.
(Ash) **£300 [≈ $534]**

- Roman Stations in Britain, according to the Imperial Itinerary. London: for J. Roberts, 1726. 8vo. Contemp MS notes. Mod qtr calf. Anon. *(Waterfield's)* **£150 [≈ $267]**

Salmon, Nicholas

- The Complete System of the French Language; or a Course of Grammatical Observations, wherein the great Deficiences of former Grammars, and even Dictionaries, are supplied. London: 1788. 1st edn. 8vo. 348, subscribers pp. Orig bds, uncut, spine worn. *(Robertshaw)* **£38 [≈ $68]**

Salmon, Thomas

- A New Historical Account of St. George for England, and the Origin of the Most Noble Order of the Garter. London: R. Janeway for Nath. Dancer, 1704. 1st edn. Sm 8vo. [8], 109, [4],[115] pp. Port, view. Lacks port of Queen Anne. Contemp calf, rebacked, sl worn.   *(D & D Galleries)* **$150 [≈ £84]**

Salmon, William

- The London and Country Builder's Vade Mecum: or, the Complete and Universal Architect's Assistant. London: J. Hodges, 1748. 2nd edn. 8vo. [2],ii,187,[1] pp. Frontis. Contemp calf, rebacked, crnrs sl bumped.
(Sotheran's) **£375 [≈ $668]**

- Pharmacopoeia Londinensis; or The New London Dispensatory. In Six Books. Eighth Edition, Corrected and Amended. London: 1716. 8vo. Title supplied in facs. Mod mor. *(Robertshaw)* **£30 [≈ $53]**

- Polygraphice: or the Arts of Drawing, Engraving, Etching, Limning, Painting ... Second Edition, with many large Additions ... London: for John Crumpe, 1673. 8vo. [8],352,8 pp. Addtnl engvd title (dated 1672), 14 engvd ills & plates. Mod calf. Wing S.445. *(Spelman)* **£650 [≈ $1,157]**

The Salopian Zealot ...

- See Sandys, John

Saluste du Bartas, Guillaume de

- Bartas His Divine Weekes & Workes. Translated ... by John Sylvester. London: [1605-06]. 1st coll edn. 4to. With all w'cuts &

blanks called for. Sm marg worm hole inner marg prelims. Contemp sheep, rebacked. STC 21649a.5. *(Vanbrugh)* **£575 [≈ $1,024]**

Sammes, Aylett

- Britannia Antiqua Illustrata: or, the Antiquities of Ancient Britain Derived from the Phoenicians ... The First Volume [all published]. London: Tho. Roycroft for the author, 1676. Folio. Map, ills. Some marg browning. Old calf, sl worn.

  (Francis Edwards) **£200 [≈ $356]**

Sampson, Thomas (editor)

- The Rule of Life: in Select Sentences, collected from the greatest Authors, Ancient and Modern. The Ninth Edition, improved. London: for J. Hinton, 1769. 12mo. ix,[i], 297, [5 advt] pp. Rec bds. Anon.

  (Burmester) **£58 [≈ $103]**

Sandby, Paul

- A Collection of One Hundred and Fifty Select Views in England, Wales, Scotland, and Ireland. London: John Boydell, 1782-83. 2nd edn. 2 vols. Folio. Large Paper. [4],33,[1]; [4], 12, 15,[1] pp. 73 + 17 + 27 + 33 plates. Contemp tree calf, gilt dec spines, contrasting labels. *(Sotheran's)* **£1,850 [≈ $3,293]**

Sandeman, Robert

- The Honor of Marriage opposed to all Impurities: an Essay. London: for T. Vernor, 1777. 1st edn. 8vo. Orig (?) wraps.

  (Waterfield's) **£125 [≈ $223]**

Sanders, Mark

- Poems on Occasional Subjects. Written between the Fourteenth and Twentieth Years, of the Author's Age. Dublin: Robert Jackson, 1778. 1st edn. 12mo. 143 pp. Subscribers. Sl water stains. Contemp calf, spine rubbed. *(Burmester)* **£350 [≈ $623]**

Sandwich, John, Earl of

- A Voyage performed by the late Earl of Sandwich round the Mediterranean in the Years 1738 and 1739. Written by himself ... prefixed Memoirs ... by John Cooke. London: Cadell & Davies, 1799. 1st edn. 4to. xl,540 pp. Fldg map, 26 plates. Contemp calf, jnts cracked but firm.

  (Frew Mackenzie) **£450 [≈ $801]**

Sandys, John

- The Salopian Zealot: or, the Good Vicar in a Bad Mood. By John the Dipper. [Bristol? London?] Sold by G. Keith, & J. Buckland, London; T. Evans, bristol ..., [1778]. 1st edn. 12mo. 52 pp. Outer ff browned & dusty.

Contemp limp leather. Anon.

  (Burmester) **£175 [≈ $312]**

Sapho to Phaon ...

- Sapho to Phaon: An Epistle from a Lady of Quality to a Noble Lord, occasion'd by the Late publication of his Miscellaneous Thoughts. London: for Jacob Robinson, 1743. 1st edn. 8vo. [4],63 pp, inc half-title. Disbound. *(Hannas)* **£75 [≈ $134]**

Sargent, John

- The Mine: a Dramatic Poem. London: for T. Cadell, 1785. 4to. Mod calf backed bds.

  (Waterfield's) **£110 [≈ $196]**

- The Mine: A Dramatic Poem ... London: for T. Cadell, 1785. 1st edn. 4to. [xv],i,63 pp. New qtr calf. Inscrbd "From the Author". Anon. *(Young's)* **£140 [≈ $249]**

- The Mine: a Dramatic Poem. London: for T. Cadell, 1785. 1st edn. 4to. [4],xvi,63 pp, inc half-title. Mod half calf.

  (Hannas) **£90 [≈ $160]**

- The Mine: a Dramatic Poem. The Second Edition. To which are added Two Historic Odes. London: for T. Cadell, 1788. 12mo. Frontis & 3 plates (sl foxed). Contemp tree calf, rebacked. *(Waterfield's)* **£70 [≈ $125]**

Sarpi, Paolo

- The Historie of the Councel of Trent ... Translated into English by Nathaniel Brent ... Third Edition ... London: for Whittaker, 1640. 3rd edn in English. Folio. [x],879,[15] pp. Lacks 1st & last blanks. Sl marg worm. Contemp calf, sl wear spine ends. STC 21763. Anon. *(Sotheran's)* **£185 [≈ $329]**

- The History of the Council of Trent ... Translated into English by Sr Nathanael Brent ... London: J. Macock ..., 1676. Folio. [xvi], cvi, [ii],889,[xliv] pp. Imprimatur leaf. Sl marg damp staining. Contemp calf, gilt spine, sl worn. Wing S.696.

  (Clark) **£140 [≈ $249]**

- The History of the Council of Trent ... Written in Italian by Pietro Soave Polano [pseudonym] ... Translated into English by Sr. Nathanael Brent ... London: 1676. 3rd edn in English. Folio. [16],cvi, 889,[1 blank], [24] pp. Contemp calf, rebacked. Wing S.696.

  (O'Neal) **£350 [≈ £197]**

- The Opinion of Padre Paolo ... given to the Lords the Inquisitors of State. In what manner the Republick of Venice ought to govern themselves both at home and abroad. London: 1689. 1st English edn. 12mo. Licence leaf. Marg worm at end. Contemp calf, rebacked, crnrs worn. Wing S.699.

  (Hannas) **£50 [≈ $89]**

Satan Disrob'd from his Disguise of Light ...
- See Leslie, Charles

Saumarez, Richard
- A Dissertation on the Universe in General, and on the Procession of the Elements in Particular ... London: T. Egerton ..., 1795. 1st edn. 8vo. xxvii,266 pp. 3 ff sl stained in margs. Old calf, rubbed, label chipped.
(Young's) £110 [≈ $196]

Savage, Richard
- The Poetical Works. In Two Volumes. With the Life of the Author. Edinburgh: at the Apollo Press, 1780. 2 vols in one. Addtnl engvd titles. Contemp half calf, jnts cracked & sl worn.   *(Claude Cox)* £15 [≈ $27]
- Various Poems. The Wanderer ... The Triumph of Mirth and Health ... The Bastard ... Preface ... London: for J. Turner, 1761. 1st coll edn. Sm 8vo. Contemp roan, rebacked, new endpapers.   *(Hannas)* £250 [≈ $445]

Savary, Claude Etienne
- Letters on Greece; being the Sequel of Letters on Egypt ... London: Elliot & Kay, 1788. 1st English edn. 8vo. viii,442,[i advt] pp. Fldg map, fldg plate. Contemp calf, hd of spine chipped, some stains to cvrs.
(Frew Mackenzie) £100 [≈ $178]
- Universal Dictionary of Trade and Commerce ... see Postlethwayt, Malachy

Savile, George
- An Argument Concerning the Militia. [London: 1762]. 1st edn. 4to. 19,[1] pp. Rec wraps. Anon.   *(Burmester)* £40 [≈ $71]

Saxe, Maurice de
- Reveries or Memoirs upon the Art of War. London: Nourse, 1758. 1st English edn. 4to. 40 fldg plates. Calf, rebacked, sl scuffed.
(Rostenberg & Stern) $450 [≈ £253]

Sayer, Joseph
- Reports of Cases adjudged in the Court of King's Bench, beginning Michaelmas Term, 25 Geo. 2 ... London: Strahan & Woodfall ..., 1775. 1st edn. Folio. [iv],317,[318-350] pp. Contemp calf, spine damaged.
(Vanbrugh) £125 [≈ $223]

Scarborough ...
- The Scarborough Guide, (a Second Edition), to which is prefixed, a Descriptive Route through Hull and Beverley ... Hull: Thomas Lee, 1796. 8vo. 178 pp, errata leaf. Blank leaf

after title. Contemp calf, rebacked, crnrs worn, inner jnts reprd.
(Spelman) £80 [≈ $142]
- See also under Historical (An Historical and Descriptive Guide to Scarborough, 1787)

Scarron, Paul
- The Comic Romance of Monsieur Scarron translated by Oliver Goldsmith in Two Volumes. London: for W. Griffin, 1775. 2 vols. 8vo. Contemp calf, front jnts cracked, sometime roughly reprd.
(Waterfield's) £300 [≈ $534]
- The Whole Comical Works ... London: for J. Nicholson ..., 1712. 3rd edn & crrctd. 8vo. [viii],560 pp. Addtnl engvd title, 3 plates. Contemp speckled panelled calf, rebacked.   *(Young's)* £85 [≈ $151]

Scarronides: or, Virgil Travestie ...
- See Cotton, Charles; Smyth, John

Scheffer, Johannes
- The History of Lapland ... Oxford: at the Theater, 1674. 1st English edn. Probably 1st issue. Folio. Addtnl engvd title, fldg map, 25 w'cuts in text. Contemp panelled calf, gilt spine (reprd), a.e.g. Wing S.851A.
(Hannas) £950 [≈ $1,691]
- The History of Lapland ... Oxford: at the Theater, sold by George West & Amos Curtein, 1674. 1st edn. Later issue. Folio. Addtnl engvd title, fldg map, 25 w'cuts in text. Few sl marg tears. Contemp mottled calf, hd of spine worn. Wing S.851.
(Hannas) £850 [≈ $1,513]

Schiefer, John Frederic
- An Explanation of the Practice of Law ... Dublin: Stockdale for Lynch ..., 1793. 8vo. [4 blank],xxxi,340,[2 blank] pp. Browning & minor soiling. Contemp sheep, rubbed, scraped, jnts splitting.
(Meyer Boswell) £350 [≈ $197]

Schiller, Johann Christoph Friedrich von
- The Ghost-Seer; or, Apparitionist ... From the German of Schiller. London: Vernor & Hood; Leeds: Binns; Hull: Rawson, 1795. 1st edn in English. 12mo. [iv],242 pp. Contemp calf, rebacked, new endpapers, edges & hd of spine worn.   *(Burmester)* £750 [≈ $1,335]

The School of Arts Improv'd ...
- The School of Arts Improv'd: or Companion for the Ingenious. Containing I. Drawing ... VI. The Art of making Porcelain ... Gainsborough: ptd by John Mozley, 1776. Fcap 8vo. [2],156 pp. Sl used. Contemp half

calf, rebacked, crnrs reprd, new endpapers.
(Spelman) £180 [≈ $320]

Scobell, Henry
- Memorials of the Method and Manner of the Proceedings in Parliament in passing Bills ... Gathered by Observation, and out of the Journal Books from the time of Edward 6. By H.S.E. C.P. London: ptd in the year, 1670. 110 pp. Rebound in qtr sheep. Wing S.924 Anon. *(C.R. Johnson)* £125 [≈ $223]

Scot, John
- An Enquiry into the Origin of the Gout ... Third Edition, Corrected and Improved. London: J.P. Cooke, [ca 1783]. 8vo. [2],216 pp. Rebound in qtr calf, vellum tips.
(Spelman) £120 [≈ $214]

Scot, Walter, Captain
- A True History of several Honourable Families of the Right Honourable Name of Scot ... Edinburgh: Printed ... 1688; & reptd by Balfour & Smellie, 1776. Sm folio. [ii], iii, [i], 3-60, [iv], 97,[iii] pp. Contemp half calf, sl rubbed, crnrs sl worn. *(Clark)* £200 [≈ $356]

The Scotch Medal Decipher'd ...
- See Defoe, Daniel.

The Scots Compendium ...
- The Scots Compendium, or Rudiments of Honour: containing the Succession of the Scots Kings ... Nobility ... Coats of Arms ... London: Millar ..., 1764. 7th edn. 546,[2 advt] pp. 86 plates, correct. Orig leather, gilt dec spine, spine ends sl worn.
(Bates & Hindmarch) £95 [≈ $169]

Scott, James
- Odes on Several Subjects. Cambridge: J. Bentham, 1761. 4to. Mod mrbld bds.
(Waterfield's) £135 [≈ $240]

Scott, Job
- Journal of the Life, Travels & Gospel Labours ... New York: 1797. 1st edn. [xiv], 360 pp. Few gatherings pulled. Calf, backstrip wormed. *(Petrilla)* $65 [≈ £37]

Scott, Sarah
- A Description of Millenium Hall, and the Country Adjacent. London: 1762. 1st edn. 12mo. 262 pp. Advt leaf at end. Frontis. Contemp calf. Anon.
(Robertshaw) £135 [≈ $240]
- The Life of Theodore Agrippa d'Aubigne, containing a Succinct Account of the most remarkable Occurrences during the Civil

Wars of France ... London: 1772. 1st edn. 8vo. 421, index pp. Orig bds, uncut, some wear to spine. Anon.
(Robertshaw) £30 [≈ $53]
- The Test of Filial Duty. In a Series of Letters between Miss Emilia Leonard, and Miss Charlotte Arlington. A Novel. London: for the author, & sold by T. Carnan, 1772. 1st edn. 2 vols. 12mo. Contemp calf gilt, backstrips relaid. Anon.
(Ximenes) $1,500 [≈ £843]

Scrope, John
- Reflections upon Tithes, seriously addressed, in behalf of the Clergy ... By a Clergyman of Wiltshire. Salisbury: E. Easton ..., 1773. 1st edn. 8vo. [2],iv,25 pp. Rec wraps. Anon.
(Fenning) £75 [≈ $134]

Scudamore, James
- Homer a la Mode. A Mock Poem upon the First, and Second Books of Homer's Iliad. Oxford: 1664. 1st edn of part 1. 12mo. 120 pp. Longitudinal title A1. Contemp sheep. Wing S.2131. Anon.
(Robertshaw) £75 [≈ $134]

Scudery, George de
- Curia Politiae: or, The Apologies of Severall Princes. London: Moseley, 1654. 1st English edn. Sm folio. Engvd title, 11 ports. Calf. Wing S.2140.
(Rostenberg & Stern) $275 [≈ £154]

Sculptura-Historico-Technica ...
- Sculptura-Historico-Technica: or the History and Art of Ingraving ... London: S. Harding, 1747. 12mo. xii,225,[i advt] pp. 10 plates. Sl browned. 19th c tan calf, mor label.
(Frew Mackenzie) £160 [≈ $285]

Seasonable ...
- A Seasonable Memento both to King and People upon this Critical Juncture of Affairs. London: Printed in the Year, 1680. 1st edn. 4to. 12 pp. Some marg browning. Sm tear in final leaf. Disbound. Wing S.2232.
(Finch) £95 [≈ $169]
- A Seasonable Recapitulation of Enormous Crimes and Grievances to help the Memory ... London: M. Cooper, 1749. Only edn. 8vo. [ii], 51 pp. Mod half calf, extrs sl rubbed.
(Blackwell's) £75 [≈ $134]

Secret ...
- The Secret History of the Calves-Head Club ... see Ward, Edward
- See Jones, David, Captain of the Horse Guards

Sedley, Sir Charles
- Bellamira, or the Mistress, a Comedy ... London: D. Mallet, for L.C. & Timothy Goodwin, 1687. 1st edn. 4to. Advt leaf. Title & last page dust soiled. Disbound. Wing S.2397.   *(Hannas)* £150 [≃ $267]
- The Miscellaneous Works ... Published from the Original Manuscripts by Captain Ayloffe. London: J. Nutt, 1702. 1st coll edn. 8vo. Half-title. Sl browned. Contemp calf, rubbed, rebacked.   *(Hannas)* £150 [≃ $267]
- The Poetical Works ... Speeches ... London: Sam. Briscoe, 1707. 1st coll edn. 8vo. [xvi],224,175,[i] pp. Some damp marking. Contemp panelled calf, rebacked, crnrs reprd, rubbed.   *(Blackwell's)* £120 [≃ $214]

Seed, Jeremiah
- Discourses upon Several Important Subjects. To which are added, Eight Sermons ... London: for R. Manby, 1743. 1st edn. 2 vols. 8vo.   [xl],436,[2];   [viii],446,[2]   pp. Subscribers. Contemp calf, lacks labels.
          (Burmester) £50 [≃ $89]

Seeley, B.
- Stowe: a Description of the Magnificent House and Gardens of the Right Honourable Richard Grenville Temple ... New Edition with Alterations ... London: Rivington, 1769. 8vo. 44 pp. 19 plates (1 lge fldg). Sl foxing. Mod qtr calf.   *(Sotheran's)* £525 [≃ $935]

Selden, John
- The Historie of Tithes ... London: 1618. 4to. [vi],xxii, [12],491,[4] pp. Some dusting. Title sl worn. Early mrbld bds, rebacked. STC 22172.3.   *(Meyer Boswell)* $350 [≃ £197]
- The Historie of Tithes ... [London]: 1618. 1st edn. Sm 4to. Red & black title. Sl dusty. Bottom crnrs of 4 prelim ff torn away, no loss of text. Contemp sprinkled calf, jnts tender, later label. STC 221272.5.
          (Georges) £250 [≃ $445]
- The Historie of Tithes ... London: 1618. 3rd edn. Sm 4to. Red & black title. Sl browned. Contemp calf, rebacked, backstrip relaid, edges rubbed. STC 22172.5
          (Frew Mackenzie) £220 [≃ $392]
- The Priviledges of the Baronage of England, When they sit in Parliament. London: T. Badger for Matthew Wallbanck ..., 1642. 1st edn. Calf, rubbed, jnts cracking but sound. Wing S.2434. *(Meyer Boswell)* $350 [≃ £197]
- Table-Talk ... The Third Edition. London: Jacob Tonson, Awnsham & John Churchill, 1716. 12mo. [viii],136 pp. Dusty at ends. Contemp half calf, extrs sl worn, jnts cracked,

lacks label.   *(Clark)* £45 [≃ $80]
- Titles of Honor. The Second Edition. London: William Stansby, 1631. Folio. [xxxvi], 941,[i] pp. Red & black title. Contemp panelled calf, reprd at hd, 5 v sm worm holes at ft, thongs lacking. STC 22178.
          (Frew Mackenzie) £380 [≃ $676]

Select ...
- A Select Collection of Poems, from the most approved Authors. Edinburgh: for A. Donaldson, 1768. 1st edn. 2 vols. 12mo (in 6s, horizontal chain-lines). Half-titles. Inserted advt leaf with catchword 'A COL' in vol 1. Contemp calf, 1 headband torn.
          (Hannas) £220 [≃ $392]

Semmedo, Alvarez
- The History of the Great and Renowned Monarchy of China ... Now put into English by a Person of Quality ... London: for John Cook, 1655. 1st edn. Folio. [x],308,[2] pp. Frontis, 2 maps, 2 plates. Contemp calf, hd of spine sl damaged. Wing S.2490.
          (Vanbrugh) £425 [≃ $757]
- The History of That Great and Renowned Monarchy of China ... London: Tyler for Crook, 1655. 1st edn in English. One vol in 2. 4to. [11],308,[2] pp. 2 ports, 2 maps (1 fldg sl trimmed at ft). Rebound in polished calf gilt.   *(Argonaut)* $1,750 [≃ £983]

Seneca
- The Works ... Newly Inlarged and Corrected by Thomas Lodge. [Colophon] London: William Stansby, 1620. 2nd edn. Lge folio. Engvd title. Lacks A1 (blank?). Text box-ruled throughout. Contemp calf, elab gilt spine, sl faded.   *(Vanbrugh)* £355 [≃ $632]

Sennertus, D.
- The Institutions of the Fundamentals of the Whole Art, both of Physick and Chirurgery ... Also the Grounds of Chemistry ... London: 1656. 494 pp. Cambridge antique calf.
          (Whitehart) £580 [≃ $1,032]

A Sentimental Journey ...
- A Sentimental Journey through France and Italy ... see Sterne, Laurence

The Sentiments of a Great Man ...
- The Sentiments of a Great Man upon Proposals for the general reduction of Interest to Three per Cent. In a Speech made to an Honourable Assembly. London: for H. Whitridge, 1751. 1st edn. 8vo. 31 pp. Disbound.   *(Hannas)* £50 [≃ $89]

Serres, Jean de
- A Generall History of France ... continued unto ... the yeare 1622. By Edward Grimston ... London: Eld & Flesher, 1624. Folio. [xvi], 1209, 335,[15] pp. Engvd title, port frontis. Lacks final blank. Contemp calf, rebacked. STC 22246.   *(Sotheran's)* **£300 [≈ $534]**

The Servitour ...
- The Servitour: a Poem. Written by a Servitour of the University of Oxford ... London: H. Hills, 1709. 1st edn. 16 pp. Lacks half-title.   *(Hannas)* **£75 [≈ $134]**

Seton, Sir Alexander
- A Treatise of Mutilation and Demembration. Edinburgh: heirs of Andrew Anderson ..., 1699. Folio. [vi],30, [ii],31-32, [4], 33-66 pp. Some foxing & browning. Contemp calf, rebacked.   *(Meyer Boswell)* **$500 [≈ £281]**

Settle, Elkanah
- Absalom Senior: or, Achitophel Transpros'd. A Poem. London: for S.E. & sold by Langley Curtis, 1682. 1st edn. Folio. [iv], 38,[2] pp. Final blank. Sm repr to title. Later half mor, gilt spine, rubbed, upper jnt cracked but secure. Wing S.2652. Anon.   *(Clark)* **£110 [≈ $196]**
- The Character of a Popish Successour, and what England may expect from Such a One. London: for T. Davies, 1681. Probably 2nd edn, set in smaller type & with reduced margs, final paragraph in v sm type. Folio. [2], 22 pp. Disbound. Wing S.2670. Anon.   *(Hannas)* **£30 [≈ $53]**
- The Character of a Popish Successor, and what England may Expect from such a One ... London: for T. Davies, 1681. 1st edn. Folio. 36 pp. Few marks on last leaf. Disbound. Anon. Wing S.2670. *(Young's)* **£120 [≈ $214]**

Seven Discourses ...
- Seven Discourses delivered in the Royal Academy by the President ... see Reynolds, Sir Joshua.

Several Years Travel through Portugal ...
- See Bromley, William

Seward, Anna
- Monody on Major Andre ... added Letters addressed to her by Major Andre ... Second Edition. Lichfield: J. Jackson, for the author, 1781. 4to. Sgnd by the author at end. Sugar paper wrappers. *(Waterfield's)* **£100 [≈ $178]**
- Monody on Major Andre ... added Letters addressed to her by Major Andre ... Second

Edition. Lichfield: J. Jackson, for the author ..., 1781. 4to. [2],vi,47 pp, inc half-title. Sgnd by the author at end, as always. Blank part of last leaf torn away. Disbound, loose.   *(Hannas)* **£35 [≈ $62]**

Seward, William
- Journal of a Voyage from Savannah to Philadelphia, and from Philadelphia to England, 1740. London: at J. Oswald's ..., 1740. 1st edn. 8vo. [6],87,[1 advt with pasted slip] pp. Sl marks. Disbound.   *(Spelman)* **£60 [≈ $107]**

Sewell, George
- A New Collection of Original Poems, never printed in any Miscellany. By the Author of Sir Walter Raleigh. London: Pemberton & Peele, 1720. 1st edn. 8vo. [8],87 pp. Disbound. Anon.   *(Hannas)* **£110 [≈ $196]**

Shadwell, Thomas
- The Scowrers. A Comedy ... London: for James Knapton, 1691. 1st edn. 4to. Final advt leaf (head-line cut into). Most page numerals cut into or cropped. Qtr calf. Wing S.2872.   *(Hannas)* **£250 [≈ $445]**
- The Squire of Alsatia. A Comedy. London: for James Knapton, 1688. One of the two 1688 edns, with 64 pp. 4to. "72" [ie 64] pp. Sl browned, few margs sl frayed. Half calf & mrbld bds. Wing S.2874A.   *(Ximenes)* **$450 [≈ £253]**
- The Woman-Captain: a Comedy ... London: for Samuel Carr, 1680. 1st edn. 4to. Paper browned. Half mor. Wing S.2887.   *(Hannas)* **£220 [≈ $392]**

Shaftesbury, Anthony Ashley Cooper, 3rd Earl of
- Characteristicks &c. London: printed in the Year, 1733. 1st 12mo edn. 3 vols. General title without imprint, sep titles in each vol. Contemp calf.   *(Hannas)* **£85 [≈ $151]**

Shakespeare, William
- The Beauties of Shakespeare; selected from his Plays and Poems. London: for G. Kearsley, 1783. 1st edn. 12mo. Engvd title. 19th c half calf, gilt spine (sl rubbed).   *(Ximenes)* **$275 [≈ £154]**
- The Works ... Collated with the Oldest Copies, and Corrected; with Notes ... by Mr. Theobald. London: for C. Bathurst ..., 1773. 8 vols. 12mo. Port, engvd plate to each play. Contemp calf, gilt ruled spines, sl wear at some spine ends, 2 jnts reprd.   *(Burmester)* **£300 [≈ $534]**

Sharp, Granville

- The Law of Passive Obedience. [London: White, 1776]. 8vo. Lacks title-page. Bds.
(Rostenberg & Stern) **$175 [≈ £98]**

Sharp, Samuel

- A Critical Enquiry into the Present State of Surgery. Second Edition. London: Tonson, 1750. 8vo. [8],294 pp. Lacks front endpaper. Contemp calf.
(Spelman) **£160 [≈ $285]**
- A Critical Inquiry into the Present State of Surgery. London: for Tonson & Draper, 1750. 1st edn. 294 pp. Contemp half calf & bds.
(Goodrich) **$395 [≈ £222]**
- Letters from Italy, describing the Customs and Manners of that Country, in the Years 1765, and 1766 ... London: R. Cave ... [for] W. Nicol, 1766. 1st edn. 8vo. iv,[errata],312 pp. Contemp calf, gilt spine, new label, upper jnt cracked. *(Frew Mackenzie)* **£100 [≈ $178]**
- Letters from Italy, describing the Customs and Manners of that Country, in the years 1765 and 1766 ... London: R. Cave ..., 1767. 2nd edn. 8vo. Contemp calf gilt, spine a little worn. *(Ximenes)* **$300 [≈ £169]**
- A Treatise on the Operations of Surgery, with a Description and Representation of the Instruments used in Performing them. London: 1761. 8th edn. 234 pp. Plates. Leather. *(Fye)* **$350 [≈ £197]**
- A Treatise on the Operations of Surgery, with a Description and Representation of the Instruments used in Performing them ... Eighth Edition. London: Tonson, 1761. 8vo. [viii], liv,234 pp. 14 plates. Contemp calf, spine sl rubbed & chipped at hd.
(Frew Mackenzie) **£265 [≈ $472]**

Sharpe, Gregory

- An Introduction to Universal History ... prefixed A Short System of Geography ... Second Edition Corrected and Enlarged. London: A. Millar, 1758. Half-title,xxi,4, 4,3, 1-341 pp. 6 maps & plates by Kitchin. Contemp calf, worn, jnts cracked.
(Jermy & Westerman) **£65 [≈ $116]**

Sharpe, Samuel

- A Critical Enquiry into the Present State of Surgery. London: Tonson, Draper, 1750. 2nd edn. 8vo. [viii],294 pp. Sm blank piece cut from title crnr. Contemp calf, jnts sl tender, hd of spine sl worn. *(Burmester)* **£95 [≈ $169]**

Sharrock, R.

- The History of the Propagation and Improvement of Vegetables by the Concurrence of Art and Nature. Oxford:

1660. 1st edn. 8vo. [xviii],150 pp. Plate. Mod half calf, a.e.g.
(Wheldon & Wesley) **£380 [≈ $676]**

Shaw, Joseph

- Parish Law: or a Guide to Justices of the Peace ... London: for F. Cogan, 1733. 1st edn. [8],367, [31],xviii pp. Contemp calf, some wear. *(C.R. Johnson)* **£95 [≈ $169]**
- Parish Law: Or, a Guide to Justices of the Peace, Ministers, Church-Wardens ... In the Savoy: Henry Lintot, 1743. 5th edn. 8vo. [vi], 374, [12] pp. Final gathering loosening. Old calf, front jnt cracking.
(Young's) **£75 [≈ $134]**
- Parish Law: or, a Guide to Justices of the Peace, Ministers, Churchwardens, Overseers of the Poor ... London: 1750. 7th edn, with addtns. 8vo. A-A8,378,table pp. Calf, edges sl rubbed, sm worm hole hd of upper jnt.
(Francis Edwards) **£45 [≈ $80]**
- Parish Law ... The Eighth Edition ... In the Savoy: Henry Lintot, 1753. [18],389,[23] pp. Contemp calf, some wear, hinges weak.
(C.R. Johnson) **£55 [≈ $98]**
- Parish Law ... The Tenth Edition ... London: Woodfall & Strahan, 1763. [20], 421, [31] pp. Contemp calf, fine.
(C.R. Johnson) **£75 [≈ $134]**

Shaw, Peter

- Chemical Lectures publickly read at London in the years 1731 and 1732, and since at Scarborough in 1733 ... London: for Shuckburgh & Osborne, [1734]. 1st edn. 8vo. xxiv, 478 pp. Tiny marg worm hole in title. Contemp calf, sl rubbed, rec label.
(Burmester) **£250 [≈ $445]**
- An Enquiry into the Contents, Virtues and Uses, of the Scarborough Spaw-Waters: with the Method of examining any other Mineral Water. London: for the author, 1734. 1st edn. 8vo. viii,[2],166 pp, advt leaf. Contemp calf, rebacked, crnrs reprd.
(Spelman) **£110 [≈ $196]**
- The Tablet, or Picture of Real Life ... In a Select Set of Essays ... London: T. Longman, 1762. 371 pp. Contemp calf. Anon.
(C.R. Johnson) **£175 [≈ $312]**

Shaw, Thomas

- Travels or Observations relating to several parts of Barbary and the Levant. Oxford: 1738. 1st edn. Folio. [vi],xvi,442, 60,[viii] pp. 12 maps & plans, 21 plates. 5 extra plates tipped-in. Sl marg worm, sl wear index ff crnr. Rec contemp style half calf.
(Frew Mackenzie) **£670 [≈ $1,193]**

Shenstone, William

- The Judgment of Hercules, a Poem ... London: for R. Dodsley, & sold by T. Cooper, 1741. 1st edn. 8vo. Lacks half-title & advt leaf. Rec wraps. Anon.
(Ximenes) **$500 [≈ £281]**
- Poetical Works. Edinburgh: for Gray & Alston, & J. Dickson, 1771. 1st edn of poems separately. 12mo. Engvd title. Contemp calf, sl rubbed. *(Hannas)* **£45 [≈ $80]**
- The Works in Verse and Prose ... London: Dodsley, 1764-69. 1st coll edn. 3 vols. 8vo. Fldg map, 2 frontis, engvd vignettes. End of vol 1 sl browned. Contemp calf, rebacked in mor gilt, black & citron labels.
(Hannas) **£120 [≈ $214]**
- The Works ... in Two Volumes with Decorations. London: for R. & J. Dodsley, 1764. 2 vols. 8vo. 2 frontis, fldg plate vol 2. Lib blind stamps, occas sl spot. Mod qtr calf.
(Waterfield's) **£185 [≈ $329]**
- The Works in Verse and Prose. London: for R. & J. Dodsley, 1764-1769. 3 vols. 8vo. Contemp calf, rebacked.
(Waterfield's) **£225 [≈ $401]**

Sheppard, William

- Englands Balme: or, Proposals by way of Grievance & Remedy; Humbly presented to His Highness and the Parliament towards the Regulation of the Law ... London: J. Cottrel, for Hen. Fletcher ..., 1657. Margs cut close. Mor. Wing S.3183.
(Meyer Boswell) **$1,500 [≈ £843]**
- The President of Presidents. Or, One General President for Common Assurances by Deeds ... Third Edition. London: for B. Pawlet ..., 1684. 8vo. Sl browned. Contemp sheep, rubbed, rebacked. Wing S.3209B.
(Meyer Boswell) **$650 [≈ £365]**
- The Second Part of the Faithfull Councellour: or, The Marrow of the Law in English ... London: Tho. Roycroft for Hen. Twyford ..., 1654. Browning. Mod qtr calf.
(Meyer Boswell) **$450 [≈ £253]**

Sheraton, T.

- The Cabinetmaker and Upholsterer's Drawing Book, with Appendix, Accompaniment, and List of Subscribers. London: Bensley, 1793-95. 115 engvd plates. 10 plates reprd in fold, frontis laid down. 19th c half mor. *(Phillips)* **£875 [≈ $1,558]**

Sheridan, Charles Francis

- A History of the late Revolution in Sweden ... preceded by a short Abstract of the Swedish History ... London: 1788. 1st edn. 8vo.

[iv],348 pp. Few ink notes. Sl foxing. Old mrbld bds, vellum foredges, later calf spine.
(Bow Windows) **£185 [≈ $329]**

Sheridan, Frances

- The History of Nourjahad. London: Dodsley, 1767. 1st edn. 12mo. [iv],240 pp. Half-title. Contemp calf, upper jnt reprd. Anon.
(Burmester) **£125 [≈ $223]**

Sheridan, Richard Brinsley

- The Critic: or, a Tragedy Rehearsed ... Dublin: for Sheppard, Wilkinson ..., 1785. 1st Dublin edn. 12mo. [viii],59,[1] pp. New bds. *(Claude Cox)* **£20 [≈ $36]**
- The Duenna: a Comic Opera ... London: Longman, 1794. 1st authorized edn. 2nd issue, with price on title. 8vo. Final blank leaf. Disbound. *(Hannas)* **£65 [≈ $116]**
- The Rivals ... Dublin: for R. Moncrieffe, 1775. 1st Irish edn. Lge 12mo. 106,[2 blank] pp. Half-title sl dusty. Rec wraps. Anon.
(Fenning) **£85 [≈ $151]**

Sheridan, Thomas

- A Complete Dictionary of the English Language ... The Second Edition, Revised, Corrected, and Enlarged by the Author. London: for Charles Dilly, 1789. 4to. Frontis port. Contemp qtr calf, rebacked.
(C.R. Johnson) **£165 [≈ $294]**
- Lectures on the Art of Reading. In Two Parts ... London: for J. Dodsley ..., 1787. 3rd edn. 8vo. 409,1 pp. Half-title. Rec contemp style half calf. *(Young's)* **£90 [≈ $160]**
- Sheridan's and Henderson's Practical Method of Reading and reciting English Poetry, elucidated by a Variety of Examples ... London: E. Newbery, 1796. 264 pp. Contemp sheep. *(C.R. Johnson)* **£95 [≈ $169]**
- A State of the Case in Regard to the Point in Dispute between Mr. Mosse and Mr. Sheridan. Dublin: 1750. 26,xix,[1] pp. Rec qtr mor. *(C.R. Johnson)* **£550 [≈ $979]**

Sherlock, Martin

- Letters on Several Subjects. London: J. Nichols, 1781. 12mo. xii,13-228, vii,[i],247 pp. Contemp tree calf, gilt spine with repeat sun device & gilt label, ft of spine sl chipped.
(Spelman) **£40 [≈ $71]**

Sherlock, Thomas

- A Letter from the Lord Bishop of London, to The Clergy and People of London and Westminster; On Occasion of the Late Earthquakes. London: for John Whiston ..., 1750. 3rd edn (?). 8vo. 20 pp. Disbound.

(Young's) £60 [≈ $107]
- The Tryal of the Witnesses of the
Resurrection of Jesus. London: for J. Roberts
..., 1729. 1st edn. 8vo. 110,[1 errata] pp.
Disbound. Anon.   *(Young's)* £150 [≈ $267]

Sherlock, William
- A Practical Discourse concerning a Future
Judgment. London: W. Rogers, 1692. 1st
edn. 8vo. [viii],541,[iii] pp. Imprimatur leaf.
Contemp calf, rubbed, label darkened, hd of
spine frayed. Wing S.3307.
(Clark) £40 [≈ $71]
- A Practical Discourse concerning a Future
Judgment. Fourth Edition. London: R.R. for
W. Rogers, 1695. 8vo. [viii],413,[iii] pp.
Contemp calf, gilt spine, no free endpapers.
Wing S.3312.   *(Blackwell's)* £45 [≈ $80]
- A Practical Discourse concerning Death.
Three and Twentieth Edition. London: J.
Walthoe, 1739. 8vo. [xii],292 pp. Contemp
calf, gilt, sm cracks in jnts.
(Blackwell's) £35 [≈ $62]
- A Practical Discourse of Religious
Assemblies. The Second Edition Corrected.
London: J.D. for Richard Chiswell, 1682.
8vo. [xvi],367,[i] pp. No free endpapers.
Contemp calf, worn, front bd almost
detached. Wing S.3323. *(Clark)* £24 [≈ $43]
- The Proceedings of the Vice-Chancellor and
University of Cambridge against Dr. Bentley,
stated and vindicated in a Letter to a Noble
Peer. London: 1719. 1st edn. Folio. 12 pp. 1
sm marg worm hole. Mod bds. Anon.
(Robertshaw) £60 [≈ $107]
- A Vindication of Both Parts of the
Preservative against Popery: In Answer to the
Cavils of Lewis Sabran, Jesuit. London: for
William Rogers ..., 1688. 1st edn. 4to. [vi],
113, [3 advt] pp. Imprimatur leaf. Disbound.
Wing S.3370.   *(Young's)* £65 [≈ $116]

Shields, Alexander
- A True and Faithful Relation of the
Sufferings of the Reverend and Learned Mr.
Alexander Shields, Minister of the Gospel.
Written with his own Hand ... N.p.: 1715. 1st
edn. 4to. 140 pp. Sl browning. Title sl dusty.
Mod qtr roan.   *(Robertshaw)* £35 [≈ $62]

Shippen, William
- Faction Display'd. A Poem. London: Printed
in the Year, 1704. 1st edn. 4to. [4],20 pp. Last
line of 'To the Reader' cropped, with loss of
1 word. Disbound. Anon.
(Hannas) £65 [≈ $116]
- Faction Display'd. A Poem. London: Printed
in the Year, 1704. Pirated edn. 4to. [4],20 pp.

Contemp ink names written in. Some notes
cut into. Disbound, wraps. Anon.
(Hannas) £40 [≈ $71]
- Moderation Display'd. A Poem. London:
1704. 1st edn. 20 pp. Mod wraps. Anon.
(Robertshaw) £20 [≈ $36]

Shirley, James
- The Grateful Servant. A Comedy ... London:
for William Leake, [after 1662]. 3rd edn. 4to.
Title & edges sl dust soiled. Stitched, uncut,
as issued. Wing S.3472.
(Hannas) £250 [≈ $445]

Shirley or Sherley, Thomas
- A Philosophical Essay: declaring the probable
Causes, whence Stones are produced in the
Greater World ... London: for William
Cademan, 1672. 1st edn. 8vo. [xvi],143 pp.
Worm track in upper crnr. Contemp sheep,
spine & crnrs worn. Wing S.3523.
(Gaskell) £350 [≈ $623]

Short ...
- A Short History of the Highland Regiment;
Interspersed with Some Occasional
Observations as to the Present State of the
Country, Inhabitants, and Government of
Scotland. London: Robinson, 1743. 1st edn.
8vo. [iv],51,[1] pp. Dusty. Later half calf,
t.e.g.   *(Georges)* £400 [≈ $712]
- A Short Introduction of Grammar ... see
Bennett, Thomas
- A Short Introduction to English Grammar ...
see Lowth, Robert
- Short Reflections upon Patents, relating to
the Abuses of that noble Privilege, and
proposing the means to reform them.
London: R. Griffiths, 1760. 8 pp. Rec cloth.
(C.R. Johnson) £165 [≈ $294]
- A Short Survey or History of the Kingdome
of Sveden ... London: for Michael Sparke,
sold by James Boler, 1632. 1st English edn. 2
parts. 4to. Intl & final blanks in 1st part.
Lacks intl blank in 1st part. Mod calf. STC
23518, 13458.   *(Hannas)* £850 [≈ $1,513]
- A Short Treatise on the Game of Whist ... see
Hoyle, Edmond
- A Short View of the continual Sufferings and
heavy Oppressions of the Episcopal Reformed
Churches, formerly in Bohemia, and now in
Poland and Polish Prussia ... London: John
Basket ..., 1716. Only edn. Folio. 4 pp.
Disbound.   *(Clark)* £100 [≈ $178]
- A Short Vindication of Marine Regiments. In
Answer to a Pamphlet, Entituled, A Letter to
a Member of Parliament, concerning the Four
Marine Regiments. London: A. Baldwin,

1699. 1st edn. Sm 4to. 11 pp. Sl browned. Disbound. Wing S.3643.

(Blackwell's) £85 [≈ $151]

Short, Thomas

- A Comparative History of the Increase and Decrease of Mankind in England and several Countries abroad ... General States of Health, Air, Seasons and Food ... London: 1767. 1st edn. 4to. [xii],213 pp. Title laid down, some soil. Mod half leather.

(Whitehart) £150 [≈ $267]

- Discourses on Tea, Sugar, Milk, Made-Wines, Spirits, Punch, Tobacco, &c. with Plain and Useful Rules for Gouty People. London: Longman & MIllar, 1750. 1st edn. 8vo. vi, [iv],424 pp. Advt leaf before title. Occas sl browning. Old calf gilt, rebacked.

(Hollett) £650 [≈ $1,157]

- The Natural, Experimental, and Medicinal History of the Mineral Waters of Derbyshire, Lincolnshire, and Yorkshire ... London: 1734. [xx], xxii,362 pp. 4 plates. Sl worm in last few ff. Reversed calf, v sl worn, inner hinges sl cracked. *(Whitehart)* £250 [≈ $445]

Shower, Sir Bartholomew

- The Reports ... Cases Adjudg'd in the Court of King's Bench in the Reign of ... King William III. London: Assigns of R. & E. Atkins, 1708. Folio. Port frontis. Occas v sl spotting & offsetting. Lacks 1 free endpaper. Contemp calf, splits in jnts.

(P and P Books) £70 [≈ $125]

- The Reports ... Cases ... in the Reign of ... King William III ... London: ... for Daniel Brown ..., 1708. 1st edn. Folio. 4 pp ctlg at end. Port. Contemp calf.

(Vanbrugh) £155 [≈ $276]

A Sicilian Romance ...

- See Radcliffe, Ann

Sidney, Algernon

- Discourses concerning Government ... London: the booksellers, 1698. 1st edn. Large Paper. Folio. [ii],462,[v] pp. Errata. Contemp calf, gilt dec spine, fine. Wing S.3761.

(Vanbrugh) £495 [≈ $881]

- Discourses concerning Government ... London: the booksellers, 1698. 1st edn. Folio. [ii],462,[v] pp. Occas faint water stain & spotting. 18th c mrbld sheep, label, jnts beginning to crack at ft, some rubbing, later endpapers. Wing S.3761.

(Blackwell's) £375 [≈ $668]

- The Essence of Algernon Sidney's Work on Government ... By a Student of the Inner Temple [William Scott, Baron Stowell].

London: J. Johnson, 1795. 1st edn. 8vo. xix, [v], 287,[i] pp. Occas spotting. Rec qtr calf.

(Clark) £65 [≈ $116]

Sidney, Sir Philip

- The Countesse of Pembrokes Arcadia ... Now the ninth time published ... London: Waterson & Young, 1638. Folio. [vi],624,[625-643] pp. Occas sl wear. Contemp calf, spine reprd. STC 22550.

(Vanbrugh) £355 [≈ $632]

Simmons, Samuel

- Elements of Anatomy and the Animal Economy. From the French of M. Person. Corrected ... augmented with Notes. London: Wilie, 1775. 1st edn. xii,396 pp, errata leaf. 3 plates. Light pencilling. Old qtr calf, worn.

(Goodrich) $75 [≈ £42]

Simon, Richard

- The History of the Original and Progress of Ecclesiastical Revenues ... written in French by a learned Priest and now done into English. London: for Henry Faithorn ..., 1685. 1st English edn. 8vo. Contemp calf, rubbed. Wing S.3802. Anon.

(Waterfield's) £75 [≈ $134]

Simpson, Thomas

- The Doctrine and Application of Fluxions ... Second Edition, revised and Carefully Corrected. London: for John Nourse, 1776. 2 vols. 8vo. xii,274,[2 advt]; [ii],275-576 pp. Name torn from vol 2 title. Contemp sheep, rebacked, sides scuffed.

(Burmester) £125 [≈ $223]

The Sixpenny Miscellany ...

- The Sixpenny Miscellany. or, a Dissertation upon Pissing. Written at Piss-at-aqua ... Printed at Pots-Dam on Superfine Pot-paper ... London: reprinted for A. Moore, 1726. Presumed 1st edn. 8vo. 32 pp. Disbound.

(Hannas) £450 [≈ $801]

Skene, Alexander (anon)

- Memorialls for the Government of the Royal-Burghs in Scotland ... Translated into English by I.B. [John Barclay]. By [in Greek] Philopoliteius. Aberdeen: John Forbes, 1685. 8vo. 288 pp, inc sep title to "A Succinct Survey". Sl used. 19th c calf, rebacked.

(Rankin) £300 [≈ $534]

Skene, John

- Regiam Majestatem. The Auld Lawes and Constitutions of Scotland. Edinburgh: Thomas Finlason, 1609. 1st edn. Folio. W'cut

on title verso. Some damp stains, p 69 soiled.
Mod half calf. STC 22624.
(Robertshaw) **£95 [≈ $169]**

Sketch(es) ...
- A Sketch of Modern France ... see Moody,
  Christopher Lake (editor)
- Sketches of the History of Man ... see Kames,
  Henry Home, Lord

Skinner, Robert
- Reports of Cases adjudged in the Court of
  King's Bench, from the Thirty-third Year of
  King Charles the Second ... London: for
  Bernard Lintot, 1728. 1st edn. Folio. [xvi],
  686, [687-766] pp. Licence leaf. Errata.
  Contemp calf, front bd detached.
  (Vanbrugh) **£125 [≈ $223]**

Skinner, Thomas
- The Life of General Monck: Duke of
  Albemarle ... Publish'd from an Original
  Manuscript ... Second Edition, Corrected.
  London: J. Graves ..., 1724. 8vo. [x], [lxviii],
  385,[vii] pp. Contemp calf, gilt dec spine, sl
  worn.
  (Clark) **£68 [≈ $121]**

Slack, Thomas
- The British Negotiator; or, Foreign
  Exchanges made perfectly easy ... The Fourth
  Edition, Corrected and Enlarged. By S.
  Thomas, Merchant. London: G. Robinson;
  Newcastle: T. Slack, 1784. Tall 12mo. [xii],
  323, [1 advt] pp. Browned, few ff frayed.
  Contemp sheep, sl worn.
  (Gaskell) **£250 [≈ $445]**

Smalridge, George
- A Poem on the Death of ... Queen Anne, and
  the Succession of ... King George. London:
  for E. Curll, 1715. 1st edn. 8vo. [8],15 pp, inc
  half-title & 2 advt ff. Errata on last page of
  prelims. Disbound.   *(Hannas)* **£65 [≈ $116]**
- A Speech to the Upper House of
  Convocation, upon the Presentment of the
  late Prolocutor. London: for J. Roberts, 1714.
  2nd edn. 8vo. [iv],19 pp. Half-title. Marg tear
  in last leaf. Some browning. Disbound.
  (Young's) **£48 [≈ $85]**

Smart, Christopher
- Poems by Mr. Smart. Viz. Reason and
  Imagination a Fable. Ode to Admiral Sir
  George Pocock ... London: for the author, &
  sold by Mr. Fletcher & Mr. Laurence, [1763].
  1st edn. 4to. [ii],22 pp, "Proposals" on last
  leaf. Sgnd by Smart. Sl water stain. Contemp
  style qtr calf. *(Burmester)* **£1,350 [≈ $2,403]**

Smeaton, John
- Experimental Enquiry concerning the
  Natural Powers of Wind and Water to turn
  Mills and Other Machines depending on a
  Circular Motion ... London: for I. & J.
  Taylor, 1794. 110 pp. 5 fldg plates. Qtr calf,
  mrbld bds.   *(C.R. Johnson)* **£260 [≈ $463]**
- A Narrative of the Building and a Description
  of the Construction of the Eddystone
  Lighthouse with Stone ... Appendix ...
  Lighthouse on the Spurn Point ... London:
  Nicol, 1793. 2nd edn. Folio. xiv,198 pp. Title
  vignette, 23 plates. 1 sm marg repr. Contemp
  half calf.   *(Sotheran's)* **£1,250 [≈ $2,225]**

Smedley, Jonathan
- Gulliveriana: or, a Fourth Volume of
  Miscellanies. Being a Sequel of the Three
  Volumes, published by Pope and Swift.
  London: for J. Roberts, 1728. 1st edn. 8vo.
  Frontis. Lib stamp. Sl browned. Lib half mor.
  Anon.   *(Hannas)* **£280 [≈ $498]**

Smellie, William
- The Philosophy of Natural History.
  Edinburgh: for the heirs of Charles Elliot,
  1790. 1st edn. 4to. xvi,547 pp. Occas marg
  damp stains, endpapers sl dusty. Sm marg
  tear in 1 leaf. Period calf, sometime rebacked.
  (Rankin) **£265 [≈ $472]**
- The Philosophy of Natural History [vol 1].
  Edinburgh: for the heirs of Charles Elliot ...,
  1790. 1st edn. 4to. xiii,[3],547 pp. Contemp
  qtr calf, uncut, sl rubbed.
  (Heritage) **$450 [≈ £253]**

Smith, Charlotte
- The Emigrants, a Poem, in Two Books.
  London: T. Cadell, 1793. 4to. Half-title, [12],
  68 pp. Disbound.
  (C.R. Johnson) **£125 [≈ $223]**
- Rural Walks: in Dialogues intended for the
  Use of Young Persons ... London: Cadell &
  Davies, 1795. 1st edn. 2 vols. 12mo. vi,[ii],
  174; [iv],183,[i] pp. Contemp green vellum
  backed bds, orig paper labels (chipped).
  (Finch) **£580 [≈ $1,032]**
- The Young Philosopher: A Novel ... London:
  Cadell & Davies, 1798. 1st edn. 4 vols in 2.
  12mo. Contemp continental marbled paper
  wraps, spines v sl faded & browned.
  (Finch) **£780 [≈ $1,388]**

Smith, Edmund
- Phaedra and Hippolitus. A Tragedy ...
  London: for Bernard Lintot, [1707]. 1st edn.
  4to. Half-title. Browned. Red half mor.
  (Hannas) **£110 [≈ $196]**

- The Works ... prefix'd, A Character of Mr. Smith by Mr. Oldisworth. London: for Bernard Lintot, 1719. 3rd edn. 8vo. [xxxvi],101 pp. Sl spotting & staining. New bds. *(Young's)* **£45 [≈ $80]**

Smith, Eliza
- The Compleat Housewife: or Accomplish'd Gentlewoman's Companion ... The Seventh Edition, with very large additions ... London: Pemberton, 1736. 8vo. [xvi],352,xv pp. 6 fldg plates. Occas soil & marg stains. Contemp style half calf. *(Burmester)* **£250 [≈ $445]**
- The Compleat Housewife: or, Accomplish'd Gentlewoman's Companion ... Receipts in Cookery ... Wines ... Seventh Edition, with very large Additions ... London: Pemberton, 1736. [xvi],352,xv pp. 5 plates (of 6). Crnr of plate 5 torn. 19th c cloth. *(Gough)* **£195 [≈ $347]**

Smith, George
- A Complete Body of Distilling, explaining the Mysteries of that Science ... London: for Bernard Lintot, 1725. 1st edn. 8vo. Intl advt leaf. 24 ctlg pp at end. Contemp calf, rebacked, trifle rubbed. *(Ximenes)* **$475 [≈ £267]**
- A Compleat Body of Distilling ... In Two Parts ... London: Printed in Fleetstreet, 1738. 3rd edn. 8vo. [vi],89,[3], 93-150,[2] pp. Frontis. Occas sl damp stains. Contemp bds, rec calf spine. *(Vanbrugh)* **£225 [≈ $401]**

Smith, Hugh
- Letters to Married Women. The Third Edition, Revised ... London: for the author, 1774. 256 pp. Contemp calf, hinges cracking. *(C.R. Johnson)* **£225 [≈ $401]**

Smith, J.E.
- Tracts relating to Natural History. London: 1798. xiv,[1],312 pp. 7 plates (6 cold). Calf, rebacked. *(Wheldon & Wesley)* **£75 [≈ $134]**

Smith, John
- The Narrative of Mr. John Smith ... Containing a Further Discovery of the Late Horrid Popish-Plot ... London: Robert Boulter, 1679. Folio. [8],35 pp. New wraps. Wing S.4127. *(O'Neal)* **$75 [≈ £42]**

Smith, John Thomas
- Remarks on Rural Scenery, with Twenty Etchings of Cottages ... London: Nathaniel Smith, 1797. 1st edn. 4to. 27,[1] pp, subscribers leaf. Dec title additionally hand cold in green, 20 etched plates (v sl stain some versos). Contemp half mor, bds renewed to style. *(Spelman)* **£500 [≈ $890]**
- Remarks on Rural Scenery; with Twenty Etchings of Cottages, from nature ... London: Nathaniel Smith & J.T. Smith, 1797. 1st edn. 4to. 27,[i blank],[ii subscribers] pp. Dec title, 20 plates (washed). Contemp half mor, new paper on sides. *(Finch)* **£750 [≈ $1,335]**

Smith or Smyth, John, 1662-1717
- Poems upon Several Occasions ... London: for H. Clements, 1713. 1st edn. 8vo. [ii], viii, vi, [iv],384,[iv] pp. Errata slip. Contemp panelled calf, rubbed, spine darkened & worn at hd, upper jnt cracked but firm. *(Finch)* **£175 [≈ $312]**

Smith, Robert
- Court Cookery: or, The Compleat English Cook ... Second Edition, with Additions. London: for T. Wotton,1725. 8vo. [viii], 218, [xiv] pp. Sm repr to title. Contemp calf, later labels. *(Gough)* **£450 [≈ $801]**

Smith, Robert, 1689-1768
- Harmonics, or The Philosophy of Musical Sounds ... The Second Edition, much improved and augmented. London: for T. & J. Merrill, Cambridge ..., 1759. 8vo. xviii,[ii], 280, [xiii] pp. 28 fldg plates. Orig bds, uncut, v sl soiled. *(Finch)* **£385 [≈ $685]**

Smith, Samuel Stanhope
- An Essay on the Causes of the Variety of Complexion and Figure in the Human Species. To which are added Strictures on Lord Kaim's Discourse, on the Original Diversity of Mankind. Phila: Robert Aitken, 1787. 1st edn. 8vo. Sl foxing. Disbound. *(Ximenes)* **$500 [≈ £281]**

Smith, Simon
- The Golden Fleece: or, the Trade, Interest, and Well-Being of Great Britain considered ... [London: 1736]. 1st edn. Folio. 26 pp. Disbound. Anon. *(Young's)* **£250 [≈ $445]**

Smith, Sir Thomas
- The Common-Wealth of England. And the Manner and Governement thereof ... London: Stansby for Smethwicke, 1633. 1st 12mo edn. [xii],285,[2 colophon] pp. Addtnl engvd title. Contemp calf, later gilt, lacks label. STC 22865. *(Vanbrugh)* **£275 [≈ $490]**

Smith, Thomas
- An Account of the Greek Church ... London: Miles Flesher for Richard Davis at Oxford, 1680. 1st edn in English. 8vo. [xxiv], 303, [xiii] pp. Blank before title, 9 advt pp at end.

Contemp calf, gilt, sl worn. Wing S.4232.
(Clark) **£120 [≈ $214]**
- Remarks upon the Manners, Religion and Government of the Turks ... London: for Moses Pitt, 1678. 8vo. Collates A-P8, (*)Q-(*)R4, S-Z8. Last leaf reprd with sl loss. Contemp calf, rebacked & reprd. Wing S.4246. *(Quest Books)* **£1,850 [≈ $3,293]**

Smollett, Tobias
- The Adventures of Ferdinand Count Fathom. London: for W. Johnston, 1753. 1st edn. 2 vols. 8vo. 262; 315 pp. Few sm reprs. Lacks half-titles, lacks (?) final blank vol 2. Early 20th c period style speckled calf gilt, gilt dentelles, mor labels, by Wallis. Anon.
(Chapel Hill) **$700 [≈ £393]**
- The Adventures of Ferdinand Count Fathom. By the Author of Roderick Random. London: W. Johnston, 1753. 1st edn. 2 vols. 12mo. [ii], viii,262; [ii],315 pp. Contemp calf, 3 jnts reprd, sl rubbed. Half mor slipcase. Anon. Buxton Forman's copy.
(Blackwell's) **£450 [≈ $801]**
- The Adventures of Peregrine Pickle. In which are included, Memoirs of a Lady of Quality ... Fifth Edition. London: T. Lowndes ..., 1773. 4 vols in 2. 12mo. Contemp calf, gilt spines, crnrs sl worn, spine ends sl chipped. Anon. *(Clark)* **£85 [≈ $151]**
- The Adventures of Roderick Random. London: for J. Osborn, 1748. 1st edn. 2 vols. 8vo. 324; 366 pp. Contemp calf, gilt borders, 1 jnt reprd, other jnts cracked but holding. Qtr mor slipcase. Anon.
(Chapel Hill) **$800 [≈ £449]**
- The Expedition of Humphry Clinker. London: for W. Johnston; Salisbury: B. Collins, "1671" [ie 1761]. 1st edn, with press figs vi-6, 2-1, 16-2 in vol 1. 3 vols. 12mo. Half-titles. Sl washed. Red crushed levant gilt, a.e.g., by Riviere. Cloth case. Anon.
(Ximenes) **$1,500 [≈ £843]**
- The Expedition of Humphry Clinker. By the Author of Roderick Random. Dublin: for A. Leathley ..., 1771. 1st Dublin edn. Issue with "London" on 2nd line of title on p iii. 2 vols. 12mo. 24 advt ff. Contemp calf, sl rubbed, jnts weak. Anon. *(Hannas)* **£240 [≈ $427]**
- The Expedition of Humphry Clinker. London: for W. Johnston; Salisbury: B. Collins, 1772. 2nd edn. 3 vols. 12mo. Half-titles. Contemp half calf, sides rubbed, rebacked. Anon. *(Burmester)* **£60 [≈ $107]**
- The Expedition of Humphry Clinker ... The Fourth Edition. London: for T. Longman & C.G.J. Robinson, 1792. 3 vols. 12mo. Sl repr to 1 title. Contemp calf, rebacked.
(Waterfield's) **£100 [≈ $178]**

- The Adventures of Peregrine Pickle. London: R. Baldwin ..., 1769. 4th edn. 4 vols. 12mo. Contemp calf, jnts sl rubbed. Anon.
(Bookpress) **$500 [≈ £281]**
- Plays and Poems ... With Memoirs of the Life and Writings of the Author. London: for T. Evans, & R. Baldwin, 1777. 1st edn. 8vo. [iv], xlvii,[ii], 4-272 pp. Half-title. Vignette port on title. Some foxing. Contemp calf, rubbed, spine ends worn, label defective.
(Burmester) **£85 [≈ $151]**
- The Present State of All Nations. Containing a Geographical, Natural, Commercial, and Political History of all the Countries in the Known World. London: Baldwin, 1768-69. 8 vols. 16 maps, 32 engvs (inc 1 not called for). Contemp calf gilt, rubbed, sl worn.
(Jermy & Westerman) **£475 [≈ $846]**
- Travels through France and Italy ... London: for R. Baldwin, 1766. 1st edn. 2 vols. 8vo. Half-titles. Contemp calf, sl worn.
(Ximenes) **$600 [≈ £337]**

Smyth, James Carmichael
- The Effect of the Nitrous Vapour in Preventing and Destroying Contagion ... made chiefly by the Surgeons of His Majesty's Navy ... with an Introduction ... on Jail or Hospital Fever ... Phila: Dobson, 1799. 8vo. 174 pp. Fldg table. Sl wear, foxed. Sheep, rebacked. *(Goodrich)* **$165 [≈ £93]**

Smyth, John
- Scarronides, or Virgil Travestie. A Mock-Poem on the Second Book of Virgil's Aenaeis [sic]. In English Burlesque. London: 1692. 1st edn. 8vo. 86 pp, advt leaf. Some marg worming. Contemp calf, rebacked. Wing S.4359A. Anon. *(Robertshaw)* **£40 [≈ $71]**

Smyth, John Ferdinand Dalziel
- A Tour in the United States of America ... London: G. Robinson, 1784. 1st edn. 2 vols. 8vo. 453; 400 pp. Contemp calf, fine.
(Chapel Hill) **$900 [≈ £506]**

Soave Polano, Pietro
- See Sarpi, Paolo

Sober and Seasonable Queries ...
- Sober and Seasonable Queries humbly offered to Good Protestants in England, in Order to a Choice of the New Parliament. [London: 1679]. 1st edn. Folio. 4 pp. drop-head title. Disbound. Wing S.4402.
(Hannas) **£30 [≈ $53]**

Society of Dilettanti
- Ionian Antiquities. London: The Society,

1769. 1st edn. Lge folio. [iv],iv,53 pp. 6, 12, 10 plates. Contemp qtr leather, worn & rubbed. *(Bookpress)* **$1,500 [≃ £843]**

The Solicitor's Compleat Guide ...

- The Solicitor's Compleat Guide ... London: for J. Williams, M. Folingsby & G. Kearsly ..., 1776. Only (?) edn. 2 vols. Post 12mo. [2], iv,276; [ii], 277-530, [x] pp. Sl marks & creases. Contemp calf, rubbed & split.
(Ash) **£250 [≃ $445]**

Somers, John, Lord

- The Security of Englishmen's Lives: Or, the Trust, Power and Duty of Grand Juries of England Explained ... London: for J. Almon, 1766. 2nd edn. 8vo. 112 pp. Stitched as issued. *(Young's)* **£45 [≃ $80]**

The Somerset Petition ...

- The Somerset Petition With an Answer in Defence of the Parliament, against the Same Petition. London: Lindsey, 1642. 4to. Title border. Stitched. Wing S.4652.
(Rostenberg & Stern) **$90 [≃ £51]**

Somervile, William

- The Chase. A Poem. London: for G. Hawkins, sold by T. Cooper, 1735. 1st edn. 4to. Errata leaf. Frontis. Contemp calf, rebacked. *(Hannas)* **£110 [≃ $196]**
- The Chace. A Poem. London: G. Hawkins, 1735. 1st edn. 4to. [xii],106,[i] pp. Final errata leaf. Frontis. Rec wraps.
(Blackwell's) **£125 [≃ $223]**
- The Chace. A Poem. London: for G. Hawkins, 1735. 1st 8vo edn. [xx],131 pp. Contemp calf, elab gilt border, gilt dec panels, sl worn. *(Young's)* **£85 [≃ $151]**
- The Chace. A Poem. Third Edition. London: 1735. 8vo. 131 pp. Mod bds.
(Robertshaw) **£12 [≃ $21]**
- Hobbinol, or the Rural Games. A Burlesque Poem, in Blank Verse. London: for J. Stagg, 1740. 1st edn. 4to. [iv],vii,64 pp. Pale damp stain across last 4 sections. Rec half mor.
(Sotheran's) **£125 [≃ $223]**
- Occasional Poems, Translations, Fables, Tales &c. London: for Bernard Lintot, 1727. 1st edn. 8vo. Contemp calf gilt.
(Hannas) **£190 [≃ $338]**

Somerville, Thomas

- The History of Great Britain during the Reign of Queen Anne ... London: Strahan & Cadell, 1798. 1st edn. Half-title, xxviii, 674,2 advt pp. Half calf, worn, lacks backstrip.
(Jermy & Westerman) **£40 [≃ $71]**

Somner, William

- A Treatise of the Roman Ports and Forts in Kent. Publish'd by James Brome ... Oxford: at the Theater, 1693. 1st edn. Sm 8vo. [x],118, [ii], 117,[15] pp. Port frontis. Contemp calf, rebacked, rubbed. Wing S.4669. *(Blackwell's)* **£115 [≃ $205]**

Sonnini, C.S.

- Travels in Upper and Lower Egypt ... Translated from the French by Henry Hunter. London: Stockdale, 1799. 1st edn. 3 vols. xix, 376; vii,368; viii,324 pp. 40 plates inc 1 fldg map. Some foxing & damp staining. Half mor, v worn. *(Worldwide)* **$280 [≃ £157]**

The Sophister. A Comedy ...

- See Zouch, Richard

Sophocles

- The Tragedies. From the Greek. By Thomas Francklin. London: for R. Francklin, 1758-59. 1st edn thus. 2 vols in one. 4to. [20],297,[3 advt]; 398,59 pp. Frontis, title vignettes, engvd plan. Contemp calf, rebacked. *(O'Neal)* **£300 [≃ $169]**

Sorrows ...

- The Sorrows of Werter ... see Goethe, Johann Wolfgang von
- Sorrows. Sacred to the ⅞Memory of Penelope ...see Boothby, Sir Brooke.

Sotheby, W.

- A Tour through Parts of Wales, Sonnets, Odes and Other Poems. London: J. Smeeton ..., 1794. 4to. Half-title. 13 aquatints. Endpapers v sl foxed. Speckled half calf gilt, mor label. *(Francis Edwards)* **£200 [≃ $356]**

Southerne, Thomas

- The Fatal Marriage: or, the Innocent Adultery, a Play. London: for Jacob Tonson, 1694. 1st edn. Sm 4to. Mottled calf, inner dentelles gilt, spine ends chipped. Wing S.4756. *(Ximenes)* **$650 [≃ £365]**
- The Maid's Last Prayer: or, any, rather than fail. A Comedy. London: for R. Bentley, & J. Tonson, 1693. 1st edn. Sm 4to. Disbound. Wing S.4760. *(Ximenes)* **$500 [≃ £281]**

Southey, Robert

- Joan of Arc, an Epic Poem. Boston: Manning & Loring, for Nancrede, 1798. 1st Amer edn. 8vo. 264 pp. Rec bds.
(Burmester) **£45 [≃ $80]**

Southey, Robert (editor)

- The Annual Anthology. Bristol: Biggs & Co., for Longman & Rees, London, 1799-1800. 1st edn. 1st issue, with C3 in vol 2 uncancelled, omitting "wicked". 2 vols. Sm 8vo. Cancellans C3 bound in. 19th c calf gilt, sl worn, 1 jnt reprd. Anon.
  (Ximenes) **$2,000 [≈ £1,124]**

Southwell, Robert

- St Peters Complainte. Mary Magdal. Teares. With other Workes ... By R.S. London: J. Haviland, sould by I. Benson, 1636 [ie 1634]. 12mo. Collates A1-Z12, Aa1-12. Engvd title, 3 sectional titles. V sl damp stains. 19th c russia gilt, a.e.g., sl worn. STC 22968.
  (Clark) **£450 [≈ $801]**

The Sovereign ...

- The Sovereign: or a Political Discourse upon the Office and Obligations of the Supreme Magistrate. London: Printed in the Year, 1680. 1st edn. 4to. [ii blank],[vi], 61, [i] pp. Disbound. Wing S.4777.
  (Finch) **£90 [≈ $160]**

Spagnuoli, Baptista, Mantuanus

- The Bucolicks of Baptist Mantuan in Ten Eclogues. Translated out of Latine into English, by Tho: Harvey Gent. London: for Humphrey Moseley, 1656. 1st edn of this translation. Sm 8vo. [viii],104 pp. Marg stains & dust soiling. Contemp sheep, rebacked. Wing S.4791.   *(Burmester)* **£120 [≈ $214]**

Sparrow, Anthony

- A Collection of Articles, Injunctions, Canons, Orders, Ordinances and Constitutions Ecclesiastical; with other Publick Records of the Church of England ... Third impression with additions. London: 1675. 4to. 406,index pp. Frontis. Contemp calf, rebacked. Anon.
  (Robertshaw) **£65 [≈ $116]**

Specimens ...

- Specimens of the Early English Poets ... see Ellis, George (ed.)

Spectacle de la Nature ...

- See Pluche, Antoine-Noel

Speculum Crape-Gownorum ...

- Speculum Crape-Gownorum: or, A Lesson of Instruction To Those Pragmatical Pr--sts, Who turn the Pulpit into a Prattling-Box ... London: for W. Hinton, 1739. 8vo in 4s. 49 pp. Blind stamp on title & last leaf. Mod calf gilt.   *(Hollett)* **£85 [≈ $151]**

Spelman, Sir Henry

- De non temerandis Ecclesiis, Churches not to be Violated. A Tract ... Oxford: H. Hall, for Amos Curteyn, 1668. 4th edn. 8vo. [xiv], 128 pp. Lacks the 2 endpapers. Old sheep. Wing S.4922.   *(Young's)* **£90 [≈ $160]**

- The English Works ... Second Edition. London: D. Browne ..., 1727. Folio. 256,[24] pp. Port frontis. Occas spotting & browning. Contemp calf, rebacked, red edges.
  (Frew Mackenzie) **£120 [≈ $214]**

- The History and Fate of Sacrilege ... London: John Hartley, 1698. 1st edn. 8vo. [x],292,40 pp. Intl advt leaf. Twisden's 'Beginners of a Monastic Life' with sep half-title at end. Minor browning. Contemp calf, extrs sl worn. Wing S.4927.   *(Clark)* **£65 [≈ $116]**

- Of the Law Terms: A Discourse ... Wherein the Laws of the Jews, Grecians, Romans, Saxons, and Normans, relating to the Subject, are Fully Explained. London: Matthew Gillyflower, 1684. 1st edn. 8vo. [4],88 pp. Sl soiling. Mod calf. Wing S.4929.
  (Meyer Boswell) **$650 [≈ £365]**

- Of the Law-Terms: A Discourse ... Wherein the Laws of the Jews, Grecians, Romans, Saxons, and Normans, relating to this Subject are Fully Explained. London: Matthew Gillyflower, 1684. Sm 8vo. [4],88 pp. A1 before title. Sl soiling. Disbound. Wing S.4929.   *(Karmiole)* **$175 [≈ £98]**

Spelman, Sir John

- Certain Considerations vpon the Dvties both of Prince and People. Written by a Gentleman of Quality ... Printed at Oxford. London: Re-printed, 1642. Sm 4to. [i],14,[7] pp. Sl soiled & browned, 2 margs sl cropped. Mod wraps. Wing S.4938. Anon.
  (Blackwell's) **£60 [≈ $107]**

Spence, Joseph

- An Account of the Life, Character, and Poems of Mr. Blacklock: Student of Philosophy, in the University of Edinburgh. London: for R. & J. Dodsley, 1754. 1st edn. 8vo. Mod wraps. *(Ximenes)* **$200 [≈ £112]**

- Polymetis: or, an Enquiry concerning the agreement between the Works of the Roman Poets and the Remains of the Antient Artists. London: R. Dodsley, 1747. 1st edn. Folio. 361 pp. Num plates. Contemp tree calf, elab gilt spine, jnts cracked but firm, spine chipped.   *(Hermitage)* **$350 [≈ £197]**

- Polymetis or, an Enquiry concerning the agreement between the Works of the Roman Poets and the Remains of the Antient Artists ... London: for R. Dodsley, 1747. Folio. Frontis port, 41 plates. Contemp calf, some

wear at crnrs, jnts cracked.
(Waterfield's) **£250 [≈ $445]**

Spencer, Edmund

- A View of the State of Ireland as it was in the Reign of Queen Elizabeth. Written by way of Dialogue between Eudoxus and Ireneus. Dublin: Flin, 1763. 8vo. xxii,258,xviii pp. Contemp calf.   *(de Burca)* **£90 [≈ $160]**

Spencer, John

- A Discourse concerning Prodigies: wherein the Vanity of Presages by them is reprehended ... Second Edition corrected and inlarged ... London: Field for Graves, 1665. 2 parts. 8vo. Lacks final blank. Marg worm affecting side notes. Contemp calf, jnt cracking. Wing S.4948, 4949.
  (Hannas) **£120 [≈ $214]**
- A Discourse concerning Prodigies, wherein the Vanity of Presages by them is reprehended ... added a short Treatise concerning Vulgar prophecies. Second Edition, corrected and inlarged. London: 1665. 2 parts in one vol. 8vo. Sl used. Contemp calf. Wing S.4948, 4949.
  (Robertshaw) **£75 [≈ $134]**

Spenser, Edmund

- Colin Clouts Come Home Againe. London: William Ponsonbie, 1595. 1st edn. 1st issue, with "worthylie" on line 24 of leaf C. Sm 4to. Collates A-K4. Last leaf supplied in facs. Later mor.   *(Bookpress)* **$2,250 [≈ £1,264]**
- The Faerie Queene. London: 1609. 1st folio edn. Sm marg reprs, occas minor soiling or spotting. Lacks final blank. Contemp calf, jnts reprd. STC 23083.
  (D & D Galleries) **$2,000 [≈ £1,124]**
- The Faerie Queen: The Shepheards Calendar: Together with other works ... Collected ... London: H.L. for Mathew Lownes, 1611. 1st coll edn, 2nd issue. 5 parts. Folio. 3 blank ff Lacks intl blank. Title dedic & last leaf stained. Contemp calf, rebacked, reprd. STC 23083.7.
  (Hannas) **£1,400 [≈ $2,492]**
- The Faerie Queen ... added, a New Life of the Author ... London: J. Brindley, 1751. 1st illust edn. 4to. 32 engvd plates after W. Kent. Minor marg dustiness, hd of titles reprd. Contemp calf, gilt rebacked.
  (Spelman) **£420 [≈ $748]**
- The Faerie Queen ... added, a New Life of the Author ... London: Brindley & Wright, 1751. Edited by Thomas Birch. 3 vols. 4to. 32 fldg plates. Some foxing throughout. Contemp mottled calf, rebacked.
  (Blackwell's) **£350 [≈ $623]**

- The Fairy Queen ... With a Glossary ... London: Tonson, 1758. 2 vols. 8vo. xxxviii, [ii], 527,[i]; 496 pp. Vignette port, 9 plates. Occas browning. Contemp tree calf, rebacked & recrnrd, dble labels, sl rubbed.
  (Clark) **£85 [≈ $151]**
- The Works ... to which is prefix'd the Life of the Author and an Essay on Allegorical Poetry by Mr. Hughes. London: 1750. 6 vols. 12mo. Contemp calf, later labels, few spine ends sl worn, 2 jnts cracked.
  (Robertshaw) **£55 [≈ $98]**
- The Works ... With a Glossary ... prefix'd the Life of the Author ... by Mr. John Hughes. London: 1750. 6 vols. Contemp speckled calf gilt, gilt dec spine, red & green labels, 2 hinges starting, hd of spines rubbed, crnrs bumped.   *(D & D Galleries)* **$225 [≈ £126]**

Spicer, John

- Tables of Interest ... Computed, and carefully examined by John Spicer, Gent. at the Exchequer. London: for J. Spicer, 1693. 1st edn. 4to. 135 pp. Contemp calf, lower part of jnts cracking. Wing S.4973.
  (Burmester) **£225 [≈ $401]**

The Spirit of Nations ...

- See Espiard de la Borde, F.I.

Spiritual Songs ...

- See Mason, John

The Sportsman's Dictionary ...

- The Sportsman's Dictionary; or, the Gentleman's Companion: for Town and Country ... London: Robinson, 1785. 3rd edn. 4to. viii, 560 pp. 17 engvs. Prelims & frontis sl water stained. Leather gilt, front bd nearly detached, spine weak.
  (Bates & Hindmarch) **£125 [≈ $223]**

Spottiswoode, John

- The History of the Church of Scotland ... London: J. Flesher for J. Royston, 1655. 1st edn. Sm folio. [xx],546,[xiv] pp. 2 ports. A few headlines cropped. Sl damp staining. Mod half calf. Wing S.5022.
  (Blackwell's) **£250 [≈ $445]**
- The History of the Church and State of Scotland ... Fourth Edition ... Appendix. London: R. Royston, 1677. Folio. [xx],546, [xx], 47,[i] pp. Half-title. 2 ports. Contemp calf, gilt spine, rubbed, spine ends reprd, new endpapers. Wing S.5021.
  (Clark) **£90 [≈ $160]**

The Spouter's Companion ...

- The Spouter's Companion; or Theatrical

Remembrancer: containing a Collection of the most esteemed Prologues and Epilogues ... London: for J. Cooke ..., [ca 1770?]. 12mo. [iv], 24, 23*-24*, 25-104, [12 advt] pp. Frontis (sl browned & offset). Contemp qtr calf, jnt weak.   *(Burmester)* **£175 [≈$312]**

Sprat, Thomas
- The History of the Royal-Society of London ... London: for Martyn & Allestry, 1667. 1st edn. 1st issue, 'of' repeated p 85 lines 6-7. 4to. [xvi],438,[1] pp. Frontis, 2 fldg plates. Faint water stain in upper marg. Contemp calf, rebacked. Wing S.5035.
        (Gaskell) **£1,250 [≈$2,225]**
- The History of the Royal Society of London, for the Improving of Natural Knowledge. London: T.R. for J. Martyn, 1667. 438 pp, errata sheet. Frontis, fldg plate. Lib stamp on title. Leather gilt. *(Key Books)* **$500 [≈£281]**
- The History of the Royal-Society of London ... London: Rob. Scot ..., 1702. 2nd edn, crrctd. 4to. Imprimatur leaf. 2 fldg plates. Water stain at start. Contemp calf, rebacked.
        (P and P Books) **£250 [≈$445]**
- The History of the Royal Society of London for the Improving of Natural Knowledge. London: Knapton ..., 1722. 3rd edn. 4to. [xvi], 438 pp. 2 fldg plates. Contemp calf.
        (Bookpress) **£375 [≈£211]**
- The Plague of Athens ... Now attempted in English ... London: for Joanna Brome, 1683. 8vo. [vi],34 pp. Occas sl staining. Rec bds. Wing S.5043.   *(Clark)* **£42 [≈$75]**
- A Sermon preach'd before the King at White-Hall, December the 22d. 1678. London: 1708. 8vo. 24 pp. Later wraps.
        (Robertshaw) **£18 [≈$32]**
- A Sermon preached before the Artillery Company of London at St. Mary Le Bow, April 20. 1681. London: for John Baker, 1682. 1st edn. 4to. [4],31 pp. Title & last leaf v dust soiled. Qtr calf. Wing S.5058.
        (Hannas) **£20 [≈$36]**
- A True Account and Declaration of the Horrid Conspiracy against the late King ... In the Savoy: Newcomb for Lowndes, 1685. 1st edn. 2 parts in one. Folio. [vi],167, [iii], 141 pp. Orig sheep, spine reprd. Wing S.5065. Anon.   *(Vanbrugh)* **£295 [≈$525]**

Sprengell, Sir Conrad
- The Aphorisms of Hippocrates and the Sentences of Celsus, with Explanations and References to the most considerable Writers in Physick and Philosophy ... Second Edition ... enlarged. London: 1735. 8vo. 435,index pp. Port. Marg worm index. Contemp calf, rebacked.   *(Robertshaw)* **£35 [≈$62]**

Squire, Samuel
- An Enquiry into the Foundation of the English Constitution; or, an Historical Essay upon the Anglo-Saxon Government both in Germany and England. London: W. Bowyer for C. Bathurst, 1745. 1st edn. 8vo. vi,291,[1] pp. Contemp calf gilt.
        (Burmester) **£85 [≈$151]**

Stackhouse, Thomas
- A Complete Body of Divinity, consisting of Five Parts. London: for J. Batley, 1729. Issue with dedic subscribed 'The Editors'. Folio. Old panelled calf, worn, jnts cracked but sound. Anon.   *(Waterfield's)* **£45 [≈$80]**
- Memoirs of the Life, Character, Conduct, and Writings of Dr. Francis Atterbury, late Bishop of Rochester ... Second Edition. London: [Curll], 1727. 8vo. xix,[iv],144,[16 ctlg] pp. Port. Contemp panelled sheep, rubbed.   *(Blackwell's)* **£80 [≈$142]**

Stanhope, George
- Parsons, his Christian Directory, Being a Treatise of Holy Resurrection. In Two Parts. Put into Modern English ... London: for Richard Sare ..., 1709. 3rd edn. 8vo. 12, 465, 3 advt pp. Contemp panelled calf, sl worn.
        (Young's) **£70 [≈$125]**

Stanhope, James, Earl Stanhope
- Mr. Stanhope's Answer to the Report of the Commissioners sent into Spain, &c. London: Richard Charret, 1714. 1st edn (?). 12mo. [2], 22, 24-40 pp. Disbound. *(Hannas)* **£35 [≈$62]**

Stanyan, Abraham
- An Account of Switzerland, Written in the Year 1714. London: for Jacob Tonson ..., 1714. Pencil marks to margs. Sev sm marg holes. Free endpapers excised. Calf, sl worn, splits hd of jnts. Anon.
        (Francis Edwards) **£125 [≈$223]**
- An Account of Switzerland. Written in the Year 1714. London: Tonson, 1714. 1st edn. Large Paper. 8vo. Title & next ff sl foxed. 19th c polished calf, rebacked. Anon.
        (Hannas) **£85 [≈$151]**
- An Account of Switzerland. Written in the Year 1714. London: Tonson, 1714. 1st edn. 8vo. [viii],247,[i] pp. 2 marg tears. Contemp calf gilt, sl rubbed, jnts cracked & internally reinforced. Anon.   *(Clark)* **£140 [≈$249]**
- An Account of Switzerland. Written in the Year 1714. London: Tonson, 1714. 1st edn. 8vo. [viii],247,[i] pp. Engvd title vignette. Contemp panelled calf, lacks label, extrs worn, jnts cracking. Anon.
        (Finch) **£100 [≈$178]**

Stanyan, Temple

- The Grecian History. From the Original of Greece, to the End of the Peloponnesian War ... London: Tonson, 1739. 2nd edn, rvsd & enlgd. 2 vols in one. 8vo. Fldg map (tear in crease), 1 plate. Worm in lower marg. Contemp calf, worn, cvrs almost detached.
(Worldwide) **$50 [≈ £28]**

Stapleton, Philip

- Speech ... Ian 15, 1641. Concerning an accusation of the Lord Digby of High Treason. London: 1641. 4to. Wraps. Wing S.5258. *(Rostenberg & Stern)* **$75 [≈ £42]**

State ...

- The State of the Nation for the Year 1747 ... see Carteret, John, Earl Granville.
- The State of the Nation, with a General Balance of the Publick Accounts ... London: for M. Cooper, 1748. 2nd edn. 8vo. [iv],55 pp. Half-title. Fldg table. Disbound.
(Young's) **£75 [≈ $134]**
- The State of the Protestants in Ireland ... see King, William
- The State Preferable to the Church: or, Reasons for making Sale of the whole present Property of the Church, in England and Ireland, for the Use of the State ... London: for M. Cooper, 1748. 1st edn. 8vo. 62 pp. Title loose. Disbound. *(Hannas)* **£50 [≈ $89]**

Staunford, William

- An Exposicion of the kinges prerogatiue collected out of the great abridgement of Iustice Fitzherbert and other olde writers of the lawes of Englande ... London: 1568. 4to. 85 ff. Occas sl marks. Old MS notes. Mod dec calf. STC 23214.
(Meyer Boswell) **$1,250 [≈ £702]**

Stearns, Charles

- The Ladies Philosophy of Love, a Poem in Four Cantos written in 1774 and now first published ... Leominster, Mass.: John Prentiss & Co. for the author, 1797. 4to. Sl browned. 1 leaf torn, no loss. Disbound.
(Waterfield's) **£200 [≈ $356]**
- The Ladies' Philosophy of Love. A Poem, in four Cantos ... Now first published ... Leominster, Mass.: John Prentiss for the author, 1797. 1st edn. Sm 4to. 76 pp. Side-stitched as issued, unopened, lower blue paper wrapper preserved.
(Finch) **£75 [≈ $134]**

Steele, Sir Richard

- The Crisis: or, a Discourse representing,

from the most Authentick Records, the Just Causes of the late Happy Revolution ... London: 1714. 1st edn. 4to. 37 pp. Title sl stained. Disbound. *(Robertshaw)* **£25 [≈ $45]**
- The Importance of Dunkirk Consider'd: in Defence of the Guardian of August the 7th ... London: for A. Baldwin, 1713. 1st edn. 4to. 63 pp. No fldg map (sometimes found). Disbound. *(Hannas)* **£85 [≈ $151]**
- The Plebeians. By a Member of the House of Commons. The Sixth Edition. London: for S. Popping, 1719. 1st coll edn. 8vo. 67,[5] pp. Old wraps. Anon. *(Burmester)* **£75 [≈ $134]**

Steele, Sir Richard (editor)

- Poetical Miscellanies, consisting of Original Poems and Translations. By the best hands. London: Tonson, MDDCXIV [1714]. 1st edn. 8vo. Final blank leaf. frontis. Cancels: A7, E4, G6, G8, P1, P1 [sic]. Browned. Contemp calf, v worn, rebacked.
(Hannas) **£180 [≈ $320]**

Stepney, George

- An Epistle to Charles Montague Esq; on His Majesty's Voyage to Holland. London: for Francis Saunders, 1691. 1st edn. Folio. [2], 10 pp. Faint water stains. Mod bds. Wing S.5467. *(Hannas)* **£75 [≈ $134]**

Sterling, Joseph

- Bombarino, a Romance: with Poems on the Four Sister Arts, viz. Eloquence, Poetry, Painting, and Music: and other Miscellaneous Poems. Dublin: George Cecil, 1768. 1st edn. Sm 8vo. Trimmed a bit close. Disbound. *(Ximenes)* **£400 [≈ £225]**
- Poems. London: G.G.J. & J. Robinson, 1789. Half-title, vii,[6],232,[2] pp. Errata. Contemp calf. *(C.R. Johnson)* **£225 [≈ $401]**

Sterne, Laurence

- Letters supposed to have been written by Yorick and Eliza ... see Combe, William.
- Sterne's Letters to his Friends on Various Occasions. To which is added, his History of a Watch Coat, with Explanatory Notes. London: Kearsly, Johnson, 1775. 1st edn. Sm 8vo. Contemp calf, rebacked. Probably edited & 'improved' by William Combe.
(Hannas) **£180 [≈ $320]**
- A Sentimental Journey through France and Italy. By Mr. Yorick. London: Becket & De Hondt, 1768. 1st edn. 2 vols in one. Sm 8vo. Subscribers. Lacks half-titles. Sl stains. Early 19th c half calf, rubbed. Anon.
(Hannas) **£380 [≈ $676]**
- A Sentimental Journey through France and

Italy. By Mr. Yorick. London: P. Miller & J. White, 1774. Pirated edn. 12mo. 328 pp. Contemp calf, extrs sl worn, 1 jnt cracked. Includes 'A Political Romance'. Anon.
(Clark) £45 [≈ $80]

- A Sentimental Journey through France and Italy. Complete in One Volume. London: Payne, Gray & Murray, 1782. Fcap 8vo. [2],267,[i] pp. Port inserted from another edn. Contemp calf, gilt spine, sl wear spine ends. Inc Hall-Stevenson's continuation.
(Spelman) £45 [≈ $80]

- A Sentimental Journey through France and Italy. By Mr. Yorick. A New Edition. London: J. Wenman, [1782]. 12mo. [2],177 pp. Frontis. Some dustiness. Contemp calf, rebacked.
(Spelman) £20 [≈ $36]

- A Sentimental Journey through France and Italy. By Mr. Yorick: and the Continuation thereof by Eugenius. The Four Volumes Complete in One. A New Edition. London: for T. Osborne, 1784. Sm 8vo. 267 pp. Frontis. Occas foxing. Period sheep, gilt spine.
(Rankin) £85 [≈ $151]

- A Sentimental Journey through France and Italy. By Mr. Yorick. London: for John Taylor, 1790. 4 vols in one. 12mo. "224" [ie 234] pp. Contemp sheep backed bds, uncut, lower jnt cracked but firm. Includes Hall-Stevenson's spurious continuation. Anon.
(Burmester) £65 [≈ $116]

- The Sermons of Mr. Yorick. London: 1769. 2 vols. 12mo. Later mor, hd of spines sl snagged. Anon. *(Robertshaw)* £25 [≈ $45]

- Sermons. A New Edition. London: J. James, 1787. Thick 8vo. xiv,[2],643 pp. Frontis. Occas foxing. Orig bds, uncut, rebacked.
(Spelman) £25 [≈ $45]

- The Life and Opinions of Tristram Shandy, Gentleman. Third Edition. London: Printed in the Year, 1769. Pirated edn. 9 vols in 2, as published. 12mo. Half-titles. Port. Contemp calf, gilt spines, contrasting labels, some wear to spines, 1 label chipped. Anon.
(Ximenes) $450 [≈ £253]

- The Life and Opinions of tristram Shandy, Gentleman. Eighth Edition. London: J. Dodsley, 1770. 6 vols. Contemp calf, red labels, rubbed, hd of some spines worn & sl chipped, few hinges sl cracked.
(Jermy & Westerman) £75 [≈ $134]

- The Works ... Dublin: Thomas Armitage, 1774. 2nd Irish coll edn. 7 vols. 12mo. Engvd titles, port in vol 1, frontises in vols 1 & 2, as called for. Clean tear in port. Few sl marks. Contemp calf, some spines sl worn.
(Burmester) £150 [≈ $267]

Stevens, George Alexander
- Songs, Comic, and Satyrical. Dublin: for W. Sleater, D. Chamberlaine ..., [1778?]. 1st Dublin edn. 12mo. [ii],ii,3-16,246 pp. Fldg frontis, plate. Half mor, upper jnt sl rubbed.
(Burmester) £225 [≈ $401]

Stevens, John
- Monasticon Hibernicum, or The Monastical History of Ireland. Containing ... all the Abbies, Priories, Nunneries ... London: for William Mears, 1722. 8vo. Fldg map, plates. BM duplicate. Rec 18th c style calf.
(de Burca) £315 [≈ $561]

- A New Spanish Grammar, more perfect than any hitherto publish'd ... The Second Edition ... London: for T. Meighan ..., 1739. 8vo. [viii], 392 pp. Title sl marked. Contemp calf, rebacked.
(Burmester) £110 [≈ $196]

Stevens, William Bagshaw
- Poems. London: for Ab. Portal ..., 1782. 1st edn. 4to. [ii],39 pp. Title vignette. Sl marked. Wraps.
(Burmester) £150 [≈ $267]

- Poems. London: for Ab. Portal, R. Faulder, G. Kearsley, 1782. 1st edn. 4to. [ii],39 pp. Title vignette. Occas sl marks. Wrappers.
(Burmester) £150 [≈ $267]

Stevenson, Henry
- The Gentleman Gardener Instructed in Sowing, Planting, Pruning, and Grafting Seeds, Plants, Flowers, and Trees; also in the Management of Bees ... London: for James Hinton, 1764. 5th edn, enlgd. 12mo. Contemp sheep gilt, spine rubbed.
(Ximenes) $175 [≈ £98]

- The Young Gard'ners Director. London: 1716. Sm 8vo. vi,144 pp. Frontis. Calf, reprd. Anon. *(Wheldon & Wesley)* £100 [≈ $178]

Stewart, Matthew
- Tracts, Physical and Mathematical. Containing, an Explication of Several Important Points in Physical Astronomy ... Edinburgh: A. Millar ..., 1761. 1st edn. 8vo. viii, 412 pp. 19 fldg plates. 19th c half calf, hinge cracked but sound.
(Karmiole) $500 [≈ £281]

Stillingfleet, Benjamin
- An Essay on Conversation. London: for L. Gilliver & J. Clarke, 1737. Folio. Title sl foxed. Cut close at top affecting a few page numbers. Disbound.
(Waterfield's) £105 [≈ $187]

- Miscellaneous Tracts relating to Natural History, Husbandry, and Physick ... The

Second Edition ... London: 1762. 8vo. xxxi, 391 pp. 11 plates. Lib stamp on title. Contemp calf, rebacked. Author's pres copy.
(Goodrich) **$145 [≈ £81]**

- Miscellaneous Tracts relating to Natural History, Husbandry, and Physick. To which is added The Calendar of Flora. London: 1762. 2nd edn. xxxi,391 pp. 11 plates. Contemp sprinkled calf, spine gilt (sl rubbed).
(Whitehart) **£130 [≈ $231]**

Stillingfleet, Edward

- An Answer to some Papers Lately Printed, concerning the Authority of the Catholick Church ... London: Ric. Chiswell, 1686. 1st edn. 4to. [vi],72 pp. Imprimatur leaf. Disbound, outer ff sl soiled. Anon.
(Clark) **£20 [≈ $36]**

- An Answer to some Papers Lately Printed, concerning the Authority of the Catholick Church ... London: Chiswel, 1686. 1st edn. Sm 4to. [v], "72" [ie 66,i advt] pp. Imprimatur leaf (discold). Loose in mod wraps. Wing S.5562. Anon.
(Blackwell's) **£40 [≈ $71]**

- The Bishop of Worcester's Answer to Mr. Locke's Second Letter ... London: Henry Mortlock, 1698. 1st edn. 8vo. 178,[vi] pp. Title sl soiled, sm tear. Some worming to lower marg. Contemp roan, upper jnt reprd. Wing S.5558.
(Frew Mackenzie) **£190 [≈ $338]**

- The Grand Question concerning the Bishops Right to Vote in Parliament in Cases Capital. London: for M.P., sold by Richard Rumball, 1680. 1st edn. 8vo. Cancel title. Some water stains. Contemp calf, v worn. Wing S.5594. Anon.
(Hannas) **£35 [≈ $62]**

- The Grand Question, Concerning the Bishops Right to Vote in Parliament in Cases Capital, Stated and Argued ... London: for M.P., & sold by Richard Rumball, 1680. 1st edn. 8vo. [iv],188 pp. New speckled calf. Wing S.5594. Anon. *(Young's)* **£95 [≈ $169]**

- Origines Britannicae, or, the Antiquities of the British Churches ... London: M. Flesher for Henry Mortlock, 1685. 1st edn. Folio. lxxiii,[6],[2 advt],364 pp. Orig calf, gilt panels, front jnt cracked. Wing S.5615.
(Young's) **£75 [≈ $134]**

- Origines Britannicae; or, the Antiquities of the British Churches ... London: M. Flesher for Henry Mortlock, 1685. 1st edn. Sm folio. [i],lxxiii, [6,2 advt],364 pp. Contemp calf, rebacked, crnrs sl worn. Wing S.5615.
(Blackwell's) **£120 [≈ $214]**

- Origines Sacrae, or a Rational Account of the Grounds of Christian Faith ... The Fifth Edition Corrected and Amended. London: M.W. for Henry Mortlock, 1680. 4to. [xxxvi],

619, [i] pp. Contemp calf, extrs sl worn, lacks label. Wing S.5620A. *(Clark)* **£32 [≈ $57]**

Stirrup, Thomas

- Horometria: Or, The Compleat Diallist ... The Second Edition with Additions ... London: R. & W. Leybourn, for Thomas Pirrepoint, 1659. 4to. [iv],181, [xi],31,[i] pp. Lacks frontis & contents leaf. Sl wear & tear. Later half vellum, darkened. Wing S.5689.
(Clark) **£150 [≈ $267]**

Stonecastle, Henry (pseudonym)

- See The Universal Spectator.

Stopford, James

- A Sermon Preached at St. Anne's Church, Dublin, on the 9th of April, 1758, before the Incorporated Society, for promoting English Protestant Schools in Ireland ... Dublin: S. Powell, 1758. 1st edn. 4to. 70 pp. Disbound.
(Young's) **£40 [≈ $71]**

Strangford, Percy Clinton Sydney Smythe, Viscount

- Poems. Dublin: Zachariah Jackson, 1796. 1st edn. Sm 8vo. vi,66 pp. MS corrections on 6 ff. Lacks half-title. Contemp mottled calf, gilt spine, a.e.g. *(Burmester)* **£350 [≈ $623]**

Strother, Edward

- Euodia: or, a Discourse on Causes and Cures. In Two Parts. Second Edition, carefully corrected, with additions. London: 1718. 8vo. 211,index pp. Lib stamp on title & at end. Contemp calf, upper cvr detached.
(Robertshaw) **£60 [≈ $107]**

Strutt, Joseph

- The Chronicle of England. London: W. Shropshire, 1777-78. 1st edn. 2 vols in one. 4to. viii,365,[3]; vi,[2],291 pp. 43 plates & maps. Sl browning. 19th c mor & mrbld bds, gilt spine, t.e.g., sl rubbed.
(O'Neal) **$275 [≈ £154]**

Strype, John

- The History of the Life and Acts of the Most Reverend Father in God, Edmund Grindal ... By J.S. M.A. London: John Wyat & John Hartley, 1710. 1st edn. Folio. [ii],xviii, 314, 108,[vi] pp. Port frontis. Some browning. Contemp calf, gilt spine, sl worn.
(Clark) **£90 [≈ $160]**

- The Life of the Learned Sir Thomas Smith, Kt., Doctor of the Civil Law ... London: A. Roper & R. Basset, 1698. 1st edn. 8vo. [24], 147, [4] pp. Frontis port, engvd map, 4 fldg engvd tables. Damp stain top of prelims.

Contemp calf, rebacked. Wing S.6023. Anon.
(O'Neal) **$275 [≈£154]**

Stuart, Gilbert
- A View of Society in Europe ... or Inquiries concerning the History of Law, Government, and Manners. Edinburgh: for John Bell; London: Murray, 1778. 1st edn. 4to. xx, 433, [3] pp. Half-title, errata leaf. 2 sm lib stamps. Contemp style half calf.
(Burmester) **£450 [≈$801]**

Sturch, John
- A View of the Isle of Wight, in Four Letters to a Friend ... Newport, Isle of Wight: for the author, 1794. 5th edn. 12mo. 84 pp. Fldg map (sl soiled). Title & last few ff soiled. Orig mrbld paper wraps, cvrs worn, backstrip defective. (Frew Mackenzie) **£25 [≈$45]**

Substance ...
- Substance of the Charge of Mismanagement in His Majesty's Naval Affairs, In the Year 1781 ... London: for J. Stockdale, 1782. 1st edn. 8vo. 55,[1 advt] pp. Stitched as issued, uncut. (Young's) **£43 [≈$77]**

Succinct ...
- A Succinct Description of France ... Sent by a Gentleman now Travelling there, to his Friend in England. London: Printed in the Year, 1700. 1st edn. 8vo in 4s. [viii],70 pp. Title browned & a few ink blots. Later wraps. Wing S.6114A. (Clark) **£85 [≈$151]**

Suckling, Sir John
- The Coppy of a Letter written to the Lower Hovse of Parliament touching divers Grievances and Inconveniences of the State &c. London: Dawson for Walkley, 1641. 1st edn. Sm 4to. [i],26 pp. Mod wraps. Wing S.6124. Anon. (Blackwell's) **£60 [≈$107]**
- The Works ... containing his Poems, Letters, and Plays. London: Jacob Tonson ..., 1709. 8vo. [viii],376 pp. Port frontis. Browned, minor stains. Contemp calf, rebacked, crnrs worn. (Clark) **£75 [≈$134]**
- The Works ... containing his Poems, Letters, and Plays. London: for Jacob Tonson ..., 1719. 3rd edn. 12mo. [x],420 pp. Port frontis. Calf, rebacked, sl rubbed.
(Young's) **£90 [≈$160]**

Sullivan, Francis Stoughton
- Lectures on the Constitution and Laws of England ... London: Dilly, 1776. 2nd edn. 4to. xxxii,415 pp. Occas sl spotting, occas sl marg water stain. Calf, rubbed, rebacked, crnrs reprd. (Francis Edwards) **£85 [≈$151]**

Sullivan, Richard Joseph
- Observations made during a Tour through Parts of England, Scotland, and Wales. In a Series of Letters. London: T. Becket, 1780. 4to. Half-title,247,[1] pp. Early 19th c qtr calf. Anon. (C.R. Johnson) **£125 [≈$223]**

Survey ...
- A Survey of the National Debts, the Sinking Fund, the Civil List, and the Annual Supplies. London: W. Webb, 1745. 1st edn. 8vo. [4],72 pp. 5 fldg tables. Disbound.
(Hannas) **£65 [≈$116]**
- A Survey of the Province of Moray ... see Grant, John & Leslie, William.

Sutherland, David
- A Tour up the Straits, from Gibraltar to Constantinople ... London:for the author, 1790. 1st edn. 8vo. xlvii,372 pp. Contemp half calf, spine worn.
(Frew Mackenzie) **£90 [≈$160]**

Swediaur, F.
- Practical Observations on Venereal Complaints. Edinburgh: 1787. 3rd edn. viii, 312 pp. Lib stamp on title. Old leather & mrbld bds, rebacked.
(Whitehart) **£85 [≈$151]**

Swift, Jonathan
- Baucis and Philemon. London: 1710. 2nd Hills edn (unauthorized). 8vo. 16 pp. Later half calf, mor label, extrs sl worn. Anon.
(D & D Galleries) **$100 [≈£56]**
- The Conduct of the Allies, and the last Ministry, in beginning and Carrying on the Present War. London: John Morphew, 1712. 1st edn. 8vo. Some words scored. Stabbed & sewn as issued, edges sl dusty, few minor folds & nicks. (Black Sun) **$450 [≈£253]**
- The Conduct of the Allies, and of the Late Ministry, in beginning and Carrying on the Present War ... London: for John Morphew ..., 1712. 7th edn. 8vo. 48 pp. Disbound. Anon. (Young's) **£60 [≈$107]**
- Gulliver Decypher'd: or Remarks On a late Book, intitled, Travels into several Remote Nations of the World. By Capt. Lemuel Gulliver ... London: for J. Roberts, n.d. [2], v-xii, [2],49,[1] pp. Disbound. Anon.
(C.R. Johnson) **£550 [≈$979]**
- The History of the last Years of the Queen. London: A. Millar, 1758. 1st edn. xvi, 392 pp. Contemp speckled calf, gilt spine, crnrs rubbed, hd of spine worn, cvrs almost detached.
(Jermy & Westerman) **£90 [≈$160]**

- The Poetical Works, of J.S. D.D. D.S.P.D. consisting of Curious Miscellaneous Pieces ... Reprinted from the Second Dublin Edition, with Notes and Additions. London: printed in the year, 1736. 1st sep coll edn. 12mo. [viii], 304 pp. Frontis. Sl marks. Contemp calf, rebacked.   *(Clark)* £200 [≃ $356]
- The Publick Spirit of the Whigs: set forth in their Generous Encouragement of the Author of the Crisis ... Third Edition. London: John Morphew, 1714. 4to. [2],'45" [ie 43],[1] pp. Rec wraps. Anon.
         (C.R. Johnson) £85 [≃ $151]
- Some Remarks on the Barrier Treaty, between Her Majesty and the States-General. London: 1712. 1st edn. 8vo. 48 pp. Disbound. Anon.   *(Robertshaw)* £38 [≃ $68]
- Some Remarks on the Barrier Treaty, between Her Majesty and the States-General. By the Author of the Allies. To which are added the said Barrier Treaty. London: John Morphew, 1712. 1st edn. Sm 8vo. Qtr mor.
         (Black Sun) $350 [≃ £197]
- Three Sermons: I. On Mutual Subjection. II. On Conscience. III. On the Trinity. London: for R. Dodsley, sold by M. Cooper, 1744. 2nd edn. Sm 4to. [ii],62 pp. Lacks final blank leaf. Title torn & backed. Rec half calf.
         (Burmester) £80 [≃ $142]
- Travels into Several Remote Nations of the World. In Four Parts. By Lemuel Gulliver. London: for Benj. Motte, 1726. 1st edn. Titles in Teerink's state B, text state AA. 2 vols. 8vo. Minor marg worm end of vol 1. Mod period style calf by Riviere.
         (Chapel Hill) $3,000 [≃ £1,685]
- The Works ... With the Author's Life and Character ... Edinburgh: for A. Donaldson, 1768. 1st issue of Donaldson's edn. 13 vols. Sm 8vo. Few lib marks. Period calf, gilt spines & labels, tiny chip 1 headcap, occas ink spots on some cvrs. *(Rankin)* £250 [≃ $445]

Swift, Jonathan & Sheridan, Thomas
- The Intelligencer. Printed at Dublin. London: reprinted, & sold by A. Moor, 1729. 1st coll edn. 8vo. [vi],217,[i] pp. Minor damp stains. Contemp calf, rebacked, crnrs worn. Anon.   *(Clark)* £200 [≃ $356]

Swift, Theophilus
- Letter to the King; in which the Conduct of Mr. Lenox, and the Minister, in the Affair with his Royal Highness the Duke of York, is fully considered. London: for James Ridgway, 1789. 1st edn. 8vo. [ii],40 pp. Lacks half-title. Disbound.
         (Burmester) £58 [≃ $103]

Swinburne, Henry
- A Brief Treatise of Testaments and Last Willes. London: Companie of Stationers, 1611. 2nd edn. 4to. Errata leaf at end. Lacks A1 blank. Occas sl marks. Contemp calf, rebacked. STC 23548.
         (P and P Books) £395 [≃ $703]
- A Treatise of Testaments and Last Wills ... The Sixth Edition, corrected and very much enlarged ... In the Savoy: ptd by Henry Lintot ..., 1748. Folio. [xviii], 567, [568-580] pp. Contemp calf.   *(Vanbrugh)* £225 [≃ $401]

Switzer, S.
- The Nobleman, Gentleman, and Gardener's Recreation: or, an Introduction to Gardening, Planting, Agriculture and the other Business and Pleasures of a Country Life. London: 1715. 8vo. [vi],xxxiv, 266,[16] pp. Frontis. 3 sm ink marks frontis & title. Contemp calf, reprd.   *(Wheldon & Wesley)* £200 [≃ $356]

Sydenham, Thomas
- The Whole Works ... Translated from the Original Latin, by John Pechey. London: Richard Wellington, 1696. 1st edn in English. 8vo. [xxiv],248, 353-592 pp. Sl used. Rec half calf. Wing S.6305.
         (Clark) £380 [≃ $676]

Sykes, Arthur Ashley
- An Essay on the Nature, Design, and Origin, of Sacrifices. London: Knapton, 1748. Only edn. 8vo. viii,354,[2 advt] pp. Contemp calf. Anon.   *(Young's)* £120 [≃ $214]

Systema Agriculturae ...
- See Worlidge, John

T., D.
- Hieraginisticon: Or, Corah's Doom, being an Answer to Two Letters of Enquiry into the Grounds and Occasions of the Contempt of the Clergy and Religion ... London: Tho. Milbourn, 1672. Only edn. 8vo. [ii],198,[1 errata] pp. Rec contemp style calf. Wing T.4.
         (Young's) £120 [≃ $214]

The Tablet ...
- See Shaw, Peter

Tacitus
- The Works ... prefixed Political Discourses Upon that Author. London: Woodward & Peele, 1728-31. Translated by Thomas Gordon. Large Paper. 2 vols. Folio. Contemp vellum, mor labels (sl defective), marked.
         (Clark) £100 [≃ $178]

Talbot, B.
- The New Art of Land Measuring; or, A Turnpike Road to Practical Surveying ... Wolverhampton: for the author, & sold by J. Smart ..., 1779. 1st edn. 8vo. xxiv,412 pp. 13 plates, fldg table. Contemp qtr calf, sl rubbed.
(Burmester) **£325 [≈$579]**

Tales for Youth; in Thirty Poems ...
- See Bewick, John (illustrator).

Tanner, Thomas
- Notitia Monastica or A Short History of the Religious Houses in England and Wales. Oxford: at the Theater, 1695. 8vo. [lxxxii], 288, [38] pp. 5 plates. Mod half mor gilt. Wing T.144.   *(Hollett)* **£85 [≈$151]**

Taplin, William
- The Gentleman's Stable Directory; or, Modern System of Farriery ... London: for G. Kearsley, 1788-91. 6th edn vol 1, 1st edn vol 2. 2 vols. 8vo. xxiii,448; viii,424 pp. Half-titles. Early 19th c calf, sometime rebacked.
(Young's) **£110 [≈$196]**
- The Gentleman's Stable Directory; or, Modern System of Farriery. The Sixth Edition, corrected, improved and considerably enlarged. London: for G. Kearsley, 1788. 8vo. Lacks free endpapers. Sm marg loss on T2. Contemp sheep, spine ends chipped, sm loss rear bd.
(Waterfield's) **£85 [≈$151]**

Tartini, Giuseppe
- A Letter from the late Signor Tartini to Signora Maddalena Lombardini, (now Signora Sirmen) published as an important lesson to Performers on the Violin ... London: for R. Bremner, by George Bigg, 1771. 1st edn. 4to. [16] pp. Later wraps, sl spotted.
(Finch) **£575 [≈$1,024]**

Tasso, Torquato
- Godfrey of Bulloigne ... Done into English Heroicall Verse by Edward Fairfax ... London: for Ric. Chiswell, 1687. Thick 8vo. [32],655 pp. Period style polished calf.
(Hartfield) **$595 [≈£334]**
- Godfrey of Bulloigne: or the Recovery of Jerusalem. Done into English Heroical Verse, by Edward Fairfax ... London: for H. Herringman, 1687. 3rd edn. 8vo. [xxxii],355 pp. Early 19th c half russia, gilt spine, sl rubbed. Wing T.174.
(Blackwell's) **£120 [≈$214]**
- Godfrey of Bulloigne; or, The Recovery of Jerusalem. Done into English Heroical Verse, by Edward Fairfax, Gent. London: 1687. 8vo.

Mod three qtr mor gilt, t.e.g. Wing T.174.
(D & D Galleries) **$225 [≈£126]**

Tate, Nahum
- A Congratulatory Poem to his Royal Highness Prince George of Denmark ... upon the Glorious Successes at Sea ... London: Henry Hills, 1708. 8vo. 16 pp. Sl browned. Disbound.   *(Hannas)* **£25 [≈$45]**
- On the Sacred Memory of our late Sovereign: with Congratulations to his Present Majesty. London: J. Playford, for Henry Playford, 1685. 1st edn. Folio. [2],6 pp. Disbound. Wing T.200.   *(Hannas)* **£110 [≈$196]**
- A Poem upon Tea; With a Discourse on its Sov'rain Virtues; and Directions in the Use of it for Health ... London: for J. Nutt, 1702. 2nd edn. 8vo. [xvi],47 pp. Stain at hd of last 3 ff. Title dusty. Disbound. Mor backed box.
(Young's) **£210 [≈$374]**

Taylor, Brook
- New Principles of Linear Perspective ... Third Edition. London: John Ward, 1749. 8vo. x, 11-80 pp. 13 fldg engvd plates, 14 decs. Contemp qtr calf, vellum crnr pieces.
(Spelman) **£180 [≈$320]**

Taylor, Henry
- The Apology of Benjamin Ben Mordecai to his Friends, for Embracing Christianity ... With Notes and Illustrations ... London: for J. Wilkie, 1771. 1st edn. 4to. viii,[1 errata], 128, v,205, v,187 pp. Calf backed bds, uncut. Anon.   *(Young's)* **£75 [≈$134]**

Taylor, I. & J.
- Ideas for Rustic Furniture proper for Garden Seats, Summer Houses, Hermitages, Cottages, Etc ... London: the Architectural Library, Holborn, [ca 1790]. 25 plates. Mod half mor.   *(Phillips)* **£875 [≈$1,558]**

Taylor, Isaac
- Specimens of Gothic Ornaments selected from the Parish Church of Lavenham in Suffolk. London: I. & J. Taylor, 1796. 1st edn. 4to. [ii], pp. 40 plates. Minor foxing. Contemp qtr calf, hinges starting.
(Bookpress) **$250 [≈£140]**

Taylor, Jeremy
- A Course of Sermons for All the Sundays of the Year ... The Fourth Edition Enlarged ... London: R. Norton for R. Royston, 1673. Folio. [xiv],270, [x],243,[iii], 79,[i] pp. Lacks port. Old calf, worn, bds detached. Wing T.332.   *(Clark)* **£48 [≈$85]**
- A Course of Sermons for all the Sundays of

the Year ... The Fourth Edition Enlarged ...
London: R. Norton for R. Royston, 1673.
Folio. 14 secondary titles. Port frontis. Later
half calf, gilt spine, extrs sl worn, jnts cracked
but firm. Wing T.332. *(Clark)* **£125 [≈ $223]**

- Doctor Dubitantium or the Rule of
Conscience in all her generall Measures
serving as a great Instrument for the
determination of Cases of Conscience.
London: Flesher for Royston, 1660. Folio.
Title rubricated. Frontis. Mod calf. Wing
T.324. *(Waterfield's)* **£200 [≈ $356]**

- Ductor Dubitantium, or the Rule of
Conscience in all her General Measures ...
The Third Edition. London: R. Norton for
R. Royston, 1676. Folio. [vi],xxx,[ii], 819,
[xxv] pp. Port frontis, title vignette. Contemp
calf, extrs worn, lower bd detached. Wing
T.326. *(Clark)* **£55 [≈ $98]**

- Ductor Dubitantum, or the Rule of
Conscience in all her general Measures ...
Third Edition. London: R. Norton for R.
Royston, 1676. Folio. [vi],xxx,[i], 818, [xxiii]
pp. Port. Final leaf creased. Sl water stain at
end. Contemp calf, rebacked, inner hinges
taped. Wing T.326.
(Blackwell's) **£125 [≈ $223]**

- Eniautos: A Course of Sermons for All the
Sundaies of the Year ... London: Richard
Royston, 1653. 1st edn. Folio. [viii], 378, [i],
55,[i],[iv], [xii],[i], "334" [ie 326], [errata] pp.
V sl marg worm few ff. Contemp calf,
backstrip relaid. Wing T.329 (405,408, 296).
(Blackwell's) **£245 [≈ $436]**

- The Great Exemplar of Sanctity and Holy
Life according to the Christian Institution ...
in Three Parts. London: R.N. for Francis
Ash, 1649. 1st edn. 4to. 3 blank ff. Contemp
calf, rebacked. Wing T.342.
(Hannas) **£90 [≈ $160]**

- Unum Necessarium. Or, the Doctrine and
Practice of Repentance ... London: James
Flesher for R. Royston, 1655. 1st edn. 8vo.
Addtnl engvd title, dble plate (sm stain in
crnr). Old style calf, a.e.g. Wing T.415.
(Hannas) **£120 [≈ $214]**

- The Worthy Communicant: or a Discourse of
the Nature, Effects, and Blessings consequent
to the Worthy Receiving of the Lords Supper
... London: for Awnsham Churchill, 1683.
8vo. Frontis. Contemp calf, rubbed,
rebacked. Wing T.421.
(Waterfield's) **£75 [≈ $134]**

Taylor, Jeremy & Cave, William

- Antiquitates Christianae; or, the History of
the Life and Death of Holy Jesus ... London:
Luke Meredith, 1703. Folio. 21 plates, 94
vignettes in text. Repr to title, few minor

tears. Calf, rebacked.
(Appelfeld) **$200 [≈ £112]**

Taylor, John

- All the Workes of John Taylor the Water-
Poet ... London: for James Boler, 1630. 1st
coll edn. Folio. [x],148, [ii],343, [i], 146 pp.
Addtnl engvd title (repr to blank marg). Text
w'cuts. 19th c elab gilt red mor. STC 23725.
(Vanbrugh) **£955 [≈ $1,700]**

Taylor, Michael

- A Sexagesimal Table, exhibiting, at sight, the
Result of any Proportion, where the Terms do
not exceed Sixty Minutes ... London: 1780.
Roy 4to. xlvi,[2],316 pp. Fldg table, tables.
Inner marg of prelims water stained.
Contemp calf, worn, rebacked.
(Weiner) **£40 [≈ $71]**

- Tables of Logarithms of All Numbers, from
1 to 101000; and of the Sines and Tangents ...
Preface ... by Nevil Maskelyne. London:
1792. Thick folio. [xiv],64 pp. Subscribers.
Old mrbld bds, mod calf spine.
(Weiner) **£50 [≈ $89]**

- Tables of Logarithms of All Numbers, from
1 to 101000; and of the Sines and Tangents ...
Preface ... by Nevil Maskelyne. London:
1792. Thick folio. [xiv],64 pp. Subscribers.
Tables. Amateur cloth backed bds.
(Weiner) **£100 [≈ $178]**

Taylor, Thomas

- A Commentarie upon the Epistle of Saint
Paul written to Titus ... Cambridge: Cantrell
Legge, 1619. 1st edn. 4to. [16],752,[18] pp.
Fldg table. Title soiled. Contemp calf, worn,
lower spine chipped. STC 23825A.
(Karmiole) **$175 [≈ £98]**

Teixeira, J.

- The Strangest Adventure that Ever
Happened ... Successe of the King of
Portugall ... London: Henson, 1601. 1st edn.
Sm 4to. Top marg trimmed rather close.
Lacks final blank leaf. 19th c half mor, sl
rubbed. Anon. STC 23864.
(P and P Books) **£990 [≈ $1,762]**

The Tell-Tale ...

- The Tell-Tale: or, Anecdotes expressive of
Characters of Persons Eminent for Rank,
Learning, Wit, or Humour ... London: for R.
Baldwin, 1756. 1st edn. 2 vols. 12mo.
Contemp calf gilt, sl worn.
(Ximenes) **$600 [≈ £337]**

Temple, Sir William

- An Introduction to the History of England ...

London: W.S., 1708. 3rd edn. 8vo. [viii], 310 pp. Contemp speckled calf, sl rubbed.
(Young's) **£34 [≈ $61]**

- An Introduction to the History of England ... The Third Edition. London: W.S. for Richard & Ralph Simpson, 1708. 8vo. Contemp panelled calf, red label.
(Waterfield's) **£80 [≈ $142]**

- Memoirs of What past in Christendom, from the War Begun 1672 to the Peace Concluded 1679. London: Chiswell, 1692. 2nd edn. 8vo. Wraps. Anon. Wing T.643.
(Rostenberg & Stern) **$125 [≈ £70]**

- Miscellanea. The Third Part ... Published by Jonathan Swift. London: Benj. Tooke, 1701. 1st edn. 8vo. [8],368 pp. Frontis. Mod mor.
(O'Neal) **$225 [≈ £126]**

- The Works. To which is prefixed The Life and Character of the Author. London: for J. Brotherton ..., 1770. 4 vols. 8vo. Few sl lib marks, occas sl browning. Period tree calf, gilt dec spines, red & green labels, 3 headcaps v sl chipped.
(Rankin) **£100 [≈ $178]**

- The Works ... to which is prefixed the Life and Character of the Author. A New Edition. London: for J. Brotherton ..., 1770. 4 vols. 8vo. Contemp calf, dble contrasting labels, jnts cracked but sound, some wear to spines.
(Waterfield's) **£95 [≈ $169]**

Tench, Watkin
- Letters written in France, to a Friend in London, between the Month of November 1794 and the Month of May 1795. London: for J. Johnson ..., 1796. iv,224 pp. Occas sl browning. Contemp half calf, minor rubbing, lacks label. *(Francis Edwards)* **£150 [≈ $267]**

Tenison, Thomas
- A Discourse Concerning a Guide in Matters of Faith ... London: ben. Tooke & F. Gardiner, 1683. 1st edn. 4to. [vi],43,[i] pp. Minor staining. Disbound. Wing T. 695. Anon. *(Clark)* **£20 [≈ $36]**

- A Sermon Preached at the Funeral of Her Late Majesty Queen Mary of Ever Blessed Memory ... London: for Ni. Chiswell ..., 1695. 1st edn. 4to. [iv],44,[2 advt] pp. New bds. Anon. Wing T.720.
(Young's) **£35 [≈ $62]**

Terry, Garnet
- A Complete Round of Cyphers for the Use of Engravers, Painters, Sculptors ... Consisting of Six Hundred Examples ... London: Bowles & Carver, [1796]. 4to. Engvd title, 25 plates. Title sl soiled. Later cloth cvrd bds, rubbed.
(Frew Mackenzie) **£150 [≈ $267]**

Tertullian, Quintus Septimus Florens
- Tertullian's Prescription against Hereticks ... Translated ... with Notes ... by Joseph Betty. Oxford: at the Theatre, 1722. 8vo. Engvd frontis & tail-piece. [viii], 313 pp. Contemp calf, rebacked, crnrs & extrs sl worn.
(Blackwell's) **£55 [≈ $98]**

The Test of Filial Duty ...
- See Scott, Sarah

Thayer, John
- An Account of the Conversion of the Reverend Mr John Thayer. Lately a Protestant Minister at Boston in North America. First Printed in London, and now in Lisbon. Lisbon: 1788. Sm 8vo. 155 pp. Contemp wraps, rather used.
(Spelman) **£30 [≈ $53]**

The Theatre ...
- The Theatre: or, Select Works of the British Dramatic Poets. To which are prefixed, The Lives ... Edinburgh: Martin & Wotherspoon, 1768. 12 vols. 12mo. 48 pieces, each with sep title. Occas worm. Contemp calf, gilt spines, worn, lacks labels, 2 bds detached.
(Clark) **£65 [≈ $116]**

Theobald, John
- Albion, a Poem. Oxford: printed in the year, 1720. 1st edn. Thick Paper copy, but cut down to 7 1/2 x 4 1/2 inches. 8vo. Title (sl soiled) on A1. Final blank leaf. Mod qtr calf. Anon. *(Hannas)* **£210 [≈ $374]**

- Every Man his own Physician. Being a complete Collection of efficacious and approved Remedies, for every Disease incident to the Human Body. New Edition. London: 1766. 8vo. 61 pp. Engvd title. Lacks final advt leaf. Mod qtr mor.
(Robertshaw) **£36 [≈ $64]**

Theobald, Lewis
- Double Falshood; or, the Distrest Lovers. A Play ... Written originally by W. Shakespeare; and now Revised ... by Mr. Theobald. London: J. Watts, 1728. 1st edn. 8vo. Half title (dust soiled). Prelim ff catchwords shaved. Mod cloth backed bds.
(Hannas) **£240 [≈ $427]**

Theocritus
- The Idylliums. Translated from the Greek, with Notes ... By Francis Fawkes. London: for the author, by Dryden Leach, 1767. 1st edn. 8vo. xlii,287 pp. Frontis port. Occas sl marg worm. Contemp polished calf, elab gilt spine, wear to jnts. *(Hartfield)* **$295 [≈ £166]**

Theophrastus

- The Characters of Theophrastus, with a strictly literal Translation of the Greek into Latin, and with Notes ... in English ... By the late R. Newton. Oxford: 1754. 8vo. xii, 268 pp. Contemp qtr calf, uncut, gilt spine, crnrs worn. *(Spelman)* **£35 [≈ $62]**

Theophrastus's History of Stones ...

- See Hill, "Sir" John.

Thevenot, Monsieur

- The Art of Swimming. Illustrated with Forty proper Copper-Plate Cuts ... London: for John Lever, 1764. 2nd edn. Sm 8vo in 12s. [xx], 60 pp, advt leaf. Frontis (worn), 39 plates. Wear & tear. Later wraps.
(Hollett) **£220 [≈ $392]**

Thevenot, Jean de

- The Travels of Monsieur de Thevenot into the Levant. In Three Parts ... London: H. Clarke, 1687. 1st edn in English. Sm folio. [xl], 291,i, [ii],200, [ii],114,4 pp. Frontis port, 3 plates. Mod half mor.
(Terramedia) **$2,000 [≈ £1,124]**

Thicknesse, Philip

- A Year's Journey through France and Part of Spain. Bath: R. Cruttwell for the author ..., 1777. 1st edn. 2 vols. 8vo. 12 pp subscribers. 9 plates (1 fldg of music, offset). Contemp calf gilt, contrasting labels, vol 1 rebacked to style, vol 2 jnts tender. *(Blackwell's)* **£375 [≈ $668]**
- A Year's Journey through the Pais Bas; or, Austrian Netherlands. Second Edition, with Considerable Additions ... London: for J. Debrett, 1786. 8vo. Fldg plate. Contemp half calf, upper jnt weak. *(Hannas)* **£140 [≈ $249]**

Thomas a Kempis

- See a Kempis, Thomas

Thomas, Antoine Leonard

- An Essay on the Character, the Manners, and the Understanding of Women, in Different Ages. Translated from the French ... by Mrs. Kindersley ... London: Dodsley, 1781. Sm 8vo. viii, 232 pp. Contemp half calf.
(Burmester) **£200 [≈ $356]**

Thomas, S.

- Britannicus Estimator: Or, the Trader's Complete Guide. In Two Parts ... London: for J. Wilson ..., 1764. 1st edn. 8vo. [vi], 13-262, [2] pp. Occas damp stains, sm marg hole. Old calf, rebacked.
(Young's) **£220 [≈ $392]**
- The British Negotiator ... see Slack, Thomas

- The Ready Calculator: or, Tradesman's Sure Guide ... Third Edition, Corrected. London: G. Robinson & T. Slack, 1777. 12mo. 251,[i] pp. No free endpapers. Minor soil. Contemp sheep, some wear, sm splits in jnts.
(Clark) **£25 [≈ $45]**

Thompson, Charles

- Rules for Bad Horsemen. Addressed to the Society for the Encouragement of Arts. London: for J. Robson, 1763. [iv],viii,84 pp. Rebound in period style bds.
(Bookline) **£180 [≈ $320]**
- Rules for Bad Horsemen. Addressed to the Society for the Encouragement of Arts, &c. London: for J. Robson, 1763. 2nd edn, "with a preface and additions." Sm 8vo. [iv],viii,84 pp. Rec bds. *(Burmester)* **£180 [≈ $320]**

Thompson, John-Weeks

- The Poor Man's Medicine Chest; or, Thompson's Box of Antibilious Alterative Pills. With a few brief Remarks on the Stomach. London: for the author, 1791. 1st edn. 8vo. 36 pp. Mod cloth.
(Robertshaw) **£40 [≈ $71]**

Thompson, William, of Queen's College, Oxon

- An Hymn to May. London: Dodsley, Waller, Cooper, [1746]. 1st edn. 4to. [2],33 pp, inc half-title. Some catchwords cut into, bottom line of 1 footnote cropped. Disbound.
(Hannas) **£75 [≈ $134]**

Thomson, George

- [Loimotomia, in Greek]: or the Pest Anatomised In these following particulars ... London: Nath. Crouch, 1666. Only edn. 8vo. [xvi], 189,[iii] pp. 3 advt pp at end. Frontis. Minor browning. Sm crnr repr. 19th c calf gilt, a.e.g., minor wear extrs. Wing T.1027.
(Clark) **£780 [≈ $1,388]**

Thomson, James

- The Castle of Indolence ... London: for A. Millar, 1748. 1st edn. Sm 4to. [ii],81,[3] pp. Lacks half-title. Sm marg tear to title. Later half calf, t.e.g., crnrs sl rubbed.
(Blackwell's) **£275 [≈ $490]**
- The Poetical Works. Glasgow: Andrew Foulis, 1784. 2 vols. Folio. Subscribers. Contemp tree calf, red & green labels, some wear at extrs. *(Waterfield's)* **£220 [≈ $392]**
- Winter, a Poem, a Hymn on the Seasons, a Poem to the Memory of Sir Isaac Newton, and Britannia, a Poem. London: for J. Millan, 1730. 8vo. frontis. Disbound.
(Hannas) **£25 [≈ $45]**

Thomson, John, accountant

- Tables of Interest ... The Sixth Edition, with Additions. Edinburgh: Murray & Cochrane, for the author, 1794. 12mo. [viii],532 pp. Mod mrbld bds. *(Waterfield's)* **£65 [≈ $116]**
- The Universal Calculator; or The Merchant's, Tradesman's, and Family's Assistant ... Edinburgh: Creech & Elliot, 1784. Tall 8vo. [viii],294 pp. Sgnd by the author on title verso as warranty. Period sheep, upper cvr sl scuffed.
  (Rankin) **£60 [≈ $107]**

Thorius, Raphael

- Hymnus Tabaci; a Poem in Honour of Tabaco [and: Cheimonopegnion, or, a Winter Song]. Made English by Peter Hausted. London: T.N. for Humphrey Moseley, 1651. 1st edn in English. 2 parts. 16mo. 18th c half russia. Wing T.1039.
  (Hannas) **£320 [≈ $570]**

Thorndike, Herbert

- A Discourse of the Right of the Church in a Christian State. London: M.F. for Octavien Pullen, 1649. 1st edn. 8vo. [viii],339,[i], clxxvii,[i] pp. Title sl dusty. Old calf, extrs sl worn, lacks label, jnts cracked but secure. Wing T.1045. *(Clark)* **£75 [≈ $134]**

Thorpe, Francis

- Sergeant Thorpe Judge of Assize for the Northern Circvit, his Charge, as it was delivered to the Grand-Jury at Yorke Assizes the twentieth of March, 1648 ... London: 1649. 1st edn. Sm 4to. [i],30 pp. Browned. Disbound. Wing T.1070.
  (Blackwell's) **£65 [≈ $116]**

Thrale (later Piozzi), Hester Lynch

- Anecdotes of the late Samuel Johnson, LL.D. During the Last Twenty Years of his Life. London: 1786. 2nd edn. 8vo. viii, 306, [1] pp. Lacks half-title & errata slip. Occas sl spotting. Cloth. *(Young's)* **£65 [≈ $116]**
- Observations and Reflections made in the Course of a Journey through France, Italy, and Germany. Dublin: Chamberlaine ..., 1789. 1st Dublin edn. 8vo. 592 pp. Calf, worn, rebacked. *(Hartfield)* **$425 [≈ £239]**

Three ...

- Three Dialogues on the Amusements of Clergymen ... see Gilpin, William
- Three Petitions Presented to the High Covrt of Parliament ... Cornwall ... Cheshire. Flint, Denbigh ... Monmouth. London: Robinson, 1642. 4to. Stitched. Wing T.408.
  (Rostenberg & Stern) **$80 [≈ £45]**

Thurston, Joseph

- The Toilette. In Three Books. London: for Benj. Motte, 1730. 1st edn. 8vo. Red & black title. F3 a cancel. Frontis. Mod cloth backed bds. *(Hannas)* **£120 [≈ $214]**
- The Toilette. In Three Books. London: for Benj. Motte, 1730. 2nd edn. 4to. 48 pp. Frontis. Rebound in tree calf.
  (Limestone Hills) **$105 [≈ £59]**

Tickell, Thomas

- Kensington Garden. London: for J. Tonson, 1722. 1st edn. Fine Paper copy, with E2 unsigned. 4to. [2],32 pp. Engv on title. Lacks half-title. Faint foxing. Mod bds. Anon.
  (Hannas) **£160 [≈ $285]**

Tijou, John

- A New Booke of Drawings invented and designed by John Tijou. Containing several Sortes of Iron Worke ... London: Louis Fondrin, 1723. Pirated edn. Folio. 20 plates. 19th c polished calf, v sl wear spine extrs & tips. *(Bookpress)* **$6,500 [≈ £3,652]**

Tillotson, John

- Sermons Concerning the Divinity and Incarnation of our Blessed Saviour ... The Second Edition. London: for Br. Aylmer & W. Rogers, 1695. 8vo. [iv],296,[iv] pp. A2 torn across. Minor marg staining. Contemp calf, rubbed, extrs worn. Wing T.1255A.
  (Clark) **£48 [≈ $85]**
- Six Sermons ... The Second Edition. London: for B. Aylmer, 1694. 12mo. [ii],vi, 208 pp. Port frontis. Some worming in outer crnrs of a few ff. Period calf, piece missing hd of spine. Wing T.1268A.
  (Rankin) **£75 [≈ $134]**

Tindal, Matthew

- New High-Church Turn'd Old Presbyterian. Utrum Horum Never a Barrel the Better Herring. London: sold by S. Bragg ..., 1709. 1st edn. 8vo. 20 pp. Disbound. Anon.
  (Young's) **£95 [≈ $169]**

To the Honovrable The House of Commons ...

- To the Honovrable The House of Commons Assembled in the High Court of Parliament: The Humble Petition of the Lord Mayor ... of London. London: Cotes, 1646. 4to. Title border. Stitched. Wing T.1445.
  (Rostenberg & Stern) **$90 [≈ £51]**

To the Kings most excellent Majestie ...

- To the Kings most excellent Majestie. The Petition of the Inhabitants of the County of

Buckingham, concerning Mr. Hampden, Mr. Hollis, Mr. Pym ... With his Majestie's Answer. London: Thomas, 1641. 4to. Stitched. Wing T.1554.
(Rostenberg & Stern) **$100 [≈ £56]**

To the Right Honorable the Lords ...
- To the Right Honorable the Lords and Commons Assembled in High Covrt of Parliament: The Humble Petition of the Lord Mayor ... of London. London: Cotes, [1646]. 4to. Title border. Stitched. Wing T.1664, variant. *(Rostenberg & Stern)* **$90 [≈ £51]**

To the Right Honourable the Lords ...
- To the Right Honourable the Lords Assembled in High Covrt of Parliament: The Humble Petition of the Lord Mayor ... of London. London: Cotes, 1646. 4to. Stitched. Wing T.1664. With alternative title: The Humble Petition of the Lord Mayor ... London: Cotes, 1646.
(Rostenberg & Stern) **$90 [≈ £51]**

The Toilet of Flora ...
- See Buch'hoz, P.J.

Toland, John
- Dunkirk or Dover; or, The Queen's Honour, The Nation's Safety, The Liberties of Europe, and The Peace of the World, All at Stake ... London: for A. Baldwin ..., 1713. 2nd edn. 8vo. 40 pp. Disbound. Anon.
(Young's) **£78 [≈ $139]**
- Letters to Serena: containing I. The Origin and Force of Prejudices ... VI. A Preface. London: for Bernard Lintot, 1704. 8vo. Mod qtr calf. *(Waterfield's)* **£380 [≈ $676]**

Tolson, Francis
- Hermathenae, or Moral Emblems, and Ethnick Tales, with Explanatory Notes. Volume I [all published]. [London: ca 1740]. 1st edn. 8vo. Engvd title, [xii],173,[5] pp, inc 2 errata ff. 60 plates. Few sm marg worm holes. Contemp sheep, rubbed & worn but sound. *(Burmester)* **£750 [≈ $1,335]**

Tomkis, Thomas
- Lingua: or the Combat of the Tongue, and the Five Senses for Superiority. A pleasant Comoedy. London: Simon Miller, [1657]. 8vo. Collates A1-I8. 4 advt pp at end. Sl loss of imprint on title, some soil & spots. Rec qtr calf. Anon. Wing T.1842.
(Clark) **£65 [≈ $116]**

Tomlinson, Ralph
- A Slang Pastoral being a Parody of a

Celebrated Poem of Dr. Byron's. London: for the editor, 1780. 4to. 11,[1] pp. Stabbed as issued. *(C.R. Johnson)* **£265 [≈ $472]**

Topographical Miscellanies ...
- See Brydges, Sir Samuel Egerton

Torr, James
- The Antiquities of York City ... York: 1719. 1st edn. Prelims,148, appendix pp. Half calf gilt, mrbld bds, extrs sl rubbed.
(Francis Edwards) **£75 [≈ $134]**
- The Antiquities of York City. York: G. White, 1719. 8vo. [8],148,[4] pp. 19th c half mor. *(Spelman)* **£90 [≈ $160]**

Tott, Baron de
- Memoirs of Baron de Tott. Containing the State of the Turkish Empire and the Crimea, during the late War with Russia ... Second Edition ... London: Robinson, 1786. 1st edn of this translation. 2 vols. 8vo. Occas spotting. Contemp qtr calf, sl rubbed.
(Frew Mackenzie) **£125 [≈ $223]**

Tour ...
- A Tour in Scotland MDCCLXIX ... see Pennant, Thomas
- A Tour thro' the Whole Island of Great Britain ... see Defoe, daniel.

Toussaint, Francois-Vincent
- Manners. Translated from the French. The Second Edition. London: for J. Payne & J. Bouquet, 1752. 12mo. (xviii),vi,251,[3 advt] pp. Occas sl water stain. Contemp calf, upper jnt cracked but firm. Anon.
(Burmester) **£45 [≈ $80]**

Townsend, Joseph
- The Physicians' Vade Mecum; being a Compendium of Nosology and Therapeutics, for the Use of Students. Second Edition. London: 1794. 2nd edn. Sm 8vo. 151 pp. Mod calf. *(Robertshaw)* **£48 [≈ $85]**

Townshend, Charles
- National Thoughts, Recommended to the Serious Attention of the Public. With an Appendix ... By a Land-Owner. London: for R. Dodsley, [1749?]. 1st edn. 8vo. [4],36 pp, inc half-title. Disbound. Anon.
(Hannas) **£65 [≈ $116]**

Townshend, Thomas
- Poems. London: Bensley, for E. & S. Harding, 1796. 1st English edn. 8vo. 14 vignettes & 8 ornaments or tail-pieces, all hand cold. Lacks frontis. Stained. A few ff

sprung. Somewhat soiled. Contemp straight grained red mor, a.e.g.
(Hannas) £80 [≈ $142]

Tractatus Navigationis et Commerciorum ...
- Tractatus Navigationis et Commerciorum ... Treaty of Navigation and Commerce Between ... Anne ... Queen of Great britain ... and ... Lewis the XIVth ... Concluded at Utrecht ... 1713. London: Baskett, 1713. 4to. English & Latin parallel text. Qtr calf.
(Rostenberg & Stern) $250 [≈ £140]

Trade catalogue
- British Plate Glass Manufactory: Tariff of the Prices of Polished Glass. London: J. March & Son, 1794. 8vo. 99 pp. Engvd title. Explanatory slip on endpaper. Contemp calf.
(Spelman) £380 [≈ $676]

Trapp, Joseph
- Abra-Mule: or, Love and Empire. A Tragedy ... London: Tonson, 1704. 1st edn. 4to. Sl browned. Half mor. Anon.
(Hannas) £120 [≈ $214]

Travestin, Mr.
- An Account of the Imperial Proceedings against the Turks: with an exact diary of the Siege of Newheusel ... London: for Sam. Crouch, & John Lawrence, 1685. 1st edn. Sm 4to. [ii],56,[2 advt] pp. Fldg map. Mrbld wraps. Wing T.2067.
(Burmester) £200 [≈ $356]

Treatise ...
- A Treatise of Humane Reason ... see Clifford, Martin
- A Treatise on the Solar Creation ... see Lowe, John

Treby, Sir George
- A Collection of Letters and other Writings, relating to the Horrid Popish Plot ... [with] The Second Part of the Collection of Letters ... London: Samuel Heyrick ..., 1681. Folio. [vi],127,[ii]; [iv],34 pp. 2 imprimatur ff. Disbound. Wing T.2102, 2104.
(Clark) £50 [≈ $89]

Trenchard, John
- An Argument, Shewing, that a Standing Army is inconsistent with A Free Government, and ... destructive to the Constitution of the English Monarchy. London: 1697. 1st edn. 4to. Stitched. Wing T.2110. Anon.
(Rostenberg & Stern) $85 [≈ £48]
- An Argument, Shewing, that a Standing Army is inconsistent with a Free

Government, and absolutely destructive to the Constitution of the English Monarchy. London: 1697. 1st edn. 4to. Stitched as issued, unopened. Wing T.2110. Anon.
(Robertshaw) £36 [≈ $64]
- A Short History of Standing Armies in England. London: 1698. 4to. Disbound. Wing T.2116. Anon.
(Rostenberg & Stern) $90 [≈ £51]

Trenck, Baron Frederic
- The Life of Baron Frederic Trenck; containing his Adventures ... Translated from the German, by Thomas Holcroft. Dublin: for Messrs Chamberlaine, Wogan ..., 1788. 1st Irish edn. 2 vols in one. 8vo. vi,220; 240, [2] pp. Port. Contemp tree calf, fine.
(Burmester) £50 [≈ $89]

Tricks of the Town Laid Open ...
- Tricks of the Town Laid Open: Or, a Companion for Country Gentlemen ... The Second Edition. London: for H. Slater; & R. Adams, 1748. 8vo. Mor backed mrbld bds.
(Hannas) £680 [≈ $1,210]

Trimnell, Charles
- A Sermon preach'd to the Societies for the Reformation of Manners ... on Monday, December the Thirty First, 1711. London: for D. Midwinter, 1712. 1st edn. 8vo. 21,[1] pp. Disbound.   *(Burmester)* £20 [≈ $36]

Troil, Uno Von
- Letters on Iceland ... London: W. Richardson, J. Robson, N. Conant, 1780. 1st English edn. 8vo. Fldg map, plate. Contemp calf, rebacked.   *(Hannas)* £200 [≈ $356]
- Letters on Iceland ... Dublin: G. Perrin, for S. Price ..., 1780. 1st Dublin edn. 8vo. [ii], xxvi,400 pp. Half-title. Plate. Half-title & intl & final blanks water stained. Contemp tree calf gilt, red mor label, green edges, gilt faded from spine.   *(Finch)* £180 [≈ $320]

Trowell, Samuel
- A New Treatise of Husbandry, Gardening, and other Matters relating to Rural Affairs ... London: Olive Payne, 1739. 164 pp. Contemp calf, sl worn. John Cator's b'plate.
(C.R. Johnson) £220 [≈ $392]
- A New Treatise of Husbandry, Gardening, and other Curious Matters ... London: for James Hodgson, 1739. 1st edn, 3rd issue. Post 8vo. [viii],164 pp. 1st few ff sl wormed in lower marg, few sl marks. Contemp gilt ruled sheep.   *(Ash)* £125 [≈ $223]

True ...

- A True Narrative of the Proceedings at Guild-Hall, London, the Fourth of this Instant February, in their Unanimous Election of their Four Members to serve in Parliament. [Colophon] London: for Francis Smith, 1681]. 1st edn. Folio broadside. Wing T.2809. *(Hannas)* £35 [≈ $62]

- A True Relation of what is discovered concerning the Murther of the Archbp. of St. Andrews. [London: 1679]. 1st edn. Folio. 4 pp. Drop-head title. Disbound. Wing T.3080. *(Hannas)* £20 [≈ $36]

Trusler, John

- Chronology; or, the Historian's Vade Mecum ... For the Library and the Use of Schools. London: for the author ..., [1782]. 10th edn, enlgd. 2 vols. 12mo. Sl browning. Contemp tree calf gilt, contrasting labels, hinges sl rubbed. *(Ximenes)* $150 [≈ £84]

- Hogarth Moralized, Being a Complete Edition of Hogarth's Works ... London: S. Hooper & Mrs. Hogarth, 1768. 1st issue, with gatherings G-H on different paper. 8vo. [4], viii, 212,v,[3] pp. Frontis port, addtnl engvd title, 75 ills. Contemp calf, rebacked, sl worn. Anon. *(O'Neal)* $500 [≈ £281]

- The London Adviser and Guide: containing every Instruction and Information useful and necessary to Persons living in London ... London: for the author, 1790. 2nd edn. 12mo. [viii], 215 pp. Rec leather. *(Burmester)* £350 [≈ $6,230]

- Modern Times, or, the Adventures of Gabriel Outcast. Supposed to be written by himself. In imitation of Gil Blas. London: for the author ..., 1785. 2nd edn, with addtns. 3 vols. 12mo. 2 half-titles, correct. Used. Contemp qtr calf, uncut, sides worn but sound. Anon. *(Burmester)* £300 [≈ $534]

Tuke, Sir Andrew

- The Adventures of Five Hours. A Tragi-Comedy. London: for Henry Herringman, 1663. 1st edn. Folio. Browned. Mod gilt panelled mor, old style. Wing T.3299. Anon. *(Hannas)* £280 [≈ $498]

Tull, Jethro

- The Horse-Hoeing Husbandry ... Dublin: A. Rhames, 1733. 1st Dublin edn. 8vo. xvii, 417, [4] pp. 6 fldg engvs. Sl foxing at ends. New qtr calf over orig pink mrbld bds. *(Blackwell's)* £200 [≈ $356]

- The Horse-Hoeing Husbandry ... Dublin: A. Rhames ..., 1733. 1st Dublin edn. 8vo. xvii, 417, [v] pp. 6 fldg plates. Few page edges dusty. Rec half calf, gilt spine.

(Clark) £285 [≈ $507]

- Horse-Hoeing Husbandry: or an Essay on the Principles of Vegetation and Tillage ... London: for A. Millar, 1762. 4th edn. 8vo. xvi, 432 pp. 7 fldg plates. New half calf. *(Egglishaw)* £240 [≈ $427]

Turberville, H.

- A Manuel of Controversies: clearly Demonstrating the truth of Catholique Religion ... Doway: Lawrence Kellam, 1654. 8vo. [xii],414 pp. Few edges sl browned. Marg blind stamp on title & last leaf. Mod half calf gilt. Wing T.3257. *(Hollett)* £85 [≈ $151]

Turnbull, George

- A Curious Collection of Ancient Paintings, accurately engraved from excellent Drawings ... London: S. Birt & B. Dod, 1744. Folio. [4], 42 pp. 55 plates (the last unnumbered & added from the 1740 edn). Occas sl foxing. Contemp calf, rebacked, reprd. *(Spelman)* £280 [≈ $498]

Turnbull, Patrick

- Analogia Legum: or, a View of The Institutes of the Laws of England and Scotland, Set One against the Other ... London: Lintot, 1725. Folio. Sl browned. New qtr calf. *(Meyer Boswell)* £850 [≈ $478]

- A Cursory View of the Ancient and Present State of the Fieffs, or Tenures, in both Parts of the United Kingdom of Great-Britain. London: for M. Cooper, [1747]. 1st edn. 8vo. iv, 55 pp. Clean tear in 1 leaf. Disbound. *(Hannas)* £55 [≈ $98]

Turner, Daniel

- The Art of Surgery. The Fifth Edition, Corrected. London: Rivington, 1736. 2 vols. 8vo. [16],576; iv,[8],520,[28] index pp. Frontis port vol 1, 1 fldg plate. Contemp calf, reprd. *(Spelman)* £260 [≈ $463]

- De Morbis Cutaneis. A Treatise of Diseases incident to the Skin. In Two Parts ... London: for R. Wilkin ..., 1736. 5th edn. 8vo. [xvi],x,524 pp. Port frontis. Contemp calf, gilt Victorian reback, front hinge cracked but firm. *(Vanbrugh)* £275 [≈ $490]

Turner, G.

- An Inquiry into the Revenue, Credit, and Commerce of France. In a Letter to a Member of this Present Parliament. The Second Edition. London: for J. Roberts, 1742. 8vo. 64 pp. Footnote on p 35. Tear in title removing 1 letter. Disbound. Anon. *(Hannas)* £75 [≈ $134]

Turner, Richard

- An Easy Introduction to the Arts and Sciences ... The Third Edition. With Considerable Additions ... Physics ... Electricity ... London: S. Crowder, 1791. xi, [1],248,[4] pp. Half-title. Contemp sheep, rebacked.   *(C.R. Johnson)* **£125 [≃ $223]**
- Easy Introduction to the Arts and Sciences ... Fifth Edition. London: 1795. 12mo. 251 pp. 8 plates, w'cuts in text. Hd of title cut with loss of 1st word. Few sm stains. Contemp sheep, jnts cracked. *(Robertshaw)* **£30 [≃ $53]**

The Tutor of Truth ...

- See Pratt, Samuel Jackson

Tuvil, Daniel

- The Dove and the Serpent. In which is conteined a large description of all such points and principles, as tend either to Conversation, or Negotiation. London: T.C. for Laurence L'Isle, 1614. 1st edn. Sm 4to. [8],92 pp. Cut sl close. Half calf. STC 24394.   *(Spelman)* **£800 [≃ $1,424]**

Twiss, Richard

- An Heroick Answer, from Richard Twiss, Esq; F.R.S. at Rotterdam, to Donna Teresa Pinna y Ruiz, of Murcia. Dublin: for W. Wilson, 1776. 1st edn. 12mo. 22 pp, inc half-title, final advt leaf. Disbound.   *(Hannas)* **£75 [≃ $134]**

Two ...

- The Two Cousins, a Moral Story ... see Pinchard, Mrs
- Two Epistles on Happiness: to a Young Lady. London: for Edward Easton, Salisbury, sold by J. & P. Knapton, 1754. 1st edn. 4to. [iv], 42 pp. Disbound.   *(Burmester)* **£225 [≃ $401]**
- Two Ordinances of the Lords and Commons ... One for the Abolishing of Archbishops and Bishops. London: Wright, 1646. 4to. Title border. Stitched. Wing E.2411.   *(Rostenberg & Stern)* **$125 [≃ £70]**
- Two Petitions of the County of Yorke. [London]: Hunscott, 1642. 4to. Title border. Stitched. Wing T.3507.   *(Rostenberg & Stern)* **$100 [≃ £56]**

Tyrrell, James

- Bibliotheca Politica: or an Enquiry into the Ancient Constitution of the English Government ... London: R. Baldwin, 1694. 1st edn. 4to. Sep titles to each of the 13 parts & the index. Sl damp stains. Contemp calf, gilt spine, sl worn. Wing T.3582. Anon.

(Clark) **£425 [≃ $757]**

Tytler, Alexander Fraser, Lord Woodhouselee

- Plan and Outlines of a Course of Lectures on Universal History, Ancient and Modern, Delivered in the University of Edinburgh ... Edinburgh: for William Creech, 1782. 8vo. [iv], 250,42 pp. 6 hand cold maps (few sl marg tears). Period sheep, sl worn.   *(Rankin)* **£125 [≃ $223]**
- Plan and Outlines of a Course of Lectures on Universal History, Ancient and Modern, Delivered in the University of Edinburgh. Edinburgh: William Creech, 1782. 1st edn. 8vo. [iv],250 pp. 6 hand cold maps (1 sl defective). Later mor.   *(Hartfield)* **$285 [≃ £160]**

Tytler, William

- An Inquiry, Historical and Critical, into the Evidence against Mary Queen of Scots ... London: for Cadell & Creech, 1790. 4th edn. 2 vols. 8vo. vii,381; viii,422,[ii errata leaf] pp. Few marg blind stamps. Mod half mor gilt.   *(Hollett)* **£85 [≃ $151]**

The Under-Sheriff ...

- The Under-Sheriff: Containing The Office and Duty of High-Sheriffs, Under-Sheriffs and Bailiffs ... By a Gentleman of the Inner-Temple ... London: Woodfall & Strahan ..., 1766. Only edn. 8vo. 601 pp. Contemp calf, some cracking jnts.   *(Meyer Boswell)* **$450 [≃ £253]**

Underwood, Thomas

- Liberty, a Poem. London: for the author ..., 1768. 1st edn. 4to. 34 pp. Half-title. Sl damp spotted. Disbound. Inscrbd by the author.   *(Burmester)* **£175 [≃ $312]**

The Universal Spectator ...

- The Universal Spectator. By Henry Stonecastle, of Northumberland, Esq. [pseudonym]. London: for Ward, Clarke ..., 1747. 1st edn. 4 vols. 12mo. Som water stains. Contemp calf, rebacked. Edited by Henry Baker & co-founded with Daniel Defoe.   *(Burmester)* **£150 [≃ $267]**

Upton, John

- Critical Observations on Shakespeare. The Second Edition. With Alterations and Additions. London: for G. Hawkins, 1748. 8vo. Contemp calf. Colquhoun of Luss b'plate.   *(Hannas)* **£75 [≃ $134]**

Urquhart, Sir Thomas
- Tracts of the Learned and Celebrated Antiquarian Sir Thomas Urquhart of Cromarty ... Edinburgh: Charles herriot, 1774. 8vo. xii, 175 pp. Occas sl foxing. Free endpapers removed. Period qtr sheep, label sl chipped, upper jnt cracked but firm.
(Rankin) **£100 [≈ $178]**

Ussher, James
- The Annals of the World. Deduced from the Origin of Time ... London: E. Tyler for J. Crook, 1658. 1st edn in English. Folio. [12], 907, [50] pp. Port, addtnl engvd title. Contemp calf, rebacked. Wing U.149.
(O'Neal) **$350 [≈ £197]**
- An Answer to a Challenge made by a Jesuite in Ireland ... Certain other Treatises of the same Author are ajoyned ... London: 1631. Sm 4to. [x],133, [xiii],12, [xxvi],538, [xiii], 50, [vi],42 pp. Sl wear. Later pigskin. STC 24544 (inc 2455A, 24548-9-55).
(Clark) **£220 [≈ $392]**
- The Principles of Christian Religion ... Now fully Corrected, and much Enlarged ... London: Nathanael Ranew, 1678. Folio. 184,[8] pp. 2 advt pp at end. Port frontis. Sl marg damp stain. Contemp calf, old reback, jnts rubbed & cracked at ends, crnrs worn. Wing U.206A.
(Clark) **£200 [≈ $356]**

V., R.
- A Restitution of Decayed Intelligence ... see Rowlands or Verstegan, Richard.

Vallavine, Peter
- Observations on the Present Condition of the Current Coin of this Kingdom ... London: R. Peny, for the author ..., 1742. 1st edn. 8vo. [2],40 pp. Few text engvs. Disbound.
(Hannas) **£120 [≈ $214]**

Valuable Secrets ...
- Valuable Secrets concerning Arts and Trades ... Engraving ... Varnishes ... Colours ... Painting ... Gilding ... Wines ... Dublin: 1778. 8vo. [viii],xxvii, [i],312 pp. Contemp calf, spine ends reprd, jnts sl cracked, new endpapers.
(Spelman) **£350 [≈ $623]**

Vanbrugh, Sir John
- The Mistake. A Comedy as it is acted at the Queen's Theatre in the Hay Market ... by the Author of The Provok'd Wife, &c. London: Tonson, 1706. 1st edn. Half-title, advt leaf. Mod qtr mor. Anon.
(Waterfield's) **£200 [≈ $356]**
- The Provok'd Wife; a Comedy ... London: J.O. for R. Wellington & Sam. Briscoe, 1697.

1st edn. 4to. [viii],78 pp. Half-title. Sl wear & tear. Disbound. Wing V.55. Anon.
(Clark) **£160 [≈ $285]**

Vancouver, George
- A Voyage of Discovery to the North Pacific Ocean, and Round the World ... London: Robinson, 1798. 1st edn. 3 vols (text only, without the atlas vol). 4to. [v],xxix,[2], [vi], 432; [vi],504; [vi],505,[3 errata] pp. Contemp russia gilt, a.e.g., sl worn.
(Gough) **£600 [≈ $1,068]**

Vane, Henry
- The Tryal of Sir Henry Vane, Kt. At the King's Bench ... June the 2d. and 6th. 1662 ... His Speech and Prayer on the Scaffold ... [London]: Printed in the Year 1662. 1st edn. Sm 4to. 134,[1] pp. Later qtr calf. Wing V.77.
(O'Neal) **$350 [≈ £197]**

Vansleb, F.
- The Present State of Egypt. Or, a New relation of a Late Voyage into that Kingdom. Performed in the Years 1672 and 1673. Englished by M.D. B.D. London: R.E. for John Starkey, 1678. 1st edn. 12mo. [vii],253,index pp. Contemp calf & bds, spine edges weak.
(Terramedia) **$700 [≈ £393]**

Van Swieten, Gerard
- The Commentaries upon the Aphorisms of Dr Herman Boerhaave ... Volumes I and II [only, of 14]. London: Knapton, 1744. 1st edns. 2 vols. 8vo. Contemp calf.
(Spelman) **£85 [≈ $151]**

Vathek ...
- See Beckford, William

Vaughan, John
- The Reports and Arguments ... London: Thomas Marriott, 1677. 1st edn. Large Paper. Folio. [xiv], 420, [421-476] pp. Errata. Licence leaf. Port. Contemp sheep, front bd detached. Wing V.130.
(Vanbrugh) **£225 [≈ $401]**

Vaughan, William
- The Church Militant, historically continued from the Yeare of Our Saviours Incarnation 33. untill this present. London: for Humfrey Blunden, 1640. 1st edn. Sm 8vo. Intl blank. Lacks final blank (errata in some copies). Contemp sheep, spine sl damaged. STC 24606.
(Hannas) **£360 [≈ $641]**

Vaurien, or, Sketches of the Times ...
- See D'Israeli, Isaac

Venables, Robert
- The Experienc'd Angler: or, Angling Improv'd ... The Third Edition much enlarged. London: Richard Marriot, 1668. 8vo. [xii], 96, [vi] pp. Addtnl engvd title. text w'cuts. Occas sl browning or spotting. Mod half calf gilt. Anon. Wing V.184.
(Hollett) **£650 [≈ $1,157]**

Veneroni, Giovanni
- The Complete Italian Master; containing the best and easiest Rules for attaining that Language ... New Edition, with considerable Additions and Improvements ... London: Nourse, 1778. 12mo. [iv],464,[208] pp. Contemp calf, elab gilt spine, extrs worn, jnts cracked but firm. *(Finch)* **£40 [≈ $71]**
- The Italian Master: or, the Easiest and Best Method for attaining that Language; revised, corrected and enlarged. The Second Edition ... Dictionary ... Translated ... by Edward Martin. London: 1729. 8vo. [viii], 298, [174] pp. Contemp calf, minor wear.
(Burmester) **£125 [≈ $223]**

Ventris, Sir Peyton
- The Reports ... in Two Parts ... In the Savoy: for D. browne ..., 1726. 4th edn. Folio. [xii],429,[430-454], [xviii],283,[i], 285-368, [369-388] pp. Licence leaf. Contemp calf, spine worn. *(Vanbrugh)* **£245 [≈ $436]**
- The Reports ... in Two Parts ... London: for Charles Harper ..., 1696. 1st edn. Folio. [xiv], 429,[28], [xx],368,[24] pp. 2 frontis ports. Occas browning, sm marg tear to title. Contemp calf, bds detached. Wing V.235.
(Vanbrugh) **£275 [≈ $490]**

Venuti, Marcello
- A Description of the First Discoveries of the Ancient City of Heraclea ... Done into English ... By Wickes Skurray ... London: for R. Baldwin, 1750. 1st edn in English. 8vo. xvi, 143 pp. New wraps.
(O'Neal) **$150 [≈ £84]**

Vergil, Polydore
- A Pleasant and Compendious History of the first Inventers and Instituters of the most famous Arts, Misteries, Laws, Customs and Manners in the whole World ... London: Harris, 1686. Sm 8vo. [xvi],159,[vii] pp, inc final blank. Old calf, rebacked, sl worn. Wing V.598. *(Hollett)* **£75 [≈ $134]**

Verstegan, Richard
- A Restitution of Decayed Intelligence ... see Rowlands or Verstegan, Richard.

Vertue, George
- A Description of the Works of the Ingenious Delineator and Engraver Wenceslaus Hollar ... With some Account of his Life. London: for Bathoe, 1759. 2nd edn, enlgd. vi, 151 pp. Frontis, port vignette on title, 2 engvd headpieces. Mod calf. *(Europa)* **£160 [≈ $285]**

A Very New Pamphlet Indeed! ...
- A Very New Pamphlet Indded! Being the Truth addressed to the People at Large. Containing some Strictures on the English Jacobins, and the Evidence ... respecting the Slave Trade. London: Printed in the Year, 1792. 1st edn. 8vo. 15 pp. Disbound.
(Blackwell's) **£185 [≈ $329]**

Veslingus, J.
- The Anatomy of the Body of Man. London: 1653. Translated by N. Culpeper. xii,194 pp. 22 engvs. Title & part of Table 1 supplied in facs. Leather antique.
(Whitehart) **£450 [≈ $801]**

Vezey, Francis
- Cases Argued and Determined in the High Court of Chancery ... From the Year 1746-7, to 1755 ... London: Strahan & Woodfall, for T. Cadell, 1771. 1st edn. 2 vols. Folio. Few sm marg tears. Contemp calf, bds detached.
(Vanbrugh) **£155 [≈ $276]**

The Vicar of Wakefield ...
- See Goldsmith, Oliver

Vicars, John
- A Discovery of the Rebels ... [London]: Printed in the Year of Our Lord, 1643. 1st edn. 4to. 44 pp, inc 'The Great Antichrist'. Stitched in plain white wraps as issued, uncut & unopened. Wing V.301. Anon.
(Young's) **£120 [≈ $214]**

Victor, Benjamin
- The Widow of the Wood. London: for C. Corbett, 1755. 1st edn. 8vo. [ii],iv,208,[1 advt] pp. 1 gathering loose. 20th c qtr calf. Anon. *(Young's)* **£180 [≈ $320]**

View ...
- A View of the Lancashire Dialect ... see Collier, John
- A View of Sir Isaac Newton's Philosophy ... see Pemberton, Henry

Villedieu, Mademoiselle
- The Exiles of the Court of Augustus Caesar ... see Desjardins, Marie Catherine Hortense

Virgil

- Georgicorum Libri Quatuor, The Georgicks ... With an English Translation and Notes By John Martyn. London: for the editor, 1741. 1st edn thus. 2 vols. 4to. xxii,403,3,[10]; xix, 280,6,[8] pp. 13 plates & 5 maps, all hand cold. Unobtrusive blind stamps. Contemp calf, rebacked.   *(Chapel Hill)* **$700 [≈ £393]**
- The Works ... translated into English Blank Verse. With ... Notes ... By Joseph Trapp. The Fourth Edition ... enlarged. London: W. Meadows, 1755. 3 vols. Fcap 8vo. Frontis vols 1 & 2. Occas sl marg worm. Contemp calf.   *(Spelman)* **£65 [≈ $116]**
- The Works of Virgil, translated into English Verse. By the Right Honourable Richard, late Earl of Lauderdale. The Second Edition. London: W. Bowyer for Bernard Lintot, [ca 1737]. 2 vols. Lge 12mo. [4],318; 320-587, [1 advt] pp. V sl marg worm vol 2. Contemp calf.   *(Spelman)* **£70 [≈ $125]**

The Virgin in Eden ...

- See Povey, Charles

Visions in Verse ...

- See Cotton, Nathaniel

Voiture, Vincent de

- The Works ... Compleat ... Made English by John Dryden [and others] ... [with] The Second Volume of the Works ... Second Edition, with Additions. London: for Sam. Briscoe, sold by J. Nutt, 1705. 2 vols in one. 8vo. Port. Contemp calf, minor wear spine ends.   *(Burmester)* **£100 [≈ $178]**

Volney, Constantin-Francois, Count

- Considerations on the War with the Turks. London: for J. Debrett, 1788. 1st edn in English. 8vo. Sewn, as issued, trifle dusty.   *(Ximenes)* **$200 [≈ £112]**

Voltaire, F.M.A. de

- The Age of Louis XV. Being the Sequel of the Age of Louis XIV. Translated from the French ... London: G. Kearsly, 1770. 1st English edn. 2 vols. Half-title. Early French tree calf, gilt dec spines, red & green mor labels.   *(D & D Galleries)* **$225 [≈ £126]**
- Critical Essays on Dramatic Poetry ... With Notes by the Translator ... London: Davis & Reymers, 1761. 1st edn in English. 12mo. xii,274,[ii] pp. Half-title, final advt leaf. Some browning page edges. Later calf.   *(Clark)* **£125 [≈ $223]**
- An Essay on the Age of Lewis XIV ... Translated from the French by Mr. Lockman.

London: Knapton, 1739. 1st edn. 8vo. 44 pp. New bds.   *(Young's)* **£50 [≈ $89]**
- The History of the War of Seventeen Hundred and Forty One. Third Edition, in which is now added a Continuation of the said History ... London: 1757. 8vo. 292 pp. Contemp calf, gilt spine.   *(Robertshaw)* **£55 [≈ $98]**
- The Philosophy of History. London: for L. Allcock ..., 1766. 1st English edn. 8vo. viii, 316 pp. Contemp tree calf, rebacked.   *(Young's)* **£150 [≈ $267]**
- The Pupil of Nature; a true History found among the Papers of Father Quesnel. London: T. Carnan, 1771. 1st edn in English. 19th c French mor, jnts & extrs rubbed, front jnt cracked but sound. *(Hermitage)* **$250 [≈ £140]**
- Le Taureau Blanc: or, The White Bull, from the French. Translated from the Syriac. London: J. Murray, 1774. 2nd edn. 8vo. 75 pp. frontis (spotted). Title sl browned, stamp on verso. Cloth backed bds, rather soiled.   *(Hollett)* **£50 [≈ $89]**

Von ...

- For all surnames commencing with "von ..." see under the primary name.

Vox Populi, Vox Dei ...

- Vox Populi, Vox Dei: being True Maxims of Government, proving 1. That all Kings, Governours, and Forms of Government proceed from the People ... London: 1709. 1st edn. 8vo. 40 pp. Later half calf. Attributed to Lord Somers or Daniel Defoe.   *(Robertshaw)* **£45 [≈ $80]**

A Voyage to the World of Cartesius ...

- See Daniel, Gabriel

Vyse, Charles

- A New Geographical Grammar: containing a Comprehensive System of Modern Geography ... London: for G. Robinson ..., 1779. 2nd edn, crrctd. 479,[8] pp. Half-title. 6 fldg maps, 5 plates. Occas foxing, sl stain to prelims. Calf, jnts split, extrs rubbed.   *(Francis Edwards)* **£40 [≈ $71]**

W., C.

- Observations on Dr. Freind's History of Physick ... see Wentingham, Clifford.

W., E.

- Reason and Religion ... see Worsley, Edward

W., G.

- A Rich Store-House or Treasury for the

Diseased ... The eighth edition, augmented and enlarged, by D.B[order]. London: Clowse, 1650. Sm 4to. [22],274 pp. Sl marg water stains & reprs, sl marg worm at end. Rec half mor. Wing W.31.
(Spelman) £650 [≈ $1,157]

W., J.
- Petition against Bishops. London: Lowndes, 1642. 4to. Stitched. Wing W.62.
(Rostenberg & Stern) $75 [≈ £42]
- Systema Agriculturae ... see Worlidge, John

W., T.
- The Natural Interest of Great-Britain, in its Present Circumstances, demonstrated in a Discourse. In Two Parts. London: for the author, 1748. 1st edn part 2, 2nd edn part 1. 2 parts in one vol. 8vo. [viii],46,[2 blank]; 64 pp. Old wraps, uncut.
(Burmester) £90 [≈ $1,602]

Wade, J.P.
- Select Evidences of a Successful Method of Treating Fever and Dysentery in Bengal. London: 1791. xi,336 pp. Pencil lib marks on title & endpaper. Some discoloration of endpapers. Contemp calf, rebacked.
(Whitehart) £180 [≈ $320]

Wadsworth, James
- The Copies of Certain Letters which have passed between Spain & England in Matter of Religion. London: 1685. 8vo. Mottled calf, a.e.g. Stirling Maxwell copy.
(Rostenberg & Stern) $200 [≈ £112]

Wagstaffe, William
- Miscellaneous Works ... prefix'd his Life and an Account of his Writings ... London: Bowyer, Isted, Worall, 1726 [ie 1725]. 1st coll edn. Ordinary paper. 8vo. Final blank leaf. Port, 2 plates. Port in earlier state, before letters. Contemp calf, upper jnt cracking.
(Hannas) £160 [≈ $285]
- Miscellaneous Works ... prefix'd his Life and an Account of his Writings ... London: Bowyer, Isted, Worall, 1726 [ie 1725]. 1st coll edn. Thick paper. 8vo. Final blank leaf. Port, 2 plates. Contemp panelled calf, rebacked.
(Hannas) £280 [≈ $498]

Wainewright, Jeremiah
- A Mechanical Account of the Non-Naturals: being a brief Explication of the Changes made in Humane Bodies, by Air, Diet, &c. The Third Edition, revis'd. London: J.H. for Ralph Smith, 1718. 8vo. [28],196 pp. Some browning. Contemp calf, jnts v sl reprd.

(Spelman) £160 [≈ $285]

Wake, William
- The Authority of Christian Princes over their Ecclesiastical Synods Asserted ... London: for R. Sare, 1697. 1st edn. 8vo. V browned. Contemp panelled calf, rebacked, reprd. Wing W.230.
(Hannas) £20 [≈ $36]
- A Discourse concerning Swearing ... London: for Richard Sare, 1696. 1st edn. Sm 8vo. Title & last leaf sl browned. Rebound in cloth. Wing W.252.
(Francis Edwards) £135 [≈ $240]
- The Principles of the Christian Religion explained: in a brief Commentary upon the Church Catechism ... The Second Edition, Corrected. London: for Richard Sare, 1700. 8vo. Lacks free endpapers. Contemp sheep, rubbed, hd of spine reprd. Wing W.259.
(Waterfield's) £45 [≈ $80]
- The Principles of the Christian Religion explained ... Fifth Edition, Corrected. London: W. Bowyer for Richard Williamson, 1731. 8vo. Contemp panelled calf Cambridge style, mor label, superficial scuffs.
(Waterfield's) £45 [≈ $80]
- Two Discourses: of Purgatory and Prayers for the Dead. London: Ric. Chiswell, 1687. 1st edn. Sm 4to. [viii],71,[i advt] pp. Imprimatur leaf. Lib stamp on title. Mod wraps. Wing W.272.
(Blackwell's) £40 [≈ $71]

Wakefield, Gilbert
- The Spirit of Christianity, Compared with the Spirit of the Times in Great Britain ... London: Kearsley, 1794. New (1st authorised) edn. 8vo. 41,[2 advt] pp. Half-title. Name cut from top marg of title. Disbound.
(Young's) £45 [≈ $80]

Walker, Sir Edward
- Historical Discourses, Upon Several Occasions: Together with Perfect Copies of all the Votes .. Treaty held at Newport, in the Isle of Wight ... London: for Sam. Keble, 1705. 1st edn. 2 parts. Folio. [xvi],369,98 pp. Plate. Lacks frontis. Old calf, jnts worn.
(Young's) £70 [≈ $125]

Walker, George
- Sermons on Various Subjects. London: for J. Johnson, & T. & J. Egerton, 1790. 1st edn. 2 vols. 8vo. xxi,[iii],408; [iv],441 pp. Subscribers. Contemp tree calf, gilt spines (sl rubbed), lacks numbering labels.
(Burmester) £120 [≈ $214]

Walker, Henry
- A Trve Copie of the Disputation held

between Master Walker and a Iesuite, in the house of one Thomas Bates ... London: Printed in the yeare, 1641. 1st edn. Sm 4to. [4] ff. Browned. Paper faults reprd. Forecrnrs cut away. Mod bds. Wing W.391.
(Blackwell's) **£80 [≈ $142]**

Walker, John
- An Attempt towards recovering an Account of the Numbers and Sufferings of the Clergy of the Church of England ... in the late Times of the Grand Rebellion ... London: for J. Nicholson ..., 1714. 1st edn. Folio. Wear & tear. Contemp calf, 19th c reback, crnrs worn.
(Blackwell's) **£165 [≈ $294]**

Walker, John
- A Critical Pronouncing Dictionary and Expositor of the English Language ... Dublin: for P. Wogan, 1794. 1st Irish edn. Contemp calf.   *(C.R. Johnson)* **£220 [≈ $392]**

Walker, Obadiah
- Of Education. Especially of Young Gentlemen. The Second Impression with Additions. Oxon: at the Theatre, 1673. 280, errata pp. Contemp panelled calf, rebacked. Wing W.400. Anon.
(C.R. Johnson) **£245 [≈ $436]**
- A Paraphrase and Annotations upon all the Epistles of St. Paul. Oxford: At the Theatre, 1684. 8vo. [16],403,[1] pp. Old panelled calf, hinges cracked but holding. Anon. Wing W.406.   *(Karmiole)* **£100 [≈ £56]**

Walker, Robert
- An Inquiry into the Small-Pox Medical and Political wherein a successful Method of treating that Diseases is proposed ... London: Murray, 1790. 8vo. xiv,499 pp. New cloth.
(Goodrich) **$150 [≈ £84]**

Walkingame, Francis
- The Tutor's Assistant; being a Compendium of Arithmetic ... A New Edition with the Addition of Book-Keeping by Single Entry ... Revised ... by William Taylor. Birmingham: M. Swinney, 1797. Fldg table frontis. Contemp sheep, rebacked.
(C.R. Johnson) **£135 [≈ $240]**

Wall, J.
- Plain Directions, &c. For the Cure of the Venereal Disease ... London: W. Griffin, 1764. Sm 8vo. [iv],45,[i] pp. Fldg leaf of Directions. V sl spotting. Qtr calf.
(Francis Edwards) **£80 [≈ $142]**

Waller, Edmund
- Works in Verse and Prose. Published by Mr. Fenton. London: Tonson, 1729. 1st edn. 4to. 450, xci pp. Engvd ills, dedic. V sl stain extreme lower crnr of ff. Old elab gilt calf, rebacked, worn & scarred.
(Argonaut) **$225 [≈ £126]**

Waller, Sir William
- Vindication of the Character and Conduct of Sir William Waller, Knight ... Written by Himself ... Now First Published ... London: Debrett, 1793. 8vo. [iii],14,[i], "126" [ie 326], [xiv],[iv] pp. Ports. Few ff creased. Contemp calf, sl worn.
(Blackwell's) **£65 [≈ $116]**

Wallis, George
- The Art of Preventing Diseases, and restoring Health ... London: Robinson, 1793. 8vo. xx,850,[12] pp. Tree calf, front jnt cracked.
(Goodrich) **$145 [≈ £81]**

Wallis, John
- London. London: for the editor, 1790. 1st edn. Post 12mo. [iv],(13)-144, *137-*144, 145-228 pp. 4 fldg plates (signs of wear on edges & folds). Orig sheep, rebacked.
(Ash) **£125 [≈ $223]**

Walpole, Horace
- A Catalogue of the Royal and Noble Authors of England ... Strawberry Hill: 1758. 1st edn. 1st issue, with 'to be partial' corrected at press to 'to have a bias'. 2 vols. 8vo. [viii], viii,219; [iv], 215,[vi] pp. Frontis vol 1. engvd titles. Contemp calf gilt, sl worn.
(Blackwell's) **£400 [≈ $712]**
- A Catalogue of the Royal and Noble Authors of England, with Lists of their Works. Second Edition. London: Dodsley, 1759. 2 vols. Frontis vol 1. Contemp black calf, rubbed, 1 jnt cracking.
(Jermy & Westerman) **£75 [≈ $134]**
- Historic Doubts on the Life and Reign of King Richard the Third. London: Dodsley, 1768. 1st edn. 4to. xv,[i],134, [i additions], [i errata] pp. Port, 1 plate (sl offset). Sl browned. Contemp speckled calf, rebacked, crnrs sl worn, hinges strengthened.
(Blackwell's) **£145 [≈ $258]**
- Historic Doubts on the Life and Reign of King Richard the Third. The Second Edition. London: Dodsley, 1768. 4to. xv,134,[2] pp. Fldg frontis, 1 full-page engv. Rebound in polished calf gilt.
(Hartfield) **$245 [≈ £138]**
- Historic Doubts on the Life and Reign of King Richard III. Dublin: G. Faulkner ...,

1768. 1st Dublin edn. 12mo. xvi,166,[2] pp.
2 fldg plates. Old calf, rebacked.
                    (Karmiole) **$185 [≈ £104]**
- Historic Doubts on the Life and Reign of
King Richard III ... Dublin: for G.
Faulkner, 1768. 1st Dublin edn. 8vo. xvi,
166, [1 directions] pp. 2 fldg plates.
Contemp speckled calf.
                    (Young's) **£110 [≈ $196]**
- Miscellaneous Antiquities; or, a Collection of
Curious Papers. Strawberry Hill: Thomas
Kirgate, 1772. Large Paper. 2 vols. Lge 4to.
Cloth.   *(Rostenberg & Stern)* **$450 [≈ £253]**
- Miscellaneous Antiquities; or, a Collection of
Curious Papers ... Strawberry Hill: Thomas
Kirgate, 1772. 1st edn. 2 parts in one vol. 4to.
1st title & last page dust soiled. Later half
calf. Anon.   *(Hannas)* **£220 [≈ $392]**
- The Mysterious Mother; A Tragedy. Dublin:
John Archer ..., 1791. Pirated edn. Later
three qtr mor, gilt spine. Anon.
                    (Hartfield) **$195 [≈ £110]**

Walpole, Horatio, 1st Baron
- An Answer to the latter Part of Lord
Bolingbroke's Letters on the Study of History
... In a Series of Letters to a Noble Lord.
London: W. Richardson, 1763. 2nd edn. 8vo.
269 pp. Title vignette. Occas spotting. Old
calf, rebacked.   *(Young's)* **£36 [≈ $64]**
- The Convention Vindicated from the
Misrepresentations of the Enemies of our
Peace. London: sold by J. Roberts, 1739. 8vo.
Mod qtr calf.   *(Waterfield's)* **£65 [≈ $116]**
- The Grand Question, whether War, or no
War, with Spain, impartially consider'd ...
London: J. Roberts, 1739. 1st edn. 8vo. 32
pp. Final leaf sl soiled. Mod wraps. Anon.
                    (Blackwell's) **£45 [≈ $80]**

Walpole, Sir Robert
- A Letter from a Member of Parliament to his
Friends in the Country, concerning the
Duties on Wine and Tobacco. London: for T.
Cooper, 1733. 1st edn. 8vo. 36 pp. Disbound,
uncut. Anon.   *(Hannas)* **£75 [≈ $134]**
- A Short History of the Parliament ... London:
for T. Warner ..., 1713. 1st edn. 8vo. xiv,33
pp. Half-title. Disbound. Anon.
                    (Young's) **£90 [≈ $160]**

Walsh, William
- A Funeral Elegy upon the Death of the
Queen. Addrest to the Marquess of
Normanby. London: Tonson, 1695. 1st edn.
Folio. 11 pp. Disbound. Wing W.646. Anon.
                    (Hannas) **£85 [≈ $151]**

Walton, Izaak
- The Life of Mr. Rich. Hooker. London: J.G.
for Rich. Marriott, 1665. 1st edn. Sm 8vo.
Licence leaf. Errata leaf. Apparently lacks an
intl blank leaf. Contemp calf, rebacked. Wing
W.670. Anon.   *(Hannas)* **£150 [≈ $267]**

The Wanderer ...
- The Wanderer: or, Memoirs of Charles
Searle, Esq.; containing his Adventures by
Sea and Land ... Dublin: for Saunders, Hoey
..., 1766. 2 vols in one. vii,134,[2]; viii, 116
pp. Contemp calf, green label.
                    (C.R. Johnson) **£650 [≈ $1,157]**

Wanley, Nathaniel
- The History of Man, or the Wonders of
Humane Nature in Relation to the Virtues,
Vices and Defects of Both Sexes ... London:
R. Basset & W. Turner, 1704. 8vo.
[10],566,[2 advt] pp. Contemp panelled calf.
Anon.   *(O'Neal)* **$200 [≈ £112]**
- The History of Man; or, the Wonders of
Humane Nature, in Relation to the Virtues,
Vices and Defects of Both Sexes ... London:
R. Basset & W. Turner, 1704. 1st edn thus.
8vo. [x],566,[2 advt] pp. Sl marg worm at edn.
Contemp panelled calf, sl worn. Anon.
                    (Clark) **£100 [≈ $178]**

Waple, Edward
- Thirty Sermons Preached on Several
Occasions. London: R. Bonwicke, 1714. [16],
416 pp. Disbound.
                    (C.R. Johnson) **£45 [≈ $80]**

Warburton, William
- The Alliance between Church and State: Or,
the Necessity and Equity of an Established
Religion and a Test Law Demonstrated ...
London: A. Millar, 1766. 4th edn. 8vo. xxvii,
355, 96,[11] pp. Contemp calf.
                    (Young's) **£50 [≈ $89]**

Ward, Edward
- Hudibras Redivivus: or, a Burlesque Poem on
the Times. London: B. Bragge, 1705-07. 1st
edn of each part. 2 vols, each with 12 monthly
parts, bound in 1 vol. 4to. Contemp calf,
rebacked. Anon.   *(Hannas)* **£750 [≈ $1,335]**
- The Republican Procession; or, the
Tumultuous Cavalcade. A Merry Poem.
[London]: printed in the Year, 1714. 1st edn.
Issue with page 44 numbered. 8vo. Browned.
Unbound, uncut. Anon.
                    (Hannas) **£85 [≈ $151]**
- The Secret History of the Calves-Head Club
... Fifth Edition, with large Additions,
Corrected ... London: the booksellers, 1705.

8vo. [iv],138[2 ctlg] pp, inc half-title. Few sm marg worm holes. Period calf, lacks label, hinges cracked but firm. Anon.
(Rankin) **£65 [≈ $116]**

- A Trip to Jamaica: with a true Character of the People and Island. By the Author of Scot's Paradise. The Seventh Edition. Londod [sic]: J. How, 1700. Folio. 16 pp. Rebound in qtr morocco-cloth & mrbld bds. Wing W.763. Anon.
(C.R. Johnson) **£650 [≈ $1,157]**

Ward, Seth

- The Christians Victory over Death. A Sermon at the Funeral of ... George Duke of Albemarle. London: Collins, 1670. 4to. Mourning band on title. Port of Monk inserted. Three qtr calf. Wing W.818.
(Rostenberg & Stern) **$75 [≈ £42]**

- A Philosophical Essay towards an Eviction of the Being and Attributes of God, the Immortality of the Souls of Men ... The Fourth Edition. Oxford: A. & L. Lichfield, 1667. 8vo. Mod calf. Wing W.825. Anon.
(Waterfield's) **£225 [≈ $401]**

Ward, Thomas

- Englands Reformation from the Time of King Henry the viiith to the End of Oates Plot. Printed at Hambourgh: 1710. 1st edn. 4 parts in one vol. 4to. Errata leaf. Lacks final blank leaf. Faint water stains. 2 sm reprs. 19th c half calf antique. *(Hannas)* **£130 [≈ $231]**

- England's Reformation ... a Poem ... London: for W.B. & sold by Thomas Bickerton, 1716. 8vo. [iv],402 pp. Contemp panelled calf, lacks label, spine ends rubbed, crnrs sl bumped.
(Finch) **£90 [≈ $160]**

Ware, Isaac

- A Complete Body of Architecture. London: T. Osborne ..., 1756. 1st edn. Folio. [xviii], 748,[4] pp. Frontis. Lacks the 115 plates. Contemp reversed calf, spine darkened & sl cracked, tips worn.
(Bookpress) **$200 [≈ £112]**

Waring, Thomas

- A Brief Narration of the Plotting, Beginning & Carrying on of that Execrable Rebellion and Butcherie in Ireland. With the unheard of Devilish Cruelties and Massacres by the Irish-Rebels ... London: Alson & Dunster, 1650. 4to. Stitched. Wing W.873.
(Rostenberg & Stern) **$125 [≈ £70]**

Warltire, John

- Analysis of a Course of Lectures in Experimental Philosophy ... The Sixth Edition. London: for the author, 1769. 8vo.

31 pp. Rec wraps. *(Fenning)* **£185 [≈ $329]**

- Tables of the Various Combinations and Specific Attraction of the Substances employed in Chemistry ... London: for the author, 1769. 1st (only?) edn. 8vo. 32 pp. Rec wraps. *(Fenning)* **£165 [≈ $294]**

Warner, Ferd.

- The History of the Rebellion and Civil War in Ireland. London: Tonson, 1767. 1st edn. 4to. xxiv,614 pp. Map. Contemp three qtr vellum, rebacked. *(de Burca)* **£315 [≈ $561]**

Warner, Richard

- A Letter to David Garrick, Esq. Concerning a Glossary to the Plays of Shakespeare ... annexed a Specimen. London: for the author, sold by T. Davies, 1768. 1st edn. 8vo. 110,[1 errata] pp. Contemp calf.
(Hartfield) **$295 [≈ £166]**

- A Letter to David Garrick, Esq. concerning a Glossary to the Plays of Shakespeare ... London: for the author, sold by T. Davies ..., 1768. 1st edn. 8vo. Final errata leaf. Contemp mottled wraps, uncut, spine renewed. Anon.
(Hannas) **£85 [≈ $151]**

- A Second Walk through Wales ... in August and September 1798 ... Bath: R. Cruttwell ..., 1799. 1st edn. 8vo. viii,365,[iii] pp. Half-title. Tinted aquatint frontis & plate, text ills. Orig bds, rebacked, remains of orig backstrip laid down, unpressed & untrimmed.
(Blackwell's) **£75 [≈ $134]**

Warren, Erasmus

- Geologia: or, a Discourse concerning the Earth before the Deluge ... London: 1690. Sm 4to. 8 ff,359 pp. Ctlg. 4 engvd ills. Occas sl marg water stain. Lib label. Contemp calf, worn, loose, leather on back bd torn.
(Weiner) **£300 [≈ $534]**

Warrington, William

- The History of Wales ... London: for J. Johnson ..., 1786. 4to. x,[ii],628 pp. Sl foxed at ends. Contemp tree calf gilt, rebacked, extrs rubbed with some loss.
(Francis Edwards) **£125 [≈ $223]**

Warton, T.

- A Description of the City, College and Cathedral of Winchester ... London: [ca 1750]. 1st edn. 12mo. 108 pp. Contemp backed bds, jnts cracked. Anon.
(Robertshaw) **£25 [≈ $45]**

Warton, Thomas

- The History of English Poetry ... Second Edition. London: Dodsley ..., 1775-81.

[With] Index. London: for Lackington, Allen, 1806. 1st edn vols 2-4. 4 vols in 3. 4to. Contemp half mor, jnts breaking. Lacks the 'Fragment' (88 pp) of 1782.
(Hannas) **£180 [≃ $320]**

- The Life of Sir Thomas Pope, Founder of Trinity College Oxford ... London: for T. davies ..., 1772. 1st edn. Thick Paper. 8vo. xii,438,[4] pp. Orig bds, uncut & unopened, spine sl worn. Custom box.
(Young's) **£120 [≃ $214]**

- Observations on the Fairy Queen of Spenser ... London: Dodsley, 1762. 2nd edn. 2 vols. 8vo. xx,228; 270 pp. Contemp speckled calf, 1 spine hd worn, 2 sm cracks in jnts.
(Young's) **£150 [≃ $267]**

- The Pleasures of Melancholy. A Poem. London: Dodsley, sold by M. Cooper, 1747. 1st edn. 4to. 24 pp. Disbound. Anon.
(Hannas) **£120 [≃ $214]**

Warton, Thomas, & others
- The Oxford Sausage: or, Select Poetical Pieces, written by the most celebrated Wits of the University of Oxford. New Edition. Oxford: 1777. New edn. Sm 8vo. W'cut frontis, w'cuts in text. Contemp calf. Anon.
(Robertshaw) **£35 [≃ $62]**

Warwick, Sir Philip
- Memoires of the Reigne of King Charles I. With a Continuation to the Happy Restoration of King Charles II ... London: Chiswell, 1701. 1st edn. 8vo. Port on verso of half-title. Contemp calf, label, spine ends worn, jnts cracked but holding.
(Blackwell's) **£50 [≃ $89]**

Waterhouse, Edward
- The Gentlemans Monitor; or, a Sober Inspection into the Vertues, Vices, and ordinary Means, of the Rise and Decay of Men and Families ... London: for R. Royston, 1665. 1st edn. 8vo. Intl blank. Final advt leaf. Port. Contemp calf, worn. Wing W.1047.
(Hannas) **£240 [≃ $427]**

- An humble Apologie for Learning and Learned Men. London: T.M. for Bedell & Collins, 1653. 1st edn. 8vo. [viii],263,[i] pp. Minor soil, errata corrected by pen. Mod half mor, a.e.g. Wing W.1048.
(Clark) **£150 [≃ $267]**

Watson, Richard
- An Address to the People of Great Britain ... London: for R. Faulder, 1798. 1st edn. 8vo. [iv],42,[i advt] pp. Half-title. Sm marg stains on 2 ff. Disbound. *(Young's)* **£45 [≃ $80]**

- An Address to Young Persons after

Confirmation. Cambridge: J. Archdeacon, 1788. 1st edn. [i],76 pp. V sm marg stain at end. Orig wraps. *(Blackwell's)* **£35 [≃ $62]**

- An Address to Young Persons after Confirmation ... London: for Thomas Evans, 1792. 4th edn. 8vo. 49 pp. Disbound.
(Young's) **£25 [≃ $45]**

Watson, Robert
- The History of the Reign of Philip the Second, King of Spain. London: Strahan ..., 1779. 3rd edn. 3 vols. 8vo. Contemp speckled calf, gilt spines, red & green labels, sl rubbed.
(Frew Mackenzie) **£80 [≃ $142]**

Watson, Samuel
- A Short Account of the Convincement, Gospell Labours, Sufferings and Service of that Faithful Servant ... Being a Collection of his Works. London: J. Sowle, 1712. 1st edn. 12mo. 260,[4 advt] pp. Sl foxing. Calf, rebacked in cloth. *(Hartfield)* **$165 [≃ £93]**

Watson, William
- An Account of a Series of Experiments, instituted with a View to ascertaining the most Successful Method of Inoculating the Small-Pox. London: J. Nourse, 1768. 1st edn. 8vo. [iv],58,[1] pp. Disbound.
(Bookpress) **$225 [≃ £126]**

- The Clergy-Man's Law: or, The Complete Incumbent ... In the Savoy: for D. Browne ..., 1725. 10th edn, enlgd. Folio. [ii], 3-4, [viii], 652,[lxii] pp. Errata. Rec half calf.
(Vanbrugh) **£255 [≃ $454]**

- The Clergy-Man's Law: or, the Complete Incumbent ... Third Edition, with large additions. London: E. & R. Nutt & R. Gosling ..., 1725. Folio. [xii],652,[62] pp. Contemp calf, upper jnt sl tender, lower crnrs worn. *(Burmester)* **£90 [≃ $160]**

Watts, Isaac
- Evangelical Discourses on Several Subjects. To which is added, An Essay on the Powers and Contests of Flesh and Spirit. London: for J. Oswald & J. Buckland, 1747. 1st edn. 8vo. Contemp calf, rubbed, sm piece missing from ft of backstrip. *(Waterfield's)* **£65 [≃ $116]**

- The First Principles of Astronomy and Geography ... London: for J. Clark & R. Hett, 1728. 2nd edn crrctd. 8vo. xii,222 pp. 6 fldg plates. Calf, spine & edges worn.
(Key Books) **$120 [≃ £67]**

- The Improvement of the Mind ... also his Posthumous Works, published from his Manuscript by D. Jennings and P. Doddridge. London: for J. Cuthell, 1794. x,412 pp. Speckled calf, gilt dec spine, extrs

worn, lower hinge tender.
(Francis Edwards) **£36 [≈ $64]**

- The Knowledge of the Heavens and the Earth made Easy; or the First Principles of Astronomy and Geography explain'd by the Use of Globes and Maps ... London: for J. Clark ..., 1726. 1st edn. 8vo. 6 fldg plates. Contemp calf, crnrs & spine ends worn, jnts cracked. *(Gaskell)* **£300 [≈ $534]**

Waugh, John
- The Duty of Apprentices and Servants. A Sermon ... London: Joseph Downing, 1713. 1st edn. 8vo. 24 pp. Disbound.
(Burmester) **£25 [≈ $45]**

- A Sermon Preached to the Societies for the Reformation of Manners ... Monday, December the 28th, MDCCCXIII. London: J. Downing, 1714. 1st edn. 8vo. 30,[2 advt] pp. Disbound. *(Burmester)* **£25 [≈ $45]**

Webb, Daniel
- An Enquiry into the Beauties of Painting; and into the Merits of the most celebrated Painters, Ancient and Modern. London: for Dodsley, 1760. 1st edn. 8vo. xv,200 pp. Pencil underlinings. Contemp calf gilt, rebacked. *(Europa)* **£75 [≈ $134]**

- An Enquiry into the Beauties of Painting ... London: for Dodsley, 1761. 2nd edn. Contemp sprinkled calf, rebacked.
(Europa) **£58 [≈ $103]**

- Observations on the Correspondence between Poetry and Music. London: Dodsley, 1769. 1st edn. 8vo. vii,[i],155,[5] pp. Half-title. 4 advt ff at end. Minor foxing early ff. Contemp calf, gilt spine, extrs sl worn, label defective. Anon. *(Clark)* **£160 [≈ $285]**

Webb, William
- An Analysis of the History and Antiquities of Ireland, Prior to the Fifth Century. To which is subjoined, a Review of the General History of the Celtic Nations. Dublin: Jones, 1791. 8vo. viii,281 pp. Contemp green half mor.
(de Burca) **£85 [≈ $151]**

Weber, Friedrich Christian
- The Present State of Russia ... and Several other Pieces ... Translated from the High-Dutch. London: W. Taylor ..., 1723-22. 1st edn in English. 2 vols. 8vo. [xlviii], 352; 432 pp. Fldg map, fldg plan. Contemp calf, sm split 1 jnt, crnrs sl worn. Anon.
(Clark) **£480 [≈ $854]**

Webster, John
- The Display of supposed Witchcraft ... London: J.M., sold by the Booksellers, 1677.

1st edn. Sm folio. [xvi],346,[iv] pp. Licence leaf, final blank. Sl marg worm at start. Contemp sheep, sometime recased, new label, crnrs sl worn. Wing W.1230.
(Blackwell's) **£875 [≈ $1,558]**

- Metallographia or, An History of Metals ... London: A.C. for Walter Kettilby, 1671. Only edn. 4to. [xvi],388 pp. Title soiled & mtd. Occas sl soil & damp stain. No advt ff. Rec half calf. Wing W.1231A.
(Clark) **£280 [≈ $498]**

The Weesils. A Satyrical Fable ...
- See Brown, Thomas

Weever, John
- Ancient Funeral Monuments within the United Monarchie of Great Britaine, Ireland, and the Islands adjacent ... London: 1631. Folio. [xvi],871,[i] pp. Lacks frontis & engvd title. Bound without index. Contemp calf, front bd detached. STC 25223.
(Clark) **£70 [≈ $125]**

Welchman, Edward
- The Duty and Reward of Charity especially as it regardeth the Education of Poor Children. A Sermon preach'd at Banbury ... London: Joseph Downing, 1707. 1st edn. 8vo. 16 pp. Disbound.
(Burmester) **£25 [≈ $45]**

Wells, Edward
- The Young Gentleman's Astronomy, Chronology, and Dialling ... London: for James & John Knapton ..., 1725. 3rd edn. 3 parts in one vol. 8vo. [viii],148, [viii],86, [viii],44 pp. 25 plates. Contemp panelled calf, sl worn. *(Young's)* **£155 [≈ $276]**

Welwood, James
- Memoirs of the most Material Transactions in England, for the last hundred years, preceding the Revolution in 1688. Fourth Edition. London: Tim. Goodwin, 1702. 8vo. [22], 405,[3 advt] pp. Half-title. Contemp panelled calf, gilt spine, jnts sl cracked.
(Spelman) **£45 [≈ $80]**

Wenderborn, G.F.A.
- A View of England towards the Close of the Eighteenth Century ... Translated from the German by the Author ... London: Robinson, 1791. 1st edn in English. 2 vols. 8vo. xiv, [ii], 442,[ii]; iv,488 pp. Half-title & errata vol 1. Occas stain. Contemp calf, 1 jnt cracked.
(Clark) **£125 [≈ $223]**

- A View of England towards the Close of the Eighteenth Century ... Translated from the

Original German by the Author ... Dublin: William Sleater, 1791. 2 vols. Contemp calf.
(C.R. Johnson) £220 [≃ $392]

Wentingham, Clifford

- Observations on Dr. Freind's History of Physick; Shewing, some False Representations of Ancient and Modern Physicians. By C.W., M.D. ... London: Strahan, 1726. 8vo. 65 pp. Period style qtr calf by Bernard Middleton. Anon.
(Goodrich) $325 [≃ £183]

Wesley, John

- A Calm Address to our American Colonies. London: R. Hawes, [1775]. 12mo. Title sl dusty. Disbound. *(Ximenes)* $450 [≃ £253]
- A Collection of Letters, on Religious Subjects, from Various Eminent Ministers, and Others; to the Rev. John Wesley. being a Supplement to the Methodist Magazine, for the Year 1797. London: Whitfield, 1797. 8vo. 55, [i] pp. Later qtr mor, spine worn.
(Clark) £28 [≃ $50]
- The Doctrine of Original Sin: according to Scripture, Reason, and Experience. Bristol: E. Farley, 1757. 1st edn. 8vo. 522,[ii] pp. Errata leaf at end. Occas staining & marg worm. Contemp calf, rebacked, crnrs sl worn.
(Clark) £110 [≃ $196]
- Some Account of the Life and Death of Matthew Lee, executed at Tyburn, October 11, 1752 ... London: at the New-Chapel, City-Road, & Mr. Wesley's Preaching-Houses, 1789. [3],4-24 pp. 19th c qtr mor, hinges worn. Anon.
(C.R. Johnson) £225 [≃ $401]

West, Gilbert

- The Institution of the Order of the Garter. A Dramatick Poem. London: for R. Dodsley, 1742. 1st edn. 64 pp. Page numerals and 1 footnote cut into. Disbound. Anon.
(Hannas) £85 [≃ $151]

West, Gilbert (translator)

- Odes of Pindar, with several other Pieces, in Prose and Verse, translated from the Greek. To which is added a Dissertation on the Olympick Games. London: Dodsley, 1753. 2nd edn. 2 vols. 12mo. Port (outer marg shaved). Contemp calf, later labels.
(Burmester) £75 [≃ $134]

West, Richard

- An Inquiry into the Manner of Creating Peers. London: 1719. 1st edn. 8vo. 74 pp. Disbound. Anon. *(Robertshaw)* £15 [≃ $27]
- An Inquiry into the Manner of Creating

Peers. London: for J. Roberts ..., 1719. 1st edn. 8vo. 74 pp. Half-title. Disbound. Anon.
(Young's) £60 [≃ $107]

West, Samuel

- Essays on Liberty and Necessity; in which the True Nature of Liberty is Stated and defended ... Boston: Samuel Hall, 1793. 1st edn. 8vo. 54,[2] pp. Sl foxed. Stabbed as issued. *(Gach)* $350 [≃ £197]

West, Thomas

- The Antiquities of Furness ... London: for the author by T. Spilsbury, 1774. 1st edn. 8vo. [xx],lvi,[ii], 288,[136] pp. Fldg map, fldg plan, 2 plates. 1 sm marg tear. Contemp calf gilt, edges worn, sl scraped, rebacked.
(Hollett) £225 [≃ $401]
- A Guide to the Lakes, in Cumberland, Westmorland, and Lancashire. The Fourth Edition. London: for W. Richardson, 1789. 8vo. xiv,311,[1 advt] pp. Half-title. Fldg frontis map. Orig bds, uncut, spine reprd, sl mark upper bd. Anon.
(Spelman) £120 [≃ $214]
- A Guide to the Lakes, in Cumberland, Westmorland and Lancashire. London: for W. Richardson ..., Kendal: W. Pennington, 1793. 5th edn. 8vo. xii,311,[3 advt] pp. Fldg hand cold map, 2 plates. Old polished calf gilt, spine sl rubbed, occas scrape, new endpapers. *(Hollett)* £140 [≃ $249]

Weston, Stephen

- Letters from Paris, during the Summer of 1791. London: for J. Debrett, & W. Clarke, 1792. 1st edn. 8vo. xx,347,[1] pp. Contemp tree calf, spine sl worn, upper jnt cracked. Anon. *(Burmester)* £120 [≃ $214]

Whaley, John

- A Collection of Original Poems and Translations. London: for the author, & sold by R. Manby & H.S. Cox, 1745. Only edn. 8vo. Sm marg damp stain. Contemp gilt ruled calf, jnts rubbed, ft of spine sl chipped.
(Sanders) £105 [≃ $187]
- A Collection of Original Poems and Translations. London: for the author, sold by R. Manby, & H.S. Cox, 1745. 1st edn. 8vo. Contemp calf, rebacked.
(Hannas) £240 [≃ $427]
- A Collection of Poems. London: for the author, by John Willis ..., 1732. 1st edn. 8vo. Subscribers. Tear in 1 leaf, no loss. Contemp calf gilt, lacks label. *(Hannas)* £280 [≃ $498]

Wheare, Degory or Diggory

- The Method and Order of Reading Both

Civil and Ecclesiastical Histories ... Third Edition, with Amendments ... Made English and Enlarged, by Edmund Bohun. London: for Charles Brome, 1698. 8vo. [74],362,[12] pp. Contemp panelled calf. Wing W.1594.
(O'Neal) **$350 [≈ £197]**

Wheatley, Charles
- A Rational Illustration of the Book of Common Prayer ... The Fourth Edition ... London: for the author, 1722. 8vo. xxvii, 559, [xx] pp. Frontis plan. Contemp calf, v sl rubbed. *(Blackwell's)* **£45 [≈ $80]**

Wheatley, Phillis
- Poems on Various Subjects, Religious and Moral. London: A. bell, 1773. 1st edn. 8vo. [128] pp, inc final advt page. Frontis port. V sl foxing. Rebound in calf, a.e.g.
(Heritage) **$4,500 [≈ £2,528]**

Wheeler, James
- The Botanist's and Gardener's New Dictionary ... London: Strahan, 1763. 8vo. viii, xxxii,480 pp. 2 plates. Contemp sprinkled calf, label, sl rubbed.
(Blackwell's) **£150 [≈ $267]**

Wheler, George
- A Journey into Greece ... in Company of Dr. Spon of Lyons ... London: 1682. 1st edn. 4to. Title, [xii],1-80, 177-483 pp. Interleaved with folio sized blanks. Fldg map, 4 pp of coins (sl damp stained), 2 sm tipped in plates, ca 70 text engvs. 19th c half calf.
(Frew Mackenzie) **£800 [≈ $1,424]**

Whichcote, Benjamin
- Moral and Religious Aphorisms. Wherein are contained, many Doctrines of truth ... Norwich: Fr. Burges, 1703. [6],144 pp. Occas sl damp staining. Contemp calf, spine rubbed. Anon. *(C.R. Johnson)* **£75 [≈ $134]**
- Moral and Religious Aphorisms ... Now republished, with very large Additions ... London: J. Payne, 1753. 8vo. [i]-viii,[iii], ix-xxxiv,[ii], 158,[i],xl, 134,[ii] pp. Sl foxing, few pencil notes. Mod buckram.
(Blackwell's) **£45 [≈ $80]**

Whiston, William
- Astronomical Principles of Religion, Natural and Reveal'd. In Nine Parts ... London: for J. Senex ..., 1725. 2nd edn. 8vo. [iv],xxxii, 304,[4] pp. 7 engvd plates. Marg worm hole 1st 19 ff. Minor damp edges of endpapers. Contemp calf. *(Burmester)* **£120 [≈ $214]**
- Memoirs of the Life and Writings of Mr. William Whiston, containing Memoirs of

several of his Friends also. Written by himself. London: for the author, 1749. 8vo. Front free endpaper loose. Contemp calf, jnts cracked, sl worn but sound.
(Waterfield's) **£90 [≈ $160]**
- A New Theory of the Earth ... [with his] A Vindication of the New Theory of the Earth ... [with his] A Second Defence of the New Theory of the Earth ... London: 1696-98-1700. 1st edns. 3 vols in one. Frontis & 7 plates in 1st work. Sl used. Old style calf. Wing 1696-8-7.
(P and P Books) **£680 [≈ $1,210]**
Original, to the Consummation of all Things ... Third Edition. London: 1722. 8vo. 95,460 pp. 8 plates (1 fldg). Occas sl spotting. Sm lib stamp title verso. Contemp calf, rebacked.
(Weiner) **£150 [≈ $267]**
- A Short View of the Chronology of the Old Testament, and of the Harmony of the Four Evangelists. Cambridge: UP for B. Tooke, 1702. 1st edn. 8vo. [viii],543,[v] pp. Final errata leaf. 4 engvd tables. Contemp calf, worn, lacks label. *(Clark)* **£50 [≈ $89]**

Whitaker, John
- The History of Manchester. London: 1773. 2nd edn, crrctd. 2 vols. xvi,385; 427 pp. Num text ills. Some browning, worming lower marg vol 1 sl affecting text. Calf, jnts cracked, spines chipped, sl worn & rubbed.
(Francis Edwards) **£55 [≈ $98]**

Whitaker, Nathaniel
- A Brief Narrative of the Indian Charity-School in Lebanon in Connecticut, New England: Founded ... by ... Eleazer Wheelock. The Second Edition, with an Appendix. London: J. & W. Oliver, 1767. 63 pp. Rec wraps. Anon.
(C.R. Johnson) **£265 [≈ $472]**

White, Gilbert
- A Naturalist's Calendar, with Observations in Various Branches of Natural History ... London: 1795. 8vo. 176 pp. Cold plate. Orig bds, spine defective.
(Wheldon & Wesley) **£140 [≈ $249]**

White, John
- A Speech of John White, Counsellor at Law, made in the Commons House of Parliament Concerning Episcopacy. London: for Thomas Nicholas ..., 1641. 1st edn. 4to. 14 pp. Sidenotes just shaved on D2v. Wraps. Wing W.1773. *(Young's)* **£75 [≈ $134]**
- A Way to the Tree of Life: Discovered in Sundrey Directions for the Profitable Reading of the Scriptures ... London: M.F.

for R. Royston, 1647. 1st edn. 8vo. [10],340 pp. Some marks. 19th c half calf. Wing W.1785.   *(O'Neal)* **$200 [≈ £112]**

White, P.

- Observations upon the Present State of the Scotch Fisheries, and the Improvement of the Interior Parts of the Highlands ... Edinburgh: for the author, 1791. 8vo. 202 pp, inc half-title. Orig mrbld bds, drab paper spine, uncut, rebacked.   *(Rankin)* **£125 [≈ $223]**

White, T.

- A Treatise on the Struma or Scrofula, commonly called The King's Evil. London: 1787. 2nd edn. viii,100 pp. Lib marks on title. Some marg pencil lines. Mod half leather.   *(Whitehart)* **£140 [≈ $249]**

Whitefield, George

- An Account of Money Received and Disbursed for the Orphan-House in Georgia. To which is prefixed A Plan of the Building. London: Strahan for Cooper, 1741. 8vo. [2],45 pp. Fldg view. Browning, sm marg repr. Rec qtr calf.   *(Spelman)* **£240 [≈ $427]**
- A Journal of a Voyage from Gibraltar to Georgia ... London: for T. Cooper, 1738. 1st edn, unauthorized. 12mo. 34 pp. Orig self-wraps, disbound.
                           (Chapel Hill) **$450 [≈ £253]**
- A Short Account of God's Dealings with the Reverend Mr George Whitefield. Written by himself ... to be published for the benefit of the Orphan-House in Georgia. London: W. Strahan ..., 1740. 1st edn. 8vo. 76 pp. Half-title. Disbound.   *(Spelman)* **£35 [≈ $62]**

Whitehead, Paul

- The Gymnasiad, or Boxing Match. A very short, but very curious Epic Poem. With the Prolegomena of Scriblerus Tertius, and Notes Variorum. London: for M. Cooper, 1744. 1st edn. 4to. [2],33 pp, inc half-title. Disbound. Anon.   *(Hannas)* **£150 [≈ $267]**
- Honour. A Satire. London: for M. Cooper, 1747. 1st edn. 4to. 22 pp. Lacks half-title. 2 edges uncut. Disbound.
                           (Burmester) **£50 [≈ $89]**
- An Hymn to the Nymph of Bristol Spring. London: for R. Dodsley, sold by M. Cooper, 1751. 1st edn. 4to. 27 pp, advt leaf. 3 vignettes. Lacks half-title. Red half roan, sl rubbed.   *(Hannas)* **£65 [≈ $116]**
- Manners: a Satire. London: for R. Dodsley [ie Edinburgh: Ruddiman], 1739. 8vo. 20 pp. Disbound.   *(Hannas)* **£85 [≈ $151]**
- The State Dunces. Inscrib'd to Mr. Pope. In

Two Parts. London: for J. Dickenson [ie Edinburgh: Fleming], 1733. 8vo. [2],29 pp. Title torn with no loss. All name blanks filled in contemp MS. Disbound. Anon.
                           (Hannas) **£90 [≈ $160]**
- The State Dunces: inscrib'd to Mr. Pope. London: J. Dickenson, 1733. 1st edn, 2nd issue. Folio. [ii],17,[i] pp. Minor soil. Sm holes in end ff, not affecting text, these 2 ff laminated. Rec bds. Anon.
                           (Clark) **£55 [≈ $98]**

Whitehurst, John

- An Inquiry into the Original State and Formation of the Earth ... Appendix ... Strata of Derbyshire ... London: for the author, & W. Bent ..., 1778. Lge 4to. [xi], iv, 199 pp. Subscribers. 9 plates on 5 sheets. Orig bds, uncut, worn.   *(Weiner)* **£500 [≈ $890]**
- An Inquiry into the Original State and Formation of the Earth deduced from Facts and the Laws of Nature ... Appendix ... On the Strata in Derbyshire. London: 1778. 1st edn. 4to. [xvi],iv,199 pp. Half-title. 9 plates (water stained) on 4 ff. Half calf, jnts worn.
                     (Wheldon & Wesley) **£325 [≈ $579]**
- An Inquiry into the Original State and Formation of the Earth ... Appendix ... Strata of Derbyshire ... London: for the author, by J. Cooper, 1778. Lge 4to. Subscribers (reset). 9 plates on 4 sheets. Mod calf.
                           (Weiner) **£400 [≈ $712]**
- The Works, with Memoirs of his Life and Writings. London: 1792. 4to. 10 plates (8 fldg). Lacks frontis port. Half calf, jnts cracking but firm.   *(Weiner)* **£110 [≈ $196]**

Whitelock, Methuselah (pseudonym)

- The Peace-Offering: An Essay ... London: for L. Raymond, sold by A. Moore, 1746. 1st edn. 8vo. 60 pp. Title stained. Disbound.
                           (Hannas) **£85 [≈ $151]**

Whitelocke, Bulstrode

- Memorials of the English Affairs ... London: Nathaniel Ponder, 1682. 1st edn. Folio. [viii],704,[xvi] pp. Contemp calf, rubbed, sl worn. Wing W.1986.
                           (Clark) **£140 [≈ $249]**
- Memorials of the English Affairs ... New Edition: with many Additions ... London: Tonson ..., 1732. Folio. [viii],[ii], 702, [xiii] pp. Few marg notes. Contemp panelled calf gilt, jnts cracked, cvrs rather worn.
                           (Blackwell's) **£75 [≈ $134]**

Whiter, Walter

- A Specimen of a Commentary on Shakespeare. London: for T. Cadell, 1794.

1st edn. 8vo. half-title, errata leaf. Mod bds, uncut. Anon.   *(Hannas)* **£95 [≈ $169]**

Whiting, John

- Judas and the Chief Priests conspiring to Betray Christ and His Followers: or an Apostate Convicted, and Truth Defended. London: T. Sowle, 1701. 4to. [12],259,1,4 pp. Foxed, Contemp calf, rebacked, worn.
          (D & D Galleries) **$100 [≈ £56]**

Whittel, John

- Constantinus Redivivus: or, a Full Account of ... William the 3d, now King of Great Britain ... London: Tho. Harbin, 1693. Only edn. 8vo. [xxviii],199,[i] pp. Imprimatur leaf. Rather used. Contemp sheep, worn. Wing W.2040.   *(Clark)* **£75 [≈ $134]**

Whitworth, Charles

- An Account of Russia as it was in the Year 1710. Strawberry-Hill, 1758. 1st edn. 8vo. Title device. Some browning at edges. Orig calf, rebacked.
          (Rostenberg & Stern) **$475 [≈ £267]**
- An Account of Russia as it was in the Year 1710. Strawberry Hill: 1758. 1st edn. One of 700. 8vo. xxiv,158,[1 errata] pp. Orig wraps, untrimmed, sl soiled.
          (Chapel Hill) **$650 [≈ £365]**
- A Collection of the Supplies, and Ways and Means; from the Revolution to the Present Time. The Second Edition. London: R. Davis, 1765. 181,6 pp. Fldg table. Contemp calf, leading hinge weak.
          (C.R. Johnson) **£45 [≈ $80]**

The Whole Duty of Man ...

- See Allestree, Richard

The Widow of the Wood ...

- See Victor, Benjamin

Wight, Thomas

- A History of the Rise and Progress of the ... Quakers in Ireland ... Introduction ... by John Rutty. Dublin: I. Jackson, 1751. 1st edn thus. 4to. 484,[8] pp. Rec qtr calf gilt.
          (Fenning) **£65 [≈ $116]**

Wight, William

- Heads of a Course of Lectures on Civil History. With a Chronological Table from the Earliest Accounts to the Present Time. Glasgow: Robert & Andrew Foulis, 1772. 8vo. 59 pp. Disbound.
          (Robertshaw) **£25 [≈ $45]**

Wilberforce, William

- A Practical View of the Prevailing Religious System of Professed Christians ... contrasted with Real Christianity. Dublin: 1797. 1st Dublin edn. 12mo. iii-xii, 354, [xvi], [2 advt] pp. Lacks half-title. Contemp tree calf gilt, some worming to jnt ends.
          (Finch) **£70 [≈ $125]**
- A Practical View of the Prevailing Religious System of Professed Christians... Fourth Edition. London: Cadell & Davies, 1797. 8vo. [iv],491,[17] pp. Orig bds, rebacked.
          (Clark) **£32 [≈ $57]**

Wild, Robert

- Iter Boreale. With other Select Poems ... London: for R.R. & W.C., 1671. 8vo. "126" [ie 128] pp. No front endpapers. Intl blank reprd. Minor browning & soiling. Contemp sheep, rebacked, edges rubbed. Wing W.2138.   *(Clark)* **£145 [≈ $258]**

Wildman, Thomas

- A Treatise on the Management of Bees ... added the Natural History of Wasps and Hornets. London: 1768. 1st edn. 4to. xx, 169, [7] pp. 3 fldg plates (some offsetting). Contemp calf, rebacked.
          (Wheldon & Wesley) **£200 [≈ $356]**
- A Treatise on the Management of Bees ... London: for the author, & sold by T. Cadell, 1768. 1st edn. 4to. xx,169 pp. 3 fldg plates. Sl offsetting onto plates. Near contemp qtr calf & paper bds, crnrs trifle rubbed.
          (Gough) **£250 [≈ $445]**
- A Treatise on the Management of Bees. London: 1770. 2nd edn. 8vo. xx,311, [8],16 pp. 3 plates. New half calf antique style.
          (Wheldon & Wesley) **£85 [≈ $151]**
- A Treatise on the Management of Bees ... London: 1778. 3rd edn. xx,325,16 pp. 3 fldg plates. Occas foxing. Mod leather backed bds.
          (Whitehart) **£140 [≈ $249]**

Wilkes, John

- A Complete Collection of the Genuine Papers, Letters, &c. in the case of John Wilkes, Esq. ... "Paris" [ie London]: chez J.W. imprimeur, 1767. 1st edn. 12mo. [iv],272 pp. Half-title. Contemp calf, jnts reprd.   *(Burmester)* **£150 [≈ $267]**
- A Letter to a Noble Member of the Club in Albemarle Street, from John Wilkes, Esq; at Paris. London: for W. Nicoll, 1764. 1st edn. 4to. [iv],19,[1] pp. Half-title. Sl fraying at beginning. Disbound.
          (Burmester) **£120 [≈ $214]**

Wilkes, Wetenhall

- A Letter of Genteel and Moral Advice to a Young Lady: in a New and Familiar Method ... London: for M. Cooper, 1744. 1st London edn. 8vo. 100 pp. Rebound in half calf.
  (Burmester) **£140 [≃ $249]**

- A Letter of Genteel and Moral Advice to a Young Lady ... The Eighth Edition, carefully revised ... London: Hawes, Clarke, Collins, 1766. 223 pp. Frontis. Contemp calf, fine.
  (C.R. Johnson) **£45 [≃ $80]**

Wilkins, John

- Ecclesiastes, or a Discourse concerning the Gift of Preaching ... The Fifth Edition. London: T.R. & E.M. for Samuel Gellibrand, 1656. Fcap 8vo. [6],133,[2],[2] pp. Some browning. Contemp calf, rebacked. Wing W.2192.   *(Spelman)* **£95 [≃ $169]**

- An Essay Towards a Real Character, and a Philosophical Language ... [with, as issued] An Alphabetical Dictionary ... London: 1668. 1st extant edn. Folio. 2 plates (1 fldg), 2 fldg tables, 3 text engvs (2 full-page). Imprimatur & errata ff. Contemp calf, rebacked. Wing W.2196.   *(Spelman)* **£850 [≃ $1,513]**

- The Mathematical and Philosophical Works ... London: for J. Nicholson ..., 1708. 1st coll edn. 8vo. viii,[vi],135, [iii],139-274, [x],90, [viii],184 pp. Plate, num w'cuts in text. Late 19th c calf, rubbed.   *(Finch)* **£425 [≃ $757]**

- The Mathematical and Philosophical Works ... prefixed the Author's Life ... London: for J. Nicholson ..., 1708. 1st coll edn. 8vo. Port, 1 plate, num w'cuts in text. Occas sl foxing. Contemp panelled calf, jnts sl rubbed.
  (Heritage) **$850 [≃ £478]**

- Mercury, or the Secret and Swift Messenger; shewing how a Man may with Privacy and Speed communicate his Thoughts to a Friend at any Distance. London: 1641. 1st edn. 8vo. xiv,170 pp. Lacks A1 (blank?). Contemp sheep, backstrip relaid. Wing W.2202.
  (Frew Mackenzie) **£400 [≃ $712]**

- Of the Principles and Duties of Natural religion ... The Ninth Edition. London: for J. Walthoe ..., 1734. 8vo. Port frontis. Contemp calf, sl rubbed.   *(Waterfield's)* **£60 [≃ $107]**

- Sermons Preach'd Upon Several Occasions before the King at Whitehall ... Second Edition. London: A.M. & R.R. for John Gellibrand, 1680. 8vo. [10],176 pp. Sep title to Discourse. Frontis port. Contemp panelled calf. Wing W.2214.   *(O'Neal)* **$125 [≃ £70]**

Wilkinson, Robert

- A Paire of Sermons Successively Preacht to a Paire of ... Princes ... London: Felix

Kyngston for William Aspley, 1614. 1st edn. 4to. [6],89 pp. 19th c calf backed bds. STC 25661.   *(O'Neal)* **$150 [≃ £84]**

Wilkinson, Tate

- The Wandering Patentee; or a History of the Yorkshire Theatres, from 1770 to the Present Time ... York: for the author, by Wilson, Spence & Mawman ..., 1795. 1st edn. 4 vols. 12mo. Lacks half-titles. Contemp half calf, fine.   *(Hannas)* **£400 [≃ $712]**

Willes, Sir John

- The Speech that was intended to have been spoken by the Terrae-Filius in the Theatre at O----d [Oxford], July 13, 1713 ... London: 1713. 1st edn. 8vo. 30 pp. Mod bds. Anon.
  (Robertshaw) **£45 [≃ $80]**

Williams, Daniel

- The Advancement of Christs Interest the governing End of a Christian Life. A Second Sermon ... January the 9th 1687/8. London: for J. Robinson, 1688. Only edn. 4to. [vi],36 pp. Calf backed bds. Wing W.2644.
  (Young's) **£120 [≃ $214]**

Williams, Helen Maria

- A Tour in Switzerland; or, a View of the Present State of the Government and Manners of those Cantons ... London: Robinson, 1798. 1st edn. 2 vols. 8vo. [xiv],354; viii,352 pp. Half-title in vol 1 only, correct. Marg tear reprd. Contemp calf, rebacked.   *(Burmester)* **£150 [≃ $267]**

Williams, John, 1582-1650

- Great Britains Salomon. A Sermon Preached at the Magnificent Funerall, of the most high and mighty King, James ... seventh of May, 1625. London: John Bill, 1625. 1st edn. Issue with 'mole' 1st word A3r. Frontis (sl shaved at ft). Disbound. STC 25723A.
  (Hannas) **£30 [≃ $53]**

Williams, John, 1636?-1709

- A Discourse Concerning the Celebration of Divine Service in an Unknown Tongue. London: for Richard Chiswell ..., 1685. 1st edn. 4to. [iv], 56 pp. Disbound. Wing W.2702. Anon.   *(Young's)* **£45 [≃ $80]**

Williams, John

- The Rise, Progress, and Present State of the Northern Governments ... made during a Tour of Five Years ... London: for T. Becket, 1777. 1st edn. 1st issue, ending with 'Finis' on p 659 vol 2. 2 vols. 4to. Mod qtr mor gilt, unopened.   *(Hannas)* **£250 [≃ $445]**

- The Rise, Progress, and Present State of the Northern Governments ... made during a Tour of Five Years ... London: for T. Becket, 1777. 1st edn. 2nd issue, with 16 pp index & advt after 'Finis' on p 659 vol 2. 2 vols. 4to. Contemp calf, jnts cracked.
(Hannas) **£110 [≃ $196]**
- The Rise, Progress, and Present State of the Northern Governments; viz. the United Provinces, Denmark, Sweden, Russia, and Poland ... London: Becket, 1777. 1st edn. 2 vols. 4to. xxii,676; [iv],659,[33] pp. Contemp calf, sl worn. *(Burmester)* **£200 [≃ $356]**

Williams, John, "Anthony Pasquin"
- The New Brighton Guide [in verse] ... With Notes ... A New Edition. London: for H.D. Symonds & T. Bellamy, 1796. 8vo. [3]-68 pp. Title vignette. Lacks half-title. Disbound. Anon. *(Hannas)* **£220 [≃ $392]**
- The Pin-Basket to the Children of Thespis. With Notes Historical, Critical, and Biographical. By John Williams, whose Public Appellation is Anthony Pasquin. London: Symonds & Bellamy, 1797. 1st edn. 12mo. Half-title. Contemp calf, gilt spine.
(Ximenes) **$350 [≃ £197]**

Williamson, John
- The British Angler. London: for J. Hodges, 1740. 1st edn. 12mo. viii,318,[x] pp. Frontis, fldg plates. Sl browning & creasing. Contemp calf, rebacked. *(Ash)* **£500 [≃ $890]**

Willich, A.F.M.
- Lectures on Diet and Regimen: being a Systematic Enquiry into the most Rational Means of preserving Health and prolonging Life ... Second Edition, Improved and Enlarged. London: 1779. 8vo. 708 pp. Contemp calf, hd of spine sl worn.
(Robertshaw) **£95 [≃ $169]**

Willis, Browne
- A Survey of the Cathedral-Church of St. Asaph ... London: for R. Gosling, 1720. Title, [viii],307,[i advt] pp. Fldg plate, fldg plan. Some browning. Contemp calf, rebacked. *(Francis Edwards)* **£50 [≃ $89]**

Willis, John
- Mnemonica; or, the Art of Memory, drained out of the Pure Fountains of Art & Nature ... London: Sowersby, 1661. Sm 8vo. [16],175 pp. 1 full-page text w'cut. Lib stamp on endpaper. Some marg browning. Contemp calf, hinges cracked but firm, crnrs sl worn. Wing W.2812. *(Spelman)* **£420 [≃ $748]**

Willis, Richard
- A Sermon Preach'd before the Queen ... 6th of February, 1708/9, being her Majesty's Birth-Day. London: for Mat. Wotton, 1709. 1st edn. 8vo. 16 pp. Disbound.
(Burmester) **£25 [≃ $45]**

Willison, John
- A Sermon Preached before His Majesty's High Commissioner to the General Assembly of the Church of Scotland ... 5th of May 1734 ... Edinburgh: Lumisden & Robertson ..., 1734. Only edn. 8vo. iv,63 pp. Disbound.
(Young's) **£140 [≃ $249]**

Willoughby, Francis
- The Ornithology of Francis Willughby, In Three Books ... London: John Martin, 1678. 1st edn. Folio. x,448 pp. 78 plates of birds. 2 plates of traps in facs. Sm marg tear 1 plate. Contemp calf, rebacked.
(Gough) **£595 [≃ $1,059]**

Willymott, William
- The Peculiar Use and Signification of certain Words in the Latin Tongue ... Sixth Edition, revised. Eton: for J. & T. Pote, 1767. 8vo. [ii],374 pp. Contemp sheep, sl scuffed.
(Clark) **£75 [≃ $134]**

Wilmot, John, Earl of Rochester
- See Rochester, John Wilmot, Earl of

Wilson, Alexander & Sons
- A Specimen of Printing Type. Glasgow: Alexander Wilson & Sons, 1783. 1st edn. Broadsheet (19 x 15 1/2 inches).
(Bookpress) **$275 [≃ £154]**

Wilson, Arthur
- The History of Great Britain, Being the Life of King James the First ... London: for Richard Lownds, 1653. 1st edn. Sm folio. [12], 292,[8] pp. Port. Damp stain throughout at hd. Old calf, rebacked. Wing W.2888.
(O'Neal) **$350 [≃ £197]**
- The History of Great Britain, being the Life and Reign of King James the First ... London: Richard Lownds, 1653. 1st edn. Folio. [xii], 290,[x], 291-2 pp. Port frontis. Contemp sheep, spine rubbed & frayed, crnrs sl worn. Wing W.2888. *(Clark)* **£100 [≃ $178]**

Wilson, Benjamin, & others
- Observations upon Lightning, and the Method of securing Buildings from its Effects, in a Letter to Sir Charles Frederick ... London: Lockyer Davis, 1773. 4to. [8],68 pp. Orig wraps, uncut, upper wrapper loose.

(C.R. Johnson) **£325** [≈ **$579**]

Wilson, John, Recorder of Londonderry
- Belphegor, or the Marriage of the Devil. A Tragi-Comedy ... London: J. Leake, sold by Randal Taylor, 1691. 1st edn. 4to. 1st word of title cut into. reprs to blank marg of title. Disbound. Wing W.2914.
(Hannas) **£110** [≈ **$196**]

Wilson, Samuel
- An Account of the Province of Carolina in America ... London: G. Larkin for Francis Smith, 1682. 1st edn. 2nd issue, with only pp 25, 26 & 27 misnumbered. Sm 4to. 26 pp [sic]. Occas sl foxing. Lacks map (not bound into all copies). 19th c half calf.
(Chapel Hill) **$6,000** [≈ **£3,371**]

Wilson, Thomas
- A Brief Journal of the Life, Travels, and Labours of Love, in the Work of the Ministry, of ... Thomas Wilson ... London: James Phillips, 1784. New edn. 12mo. xlviii,98,[2] pp. Old sheep, rebacked.
(Young's) **£35** [≈ **$62**]
- A Christian Dictionary. Opening the signification of the chief Words dispersed generally through Holy Scriptures ... London: William Iaggard, 1622. 3rd edn. 4to. Unpaginated. Title marg reprd, last few ff damp marked & reprd, sl loss. 17th c calf. STC 25788.   *(Young's)* **£240** [≈ **$427**]
- A Complete Christian Dictionary ... Eighth Edition. London: for Thomas Williams & Mary Clark, 1678. Folio. [xvii,670] pp. Port frontis. Lacks 4P4 (blank?). New half calf. Wing W.2945.   *(Blackwell's)* **£185** [≈ **$329**]
- The Principles and Duties of Christianity. A New Edition. To which is now prefixed The True Christian Method of Educating the Children both of the Rich and Poor. Egham: C. Boult, 1791. 232 pp. Contemp sheep, jnt broken. Anon. *(C.R. Johnson)* **£125** [≈ **$223**]

Wilson, William
- Elements of Navigation: or the Practical Rules of the Art, plainly laid down ... Edinburgh: for the author ..., 1773. 1st edn. Lge 8vo. xvi,510 pp. Errata leaf pasted inside upper cvr. 14 fldg plates. Lacks half-title. Some signs of use. Contemp sheep, sl worn.
(Burmester) **£150** [≈ **$267**]

Winchester, Elhanan
- The Universal Restoration exhibited in a Series of Dialogues ... The Fourth Edition, revised and corrected ... by W. Vidler. London: W. Burton ..., 1799. Lge 12mo. xvi,

195 pp. Port. Rec wraps, uncut.
(Fenning) **£14.50** [≈ **$27**]

Wing, Vincent & John
- Geodaetes Practicus Redivivus. The Art of Surveying ... Now much augmented and Improv'd ... London: Matthews for Churchill, 1700. Folio. [viii],384, 134,[iv] pp. 6 plates. Occas sl marks to text. Contemp sheep, rebacked. Wing W.2991.
(Vanbrugh) **£455** [≈ **$810**]

Wingate, Edmund
- Mr. Wingate's Arithmetick ... The Seventh Edition, very much enlarged ... revised ... By John Kersey ... London: sold by J. Williams, 1678. 8vo. [xii],544 pp. Contemp calf, gilt dec spine, minor wear extrs, sm splits in jnts. Wing W.3001.   *(Clark)* **£270** [≈ **$481**]

Winslow, J.B.
- An Anatomical Exposition of the Structure of the Human Body. Translated from the French Original by G. Douglas. Edinburgh: 1772. 6th edn. 2 vols. xxxii,428; 470 pp. 4 engvs. Some ink scribbles on vol 2 title. Old calf, rather worn & torn in places.
(Whitehart) **£150** [≈ **$267**]

Wisdom in Miniature ...
- Wisdom in Miniature; or the Young Gentleman and Lady's Pleasing Instructor ... Intended not only for the use of Schools, but as a Pocket Companion for the Youth of both Sexes. A New Edition. London: Minerva Press, 1794. 12mo. viii,240 pp. Frontis. Contemp sheep, rebacked.
(C.R. Johnson) **£175** [≈ **$312**]

Wither, George
- Speculum Speculativum: or, a Considering-Glass: being an Inspection into the present and late sad Condition of these Nations. London: 1660. 2nd edn, with errata corrected. Sm 8vo. Margs browned at ends. 18th c calf, rebacked. Wing W.3192.
(Hannas) **£170** [≈ **$303**]

Withers, John
- The Dutch better Friends than the French, to the Monarchy, Church, and Trade of England. In a Letter from a Citizen to a Country Gentleman. Fourth Edition. London: 1713. 8vo. 36 pp. Title sl soiled. Disbound. Anon.   *(Robertshaw)* **£40** [≈ **$71**]

Withers, Thomas
- Observations on Chronic Weakness. York: Ward, 1777. 8vo. ix,[1],169 pp. Rec contemp style bds.   *(Goodrich)* **$165** [≈ **£93**]

- Observations on the Abuse of Medicine. London: 1775. 1st edn. x,356 pp. Title dusty, occas foxing. Three qtr calf & mrbld bds. *(Whitehart)* **£240 [≈ $427]**

Witherspoon, John
- A Practical Treatise on Regeneration. The Third Edition. London: for Charles Dilly & J. Buckland, 1789. 8vo. Mod qtr calf. *(Waterfield's)* **£65 [≈ $116]**

Wogan, Charles
- Female Fortitude; exemplify'd, in an impartial Narrative of the Seizure, Escape and Marriage, of the Princess Clementina Sobieski. London: Printed in the Year, 1722. 12mo. v,[1],40 pp. Some stains, sl marg tears. Mod bds. *(Hannas)* **£100 [≈ $178]**

Wolcot, John
- The Remonstrance. To which is added, An Ode to My Ass ... By Peter Pindar ... J. Evans, 1791. 1st edn. 4to. [iv],63,[i] pp. Half-title. Minor damp stains. Disbound. *(Clark)* **£20 [≈ $36]**

Wollaston, William
- The Religion of Nature Delineated. London: S. Palmer for B. Lintot ..., 1725. 3rd (2nd published) edn. 4to. 219,[1] pp. Contemp calf, mor label, jnts cracked but holding, spine ends & crnrs worn. *(Gaskell)* **£250 [≈ $445]**
- The Religion of Nature Delineated ... London: Samuel Palmer, 1726. 4th edn. 4to. 219, 11 pp. Contemp calf, sl rubbed, front jnt partly cracked. Anon. *(Young's)* **£75 [≈ $134]**
- The Religion of Nature Delineated ... Dublin: 1726. 1st Dublin edn. Sm 4to. viii, 219 pp. Sl foxing. Rebound in mor. Anon. *(Francis Edwards)* **£60 [≈ $142]**
- The Religion of Nature Delineated ... The Sixth Edition, to which is added a Preface containing a general Account of the Life ... of the Author. London: Knapton, 1738. 4to. Port. Contemp calf. Anon. *(Waterfield's)* **£80 [≈ $142]**

Wollstonecraft, Mary
- Thoughts on the Education of Daughters: with Reflections on Female Conduct, in the More Important Duties of Life. London: for J. Johnson, 1787. 1st edn. 12mo. iv,160 pp. G6 a cancel. Sl stain crnr of a few ff. Contemp style half calf, gilt spine. *(Burmester)* **£2,000 [≈ $3,560]**
- A Vindication of the Rights of Woman. London: J. Johnson, 1792. 1st edn. Perf stamp on title & next leaf. Orig tree calf, rebacked. *(Mac Donnell)* **$1,250 [≈ £702]**
- A Vindication of the Rights of Woman. Boston: Edes for Thomas & Andrews, 1792. 2nd Amer edn. 8vo. W'cut on p 27. Half-title. Sm ink mark title marg, lib release stamp. Cloth. *(Rostenberg & Stern)* **$425 [≈ £239]**
- A Vindication of the Rights of Woman ... Second Edition. London: J. Johnson, 1792. 8vo. xiv,452,[1 advt] pp. Minor repr to title. Mor, rebacked. *(Hartfield)* **$1,095 [≈ £615]**
- A Vindication of the Rights of Woman. Phila: Carey, 1794. 3rd Amer edn. 8vo. Foxed. Sl marg tears on H5. Calf, scuffed. *(Rostenberg & Stern)* **$375 [≈ £211]**

Wood, Edward
- A Complete Body of Conveyancing, In Theory and Practice ... London: for J. Johnson, 1791. 5th edn, rvsd. 3 vols. Folio. Contemp calf, bds detached. *(Vanbrugh)* **£255 [≈ $454]**

Wood, Robert
- The Ruins of Palmyra, otherwise Tedmor, in the Desart. London: [for the author], 1753. Lge folio. [vi],50 pp, inc 3 pp of inscriptions. 57 plates (the 1st a 3-sheet panorama). Red ruled margs. Occas sl marg spots. Contemp qtr mor gilt, edges worn. Anon. *(Hollett)* **£1,500 [≈ $2,670]**

Wood, Thomas
- An Institute of the Laws of England ... In Four Books. Fourth Edition. In the Savoy: E. & R. Nutt, 1728. xi,663,contents,1 advt pp. Port. Contemp calf, worn, cvrs almost detached. *(Jermy & Westerman)* **£120 [≈ $214]**
- An Institute of the Laws of England ... London: Strahan & Woodfall ..., 1772. 10th edn. Folio. [ii],vii,[i], vii-x,216, 193, 218-402, 303,405-657,[xli] pp. Minor spotting at end. Contemp calf, hinges cracked, cvrs worn, lacks label. *(Vanbrugh)* **£255 [≈ $454]**

Woodhead, Abraham
- A Compendious Discourse of the Eucharist. With Two Appendixes. Oxford: ptd in the year, 1688. 1st edn. Sm 4to. Contemp unlettered calf, sl rubbed. Anon. *(Ximenes)* **$175 [≈ £98]**

Woodhouse, James
- Poems on Several Occasions. The Second Edition, Corrected, with several additional pieces ... London: for the author, sold by Dodsley ..., 1766. Thick Paper. 8vo. Subscribers. Contemp calf, gilt fillets. *(Hannas)* **£180 [≈ $320]**

Woodward, John
- An Essay towards a Natural History of the Earth and Terrestrial Bodies, especially Minerals. London: 1702. 2nd edn. 8vo. xiv,277 pp. Contemp calf.
(Wheldon & Wesley) £120 [≃ $214]

Woodward, Josiah
- An Account of the Societies for Reformation of Manners ... for the Effecting a National Reformation. London: for B. Aylmer, 1699. 2nd edn (?). 8vo. Port. Addtnl half-sheet at end "Abstract of the Penal-Laws ...". Contemp panelled calf. Wing W.3512. Anon.
(Hannas) £65 [≃ $116]
- An Account of the Societies for Reformation of Manners, in England and Ireland ... London: for B. Aylmer & A. Bell ..., 1700. 3rd edn. 8vo. (xxxii),132,(xii) pp. Port (sl weakened by damp in marg). Contemp calf, sl worn. Wing W.3514A. Anon.
(Burmester) £60 [≃ $107]
- The Soldier's Monitor, being Serious Advice to Soldiers, to behave themselves with a just regard to Religion and true Manhood. London: 1722. 1st edn. 12mo. 70 pp. Contemp calf.   *(Robertshaw)* £40 [≃ $71]
- Some Thoughts concerning the Stage in a Letter to a Lady. London: J. Nutt, 1704. 13, [2 blank] pp. Mod sheep. Anon.
(C.R. Johnson) £320 [≃ $570]

A Word in Season ...
- A Word in Season to the Traders & Manufacturers of Great Britain ... see Combe, William

Worsley, Edward
- Reason and Religion ... Wherein the Infallibility of the Roman Catholick Church is asserted ... By E.W. ... Antwerp: Michael Cnobbaert, 1672. 1st edn. 4to. [xxxviii], 681, [i] pp. Title sl dusty. Contemp calf, lacks label, sm hole in backstrip. Wing W.3617.
(Clark) £100 [≃ $178]

Worster, Benjamin
- A Compendious and Methodical Account of the Principles of Natural Philosophy ... London: for the author ..., 1722. 1st edn. 8vo. xviii,[iv],239,[1 advt] pp. Text diags. Some dust soiling & worm tracks in inner marg. Contemp calf, v worn, jnts cracked.
(Gaskell) £450 [≃ $801]
- A Compendious and Methodical Account of the Principles of Natural Philosophy ... London: for Stephen Austen, 1730. 2nd edn, rvsd. 8vo. xviii,[ii], 269,[3 advt] pp. Text diags. Some dust soiling & worm tracks in

inner marg. Contemp calf, v worn, jnts cracked.   *(Gaskell)* £300 [≃ $534]

Wortley, Sir Francis
- A Declaration from York, in Vindication of himself from divers Aspersions and Rumours ... London: A.N. for Thomas Warren, 1642. 1st edn. Sm 4to. [ii],6 pp. Faintly browned. Mod wraps. Wing W.3635.
(Blackwell's) £55 [≃ $98]

Wotton, Sir Henry
- A Parallel betweene Robert late Earle of Essex, and George late Duke of Buckingham. London: 1641. 4to. [2],14 pp. Disbound. Wing W.3646. *(C.R. Johnson)* £150 [≃ $267]
- Reliquiae Wottonianae. or, a Collection of Lives, Letters, Poems ... London: for R. Marriot ..., 1651. 1st edn. 12mo. [ix],540 pp. Errata. Sep title dated 1651 to Panegyrick. Port frontis, 3 other ports. Early 20th c elab gilt mor. Wing W.3648.
(Vanbrugh) £375 [≃ $668]
- Reliquiae Wottonianae: A Collection of Lives, Letters, Poems ... London: Marriott ..., 1672. 3rd edn. 8vo. 582 pp. Frontis, port. Orig calf, sometime rebacked, some wear.
(Hartfield) $395 [≃ £222]
- The State of Christendom ... London: for Humphrey Moseley, 1657. 1st edn. Folio. [viii], 262, [iv],32,[33-34] pp. Port. Table bound in rear. Contemp calf, rebacked. Wing W.3654.   *(Vanbrugh)* £295 [≃ $525]

Wotton, Thomas
- The English Baronetage. London: for Thomas Wotton, 1741. 2nd edn, rvsd. 5 vols. 8vo. 60 engvd sheets of arms, many ptd on both sides. Mod qtr calf. *(Ash)* £500 [≃ $890]

Woty, William
- The Shrubs of Parnassus. Consisting of a Variety of Poetical Essays, Moral and Comic. By J. Copywell, of Lincoln's-Inn [pseudonym] ... London: for the author, & sold by J. Newbery, 1760. 1st edn. 12mo. [xxiv],154 pp. 17 pp subscrs. Some stains. Contemp calf, worn.   *(Clark)* £60 [≃ $107]

Wraxall, Sir Nathaniel William
- Memoirs of the Kings of France ... added, a Tour through the Western, Southern, and Interior Provinces of France ... London: Dilly, 1777. 1st edn. 2 vols. 8vo. Contemp half calf, jnts beginning to crack but firm, hd of spines sl worn, sl rubbed.
(Blackwell's) £130 [≃ $231]
- A Tour through some of the Northern Parts of Europe, particularly Copenhagen,

Stockholm, and Petersburgh ... Second Edition, Corrected. London: for T. Cadell, 1775. 8vo. Fldg map. Contemp calf, rebacked.   *(Hannas)* **£75 [≈$134]**

- Tour through the Western, Southern, and Interior Provinces of France, in a Series of Letters. Dublin: James Moore Davis, 1786. 12mo. 231 pp. Contemp calf, new label.
       (Frew Mackenzie) **£60 [≈$107]**

Wright, George

- Pleasing Melancholy, or a Walk among the Tombs in a Country Church Yard ... London: Chapman & Co., 1793. 1st edn. 8vo. [ii],v,[i], 208 pp. Engvd frontis & title. Sl marg stain last 50 ff. Contemp vellum, uncut, ft of spine sl worn.   *(Burmester)* **£65 [≈$116]**

Wroth, Sir Thomas

- A Speech ... in the honourable House of Commons ... Delivery of a Petition ... County of Somerset ... February 25, 1642 ... London: H.S., 1642. 1st edn. Sm 4to. [8] pp. Mod wraps. Wing W.3731. *(Blackwell's)* **£50 [≈$89]**

Wyld, Samuel

- The Practical Surveyor, or the Art of Land-Measuring made Easy ... Fifth Edition, corrected and enlarged by a Careful Hand. London: W. Johnston, 1764. 8vo. viii,191 pp. Frontis, 6 plates (1 with marg tear). Some soiling throughout. New qtr calf.
       (Blackwell's) **£125 [≈$223]**

Wyndham, Henry Penruddocke

- Wiltshire, Extracted from Domesday Book. Salisbury: E. Easton, 1788. 1st edn. Demy 8vo. [2],xlii,(536) pp. Faint marks, sl spotting, 1 leaf torn without loss. Mod half calf.
       (Ash) **£100 [≈$178]**

Wynne, John

- A Sermon Preached to the Societies for the Reformation of Manners ... January the 3d, 1725 ... London: Joseph Downing ..., 1727. 1st 8vo edn. 24,8 pp. Disbound.
       (Young's) **£60 [≈$107]**

Wyvill, Christopher

- A Summary Explanation of the Principles of Mr. Pitt's intended Bill for amending the Representation of the People in Parliament. Second Edition. London: 1785. 8vo. 31 pp. Mod bds. Anon.   *(Robertshaw)* **£24 [≈$43]**

Xenophon

- [Greek title Cyropaedia, then] or the Institution and Life of Cyrus the Great ... Made English ... by Francis Digby and John

Norris. London: M. Gilliflower, 1685. 1st edn thus. 8vo. [16],190 pp. Frontis. V sm worm hole without loss of text. 19th c calf. Wing X.10.   *(O'Neal)* **$200 [≈£112]**

- History of the Affairs of Greece. London: 1770. 4to. Fldg map. Contemp calf, sl worn.
       (Robertshaw) **£40 [≈$71]**

- Xenophon's History of the Affairs of Greece ... Being a Continuation of the Peloponnesian War ... London: R.H. for William Freeman, 1685. 1st edn in English. 8vo. [46],459,[3 ctlg] pp. Piece torn from title with sm loss. Contemp calf. Wing X.19.
       (O'Neal) **$300 [≈£169]**

- Xenophon's Memoirs of Socrates ... see Fielding, Sarah

Y-Worth, William

- Introitus Apertus ad Artem Distillationis; or the Whole Art of Distillation Practically Stated ... London: Joh. Taylor, 1692. Only edn. 8vo. [xvi],189,[iii] pp. Frontis, 4 plates. Sl wear & marg worm. Contemp calf, crnrs worn, jnts split at ends. Wing Y.218.
       (Clark) **£500 [≈$890]**

Yates, William & MacLean, Charles

- A View of the Science of Life; on the Principles established in the Elements of Medicine, of the late celebrated John Brown ... Phila: 1797. 232 pp. Foxing. Old bds, rebacked.   *(Goodrich)* **$65 [≈£37]**

Yonge, Sir William

- Sedition and Defamation Display'd: In a Letter to the Author of The Craftsman ... London: for J. Roberts, 1731. 1st edn. 8vo. [4], viii,48 pp. Half-title. Anon.
       (Young's) **£45 [≈$80]**

- Sedition and Defamation Display'd: In a Letter to the Author of the Craftsman. London: for J. Roberts, 1731. 1st edn. 8vo. [4],viii,48 pp, inc half-title. Disbound. Anon.
       (Hannas) **£40 [≈$71]**

Yorick, Mr. (pseudonym)

- See Sterne, Laurence.

The York Guide ...

- The York Guide: containing a Description of the Cathedral, with other Public Buildings in the City ... Directory ... London: A. Ward, 1787. Lge 12mo. [4],53 pp. Lge fldg plan (reprd), 5 fldg plates. Some foxing & marks. Rec half calf.   *(Spelman)* **£200 [≈$356]**

Yorke, Philip

- The Royal Tribes of Wales. Wrexham: John Painter, 1799. 4to. 192,[2 errata],[i] pp.

Half-title. 12 plates (sl offset, sl marg foxing). Margin of errata leaf reprd. Crushed red mor gilt, a.e.g., sev sm reprs upper jnt, some discolouring. *(Francis Edwards)* **£100 [≈ $178]**

Young ...

- The Young Gard'ners Director ... see Stevenson, H.
- The Young Secretary's Polite Guide to an Epistolary Correspondence in Business, Friendship, Love and Marriage ... Newcastle upon Tyne: T. Saint, for W. Charnley ..., 1778. 1st edn (?). 12mo. [ii],vii, [iii],180 pp. Contemp sheep, spine reprd.
  (Burmester) **£100 [≈ $178]**

Young, Arthur

- The Example of France, a Warning to Britain. The Second Edition. Bury St. Edmund's: J. Rackham, for W. Richardson, 1793. 8vo. [2],182,[2] pp, errata leaf, advt leaf. Disbound. *(Hannas)* **£130 [≈ $231]**
- The Farmer's Guide in Hiring and Stocking Farms ... London: 1770. 1st edn. 2 vols. 8vo. [iv],viii, 458,[ii]; [iv],500 pp. Advt leaf vol 1. 10 plates vol 2. Occas sl foxing. Contemp calf, gilt spines, rubbed, lacks secondary labels. Anon. *(Clark)* **£250 [≈ $445]**
- The Farmer's Letters to the People of England ... added, Sylvae; or, Occasional Tracts on Husbandry and Rural Oeconomics. London: for W. Nicoll, 1767. 1st edn. 8vo. [iv],324 pp. Period calf, sl ink stains upper cvr, sm worm hole lower cvr. Anon. *(Rankin)* **£125 [≈ $223]**
- A Six Weeks' Tour, through the Southern Counties of England and Wales. London: W. Nicoll, 1768. 1st edn. 8vo. [2],284 pp. Half-title. Sev text ills. Marg ink mark 1 page. Contemp half calf, spine ends reprd, crnrs sl worn. *(Spelman)* **£120 [≈ $214]**

Young, David

- National Improvements upon Agriculture in Twenty-Seven Essays. Edinburgh: the author & John Bell, 1785. 403 pp. 3 plates. Contemp sheep, brown label.
  (C.R. Johnson) **£125 [≈ $223]**

Young, Edward

- Love of Fame, the Universal Passion. In Seven Characteristical Satires. The Second Edition Corrected, and Alter'd. London: Tonson, 1728. 8vo. Contemp calf gilt, lacks label. Anon. *(Hannas)* **£45 [≈ $80]**
- Love of Fame, the Universal Passion. In

Seven Characteristical Satires ... Fourth Edition. London: Tonson, 1741. 8vo. [xii], 175, [i] pp. 1 blank crnr torn. Contemp calf gilt. Anon. *(Finch)* **£60 [≈ $107]**
- Night Thoughts ... With the Life of the Author, and Notes Critical and Explanatory. London: C. Whittingham for T. Heptinstall, 1798. 4to. 364 pp. Frontis port, pict title, plates. Occas foxing. Contemp calf, poorly rebacked. *(Wreden)* **$95 [≈ £53]**
- Ocean. An Ode ... prefix'd, an Ode to the King ... By the Author of the Universal Passion. London: for Tho. Worral, 1728. 1st edn. 8vo. [4],55 pp, inc half-title. Last leaf reprd, no loss. Disbound. Anon.
  (Hannas) **£110 [≈ $196]**
- A Poem on the Last Day. Oxford: at the Theatre, 1713. 8vo. Browned. Name erased from title. Disbound.
  (Waterfield's) **£40 [≈ $71]**
- A Poem on the Last Day. Second Edition. Oxford: 1713. 8vo. 74 pp. Title vignette. Mod wraps. *(Robertshaw)* **£15 [≈ $27]**

Young, John

- Essays on the following Interesting Subjects: viz. I Government ... VI Liberty and Equality ... Fourth Edition. Glasgow: David Niven, 1794. 160 pp. Contemp half calf.
  (Robertshaw) **£65 [≈ $116]**

Zimmerman, M.

- Solitude Considered with respect to its Influence upon the Mind and Heart. Written originally in German. Translated from the French of J.B. Mercier. London: 1792. 2nd edn. xii,420 pp. Frontis. Some foxing. Contemp leather, rebacked, crnrs worn.
  (Whitehart) **£55 [≈ $98]**

Zosimus, the Historian

- The New History of Count Zosimus, Sometime Advocate of the Treasury of the Treasury of the Roman Empire ... Newly Englished. London: for Joseph Hindmarsh, 1684. Sm 8vo. [34],416 pp. 18th c tree calf, gilt spine, red & green labels. Wing Z.16.
  (Karmiole) **$250 [≈ £140]**

Zouch, Richard

- The Sophister. A Comedy. London: J.O. for Humphrey Mosley, 1639. Only edn. 4to. [70] pp. Lacks intl blank. Cropped at hd, marg worm damage reprd. Later qtr mor, jnts rubbed. STC 26133. Anon.
  (Clark) **£480 [≈ $854]**

Catalogue Booksellers Contributing to IRBP

The booksellers who have provided catalogues during 1991 specifically for the purpose of compiling the various titles in the *IRBP* series, and from whose catalogues books have been selected, are listed below in alphabetical order of the abbreviation employed for each. This listing is therefore a complete key to the booksellers contributing to the series as a whole; only a proportion of the listed names is represented in this particular subject volume.

The majority of these booksellers issue periodic catalogues free, on request, to potential customers. Sufficient indication of the type of book handled by each bookseller can be gleaned from the individual book entries set out in the main body of this work and in the companion titles in the series.

Alphabet	=	Alphabet Bookshop, 145 Main Street West, Port Colborne, Ontario L3K 3V3, Canada (416 834 5323)
Antic Hay	=	Antic Hay Rare Books, P.O. Box 2185, Asbury Park, NJ 07712, U.S.A. (908 774 4590)
Any Amount	=	Any Amount of Books, 62 Charing Cross Road, London WC2H 0BB, England (071 240 8140)
Appelfeld	=	Appelfeld Gallery, 1372 York Avenue, New York, NY 10021, U.S.A. (212 988 7835)
Argonaut	=	Argonaut Book Shop, 786-792 Sutter Street, San Francisco, California 94109, U.S.A. (415 474 9067)
Armchair Traveller	=	The Armchair Traveller, 1 Sea View Terrace, Emsworth, Hampshire PO10 7EN, England (0243 371203)
Ars Libri	=	Ars Libri, Ltd., 560 Harrison Avenue, Boston, Massachusetts 02118, U.S.A. (617 338 5763)
Ash	=	Ash Rare Books, 25 Royal Exchange, London EC3V 3LP, England (071 626 2665)
Bates & Hindmarch	=	Bates and Hindmarch, Antiquarian Bookseller, Fishergate, Boroughbridge, North Yorkshire Y05 9AL, England (0423 324258)
Between the Covers	=	Between the Covers, 132 Kings Highway East, Haddonfield, NJ 08033, U.S.A. (609 354 7665)
Blackwell's	=	Blackwell's Rare Books, B.H. Blackwell Ltd., Fyfield Manor, Fyfield, Abingdon, Oxon OX13 5LR, England (0865 791438)
Black Sun	=	Black Sun Books, 157 East 57 Street, New York, NY 10022, U.S.A. (212 688 6622)
Blakeney	=	Adam Blakeney, Apartment 313, Butlers Wharf Building, 36 Shad Thames, London SE1 2YE, England (071 378 1197)
Book Block	=	The Book Block, 8 Loughlin Avenue, Cos Cob, Connecticut 06807, U.S.A. (203 629 2990)
Bookline	=	Bookline, 35 Farranfad Road, Downpatrick BT30 8NH, Northern Ireland (039687 712)
Bookmark	=	Bookmark, Children's Books, Fortnight, Wick Down, Broad Hinton, Swindon, Wiltshire SN4 9NR, England (0793 731693)
Bookpress	=	The Bookpress Ltd., Post Office Box KP, Williamsburg, Virginia 23187, U.S.A. (804 229 1260)
Bookworks	=	Bookworks, "Gernon Elms", Letchworth Lane, Letchworth, Hertfordshire SG6 3NF, England (0462 673189)
Bow Windows	=	Bow Windows Book Shop, 128 High Street, Lewes, East Sussex BN7 1XL, England (0273 480780)
Bromer	=	Bromer Booksellers, 607 Boylston Street, at Copley Square, Boston, MA 02116, U.S.A. (617 247 2818)

Burmester	=	James Burmester, Manor House Farmhouse, North Stoke, Bath BA1 9AT, England (0272 327265)
Chalmers Hallam	=	E. Chalmers Hallam, "Trees", 9 Post Office Lane, St. Ives, Ringwood, Hampshire BH24 2PG, England (0425 470060)
Chapel Hill	=	Chapel Hill Rare Books, P.O. Box 456, Carrboro, NC 27510, U.S.A. (919 929 8351)
Clark	=	Robert Clark, 6a King Street, Jericho, Oxford OX2 6DF, England (0865 52154)
Clearwater	=	Clearwater Books, 19 Matlock Road, Ferndown, Wimborne, Dorset BH22 8QT, England (0202 893263)
Claude Cox	=	Claude Cox, The White House, Kelsale, Saxmundham, Suffolk IP17 2PQ, England (0728 602786)
Dalian	=	Dalian Books, David P. Williams, 81 Albion Drive, London Fields, London E8 4LT, England (071 249 1587)
de Burca	=	de Burca Rare Books, "Cloonagashel", 27 Priory Drive, Blackrock, Co. Dublin, Eire (01 2882159)
Deja Vu	=	Deja Vu, 31 Trafalgar Street, Brighton BN1 4ED, England (0273 600400)
Dermont	=	Joseph A. Dermont, 13 Arthur Street, P.O. Box 654, Onset, MA 02558, U.S.A. (508 295 4760)
D & D Galleries	=	D & D Galleries, Box 8413, Somerville, New Jersey 08876, U.S.A. (201 874 3162)
Edrich	=	I.D. Edrich, 17 Selsdon Road, London E11 2QF, England (081 989 9541)
Francis Edwards	=	Francis Edwards, The Old Cinema, Castle Street, Hay-on-Wye, via Hereford HR3 5DF, England (0497 820071)
Egglishaw	=	H.J. Egglishaw, Bruach Mhor, 54 West Moulin Road, Pitlochry, Perthshire PH16 5EQ, Scotland (0796 2084)
Egret	=	Egret Books, 6 Priory Place, Wells, Somerset BA5 1SP, England (0749 679312)
Ellis	=	Peter Ellis, 31 Museum Street, London WC1A 1LH, England (071 637 5862)
Europa	=	Europa Books, 15 Luttrell Avenue, Putney, London SW15 6PD, England (081 788 0312)
Fenning	=	James Fenning, 12 Glenview, Rochestown Avenue, Dun Laoghaire, County Dublin, Eire (01 2857855)
Finch	=	Simon Finch Rare Books, 10 New Bond Street, London W1Y 9PF, England (071 499 0974)
Frew Mackenzie	=	Frew Mackenzie plc, 106 Great Russell Street, London WC1B 3NA, England (071 580 2311)
Fye	=	W. Bruce Fye, Antiquarian Medical Books, 1607 North Wood Avenue, Marshfield, Wisconsin 54449, U.S.A. (1 715 384 8128)
Gach	=	John Gach Books, 5620 Waterloo Road, Columbia, Md. 21045, U.S.A. (301 465 9023)
Gaskell	=	Roger Gaskell, 17 Ramsey Road, Warboys, Cambridgeshire PE17 2RW, England (0487 823059)
Gekoski	=	R.A. Gekoski, 33B Chalcot Square, London NW1 8YA, England (071 722 9037)
Gemmary	=	The Gemmary, Inc, PO Box 816, Redondo Beach, CA 90277, U.S.A. (213 372 5969)
Georges	=	Georges, 52 Park Street, Bristol BS1 5JN, England (0272 276602)
Glyn's	=	Glyn's Books, 4 Bryn Draw Terrace, Wrexham, Clwyd LL13 7DF, Wales (0978 364473)
Goodrich	=	James Tait Goodrich, Antiquarian Books and Manuscripts, 214 Everett Place, Englewood, New Jersey 07631, U.S.A. (201 567 0199)

Gough	=	Simon Gough Books, 5 Fish Hill, Holt, Norfolk, England (0263 712650)
Green Meadow	=	Green Meadow Books, Kinoulton, Nottingham NG12 3EN, England (0949 81723)
Hannas	=	Torgrim Hannas, 29a Canon Street, Winchester, Hampshire SO23 9JJ, England (0962 862730)
Hartfield	=	Hartfield, Fine and Rare Books, 117 Dixboro Road, Ann Arbor, MI 48105, U.S.A. (313 662 6035)
Hazeldene	=	Hazeldene Bookshop, A.H. & L.G. Elliot, 61 Renshaw Street, Liverpool L1 2SJ, England (051 708 8780)
Henly	=	John Henly, Bookseller, Brooklands, Walderton, Chichester, West Sussex PO18 9EE, England (0705 631426)
Heritage	=	Heritage Book Shop, Inc., 8540 Melrose Avenue, Los Angeles, California 90069, U.S.A. (213 659 3674)
Hermitage	=	The Hermitage Bookshop, 290 Fillmore Street, Denver, Colorado 80206-5020, U.S.A. (303 388 6811)
High Latitude	=	High Latitude, P.O. Box 11254, Bainbridge Island, WA 98110, U.S.A. (206 598 3454)
Hollett	=	R.F.G. Hollett and Son, 6 Finkle Street, Sedbergh, Cumbria LA10 5BZ, England (05396 20298)
Horowitz	=	Glenn Horowitz, 141 East 44th Street, Suite 808, New York, New York 10017, U.S.A. (212 557 1381)
Hortulus	=	Hortulus, 139 Marlborough Place, Toronto, Ontario, Canada (416 920 5057)
Carol Howard	=	Carol Howard Books, Jubilee Cottage, Leck, Cowan Bridge, Carnforth, Lancashire LA6 2JD, England (05242 71072)
James	=	Marjorie James, The Old School, Oving, Chichester, West Sussex PO20 6DG, England (0243 781354)
Janus	=	Janus Books, Post Office Box 40787, Tucson, Arizona 85717, U.S.A. (602 881 8192)
Jarndyce	=	Jarndyce, Antiquarian Booksellers, 46 Great Russell Street, Bloomsbury, London WC1B 3PA, England (071 631 4220)
Jermy & Westerman	=	Jermy & Westerman, 203 Mansfield Road, Nottingham NG1 3FS, England (0602 474522)
C.R. Johnson	=	C.R. Johnson, 21 Charlton Place, London N1 8AQ, England (071 354 1077)
Karmiole	=	Kenneth Karmiole, Bookseller, Post Office Box 464, Santa Monica, California 90406, U.S.A. (213 451 4342)
Key Books	=	Key Books, P.O. Box 58097, St. Petersburg, FL 33715, U.S.A. (813 867 2931)
King	=	John K. King, P.O. Box 33363, Detroit, Michigan 48232, U.S.A. (313 961 0622)
Lame Duck Books	=	Lame Duck Books, 90 Moraine Street, Jamaica Plain, MA 02130, U.S.A. (617 522 7827)
Larkhill	=	Larkhill Books, Larkhill House, Tetbury, Gloucestershire GL8 8SY, England (0666 502343)
Levin	=	Barry R. Levin, 726 Santa Monica Blvd., Suite 201, Santa Monica, California 90401, U.S.A. (213 458 6111)
Lewton	=	L.J. Lewton, Old Station House, Freshford, Bath BA3 6EQ, England (0225 723351)
Limestone Hills	=	Limestone Hills Book Shop, P.O. Box 1125, Glen Rose, Texas 76043, U.S.A. (817 897 4991)
Lopez	=	Ken Lopez, Bookseller, 51 Huntington Road, Hadley, MA 01035, U.S.A. (413 584 2045)
McBlain	=	McBlain Books, P.O. Box 5062 Hamden, CT 06518, U.S.A. (203 281 0400)

Mac Donnell	=	Mac Donnell Rare Books, 9307 Glenlake Drive, Austin, Texas 78730, U.S.A. (512 345 4139)
Martin	=	C.J. Martin, 76 Raylawn Street, Mansfield, Nottinghamshire NG18 3ND, England (0623 20691)
Meyer Boswell	=	Meyer Boswell Books, Inc., 2141 Mission Street, San Francisco, CA 94110, U.S.A. (415 255 6400)
Ming Books	=	Ming Books (UK) Ltd., 1 Penrose Avenue, Carpenders Park, Watford, Hertfordshire WD1 5AE, England (081 428 5034)
Moorhouse	=	Hartley Moorhouse Books, 142 Petersham Road, Richmond, Surrey TW10 6UX, England (081 948 7742)
Mordida	=	Mordida Books, P.O. Box 79322, Houston, Texas 77279, U.S.A. (713 467 4280)
Northern Books	=	Northern Books, PO Box 211, Station P, Toronto, Ontario M5S 2S7, Canada (416 531 8873)
Nouveau	=	Nouveau Rare Books, Steve Silberman, P.O. Box 12471, 5005 Meadow Oaks Park Drive, Jackson, Mississippi 39211, U.S.A. (601 956 9950)
O'Neal	=	David L. O'Neal, 234 Clarendon Street, Boston, Massachusetts 02116, U.S.A. (617 266 5790)
Oak Knoll	=	Oak Knoll Books, 414 Delaware Street, New Castle, Delaware 19720, U.S.A. (302 328 7232)
Parmer	=	J. Parmer, Booksellers, 7644 Forrestal Road, San Diego, CA 92120, U.S.A. (619 287 0693)
Petrilla	=	R & A Petrilla, Roosevelt, NJ 08555-0306, U.S.A. (609 426 4999)
Phillips	=	Phillips of Hitchin, (Antiques) Ltd., The Manor House, Hitchin, Hertfordshire, England (0462 432067)
Polyanthos	=	Polyanthos Park Avenue Books, P.O. Box 343, Huntington, NY 11743, U.S.A. (516 271 5558)
P and P Books	=	P & P Books, J.S. Pizey, 27 Love Lane, Oldswinford, Stourbridge, West Midlands DY8, England (0384 393845)
Quest Books	=	Quest Books, Harmer Hill, Millington, York YO4 2TX, England (0759 304735)
Rankin	=	Alan Rankin, 72 Dundas Street, Edinburgh EH3 6QZ, Scotland, Scotland (031 556 3705)
Reese	=	William Reese Company, 409 Temple Street, New Haven, Connecticut 06511, U.S.A. (203 789 8081)
David Rees	=	David Rees, 18A Prentis Road, London SW16 1QD, England (081 769 2453)
Robertshaw	=	John Robertshaw, 5 Fellowes Drive, Ramsey, Huntingdon, Cambridgeshire PE17 1BE, England (0487 813330)
Rostenberg & Stern	=	Leona Rostenberg and Madeleine, Stern, Rare Books, 40 East 88th Street, New York, N.Y. 10128., U.S.A. (212 831 6628)
Sanders	=	Sanders of Oxford Ltd., 104 High Street, Oxford OX1 4BW, England (0865 242590)
Savona	=	Savona Books, 9 Wilton Road, Hornsea, North Humberside HU18 1QU, England (0964 535195)
Schoen	=	Kenneth Schoen, Bookseller, One Cottage Street, Easthampton, MA 01027, U.S.A. (413 527 4780)
Sclanders	=	Andrew Sclanders, 73 Duckett Road, London N4 1BL, England (081 340 6843)
Sheppard	=	Roger Sheppard, 117 Kent House Road, Beckenham, Kent BR3 1JJ, England (081 778 0534)
Sklaroff	=	L.J. Sklaroff, The Totland Bookshop, The Broadway, Totland, Isle of Wight PO39 0BW, England (0983 754960)
Alan Smith	=	Alan Smith, 15 Oakland Avenue, Dialstone Lane, Stockport, Cheshire SK2 6AX, England (061 483 2547)

Sotheran's	=	Henry Sotheran Ltd., 2 Sackville Street, Piccadilly, London W1X 2DP, England (071 439 6151)
Spelman	=	Ken Spelman, 70 Micklegate, York YO1 1LF, England (0904 624414)
Monroe Stahr	=	Monroe Stahr Books, 166 1/2 S. Sycamore Ave., Los Angeles, CA 90036, U.S.A. (213 931 9919)
Stewart	=	Andrew Stewart, 11 High Street, Helpringham, Sleaford, Lincolnshire NG34 9RA, England (052 921 617)
Sumner & Stillman	=	Sumner & Stillman, P.O. Box 225, Yarmouth, ME 04096, U.S.A. (207 846 6070)
Terramedia	=	Terramedia Books, 19 Homestead Road, Wellesley, MA 02181, U.S.A. (617 237 6485)
Thelema	=	Thelema Publications, P.O. Box 1393, Kings Beach, California 95719, U.S.A.
Tiger Books	=	Tiger Books, Yew Tree Cottage, Westbere, Canterbury Kent CT2 0HH, England (0227 710030)
Trophy Room Books	=	Trophy Room Books, Box 3041, Agoura, CA 91301, U.S.A. (818 889 2469)
Turtle Island	=	Turtle Island Booksellers, 2067 Center Street, Berkeley, CA 94704, U.S.A. (415 540 5422)
Ulysses Bookshop	=	Ulysses Bookshop, 41 Museum Street, London WC1A 1LH, England (071 637 5862)
Vanbrugh	=	Vanbrugh Rare Books, 'Ruskin House', 40a Museum Street, Bloomsbury, London WC1A 1LT, England (071 404 0733)
Virgo	=	Virgo Books, Little Court, South Wraxall, Bradford-on-Avon, Wiltshire BA15 2SE, England (02216 2040)
Walcot	=	Patrick Walcot, 60 Sunnybank Road, Sutton Coldfield, West Midlands B73 5RJ, England (021 382 6381)
Washton	=	Andrew D. Washton, 411 East 83rd Street, New York, New York 10028, U.S.A. (212 751 7027)
Waterfield's	=	Waterfield's, 36 Park End Street, Oxford OX1 1HJ, England (0865 721809)
Weiner	=	Graham Weiner, 78 Rosebery Road, London N10 2LA, England (081 883 8424)
Wheldon & Wesley	=	Wheldon & Wesley Ltd., Lytton Lodge, Codicote, Hitchin, Hertfordshire SG4 8TE, England (0438 820370)
Whitehart	=	F.E. Whitehart, Rare Books, 40 Priestfield Road, Forest Hill, London SE23 2RS, England (081 699 3225)
David White	=	David White, 17 High Street, Bassingbourn, Royston, Hertfordshire SG8 5NE, England (0763 243986)
Nigel Williams	=	Nigel Williams (Books), 196 Court Lane, Dulwich, London SE21 7ED, England (081 693 0464)
Susan Wood	=	Susan Wood, 24 Leasowe Road, Rubery, Rednal, Worcestershire B45 9TD, England (021 453 7169)
Woolmer	=	J. Howard Woolmer, Revere, Pennsylvania 18953, U.S.A. (215 847 5074)
Words Etcetera	=	Words Etcetera, Julian Nangle, Hod House, Child Okeford, Dorset DT11 8EH, England (0258 860539)
Worldwide	=	Worldwide Antiquarian, Post Office Box 391, Cambridge, MA 02141, U.S.A. (617 876 6220)
Wreden	=	William P. Wreden, 206 Hamilton Avenue, P.O. Box 56, Palo Alto, CA 94302-0056, U.S.A. (415 325 6851)
Ximenes	=	Ximenes: Rare Books, Inc., 19 East 69th Street, New York, NY 10021, U.S.A. (212 744 0226)
Young's	=	Young's Antiquarian Books, Tillingham, Essex CM0 7ST, England (0621 778187)